Baroque Sculpture in Germany and Central Europe 1600–1770

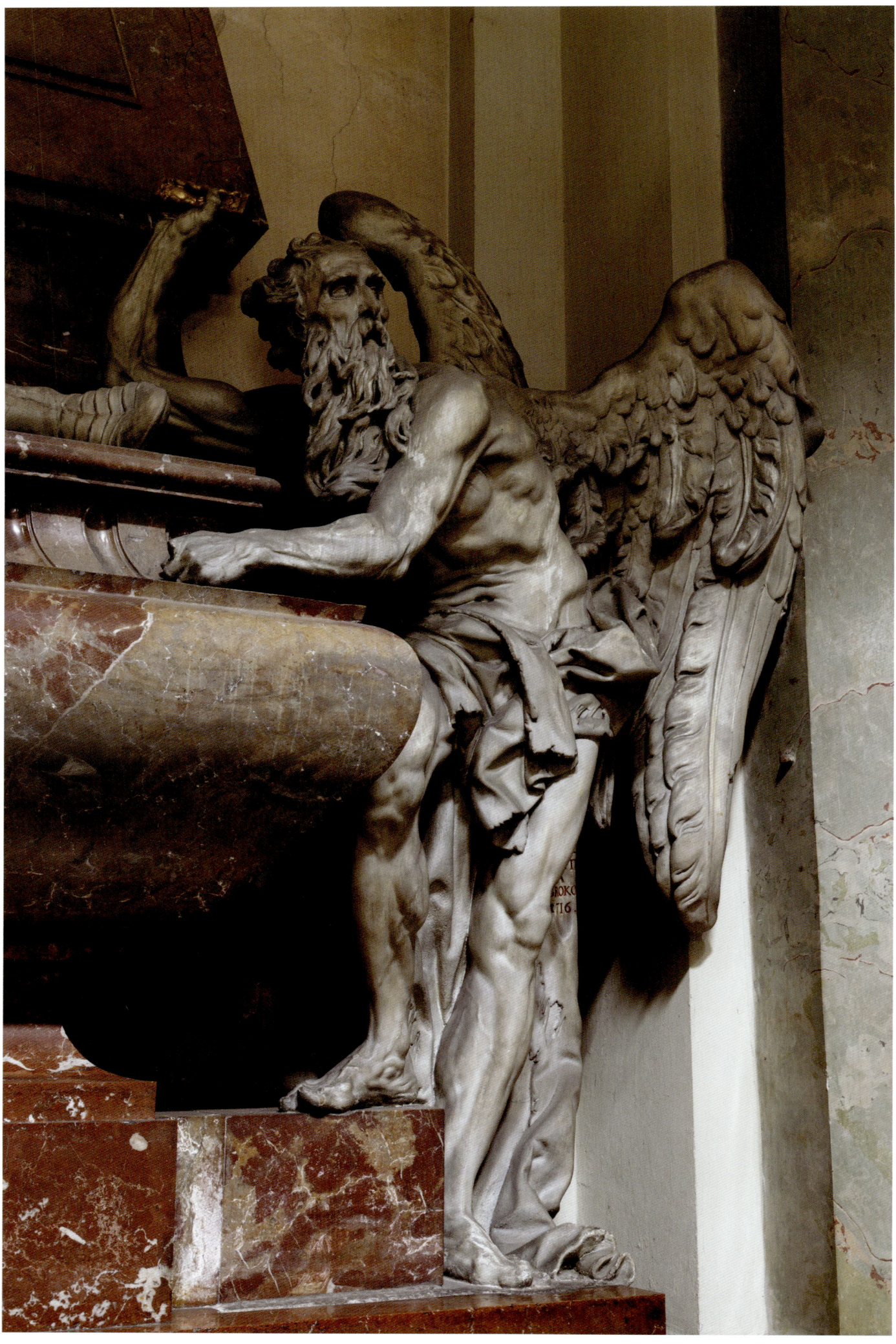

BAROQUE SCULPTURE IN GERMANY AND CENTRAL EUROPE 1600—1770

MARJORIE TRUSTED

Generously sponsored by
the Reiner Winkler Stiftung

and Joanna Barnes, Daniel Katz, Stuart Lochhead,
the Tomasso Brothers and Patricia Wengraf

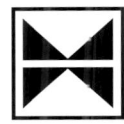

HARVEY MILLER PUBLISHERS

HARVEY MILLER PUBLISHERS
An Imprint of Brepols Publishers
London/Turnhout

British Library Cataloguing in Publication Data
A catalogue record for this book
is available from the British Library

ISBN 978-1-909400-95-5
D/2022/0095/115

Cover: Egid Quirin Asam, *The Assumption of the Virgin*,
painted and gilt stucco; 1717/23. Benedictine Abbey of
Rohr, Bavaria. Photo: Image Professionals GmbH/Alamy
Stick Photo.

Backcover: Johann Christoph Ludwig Lücke, *Poltrone*,
ivory on wood socle, c. 1730, height 10.5 cm. Victoria
and Albert Museum, London (inv. no. A. 17-1949).
Photo: Victoria and Albert Museum.

Frontispiece: 0.01. Detail of *Time* from Johann Bernhard
Fischer von Erlach and Ferdinand Maximilian Brokoff,
Tomb of Count Johann Wenzel Wratislaw von Mitrowitz,
marble and limestone, signed and dated 1716. Church
of St James the Greater, Prague. Photo: Josef Goryl.

For Cassius, Arthur, Cecily and Clara

CONTENTS

7

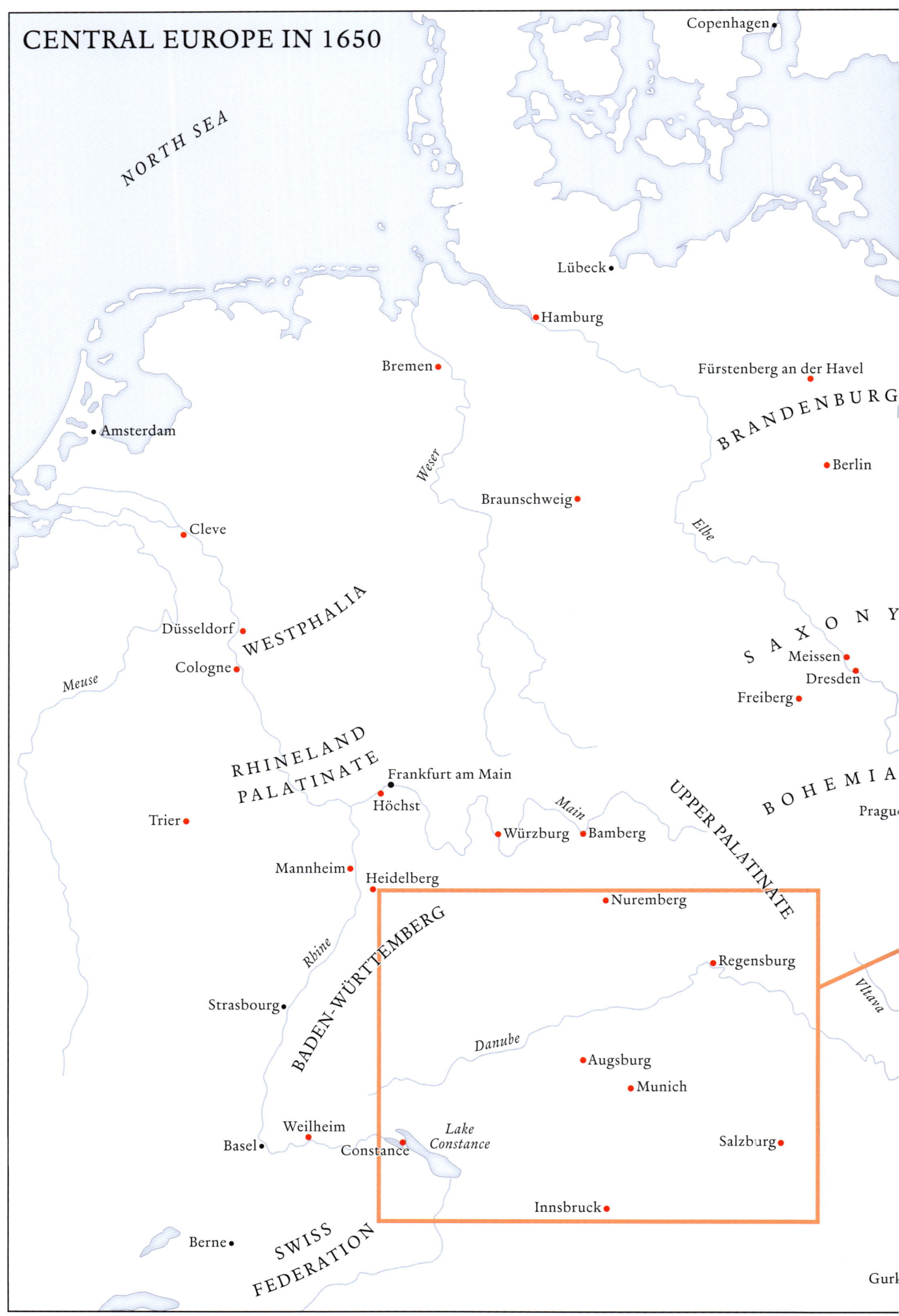

CENTRAL EUROPE IN 1650

NORTH SEA

Copenhagen•

Lübeck•

•Hamburg

Bremen•

Fürstenberg an der Havel•

B R A N D E N B U R G

•Berlin

•Amsterdam

Weser

Braunschweig•

Elbe

Cleve•

S A X O N Y

W E S T P H A L I A

Düsseldorf•

Meissen•

•Dresden

Cologne•

Freiberg•

Meuse

R H I N E L A N D
P A L A T I N A T E

Frankfurt am Main•

Höchst•

Main

U P P E R   P A L A T I N A T E

B O H E M I A

Prague•

Trier•

•Würzburg •Bamberg

Mannheim• Heidelberg•

•Nuremberg

B A D E N - W Ü R T T E M B E R G

•Regensburg

Rhine

Vltava

Strasbourg•

Danube

•Augsburg

•Munich

Weilheim•

Lake Constance

•Salzburg

Basel• Constance•

Berne•

S W I S S
F E D E R A T I O N

Innsbruck•

Gurk

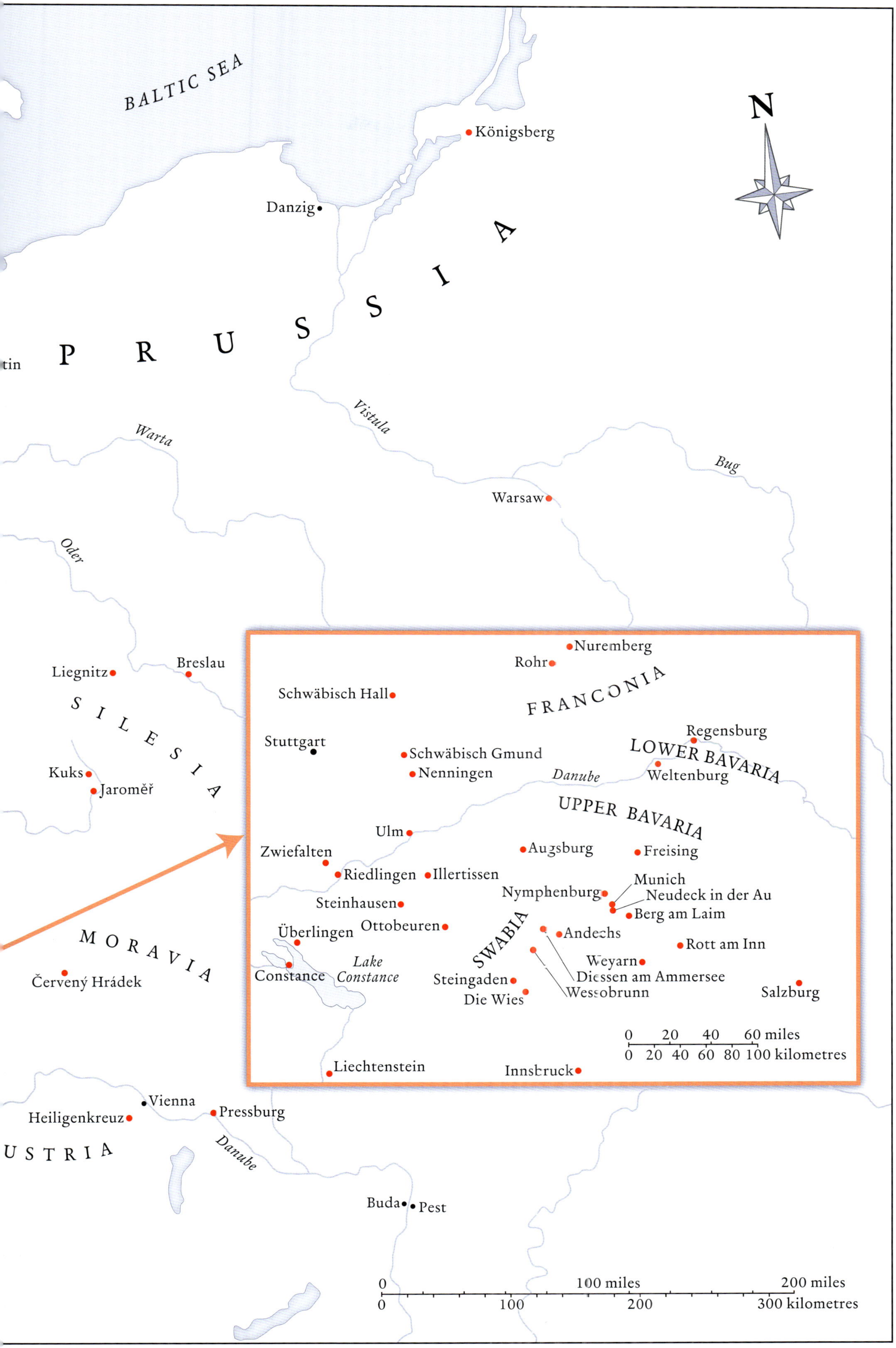

BALTIC SEA

Königsberg

Danzig

P R U S S I A

Warta

Vistula

Bug

Oder

Warsaw

Liegnitz

Breslau

Nuremberg

Rohr

FRANCONIA

S I L E S I A

Schwäbisch Hall

Stuttgart

Regensburg

LOWER BAVARIA

Kuks

Jaroměř

Schwäbisch Gmund

Nenningen

Danube

Weltenburg

UPPER BAVARIA

Ulm

Zwiefalten

Augsburg

Freising

Riedlingen

Illertissen

Munich

Nymphenburg

Neudeck in der Au

Steinhausen

Berg am Laim

M O R A V I A

Überlingen

Ottobeuren

SWABIA

Andechs

Rott am Inn

Červený Hrádek

Constance

Lake
Constance

Steingaden

Die Wies

Weyarn

Diessen am Ammersee

Wessobrunn

Salzburg

0   20   40   60 miles
0   20 40 60 80 100 kilometres

Liechtenstein

Innsbruck

Vienna

Heiligenkreuz

Pressburg

Danube

U S T R I A

Buda Pest

0   100 miles   200 miles
0   100   200   300 kilometres

Map by Martin Lubikowski, ML Design 2022

ACKNOWLEDGEMENTS

I am most grateful to a number of people who have helped bring this book to fruition. Most importantly I received extraordinarily generous sponsorship from the Rainer Winkler Stiftung, as well as from Joanna Barnes, Daniel Katz, Stuart Lochhead, the Tomasso Brothers and Patricia Wengraf. Their munificence enabled me to pay for the illustrations, and this financial assistance has helped keep the retail price of the book somewhat lower than it might otherwise have been. Since I wanted it to be available for students, amongst others, this sponsorship has unquestionably shaped the book, which partly depends on the quality and profusion of the illustrations. My particular thanks to Johan van der Beke at Brepols who has been a great support throughout, helping to steer the publication through to completion.

I want to thank, too, colleagues in Britain, Austria, Germany and the United States whose comments and encouragement have been fundamental to my text reaching completion. Several patiently read through some of my text, answered queries and gave me much appreciated suggestions, as well as bibliographical pointers: Malcolm Baker, Jens Burk, Uta Coburger, Ann Compton, Dorothea Diemer, Katharina Hantschmann, Jutta Kappel, Hans-Ulrich Kessler, Patrick Lenaghan, Regine Marth, Jennifer Montagu, Petr Přibyl, Konrad Schlegel and David Wilson.

Many people assisted in my extensive searches for photographs and provided more general support for my research and writing. Berthold Kress not only donated his stunningly good photographs of sculptures in numerous churches in Bavaria, but shared with me his expert knowledge and appreciation of German baroque sculpture. I am especially grateful to Giedymin Jablonski, whose excellent photographs of Rauchmiller's sculptures in the Piastów Chapel at Legnica were crucial. Additionally I should like to thank Suzanne Bardgett, Joanna Barnes (who also helped sponsor the illustrations, as mentioned above), Maraike Bückling, Ulrike Fladerer, Maria Geppert, Josef Goryl, Alexandra Hanzl, Georg Hartmetz, Stephanie Herrmann, Joachim Hiltmann, Wolfgang Christian Huber, Christine Kitzlinger, Daniel Kofler, Iveta Kovaříková, Vojtěch Krátký Claudia Kryza-Gersch, Mariana Kučerová, Martin Lubikowski, Georg Laue, Anette Loesch, David Lown, Alison Luchs, Angelika Neumann, Joanna Norman, Annette Otterbach, Martin Pavlis, Nicholas Penny, Daniel Rimsl, Saskia Rupp, Abbot Johannes Schaber, Antje Scherner, Nicolas Schnall, Karin Schnell, Magdalena Schnöll, Jacques Schuhmacher Danuta Solowiej, Christian Theuerkauff (†), Thomas Throckmorton, Kate Tranter, Jeremy Warren, Julia Weber, Hugh Wedderburn, Matthias Weniger, Paul Williamson, Tom Windross and Matthew Winterbottom.

All of these colleagues generously shared their knowledge and expertise, without which I could not have achieved this book. Any errors are of course my own. Much was written during periods of lockdown when the COVID-19 pandemic was at its height in 2020 and 2021, and I should particularly like to mention Bill Dunn, who steadfastly supported and encouraged my work, as well as my family: Thomas and Jess, Isabella and Edward, and their respective children, Cassius, Arthur, Cecily and Clara, three of whom were born during the time I was working on this book.

Marjorie Trusted (aka Holly Trusted)
Duns Tew, October 2022

LIST OF ILLUSTRATIONS

Frontispiece

0.01 Detail of *Time* from Johann Bernhard Fischer von Erlach and Ferdinand Maximilian Brokoff, *Tomb of Count Johann Wenzel Wratislaw von Mitrowitz*, marble and limestone, signed and dated 1716. Church of St James the Greater, Prague. Photo: Josef Goryl.

Introduction

0.1 Ignaz Günther, *St Joachim*, painted limewood, 1765-72 (once part of an altarpiece), height 179 cm. Bayerisches Nationalmuseum, Munich (inv. no. 55/168). Photo: Bastian Krack.

0.2 Interior of the Marienmünster church at Diessen am Amersee, Bavaria, designed by Johann Michael Fischer, 1732 onwards. Photo: Image Professionals GmbH / Alamy Stock Photo.

0.3 Interior of St Mary's Cathedral and St Corbinian, Freising, Bavaria, thirteenth-century structure renovated in 1724 by Cosmas Damian Asam and Egid Quirin Asam. Photo: imageBROKER / Alamy Stock Photo.

0.4 Adam Lenckhardt, *Apollo Flaying Marsyas*, ivory, 1644, height 27.2 cm. Bayerisches Nationalmuseum, Munich (inv. no. 92/145). Photo: Walter Haberland.

Chapter 1

1.1 Hubert Gerhard, *Augustus Fountain*, bronze, 1589-94. Maximilianstrasse, Augsburg. Photo: B. O'Kane / Alamy Stock Photo.

1.2 Hubert Gerhard, *St Michael*, bronze, 1588. Church of St Michael, Munich. Photo: Vladislav Gajic / Alamy Stock Photo.

1.3 East end of the church of SS. Ulrich and Afra, Augsburg, showing Hans Degler's three altarpieces and Hans Reichle's bronze crucifix. Photo: Mauritius images GmbH / Alamy Stock Photo.

1.4 Hans Degler, High Altarpiece, painted and gilt limewood, signed and dated 1604. Church of SS. Ulrich and Afra, Augsburg. Photo: imageBROKER / Alamy Stock Photo.

1.5 Tilman Riemenschneider, Altarpiece of the *Assumption of the Virgin* (the *Marienaltar*), limewood, c. 1505-10. Church of Our Lord, Creglingen. Photo: Azoor Photo Collection / Alamy Stock Photo.

1.6 Detail of Degler, South Altarpiece [1.8], the *Resurrected Christ*

1.7 Hans Degler, North altarpiece dedicated to St Afra (*Pentecost*), painted and gilt limewood, 1607. Church of SS. Ulrich and Afra, Augsburg. Photo: B. O'Kane / Alamy Stock Photo.

1.8 Hans Degler, South altarpiece dedicated to St Ulrich (*The Resurrection*), painted and gilt limewood, 1607. Church of SS. Ulrich and Afra, Augsburg. Photo:B. O'Kane / Alamy Stock Photo.

1.9 Hans Degler, Pulpit, painted and gilt limewood, 1608. Church of SS. Ulrich and Afra, Augsburg. Photo: B. O'Kane / Alamy Stock Photo.

1.10 Detail of Degler, High Altarpiece [1.4], *The Nativity*. Photo: Nicolas Schnall pba.

1.11 Christoph Rodt, High Altarpiece, polychromed and gilt wood, 1604. Church of St Martin, Illertissen. Photo: Josef Seitz.

1.12 Detail of Rodt, High Altarpiece [1.11], *The Coronation of the Virgin*. Photo: Josef Seitz.

1.13 Hubert Gerhard (gilder Johann Müller; caster Carlo di Cesari del Pelagio), *Seated Prophet* from the Fugger altarpiece, gilt bronze, c. 1581-4, height 23.8 cm. Victoria and Albert Museum, London (inv. no. A. 28-1964). Photo: Photo: Victoria and Albert Museum.

1.14 Jörg Zürn, High Altarpiece, limewood, 1613-16. St Nicholas Minster at Überlingen. Photo: INTERFOTO / Alamy Stock Photo.

1.15 Detail of Zürn, High Altarpiece, Überlingen [1.14], *The Nativity*. Photo: INTERFOTO / Alamy Stock Photo.

1.16 Cornelis Floris, *Decorative Ornament*, etching and engraving, dated 1557, 20.7 × 30.5 cm. National Gallery of Art, Washington DC., Ailsa Mellon Bruce Fund (inv. no. 1971.67.5). Photo: Photo: National Gallery of Art Washington DC.

1.17 Hans Morinck, *Throne of Mercy*, stone, c. 1612. Badisches Landesmuseum Karlsruhe (inv. no. C 3247). Photo: Thomas Goldschmidt.

1.18 Hans Reichle, Crucifixion group, bronze, 1605, cast by Wolfgang Neidhart the Younger. Church of SS. Ulrich and Afra, Augsburg. Photo: Nicolas Schnall pba.

1.19 Detail of Reichle, Crucifixion group [1.18], crucifix. Photo: Nicolas Schnall pba.

1.20 Detail of Reichle, Crucifixion group [1.18], Mary Magdalene and the Virgin. Photo: Nicolas Schnall pba.

1.21 Hans Reichle, *Mary Magdalene*, bronze, 1595. Church of St Michael, Munich. Photo: Markus Huber.

2.17 Artus Quellinus the Elder, *Goblet with the Birth of Venus*, ivory with silver gilt mounts, height 13.2 cm. Musées royaux d'Art et d'Histoire, Brussels (inv. no. 29). Photo: Creative Commons CC BY– MRAH/KMKG.

2.18 Matthias Rauchmiller, *Duke Georg Wilhelm von Liegnitz-Wohlau*, alabaster, after 1677. Piastów Chapel, church of St John the Baptist, Legnica. Photo: Giedymin Jablonski.

2.19 Matthias Rauchmiller, *Princess Charlotte von Liegnitz-Wohlau*, alabaster, after 1677. Piastów Chapel, church of St John the Baptist, Legnica. Photo: Giedymin Jablonski.

2.20 Matthias Rauchmiller and others, The Trinity at the top of the *Pestsaule* (Plague Column), gilt bronze and marble, 1694. Graben, Vienna. Photo: Hervé Champollion / akg-images.

2.21 Matthias Rauchmiller and others, *Pestsaule* (Plague Column), detail of marble figures, 1694. Graben, Vienna. Photo: Hervé Champollion / akg-images.

2.22 Matthias Steinl, *Allegory of the Elements: Water and Air*, walrus tusk, c. 1688, height 43.4 cm. Kunsthistorisches Museum, Vienna (inv. no. KK 4533). Photo: Kunsthistorisches Museum, Vienna.

2.23 Jacob Auer, *Apollo and Daphne*, ivory, c. 1688/90, height 43.9 cm. Kunsthistorisches Museum, Vienna (inv. no. KK 4537). Photo: Kunsthistorisches Museum, Vienna.

2.24 Matthias Steinl, *Emperor Leopold I Conquering a Turk*, ivory on wood base, c. 1690/93, height 74 cm. Kunsthistorisches Museum, Vienna (inv. no. KK 4662). Photo: Kunsthistorisches Museum, Vienna.

2.25 Matthias Steinl, *King Joseph I Overcoming a Fury*, ivory on wood base, signed and dated 1693, height 70.8 cm. Kunsthistorisches Museum, Vienna (inv. no. KK 4663). Photo: Kunsthistorisches Museum, Vienna.

2.26 Matthias Steinl, *Emperor Charles VI with the Personification of the Holy Roman Empire*, ivory on wood base, c. 1711/12, height 73.7 cm. Kunsthistorisches Museum, Vienna (inv. no. KK 4664). Photo: Kunsthistorisches Museum, Vienna.

2.27 Andreas Schlüter, *Head of a Dying Warrior*, stone, 1696-7. Armoury, Berlin. Photo: Ulrich Schwarz.

2.28 Andreas Schlüter, *Head of a Dying Warrior*, stone, 1696-7. Armoury, Berlin. Photo: Ulrich Schwarz.

2.29 Andreas Schlüter, *Equestrian Monument to the Great Elector, Frederick William*, bronze, designed 1696, cast 1700, installed 1703, as seen c. 1900 on the Lange Brücke, Berlin. Photo: Levy / akg-images.

2.30 Andreas Schlüter, *Equestrian Monument to the Great Elector, Frederick William*, bronze, designed 1696, cast 1700, installed 1703. Schloss Charlottenburg, Berlin. Photo: John Clark / Alamy Stock photo.

2.31 Schlüter, *Equestrian Monument* [2.29], detail of chained slaves. Photo: Eye Ubiquitous / Alamy Stock Photo.

2.32 Andreas Schlüter, *Tomb of Daniel Männlich and his Wife*, marble and bronze, c. 1701. Church of St Nicholas, Berlin. Photo: Markus Hilbich.

2.33 Andreas Schlüter, *Pulpit*, wood, sandstone and alabaster, 1703. Church of St Mary, Berlin. Photo: Yvan Travert / akg-images.

Chapter 3

3.1 Giovanni Maria Nosseni, Carlo di Cesare del Palagio and others, *The Wettin Burial Chapel in the Choir of Freiberg Cathedral*, 1590-3. Photo: akg-images / Bildarchiv Monheim.

3.2 Augustus I Elector of Saxony, *Turned covered beaker*, ivory, signed 'AHVCZS' (Augustus Herzog und Churfürst zu Sachsen), before 1586, height 17.2 cm. Grünes Gewölbe, Staatliche Kunstsammlungen Dresden (inv. no. II. 65). Photo: Jürgen Karpinski.

3.3 Jacob Zeller, *The Great Frigate*, ivory, signed and dated 1620, height 51 cm. Grünes Gewölbe, Staatliche Kunstsammlungen Dresden (inv. no. II. 107). Photo: Jürgen Karpinski.

3.4 Balthasar Permoser, *Apollo Flaying Marsyas*, ivory, c. 1680, height 17.5 cm, width 10.5 cm. Herzog Anton Ulrich-Museum, Braunschweig (inv. no. EL 233). Photo: bpk / Herzog Anton Ulrich-Museum / C. Cordes.

3.5 Francis van Bossuit, *Apollo Flaying Marsyas*, ivory, c. 1680, height 21.1 cm, width 11.5 cm. Thomson Collection, on long term loan to the Art Gallery of Ontario, Toronto (inv. no. AGO ID 29173). Photo: Art Gallery of Ontario Toronto.

3.6 Balthasar Permoser, *Princess Violante-Beatrice of Bavaria*, ivory in silver gilt frame, 1689, height 10.5 cm, width 7.8 cm (with frame). Museo degli Argenti, Palazzo Pitti, Florence (inv. Bargello 1879 no. 80). Photo: Fratelli Alinari.

3.7 Balthasar Permoser, *Anthony Ulrich, Duke of Brunswick-Lüneburg*, marble, c. 1630/5, height 99.5 cm, with socle. Herzog Anton Ulrich-Museum, Braunschweig (inv. no. Ste 4). Photo: bpk / Herzog Anton Ulrich-Museum / C. Cordes.

3.8 Balthasar Permoser, *The Four Seasons*, ivory, signed and dated 1695, height 22/24 cm. Herzog Anton Ulrich-Museum, Braunschweig (inv. nos. Elf 78, Elf 79, Elf 821, Elf 822). Photo: bpk / Herzog Anton Ulrich-Museum / C. Cordes.

3.9 Johann Melchior Dinglinger and Balthasar Permoser, *Diana's Bath*, ivory, chalcedony, silver, steel, enamel, diamonds and pearls, 1704, height 38 cm. Grünes Gewölbe, Staatliche Kunstsammlungen Dresden (inv. no. VIII. 305). Photo: Jürgen Karpinski.

3.10 Detail of Dinglinger and Permoser, *Diana's Bath* [3.9], ivory; *Diana and Putto* by Permoser.

3.11 Matthäus Daniel Pöppelmann, Balthasar Permoser and others, *The Zwinger*, Dresden, sandstone, 1710-18. Photo: Maciej Bledowski / Alamy Stock Photo.

3.12 Balthasar Permoser, *Ceres on the Kronentor*, sandstone, 1714/15. Zwinger, Dresden. Photo: Wiki Commons.

3.13 Balthasar Permoser with assistants, *Herms on the Wallpavilion*, sandstone, copies after the originals of 1717-19. Zwinger, Dresden. Photo: demonabikeGermany / Alamy Stock Photo.

3.14 Balthasar Permoser, *The Apotheosis of Prince Eugene of Savoy*, marble, 1718-21, height 230 cm. Österreichische Galerie Belvedere, Vienna (inv. no. 4219). Photo: © Fritz Simak, Vienna.

3.15 Balthasar Permoser, *Christ at the Column*, marble, 1728, height 79.5 cm. Staatliche Kunstsammlungen, Dresden (inv. nr. ZV 4090). Photo: © Staatliche Kunstsammlungen Dresden (Hans-Peter Klut / Elke Estel).

3.16 Detail of Permoser, *Christ at the Column* [3.15], Permoser's signature and self portrait.

3.17 Johann Christoph Ludwig Lücke, *Poltrone*, terracotta, monogrammed and dated 1729, height 11.4 cm, width 7.1 cm. Museum für Kunst und Gewerbe, Hamburg (inv. no. 1928. 213). Photo: Photo: Museum für Kunst und Gewerbe, Hamburg.

3.18 Johann Christoph Ludwig Lücke, *Poltrone*, ivory on wood socle, c. 1730, height 10.5 cm (ivory alone). Victoria and Albert Museum, London (inv. no. A. 17-1949). Photo: Victoria and Albert Museum.

3.19 Johann Christoph Ludwig Lücke, *King George II*, ivory, signed and dated 1760, height 18.7 cm, width 14 cm. Victoria and Albert Museum, London (inv. no. A. 18-1932). Photo: Victoria and Albert Museum.

3.20 Paul Egell, *Nymph*, sandstone, 1717/18, height c. 250 cm. The Zwinger, Dresden. Photo: annete / Alamy Stock Photo.

3.21 Gabriel Grupello, *Equestrian Monument to Elector John William*, bronze, c. 1703-13. Düsseldorf, Marketplace. Photo: Panther Media GmbH / Alamy Stock Photo.

3.22 Ignaz Elhafen, *The Childhood of Jupiter*, ivory, c. 1697-1705/10, height 10.1 cm, width 19.8 cm. Victoria and Albert Museum, London (inv. no. A.49-1949). Photo: Victoria and Albert Museum.

3.23a and b Paul Egell, *Satyr Heads*, sandstone, c. 1729/30, height c. 70 cm. Mannheim Palace. Photo: © Reiss-Engelhorn-Museen Mannheim (Germany).

3.24 Paul Egell, *The Trinity*, sandstone, 1727-30, height 430 cm, width 1460 cm. Church at Mannheim Palace. Photo: MARCHIVUM, Image Collection, ABKS01378; Photographer: Keese / Steiger.

3.25 Paul Egell, *Sorrowing Children (Adam and Eve after the Fall)*, gilded limewood, height 950 cm. Formerly from the High Altarpiece of the Catholic church of St Sebastian, Mannheim, now the Bode Museum, Berlin (inv. no. 8443). 3.25 Bode Museum, Berlin.

3.26 Paul Egell, *The Lamentation, or Allegory of the Redemption from Sin*, ivory in pearwood frame, c. 1723-5, height 18.5 cm, width 10.8 cm (ivory alone); height 26 cm, width 18.5 cm (frame). Museum für Angewandte Kunst, Cologne (inv. no. B 73). Copyright: Rheinisches Bildarchiv,

rba_c003608. Photo: Rheinisches Bildarchiv.

3.27 Paul Egell, *Christ as Man of Sorrows*, ivory, c. 1740-50, height 24.7 cm. Museum für Kunst und Gewerbe, Hamburg (inv. no. 1960.50). Photo: Joachim Hiltmann.

3.28 Paul Egell, *St Ignatius Loyola and St Francis Xavier*, limewood, 1744, height 73.5 cm, width 59 cm (without frame). Liebieghaus Frankfurt am Main, on permanent loan from the Historisches Museum, Frankfurt am Main (inv. no. X 1902). Photo: © Liebieghaus Skulpturensammlung.

Chapter 4

4.1 Johann Michael Fischer (architect), Interior of the church of St John Nepomuk (known as the Asamkirche), Munich, 1733-46. View towards the east end. Photo: Bildagentur-online/Moreno / Alamy Stock Photo.

4.2 Balthasar Ableithner, *St Mark*, painted wood (the paint restored), 1670/3. Church of St Kayetan (Theatine church), Munich. Photo: Dorothea Diemer.

4.3 Andreas Faistenberger, *The Annunciation*, silvered and gilt wood, 1710-11. Burgher's Hall (Bürgersaal), Munich. Photo: Siegfried Wameser, Munich.

4.4 Egid Quirin Asam, *The Assumption of the Virgin*, painted and gilt stucco, 1717/23. Benedictine Abbey of Rohr, Bavaria. Photo: Image Professionals GmbH/Alamy Stick Photo.

4.5 Detail of Asam, *Assumption of the Virgin* [4.4], the Virgin. Photo: Image Professionals GmbH / Alamy Stock Photo.

4.6 Detail of Asam, *Assumption of the Virgin* [4.4], Apostles. Photo: Image Professionals GmbH / Alamy Stock Photo.

4.7 Egid Quirin Asam, *St George and the Dragon*, painted and gilt stucco *in situ*, 1734-6. Benedictine Abbey of Weltenburg, Bavaria. Photo: Bildarchiv Monheim GmbH / Alamy Stock Photo.

4.8 Egid Quirin Asam, *St George and the Dragon* [closer view of 4.7]. Photo: Bildarchiv Monheim GmbH / Alamy Stock Photo.

4.9 Egid Quirin Asam, *St George and the Dragon* with *St Martin* and *St Maurus* (closer view of 4.7). Photo: Bildarchiv Monheim GmbH / Alamy Stock Photo.

4.10 Egid Quirin Asam, *Portrait of Cosmas Damian Asam*, painted stucco, c. 1736. Benedictine Abbey of Weltenburg, Bavaria. Photo: imageBROKER / Alamy Stock Photo.

4.11 Egid Quirin Asam, *St Jerome*, painted stucco, c. 1735-40. Church of St John Nepomuk (known as the Asamkirche), Munich, looking towards the east end. Photo: Davidzfr / Alamy Stock Photo.

4.12 Ignaz Günther, *Epitaph to Johann Nepomuk Joseph Freiherr von Zech*, gilt wood and stone, c. 1758. Entrance Lobby of the church of St John Nepomuk (known as the Asamkirche), Munich. Photo: John Warburton-Lee Photography / Alamy Stock Photo.

4.13 Johann Michael Fischer (architect), Interior of the church of St John Nepomuk (known as the Asamkirche), Munich, 1733-46. View towards the west end [see also 4.1]. Photo: Sueddeutsche Zeitung Photo / Alamy Stock Photo.

4.14 East end of the church of St John Nepomuk (known as the Asamkirche), Munich showing Egid Quirin Asam's *The Trinity or Throne of Mercy*, gilt and silvered stucco, c. 1735-40. Photo: Carol Barrington / Alamy Stock Photo.

4.15 François de Cuvilliés the Elder and Johann Baptist Zimmermann, interior decoration of the Amalienburg, coloured stucco, 1734-9. Park at Nymphenburg, near Munich. Photo: Menigault Bernard / Alamy Stock Photo.

4.16 Dominikus and Johann Baptist Zimmermann, Interior view of the pilgrimage church of St Peter and St Paul (dedicated also to the Virgin of Sorrows), 1727-33, Steinhausen, Bavaria. Photo: imageBROKER / Alamy Stock Photo.

4.17 Dominikus and Johann Baptist Zimmermann, *The Assumption of the Virgin* (detail), fresco and stucco, dated 1731. Church of St Peter and St Paul, Steinhausen, Bavaria. Photo: INTERFOTO / Alamy Stock Photo.

4.18 Dominikus Zimmermann, Herms under the organ loft, stucco, c. 1730-3. Church of St Peter and St Paul, Steinhausen, Bavaria. Photo: Matthias Weniger.

4.19 Dominikus and Johann Baptist Zimmermann, interior view of the pilgrimage church of Die Wies, 1745-54. Steingaden, Bavaria. Photo: Angelo Hornak / Alamy Stock Photo. ˉWieskirche to be decided Photo:

© Wolfgang Filser Panther Media GmbH / Alamy Stock Photo]

4.20 Anton Sturm, *St Jerome*, wood, 1753/6. Church of Die Wies, Steingaden. Photo: Berthold Kress; photographed by kind permission of the parish.

4.21 Aegid Verhelst, *St John*, wood, 1748/9. Church of Die Wies, Steingaden. Photo: Berthold Kress; photographed by kind permission of the parish.

4.22 Dominikus Zimmermann (designer), carving attributed to Palier Pontian Steinhauser; polychromed and gilded by Bernhard Ramis and Judas Thaddäus Ramis, *Pulpit*, wood, c. 1750-54. Church of Die Wies, Steingaden. Photo: Bildarchiv Monheim GmbH / Alamy Stock Photo.

Chapter 5

5.1 West front of the church of Our Lady at Zwiefalten, Baden-Württemberg, 1750-3, designed by Johann Michael Fischer, sculpture by Johann Joseph Christian. Photo: Mauritius images GmbH / Alamy Stock Photo.

5.2 Interior of the church of Our Lady at Zwiefalten, Baden-Württemberg, c. 1747-73, designed by Johann Michael Fischer, sculpture by Johann Joseph Christian, stucco by Johann Michael Feichtmayr. Photo: Johannes Oehl / Alamy Stock Photo.

5.3 Johann Joseph Christian and Johann Michael Feichtmayr, *Ezekiel with God the Father and Angels*, painted and gilt wood and stucco, c. 1749-67, pulpit on the north pillar at the east end of the nave. Church of Our Lady at Zwiefalten, Baden-Württemberg. Photo: © Bildarchiv Foto Marburg / Erika Groth-Schmachtenberger.

5.4 Detail of the prophet Ezekiel on the north pillar at Zwiefalten [5.3]. Photo: © Bildarchiv Foto Marburg / Helga Schmidt-Glassner.

5.5 Interior of the Benedictine abbey at Ottobeuren, Bavaria, c.1748-67, designed by Johann Michael Fischer, sculpture by Johann Joseph Christian, stucco by Johann Michael Feichtmayr. Photo: akg-images / Bildarchiv Monheim.

5.6 Johann Joseph Christian and Johann Michael Feichtmayr, Font with *The Baptism*, painted and gilt wood and stucco, c. 1756-66. North transept of the Benedictine abbey at Ottobeuren, Bavaria. Photo: Berthold Kress by kind permission of the abbey.

5.7 Johann Joseph Christian and Johann Michael Feichtmayr, Pulpit with *The Transfiguration*, painted and gilt wood and stucco, c. 1756-66. West side of the nave of the Benedictine abbey at Ottobeuren, Bavaria. Photo: akg-images / Erich Lessing.

5.8 Johann Baptist Straub, *Diana Sleigh* (detail of putto blowing a horn), painted wood, c. 1737-45. Stables (Marstall) Museum, Schloss Nymphenburg. Photo: akg-images / Bildarchiv Monheim.

5.9 Johann Baptist Straub (attributed), *Atlante (Herm)*, painted and gilt wood, 1753, under the Elector's Box. Residenz Theatre (Cuvilliés Theatre), Munich. Photo: © Bayerische Schlösserverwaltung, Philipp Mansmann, Munich.

5.10 François de Cuvilliés the Elder (designer), carved by Joseph Joachim Dietrich, *High Altarpiece*, painted and gilt wood, c. 1738. Church of the Assumption of the Virgin, Diessen am Ammersee. Photo: Süddeutsche Zeitung Photo / Alamy Stock Photo.

5.11 Joseph Joachim Dietrich, *St Ambrosius* and *St Jerome*, painted and gilt wood, c. 1738. High Altarpiece, church of the Assumption of the Virgin, Diessen am Ammersee [detail of 5.10]. Photo: akg-images.

5.12 Johann Baptist Straub, *Altarpiece dedicated to St Sebastian*, with painting by Giovanni Battista Tiepolo, dated 1739 Frame and figures of *St Thomas* and *St Matthew* painted and gilt wood. Church of the Assumption of the Virgin, Diessen am Ammersee. Photo: Berthold Kress, by kind permission of the church.

5.13 Johann Baptist Straub, *Pulpit*, painted and gilt wood, c. 1738-40. Church of the Assumption of the Virgin, Diessen am Ammersee. Photo: Berthold Kress, by kind permission of the church.

5.13a Johann Baptist Straub, *St Paul* at the apex of the pulpit [detail of 5.13]. Photo: Berthold Kress, by kind permission of the church.

5.14 Johann Baptist Straub, High Altar with *God the Father on the Globe*, painted and gilt wood, c. 1767. Church of St Michael, Berg am Laim. Photo: The Warburg Institute Iconographic Database; photographed by kind permission of the parish.

5.15 Johann Baptist Straub, *God the Father on the Globe* [detail of 5.13]. Photo: Berthold Kress; photographed by kind permission of the parish.

5.16 Johann Baptist Straub, *God the Father on the Globe*, painted terracotta, c. 1750/5, height 29.5 cm. Bode Museum, Berlin (inv. no. 7068). Photo: Bode Museum, Berlin.

5.17 Johann Baptist Straub, *Mars*, terracotta, c. 1772, height 45.3 cm. Bayerisches Nationalmuseum, Munich (inv. no. R 7817). Photo: Bayerisches Nationalmuseum, Munich.

5.18 Ignaz Günther (after Paul Egell), *St John the Baptist*, limewood relief, signed and dated 1751, height 16.8 cm. Bayerisches Nationalmuseum, Munich (inv.no. 20/16). Photo: Bastian Krack.

5.19 Ignaz Günther, *Design for the High Altarpiece at Berg am Laim*, graphite and wash, 1760, height 64.2 cm, width 41 cm. Staatliche Graphische Sammlung, Munich (inv. no. 14605). Photo: © Staatliche Graphische Sammlung München.

5.20 Ignaz Günther (workshop), *Squeeze after a Model for Ornamentation on a bell. Crucifix with Two Putti*, terracotta, before 1770, height 27.5 cm, width 20.8 cm. Bayerisches Nationalmuseum, Munich (inv. no. 13/262). Photo: Bayerisches Nationalmuseum, Munich.

5.21 Ignaz Günther, *Crucifixion with Two Mourning Putti*, painted wood, before 1770. Bayerisches Nationalmuseum, Munich (inv. no. 2017/118.1-2). Photo: Bayerisches Nationalmuseum, Munich.

5.22 Ignaz Günther, *Model for Starnberg Female Saint*, limewood, 1755, height 20.9 cm. Bayerisches Nationalmuseum, Munich (inv. no. H 724). Photo: Bayerisches Nationalmuseum, Munich.

5.23 Ignaz Günther, *Female Saint*, painted limewood, signed and dated 1755, height 155 cm. Museum Starnberger See, Starnberg (inv.no. L 73/207). Photo: Bayerisches Nationalmuseum, Munich.

5.24 Johann Michael Fischer, Interior of the Benedictine church of Rott am Inn, Bavaria, with stucco work by Jakob Rauch, 1759 onwards. Photo: ImageBROKER / Alamy Stock Photo.

5.25 Matthäus Günther, *The Glory of the Benedictine Order* on the central dome of the church of Rott am Inn, fresco, c. 1765-7. Benedictine church of Rott am Inn, Bavaria. Photo: imageBROKER / Alamy Stock Photo.

5.26 Interior of the Benedictine church at Rott am Inn, c. 1761-5. Benedictine church of Rott am Inn, Bavaria. Photo: Westend61 GmbH / Alamy Stock Photo.

6.17 Matthias Bernhard Braun, *St Luke*, stone painted white, after 1715. Church of St Clement, Prague. Photo: © Jitka Walterová – Institute of Art History of the Czech Academy of Sciences.

6.18 Copies made 1980-88 of Matthias Bernhard Braun, *Figures of Virtues and Vices*, after the sandstone originals of c.1719. Hospital at Kuks. Photo: Frank 11 Alamy/Stock photo.

6.19 Matthias Bernhard Braun, *Envy*, sandstone, c. 1719. Hospital at Kuks. Photo: Jan Pavlíček.

6.20 Matthias Bernhard Braun, *St Hubert*, sandstone, 1726. Bethlehem Wood near Kuks. Photo: Jan Pavlíček.

6.21 Matthias Bernhard Braun, *St Onuphrius*, sandstone, 1726. Bethlehem Wood near Kuks. Photo: Jan Pavlíček.

6.22 Matthias Bernhard Braun, *St Garin*, sandstone, 1726. Bethlehem Wood near Kuks. Photo: Jan Pavlíček.

6.23 Matthias Bernhard Braun, *Tomb of Anna Miselius*, sandstone, c. 1722-3. Cemetery at Jaroměř. Photo: Dr. Iveta Kovaříková.

6.24 Matthias Bernhard Braun, *Tomb of Anna Miselius*, view of inscription. Photo: Dr. Iveta Kovaříková.

Chapter 7

7.1 Georg Raphael Donner, *The Pietà*, terracotta painted black, signed and dated 1721, height 36 cm. National Gallery, Prague (inv. no. P 5189). Photo: National Gallery Prague.

7.2 Georg Raphael Donner, *Mercury and Cupid*, lead, monogrammed 'R.D.', height 44.5 cm. Abbey Museum, Klosterneuburg (inv. no. KG 176). Photo: Michael Himml, Vienna.

7.3 François Du Quesnoy, *Mercury*, bronze, 1629/30. Schloss Vaduz, Liechtenstein Collection (inv. no. SK 611). Photo: © LIECHTENSTEIN. The Princely Collections, Vaduz-Vienna.

7.4 Georg Raphael Donner, *Paris*, marble, signed and dated 1726. Schloss Mirabell, Salzburg. Photo: Stadtarchiv Salzburg, Fotosammlung.

7.5 Georg Raphael Donner, *St Martin and the Beggar*, lead, 1735. Bratislava Cathedral. Photo: Bratislava Cathedral.

7.6 Georg Raphael Donner, *Providentia* (from the fountain formerly in the Flour Market/New Market, Vienna), lead, 1737-9 (signed and dated 1738), height

337 cm. Wien Museum, Vienna (inv. no. 145040/1). Photo: Birgit and Peter Lanz, Wien Museum.

7.7 Georg Raphael Donner, *The River Enns*, lead, 1739, height 207 cm, width 235 cm. Wien Museum, Vienna (inv. no. 145040/6). Photo: Birgit and Peter Lanz, Wien Museum.

7.8 Georg Raphael Donner, *Perseus and Andromeda*, lead, 1740/1. Old Town Hall, Vienna. Photo: akg-images / Erich Lessing.

7.9 Georg Raphael Donner, *Pietà*, lead, 1741. Gurk Cathedral. Photo: © Diözese Gurk – Stift Gurk / Marcel Peda.

7.10 Detail of Donner, *Pietà* [detail of 7.9]. Gurk Cathedral. Photo: © Diözese Gurk – Stift Gurk / P. Dietmar Hynek SDS.

7.11 Johann Joachim Kändler, *Heron with Small Carp in its Beak*, Meissen porcelain, 1731, height 62.9 cm. Staatliche Kunstsammlungen Dresden (inv. no. PE 685). © Porzellansammlung, Staatliche Kunstsammlungen Dresden. Photo: Adrian Sauer.

7.12 Johann Gottlieb Kirchner, *Bust of the Court Jester Joseph Fröhlich*, Meissen porcelain, c. 1730-3, height 53 cm. Staatliche Kunstsammlungen Dresden (inv. no. PE 247). © Porzellansammlung, Staatliche Kunstsammlungen Dresden. Photo: Adrian Sauer.

7.13 Johann Joachim Kändler, *Bust of the Court Jester Gottfried Schmiedel*, Meissen porcelain, 1739, height 48.5 cm. Staatliche Kunstsammlungen Dresden (inv. no. PE 248). © Porzellansammlung, Staatliche Kunstsammlungen Dresden. Photo: Adrian Sauer.

7.14 Johann Joachim Kändler, *St Peter* (part of the altar garniture made for the Japanese Palace, Dresden), Meissen porcelain, 1731, height 115.7 cm. Staatliche Kunstsammlungen Dresden (inv. no. PE 498). © Porzellansammlung, Staatliche Kunstsammlungen Dresden Photo: Adrian Sauer.

7.15 Johann Joachim Kändler, *St Peter* (part of the altar garniture made for Cardinal Albani), Meissen porcelain, 1737, height 48.4 cm. Staatliche Kunstsammlungen Dresden (inv. no. PE 131). © Porzellansammlung, Staatliche Kunstsammlungen Dresden. Photo: Adrian Sauer.

7.16 Johann Joachim Kändler, *Harlequin with Ram-Piper* (height 14.2 cm) and *Harlequin with a Goat as Bagpipes* (height 15 cm), Meissen porcelain, c. 1740.

Staatliche Kunstsammlungen Dresden (inv. nos. PE 114 and PE 118). © Porzellansammlung, Staatliche Kunstsammlungen Dresden. Photo: Herbert Jaeger.

7.17 Franz Anton Bustelli, *Count Sigismund von Haimhausen*, Nymphenburg porcelain partly coloured and gilt, c. 1761, height 45 cm. Bayerisches Nationalmuseum, Munich (inv. no. Ker 4369). Photo: Bayerisches Nationalmuseum, Munich.

7.18 Franz Anton Bustelli, *Courting Couple among the Ruins*, Nymphenburg porcelain partly coloured, c. 1760, height 26.4 cm. Bayerisches Nationalmuseum, Munich (inv. no. Ker 4205). Photo: Walter Haberland.

7.19 Ferdinand Tietz, *Mars*, sandstone, c. 1747-53, height 198 cm. Badisches Landesmuseum Karlsruhe (inv. no. 65/33). Photo: Peter Gaul.

7.20 Johann Balthasar Neumann with sculpture by Ferdinand Tietz, The High Altar of the church of St Paulinus, Trier, painted limewood and stucco, c. 1755-60. Photo: Michael Stubbs by kind permission of the church.

7.21 Ferdinand Tietz, *The Virgin of the Immaculate Conception* from the High Altar of the church of St Paulinus, Trier, painted limewood and stucco, c. 1755-60 [detail of 7.20]. Photo: Michael Stubbs, by kind permission of the church.

7.22 Ferdinand Tietz, *Parnassus Fountain*, sandstone, 1765-6 (restored 1958-61). Veitshöchheim Park, Würzburg. Photo: akg-images / Bildarchiv Monheim.

7.23 Ferdinand Tietz, *Saturn*, sandstone, 1765-8, height 160 cm. Formerly Veitshöchheim Park, Würzburg, now on loan from the Bayerisches Verwaltung der Staatlichen Schlösser, Gärten und Seen to the Museum für Franken in Würzburg (inv. no. 33000). Photo: Museum für Franken Staatliches Museum für Kunst- und Kulturgeschichte in Würzburg.

7.24 Ferdinand Tietz, *Female Bagpipe Player*, sandstone, 1765-6, height 165 cm. Formerly Veitshöchheim Park, Würzburg, now on loan from the Bayerisches Verwaltung der Staatlichen Schlösser, Gärten und Seen to the Museum für Franken in Würzburg (inv. no. 32993). Photo: Museum für Franken Staatliches Museum für Kunst- und Kulturgeschichte in Würzburg.

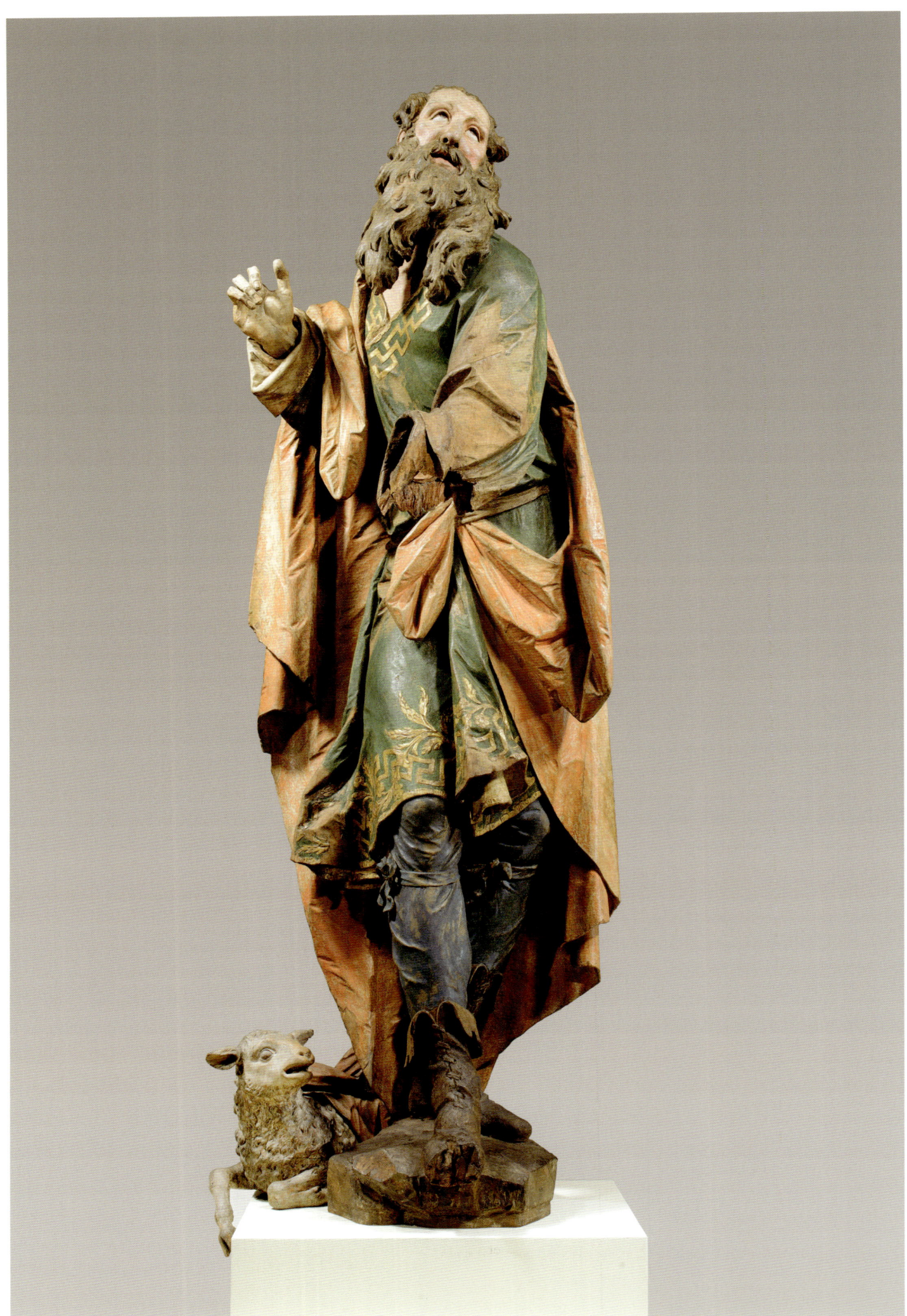

INTRODUCTION

Around 1600 a new style of sculpture began to evolve and flourish in the German-speaking lands. Dramatic wood and stone figures peopled the palaces, gardens and churches of Munich, Berlin, Dresden, Düsseldorf, Mannheim, Vienna and Prague. These great works of art are little known outside Germany and Austria, partly because their colour and vivacity are so astoundingly different from the sculpture that was being produced in Italy, France and Northern Europe at that time. Ignaz Günther's sculpture can be seen as exemplifying this style [0.1; see also Chapter 5]. This, despite the fact that the origins of the German and Central European baroque can on occasion stem from Italian, French and Netherlandish works.[1] German baroque sculptures are however amongst the greatest works of art produced in seventeenth- and eighteenth-century Europe. This book will describe some of them, looking at their contexts and history, focusing on the leading artists, and attempting to convey the compelling visual power of their works. It concentrates on sculptures made in Berlin, Dresden, Vienna, and above all in Munich and Bavaria, from about 1600 to 1770. Although German and Austrian baroque dominate the narrative outlined here, Central European sculpture is part of this story. These great Central European sculptures figure above all in those works of art made in Prague by Bohemian sculptors (see Chapter 6). Their work both complements and on occasion contrasts with the sculptures produced elsewhere in the Habsburg Empire and Bavaria.

Many profound ideas lie behind and within the forms of these sculptures, which frequently embody intense religious concepts, designed to appeal to worshippers and pilgrims. Those made for Catholic territories are brightly polychromed and gilt, expressing emotions in more forceful ways than contemporary Protestant images, in spectacular architectural settings, such as the church at Diessen am Ammersee in Bavaria [0.2; see Chapter 5]. It is no accident that we use a German word for an ensemble of works of art in different materials in one location, frequently created by different artists in one overarching scheme: a *Gesamtkunstwerk*. Baroque sculpture is theatrical, whether religious or secular. Strikingly realist marble portrait busts of German princes, swathed in dramatic classicizing drapery, were being executed, their expressiveness and movement indebted to Gian Lorenzo Bernini (1598-1680) and the Roman baroque. These likenesses form a vibrant counterpoint to the religious works of art that these self-same rulers, as well as abbots and prince-bishops, were commissioning.

Present-day Germany did not exist in the seventeenth and eighteenth centuries. But innumerable Germanic princely states flourished, the most important of which were Prussia, Saxony, Bavaria, Württemberg, Westphalia and Austria, as well as the Swiss Federation, and the kingdoms of Bohemia and Poland, which were interlinked in manifold ways to German dynasties (see map on pp. 7–8). The rulers of some of these territories were or became prince-electors, who could elect—or be elected—Holy Roman Emperor. The vast and multifaceted Holy Roman Empire (the *Sacrum Imperium*

0.1
Ignaz Günther, *St Joachim*, painted limewood, 1765-72 (once part of an altarpiece), height 179 cm. Bayerisches Nationalmuseum, Munich (inv. no. 55/168).

>> 0.2
Interior of the Marien-münster church at Diessen am Amersee, Bavaria, designed by Johann Michael Fischer, 1732 onwards.

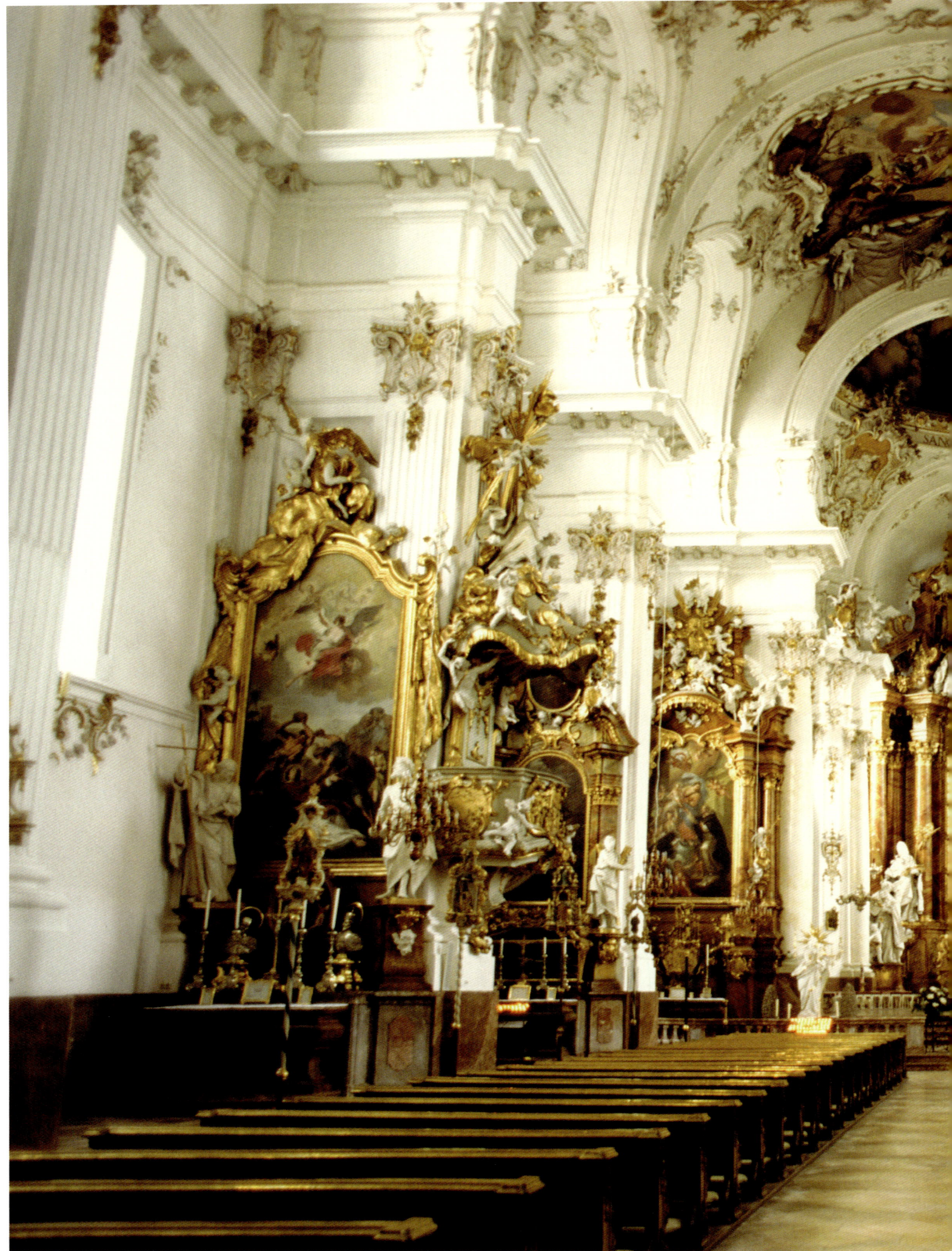

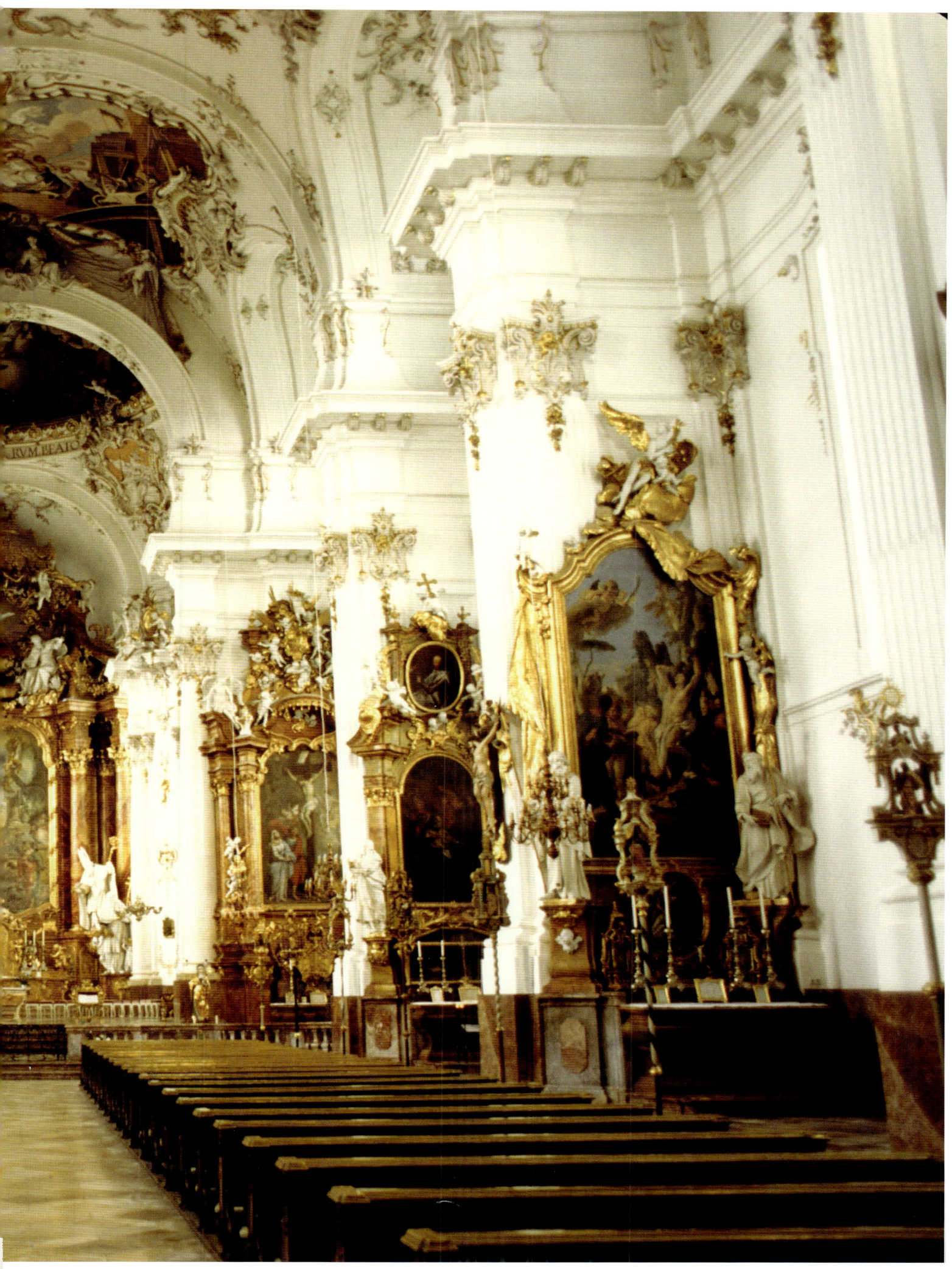

Romanum) was in existence from the middle ages until 1806, incorporating numerous separate countries. Powerful though it seemed, it lacked a stable heartland, a capital city, centralized political institutions or even a single nation. Its aims were to provide a stable political order for all Christians, and to defend them against heretics and infidels, the emperor being the chief advocate and guardian of the pope. Although the empire's origins could be traced back to Charlemagne (748-814), its college of prince-electors was only established in a Golden Bull of 1356.[2] Perhaps the most important area in terms of baroque sculpture was Bavaria, which itself comprised further territories in the eighteenth century: Upper Bavaria was centred on Munich and areas and towns along the upper reaches of the river Danube, including Freising and Rohr. Elsewhere in Bavaria the cities of Nuremberg (in Franconia), Augsburg (in Swabia) and Regensburg (in the Upper Palatinate) were Free Imperial Cities (under the direct rule of the Holy Roman Emperor). Meanwhile, Lower Bavaria was located in the east of the country, and bordered the Upper Palatinate in the north, South Bohemia (today the Czech Republic) in the northeast, Upper Austria (Innviertel, Mühlviertel) in the southeast, and Upper Bavaria in the southwest. The term 'Lower Bavaria' appeared for the first time in 1255 when the Bavarian state was divided.[3] Much later, Germany's modern borders were effectively created by Otto von Bismarck (1815-98) in 1871.[4] This book will focus on a few of the historical princely states, but will nevertheless on occasion use the term 'German' to apply to a range of German-speaking lands, when analysing some of the sculpture in other areas, notably Austria, Bohemia (today the Czech Republic) and Poland.

Stylistic Terms: Baroque and Rococo Sculpture

Baroque (*Barock* in German) is a helpful umbrella word for the style of sculpture executed/created during the period 1600-1770. This word is probably derived from the Portuguese 'barroco' or the Italian 'barocco', an irregular pearl, via the French 'baroque'.[5] It seems to have been first employed in the sixteenth century, when it was applied to jewellery. In the eighteenth century it was used in various French publications to describe music with dissonant harmonies, or when alluding to highly adorned architecture.[6] Although the adjective is now generally applied to European art and architecture or music of the seventeenth and eighteenth centuries, its meaning—implying something irregular, flamboyant, dramatic and decorative—can extend beyond chronological parameters, to art or music produced before or after that period. Moreover, while the term baroque can be applied to art of the early seventeenth century, without question in the mid-seventeenth century there was a fracture in artistic output in Germany caused by the Thirty Years' War (1618-48) [see especially Chapter 3]. Sculpture produced in Germany before this violent hiatus is inextricably connected with European mannerism, notably the art of the Netherlands, whereas after about 1650 it evolved in the wake of Bernini's sculpture and architecture in seventeenth-century Rome, reaching its peak in the eighteenth century. The later flowering of the baroque is thus closely associated with artistic currents emanating from Rome in the late seventeenth and early eighteenth century.

German art of the mid- to late eighteenth century also embraces the rococo. Rococo (*Rokoko* in German) was a term first used in the nineteenth century pejoratively, and is derived from the French 'rocaille', pebble or shell work.[7] Rococo sculpture and rococo engravings regularly incorporate decorative features such as rocks, shells, scrolls and falling water.[8] While baroque art is considered weighty and solemn, rococo art is deemed to be light and airy, even frivolous and brittle.[9] Possibly somewhat paradoxically, the evolution of German sculpture in the eighteenth century means that these styles overlap, and the term baroque can and should on occasion incorporate the rococo. French influence seen in much Bavarian sculpture and architecture of the mid- to late eighteenth century is more allied with the rococo of Versailles and art at the court of Louis XV (1710-74), as well as the art produced during the previous reign of Louis XIV (1638-1715).

Sculpture and architecture in Mannheim, Dresden, Munich and elsewhere became imbued with the spirit of French art as the eighteenth century progressed. The exile of Maximilian II Emmanuel (1662-1726), the Elector of Bavaria, at the court in France from 1706 to 1714 during the War of Spanish Succession was a crucial factor in this development of art in Bavaria. The elector brought back to Munich leading artists who had worked at the French court, including François de Cuvilliés the Elder (1695-1768) and Guillielmus (Wilhelm) de Grof (1676-1742). These artists introduced architectural and decorative styles and forms that were to inspire contemporary and later sculptors in Germany (see below and Chapter 5).

This mingling of styles means that it can be somewhat problematic to establish what is baroque and what is rococo during the eighteenth century. Arguably it is ultimately sterile to define and distinguish the two terms baroque and rococo too rigidly; a study of seventeenth- and eighteenth-century sculpture that excluded the work of the later period would be truncated.[10] Much of the art of the 1680s up to the 1720s heralds the later period and cannot be divorced from it. This study will therefore incorporate what is notionally rococo as well as baroque sculpture, and the word baroque may on occasion comprise the rococo.

Adding a further layer of intricacy, some have argued that while the sculpture of the seventeenth century in Germany and Austria evolved from mannerism, at the same time baroque sculpture formed an unbroken tradition with the gothic and medieval. Indeed, baroque and gothic winged carved wood altarpieces and individual figures alike share an angular style, conveying emotions both devout and expressionistic.[11] The winged altarpiece is a fundamental element in church architecture and decoration throughout the baroque period, drawing on earlier traditions. But unlike the antecedent medieval structures, baroque and rococo altarpieces are fully and powerfully integrated into the architecture, stucco, murals and paintings within church interiors, such as those at the Cathedral of St Mary and St Corbinian in Friesing, renovated in 1724 by the Asam

brothers [0.3, on which see Chapter 4]. As indicated above, by the first half of the eighteenth century this notion of *Gesamtkunstwerk* (total work of art) had become fundamental to the art produced in Germany and Austria. Churches such as those at Berg am Laim, Ottobeuren or Diessen am Ammersee typify this integrated virtuosity, incorporating sculpture, architecture and decoration harmoniously and indissolubly.

'Sculpture' seems to be a less ambiguous term, free of the potentially confusing geographical history of Germany's borders, or the manifold etymological roots of the baroque and its relation to gothic or the rococo. But it is useful to clarify at the outset what forms of art are covered here, and at the same time what is conceived of as sculpture. German sculptures made during this period were often of wood, whether painted, gilded or monochrome. But they might also be terracotta, stone (including marble), stucco, bronze, lead, iron, ivory or amber. Moreover, many of the churches were furnished with elaborate architectural decorations, as well as items such as pulpits, lecterns or choirstalls, which are undeniably sculptural. Sculptors frequently produced such objects, in addition to designing or making models for ceramics, medals, silver and church bells, such as Ignaz Günther's models for church bells [see Chapter 5; 5.20]. The extensive range of these plastic works means that the term sculpture can cover a wide gamut of objects made for churches and palaces. Examining properly such a broad array of art is regrettably beyond the scope of this book, and so most of the sculptures examined here in any depth will be of wood, stone, bronze, stucco or ivory. Such sculpture must also inevitably be studied in its architectural context, although architecture as such will not be the focal point of this book. I have, however, included a brief discussion of ceramic sculptures from Meissen and Nymphenburg in Chapter 7.

The Historical Context

The patronage and taste of both secular rulers and senior churchmen inevitably informed the sculpture and architecture of palaces and churches. Wider historical European events

>> 0.3
Interior of St Mary's Cathedral and St Corbinian, Freising, Bavaria, thirteenth-century structure renovated in 1724 by Cosmas Damian Asam and Egid Quirin Asam.

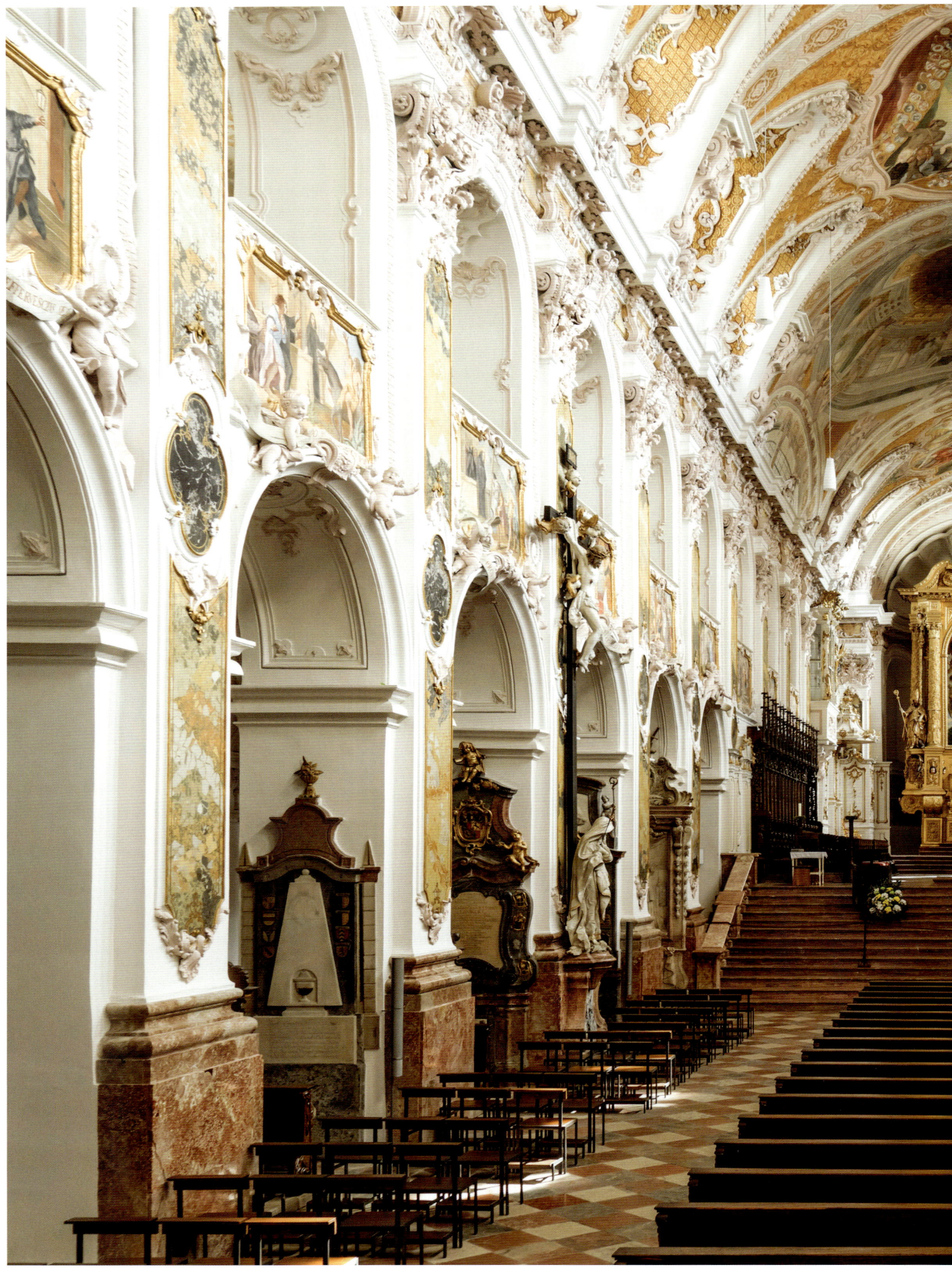

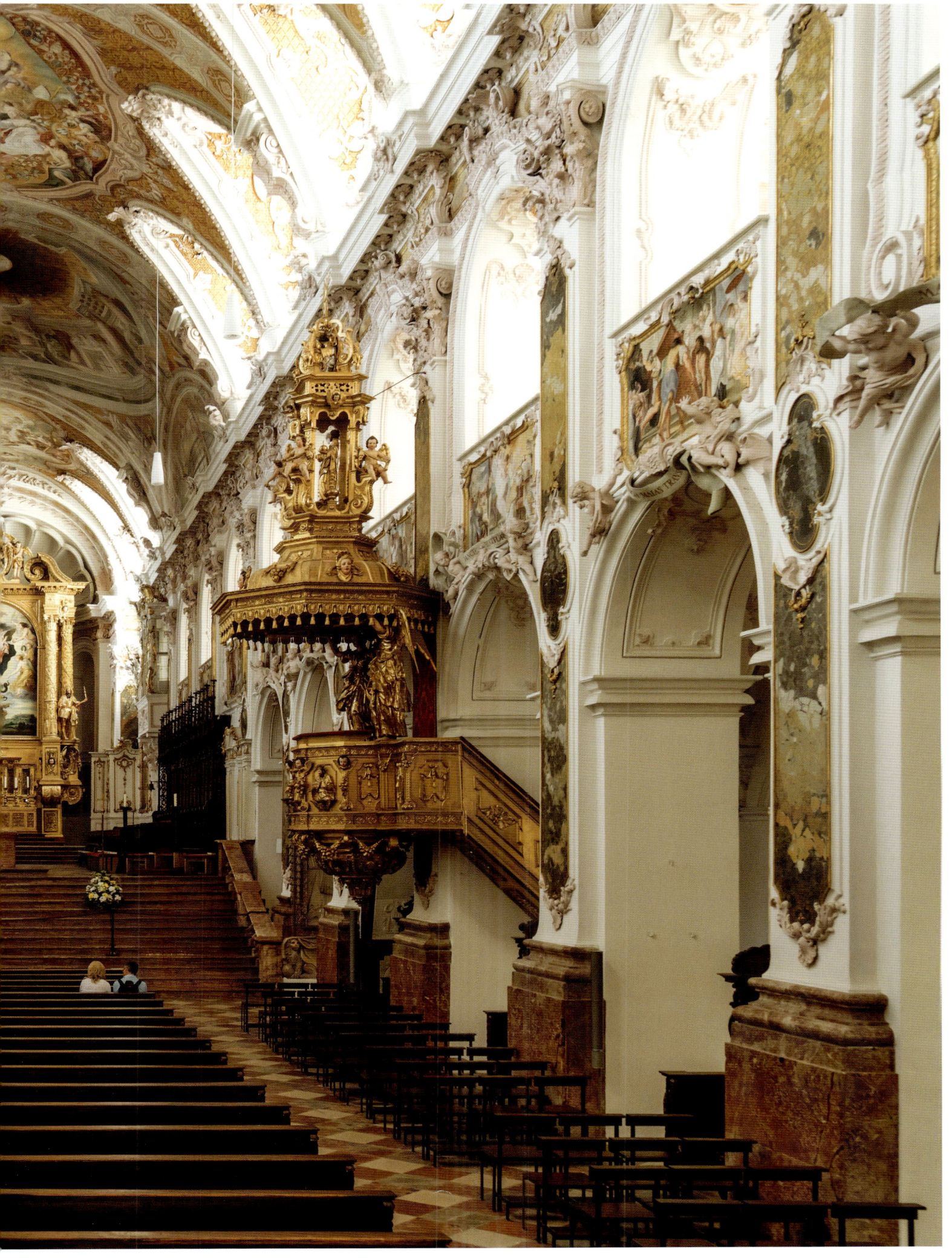

0.4
Adam Lenckhardt,
Apollo Flaying Marsyas,
ivory, 1644, height
27.2 cm. Bayerisches
Nationalmuseum,
Munich
(inv. no. 92/145).

affected not only forms of patronage, but attitudes to art, iconography, and the nature of sculpture commissions.

The Catholic Reformation and the conclusions of the Council of Trent (1545-63) influenced the development of art all over Europe, in terms of imagery and even style.[12] Sacred sculpture in Catholic churches was seen as desirable for religious reasons, and commissions were abundant in the late sixteenth and early decades of the seventeenth century. The monastic orders, notably the Jesuits and Benedictines, commissioned numerous important works of art and architecture during this period. Sculpture workshops, such as those of the Zürn dynasty around Lake Constance in southwest Bavaria, were active in numerous South German and Austrian towns.[13] That vernacular tradition paralleled the art commissioned for the court. The major cities attracted artists of international renown: the court in Munich was dominated by commissions for Hubert Gerhard (1540/50-1620). In Augsburg Adriaen de Vries (1556-1626) was given prestigious commissions, while Georg Petel (1601/2-34), who had travelled to Paris, Rome and Antwerp, was regarded as one of the leading European sculptors of his day. Vienna was to attract, amongst others, Matthias Rauchmiller (1645-86), Matthias Steinl (c. 1644-1727) and Johann Baptist Straub (1704-84).

But the battles between Protestants and Catholics during the Thirty Years' War (1618-48) caused widespread destruction, exerting an incalculable impact on art. Individual sculptors sometimes had to seek other types of religious imagery, and on occasion had to flee to other cities.[14] Smaller sculptures (*Kleinplastik*) were produced, for example in boxwood, ivory and amber, since they were less vulnerable and less costly than large monuments, and they could be transported more easily during troubled times. Adam Lenckhardt's work produced in the mid-seventeenth century epitomizes this shift in artistic production [0.4]. They could also be speculative, sometimes made to be sold at fairs, rather than to commission. The war's devastation led to a resurgence of artistic creativity in the following century, in the form of ambitious new building programmes from 1700 onwards

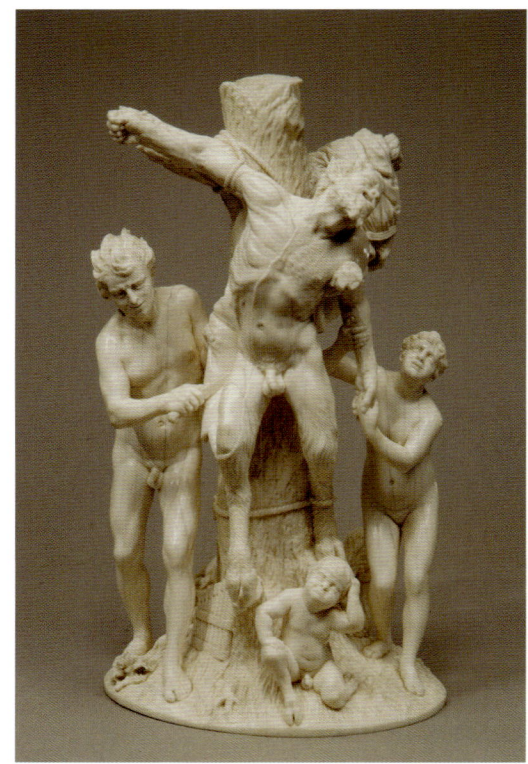

for churches and abbeys in Bavaria, Austria and elsewhere to replace the ruins and destruction caused by the conflicts. The sculptures in wood and stucco made for these monumental Bavarian and Austrian basilicas are central to the history of German baroque sculpture.

In the early eighteenth century the War of the Spanish Succession led the Elector of Bavaria, Maximilian II (Max Emmanuel) (1662-1726; r. 1679-1726), to take refuge at the French court at Versailles from 1706 to 1715. On his return to Munich, he set about rebuilding and reforming artistic taste, importing artists such as the Flemish architect François de Cuvilliés the Elder (1695-1768), who had worked in France, and whose style was to transform court architecture in Bavaria. The ornamental language of the late baroque was transformed into that of early rococo as a result. The War of Austrian Succession (1740-48) created further unrest in Austria and elsewhere, and caused financial difficulties for many, including sculptors such as Joseph Matthias Götz (1696-1760).

Taste and Attitudes from the Nineteenth Century Onwards

German baroque sculpture is not studied as intently as numerous other European sculptural traditions outside Germany and Austria. It can be perceived as challenging for various reasons, both aesthetic and historical. Like Spanish baroque sculpture, it is habitually both highly emotional and highly coloured, qualities that are not always valued elsewhere in Europe. Additionally, the religious sculptures in both Germany and Spain are frequently imbued with Catholic sentiments and were designed to appeal to devout worshippers and pilgrims, rather than to be viewed as aesthetic objects. They are generally only to be seen in churches that may be relatively isolated, far from major cities. The sculptures' passionate and theatrical qualities, manifestly potent and moving, whether they are judged as works of art or as devotional sculptures, are not always appreciated. They sit effectively outside traditions in art history that incorporate more restrained works of art, notably those created in Rome or Florence. Even within Germany during the nineteenth century, the rise of classicism led to a decline in the demand for such resplendent works. The change in mood can be dated back to 1770, when Elector Maximilian III Joseph (1727-77) of Bavaria condemned—in part for economic reasons—the church's extravagance, leading to decreasing rococo decoration in Bavarian churches.[15] German dictionaries of artists would mention German artists of this era in the first half of the nineteenth century, but the period was not studied or valued in its own right.[16] However by the late nineteenth and early twentieth centuries responses to baroque art in Germany and Austria became more positive. Art historians such as Cornelius Gurlitt (1850-1938), Heinrich Wölfflin (1864-1945), Julius von Schlosser (1868-1938), Wilhelm Pinder (1878-1947), Hans Werner Hegemann (d. after 1945), Georg Biermann (1880-1949), Albert Erich Brinckmann (1881-1958), Adolf Feulner (1884-1945) and Theodor Müller (1905-96) were re-assessing the period. They debated the nature of the baroque style in sculpture and architecture, valuing its distinctiveness in relation to renaissance or neo-classical art.[17] As the twentieth century progressed, scholars such as Hans Sedlmayr (1896-1984), Hugo Karl Maria Schnell (1904-81), Heinrich Decker (b. 1899) and Norbert Lieb (1907-94) published seminal

studies of German baroque sculpture and architecture.[8] Nevertheless nationalist feelings and the political situation within Bavaria continued to affect art history. Schnell's book *Der Baierische Barock* was published in Munich in 1936, during the Nazi era. A high gothic script was used for the typeface, while the underlying theme of the book is at times assertively nationalistic, despite the ostensibly historical subject matter. This is unsurprising, given that the book appeared during Hitler's tyranny. But Schnell's book is nonetheless a meticulous scholarly study of the baroque in Bavaria, albeit poorly illustrated, a fault sadly typical of many art books produced all over Europe at that date, regardless of the political complexion of the author. Schnell went on to found a publishing house with his business partner Johannes Steiner (1902-95). Amongst their publications were serious art historical works and relatively well-illustrated, inexpensive booklets on church architecture, widely sold in churches and elsewhere even today. Although Schnell was not sympathetic to the Nazi cause, and his 1936 publication was an academic study of the subject rather than skewed by nationalism, it would have been a difficult book for non-German readers, and indeed for many German readers. Neither the format nor the content was designed to appeal to the non-specialist, nor to anyone who could not read German. In fact, the later Schnell and Steiner booklets are far more approachable, even if normally only available in German, while their range of academic publications are valuable works of reference for both students and the educated layman.[19]

Germany self-evidently suffered from the damage caused by both world wars and Hitler's totalitarian dictatorship during the twentieth century. Austrian and German art history were perceived by others, not always fairly, as susceptible to fascist ideas. Hans Sedlmayr, mentioned above, was a member of the Nazi party, condemned by his intellectual peers after the war.[20] Few travellers visited Germany or Austria as tourists or scholars in the 1930s and 1940s, whilst in the aftermath of the Second World War retrospective revulsion for Hitler's destructive dictatorship tended to pervade attitudes to

German art in general. Bavarian sculpture was seen, again unfairly, to be symptomatic of German nationalism. As noted above, because many sculptures were generally housed in churches and monasteries that were sometimes far from cities, viewing them could be problematic. Moreover, museums elsewhere in Europe and in the US tended not to acquire German baroque sculpture.[21]

There were exceptions to this negative attitude towards the art of this place and time, and some recognition that it had been unjustly overlooked. In 1938 Sacheverell Sitwell (1897-1988) published in London *German Baroque Sculpture*, with descriptive notes by Nikolaus Pevsner (1902-83), who had arrived in Britain virtually as a refugee from Germany five years previously, in 1933. As Sitwell noted regretfully in his Introduction, 'there is hardly a book in the English language which touches upon the subject [of the eighteenth century in Austria and Bavaria]'.[22] Similarly, after the war, in 1958, *Baroque Churches of Central Europe* by John Bourke (1909-90) was published in London, because, Bourke said, 'the church art and architecture [in Bavaria and elsewhere in Central Europe] has been as good as ignored'. He had found that there was 'nothing at all in the way of a handbook that would introduce the ordinary interested and educated English or American traveller to the subject', and so he decided, 'greatly daring', to 'compile a book that . . . might provide a welcome introduction'.[23] Bourke's comparatively modest volume not only clearly paints a vivid picture of the art he had seen for anglophone readers, but also conveys his expertise and personal enthusiasm for his subject. The *Pelican History of Art* volume dedicated to baroque art and architecture in Central Europe (in the series edited by Pevsner) appeared a few years later in 1965. The author, Eberhard Hempel (1886-1967), was an academic in Dresden, and his text was given as an English translation. His book gives a comprehensive overview of painting, sculpture, architecture and some of the decorative arts in Central Europe during the baroque period, and undoubtedly provided students and scholars with a firm understanding of the topic.[24] But, as F.J.B. Watson pointed out

in his review at the time, no publication written in English was cited in the bibliography, indicating the paucity of non-German scholarship on the baroque at that date.[25] Revealingly the volume had to be commissioned from a German scholar, since no one outside Germany or Austria would have been equipped to undertake it.

Numerous outstanding books on German baroque sculpture have appeared in Germany, Canada and the US in the last twenty or thirty years, but it has generally been less favoured as a subject by anglophone scholars or students, unlike German sculpture of the early renaissance.[26] This means that sculpture of this era from Germany and Austria is comparatively rarely studied, even within those countries. Such emotive, melodramatic sculptures are seen as stylistically outlandish after the purity of the neo-classical style that held sway from the nineteenth century onwards. Indeed, some German baroque churches were stripped of their gaudier sculptures (as they would have been perceived) in the nineteenth century. A number of these were however rescued and are today housed in museums.[27]

There are some reassuring exceptions to this apparent neglect. Major exhibitions of German baroque sculpture were held in 1968, 1977, 1980 and 1981.[28] An important exhibition of German baroque and rococo sculpture was staged in Munich in 2014, precisely a century after the ambitious exhibition of baroque and rococo art held in Darmstadt in 1914.[29] Even more significantly, the reason the 2014 exhibition took place was that several of the churches in the region around Munich were being renovated; the sculptures had been removed in order to allow the restoration work to take place. Visitors to churches in Bavaria today will be impressed by the care and sensitivity with which such buildings and works of art have been recently restored and conserved. The sculptures are now cherished, rather than denigrated. Meanwhile, the major exhibition devoted to Andreas Schlüter in Berlin, also in 2014, on the tercentenary of his death, highlighted this baroque artist's profound contribution to European art, considering his work in relation to the wider context of baroque sculpture in Berlin.[30]

Themes

This book has been written as a relatively concise introduction to this complex subject matter and will simultaneously aim to explore some themes that can both illuminate the meanings and functions of sculptures. It will also attempt to clarify their historical and artistic contexts. The themes include the relationship between German baroque sculpture and sculpture produced in Italy and the Netherlands at that time; artists' training and workshop practices; the cross-fertilisation of styles and ideas brought about by the movement of artists and works of art across

territories and countries, sometimes as part of their training, and sometimes due to political events; the different genres, or types of sculpture; materials and techniques, including models and sketches; the power and propaganda of secular sculpture at court; and the playfulness and drama in later sculpture, including garden sculpture. Each chapter, while looking at specific topics in broad chronological order, will contain case studies of particular artists and works to enable a discussion of some of these themes. Maps are included at the start of each chapter, while a biographical list of artists and a summary list of rulers and patrons are provided as appendices, to help the reader navigate the subject.

Notes

1   Perhaps the sculptures of Spain and Portugal are closest in style to some of the more extreme German baroque works.
2   Whaley 2012a/b and 2018; Wilson 2016.
3   See https://en.wikipedia.org/wiki/Upper_Bavaria and https://en.wikipedia.org/wiki/Lower_Bavaria; and Volk 1981, pp. 40-1.
4   Steinberg 2011; Hawes 2018, pp. 110-11.
5   *Oxford English Dictionary* 1972, p. 170 (678).
6   Pinder n.d. [1912]; Decker 1943, p. 9.
7   Bauer 1962, pp. 18-20; Ward-Jackson 1969.
8   See Park 1992.
9   Fleming and Honour 1989, pp. 691-3; Bailey 2014, p. 109.
10   The art historical literature sometimes implicitly conflates the two stylistic terms, for example the title of Norbert Lieb's seminal 1953 book covering the period well into the eighteenth century: *Barockkirchen zwischen Donau und Alpen*.
11   Feulner 1922, p. I and p. xii.
12   Chipps Smith 1994.
13   Fischer 1986, pp. 9-10.
14   Bussmann and Schilling 1998; Bedürftig 2006.
15   Park 1992, p. 14.
16   For example, Lipowsky 1810; Brulliot 1832; Nagler 1872-85. Bode 1886 (a history of German sculpture) gives the baroque little space, only discussing the work of Andreas Schlüter and Georg Raphael Donner in any detail.
17   Wölfflin 1926; Pinder n.d. [1912] (see Halbertsma 1992 on Pinder); Biermann 1914; Brinckmann 1919;

Feulner 1926 and 1929, and Feulner and Müller 1953 (Theodor Müller completed this last book after Feulner's untimely death in 1945; see pp. 640-1 of that publication); Hegemann 1958. For a discussion of an emerging national German identity in the late nineteenth century, see Kaufmann 2004, p. 56.
18   Sedlmayr 1930; Schnell n.d. [1936]; Decker 1943; Lieb 1953; Dilly 1988. See also Pevsner 1990, his doctoral thesis of 1928 on the architecture of Leipzig, written before he left Germany.
19   See for example Grünwald 1975; Pfister 2013. Their website indicates the long tradition of art historical publishing: https://www.schnell-und-steiner.de/index.ahtml, accessed 8 February 2020.
20   See Wood 2003, pp. 12-13 and pp. 36-8.
21   There are some exceptions: the Victoria and Albert Museum acquired a number of major or small-scale German ivory and amber sculptures in the twentieth century (see Trusted 1985 and Trusted 2013), while the Busch-Reisinger Museum at Harvard houses an important collection of German sculpture (see Kuhn 1965). The Cleveland Museum of Art in Ohio acquired German baroque sculpture in the twentieth century; see Ditner 1986. See also Harding 1972 for German sculpture in New England museums.
22   Sitwell 1938, p. 9.
23   Bourke 1962, pp. 9-10. From the late 1940s onwards John Bourke (awarded the OBE in 1975) taught English at the University of Munich. He died in Munich in 1990.

24   Hempel 1965.
25   Watson 1965.
26   Baxandall 1981 exemplifies the serious study of earlier German art in Britain. For some relatively recent German publications on the baroque period, see Rasmussen 1977; Volk 1981; Fischer 1986, Maué 1997-2005; Poche and Kořán 2003, and many others listed in the bibliography. A number of outstanding books on German and Austrian baroque ivories have been published this century, for example Haag 2007b and Kappel 2017. For the US and Canada see Harries 1983; Chipps Smith 2002; Hertel 2007; Bailey 2014. See also Kuhn 1965. Kuhn pointed out that refugees from Nazi Germany brought to the US a knowledge of German sculpture, and even on occasion German works of art themselves. In Britain, Pevsner's expertise undoubtedly helped raise the profile of the subject.
27   Notably the Bayerisches Nationalmuseum in Munich and the Bode Museum in Berlin.
28   *Augsburger Barock* 1968; Rasmussen 1977; *Welt im Umbruch* 1980; *Barock in Baden-Württemberg* 1981. In addition, the 1971 exhibition (*Europäische Barockplastik* 1971) highlighted the importance of the Netherlandish sculptor Gabriel Grupello who spent much of his career working in Germany in the late seventeenth and early eighteenth century.
29   Diederen and Kürzeder 2014. For the Darmstadt exhibition, see Biermann 1914.
30   *Andreas Schlüter* 2014.

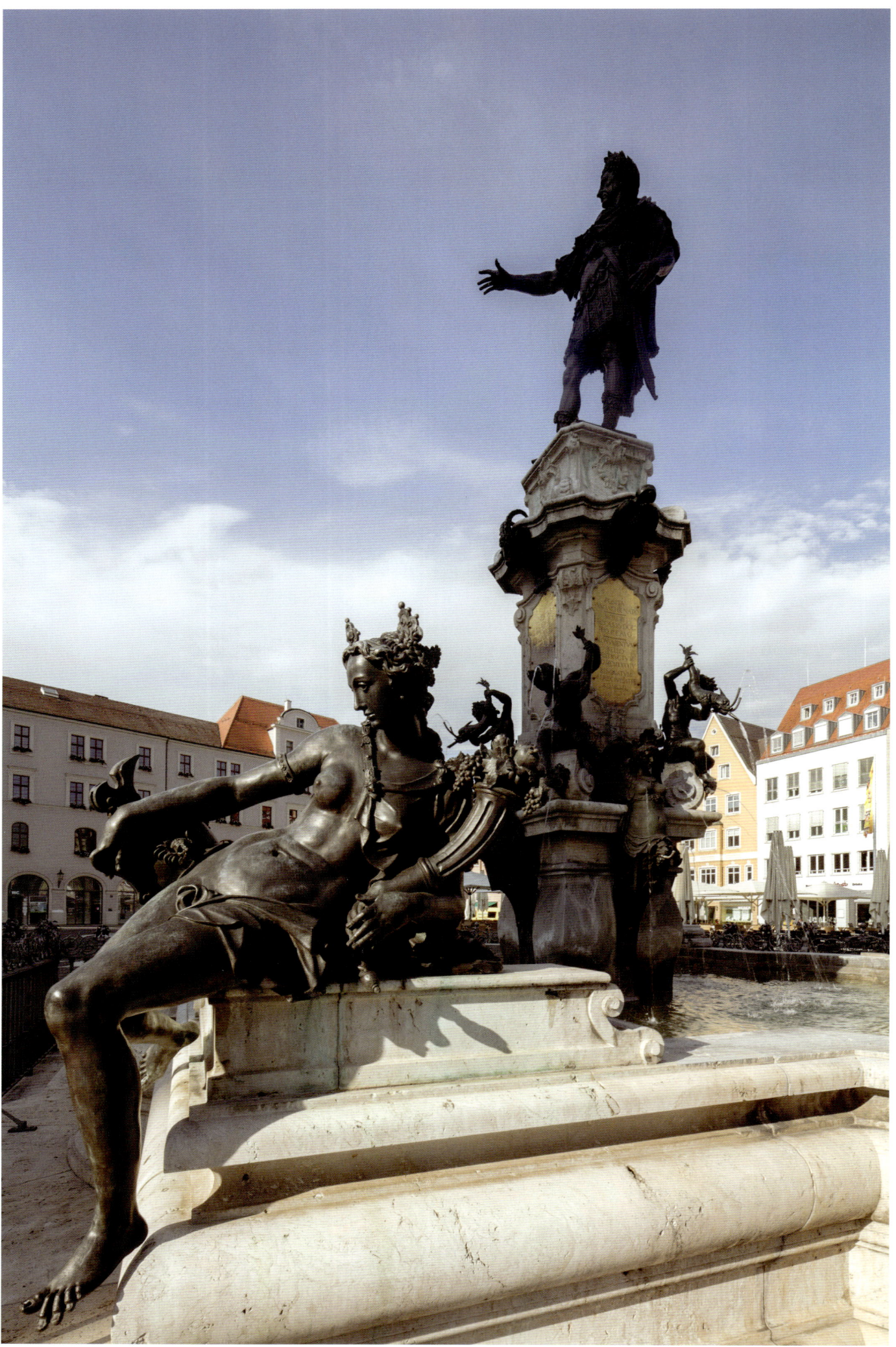

CHAPTER 1

SCULPTURE IN
SOUTH GERMANY
1600-40:
ANTECEDENTS AND
INTERNATIONAL
CURRENTS

The trajectory of South German sculpture in the first four decades of the seventeenth century, from approximately 1600 to 1640, was largely determined by three Netherlandish artists: the sculptors Hubert Gerhard (c. 1550-1620) and Adriaen de Vries (c. 1556-1626), and the painter Peter Paul Rubens (1577-1640). The bronzes by De Vries and Gerhard made in South Germany inspired in particular the Weilheim sculptors Hans Reichle (1565/70-1634) and Hans Krumper (c. 1570-1634), who both worked with Gerhard. Weilheim, a small Upper Bavarian town just over 50 kilometres southwest of Munich, exceptionally produced a number of prominent sculptors in the early seventeenth century.[1]

Rubens's paintings were avidly collected by European monarchs (including the Wittelsbach Duke of Bavaria Maximilian I (1573-1651; r. 1597-1651) and were widely known to artists from engravings. The Flemish painter was a particular source of inspiration to another Weilheim sculptor, Georg Petel (1601/2-1635), the most noteworthy German artist in Rubens's shop in Antwerp, where he worked in the 1620s; Petel's work will be discussed more fully at the end of this chapter. This Netherlandish strand in German sculpture, the legacy of all three artists, endured throughout the seventeenth century and beyond, despite political and social upheavals. Like Rubens, Gerhard and De Vries were sophisticated artists of renowned abilities. They brought an international perspective to the existing Germanic tradition of sculpture in Bavaria, especially Munich and Augsburg, as well as fuelling court patronage and the recognition of the prestige of art at the highest level of society. Crucially, they had both worked in Florence with Giambologna (1629-1608) for Duke Cosimo III Medici (1640-1723). For these reasons their bronze figures exhibit an undeniable Italianate, mannerist inflexion, with smooth surfaces and sinuous forms, expressing an ideal of elegant beauty derived from the very material [1.1 and 1.2]. Italianate elements in Bavarian sculpture are in fact evident in many of the altarpieces and small-scale sculptures produced in Germany in the early seventeenth century, as will be seen. Gerhard came to work in Munich from 1584 to 1599, after which he was employed in Innsbruck by Archduke Maximilian III of Austria (1558-1616). He returned to Munich in 1613, remaining there until his death in 1620. De Vries was in Augsburg from 1595 to 1602, having been employed in Prague at the court of Archduke Maximilian's older brother, Emperor Rudolph II (1552-1612), from 1589 to 1594. By 1603 De Vries had returned to Prague, where he spent the rest of his life, dying there in 1626.

1.1

Hubert Gerhard, Augustus Fountain, bronze, 1589-94. Maximilianstrasse, Augsburg.

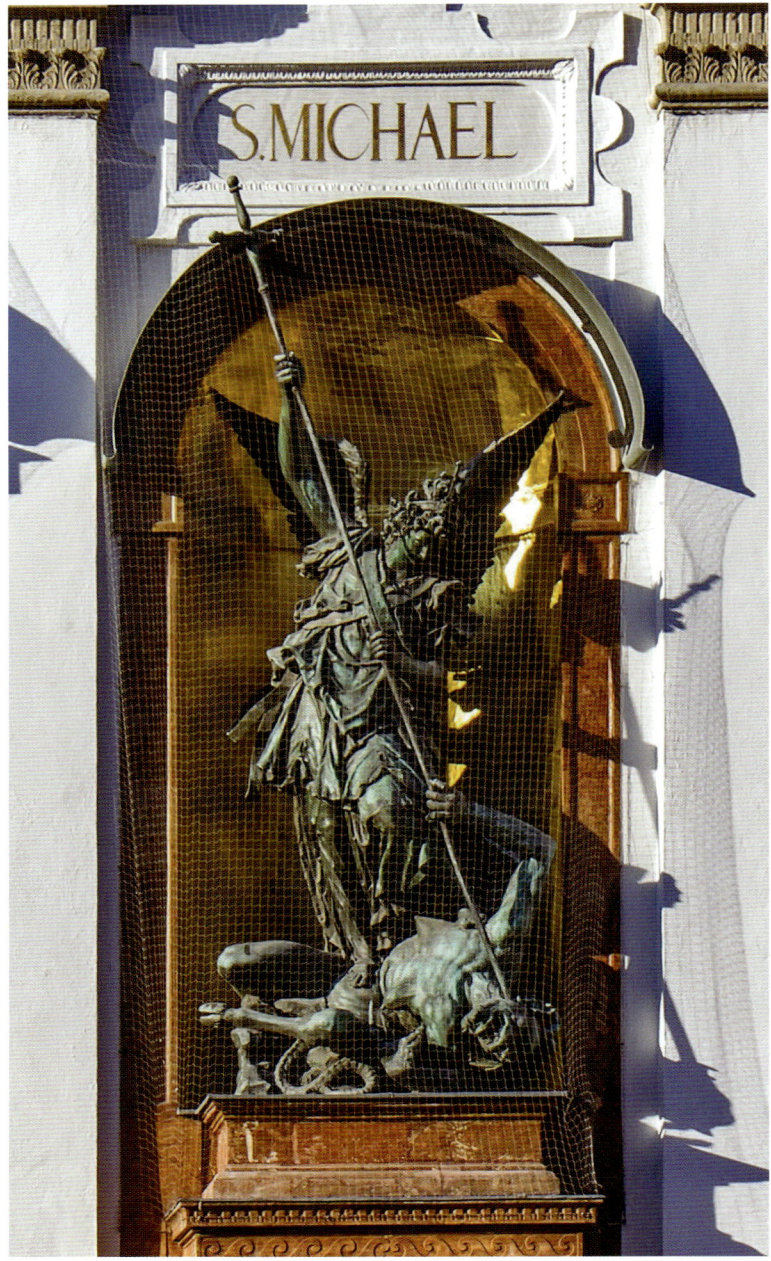

sculptures in Munich and Augsburg, should be considered in parallel with the contemporary vernacular art being produced in Germany. Massive carved polychromed and gilt wood altarpieces were being created by numerous artists, including Hans Degler (1564/5-1635), Christoph Rodt (c. 1578-1634), and Jörg Zürn (1583/4-1635/8) for Bavarian churches, sometimes in relatively small towns far from the big cosmopolitan cities. Such altarpieces were in the still robust tradition of medieval and later German wood carving, such as the early sixteenth-century altarpieces of the Franconian sculptors Tilman Riemenschneider (1460-1531) and Veit Stoss (1447-1533).[3]

This chapter will start by focussing on altarpieces by Degler, Rodt and Zürn, and then examine some major large-scale bronzes by Reichle and Krumper. These works illustrate in parallel ways how sculptures at this time reflected and expressed myriad traditions, and the complex society in which they were created. The chapter will close with a discussion of two prominent Bavarian sculptors of the first half of the century: Christoph Angermair (c. 1580-1633) and Angermair's pupil Georg Petel, concentrating especially on ivories and small-scale sculpture. Brief biographies of the key artists mentioned in this chapter—as throughout—are also provided in the biographical appendix at the end of the book.

The Basilica of SS. Ulrich and Afra, Augsburg: Altarpieces by Hans Degler

The high altarpiece and two side altarpieces by Hans Degler at the east end of the basilica of SS. Ulrich and Afra in Augsburg flank a crucifixion group in bronze by Hans Reichle [1.3]. All date from the first years of the seventeenth century. Degler was born perhaps in Munich, and worked with Adam Krumper, the father of the architect and sculptor Hans Krumper (for whose work see below), from 1590 to 1595 for Duke William V (William the Pious) (1548-1626; r. 1579-1597) at the court in Munich. Degler was to marry Adam Krumper's daughter in 1590, taking over his father-in-law's workshop in Weilheim at his death, settling there in the early seventeenth century. He is therefore known

1.2
Hubert Gerhard,
St Michael, bronze,
1588. Church of
St Michael, Munich.

> 1.3
East end of the church
of SS. Ulrich and Afra,
Augsburg, showing
Hans Degler's three
altarpieces and Hans
Reichle's bronze
crucifix.

De Vries and Gerhard were employed by Duke Maximilian I of Bavaria (a cousin of Archduke Maximilian III and Emperor Rudolph II) in Munich, which became a vibrant centre of art and patronage in the late sixteenth and early seventeenth century.[2] The duke had an active interest in the arts, employing numerous other artists at the Bavarian court, notably Krumper and Petel. He also instigated building projects, including the extension of the Munich Residenz in 1611, and he acquired paintings by Rubens.

But this new international court style, flowering in the early years of the century, and to be seen especially in fountains and public

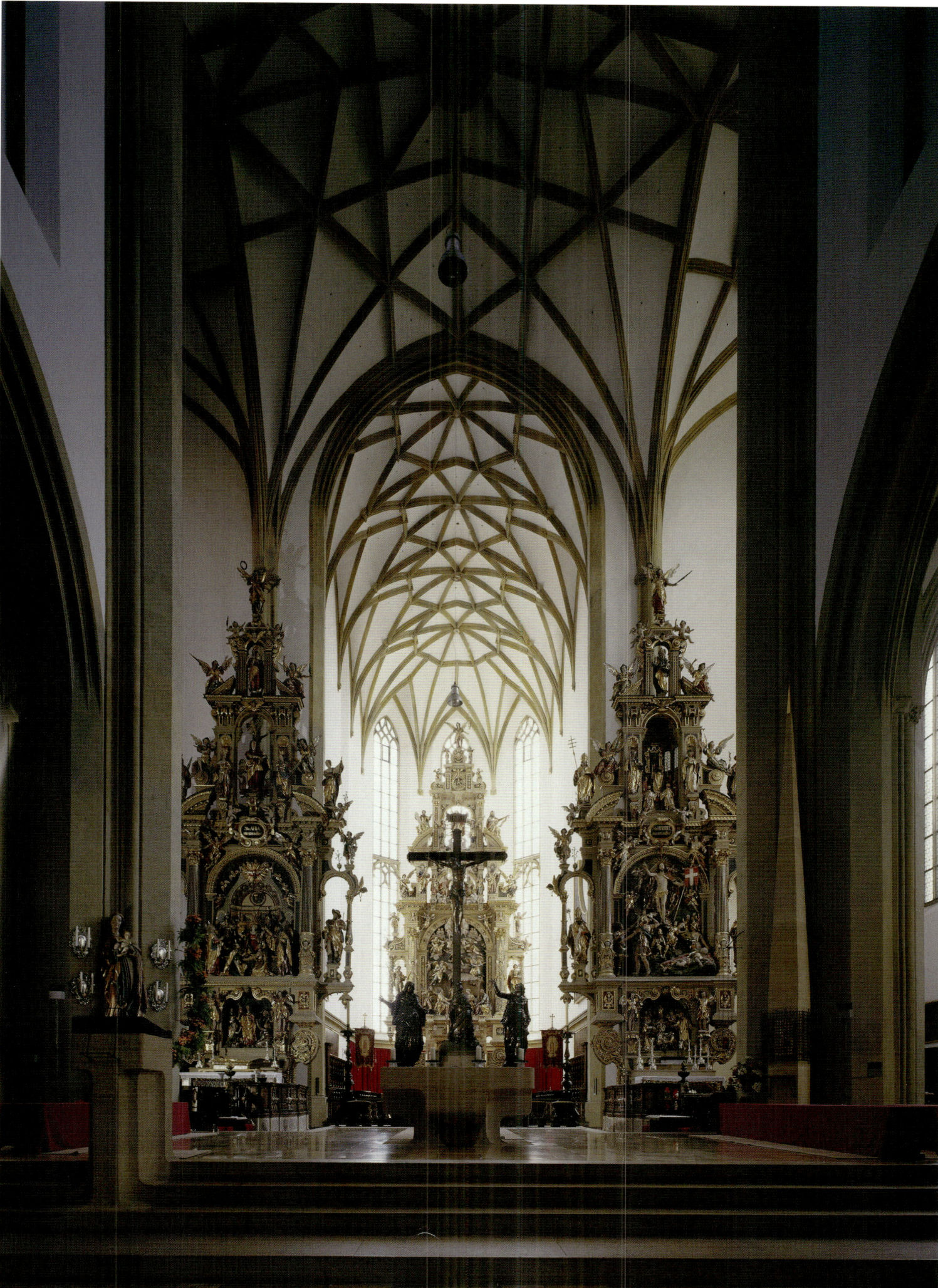

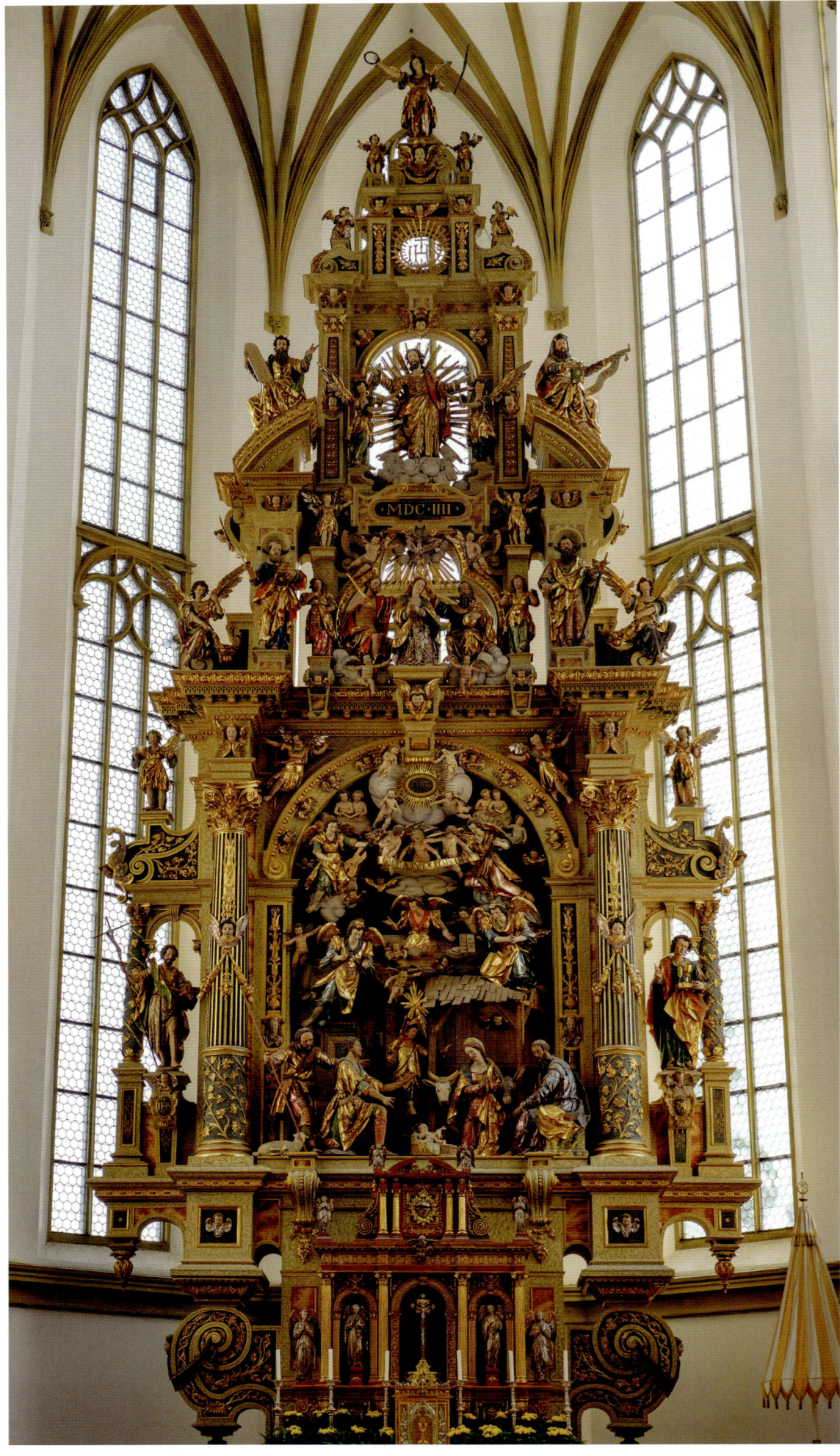

1.4
Hans Degler, High
Altarpiece, painted and
gilt limewood, signed
and dated 1604.
Church of SS. Ulrich
and Afra, Augsburg.

> 1.5
Tilman
Riemenschneider,
Altarpiece of the
Assumption of the Virgin
(the *Marienaltar*),
limewood, c. 1505–10.
Church of Our Lord,
Creglingen.

> 1.6
Detail of Degler,
South Altarpiece [1.8],
the Resurrected Christ

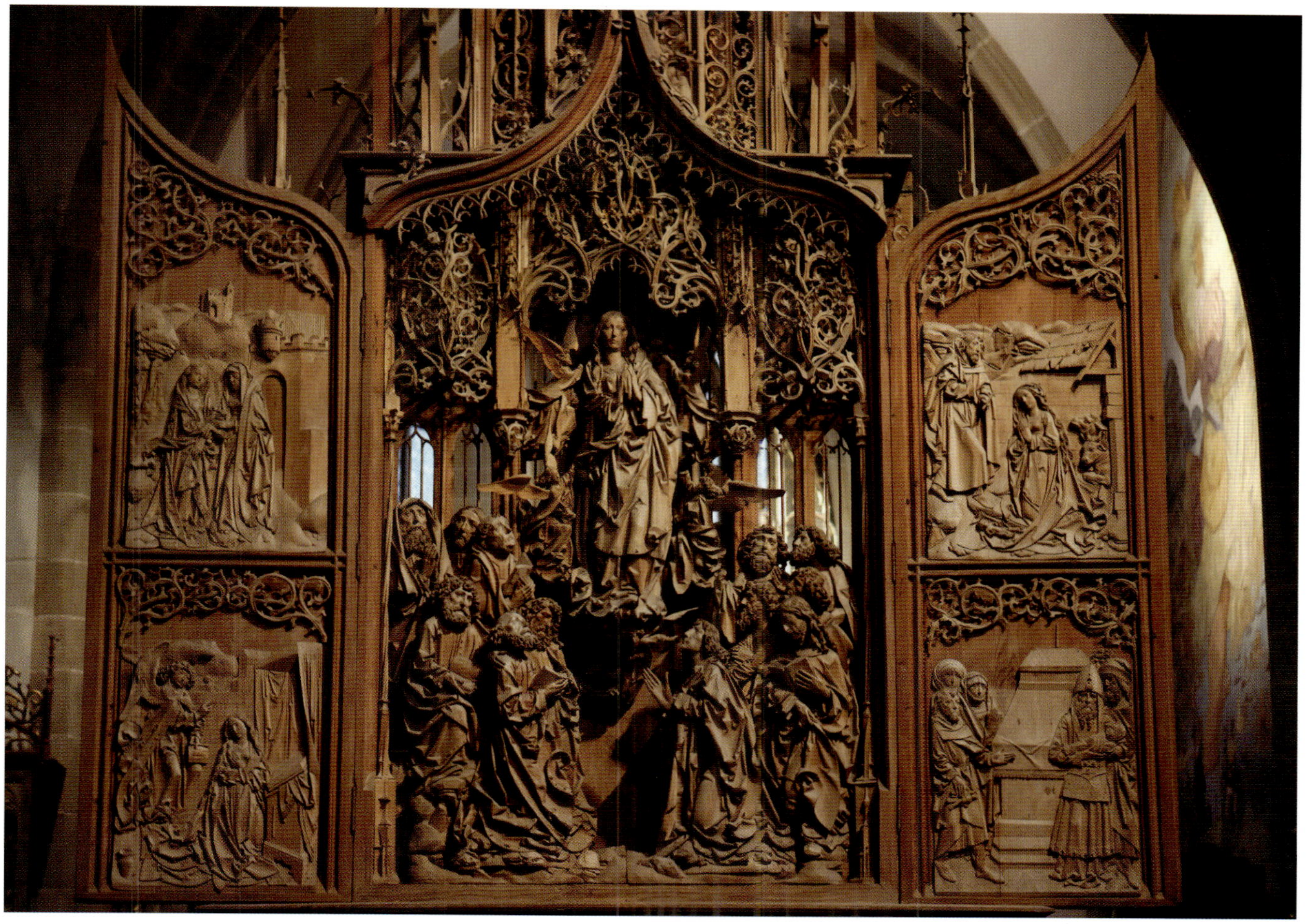

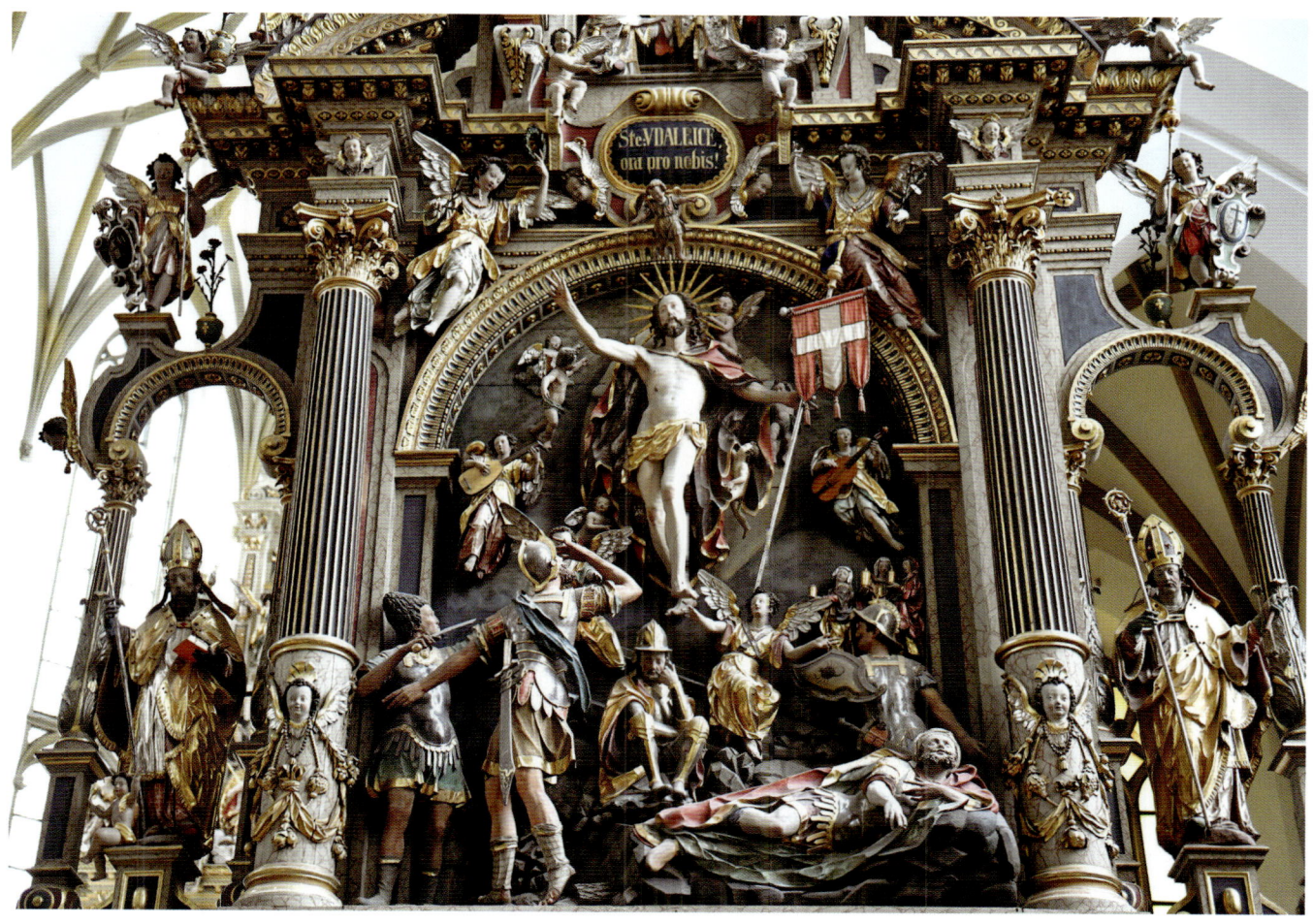

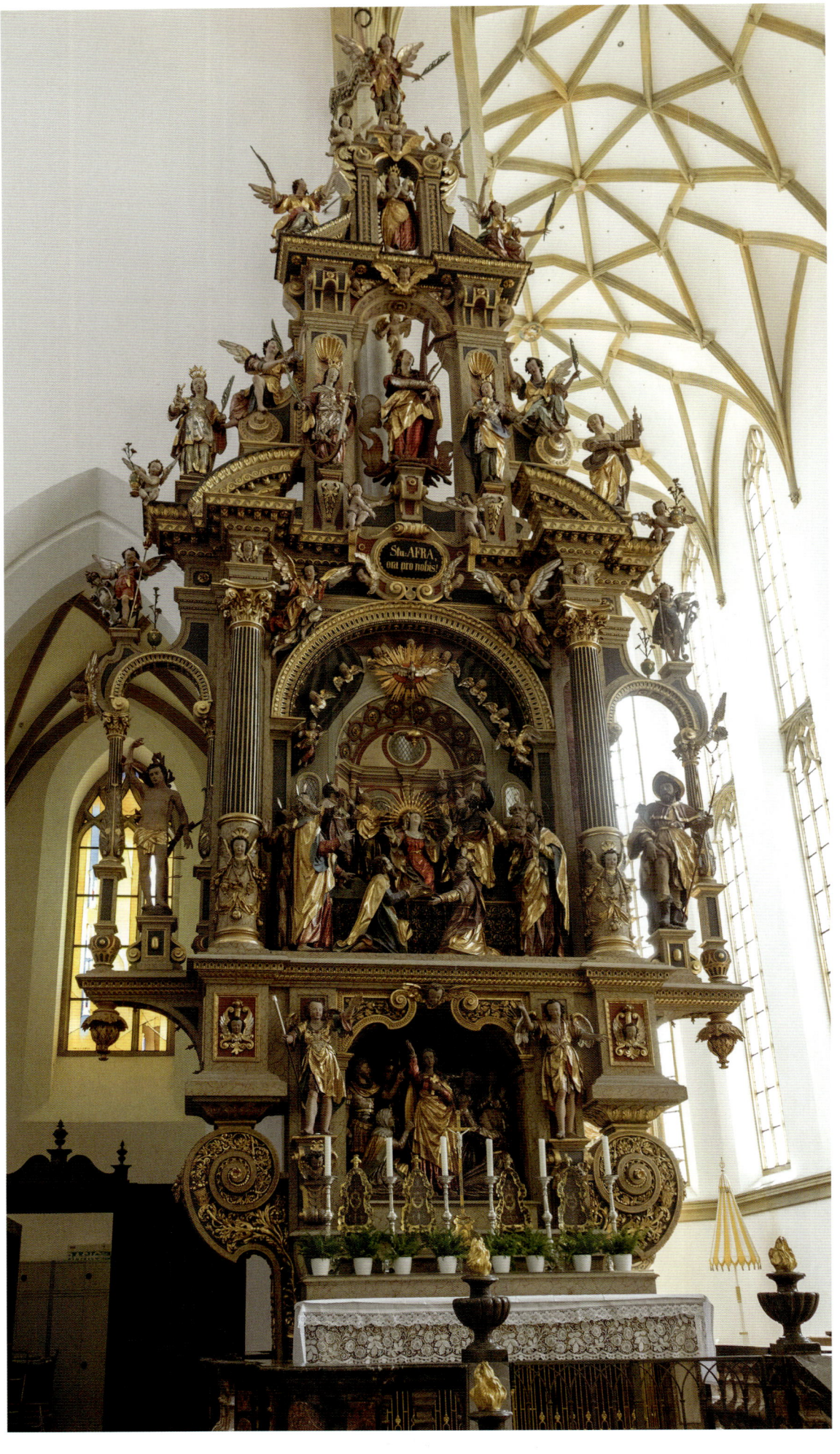

1.7
Hans Degler, North altarpiece dedicated to St Afra (*Pentecost*), painted and gilt limewood, 1607. Church of SS. Ulrich and Afra, Augsburg.

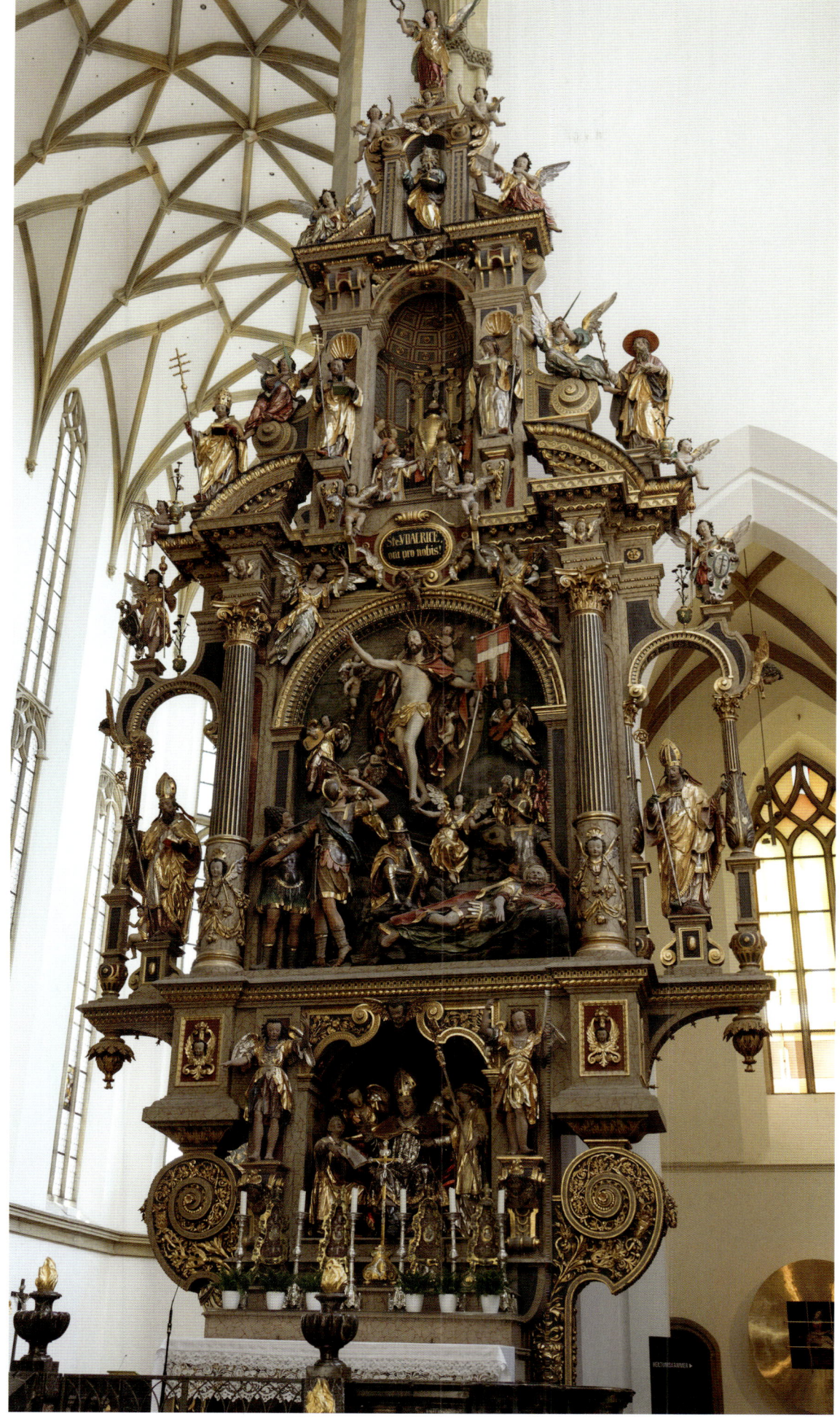

1.8
Hans Degler, South altarpiece dedicated to St Ulrich (*The Resurrection*), painted and gilt limewood, 1607. Church of SS. Ulrich and Afra, Augsburg.

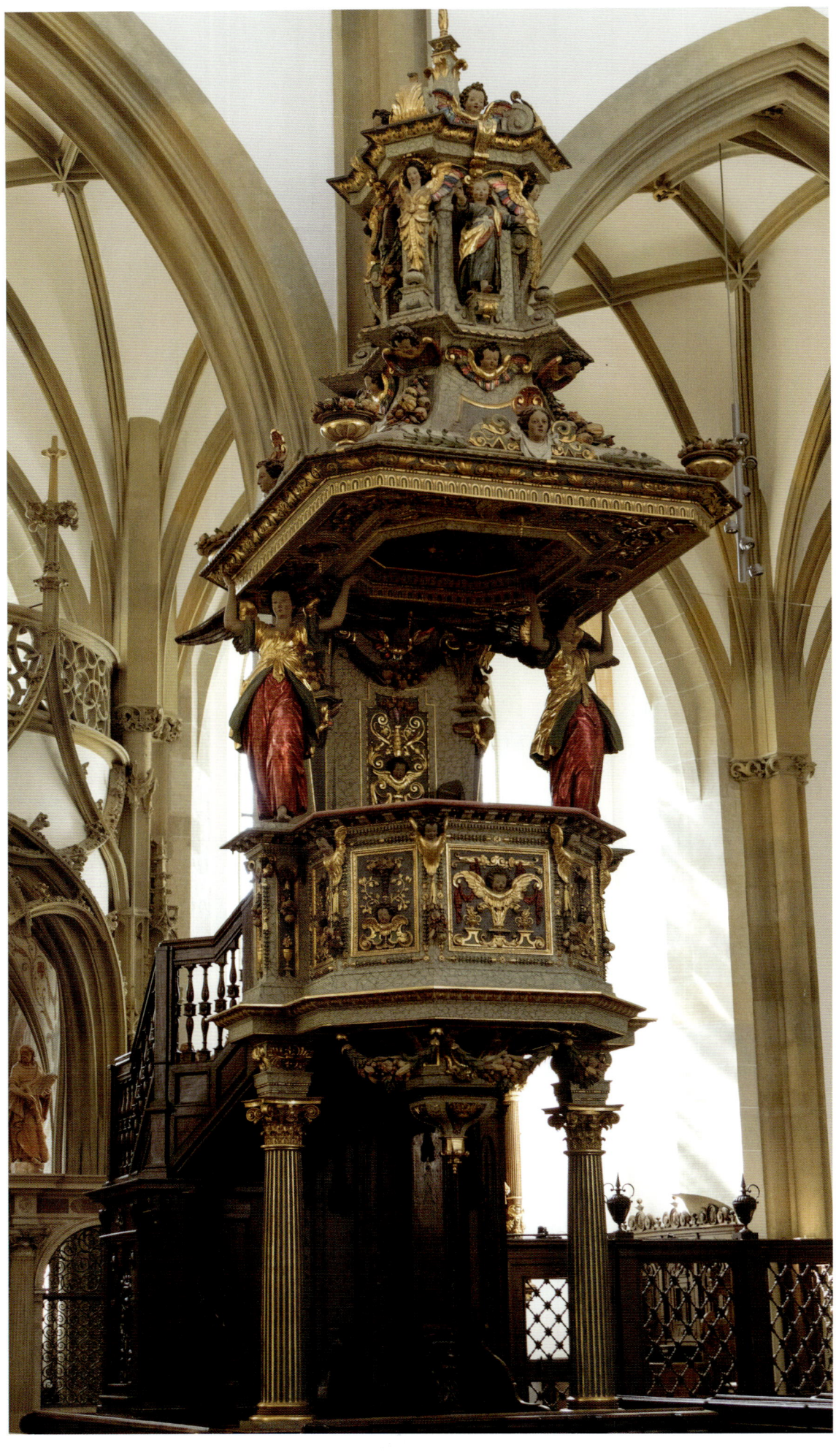

1.9
Hans Degler, Pulpit,
painted and gilt
limewood, 1608.
Church of SS. Ulrich
and Afra, Augsburg.

primarily as a Weilheim sculptor, often collaborating with his brother-in-law, Hans Krumper.[4]

The three altarpieces that Degler executed for the basilica in Augsburg are towering structures, measuring over 20 metres high, and peopled with many figures, some life size [1.3].[5] Whilst being very much of their time, these retables recall earlier German ones, such as Tilman Riemenschneider's altarpiece of the *Assumption of the Virgin*, known as the *Marienaltar*, at Herrgottskirche, Creglingen, Baden-Württemberg a century before, c. 1505-10 [1.5].[6] In both Degler's and Riemenschneider's altarpieces a powerful central scene dominates the work. But there are multiple differences: the elaborate frameworks of Degler's retables are replete with classicizing motifs, rounded triumphal arches and ornate pilasters and columns, and are animated by profuse colour and gilding. Conversely, the pinnacled gothic tracery of the *Marienaltar* was never polychromed, so that, as can be clearly seen in the unpainted central figures and the reliefs on the wings, the natural colouring of the limewood draws attention to the virtuoso carving. Degler's dazzling figurative scenes are likewise stylistically of their time, consisting of freestanding figures in theatrical narratives within highly decorated and intricate classicizing frameworks, rather than conforming to the simpler early sixteenth-century triptych format evident in Riemenschneider's work.

Degler's high altarpiece is prominently dated 1604 in a cartouche beneath the resurrected Christ, above the central scene of the *Nativity* in the main body of the work [1.4].[7] The two side altarpieces date from 1607: that dedicated to St Afra on the north side of the nave depicts the *Pentecost*, with the martyrdom of St Afra, patron saint of the city, and other martyred female saints, shown in the crowning fixture at the top (the *Auszug*) [1.7]. Until the secularization of the monastery in 1804 the relics of St Afra (now in an antique stone sarcophagus in the crypt) were incorporated into the altarpiece.[8] The altarpiece dedicated to St Ulrich on the south side shows the *Resurrection*, with scenes from the life and death of St Ulrich in the predella and in the *Auszug* [1.6 and 1.8].[9] The three altarpieces thus

celebrate the three prime festivals of the church: Christmas, Easter and Pentecost. Degler executed the ornate painted wood pulpit in the nave in 1608, its sounding board held aloft by two angels serving as caryatids [1.9]. The altarpieces and pulpit may all have been designed by Degler's brother-in-law, Hans Krumper, whilst the polychromy was carried out by another artist from Weilheim, the painter Elias Greither I (1565/70-1646), as indicated by the inscription on the altarpiece, naming Degler as sculptor and Greither as polychromist.[10]

Degler's theatrical style is most apparent in the central scene of the high altarpiece. The life size, naturalistically painted figures of the Virgin, St Joseph and the shepherds, carved in limewood, appear as if on a stage [1.10]. Above these protagonists hovers a host of angels within the triumphal arch. Near the apex of the altarpiece is the gilded and polychromed figure of the resurrected Christ, his arms outstretched in a welcoming gesture. He stands, or rather walks forward, over a cluster of clouds, with a sunburst behind, flanked by two angels, within another triumphal arch [1.4]. The pierced frameworks of Degler's altarpieces enhance their impact, the natural light from the apse shining through the openwork backs, giving to the altarpiece what could be called a monumental *ajouré* effect. The expansive gestures seen in the *Nativity* scene and in the resurrected Christ not only convey the Christian story to the unlettered, but look forward to the emotion expressed in sculptures of over a century later by Johann Baptist Straub (1704-1784) and Ignaz Günther (1725-1775).

The City of Augsburg and the Basilica of SS. Ulrich and Afra

Degler's altarpieces reflect both Augsburg's prosperity and the city's recent history. The sculptures at SS. Ulrich and Afra were costly works of art, reflecting the city's affluence. The Fugger and Welser merchant banking families, who had risen to prominence in the sixteenth century, remained a strong presence, contributing to the city's prosperity with international trading links, to Italy above all.[11] Moreover Augsburg was a Free Imperial City under the

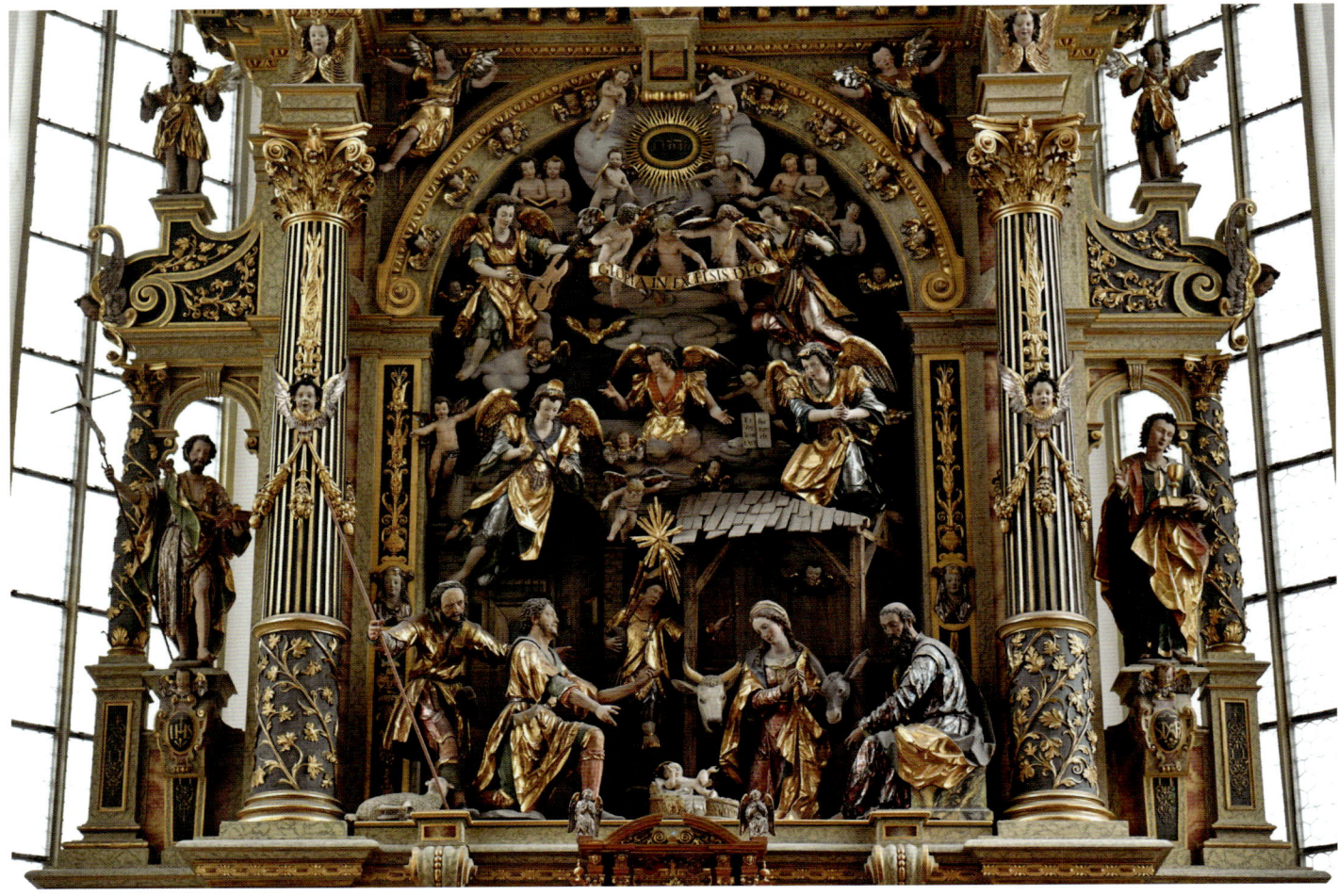

authority of the Holy Roman Emperor, rather than being directly ruled by the Prince-Bishop of Augsburg.

Largely Protestant, the city was the place of origin of the Augsburg Confession, which in 1530 had set out the principles of the Lutheran reformers in an attempt to reconcile the Catholic and Lutheran churches. But following Charles V's imperial decree condemning Lutheranism in 1547/48, the Schmalkaldic War was waged by Lutheran princes against the Catholic forces led by the emperor. The tensions between Charles V and the German rulers were finally resolved with the Peace of Augsburg in 1555. This agreement formally acknowledged Protestantism as a legitimate religion of the Holy Roman Empire. Running parallel to these events, the sessions of the Council of Trent (1545-1563) were forceful responses to the expanding Lutheran church, asserting Catholic doctrine, and articulating the tenets of the Counter Reformation. The Council's decrees were acknowledged by the Catholic princes of

Germany at the Diet of Augsburg held in 1566.[12]

Although Augsburg was predominantly Protestant, the Catholic faith of the city remained strong. The basilica of SS. Ulrich and Afra formed part of the Benedictine monastery in the city, having been rebuilt in the mid-sixteenth century.[13] The abbot at that time, Jakob Köplin (abbot 1548-1600), succeeded in having the claim of the church to 'Imperial immediacy' (*Reichsfreiheit*) recognized in 1577, confirming the abbey as an Imperial estate, under the jurisdiction of the Holy Roman Emperor, without the intermediary of the Prince-Bishop of Augsburg, an even more privileged status than the city itself enjoyed as a Free Imperial City. This status was however contested by the Prince-Bishop, the legal dispute only being resolved in favour of the abbey in 1643/4.[14]

Building was carried out at the basilica in the early seventeenth century under Abbot Johann Merk (b. c. 1555; abbot 1600-32), who wished to reaffirm the Catholic faith. It was he who commissioned the three altarpieces and

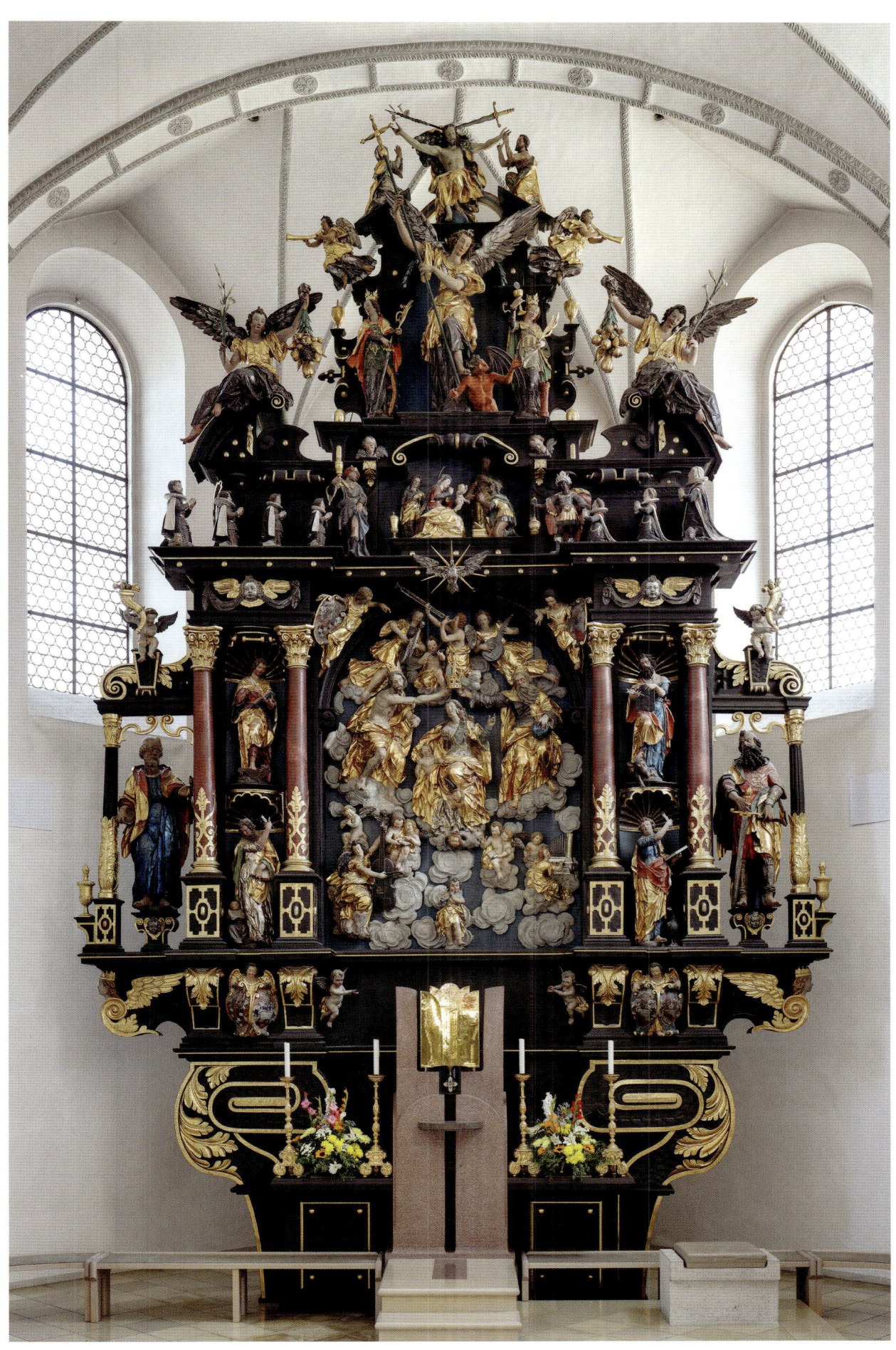

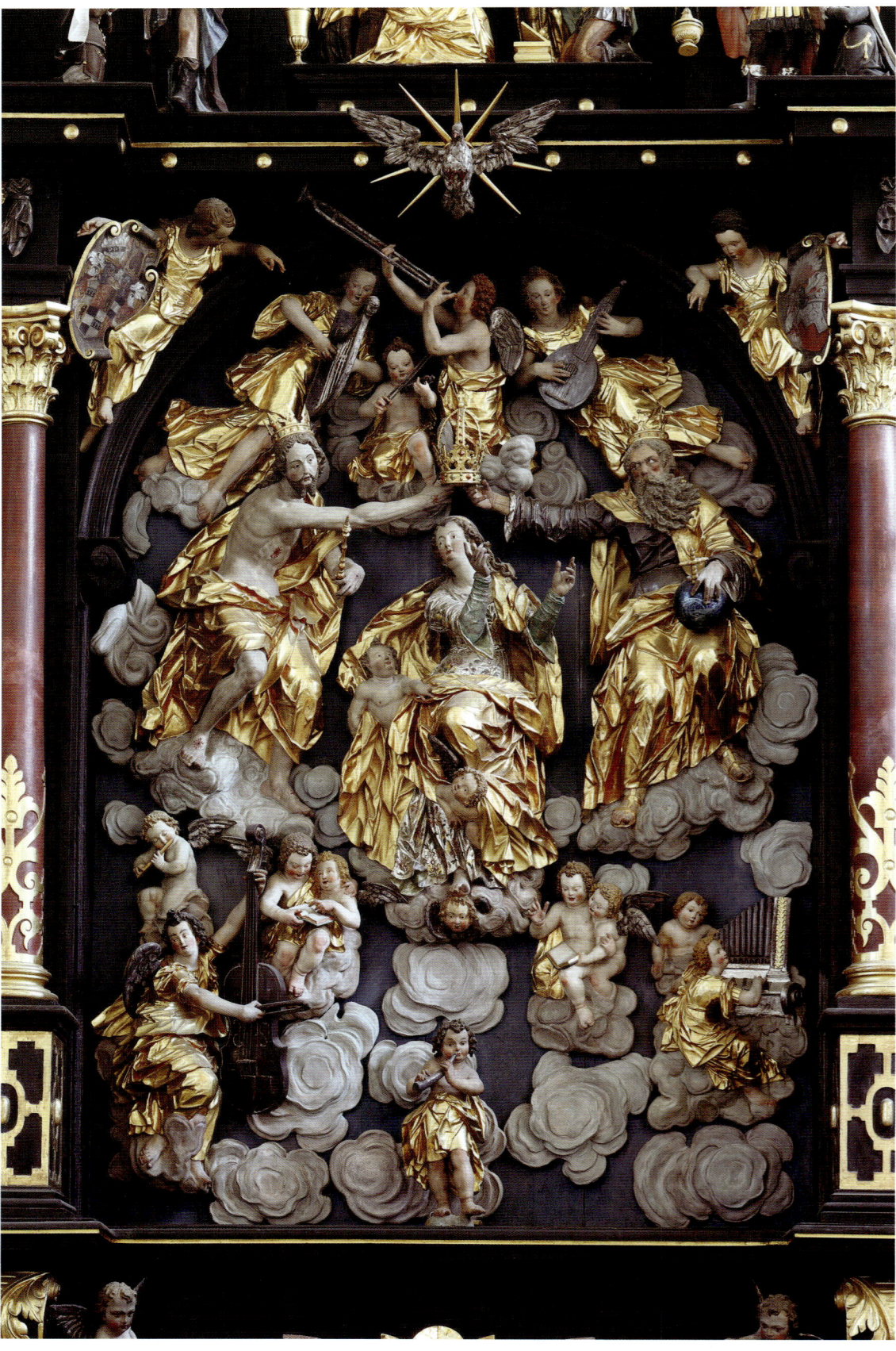

1.12
Detail of Rodt,
High Altarpiece [1.11],
*The Coronation of
the Virgin.*

pulpit from Degler, as well as the bronze crucifixion group from Reichle (to be discussed later on in this chapter).[15] Merk commissioned Reichle to produce a series of thirty-two over-life-size (over three metres high) terracotta figures of saints, some of whose relics were owned by the church.[16] They were once installed high up in the choir and transepts of the church, echoing those that had been produced for the Jesuit church of St Michael in Munich by Carlo di Cesare del Palagio (1538-1598/1600) in the 1580s and 1590s.[17] However Reichle's figures were unfortunately mostly destroyed in 1873, when the church was renovated; their original positioning can be seen in Bernhard Hertfelder's engraving of the church interior, dating from 1627.[18]

Despite the juxtaposition of different styles, Hans Reichle's crucifixion group and Degler's three altarpieces convey essentially the same doctrinal ideas of redemption through Christ's sacrifice. Their triumphant assertion of Catholic imagery evinces the religious tensions of the city in the wake of the Counter Reformation. Their works must be viewed in the context of the basilica's somewhat vexed ecclesiastical and civic history.

Altarpieces by Christoph Rodt at Illertissen and by Jörg Zürn at Überlingen

Degler's retable in Augsburg should be compared with two contemporary altarpieces elsewhere in Bavaria: that by Christoph Rodt at Illertissen, and Jörg Zürn's altarpiece at Überlingen, testaments to the profusion of altarpieces being commissioned in Bavaria in the early seventeenth century.

Christoph Rodt's altarpiece of 1604 at the parish church of St Martin in Illertissen in the south of Bavaria is exactly contemporary with Degler's at Augsburg [1.11]. Like Degler's, it is a soaring construction of polychromed and gilt wood, designed to create an impact from a distance, impressive above all because of its size.[19] The Illertissen retable is signed and dated on the back. Another inscription also on the back records that it was erected as an epitaph to his family by Freiherr Ferdinand Vöhlin von Frickenhausen (d. 1603) and his wife Anna Maria (d. 1615). The two donors and their five children

are somewhat unconventionally shown in the upper tier, kneeling on either side of the *Adoration of the Magi*. Thus the family too is adoring the Christ child. Above this scene is the figure of St Michael overcoming the devil, with accompanying angels, and the slightly smaller figures of St Catherine of Alexandria and St Barbara. Two larger angels holding garlands of fruit and flowers are perched on the volutes at the sides. Crowning the whole is Christ as Redeemer, seated over the globe, his arms outspread, revealing his wounds, with the symbols of the Passion behind him. Adoring him are the kneeling figures of the Virgin and St John the Baptist. The main scene depicts a highly animated *Coronation of the Virgin*, filled with music-making angels on clouds [1.12]. Between the main columns stand the four Evangelists, while larger figures of St Peter and St Paul are positioned in the wing-like structures to the left and right sides. The classical composition of the whole, in the form of a triumphal arch, recalls Degler's high altarpiece in Augsburg, and is indebted to a design of 1551

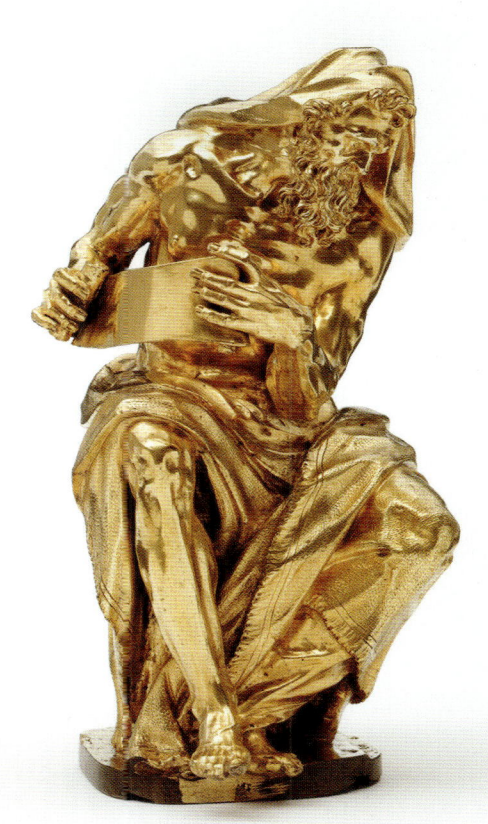

1.13
Hubert Gerhard (gilder Johann Müller; caster Carlo di Cesari del Pelagio), *Seated Prophet* from the Fugger altarpiece, gilt bronze, c. 1581-4, height 23.8 cm. Victoria and Albert Museum, London (inv. no. A. 28-1964).

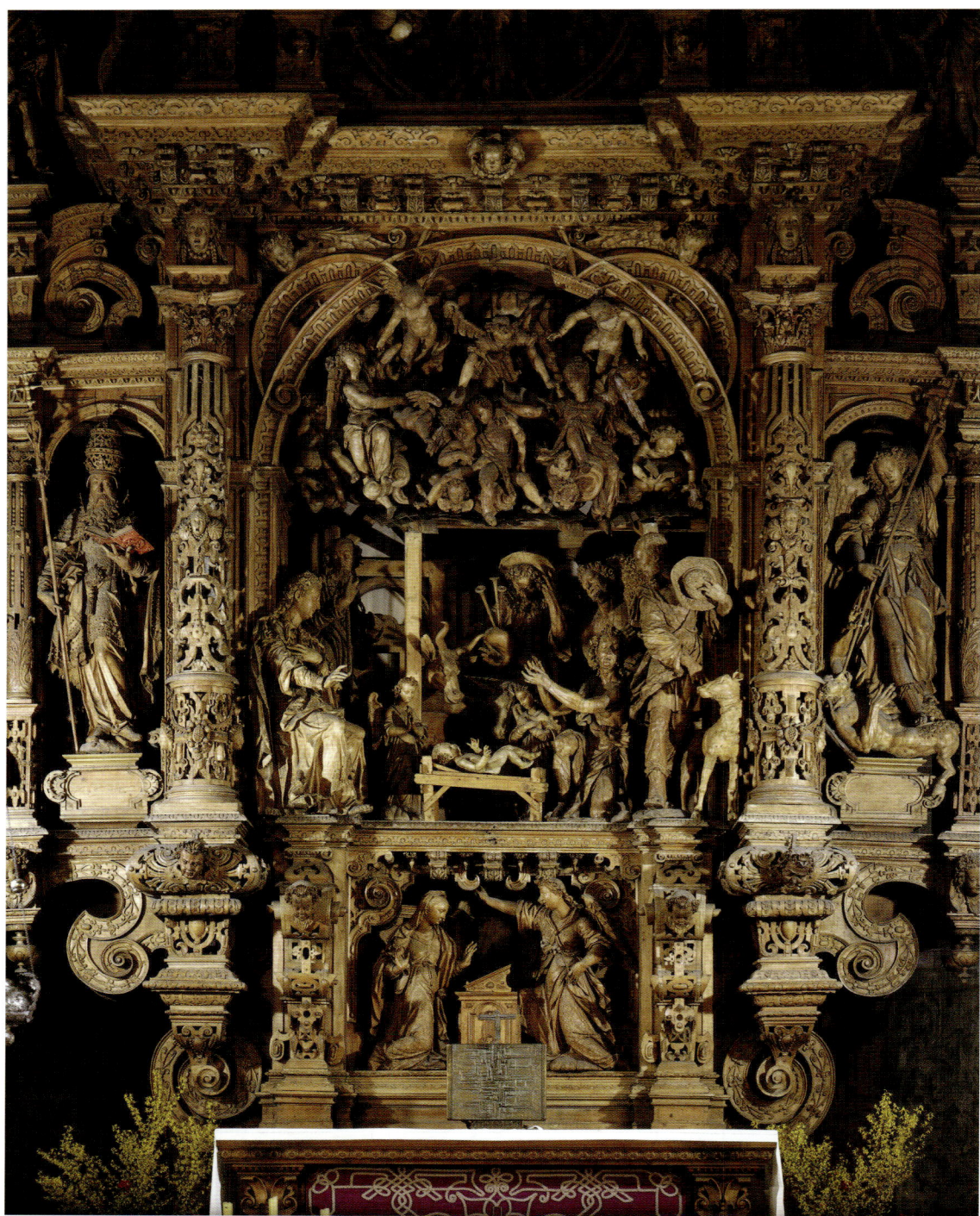

1.14
Jörg Zürn, High
Altarpiece, limewood,
1613-16. St Nicholas
Minster at Überlingen.

from Sebastiano Serlio's (1475-c. 1554) multi-volume treatise on architecture and architectural proportions (*Tutte l'opere d'architettura et prospetiva*). Rodt may also have been inspired by the form of the high altarpiece in the Jesuit church of St Michael (the Michaelskirche), Munich, of the 1590s, probably designed by the Italo-Dutch court architect Friedrich Sustris (c. 1540-99).[20] The Jesuit church of St Michael had been founded by Duke William V in 1583 and became the prototype for later buildings in Bavaria.[21]

The classical format of Rodt's retable is however dominated by decorative scroll motifs, redolent of mannerism, and vibrant polychromy—the black background, red columns, gilt architectural ornaments, as well as the figures' brightly coloured drapery. As a result, the altarpiece resembles a giant monstrance, and at the same time the black structure gives it a weight and monumentality associated with sixteenth-century German stone epitaphs, rather than wood retables.[22] The drapery and faces of the figures are stylistically allied to sculpture of the Weilheim school, in particular the work of Hans Degler, who may have been

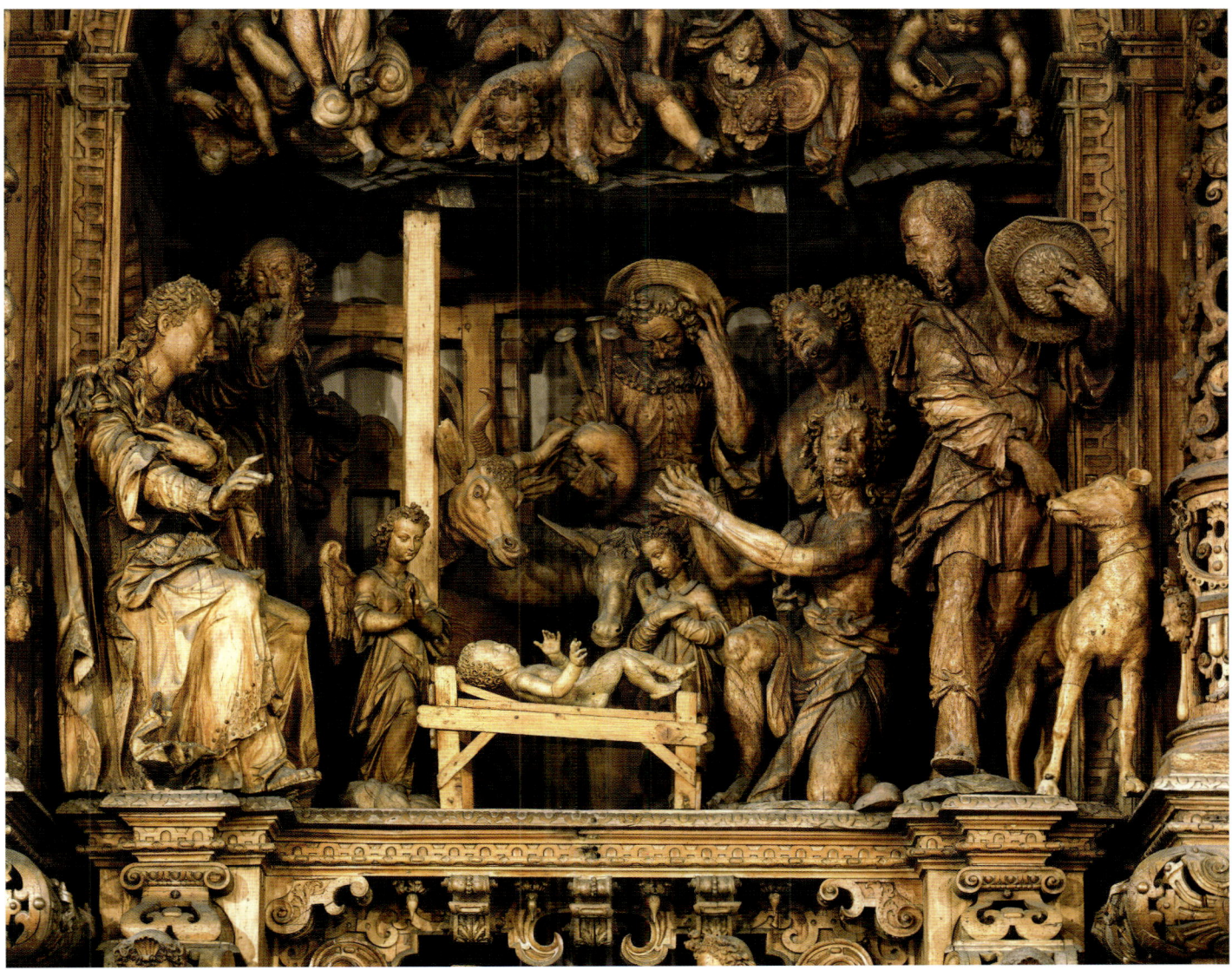

Rodt's teacher. The *St Michael* additionally recalls Hubert Gerhard's bronze of the same saint on the façade of St Michael's church of the 1590s [1.2], whilst the contrapposto poses of the Evangelists are reminiscent of Gerhard's much smaller seated gilt bronze figures of c. 1581-4 for the altarpiece made as a memorial to Christoph Fugger, commissioned by Hans Fugger (1531-98) for the church of the Magdalene in Augsburg (now in the Victoria and Albert Museum) [1.13].[23]

The altarpiece by Jörg Zürn and his workshop was produced only a few years later, from 1613 to 1616, at the Minster of St Nikolaus in Überlingen on the shores of Lake Constance, in the southwest of Bavaria [1.14 and 1.15].[24] Zürn was the most gifted member of a dynasty of sculptors working on the shores of Lake

Constance. His son, Hans Jakob Zürn, was to train in Degler's workshop in 1616. Their work in the late sixteenth and early seventeenth century illustrates the continuation and evolution of fifteenth- and sixteenth-century carved wood altarpieces in Bavaria into the seventeenth century. At the same time, certain features in Zürn's work epitomize international links within Bavaria, both Flemish and Italian. Like Degler's high altarpiece, Zürn's depicts the *Nativity* as the main scene, set within an even more exuberant classicising framework. Beneath this scene is the *Annunciation*, and above is the *Coronation of the Virgin*. The language of Zürn's altarpiece—again recalling mannerism—with its elaborate decorative motifs is evidently indebted to the Antwerp sculptor and printmaker Cornelis Floris (1514-75), whose engravings of

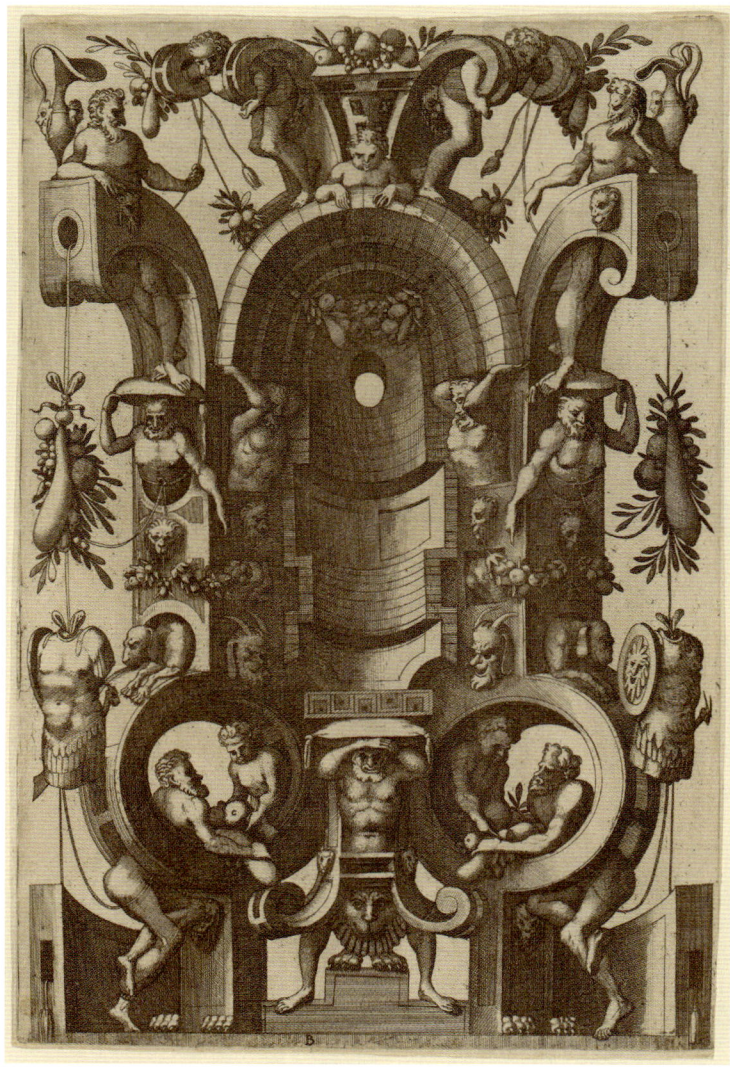

reliefs and epitaphs, and whose sculpture was in turn inspired by the Italian high renaissance [1.17].[25]

Bronzes in Augsburg and Munich: *The Crucifixion* by Hans Reichle at SS. Ulrich and Afra, Augsburg

As well as being seen in comparison with contemporary altarpieces elsewhere in Bavaria, Degler's altarpieces in Augsburg should also be considered in the immediate context of the basilica in which they were placed. They seem almost to embrace the bronze crucifixion group of 1605 by Hans Reichle, which was moved to its present position one bay nearer the choir at the east end of the church in the early nineteenth century. This bronze group was a costly and prestigious work, originally on a stone plinth, with Latin devotional inscriptions, lost when the group was moved in the nineteenth

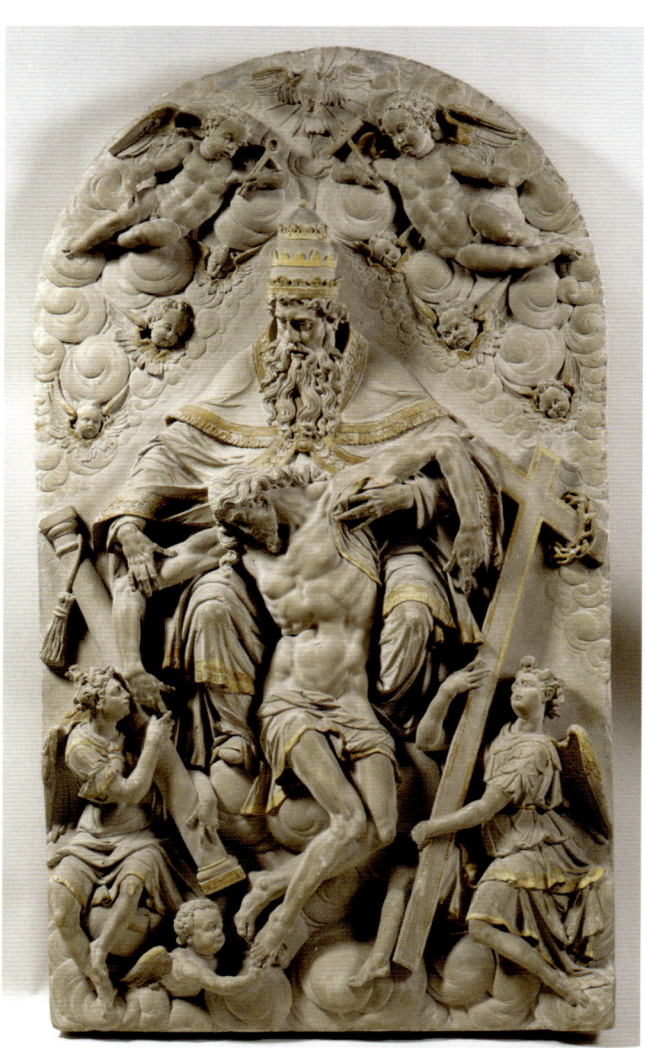

1.16
Cornelis Floris, *Decorative Ornament,* etching and engraving, dated 1557, 20.7 x 30.5 cm. National Gallery of Art, Washington DC., Ailsa Mellon Bruce Fund (inv. no. 1971.67.5).

1.17
Hans Morinck, *Throne of Mercy,* stone, c. 1612. Badisches Landesmuseum Karlsruhe (inv. no. C 3247).

grotesque ornament were disseminated throughout Europe [1.16]. As in Degler's work, the central scene with its pierced surrounding framework allows the light from behind to penetrate and illuminate the sculptures. Zürn's is a vivid rendering of the Biblical story, with life size gesticulating figures, but it differs in critical respects from the Augsburg and Illertissen altarpieces. Most obviously it is unpainted, like Riemenschneider's Creglingen triptych, and the figurative sculpture is more muscular than Degler's or Rodt's, the shepherd holding his hat on the right side for instance clearly recalling sixteenth-century precedents in the style of Michelangelo. These prototypes may have been conveyed via the work of the leading sculptor active in the city of Constance in the sixteenth century, the Netherlandish artist Hans Morinck (c. 1555-1616), who specialised in carved stone

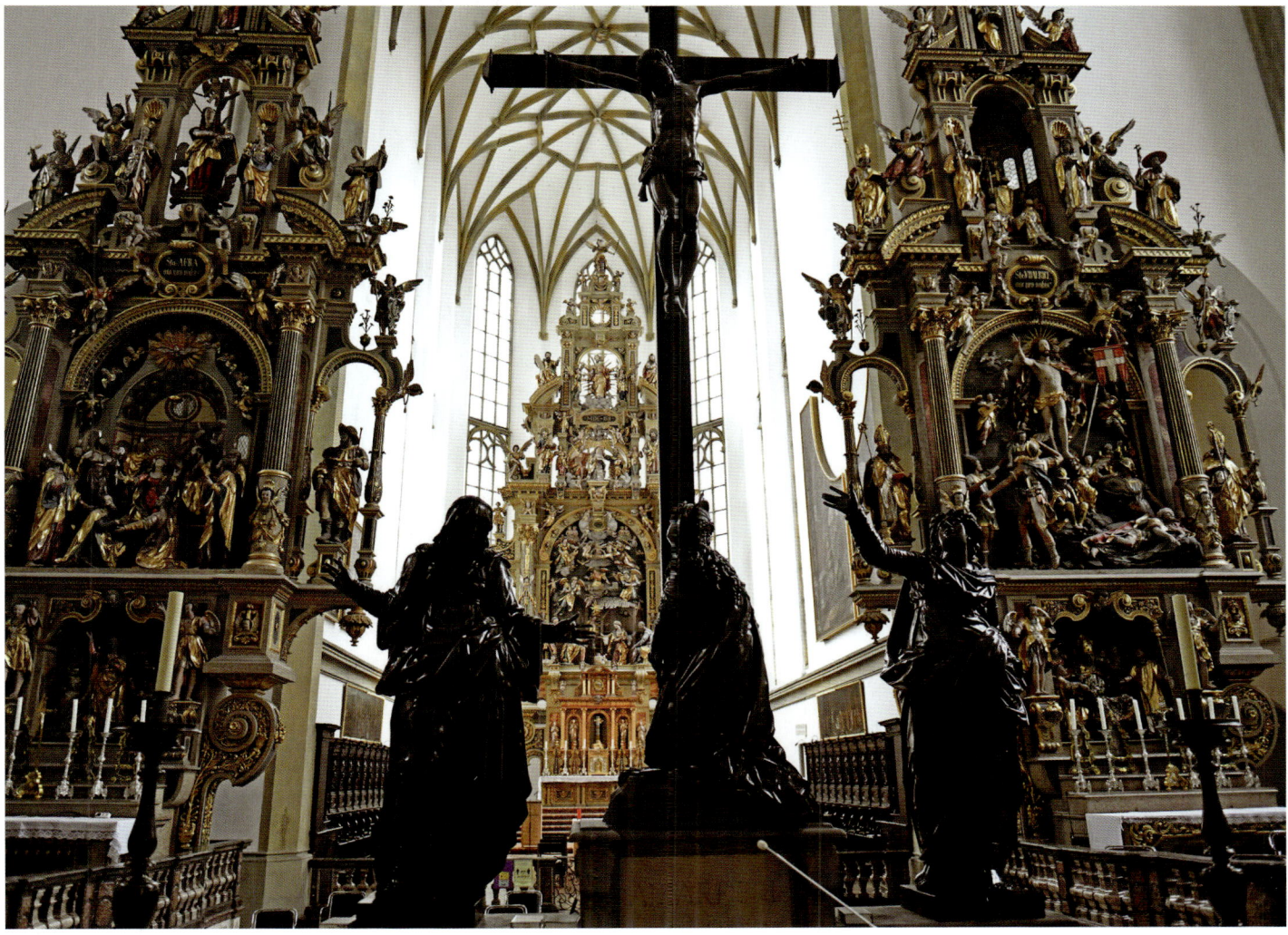

century.[26] It was cast by the Augsburg founder Wolfgang Neidhart the Younger (1575-1632) and was intended to be seen as part of the ensemble of altarpieces and architecture [1.3]. Reichle's group stood at the east end of the nave behind the altar used by the lay congregation. The choir and the high altar were reserved for the clergy. Similarly, the prototype for Reichle's group, Giambologna's crucifix at St Michael's church in Munich, stood at the entrance of the choir.[27]

At the foot of the cross are the three figures of the mourning Virgin, Mary Magdalene and St John the Evangelist [1.18]. The simultaneously graceful and pitiful figure of Christ on the cross recalls the work of Giambologna, with whom Reichle had worked in Florence from 1588 to 1595 [1.19]. The monochrome bronze, its surface smooth and luminous, renders not only Christ's body but the voluminous drapery on all three figures in an almost liquid fashion, seen for

example in the generous cascade of the Magda-lene's robe falling over the base of the cross [1.20]. The Magdalene recalls Reichle's own earlier rendition of the same subject made for the foot of Giambologna's bronze crucifix figure for St Michael's church in Munich in 1595, a gift from Ferdinando de' Medici, Grand Duke of Tuscany (1549-1609; r. 1587-1609) to William V [1.21 and 1.22]. Reichle had himself brought the crucifix from Florence to Munich in 1595.[28] These assured sculptures are also in the tradition of the bronzes of Adriaen de Vries and Hubert Gerhard in Augsburg, such as the *Augustus Fountain* by Gerhard of 1589-94 [1.1]. Abbot Merk may have been inspired by the Giambologna crucifix and Riechle's *Magdalene* in Munich to commission the crucifixion group for SS. Ulrich and Afra from Reichle. Like the figures on Degler's altarpieces, the dramatic gestures of the Virgin and St John in Reichle's bronze crucifixion

1.18
Hans Reichle, Crucifixion group, bronze, 1605, cast by Wolfgang Neidhart the Younger. Church of SS. Ulrich and Afra, Augsburg.

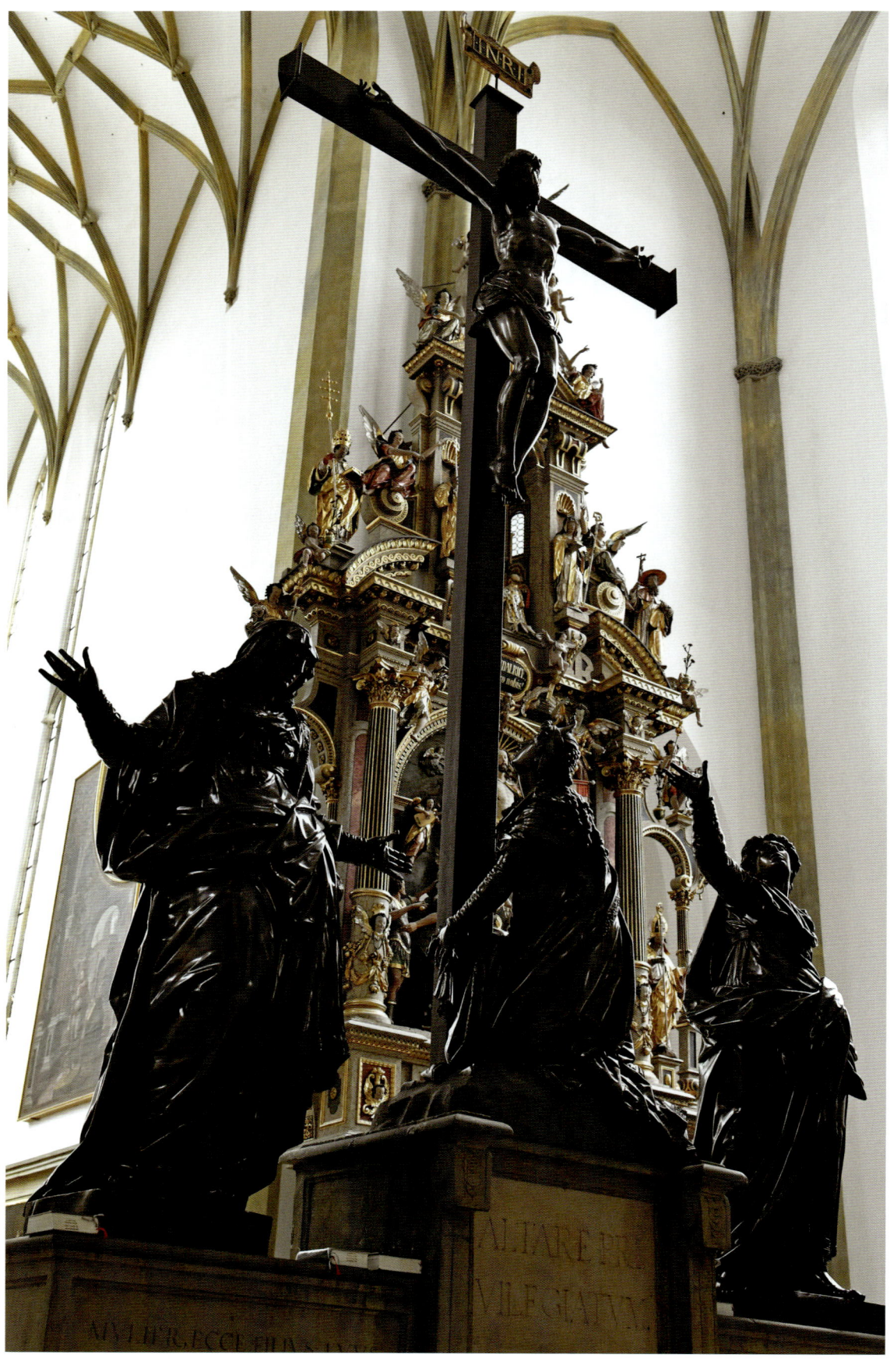

1.19
Detail of Reichle,
Crucifixion group [1.18],
crucifix.

> 1.20
Detail of Reichle,
Crucifixion group [1.18],
Mary Magdalene, St
John and
the Virgin.

> 1.21
Hans Reichle, *Mary
Magdalene*, bronze, 1595.
Church of
St Michael, Munich.

> 1.22
Detail of Reichle, *Mary
Magdalene* [1.21], head.

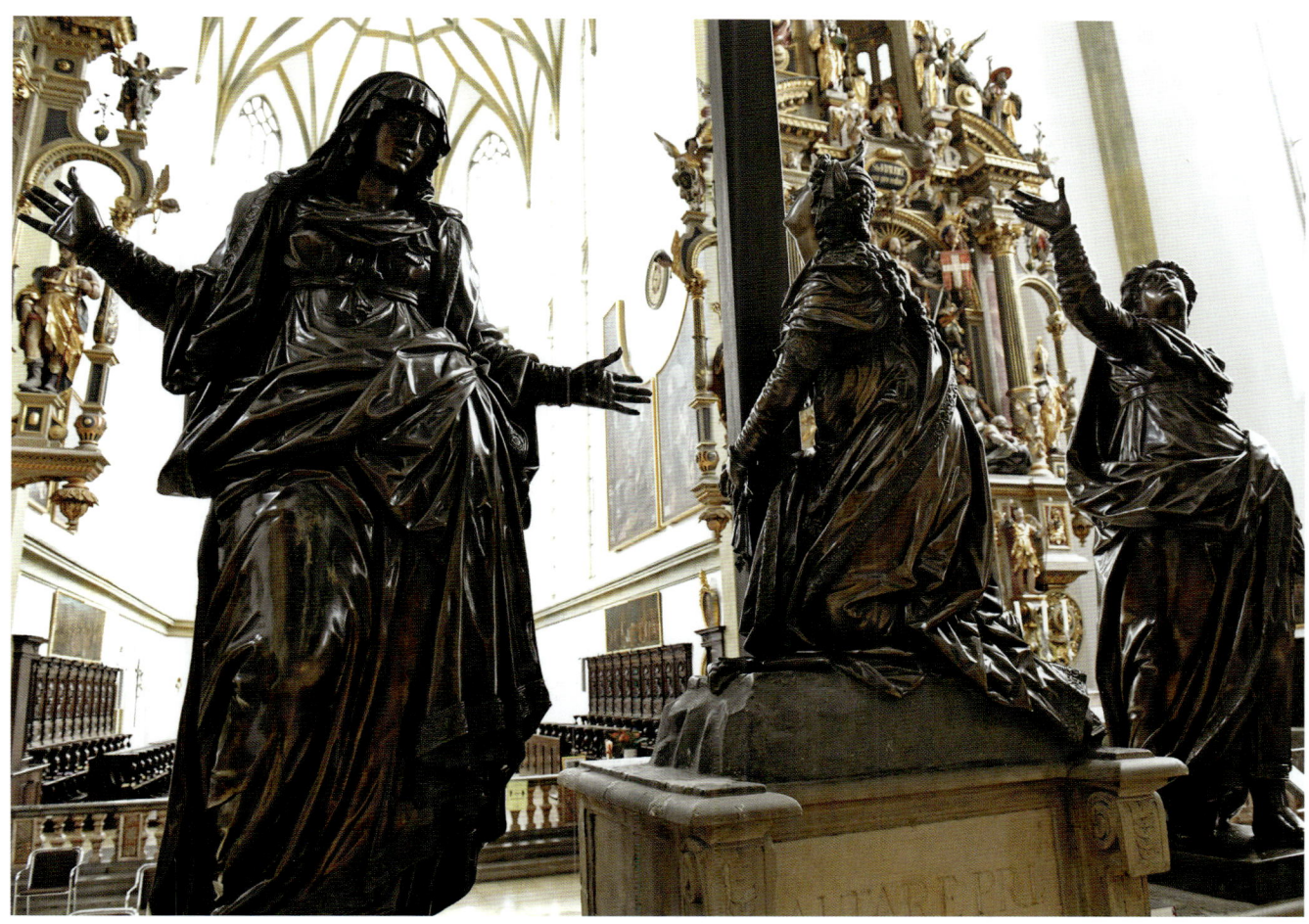

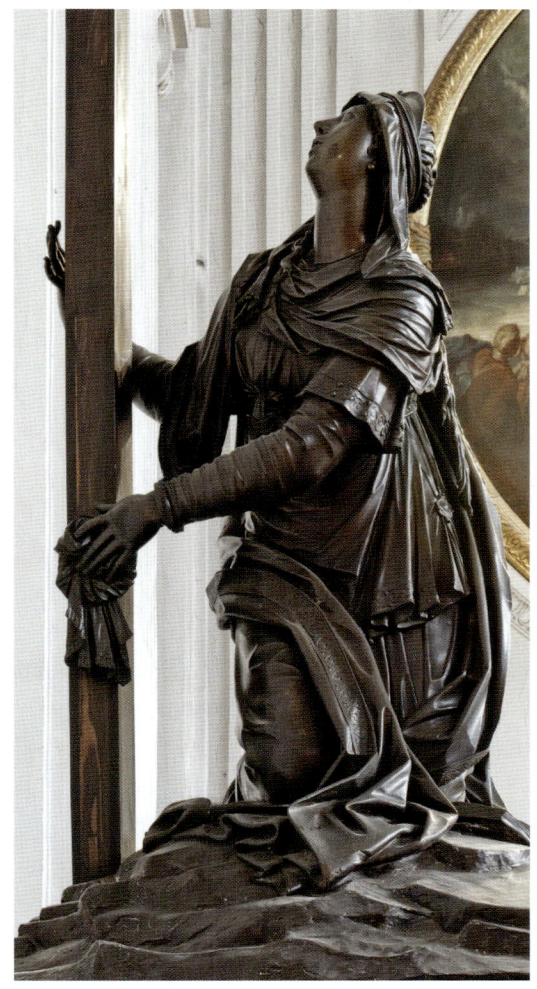

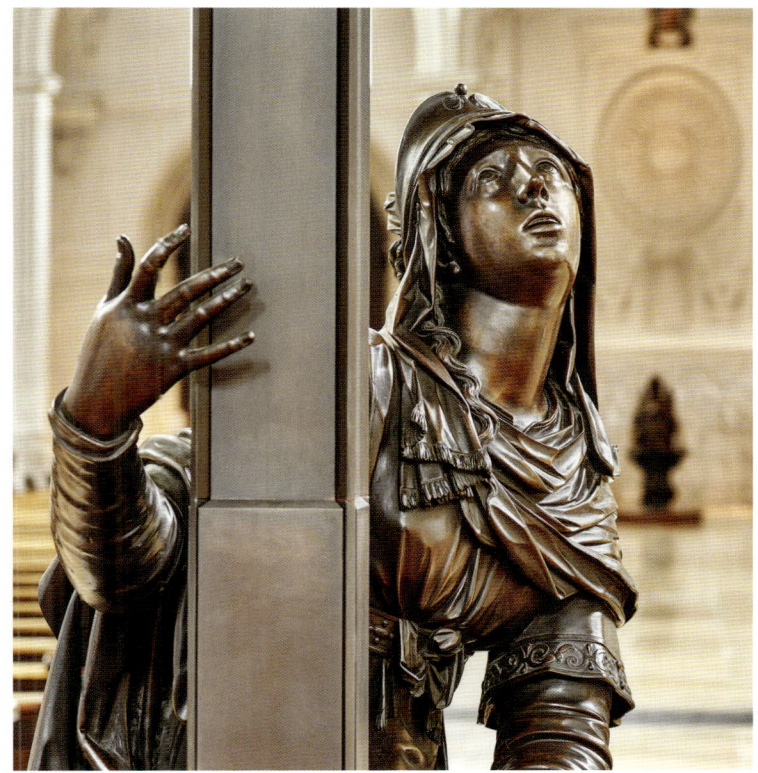

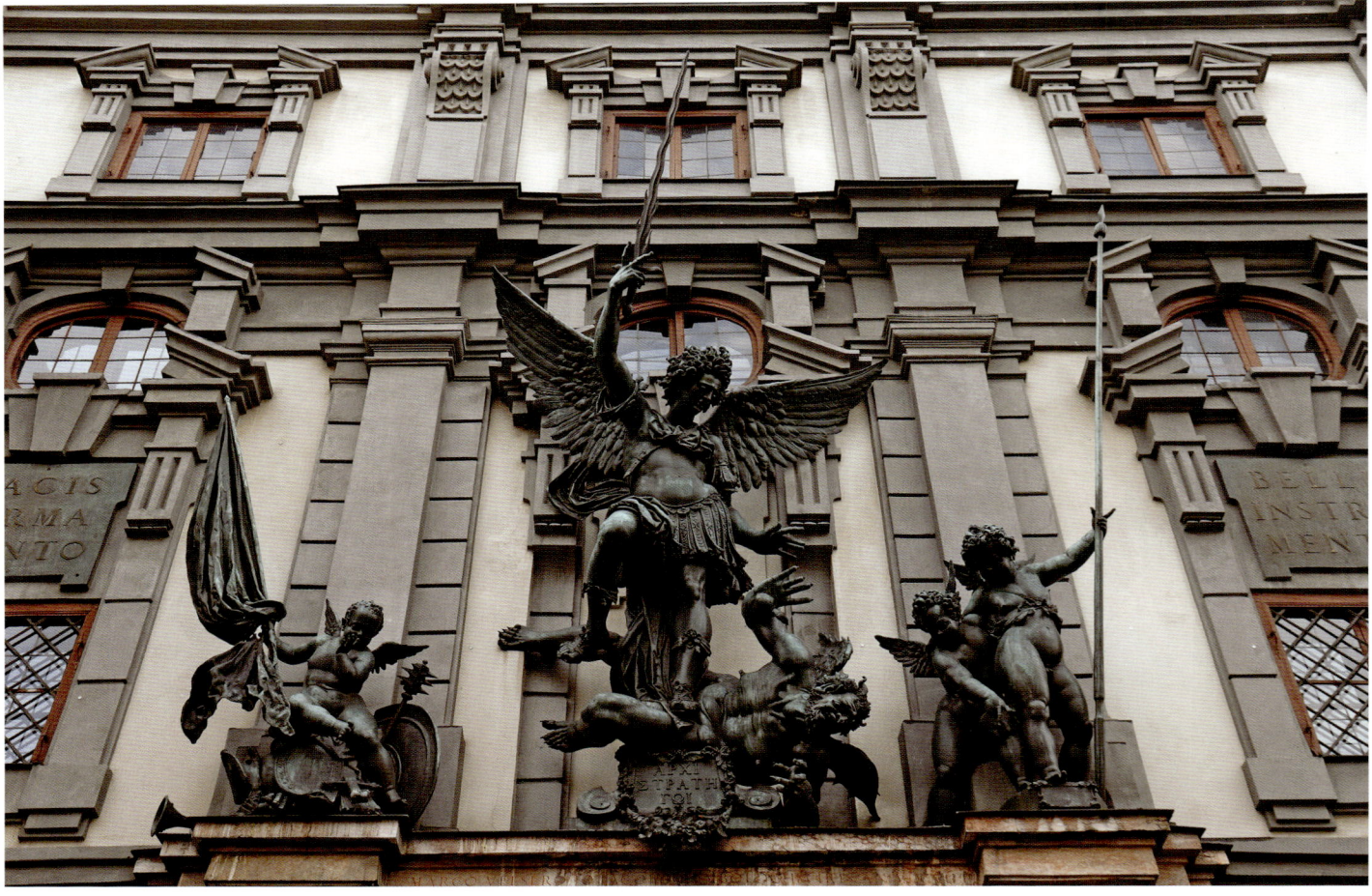

command the viewer's attention. St John's upraised right hand directs us to the pathos of the crucified Christ, while the outstretched arms of the Virgin echo the resurrected saviour's same gesture on the high altarpiece behind, expressing the sorrows of the Passion [1.20].

The three altarpieces by Degler are polychromed and gilt limewood, whilst Reichle's crucifixion was cast in bronze. Although they were commissioned at the same time, and are more or less contemporary with one another, Degler's sculptures illustrate and represent the continuation of the vernacular tradition of altarpieces going back to the fifteenth and sixteenth centuries, whereas Reichle's crucifixion points to an entirely different tradition. The use of bronze for works of art was hardly a new idea, but a life-size bronze group within a church was novel in South Germany. In both style and material the crucifixion is more akin to the sculpture being produced in Italy in the late sixteenth century, via the artistic language used by De Vries and Gerhard, rather than contemporary and earlier

German works of art. Yet at the same time it expresses the new baroque style, and could not be mistaken for an Italian mannerist work.

St Michael by Hans Reichle, The Armoury, Augsburg

Contemporary with Reichle's work on the crucifixion for SS. Ulrich and Afra is his remarkable bronze group of St Michael defeating the devil for the façade of the Armoury (*Zeughaus*) in Augsburg from 1602-7 [**1.23 and 1.25**]. The archangel is a suitable subject to embellish the Armoury, combining martial triumph with religious fervour. St Michael, holding aloft a giant flaming sword, overpowers the defeated faun-like devil, a magnificent male nude, whose grotesque face and spiky bat-like wings contrast with the noble mien and graceful feathered wings of his conqueror. To the left, a nude winged putto seated on a heap of weaponry holds a furled banner. One of the two smiling putti standing on the right clasps a lance, while the other points down to the doorway of the Arsenal below. Like

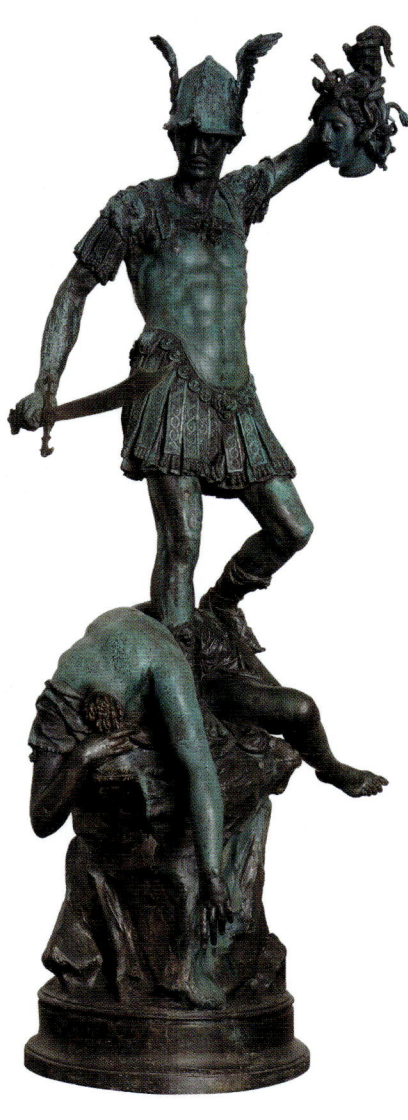

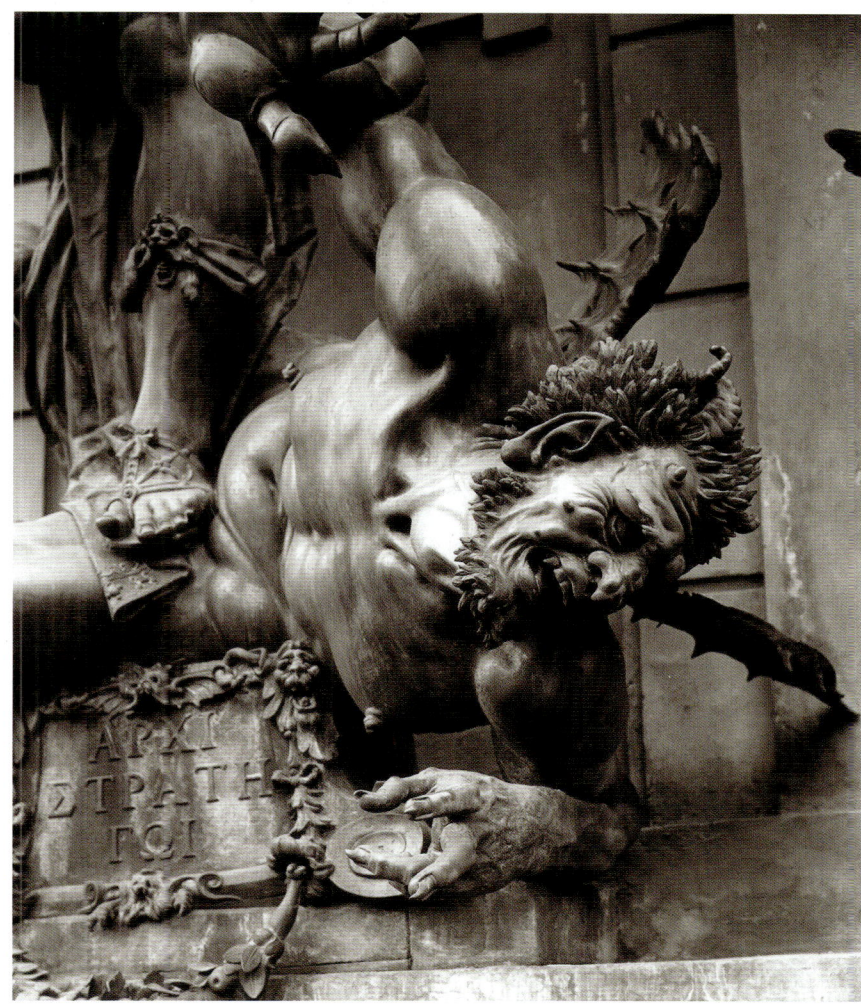

1.24
Hubert Gerhard (based on a
design by Friedrich Sustris),
Perseus Fountain, bronze,
c. 1585-90. The Residenz,
Munich.

1.25
Detail of Reichle, *St Michael*
[1.24], figure of Satan
(photograph of 1926).

1.26
Christoph Angermair,
Satyr head, ivory, c. 1623-7,
height 27.3 cm. Bayerisches
Nationalmuseum, Munich
(inv. no. R 4708).

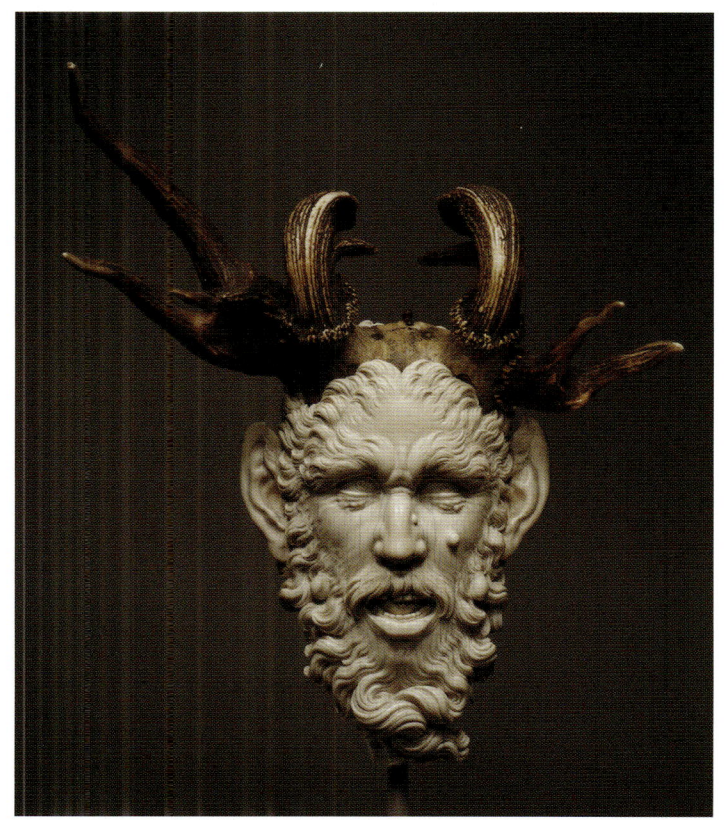

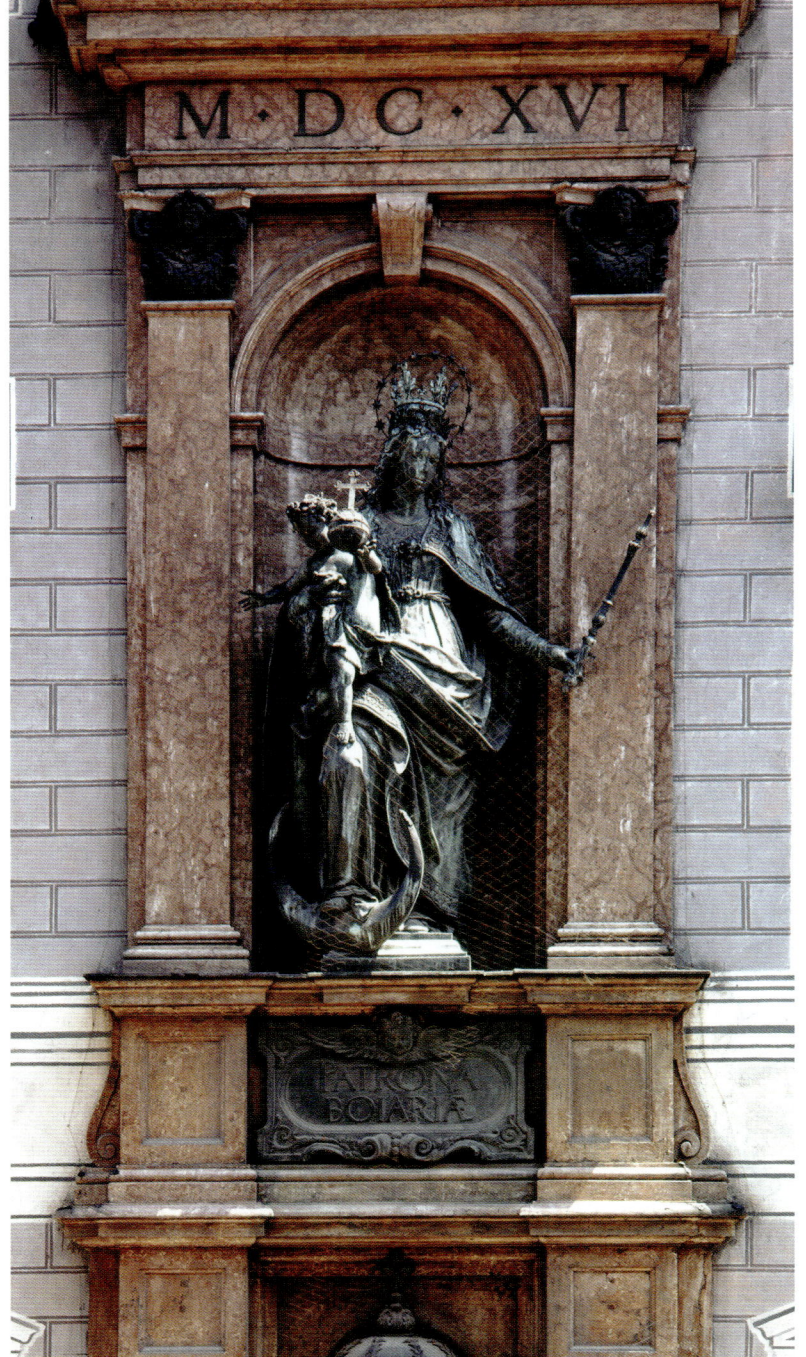

the crucifixion in the basilica of SS. Ulrich and Afra, this ensemble was cast by the founder Wolfgang Neidhart.

The majestic baroque Armoury in Augsburg was built for the Imperial Free City by Elias Holl (1573-1646) from 1602 to 1607; Reichle's military bronze was conceived as part of the architectural ensemble.[29] The over-life-size St Michael is partly dressed in classical armour, though barefoot. The pose and costume are reminiscent of Hubert Gerhard's *Perseus Fountain* at the Munich Residenz of 1585-90 [1.24], as well as the same artist's *St Michael* of 1588 on St Michael's church [1.2].[30] The grotesque head of Reichle's Satan is however distinctive, his agonized pose and claw-like hands contrasting with St Michael's graceful contrapposto and the supple Italianate putti at each side [1.25). Reichle's work indubitably laid the foundation for subsequent sculpture in Germany in the seventeenth century. The devil's idiosyncratic head may have inspired the ivory heads of satyrs of 1623-7, carved for the Munich court by Christoph Angermair, Reichle's slightly younger contemporary, to be discussed in more detail below [1.26].[31] Angermair's work suggests that the almost caricature-like earthy flourish of the bronze devil could be transmogrified into an ivory carving on a far smaller scale made for the urbane and refined Wittelsbach court.

Hans Krumper: *Patrona Boiariae*, The Residenz, Munich, 1615

Shortly after Reichle produced his monumental bronzes for Augsburg, the figure of the Virgin as *Patrona Boiariae*, the Protector of Bavaria (the archaic use of the name 'Boariae' rather than

1.27
Hans Krumper, *Patrona Boiariæ*, bronze, 1615, cast by Bartolomäus Wenglein. West façade of The Residenz, Munich.

1.28
Detail of Krumper, *Patrona Boiariæ* [1.27], cartouche.

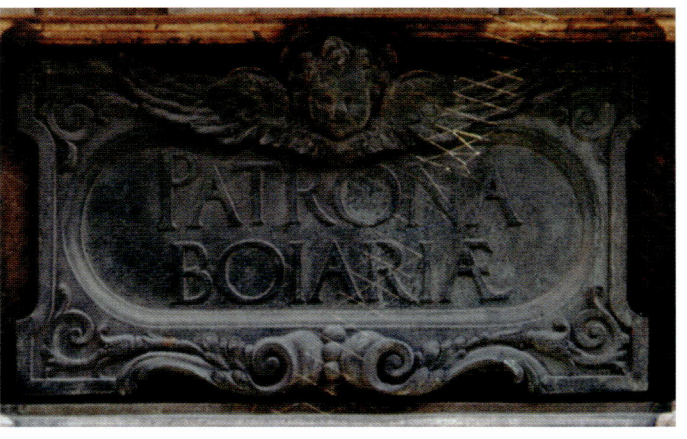

'Bavariae' referred specifically to the Bavaria ruled by the medieval duke Theodo), was designed for the façade of the Munich Residenz in 1615.[32] This bronze was produced by Hans Degler's brother-in-law, Hans Krumper, who had himself married the architect Friedrich Sustris's daughter. Krumper submitted the wax model for the bronze in 1614; the following year it was cast by the Munich founder Bartolomäus Wenglein, and chased by the goldsmith Georg Mair [**1.27 and 1.28**].[33] In a red marble aedicule, the Virgin—crowned as Queen of Heaven with a halo of twelve stars—rests her bent right leg on the crescent moon, both allusions to the Immaculate Conception of the Virgin. The Christ child, standing on the Virgin's right knee, presents the orb, holding out his right hand in an answering gesture to his mother's out-stretched left hand holding the sceptre. Beneath the figures is a large lantern in which burns the eternal light, another symbol of the Immaculate Conception. A shield serving as a cartouche, adorned with laurels and cherubim heads, is held by two angels above the architrave. It is inscribed with an antiphon, 'Sub tuum praesidium confugimus, sub quo secure laetique degimus' (we take refuge under your protection, under which we live safely and joyfully). The current shield and putti are copies of the original bronzes, which were lost during the Second World War.[34]

Just as Reichle's *St Michael* for the Arsenal at Augsburg was a statement of secular power, using the imagery of an archangel, so the *Patrona Boiariae* asserts the indivisibility of earthly and sacred power, representing the authority of the ruler of Bavaria, Duke Maximilian, and his lifelong devotion to the Virgin. The duke made numerous pilgrimages to Marian shrines in Germany, decreeing that after his death his heart should be buried at the Shrine to Our Lady at Altötting, to which he was particularly devoted. The hearts of all subsequent kings of Bavaria were to be buried at the shrine.[35] In fact, Maximilian declared the Virgin as the Protector of Bavaria not only through Krumper's sculpture, but in other ways, such as ordering a gold coin to be struck in 1610 with an image of the Virgin and the legend 'sub tuum praesidium' above a

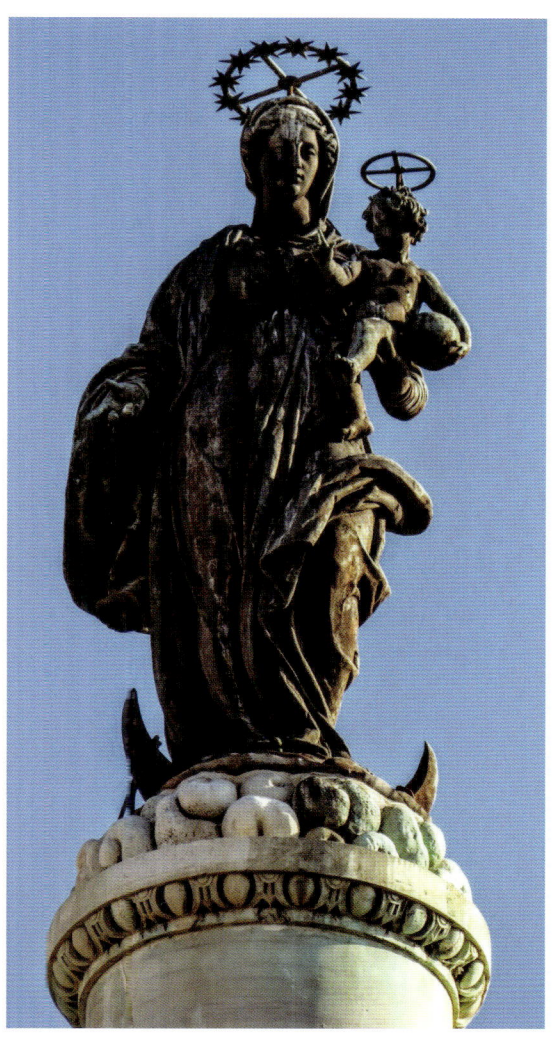

1.29
Guillaume Berthelot, *Virgin and Child*, bronze, 1613, cast by Domenico Ferrerio. Piazza S. Maria Maggiore, Rome.

silhouette of the city of Munich, and a four volume publication, *Bavaria sancta*, issued from 1615 onwards, narrating the lives of saints in Bavaria with a foreword overtly stating that Bavaria was under the protection of the Virgin.[36]

The composition of the Virgin and Christ child can be compared with the swaying pose of Guillaume Berthelot's (d. 1648) bronze *Virgin and Child* of 1613 in the Piazza S. Maria Maggiore, Rome [**1.29**]. Both were positioned in prominent public places for citizens to see and revere, in Munich and Rome respectively. While Berthelot's and Krumper's bronzes assert the Virgin's supremacy, the differences between them reveal clear distinctions between the Bavarian and Roman styles. Although Berthelot was a native of France, his work in Rome is effectively Roman, and the founder of that particular statue was an Italian, Domenico Ferrerio.[37] Stylistically, the sweep of the drapery and the serene facial features seen in Berthelot's bronze contrast with

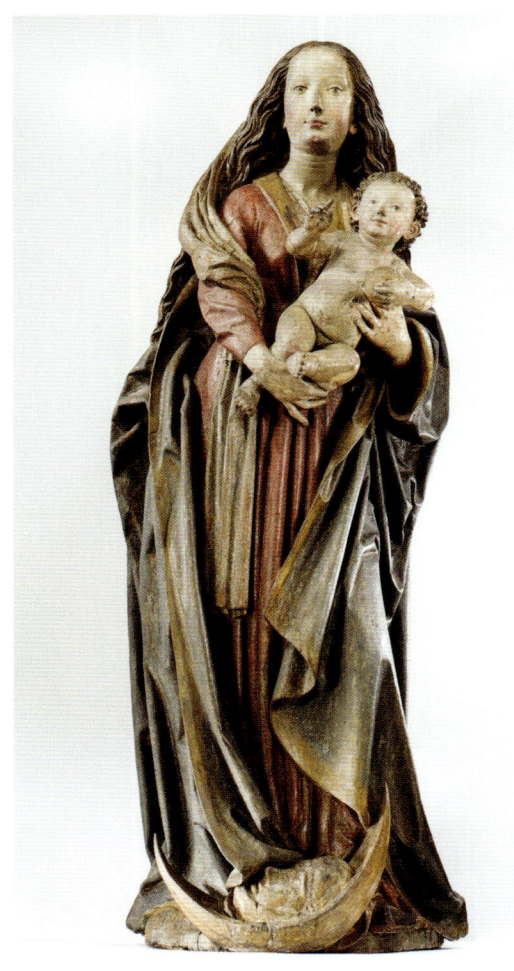

initially because of the clash between Protestant and Catholic factions, and ultimately became a conflict between the major European powers, leading to widespread violence and disruption. Not only was there looting and the destruction of existing buildings and works of art, but the fighting and its attendant financial implications for both church and state inevitably meant that there was a comparative dearth of commissions for large-scale sculptures and altarpieces until well into the second half of the century. One apparent exception was the Marian Column (*Mariensäule*), a gilt bronze figure of the Virgin and Child on a marble column in the Schrannenplatz (now the Marienplatz) in Munich, constructed in 1639-41 [1.31]. This was erected at the behest of Duke Maximilian as a votive offering to the Virgin for the redemption of the city after Swedish troops under King Gustav Adolph (1594-1632) had invaded Bavaria in 1632, defeated only in 1635/ not to be defeated until 1635.[39] The inauguration of the Marian Column, the first of its kind north of the Alps, not only celebrated the gratitude of the Bavarian people for the triumph over/ defeat of foreign invaders, but simultaneously commemorated the end of an attack of the plague in the city. Nevertheless, although it was a new installation, tellingly the gilt bronze sculpture of the Virgin was repurposed, having originally been made some years before by Hubert Gerhard in 1593 for the (never completed) tomb of Duke William V, Maximilian's father, in the church of St Michael.[40] It was subsequently placed on the high altar of the church of Our Lady (the *Frauenkirche*) in Munich from 1603 to 1620, until its repositioning on the column.[41] The Marian Column in Munich may have been inspired by Berthelot's monument in front of S. Maria Maggiore in Rome of 1614, mentioned earlier in relation to Hans Krumper's sculpture of the Virgin on the façade of the Residenz [1.27]. As in Krumper's figure, the Virgin is shown as Queen of Heaven and as the Virgin of the Immaculate Conception, a further demonstration of Duke Maximilian's devotion to the Virgin. But Gerhard's sculpture, with its fluid, Italianate drapery, clearly embodies an imported Florentine style. Again, the public and political dimension was indissolubly fused with

the heavier—indeed Germanic—proportions seen in Krumper's group. The long flowing h air of the Munich Madonna echoes that seen on any number of earlier German depictions of the Virgin, such as the polychromed poplar figure of the *Virgin and Child* by Michel Erhart (c. 1440/ 5-1522) of around 1480 (1.30).[38] Krumper's work then recalls Italianate bronzes, such as those by Gerhard and De Vries, and even parallels the Roman baroque, as seen in Berthelot's monumental figure. But the *Patrona Boiariae* is at the same time unmistakably rooted in the traditional forms of Krumper's native land.

The Marian Column in Munich

The first two decades of the century were artistically the end of an era, as well as heralding the distant beginning of a new one. This fertile era in South Germany was to be interrupted by the outbreak of the Thirty Years' War in 1618, shortly after Krumper's figure was created for Munich. The long-fought war came about

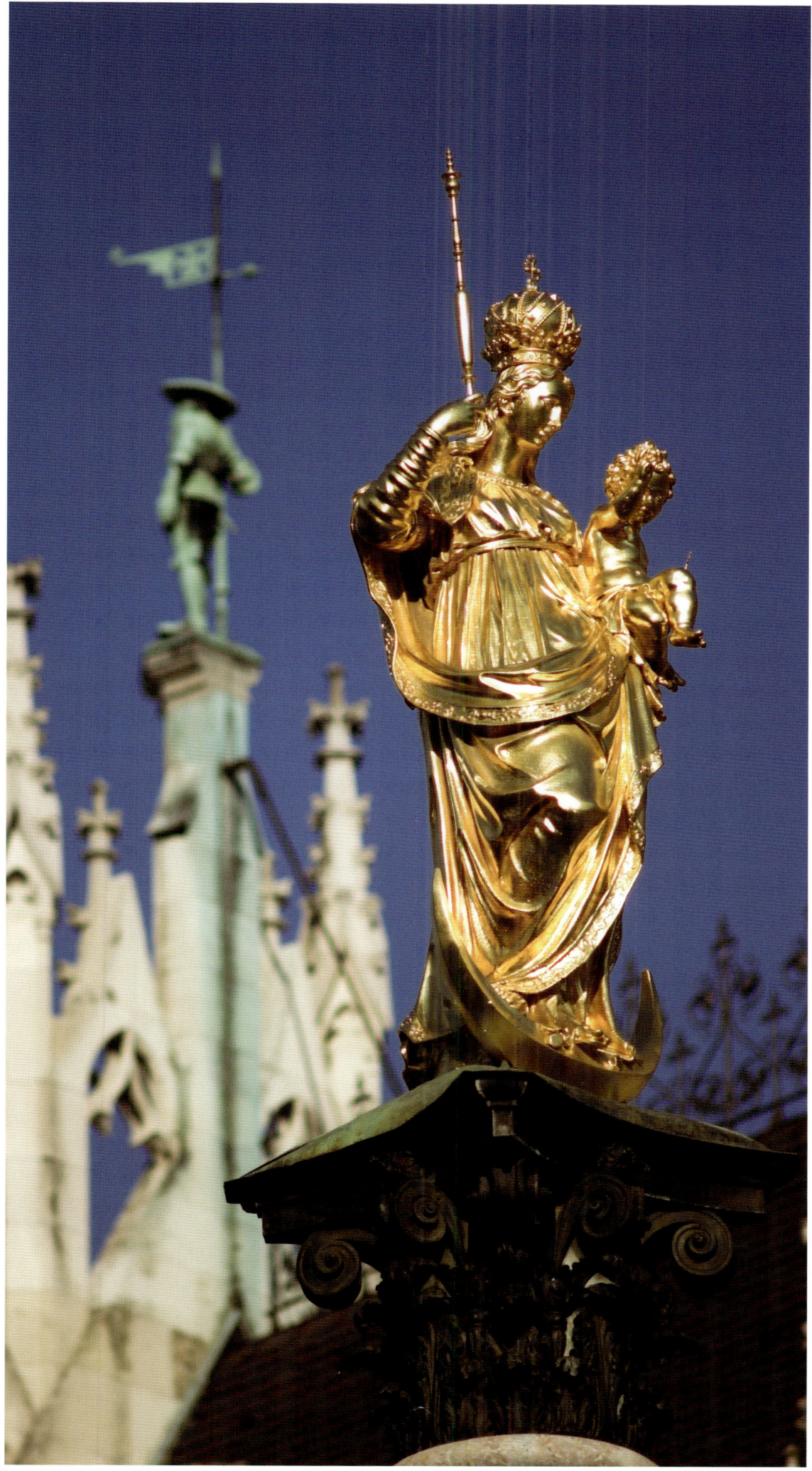

1.31
Hubert Gerhard,
The Virgin, Marian
Column (*Mariensäule*),
gilt bronze on marble
column, erected 1638.
Marienplatz (Schrannen-
platz), Munich.

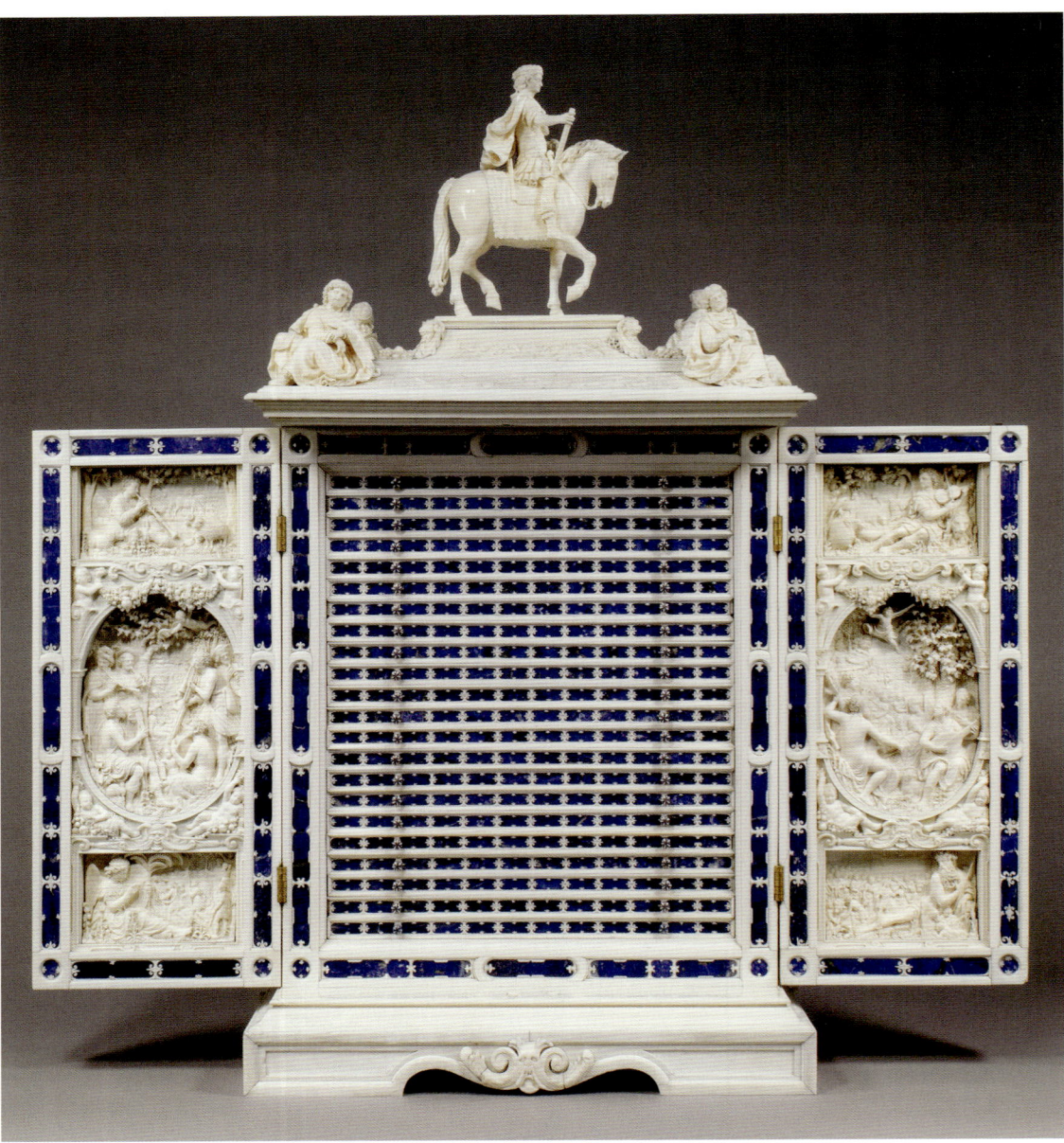

religious meaning. Relics were placed under the figure's crown, and at the base four armed angels, each fighting a different beast, symbolise the overcoming of adversities: war, pestilence, famine and heresy. The bronze angels may have been cast from models made in Georg Petel's former workshop, and were produced by the founder Bernhard Ernst, who apparently suffered enormous technical difficulties in bringing them to fruition. With the advent of the Thirty Years' War much expertise in the art of bronze casting had been lost.[42]

Ivories by Christoph Angermair

It is fitting to end this chapter on the early decades of the seventeenth century with Christoph Angermair and Georg Petel, two of the greatest sculptors and practitioners of ivory of their time. Like Degler and Krumper, they were both of the Weilheim school of sculptors. Angermair, who was slightly older than Petel, was to teach the younger man the art of ivory carving in Munich.[43] Although Angermair's workshop produced polychromed wood figures for altarpieces, and indeed he had been apprenticed to Hans Degler, he subsequently worked for the court at Munich, where his chief works were ivory [see also 1.26]. This prized material had been of immense importance for sculpture in the medieval period but became less easily obtainable in the fifteenth and sixteenth centuries. In the seventeenth century ivory sculpture prospered gained popularity once more, especially at the German courts.[44]

Angermair's most significant work is the magnificent coin cabinet, signed and dated 1618, commissioned by Duke Maximilian, and now in the Bayerisches Nationalmuseum, Munich [1.32].[45] The cabinet is an intricately fashioned work of art of carved ivory, adorned with lapis lazuli and silver gilt mounts. It held the ducal collection of antique coins, modern gold copies of antique coins, renaissance medals, and other treasured objects, including a chess set. Ivory panels sculpted with virtuoso reliefs of classical subjects are mounted on an oak core, and the whole is surmounted by an equestrian figure of Emperor Constantine, surrounded by four shackled kings in classical robes seated at the corners. The complex iconography of the reliefs around the cabinet is ambitious and multifarious, depicting allegories of knowledge and belief, Christian thought and pagan philosophy, the legendary past and the political present, all with the aim of glorifying the ruling house of the Wittelsbachs. Two allegorical reliefs on the front of the cabinet complement each other [1.33 and 1.34]. One is an allegorical figure of an old woman representing the ancient history: she holds a scroll with Greek lettering, standing before a plinth inscribed in Latin. The pendant relief shows a young woman, representing coinage and humanist learning in the present. In her right hand she holds a coin she has picked up—or perhaps excavated—from the earth at her feet. She stands on a pile of discarded ancient coins to be given new life in the present. Beneath, two putti hold the Wittelsbach coat of arms.

After the start of the Thirty Years' War in 1618, small-scale, portable sculptures became more desirable for both patrons and artists. Angermair's coin cabinet was hardly a portable item, but it was designed to contain small precious works, and illustrates the high value placed on ivory and on other small-scale works of art (*Kleinkunst*) at Maximilian's court. This

1.33
Detail of Angermair, *Coin Cabinet* [1.32], relief, *Intellectual History*.

1.34
Detail of Angermair, *Coin Cabinet* [1.32], relief, *Coinage and Humanist Learning*.

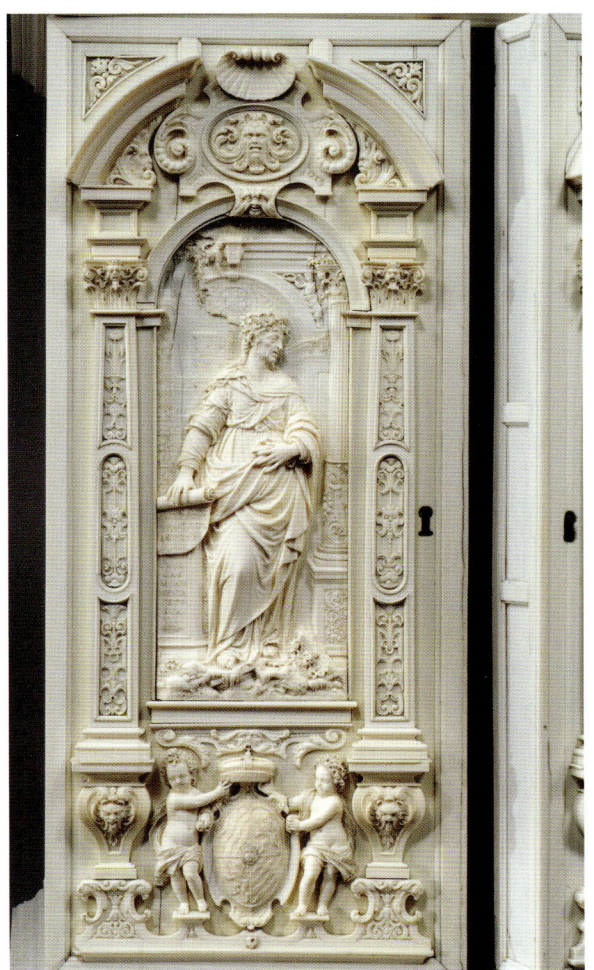

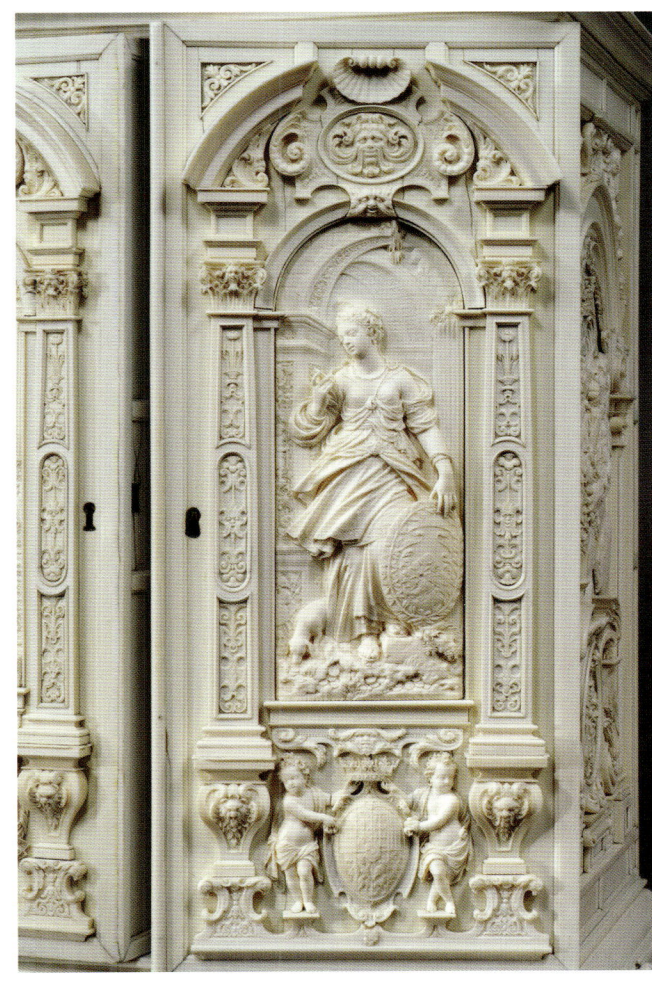

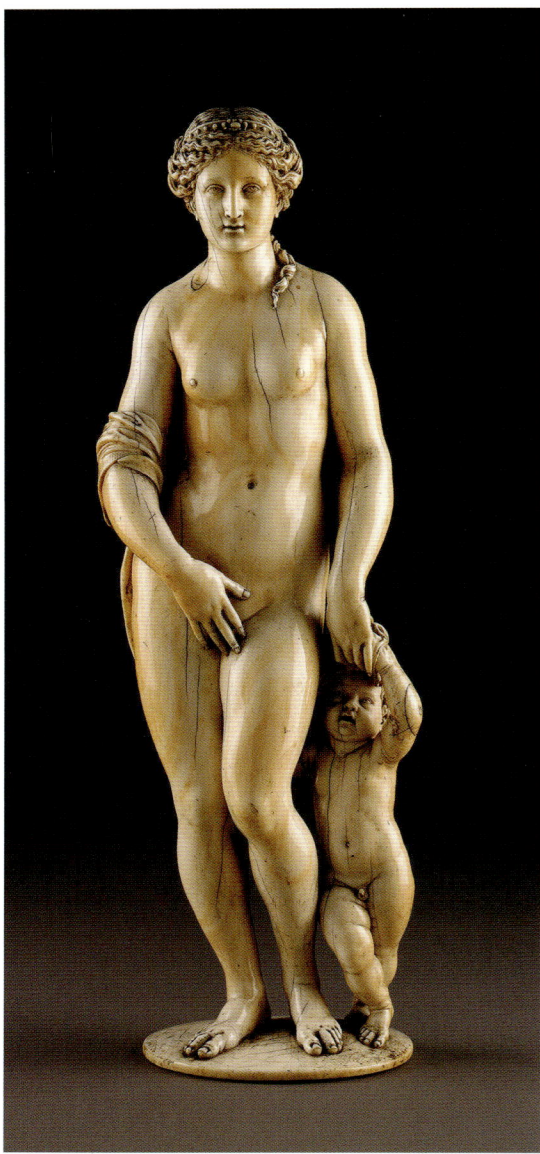

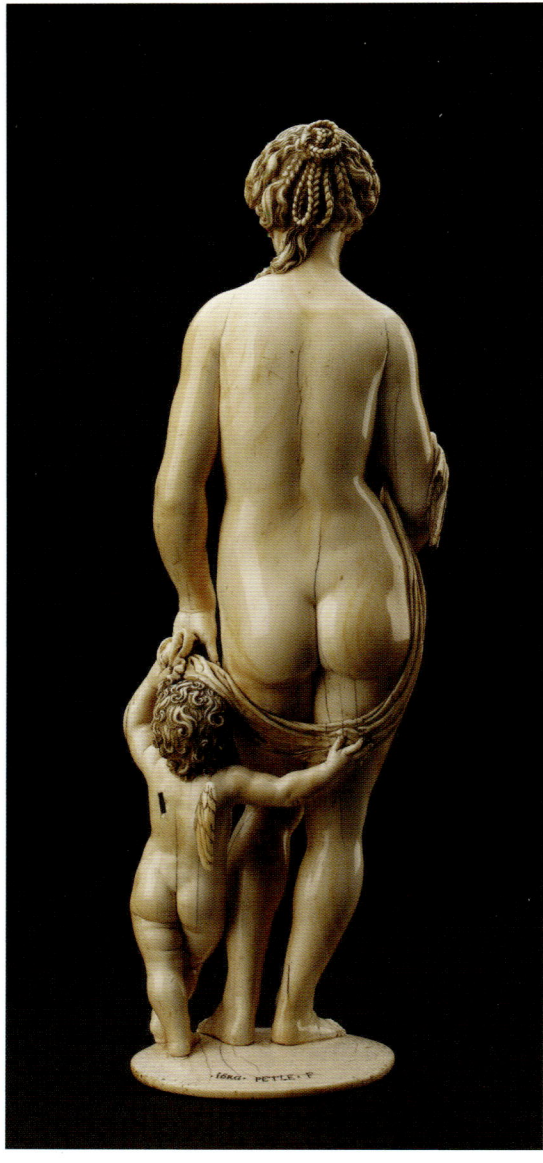

1.35
Georg Petel, *Venus and Cupid*, ivory, c. 1624, height 40 cm. Ashmolean Museum, Oxford.

1.36
Petel, *Venus and Cupid* [1.35], back.

was the period when cabinets of curiosities (*Kunstkammern*) were being assembled by monarchs, aristocrats and scholars all over Europe. The Munich *Kunstkammer* was largely created by Duke Maximilian's grandfather, Albert V, Duke of Bavaria (1528-79; r. 1550-79), who also collected coins, along with Maximilian's father, William V.[46] *Kunstkammer* collections comprised finely made small works in materials, such as boxwood, amber or ivory, and coins and medals, cast or struck in silver gold or bronze, as well as wonders of nature, such as ostrich eggs and shells. Angermair's coin cabinet was not only a valuable item in itself, but contained further treasures within, in the tradition of the *Kunstkammer*.[47] One of the most famous examples of a similarly finely-worked cabinet made to contain smaller works of art was the Pomeranian art cabinet (*Pommersche Kunstschrank*), an ebony cabinet adorned with silver gilt, enamels and

precious stones. Produced in Augsburg in 1611-18 by a number of artists, including Ulrich Baumgartner (c. 1580-1652) and Matthias Walbaum (c. 1554-1634), the cabinet's production was coordinated by the patrician and art agent Philipp Hainhofer (1578-1647) for Philip II, Duke of Pomerania-Stettin (1573-1618). It later entered the Berlin *Kunstkammer* at an unknown date between 1684 and 1689, but was sadly destroyed in the Second World War.[48]

Ivory, Terracotta, Bronze and Wood Sculpture by Georg Petel

Like Angermair, Georg Petel was born in Weilheim, where he first trained under the sculptor Bartholomäus Steinle (c. 1580-1628), though he subsequently studied ivory carving under Angermair in Munich.[49] As a young man in his twenties Petel's travels (*Wanderschaft*) in the Netherlands and Italy gave him an international

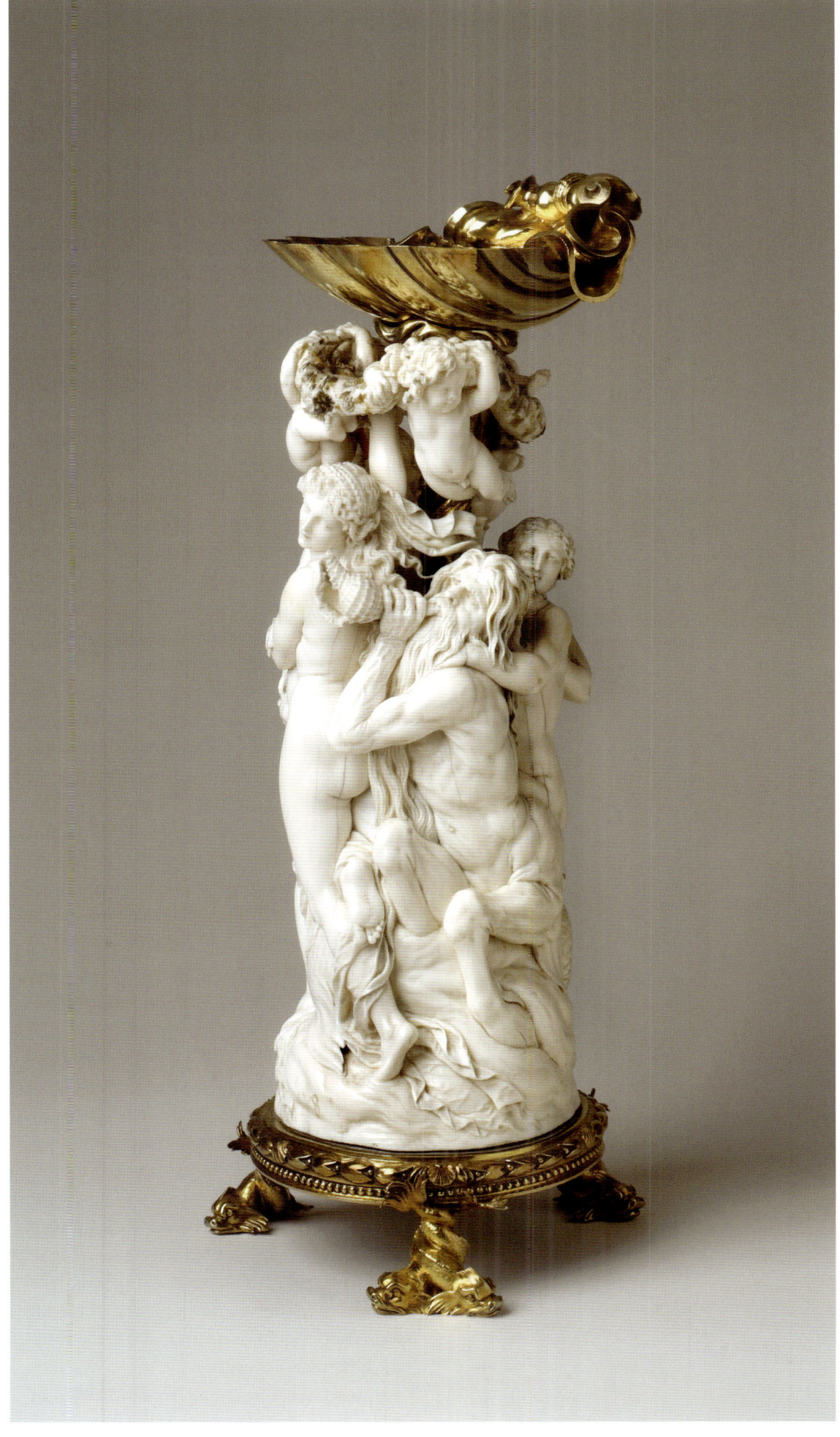

1.37
Georg Petel, *Salt Cellar with the Triumph of Venus*, ivory with silver gilt mounts (Amsterdam marks of 1627/8), monogrammed, height: 43.8 cm (with mounts), 32 cm (ivory alone). The Royal Household Chamber (Kungl. Husgerådskammaren), Stockholm (inv. no. S.S. 143).

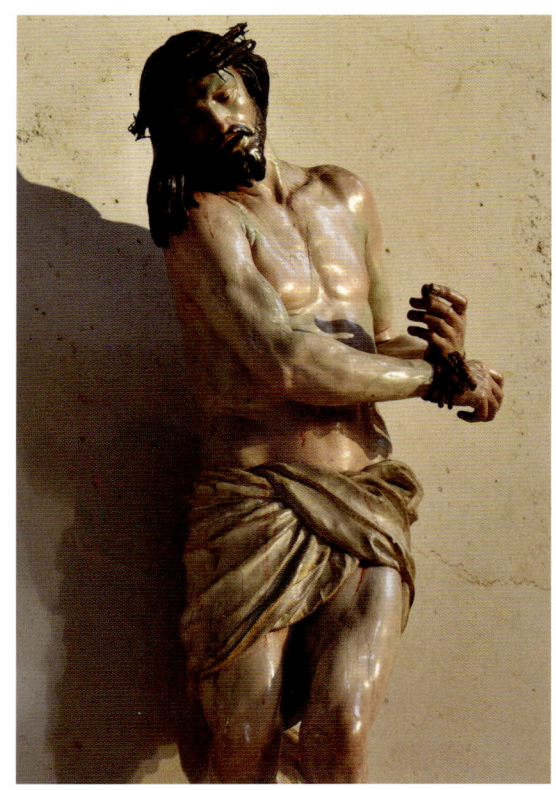

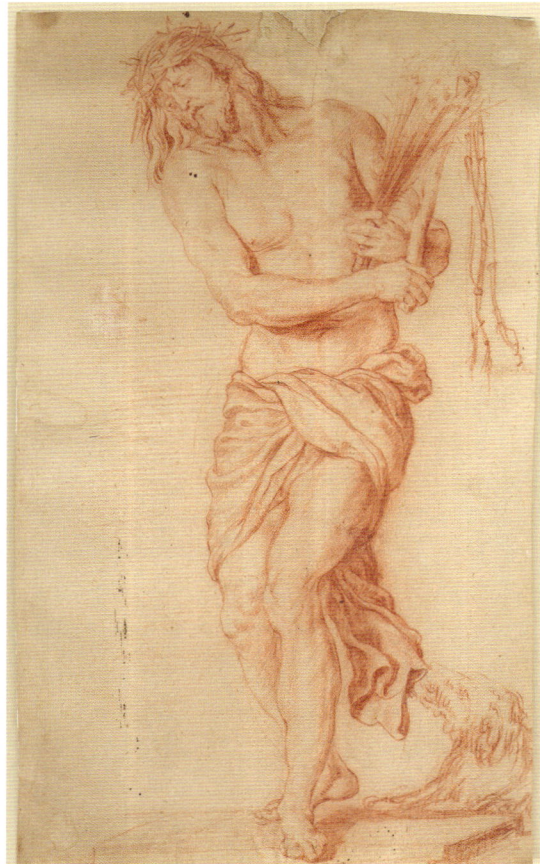

1.38
Georg Petel, *Ecce Homo*, polychromed wood, c. 1630/31 (detail). Augsburg Cathedral.

1.39
Georg Petel, *Ecce Homo*, chalk drawing, c. 1630. Royal Print Collection (Kongel. Kobberstiksamling), Copenhagen.

perspective. In 1620/1 he went to Antwerp, where he spent time in Rubens's workshop, as mentioned above. Subsequently he went to Rome, and there met the Flemish artists François Du Quesnoy (1597-1643) and Anthony van Dyck (1599-1641), before travelling to Genoa and Livorno, and returning to Germany in late 1624. He settled in Augsburg and resided there for the rest of his relatively short life, apart from occasional trips to the Netherlands.

The extensive range of Petel's art embraced religious and secular art, large-scale and small-scale pieces, and various different materials: wood, bronze and ivory. Angermair's tuition of Petel in ivory in Munich led to the production of some of Petel's most important masterpieces. A figure of *Venus and Cupid*, now in the Ashmolean Museum, Oxford, signed on the integral socle, 'IÖRG . PETLE . F .', could date from the artist's second visit to Antwerp in 1624 [**1.35 and 1.36**].[50] Acquired by the Ashmolean Museum in 1932, it may have been sold by Rubens to George Villiers, 1st Duke of Buckingham (1592-1628) when the duke was in Antwerp in 1625. The goddess stands contrapposto, nude, except for a loop of drapery held in her left hand, draped under her buttocks and over her right arm. She covers her pubis with her right hand, her left holding Cupid's right hand and the end of the drapery. Her hair is elaborately coiffured in a plaited bun on top of her head, one loose strand falling over her left shoulder. The little winged Cupid, also in a contrapposto pose, stands at her side, touching the drapery at the back of his mother's thighs with his right hand, and clasping her hand in his other small fist. Venus's pose is partly indebted to that of the ancient Cnidian Venus (the Aphrodite of Knidos), two versions of which were in the Vatican, which Petel could therefore have seen in Rome.[51] The sculpture is a fusion of European sources, not least the work of Rubens, whose buxom forms are echoed in the seemingly soft flesh of Venus's body. Petel's figure is simultaneously a remarkable example of baroque ivory carving, exemplifying the keen interest in small-scale sculptures in Germany in the first half of the seventeenth century.

Another outstanding ivory by Petel is the salt cellar with silver gilt mounts now in

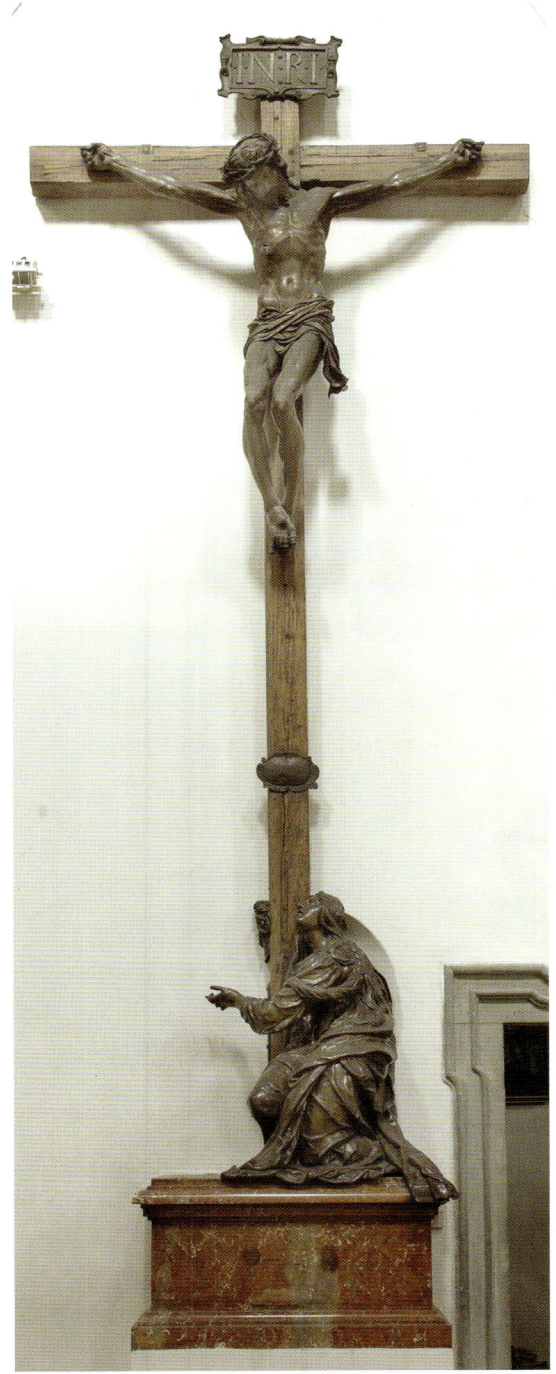

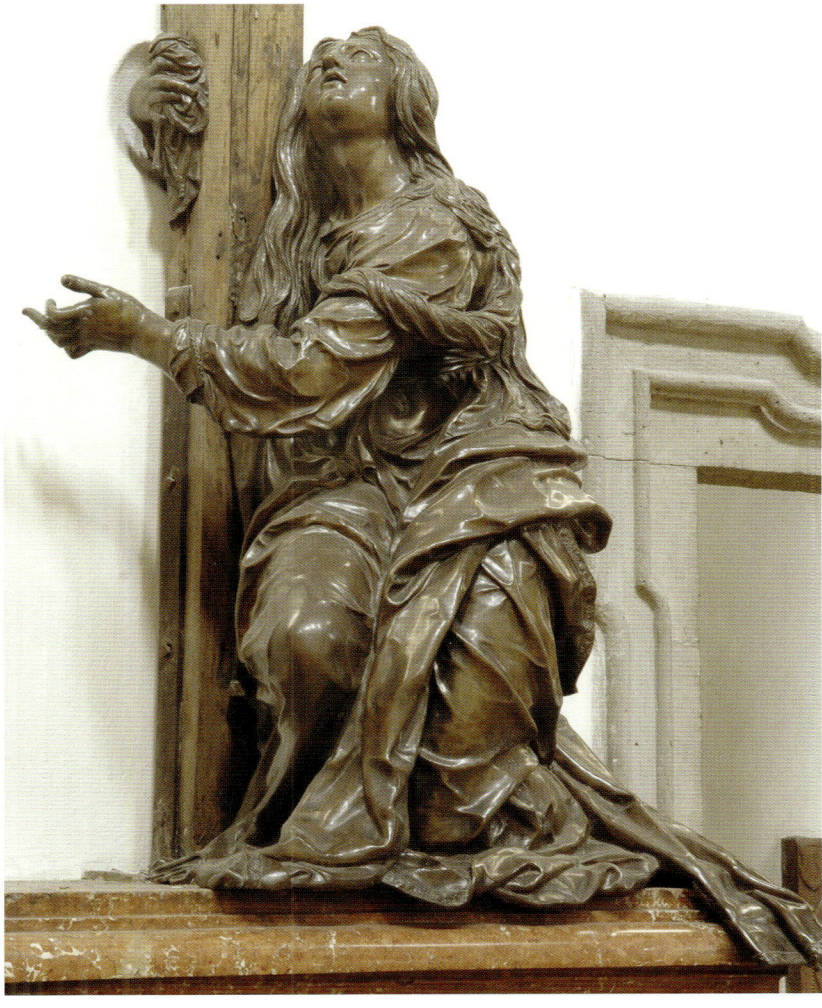

Stockholm, later purchased for Queen Christina of Sweden (1626-89) in 1649 from Rubens's own collection [1.37]. The salt cellar, carved from one cylindrical ivory tusk, and depicting the Triumph of Venus, is monogrammed with Petel's initials and can be dated from its silver gilt mounts to 1628; it must have been carved in Antwerp by Petel in that year, when he was visiting the Flemish master.[52]

Petel was an extraordinary sculptor in wood, seen for instance in his Christ as *Ecce Homo* (a fusion of *Christ as Man of Sorrows* and *Christ at the Column*) in Augsburg. The polychromed limewood sculpture, about half life size, was made towards the end of his life, around 1630/1, for the Dominican church of St Magdalena in the city, and is now in the Cathedral [1.38].[53] Christ stands leaning his head to his right, his hands bound, probably originally holding the scourge and rods, which appear in Petel's preparatory red chalk sketch for the figure. The drawing, Rubensian in character, is a fully realized study of a muscular male nude, exhibiting draughtsmanship that seems both spontaneous and yet firmly controlled [1.39].[54] The heavy drapery of the loincloth in the sculpted Christ is likewise reminiscent of Rubens, while the quiet pathos of the face movingly evokes the sorrow of the Passion. The luminous polychromy of the sculpture, with its pale skin, blotches of red for blood, and green for bruised flesh, also recalls

1.40
Georg Petel, *Crucifixion group*, bronze, c. 1630, probably cast by Wolfgang II Neidhardt. Niedermünster, Regensburg.

1.41
Detail of Petel, *Crucifixion group* [1.40], Mary Magdalene.

Rubens's work as a painter. The polychromist of Petel's figure was probably the Augsburg painter Caspar Strauss. Italo-Flemish precedents, such as the bronzes of Giambologna, as well as the work of Du Quesnoy, can be seen in the figure's twisting pose.[55] The sculpture thus fuses Italian, Flemish and German elements, whilst being at one and the same time indisputably a distinctive work executed by Petel in his maturity.

The confluence of both Italian and Flemish traditions can be detected in the impressive bronze crucifixion group convincingly attributed to Petel in the Niedermünster, Regensburg of c. 1630, comprising the crucified Christ and the kneeling figure of Mary Magdalene [1.40 and 1.41].[56] This was made a generation after Hans Reichle's *Magdalene* of 1595 in St Michael's church in Munich [1.21 and 1.22], and his crucifixion group of 1605 in the church of SS. Ulrich and Afra in Augsburg [1.18]. As in Reichle's figures, the robes of Petel's Magdalene

spill over the base. Petel's Magdalene looks upwards to the bronze crucified Christ with a tear-stained face, and at the same time functions as an autonomous bronze sculpture. Her copious drapery recalls the paintings of Van Dyck or Rubens, while the monumentality of the figure parallels the work in Rome of Du Quesnoy, and even Bernini.

The Thirty Years' War came to an end in 1648 with the Peace of Westphalia. Economic hardship continued more or less until the end of the century, but after the disruption and financial difficulties suffered all over Germany, small-scale sculptures, especially ivories, began to be made once more. The Brandenburg court in Berlin, as well as the Habsburgs in Vienna and aristocrats in Silesia (now Poland), collected and commissioned works of art and sculpture. The following chapter will look at sculpture from the second half of the century in Berlin, Vienna and Silesia.

Notes

1 Sauermost 1988. For Krumper, see Diemer 1980a.
2 Volk-Knüttel 1980.
3 For Riemenschneider and Stoss, see Baxandall 1981.
4 For Degler, see Zohner 1977.
5 See Lieb 1984 and the entry on Degler by Jeffrey Chipps Smith in Grove Art Online, accessed April 2020. See also http://st-ulrich-und-afra.de/rundgang-und-schaetze.html, accessed April 2020.
6 Baxandall 1981, plates 27 and 28.
7 The altarpiece is sometimes called the St Narcissus altarpiece, after the saint who converted Afra of Augsburg (later St Afra) to Christianity in the fourth century. See Zohner 1977, p. 78, and an unnumbered plate of engravings by Daniel Manasser of the three altarpieces, published in 1627.
8 St Afra (d. 304) was a Christian saint martyred in Augsburg.
9 St Ulrich (890-973) was Bishop of Augsburg from 923 onwards.
10 Zohner 1977, p. 79; Diemer 2012, p. 25. For Greither, who was also a painter of ceilings, see Bauer and Rupprecht 1976, pp. 305, 553.
11 Hartmetz 2019, p. 17; Kluger 2014; Haberlein and Burkhardt 2002.

12 See Forster 2001; Chipps Smith 1994, pp. 39-41, 111-16.
13 Lieb 1984; Wendel 2010; Corpis 2010.
14 Wendel 2010; Corpis 2010.
15 Diemer 2012, pp. 23-5.
16 Diemer 1988, p. 20; Diemer 2012, pp. 36-41.
17 Diemer 1988, p. 62.
18 Diemer 2012, p. 35. Five fragmentary heads from the cycle are now in the Maximilian Museum, Augsburg; for two of them, see *Welt in Umbruch* 1980, Vol. II, cat. nos. 575 and 576, pp. 200-1.
19 The altarpiece may have been originally installed unpainted; Hartmetz 2019, p. 40.
20 Plate XVIIII in Serlio, cited in Hartmetz 2019, note 282 on p. 60. For Sustris, see Hartmetz 2019, p. 61.
21 Lieb 1953, p. 8.
22 Hartmetz 2019, p. 61.
23 For the Gerhard altarpiece now at the Victoria and Albert Museum, see Diemer 2004, Vol. I, pp. 73-82; Vol. II, pp. 141-2, cat. no. G1. See also Hartmetz 2019, p. 63. Rodt could have seen Gerhard's figures in the print by Lukas Kilian (1579-1637) of 1598.
24 Zoege von Manteuffel 1998.
25 For Morinck, see Ricke 1973.
26 Diemer 2012, pp. 30-34. Diemer notes that the bronze candelabra in

the church should also be attributed to Reichle.
27 I am most grateful to Dorothea Diemer for her comments on Reichle's crucifixion group.
28 Diemer 1980a/b; Zikos 2015, p. 93; *Bella Figura* 2015, cat. no. 37 on pp. 264-7.
29 For Holl, see *Elias Holl* 1985; Roeck 2004; Haberstock 2016.
30 Gerhard's figure is based on a design after the Italo-Dutch artist Friedrich Sustris (1540-99).
31 See Volk 1980b.
32 See Glaser and Werner 1998, p. 149.
33 The architrave above the figures is dated 1616, the year in which they were installed.
34 See Heal 2011; Albrecht 2014, p. 295; Diemer 1980a, p. 291.
35 Albrecht 2014, p. 292.
36 Albrecht 2014, pp. 294-5.
37 Montagu 1989, p. 60. I am most grateful to Jennifer Montagu for suggesting this comparison.
38 Baxandall 1981, plate 17.
39 Bussmann and Schelling 1998, pp. 149-50.
40 Diemer 2015, fig. 22.
41 Diemer 2004, Vol. I, p. 312.
42 Diemer 2015, p. 49; Albrecht 2014, pp. 295-6.
43 For Angermair, see Grünwald 1975. For Petel, see Feuchtmayr and

Schädler 1973; Schädler 1985; Krempel and Söding 2009.

44 Trusted 2013, p. xxiii, discussing the carving of ivory from the mid-sixteenth century onwards.

45 Grünwald 1975, pp. 32-41.

46 Diemer et al. 2008.

47 For cabinets of curiosities, see Schlosser 1908; MacGregor and Impey 1985.

48 Hildebrand and Thuerkauff 1981, pp. 64-8; *Wunderwelt* 2014.

49 For Steinle, who also worked in Munich, see Zohner 1993.

50 Feuchtmayr and Schädler 1973, pp. 85-7; Penny 1992, Vol. 2, pp. 145-7; Riccardi-Cubitt 2000, p. 84.

51 They later entered the Pio-Clementine Museum at the Vatican; see Haskell and Penny 1982, pp. 330-1.

52 Feuchtmayr and Schädler 1973, cat. no. 14, pp. 98-102.

53 Feuchtmayr and Schädler 1973, pp. 119-20.

54 Kongel. Kobberstiksamling, Copenhagen; Schädler 1985, p. 65.

55 For Giambologna, see Avery and Radcliffe 1978; Avery 1987.

56 In fact, earlier scholars ascribed the group to Reichle. See Feuchtmayr and Schädler 1973, pp. 114-16.

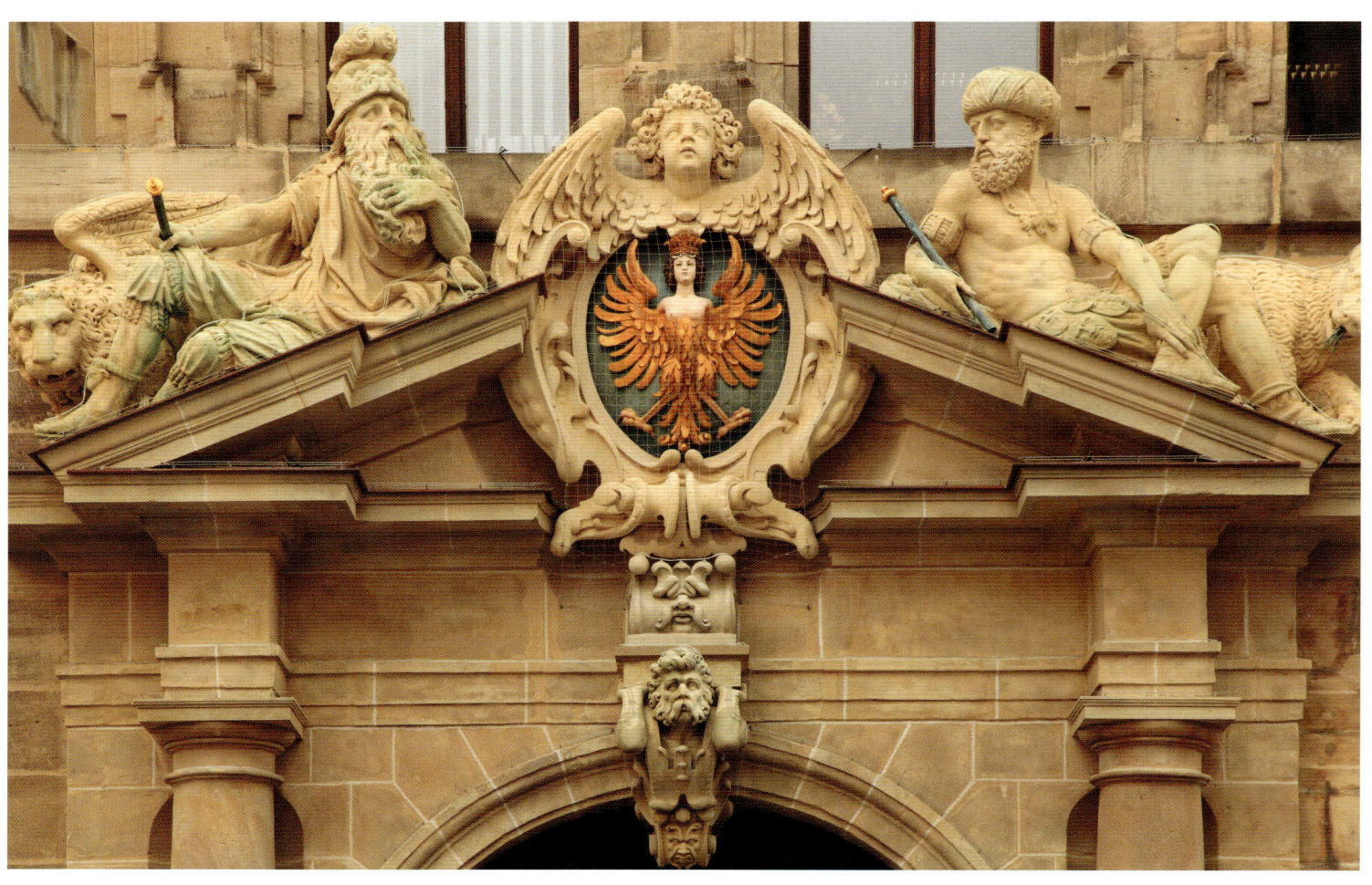

CHAPTER 2

SMALL-SCALE SCULPTURE AND PATRONAGE IN BERLIN AND VIENNA: 1630-1700

This chapter will focus on the sculpture, much of which was small-scale, produced mainly in the mid- to late seventeenth century in the aftermath of the Thirty Years' War, primarily for the courts in Prussia and Vienna. It will conclude with the monumental sculptures by Andreas Schlüter (c. 1659-c. 1714) in Berlin. The impact of wars on German baroque sculpture in both the seventeenth and the twentieth centuries will become apparent. In the mid-seventeenth century, commissions for sculpture were affected by conflict, while in the mid-twentieth century sculpture and buildings in Berlin—as well as elsewhere in Germany—suffered losses and damage during and after the Second World War.

Sculpture of the Mid-Seventeenth Century in Schwäbisch Hall and at the Brandenburg Court: Leonhard Kern

Both the practice and patronage of sculpture in Germany from the 1620s to the 1650s and beyond were severely affected by the disruptions of the Thirty Years' War. Some sculptors turned to works on a smaller scale that could be sold more readily, because they were generally less costly and more portable. At the same time, the burgeoning *Kunstkammer* collections (cabinets of curiosities) being formed at various princely courts, including the Brandenburg court, led to a demand for virtuoso works of art in exotic

or precious materials, as noted in the previous chapter.[1] The Brandenburg *Kunstkammer* flourished in the mid-seventeenth century during the rule of Great Elector Frederick William (1620-88), who acquired numerous ivories, ambers, waxes and bronzes, as well as many other small-scale works of art. The origins of the *Kunstkammer* can effectively, however, be dated to the rule of Joachim II (1505-71; r. 1535-71), Elector of Brandenburg, and that of his son Joachim Frederick (1546-1608; r. 1598-1608). Both those electors acquired unusual and noteworthy objects for the Brandenburg collection, including ancient coins.[2]

One artist who specialized in small-scale sculpture, perhaps because of the turmoil caused by the Thirty Years' War, was the successful and productive Schwäbisch-Hall sculptor Leonhard Kern (1588-1662), who, like Georg Petel, worked in a number of different materials, including stone, bronze, wood and ivory. Kern, again like Petel, was a 'freier Künstler', an artist not tied down to a guild, and who—at the same time— for most of his career did not have a permanent court appointment.[3] The earliest mention of him, in 1675, appears in a publication by the contemporary German artist, writer and traveller Joachim von Sandrart (1606-88): the *Teutsche Academie* (biographical dictionary of German artists).[4] Sandrart recorded the sculptor's sojourn in Italy, noting that much of his

2.1
Leonhard Kern, *Ninus* and *Cyrus*, stone, 1617, Portal of Nuremberg town hall.

65

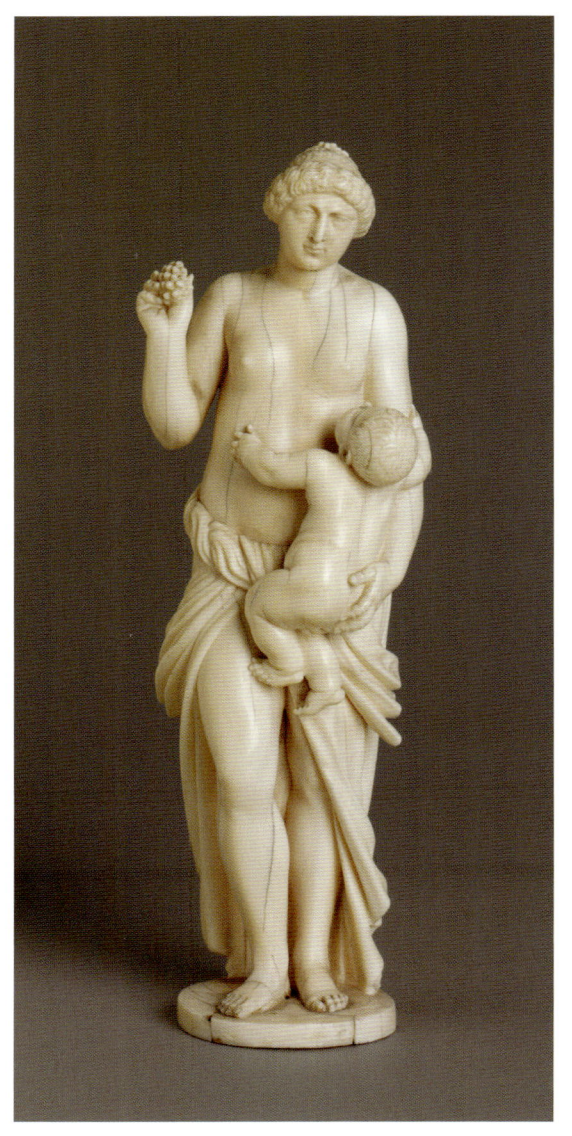

2.2
Leonhard Kern, *Charity*,
ivory, c. 1620-45,
height 23.2 cm.
Victoria and Albert
Museum, London
(inv. no. A. 37-1949).

The ivory sculpture of *Venus and Cupid* by Petel seen in the last chapter [**1.35 and 1.36**] can be compared with Kern's ivory figures dating from around the same time. Kern's nude female figure of *Charity*, dating probably from the 1620s or 1630s, and carved from one large tusk, albeit a stockier, less classicizing rendition than Petel's *Venus*, is likewise Rubensian [**2.2**], the bulky proportions and finely carved elaborate coiffure typical of Kern's nudes. Although his years working in Italy can be detected in the Italianate style—and often the classical subjects—of his work, the generous rounded forms of his figures are fused with Flemish qualities, as seen here.

One of Kern's most celebrated ivories is his double portrait of the Great Elector and his consort Louise Henrietta (1627-67) [**2.3**]. The sovereigns are extraordinarily portrayed nude as Adam and Eve. On the integral socle, a small dog symbolizes fidelity, while the tortoise depicted there may signify domesticity. Although Kern was at the Brandenburg court at Cleve in Prussia for three months in 1648, when he was apparently appointed court sculptor for one year, the group may pre-date that stay. It could have been made at the time of the couple's marriage in 1646.[7] Known to have entered the Brandenburg *Kunstkammer* collectionin Berlin by 1695, it was almost certainly kept in the Great Elector's private rooms before that date. Like Kern's figure of *Charity* and Petel's *Venus*, it is carved from one large piece of ivory, the couple shown in the seemingly intimate yet almost humorous context of a depiction of the Fall: Louise/Eve as temptress, and Frederick William/Adam accepting his fate as a fallen man willingly succumbing to earthly love.

The Thirty Years' War came to an end in 1648 with the Peace of Westphalia. Economic hardship continued, however, in various parts of Germany until the end of the century. An alabaster group convincingly attributed to Kern, now known as a *Scene from the Thirty Years' War*, probably dates from about 1656-9 [**2.4**].[8] A finely dressed officer seizes a naked woman from behind, grasping her long hair, whilst holding a threatening dagger at her arched back. The clash of the dandified soldier and his vulnerable victim evokes the violence of the invader. But

work in Germany had survived, despite the unrest caused by the war ('*Kriegs-Unruh*'). Elsewhere, the writer deplored the devastation wrought by the struggles: 'Queen Germania saw her palaces and churches . . . go up in flames . . . whilst her eyes were so blinded by smoke and tears that she no longer had the power or will to attend to art . . . . So art was forgotten, and its practitioners overcome by poverty and contempt . . .'.[5] The implication is that *Kleinkunst* (small-scale art) could perhaps escape the destruction of war. Kern had in fact carved larger architectural sculptures in sandstone for the town hall of Nuremberg shortly before the outbreak of the war in 1617, and these do remarkably survive today [**2.1**].[6] But his reputation rests primarily on numerous small-scale sculptures, notably his ivories.

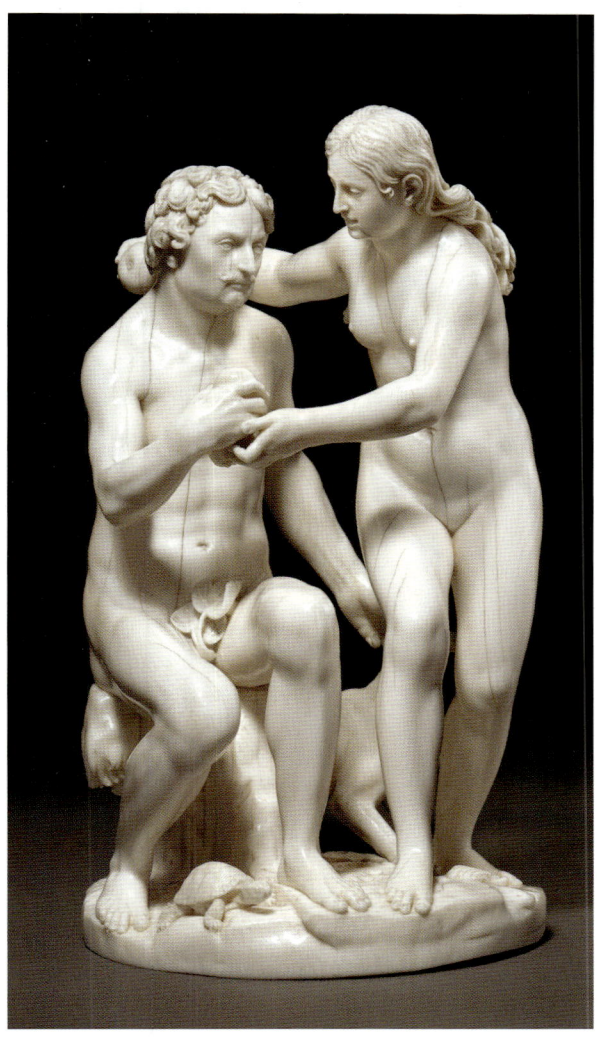

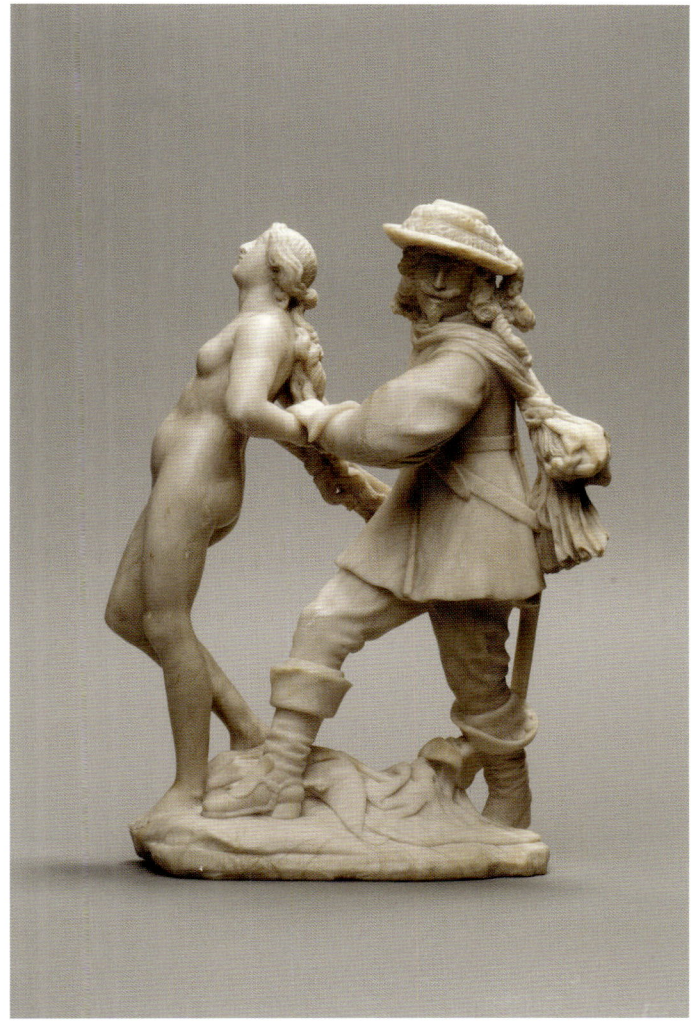

the group may have a larger political, symbolic meaning, rather than being a depiction of an actual scene from the war. The three roses carved on the soldier's sash could refer to the Von Rosen family, and the soldier himself may be a portrait of Reinhold von Rosen (1605-67), a general who fought with the Swedish/French troops against the Austrian Habsburg forces. The woman's face is calm, and her features generalized; she seems almost to be a passive victim of her tormentor. Rather than a portrait of a specific woman, it has been plausibly suggested that she could be an allegorical personification of Schwäbisch Hall. This was the town in Baden-Württemberg where Kern was based for most of his working life; it was invaded by troops on both sides of the conflict during the Thirty Years' War at various times. The first owner of the alabaster group is likely to have been the Habsburg Archduke Leopold Wilhelm of Austria (1614-62), an adversary of Reinhold von Rosen in the war.

It is not known whether the archduke commissioned it, but it was recorded in his collection as early as 1659, during Kern's lifetime. Apart from the topical subject, the artistic parallels are also intriguing. Kern would have known Giambologna's monumental marble *Rape of a Sabine Woman* in Florence, dating from 1581-2, a rendition of a nude male figure seizing a nude woman, though with fewer overtly threatening overtones, because of its classicizing format and subject [**2.5**].[9] Whilst it is a much smaller cabinet piece, Kern's harsher depiction of a painful seventeenth-century subject has the immediacy of the present, undeniably Germanic rather than Italianate in style, the man clearly in contemporary costume. Kern's alabaster thus chillingly evokes the horrors of recent war, rather than illustrating classical myth, paralleling contemporary prints, such as *Les Misères et les Malheurs de la Guerre*, the etchings published in 1633 by Jacques Callot (1592-1635), or the *Schrecken*

2.3
Leonhard Kern, *Frederick William Great Elector of Brandenburg, and his consort Louise Henrietta as Adam and Eve*, ivory, signed, c. 1646, height 23 cm. Bode Museum, Berlin (inv. no. 713).

2.4
Leonhard Kern, Scene from the Thirty Years' War, alabaster, c. 1656-9, height 34.3 cm. Kunsthistorisches Museum, Vienna (inv. no. KK 4363).

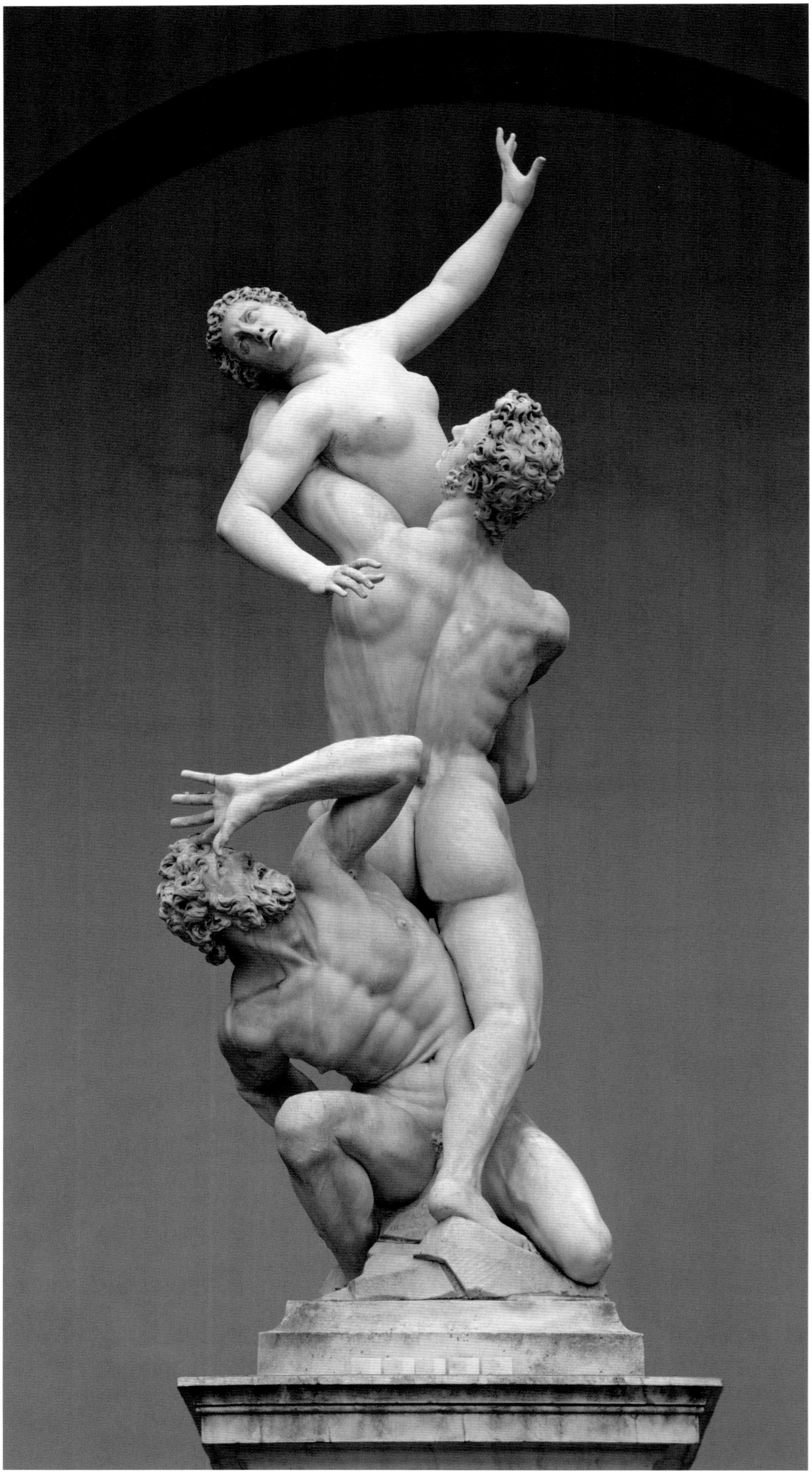

2.5
Giambologna, *Rape of a Sabine Woman*, marble, 1581-2. Loggia dei Lanzi, Florence.

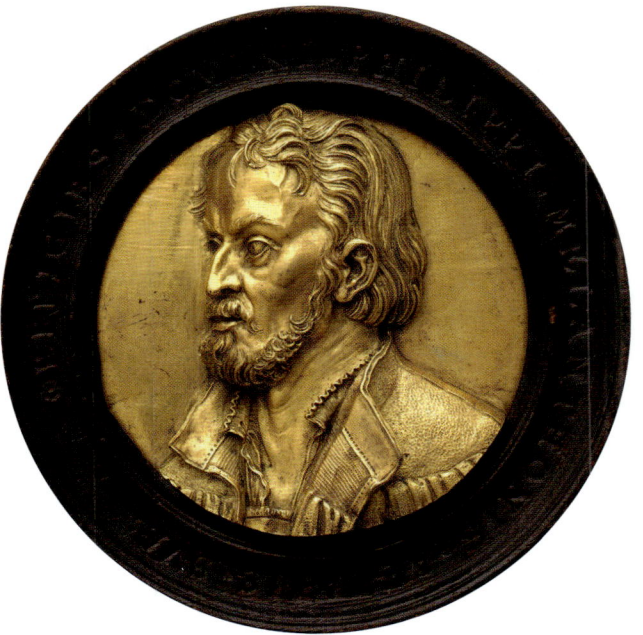
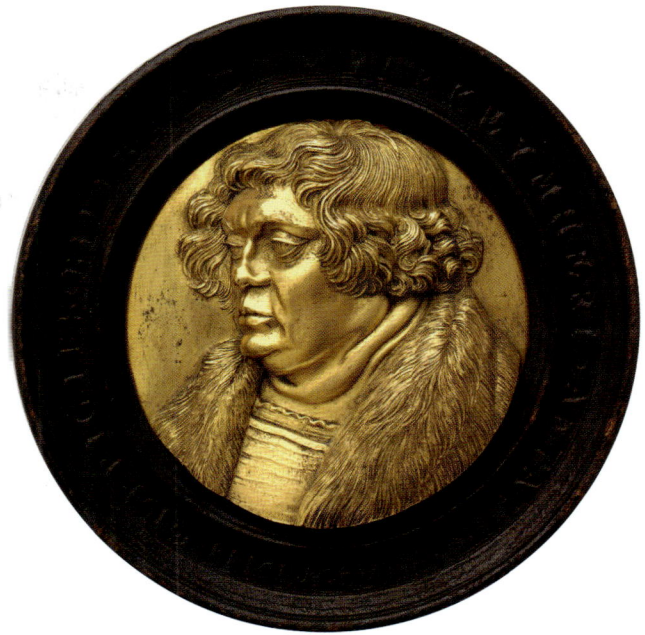

des Dreißigjährigen Krieges, prints of the 1640s and 1650s by the Augsburg artist Hans Ulrich Franck (1603-75).[10]

Sculpture of the Mid-Seventeenth Century in Nuremberg and at the Brandenburg Court: Georg Schweigger

The Bavarian city of Nuremberg remained a centre for art throughout the seventeenth century, albeit intermittently, despite the uncertainties of war. As a Protestant city it was occupied by both Swedish and Catholic League troops during the Thirty Years' War, suffering considerable damage and loss of life—although, as has been seen, Kern's sculptures on the town hall endured the ravages of war. Other artists continued their activity there, especially those who worked in metal. Like Augsburg, it had a long tradition of practitioners and founders in bronze, as well as goldsmiths.

The sculptor Georg Schweigger (1613-90) was based in Nuremberg, and worked in numerous materials, including stone, terracotta and bronze, producing for example the monumental bronze Neptune fountain in 1656 for the Hauptmarkt as a memorial to Peace after the Thirty Years' War.[11] During the war, Schweigger specialised in smaller works, sometimes with Protestant overtones. His medallic portraits of

the Lutheran reformer Philipp Melanchthon (1497-1560) of 1636, and of Willibald Pirckheimer (1470-1530), the humanist patrician and friend of Dürer, probably also of 1636, are based on copper engravings by Albrecht Dürer (1471-1528) dating from 1524 and 1526 respectively [**2.6 and 2.7**]. Made of cast bronze, they are gilded and finely chased, the detail of both the faces and the costume meticulously rendered in a manner recalling goldsmiths' work. They exemplify the so-called Dürer revival that took place in Germany in the seventeenth century, when many of the revered Nuremberg master's prints were transformed into other works of art, especially sculpture.[12] Schweigger's medallions were recorded in the Brandenburg *Kunstkammer* collection by 1688; that of Melanchthon may have been acquired by the Great Elector because of its explicit Protestant subject matter. Not only do they look back to the German renaissance of Dürer, they also represent the sixteenth-century tradition of the cast portrait medal in Germany, dating back to the sixteenth century, when monarchs, aristocrats, merchants and scholars collected and treasured bronze and silver likenesses of eminent historical figures and their friends and contemporaries.[13]

2.6
Georg Schweigger, *Philipp Melanchthon*, gilt bronze in wood frame, c. 1636, diameter 11 cm (with frame). Bode Museum, Berlin (inv. no. 5856).

2.7
Georg Schweigger, *Willibald Pirckheimer*, gilt bronze in wood frame, signed and dated 1636, diameter 11 cm (with frame). Bode Museum, Berlin (inv. no. 5855).

2.8
Gottfried Leygebe,
*Frederick William, the
Great Elector*, bronze,
signed and dated 1671,
height 72 cm, width
64 cm. Schloss Caputh,
Stiftung Preussische
Schlösser und Gärten
Berlin-Brandenburg
(SPSG) (inv. no. Skulpt.
Slg. 1552, GK III 3710).

> 2.9
Gottfried Leygebe,
*Frederick William,
the Great Elector as
St George*, iron, signed
and dated 1680, height
27.7 cm (including
base). Bode Museum,
Berlin (inv. no. 856).

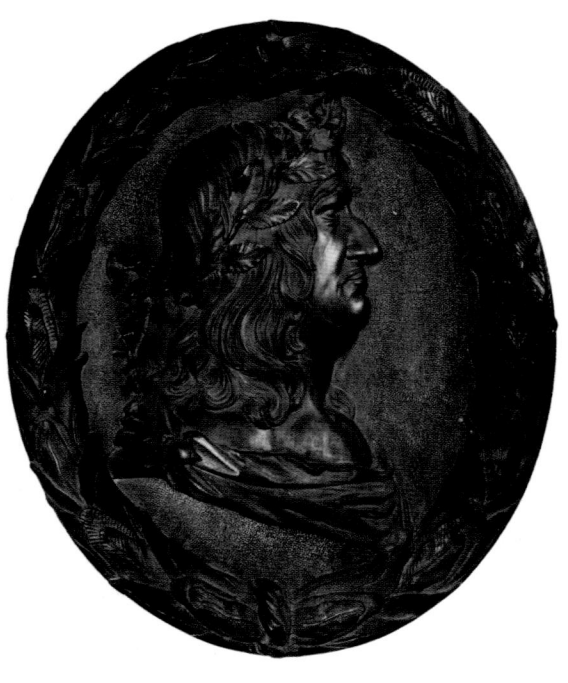

Sculpture of the Mid-Seventeenth Century for the Brandenburg Court: Gottfried Leygebe

Nuremberg was also initially the base for the workshop of Gottfried Christian Leygebe (1630-83), a die-cutter, medallist and sculptor who trained in the city with the armourer Albrecht Liechtmann. In 1653 Leygebe set up his own shop in the city, specialising in engraving on iron. Appointed court sculptor, die-cutter and medallist at the Brandenburg court in 1668, Leygebe then moved to Berlin, where he executed numerous commissions for the court, including portraits in clay and wax, medals, decorative motifs for cannons, and a games board made of silver and gold. He produced commemorative coins and a large oval bronze relief of the Great Elector in 1671 [2.8]. This finely worked profile bust portrait, dated and signed by the artist 'AD VIV: FECIT' (done from life), is a vivid likeness of the elector, communicating his worldly power, as well as being a naturalistic portrait. He is shown with his own long hair, rather than a wig or cropped hair in the classical style. But classicising imagery is nevertheless present: he wears a toga and is crowned with a laurel wreath, while the surround of the relief is also of laurel. The bronze was possibly made for the palace at Potsdam, where it was recorded in 1682.[14]

Leygebe's small equestrian figure in iron of a few years later depicts the elector clad in armour as St George fighting a three-headed chimera; it is signed and dated 1680 [2.9]. A portrait of the Prussian ruler overcoming a monstrous foe had been prefigured in an engraving by the artist of 1672, when the elector was shown as the Greek hero Bellerophon mounted on the winged horse Pegasus conquering the chimera.[15] Here the horse is not winged, and the elector is identified as St George, rather than Bellerophon. He is wearing the English Order of the Garter, with a medallion of St George and the Order's motto, 'Honi soit qui mal y pense', while the initials 'FWC' on the engraved saddle cloth stand for 'Frederick William Churfürst' (Kurfürst, the Elector). The raw material for the statuette had been acquired a couple of years before. In 1678 the artist purchased a consignment of iron from the Master of the Mint, Heinrich Bonhorst of Clausthal, noting later that he was to work on the equestrian group portraying the elector for over three years, costing him his health.[16] As Leygebe's lament implies, iron is a good deal more difficult to work than bronze or silver, and is rarely used for small-scale sculpture. He had to develop a technique for working the cast iron with specially hardened tools.[17] Iron is a typically Prussian material, later to be much used in Brandenburg for decorative ironwork, and even jewellery, into the nineteenth century.[18] The metal would therefore have had immense symbolic significance for Frederick William, with its overtones of strength. It would also have been regarded as a local material, unlike precious metals or bronze, which were more readily associated with Italy. Like Schweigger's medallions, this cabinet piece of the Brandenburg ruler as St George is meticulously worked, and, like Kern's ivory group of Frederick William and his consort, is a remarkably original portrait, here an allegorical portrait of the monarch overcoming his symbolic foes. Despite its small size, it has a forceful, monumental presence. The sculpture was probably in the Brandenburg *Kunstkammer* by 1688, one of a series of three equestrian iron statuettes produced by Leygebe, the other two being sent as diplomatic gifts by the Great Elector to Denmark and Saxony respectively. An iron statuette

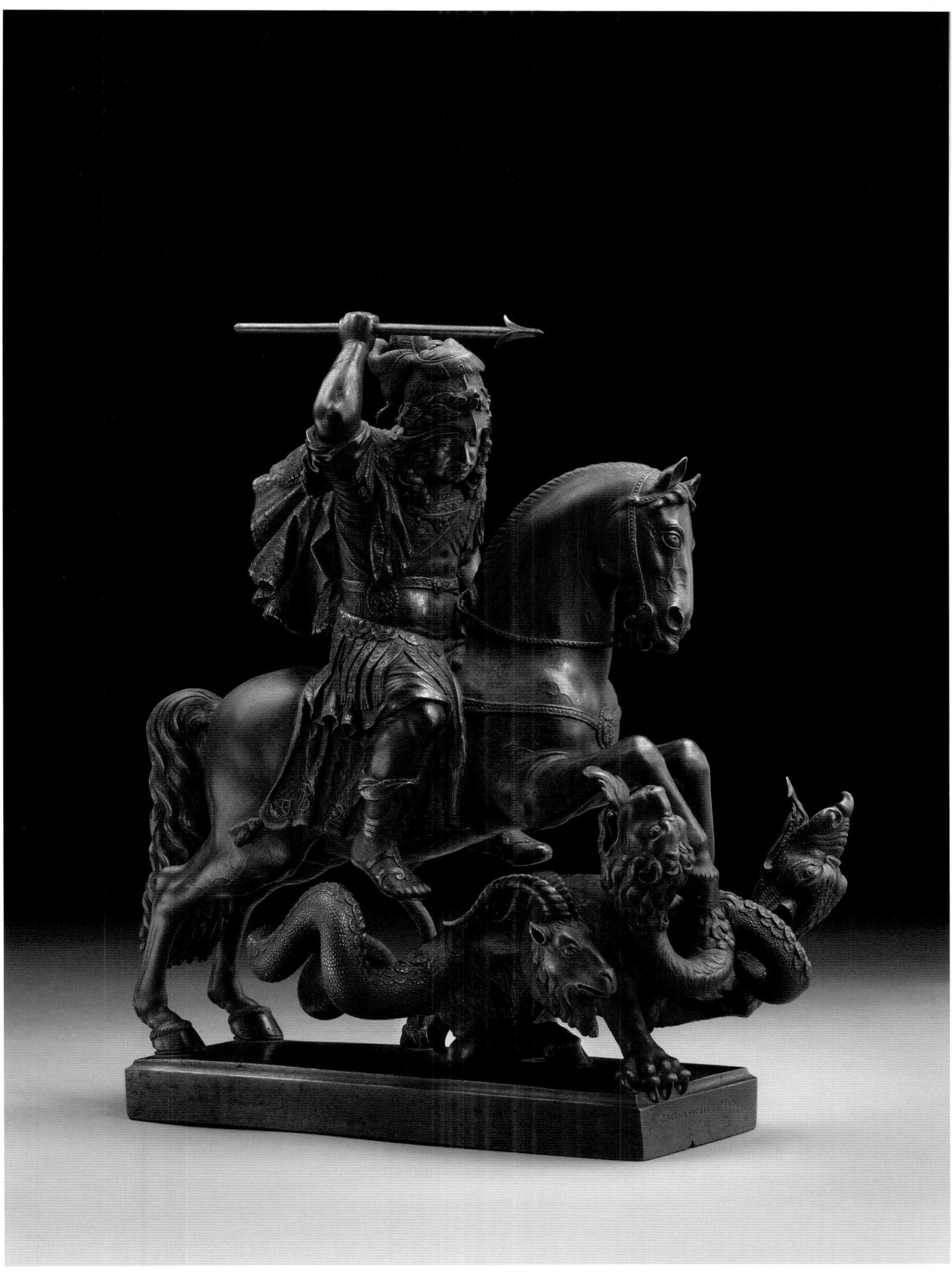

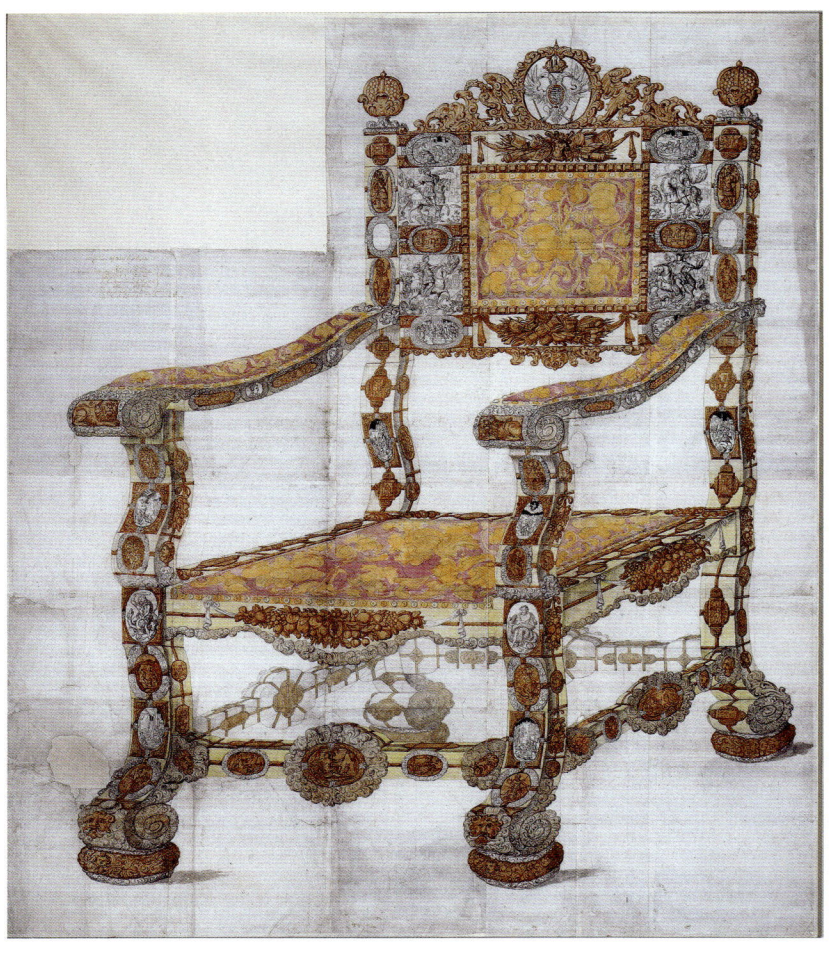

2.10
Anonymous, Gdańsk, *Drawing for the amber throne for Emperor Leopold I*, pencil, brush and red, yellow and grey ink on paper, c. 1677/8, height 170.3 cm, width 149.6 cm. Staatliche Museen Berlin, Kupferstichkabinett (inv. no. 3135).

would be considered a highly appropriate diplomatic gift to be made from Prussia to other European monarchs. The other two statuettes depicted the Habsburg Emperor Leopold I (1640-1705) (Rosenborg, Copenhagen), and the English monarch King Charles II (1630-85) (Grünes Gewölbe, Dresden)—in the latter case, one of the conquered foe's heads depicting Oliver Cromwell (1599-1658).[19]

Sculpture of the Mid- to Late Seventeenth Century at the Courts of Brandenburg and Vienna: Christoph Maucher

As already noted in Chapter 1, and as seen in the work of Kern, Schweigger and Leygebe discussed above, smaller secular sculptures were increasingly in demand in Germany during the seventeenth century, especially by regal and aristocratic collectors, such as the Great Elector. Moreover, an array of materials, including ivory and iron, could be used for sculpture and were valued in their own right, the very substances being of as much interest as the artifice of the

sculptor. Amber was another of these prized materials. Christoph Maucher (1642-1706/7), a sculptor in amber and ivory originally from Schwäbisch Gmund, Baden-Württemberg, was based from 1670 onwards in Gdańsk (Danzig), a major centre for amber working at this date. His younger brother Johann Michael Maucher (1645-1701) was also active as an ivory sculptor in Schwäbisch Gmund.[20]

Christoph Maucher was a 'freier Künstler', like Petel and Kern, employed on occasion by both the Great Elector in Berlin and the Habsburg Emperor Leopold I in Vienna, although he never held a court appointment. In 1677 he probably worked with the craftsman Nikolaus Turau (Turow) (1623-85?) on the great amber throne commissioned by Frederick William to be presented as a diplomatic gift to the emperor in 1678 [2.10 and 2.11]. Amber, a fossilized resin found in quantities along the Baltic coast, was—like iron—considered to be very much a Prussian material; an amber throne was therefore both a suitable and generous diplomatic gift to be presented to the Habsburg Emperor by the Prussian Elector. The throne, which today survives sadly only in fragmentary form, was encrusted with a rich array of relief amber carvings mounted on wood. The reliefs depicted classical subjects: the four so-called 'Ancient Kings', Ninus, Cyrus, Julius Caesar and Alexander the Great, derived from engraved sources, as well as scenes of the Labours of Hercules, and numerous other decorative panels, amounting to a panoply of imperial imagery.[21] Maucher was permitted by the city of Danzig to work as a sculptor in 1684, despite objections from the amber guild, since he was not a guild member. He had clearly acquired an international reputation, not only through the making of the throne, but from having previously worked as a sculptor for nine months at the court of Charles Eusebius von Liechtenstein (1611-84) in 1667.

Among Maucher's amber sculptures in Berlin is *The Judgement of Paris*, presumably made for Frederick William, and first recorded in an inventory of the Brandenburg *Kunstkammer* of 1690 [2.12]. This small group, carved in the round, shows Maucher's exceptional skill,

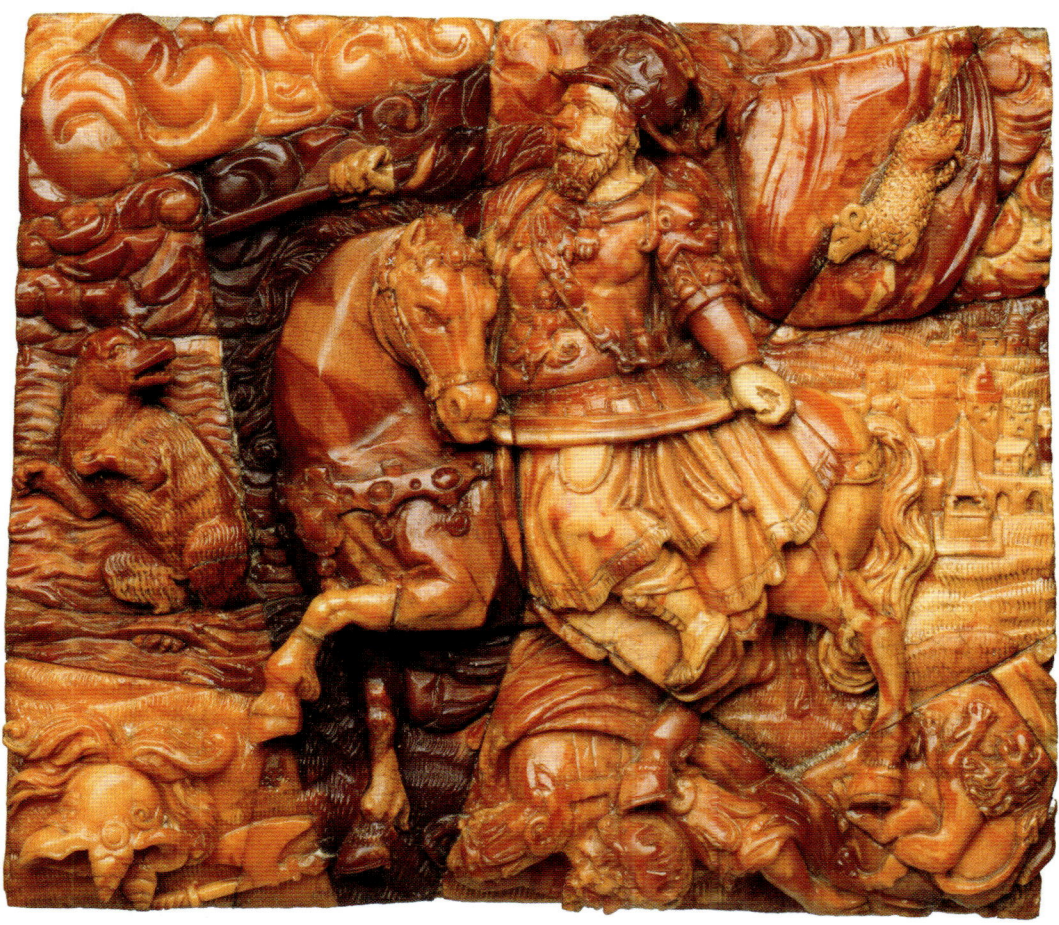

2.11
Christoph Maucher,
King Cyrus, amber, one
of the panels made for
the throne presented
to Emperor Leopold I,
c. 1677, height 10.9 cm,
width 12.4 cm.
Kunsthistorisches
Museum, Vienna
(inv. no. KK 3558).

and surely his sense of humour. The group enacts a drama, but of a very different kind from that seen on Hans Degler's or Christoph Rodt's earlier monumental wood altarpieces [1.3 and 1.11], which were of course sacred, and made for large public spaces. In Maucher's amber we see a dramatic scene taking place between figures on a much smaller scale. It depicts, moreover, a classical myth (though it is arguably not classical in style) rather than a religious narrative, and was intended for a courtly audience—a luxury item, rather than a visual tool by which a biblical story could be understood. The semi-nude shepherd Paris, wearing a swathe of classical drapery, a floppy hat and rustic boots, is seated hunched over the small dog at his feet, judging the beauty of the three goddesses, Juno, Minerva and Venus, in a leafy arbour. Venus leans forward to seize the prize apple from him in a lively pastoral scene that is far from classicizing. Like Maucher's two other amber groups of the sam e subject, the sculpture captures the humanity of the situation, the goddesses themselves portrayed as almost rustic characters.[22]

Maucher's signed ivory sculpture of the *Apotheosis of Leopold I* of 1700 (Kunsthistorisches Museum, Vienna) [2.13] is his masterpiece.[23] The emperor is shown seated at the centre beside his son and heir, King (and future Emperor) Joseph I (1678-1711), under a canopy of music-making putti perched on clouds, supported by the double-headed Habsburg eagle, and flanked by two standing allegorical figures, Providence and Nemesis. Beneath their feet are their conquered enemies, turbaned Turks, the Siege of Vienna having taken place in 1683. Seated at the side are two further allegories, Peace and Fame, while the relief on the base below shows the emperor and his son in a triumphal carriage, with more conquered Turks chained in thrall. The monumentality and energy of this ivory is remarkable, seemingly imitating marble or bronze sculpture on a much larger scale, such as the contemporary work of the court sculptor at Berlin, Andreas Schlüter (to be discussed below), or the great tradition of the Roman baroque seen in Bernini's work. Almost certainly commissioned by the emperor himself, it is the

>> 2.12
Christoph Maucher,
The Judgement of Paris,
amber, before 1690,
height 20.5 cm. Bode
Museum, Berlin
(inv. no. 859).

>> 2.13
Christoph Maucher,
*The Apotheosis of
Leopold I*, ivory on ebony
wood base, height
68 cm, width 47 cm,
depth 41.5 cm. Kunst-
historisches Museum,
Vienna (inv. no.
KK 4560).

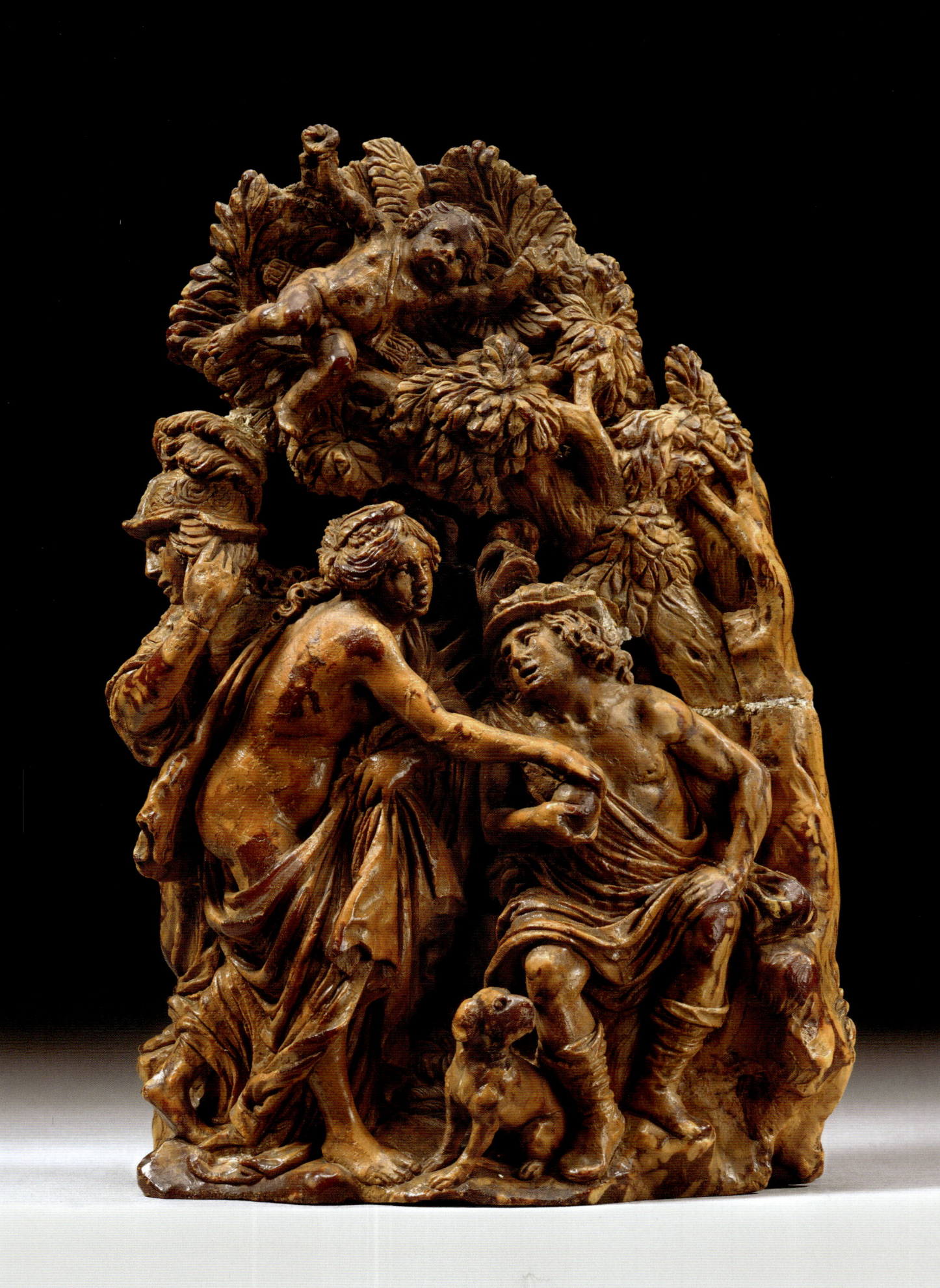

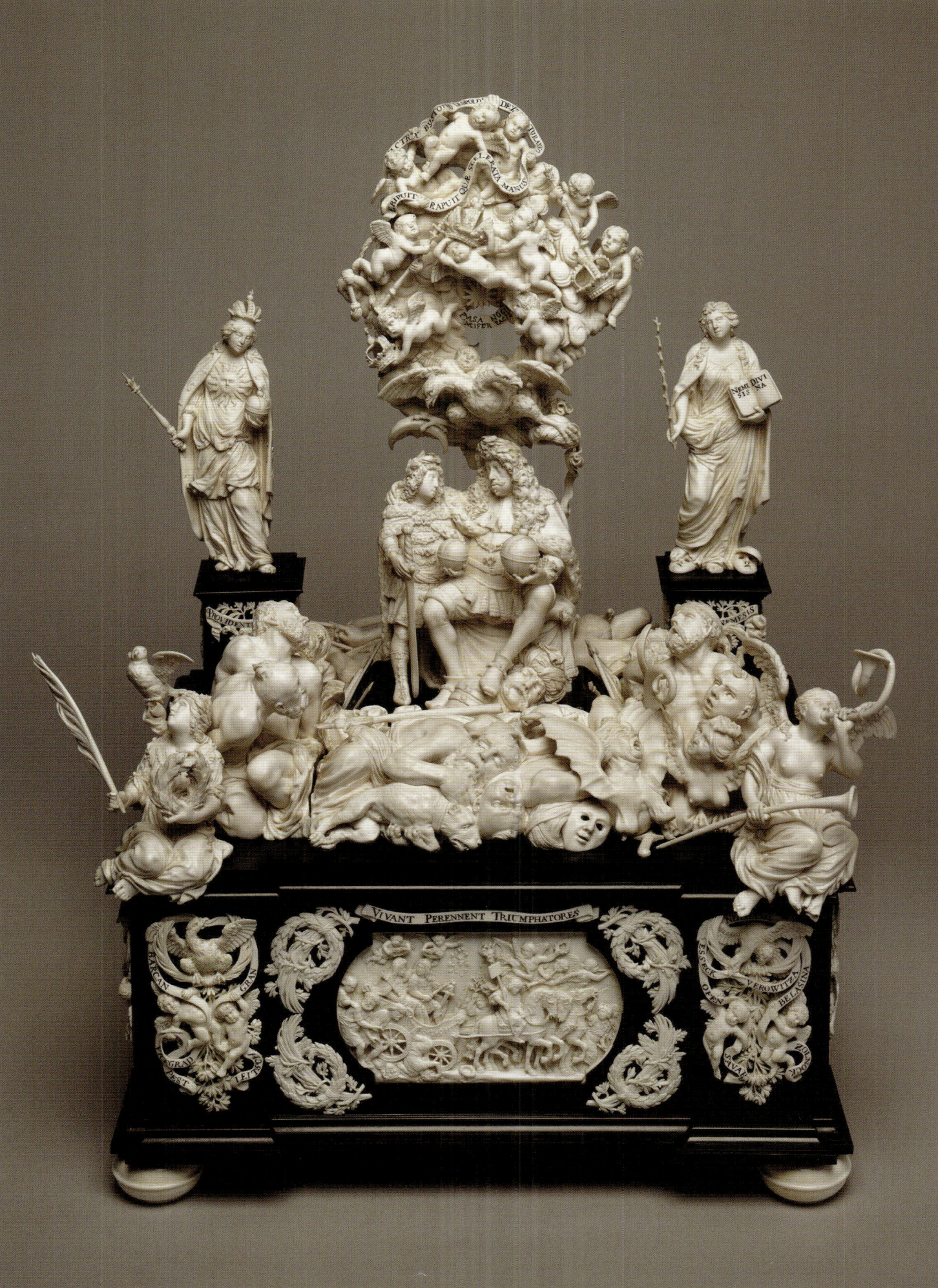

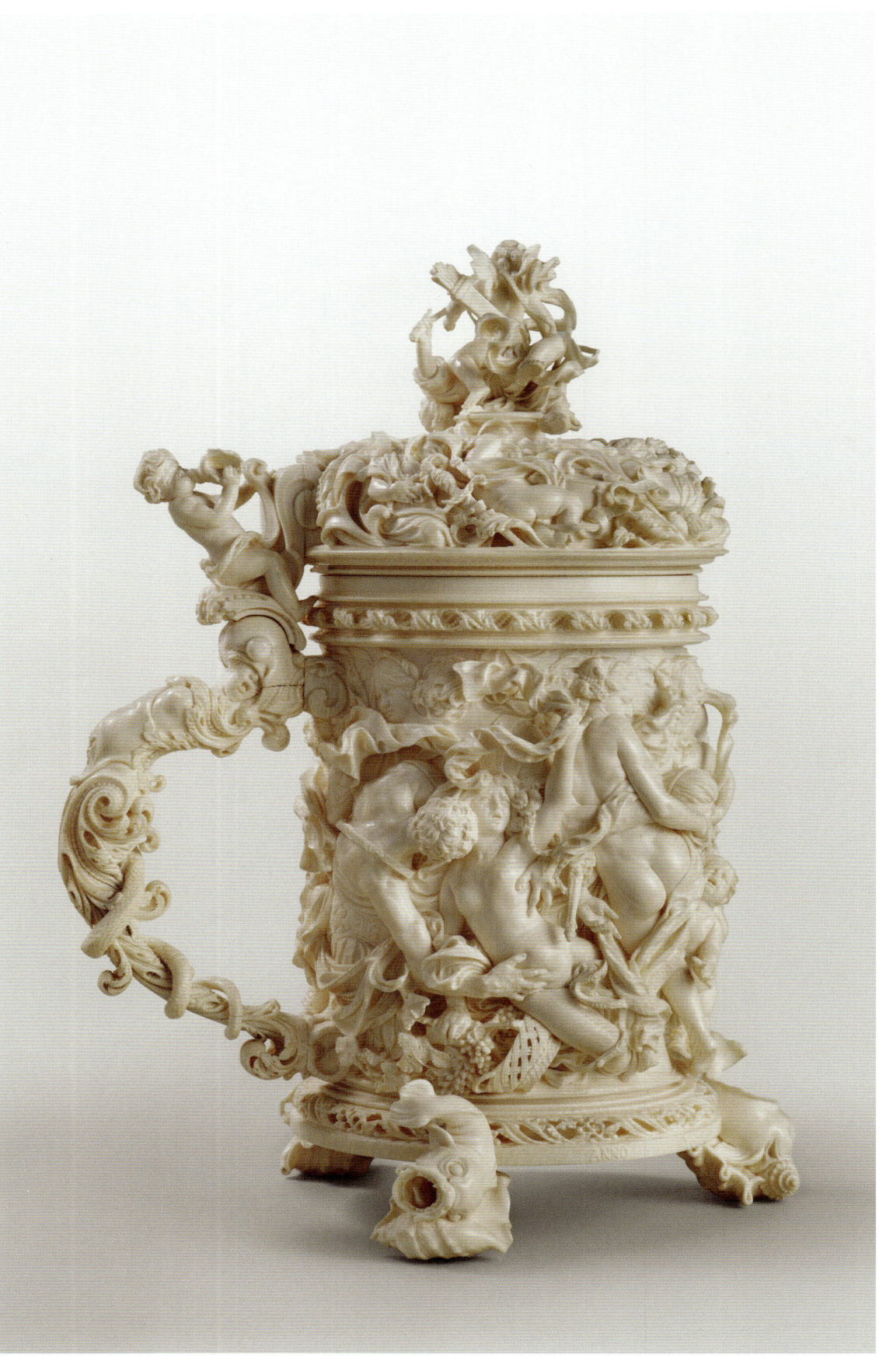

2.14
Matthias Rauchmiller,
Rape of the Sabines,
ivory tankard with silver
gilt lining, signed
and dated 1676,
height 34.9 cm.
Liechtenstein Collec-
tion, Vaduz-Vienna
(inv. no. SK 326).

> 2.15
Rauchmiller, *Rape of
the Sabines* [2.14],
detail.

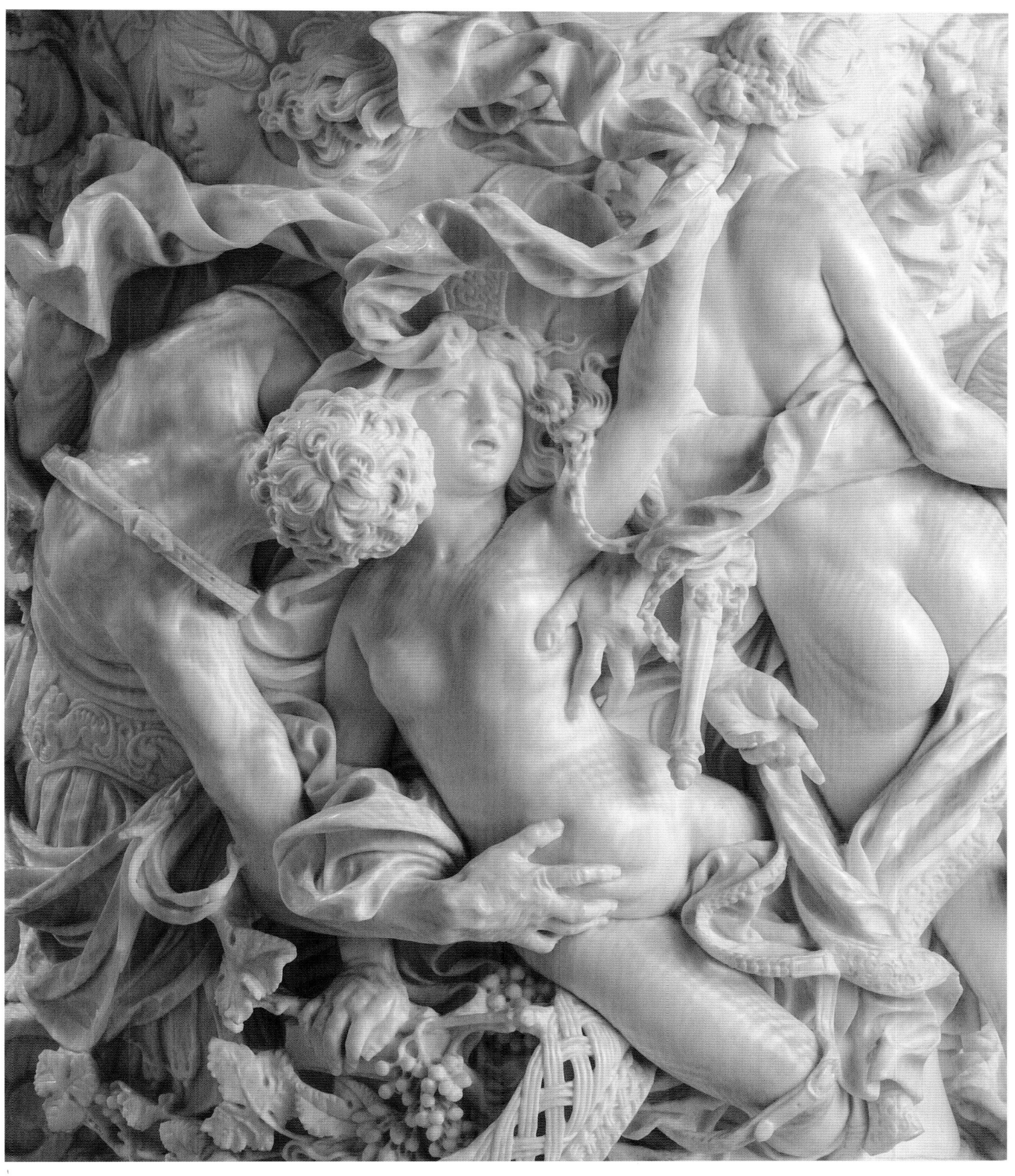

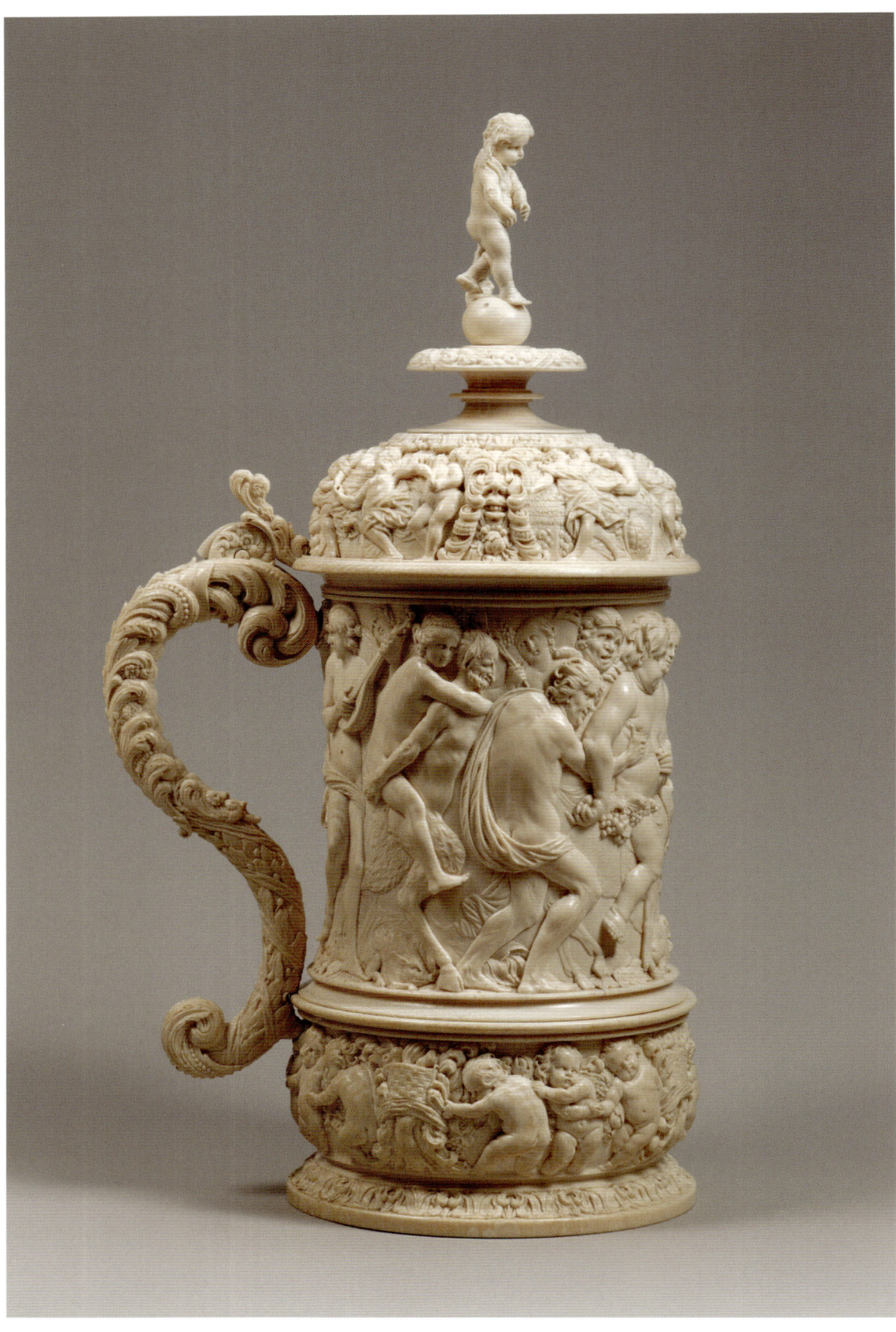

2.16
Johann Caspar
Schenck, *Bacchic
Scenes (King Pentheus
and Bacchus)*, ivory
tankard, mono-
grammed, c. 1665/74,
height 35.8 cm.
Kunsthistorisches
Museum, Vienna
(inv. no. KK 4467).

only known signed and dated piece by Maucher, an explicit indication of the artist's pride in his work.[24]

Sculpture of the Mid-Seventeenth Century at the Court of Vienna: Matthias Rauchmiller

In the mid- to late seventeenth century, the patronage of both the Brandenburg court and the imperial court in Vienna was paralleled by commissions from aristocratic families in Silesia (now Poland). Many outstanding and costly works of art were created there in the seventeenth century, despite the recent ravages of war.

An ivory tankard signed and dated 1676 by Matthias Rauchmiller (1645-86), depicting *The Rape of the Sabine Women*, is one such work, monumental despite its modest size [**2.14 and 2.15**]. Rauchmiller was both a painter and sculptor, originally from the area around Lake Constance; he had been appointed court painter in Vienna in 1675. The frieze of the figures on the tankard, though fully sculptural, suggests painted compositions or engravings, notably those by or after Rubens, although the earlier Flemish master was not a direct source. The ivory was acquired by Johann Adam Andreas, Prince of Liechtenstein (1690-1732) in 1707, and it remains in the Liechtenstein Collection, but it may have been previously owned, or even commissioned, by the Silesian diplomat, lawyer and playwright Daniel Caspar von Lohenstein (1635-83). Von Lohenstein, who was of an aristocratic family from Breslau (Wrocław) in Silesia, had been sent to Vienna to negotiate with the emperor on behalf of the Protestant population in Breslau in 1675, Silesia being under the rule of the Habsburgs in Vienna at that date. He was a friend of Rauchmiller, publishing an adulatory poem on the tankard soon after it was created. The ivory carvings depict a frenzied pursuit, dramatically conveyed in the virtuoso working of the intertwined figures. The handle, lid and feet are intricately carved with figures, animals and plant forms, all in ivory. Just as Kern's alabaster group differed in feeling and style from Giambologna's *Rape of a Sabine Woman* in Florence [**2.5**], so this tankard presents a distinctly baroque perspective on this classical subject. Indeed, in this

instance the subject, known from the title of Von Lohenstein's contemporary poem ('Herr Matthias Rauchmiller's artfully carved Rape of the Sabines in ivory'), is conveyed with such complexity—even with conflicting details in relation to the ostensible narrative—that without the confirmation of the title in Von Lohenstein's poem it might have been difficult to construe it.[25] The virtuoso carving recalls the work of the Schenck family of ivory carvers of Constance, with whom Rauchmiller may have trained [**2.16**]. The Flemish quality of the figures with their rounded forms is reminiscent of the work of Rubens, and possibly the Netherlandish sculptor Artus Quellinus the Elder (1609-68), whose sculpture Rauchmiller might have seen in the Netherlands in his youth [**2.17**].[26] But the ivory also seems to emulate Rauchmiller's earlier compatriot Georg Petel,

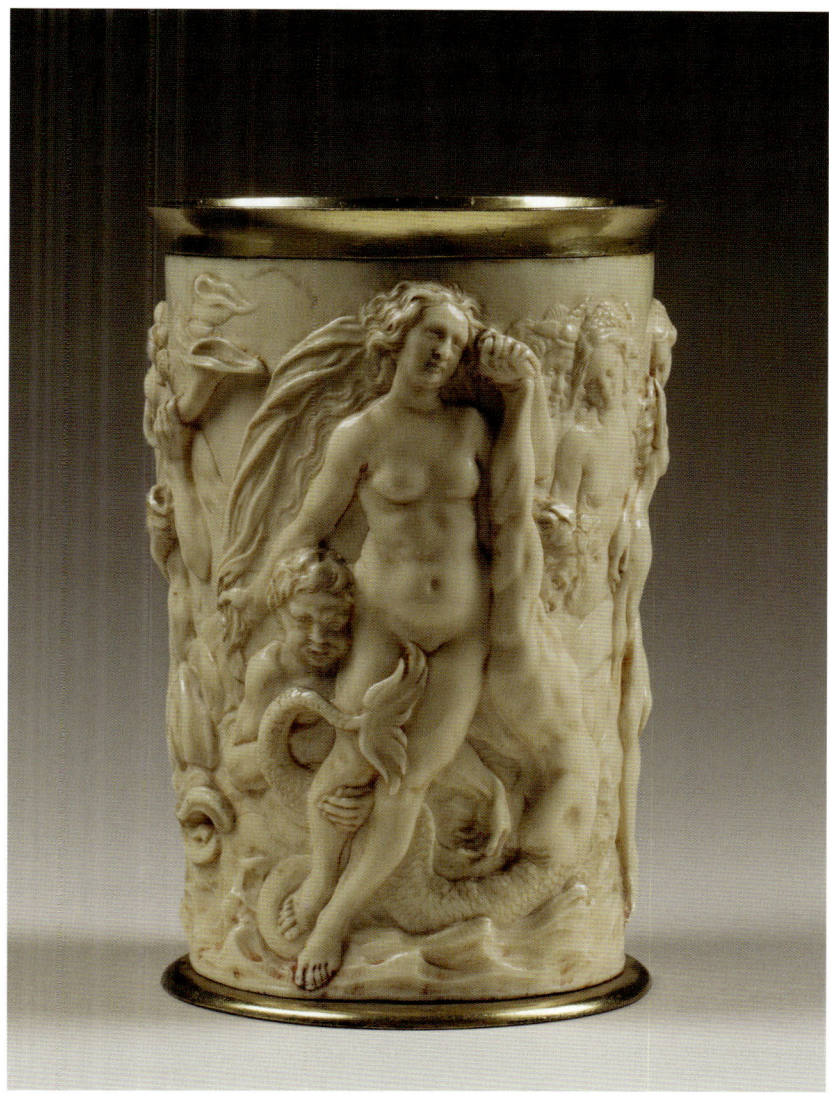

2.17
Artus Quellinus the Elder, *Goblet with the Birth of Venus*, ivory with silver gilt mounts, height 13.2 cm. Musées royaux d'Art et d'Histoire, Brussels (inv. no. 29).

2.18
Matthias Rauchmiller, *Duke Georg Wilhelm von Liegnitz-Wohlau*, alabaster, after 1677. Piastów Chapel, church of St John the Baptist, Legnica.

2.19
Matthias Rauchmiller, *Princess Charlotte von Liegnitz-Wohlau*, alabaster, after 1677. Piastów Chapel, church of St John the Baptist, Legnica.

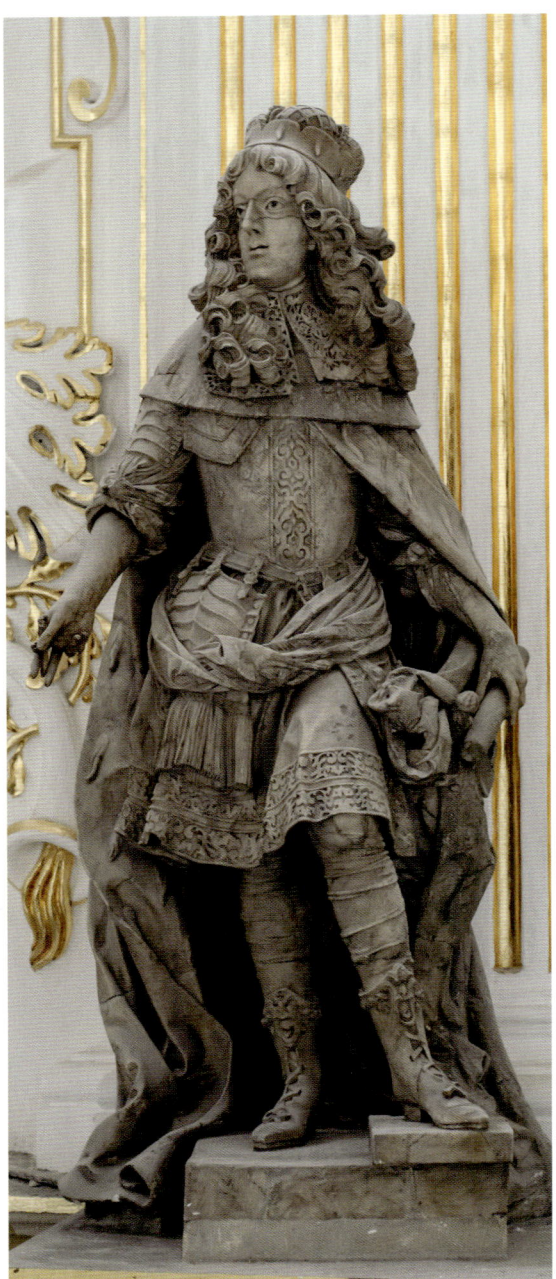

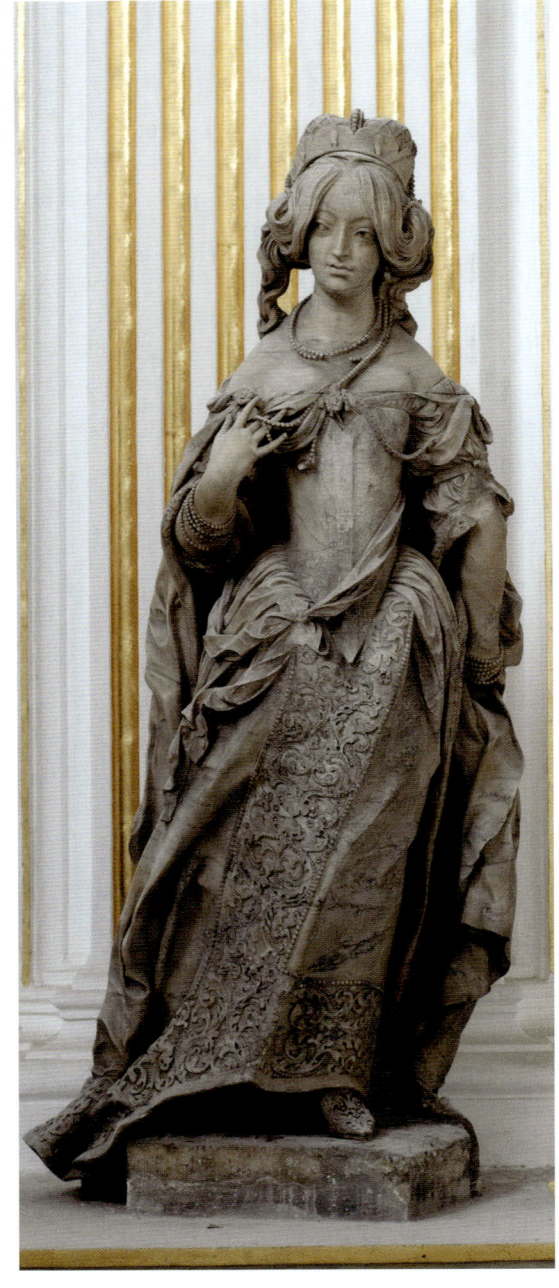

for example Petel's salt cellar of 1628, once owned by Rubens [1.37].[27] Rauchmiller's tankard is the only surviving work known by him in ivory, but several of his other large-scale sculptures are extant.

The four alabaster statues of the Liegnitz family for their mausoleum, the Piast Chapel (Piastów Chapel) in the church of St John the Baptist, Liegnitz, Silesia (now Legnica, Poland), were produced by Rauchmiller in 1677-9 [2.18 and 2.19].[28] They were commissioned by Duchess Louise von Anhalt Dessau (1633-80) to commemorate herself, her husband Duke Christian II (1618-72), her son Duke George William

(1660-75), and her daughter Princess Charlotte, Duchess of Holstein (1652-1707). George's premature death extinguished the male line of the family, and the chapel was seen as a lasting memorial to them for posterity. Rauchmiller's friend Von Lohenstein advised on the iconographic programme, writing poetic lines for the arches in the mausoleum, and Rauchmiller also painted the frescoes in the space.[29] The statues of George William and his sister Charlotte, just under life size, with their youthful faces, exquisitely detailed fashionable costumes and dance-like poses conveying a light, animated movement, look forward to the rococo. Although commemorating the end of the hereditary line and set in the religious context of a mausoleum, all four figures seem superbly confident secular portraits of the final members of this ducal family.

Towards the end of his short life Rauchmiller designed the *Pestsaule* (Plague Column) in Vienna in 1679, celebrating the end of the attack of bubonic plague in the city. Because of his early death, however, he was unable to complete the project. Only the overall design of the monument and the three life-size angels are by him. The complex polygonal column with elaborate sculpted reliefs, surmounted by a group of the Trinity, was completed by others in 1694 [**2.20 and 2.21**]. Although the ivory tankard, the alabaster figures and the marble angels seem so diverse, Rauchmiller's distinctive style can be perceived in all of them: his fascination with movement and figurative form, his seemingly effortless handling of diverse materials, and his mastery of carving surface details.

Sculpture of the Late Seventeenth and Early Eighteenth Centuries at the Court of Vienna: Matthias Steinl

The ivory sculptures of the seventeenth century and early eighteenth century in Germany and Austria are amongst the most impressive works of art to be produced anywhere in Europe, as Rauchmiller's tankard [**2.14**] and Maucher's *Apotheosis of Leopold I* [**2.13**] make clear. These two works can be paralleled by the extraordinary sculptures made for the imperial court in Vienna by the Austrian sculptor and architect Matthias Steinl (c. 1644-1727). In 1688 Steinl was appointed court ivory sculptor (*Kammerbeinstecher*) at Vienna, an appointment that lasted thirty-nine years, until his death. During that time he carved the three great ivory equestrian groups to be discussed below, as well as designing numerous churches, altarpieces, pulpits and monstrances for Vienna and elsewhere.[30]

Steinl's *Allegory of the Elements, Water and Air*, was executed in about 1688 in walrus ivory, an exotic material comparable to elephant ivory and with similar qualities: an organic substance that can be carved with great precision. The sculptor has exploited its crystalline surface and the spiralling forms inherent in the tapering shape of the tusk [**2.22**]. The *Allegory of the Elements* was probably carved at the time of Steinl's appointment to the court, a resounding proof of his superlative skill in carving. Three intertwined figures, with a putto hovering above, rise up from a base of shells and water creatures, every part of the figurative group fusing characteristics of water and air. A triton, the lower half of whose body is that of a fish, blows a conch shell, while supporting a young semi-nude male figure who wears tendrils of leaves around his hips and carries a fish slung over his shoulder. The youthful male figure in turn lifts another semi-nude figure, a woman wearing a skimpy swathe of seaweed-like drapery around her waist. She holds up a shell with both hands stretched above her head. Floating above them all, the putto grasps a furled banner, while delicate scrolls stream out in the air around him. Like Giambologna's sculpture [**see 2.5**], Steinl's group embodies a complex serpentine movement, leading the viewer continually to move around a sculpture that has no single frontal view. This virtuoso piece was apparently once displayed in the imperial Treasury (*Schatzkammer*) on an oval socle alongside a contemporary ivory group of *Apollo and Daphne*, also carved from one tusk, in this case that of an elephant rather than a walrus, by the Tyrolean sculptor Jacob Auer (1645-1706) [**2.23**]. Auer worked in a variety of materials, including large-scale stone sculpture, but specialized in ivory. His *Apollo and Daphne* illustrates a story from Ovid's *Metamorphoses*: the nymph Daphne, fleeing the god Apollo, is transformed into a laurel tree in order to escape the god's advances. The surfaces of the sculpture imitate varied textures: the soft flesh and drapery of the nymph and the god pursuing her, and the delicate twigs and leaves of the emerging laurel tree, Daphne's hands and feet disappearing as they become branches and roots. Her body leans gracefully backwards, reflecting the curve of the tusk. The most celebrated interpretation of the subject in the baroque era was Bernini's marble group of the same subject of 1622-5 in Rome, similarly using the material of the sculpture (in that case marble) to imitate

>> **2.20**
Matthias Rauchmiller and others, The Trinity at the top of the Pestsaule (Plague Column), gilt bronze and marble, 1694. Graben, Vienna.

>> **2.21**
Matthias Rauchmiller and others, *Pestsaule* (Plague Column), detail of marble figures, 1694. Graben, Vienna.

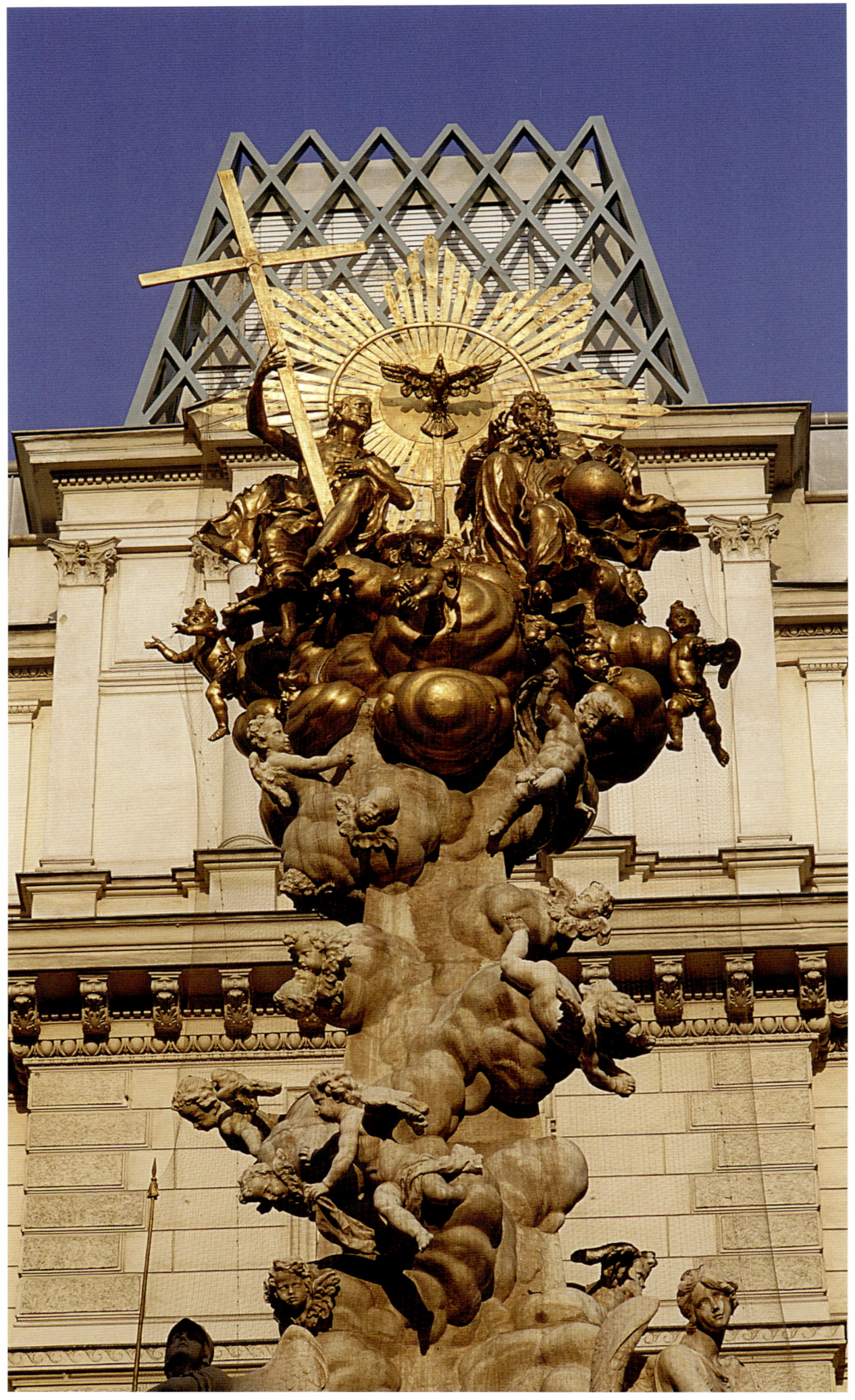

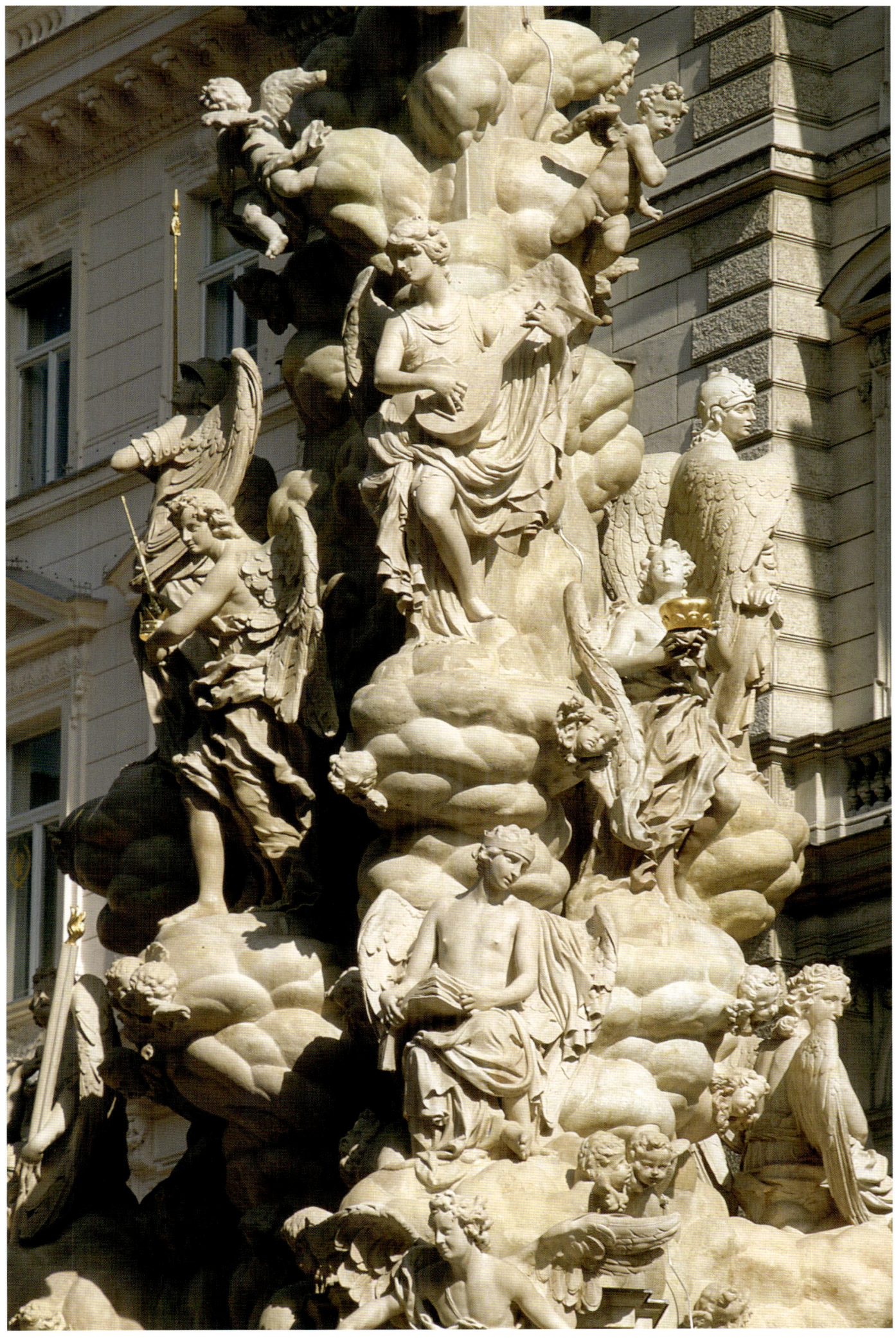

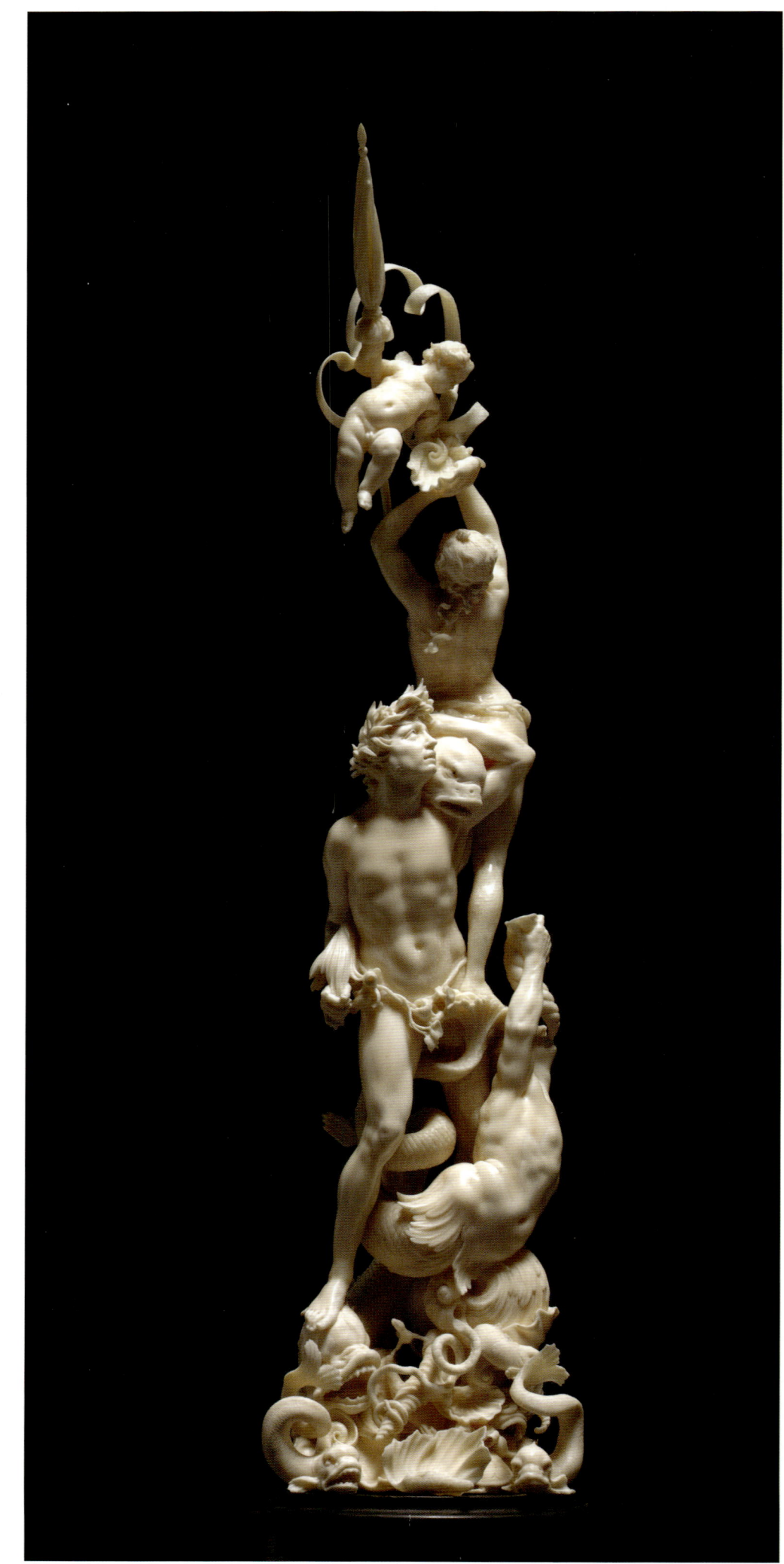

2.22
Matthias Steinl, *Allegory
of the Elements: Water
and Air*, walrus tusk,
c. 1688, height
43.4 cm. Kunst-
historisches Museum,
Vienna
(inv. no. KK 4533).

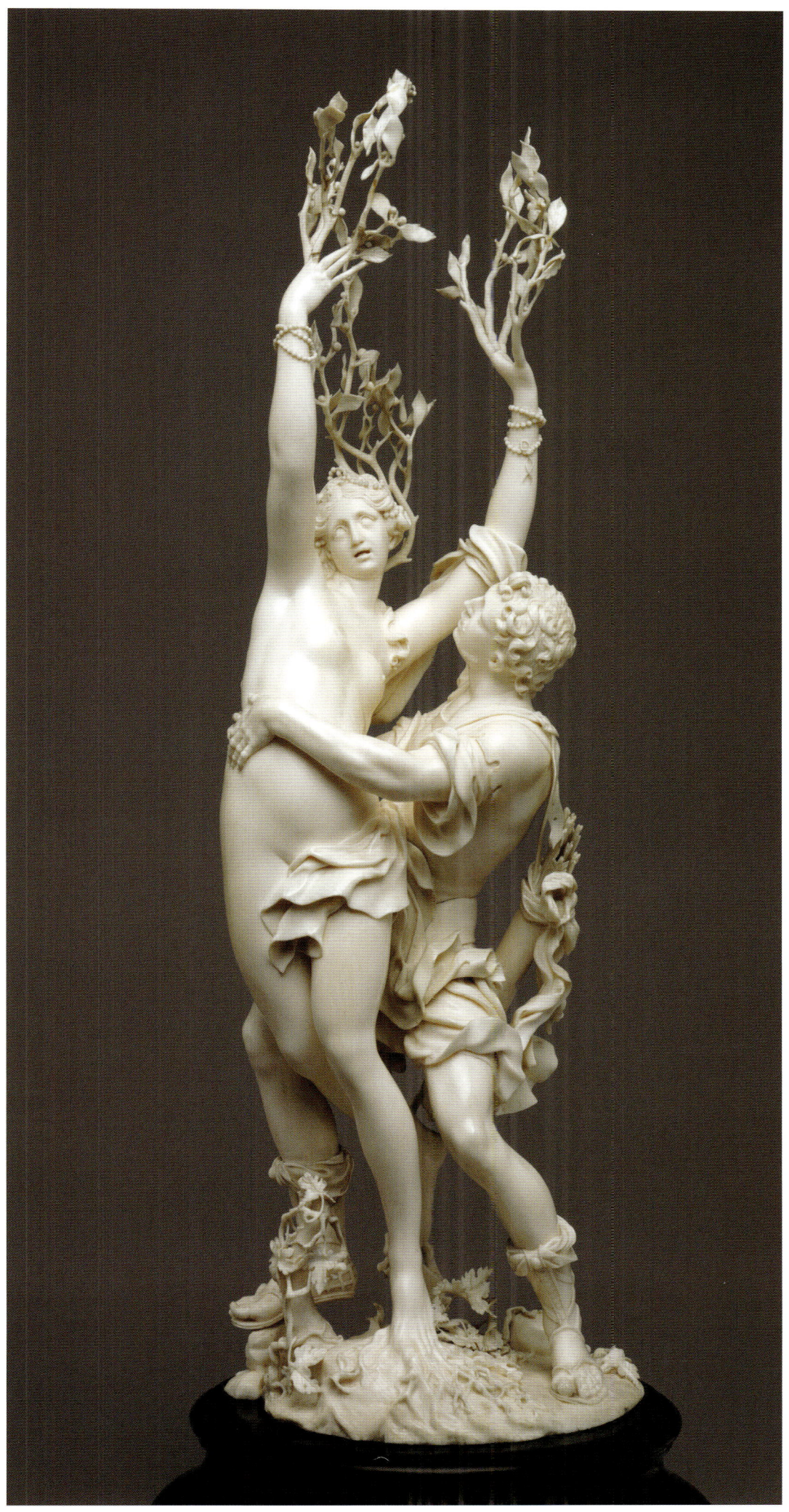

2.23
Jacob Auer, *Apollo and Daphne*, ivory, c. 1688/90, height 43.9 cm. Kunsthistorisches Museum, Vienna (inv. no. KK 4537).

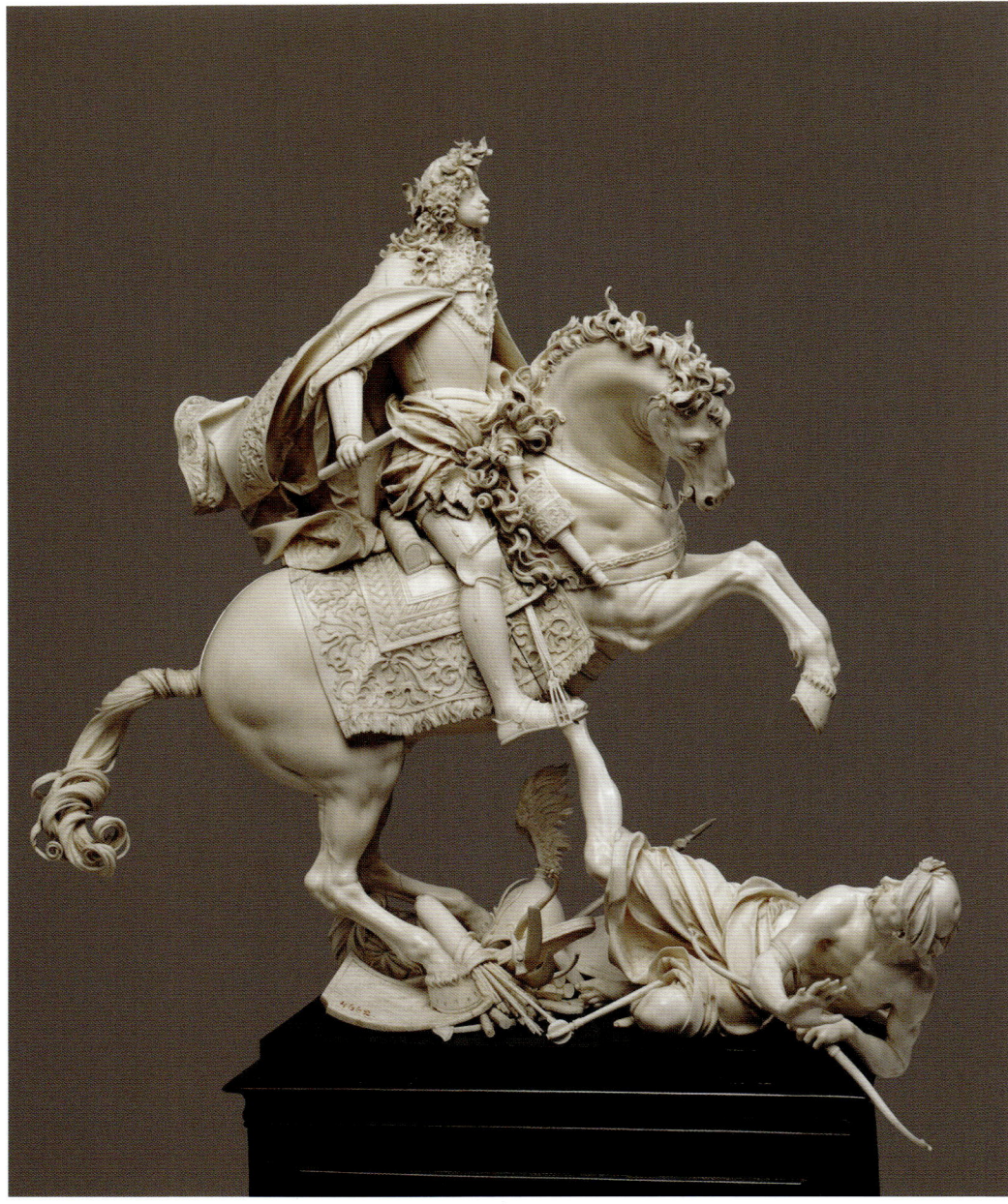
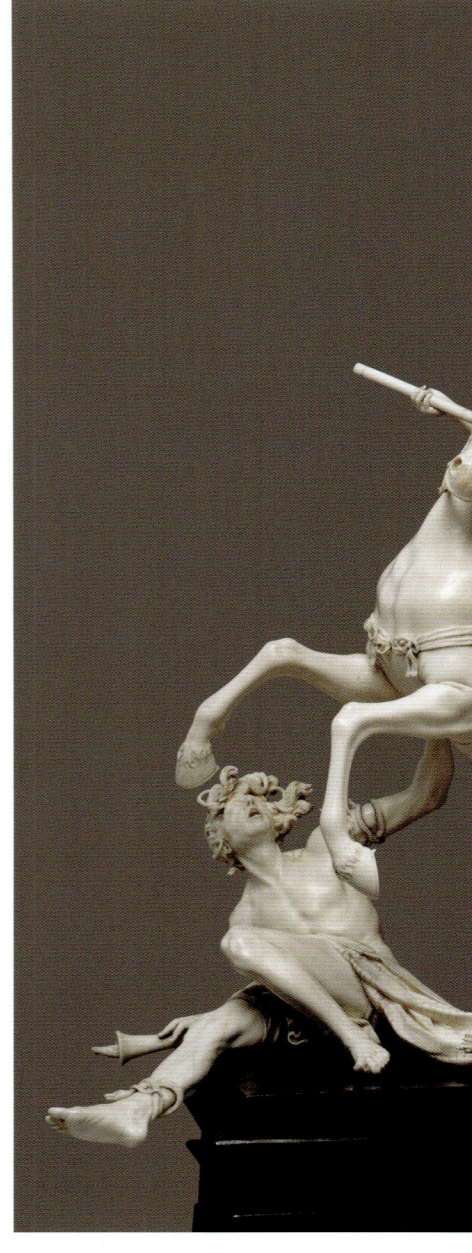

2.24
Matthias Steinl, *Emperor Leopold I Conquering a Turk*, ivory on wood base, c. 1690/93, height 74 cm. Kunsthistorisches Museum, Vienna (inv. no. KK 4662).

2.25
Matthias Steinl, *King Joseph I Overcoming a Fury*, ivory on wood base, signed and dated 1693, height 70.8 cm. Kunsthistorisches Museum, Vienna (inv. no. KK 4663).

the dramatic transformation of flesh into a tree. Auer must have known this Roman work. However Bernini's sculpture has one clear frontal view, whereas Auer's—like Steinl's *Allegory*—has multiple viewpoints.[31] The swirling composition means the viewer has to look at the group from every angle. Not only in its serpentine movement and the exquisite carving of the ivory but in its dimensions, Auer's ivory seems to be a fitting pendant to Steinl's *Allegory of the Elements*; the two sculptures are virtually the same height.

Steinl also produced three exceptional equestrian monuments in ivory. The first two, dating from the 1690s, depict Leopold I and his oldest son and heir Joseph I, who inherited the imperial throne in 1705 [**2.24 and 2.25**]. When

Joseph died prematurely in 1711 his younger brother Charles (1685-1740) became Emperor Charles VI; Steinl's third equestrian group dates from that time [**2.26**].[32] The first two groups of Leopold and Joseph, made just a few years before Maucher's *Apotheosis of Leopold I* of 1700 [**2.13**], demonstrate—like Maucher's work— the fact that ivory can be used to create seemingly colossal works, even though these groups are only about half life size. The ivory group of Charles VI, made nearly twenty years later, because of the unexpected death of Joseph I, is on the same impressive, imperial scale as the preceding pendant works of the new emperor's father and brother. Steinl's technique surpasses even Maucher's: the movement of the great rearing horses with their windswept manes and

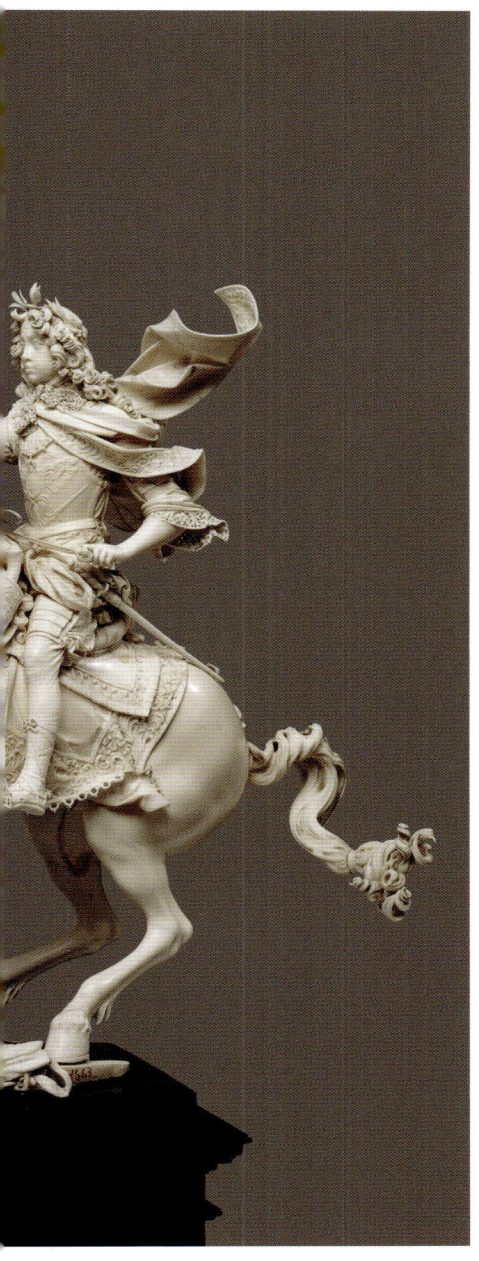

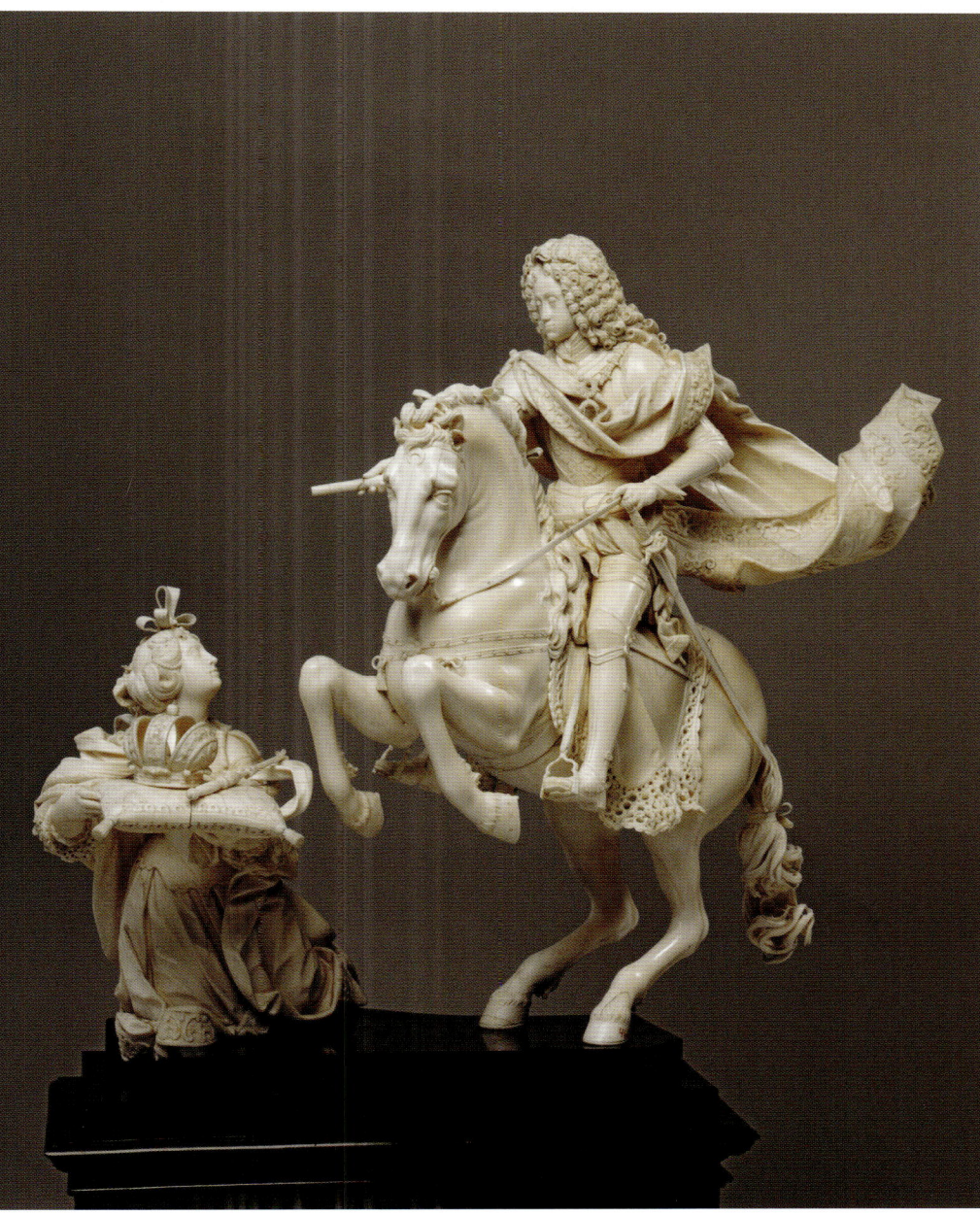

tails complement the billowing cloaks of the three monarchs. At the same time, the portraits of Leopold (the proud emperor), Joseph (the youthful future emperor), and Charles (the new emperor) are assertive and naturalistic likenesses of the Habsburg rulers, Charles resplendent in an elegant flowing wig, receiving the crown and sceptre of the Holy Roman Empire from a kneeling handmaiden. All three hold batons, Charles holding out his in a manner echoing the outstretched arm of the Roman emperor Marcus Aurelius. Unlike his father and brother, who needed to overcome hostile forces, Charles VI's rule is assured: despite his armour, he seems to be first and foremost a courtier.

Sculpture of the Late Seventeenth and Early Eighteenth Centuries at the Brandenburg Court: Andreas Schlüter

Sculptures on a small scale have dominated this chapter, but the work of the architect and sculptor Andreas Schlüter (c. 1659-1714) was grander and larger, designed for specific architectural contexts in Warsaw and Berlin. Schlüter's place and exact date of birth are uncertain, though he was probably born in about 1659 in Gdańsk (Danzig), where he trained under David (Christoph) Sapovius (d. 1710). By 1689, and perhaps as early as 1681/2, he was working at the court of the Polish king John Sobieski III (1629-96), where he became aware of international artistic currents, especially Italian and Netherlandish, through the work of the Netherlandish

2.26
Matthias Steinl, *Emperor Charles VI with the Personification of the Holy Roman Empire*, ivory on wood base, c. 1711/12, height 73.7 cm. Kunsthistorisches Museum, Vienna (inv. no. KK 4664).

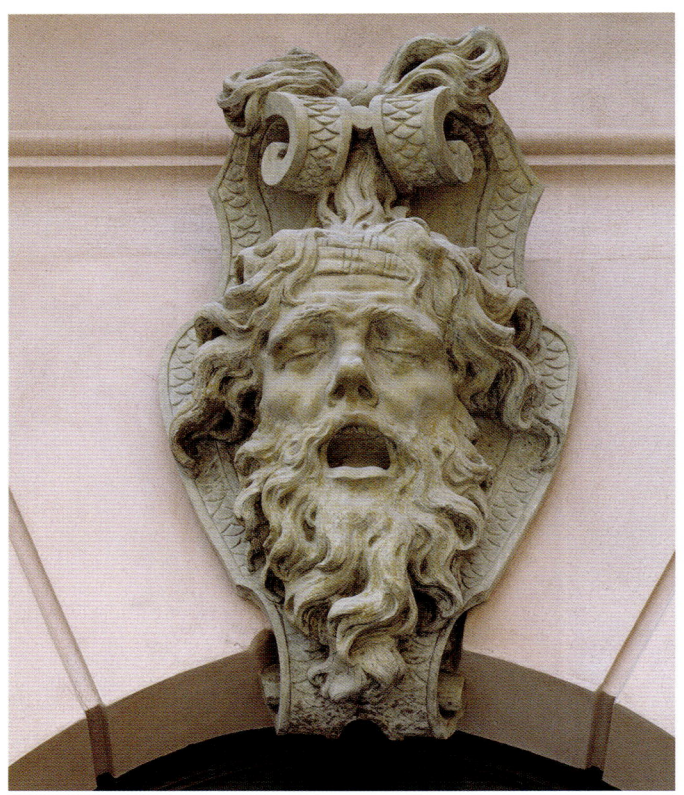

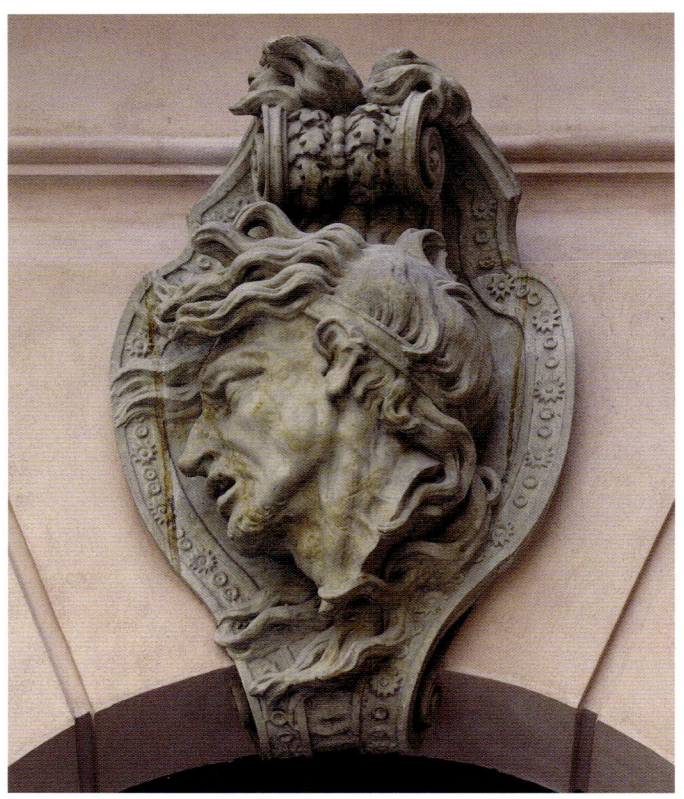

2.27
Andreas Schlüter,
*Head of a Dying
Warrior*, stone, 1696-7.
Armoury, Berlin.

2.28
Andreas Schlüter,
*Head of a Dying
Warrior*, stone, 1696-7.
Armoury, Berlin.

architect Tylman van Gameren (1632-1706), whose work had transformed baroque architecture in Poland. In 1691 Schlüter was appointed court sculptor in Warsaw, but three years later in 1694 he was summoned to Berlin as court sculptor by Elector Frederick III (1657-1713) (from 1701 King in Prussia), the son of the Great Elector Frederick William.[33] He was probably sent to the Netherlands and France by the elector in 1695, and to Italy in 1696. The Academy of Arts in Berlin was established in 1696, the third after those that had been founded in Rome and Paris, and in 1698 he was appointed Rector, a post he retained until 1713. He acquired plaster casts of antique busts from Rome for the Academy, although a later fire in 1743 destroyed not only the collections but important archival records.[34] His appointment to the Brandenburg court was part of Frederick III's own ambitious building programme and his wish to transform Berlin into a truly royal city.

Schlüter's *Masks of Dying Warriors* are keystones, made from 1696 onwards for the Armoury (Zeughaus) in Berlin, a building initially designed by the court architect Johann Arnold Nering (1659-95) and that Schlüter was to bring to completion in 1712 [**2.27 and 2.28**]. Schlüter designed other keystones in the form of helmet trophies for this new edifice. All are carved in sandstone, made with the assistance of Georg Gottfried Weihenmeyer (1666-1715). The helmet trophies were based on engravings by Giovanni Battista Galestruzzi (1619-after 1678) after paintings by Polidoro da Caravaggio (c. 1492-1543). Schlüter modelled clay bozzetti for the keystones, which would then be carved in stone. Some of these bozzetti were to be cast in plaster later in the eighteenth century, and were subsequently engraved by Christian Bernhardt Rode (1725-97). Three of these aftercasts, showing signs of the sculptor's original clay modelling, are extant today in the collections of the Academy in Berlin, on loan to the Bode Museum.[35] Each of the warriors' heads rests against the backing of a shield, forming a border. Their anguished expressions recall the contemporary engravings by Charles Le Brun (1619-90) of 'expressive heads'. Schlüter's heads are also reminiscent of antique prototypes, such as the *Dying Gaul* or those from the *Laocoön* group.[36] They also form a continuum in the history of German sculpture, paralleling the heads of the defeated warriors

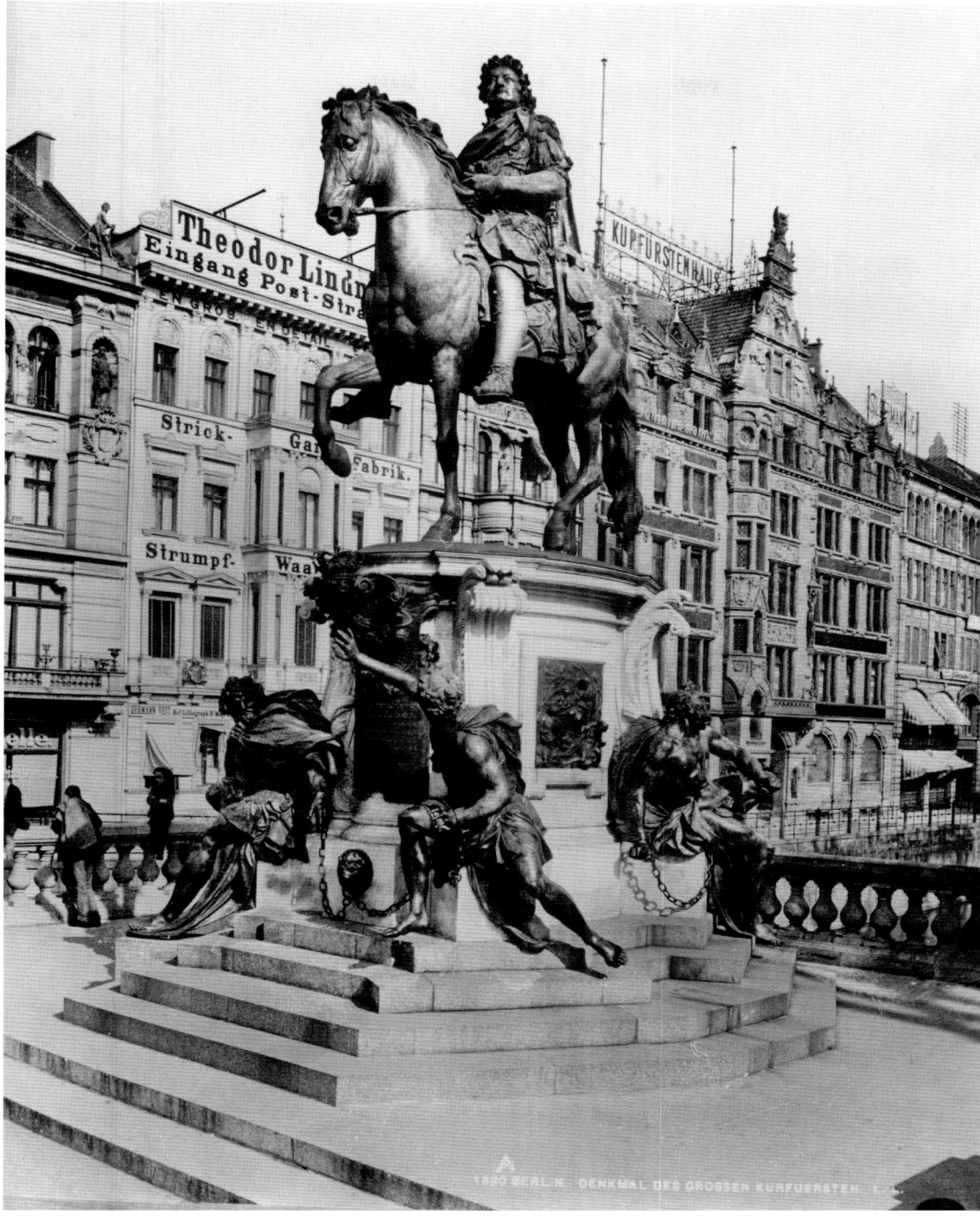

2.29
Andreas Schlüter,
*Equestrian Monument
to the Great Elector,
Frederick William*,
bronze, designed 1696,
cast 1700, installed
1703, as seen c. 1900
on the Lange Brücke,
Berlin.

seen on Steinl's contemporary ivory equestrian groups in Vienna [2.24 and 2.25], and even distantly echoing the face of the devil overcome by St Michael on Hans Reichle's bronze group in Augsburg of nearly a century before [1.25].

Schlüter's bronze equestrian monument of the Great Elector (designed 1696, cast 1700, installed 1703) originally stood on the Lange Brücke in Berlin, the bridge linking the former independent town of Cölln to Berlin, before they were combined as one in the new baroque

city of Berlin being created for Frederick III [2.29, 2.30 and 2.31]. The equestrian monument, cast in one piece by the founder Johann Jacobi (1661-1726), using the lost wax process, was the first of its kind in Germany, an extraordinary artistic and technical achievement.[37] Although a triumphal equestrian monument of this sort was unprecedented in Germany, it originated in a rich European tradition of such sculptures, and the impetus to erect such a prestigious public sculpture to his father must

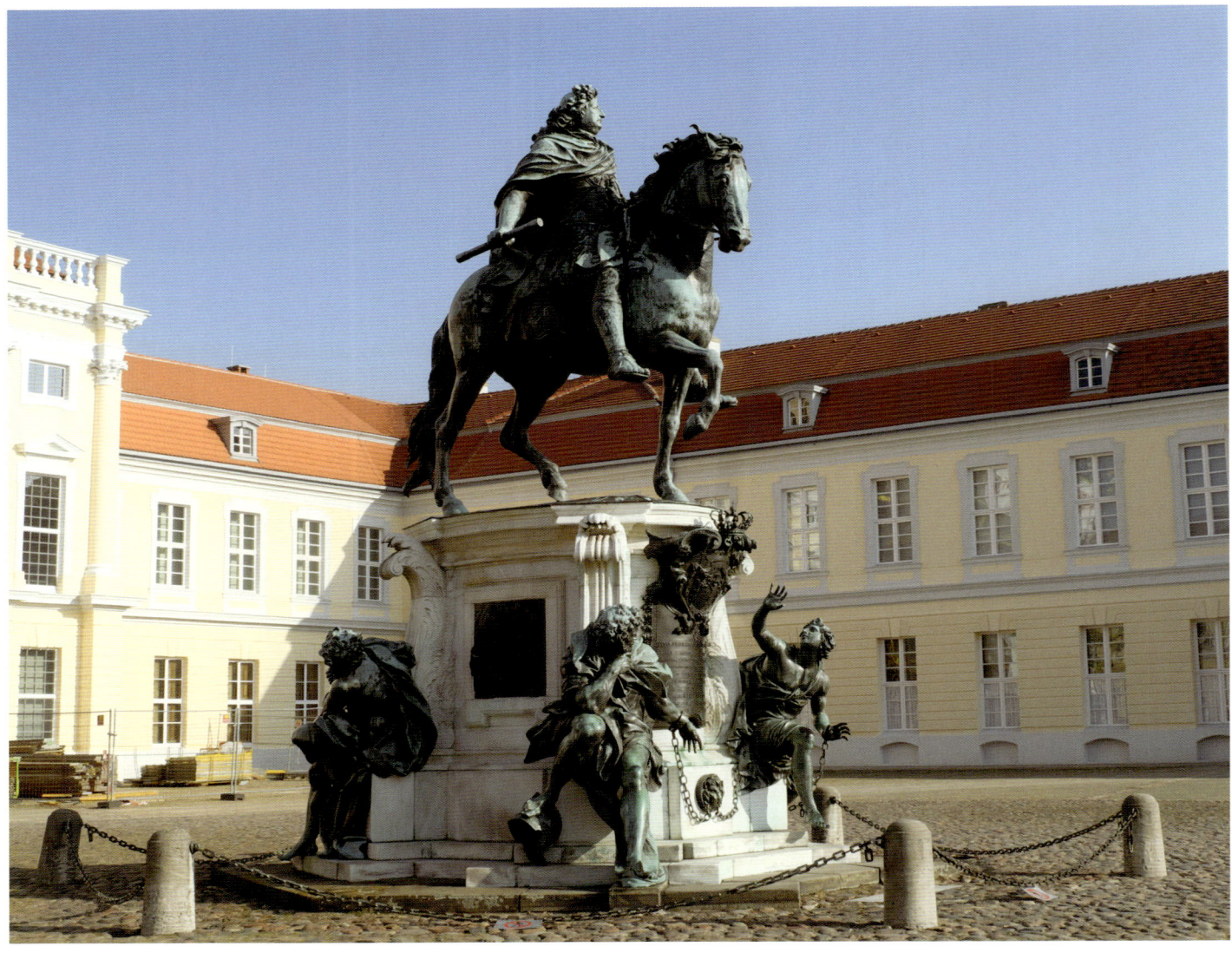

2.30
Andreas Schlüter,
*Equestrian Monument to
the Great Elector,
Frederick William,*
bronze, designed 1696,
cast 1700,
installed 1703.
Schloss Charlottenburg,
Berlin.

have been linked to Frederick's desire to raise his own and Prussia's status, culminating in his coronation as King in Prussia in 1701. Leygebe's iron statuette of the Great Elector of twenty years earlier/prior [2.9] could be said to have been a preliminary small local prototype, but other far grander equestrian monuments in France and Italy must have inspired both the patron Frederick III and the artist himself. Schlüter's great bronze is in the tradition of other equestrian monuments, such as that to Louis XIV by François Girardon (1691-99), originally in the Place Vendôme, Paris, destroyed in the French Revolution. Schlüter and Jacobi may well have studied Girardon's equestrian figure (then in process) when they were in Paris in 1694.[38] Francesco Mochi's bronze statues of Ranuccio and Alessandro Farnese in Piacenza

(1612-20) may have provided further prototypes, and Schlüter would undoubtedly have known both the second-century monument to Marcus Aurelius in Rome and Giambologna's equestrian statue of Cosimo I de' Medici of 1598 in Florence.[39]

The Great Elector, wearing antique armour and a flowing cloak, rides his pacing horse without stirrups in classical mode, holding out his baton, though his long hair is uncropped. The four chained slaves at the corners of the high marble plinth were added in 1708/9, recalling the four Barbary pirates by Pietro Tacca (1577-1640) of 1620-24 at the foot of the monument to Ferdinando I de' Medici (1549-1609) in Livorno [2.30].[40]

Equestrian monuments to rulers are public symbols of their power, and for that reason become more vulnerable as the political climate changes, a phenomenon epitomized by the

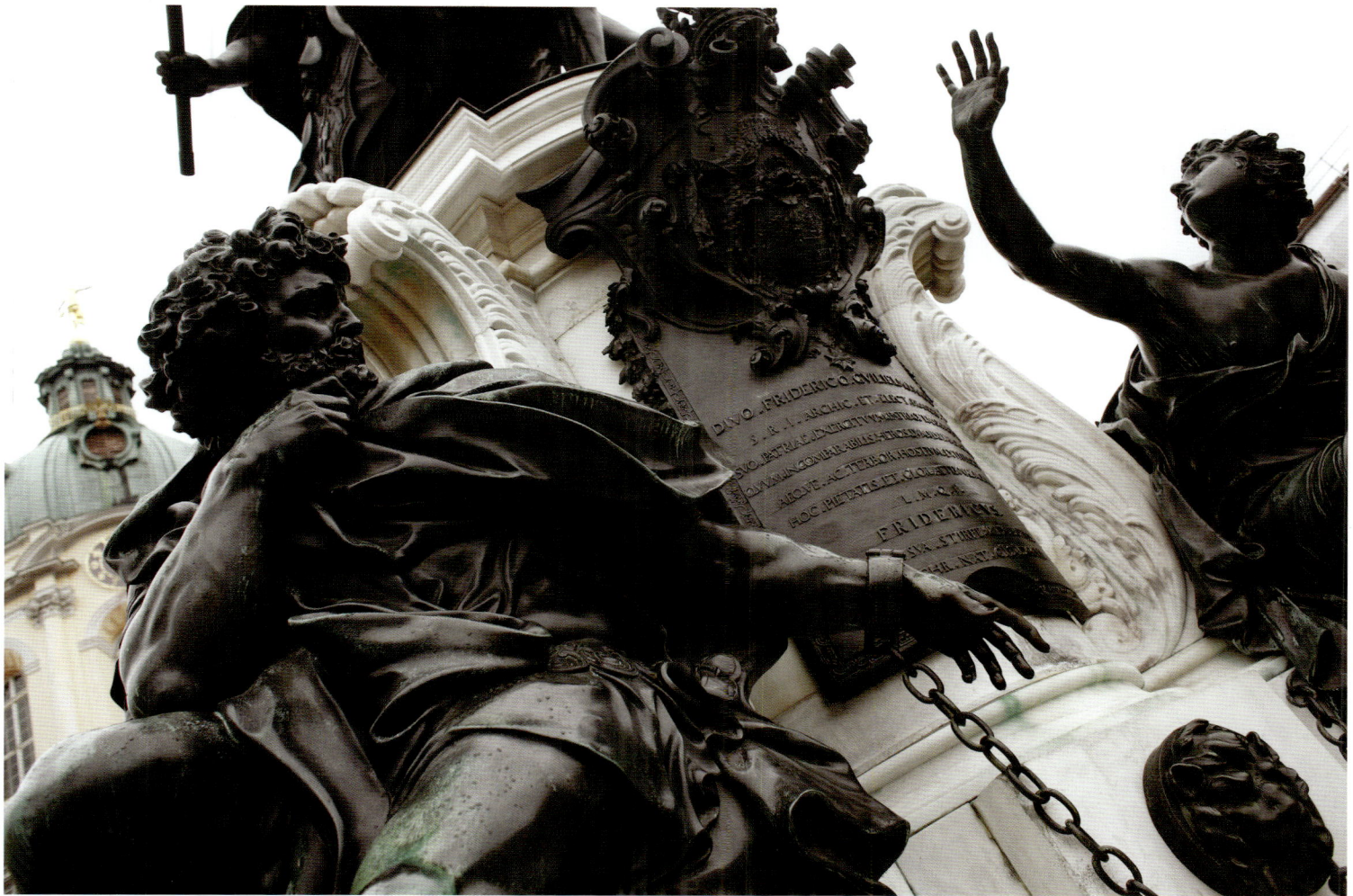

destroyed statues of the kings in France during the French Revolution. The equestrian statue of the Great Elector has suffered a somewhat remarkable history, enduring the vagaries of the twentieth century. It is now at Charlottenburg Palace in Berlin, for the Lange Brücke did not survive the bombing of Berlin in the Second World War. Although the monument had exceptionally survived the war relatively un-scathed, in 1947 it was sunk in Lake Tegel in the suburbs of East Berlin, probably in order to hide it from government authorities, since (like the French revolutionaries' attitude towards the public portraits of their kings) it was feared that the East German government might destroy it for ideological reasons, as a symbol of Germany's autocratic history. Two years later in 1949, however, the climate had changed somewhat,

and it was dredged up from the lake. The surface of the bronze had been corroded by the water, but otherwise the sculpture was in a relatively stable condition. It was restored and was installed on a marble plinth (a copy of the original) at Charlottenburg in July 1952.[41] Although there was clearly some change of heart about Berlin's baroque past, in 1950 the Berlin Palace (*Schloss*) and the baroque architectural centre of the city, much of it created by Schlüter, were demolished by the East German govern-ment, again for ideological reasons.[42]

Schlüter's commemorative monument to the court goldsmith Daniel Männlich (1625-1701) and his wife Anna Katherina (1636-98) in St Nicolas's church in Berlin, dating from 1700/1 [2.32], though now compromised by losses, is as arresting as the bronze royal sarcophagi he

2.31
Schlüter, *Equestrian Monument* [2.29], detail of chained slaves.

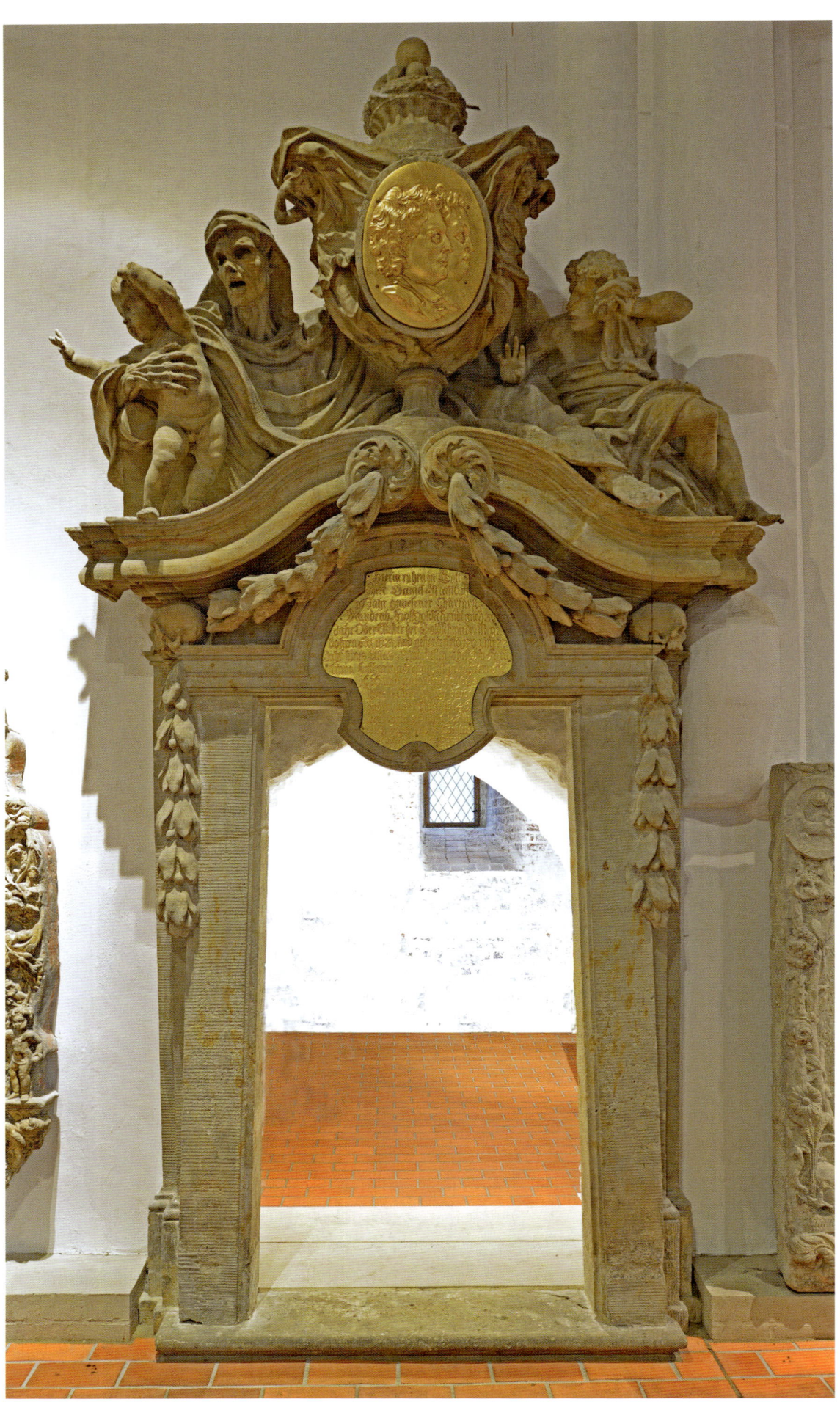

2.32
Andreas Schlüter, *Tomb of Daniel Männlich and his Wife*, marble and bronze, c. 1701. Church of St Nicholas, Berlin.

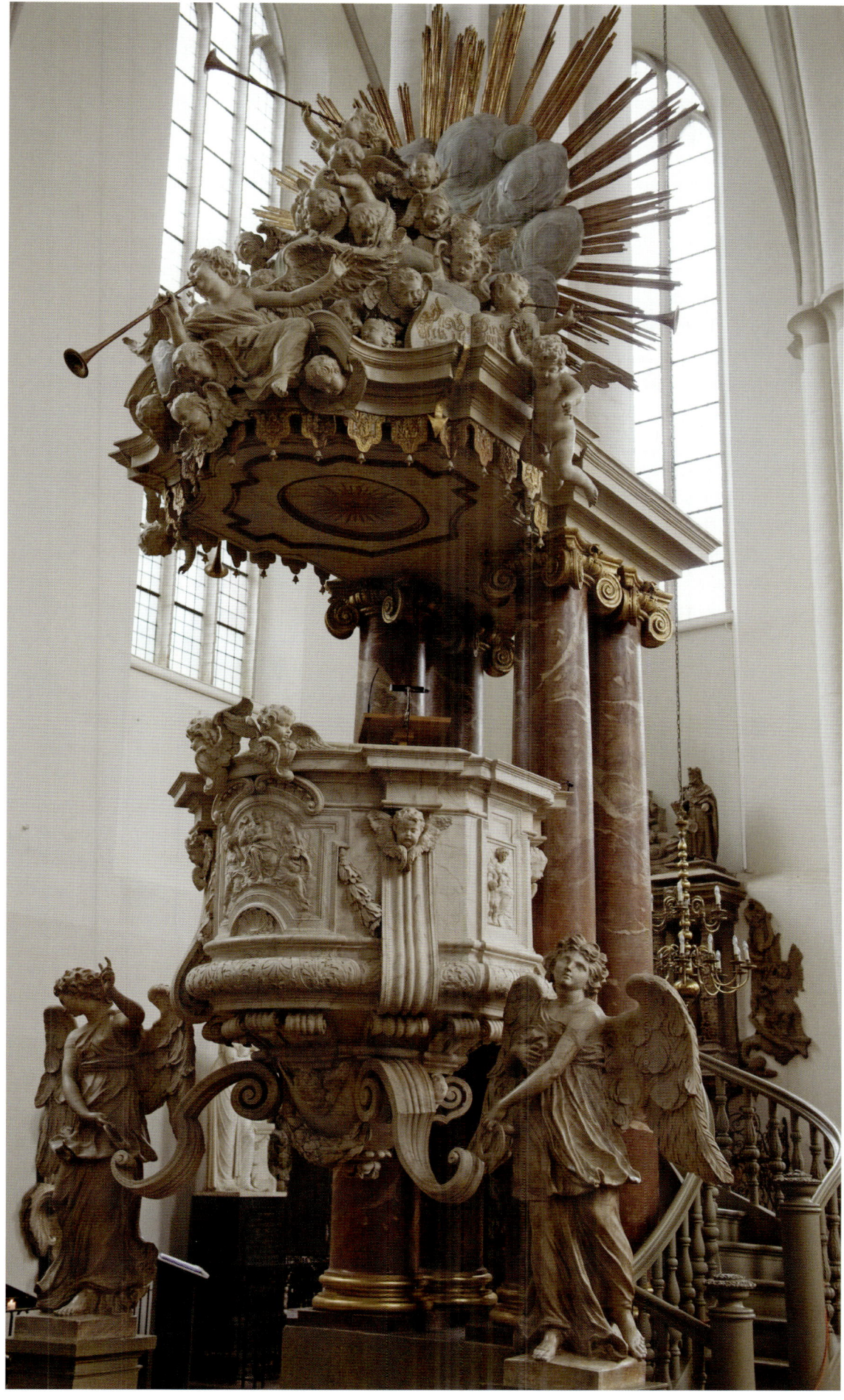

2.33
Andreas Schlüter,
Pulpit, wood, sandstone
and alabaster, 1703.
Church of St Mary,
Berlin.

was to produce for the Prussian royal family in the first decade of the eighteenth century.[43] The Männlich memorial was exceptional for Berlin at that date: it is a major monument in one of the most important churches in the city, but commemorates an artist (and friend of Schlüter)—someone who was neither an aristocrat nor of royal blood. It takes the form of a stone portal: a massive, draped urn and three allegorical figures rest on a Palladian pediment, below which garlands of laurel are draped over the upper half of the erstwhile entrance to the crypt, two skulls positioned at the corners. Between the figures, and in front of the urn, is an oval gilt medallion with a double profile portrait of the couple in a form recalling a medal or a cameo. Below the medallion is an inscribed gilt metal tablet recording the names and dates of the deceased. However, like the equestrian monument to the Great Elector, this memorial has been the victim of twentieth-century conflict. The original iron doors, in the form of a grill decorated with rich foliate decoration, which would have led to the crypt, have been lost since 1945; the crypt itself collapsed during the Second World War and has not been rebuilt. Similarly, the oval medallion and the inscribed metal plaque are modern copies made in 1988 based on earlier photographs, the originals having again been missing since the end of the war.[44] The overall dramatic design of the monument and stone sculptures testify, however, to Schlüter's extraordinary genius as a sculptor. The stone carvings enact a dramatic allegory of the passage of time: on one side of the pediment a skeletal draped half-figure of Death, or perhaps old age, holds a struggling child, representing childhood. On the other side a draped figure of Youth looks over at those two figures, holding out his right hand as if trying to stop the passage of time, whilst with his left he grasps some drapery, perhaps vainly trying to hide from impending mortality. Schlüter's monument, though for a Protestant setting, must surely be partly inspired by Bernini's funerary monuments in Rome, in particular the tomb of Pope Alexander VII Chigi in St Peter's Basilica of 1671-8, where a draped doorway is also framed by dramatic figures.[45]

Schlüter's great pulpit in the church of St Mary in Berlin was installed in 1703, having been commissioned by Anna Maria Lehmans, the widow of the elector's secretary, Georg Friedrich Fehr [**2.33**].[46] In terms of both engineering and artistic design it was an extraordinary achievement, with an elaborate sounding board populated by jubilant angels, supported by four ionic columns, the whole reaching a height of 6.5 metres. It cost 6000 thalers, in addition to further expenses, which Schlüter paid himself, surely a sign of the pride he took in this ambitious work. The columns are of sandstone, while the body and sounding board above are of wood and alabaster. Trumpet-blowing angels and cherubim, one holding the tablets of the Covenant presented to Moses, are positioned on the sounding board against a sunburst and clouds. Perhaps paradoxically for a pulpit in a Lutheran church, this exuberant sculpture was unquestionably inspired by Bernini's *Cathedra Petri* of 1625-33 at St Peter's Basilica in Rome. In a more Protestant mode, on the main body of the pulpit is a central relief in alabaster of St John the Baptist flanked by allegorical figures, emphasizing the authority of preaching and the word as a tool for Christian teaching. Allegories of Hope and Charity respectively are depicted on two reliefs on the sides of the pulpit, while two angels are standing on separate plinths on either side. The pulpit was originally positioned against a pillar halfway up the nave, at right angles to the congregation, because its placing had to be adapted to the existing architecture of the medieval church. However in 1949 it was moved to a more commanding position facing the congregation at the east end of the nave, where it is now satisfyingly assertive, a superb demonstration of Schlüter's sculptural powers, fusing Italianate forms into a harmonious whole. Some of the decorative motifs, such as the carved garlands, scrolls and shells, may stem from models for architectural ornaments the artist used for the Berlin Palace, which was being constructed at around the same time.

When the new King Frederick William I (1688-1740) came to the throne in 1713 he dismissed the current artists at court, and Schlüter went to the newly emerging city of

St Petersburg, where he became building director for Czar Peter I (Peter the Great) (1672-1725). However he was to die in Russia after only one year. Despite the truncation of his career, Schlüter can be said to be one of the most important sculptors of his era, combining sculpture with architecture in a way previously unseen in Germany and ultimately responsible for the renaissance of Berlin as a great baroque city.

The imposing sculptures executed in Berlin, Vienna and Silesia were paralleled by works of art being produced in Dresden in the late seventeenth and early eighteenth centuries, when the electors of Saxony were rivalling the Brandenburg court in sculptural and architectural projects to enhance and reinforce their prestige and status. The next chapter will focus on the sculptures being produced for the Wettin dynasty at the Dresden court at this time.

Notes

1   See Hildebrand and Theuerkauff 1981; MacGregor and Impey 1985.
2   Hildebrand and Theuerkauff 1981, p. 13.
3   He was, however, appointed as sculptor to the Brandenburg court for one year in 1648. See below.
4   See http://ta.sandrart.net/en/, accessed 9 May 2020.
5   'Die Königin Germania sahe ihre . . . gezierte Paläste und Kirchen hin und wieder in der Lohe aufliegen und ihre Augen wurden von Rauch und Weinen dermassen verdunkelt dass ihre keine Begiede oder Kraft übrig bleiben konte nach dieser Kunst zu sehen . . . . Also geriethe solche in vergessenheit und die jenigen so hiervon Beruff macheten in Armut und Verachtung . . .'. Cited in Kauffmann 1998, p. 163, and Tacke 1998, p. 245. Sandrart also mentioned Kern's activity as an architect, though no works of architecture by him are now known.
6   Maué 1997-2005, Vol. 1, pp. 35-7.
7   Hildebrand and Theuerkauff 1981, pp. 172-5.
8   Schraut 1990. I am indebted to Elisabeth Schraut's detailed discussion of this alabaster group.
9   Avery 1987, pp. 109-12.
10   Also comparable are the engravings by the monogrammist CR of 1642. See Thon 1977, p. 105; Knauer 1998; Richard 1998; Tacke 1998.
11   This is now replaced by a copy in Nuremberg. The original is in the Peterhof Palace Garden, St Petersburg, having been purchased by Czar Paul I in 1707.
12   *Dürers Verwandlung* 1981. A third medallion by Schweigger depicting the Swiss alchemist and natural philosopher Paracelsus (1493-1541), probably based on a Netherlandish engraving, was also in the Brandenburg collection; see Hildebrand and Theuerkauff 1981, pp. 138-42.

13   Trusted 1990.
14   *Andreas Schlüter* 2014, p. 62.
15   Hildebrand and Theuerkauff 1981, p. 137.
16   'das ich dabey meine Gesundheit (mit Antrücken des Leibes) verloren'; Hildebrand and Theuerkauff 1981, p. 136.
17   *Andreas Schlüter* 2014, p. 61.
18   Schreiter and Pyritz 2007.
19   Falcke 2006.
20   Ehmer 1992.
21   *Bernstein für Thron und Altar* 2005, pp. 76-83.
22   Maucher's two other ambers depicting *The Judgement of Paris* are in the Victoria and Albert Museum; Trusted 1985, cat. nos. 12 and 13, pp. 59-63.
23   *Bernstein für Thron und Altar* 2005, pp. 86-90.
24   'Christophorus Maucher Sculptor Gedani [of Gdańsk] A D. 1700'; Haag 2007b, p. 146.
25   'Herrn Matthias Rauchmillers Künstlich erhöheter Raub der Sabinen in Helffenbein'. See Johanna Hecht's comprehensive entry on the tankard in *Liechtenstein* 1985, pp. 100-4.
26   For Quellinus, see *Sculpture* 1977, pp. 142-57, especially cat. no. 117, the ivory goblet in the Musées royaux d'Art et d'Histoire, inv. 29 on pp. 155-6.
27   Feuchtmayr and Schädler 1973, cat. no. 14, pp. 98-102.
28   For the chapel, see https://legnica. franciszkanie.pl/, accessed 16 December 2021.
29   Birke 1981, pp. 61-9.
30   Pühringer-Zwanowetz 1966.
31   Bernini's marble is in the Borghese Gallery in Rome; Wittkower 1999b, p. 6.
32   Haag 2007a.
33   The title 'King in Prussia' rather than 'King of Prussia', a title held from 1701 to 1772 by the rulers of Prussia, reflected the fiction that Frederick III was only a king over

his former duchy (Prussia). In Brandenburg and the other Hohenzollern domains within the borders of the Holy Roman Empire he was legally still just an elector, rather than a king, under the ultimate overlordship of the Holy Roman Emperor. Although Prussia's royal title gave the Hohenzollern rulers higher status, Brandenburg was the wealthier and more populous portion of the combined realm, and Brandenburg's capital Berlin remained the primary residence of the King and his administration. See Beier and Wahnschaffe 2009.
33   Hannesen 2014, pp. 120-1.
34   Keller 2014, p. 142.
35   Keller 2014, pp. 148-9.
36   Kessler 2014a, p. 208.
37   Kessler 2014a, p. 210.
38   Kessler 2014b, p. 231.
39   Wittkower 1999a, p. 93.
40   The original marble plinth on the Lange Brücke was found to be unstable in c. 1900 and was replaced by a copy in 1901. An electrotype copy of the equestrian figure was made at that date; this is now in the Bode Museum. This means that the original bronze at Charlottenburg is displayed on a marble copy of the original plinth, while the electrotype copy of the equestrian monument is displayed on the original marble plinth in the Bode Museum; Kessler 2014b, p. 234.
41   Kessler 2014b, pp. 222-4. For the Berlin Palace, see Hinterkeuser 2014.
42   Kühn 1977, pp. 161-8; Lindemann 2014, pp. 400-15.
43   Zitzelsperger 2014, p. 338, note 10. For the original appearance of the monument, see Ladendorf 1937, fig. 127 on p. 103.
44   Wittkower 1999b, fig. 20 on p. 17.
45   Guinomet 2014.

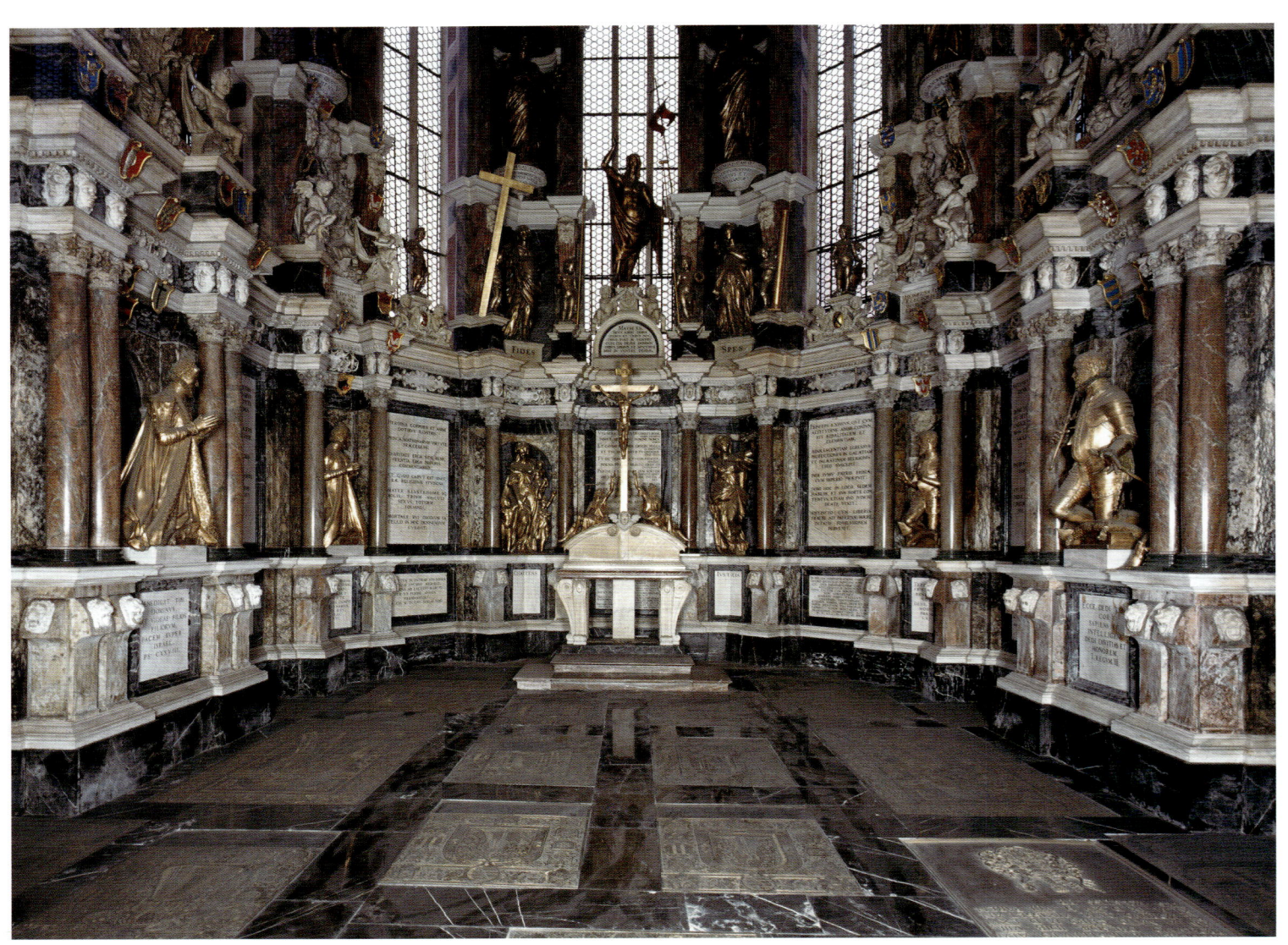

CHAPTER 3

THE COURT OF SAXONY IN THE LATE SIXTEENTH AND EARLY SEVENTEENTH CENTURIES

Just as the Electors of Brandenburg were the leading patrons of sculpture in Berlin in the late seventeenth and early eighteenth centuries, so the Saxon Electors at the court in Dresden, in particular Augustus II the Strong (1670-1733; r. 1697-1733; King of Poland 1709-33), both commissioned and collected major works of sculpture and other works of art during that period. And just as Andreas Schlüter could be said to dominate the sculpture produced in Berlin at that time, so in Dresden was Balthasar Permoser (1651-1732) the single most influential artist in the first third of the eighteenth century. Additionally, turned and carved ivories were a vital aspect of the sculptures produced in Dresden in the seventeenth century, as in contemporary Munich and Vienna. Like Georg Petel nearly a century before, Permoser worked on both large- and small-scale sculptures, and his carved ivories are as remarkable as his stone figures. Johann Christoph Ludwig Lücke (1703-80) was to continue the tradition of carved ivories of the highest quality. The city of Mannheim in the Rhineland Palatinate became another centre of art and architecture under the rule of Charles III Philip, Elector Palatine (1661-1742; r. 1716-42), once Paul Egell (1691-1752) had been appointed court sculptor in 1729.

The Court of Saxony in the Late Sixteenth and Early Seventeenth Centuries

Saxony was at the crossroads of Europe: to the north, Copenhagen; to the west, Paris; to the east, Warsaw and Prague; to the south, Venice, Florence and Rome. The diplomatic and dynastic ties that Dresden enjoyed with Berlin, Munich, Braunschweig, Mannheim, Vienna, Prague, Florence and Copenhagen led to fertile artistic and cultural crosscurrents. Artists travelled to Dresden from elsewhere, specifically Italy, and were employed at the Saxon court from the sixteenth century onwards. Works of art were received from, and sent to, other European rulers as ambassadorial gifts, such contacts extending even as far as Asia.[1] Already in the 1590s prestigious sculptures were being created in Saxony. Christian I, Elector of Saxony (1560-91; r. 1586-91), had commissioned the Italian architect Giovanni Maria Nosseni (1554-1620) to re-design the choir of Freiberg Cathedral to provide a suitable setting for the tombs of the Albertine line of the Wettin dynasty, and Carlo di Cesare del Palagio (1538-98/1600) was commissioned to make sculptures in bronze, terracotta and stucco for the burial chapel there in 1590-93 [**3.1**].[2] As in Augsburg and Munich, the complex technique of casting bronze had to be imported from Florence.

3.1
Giovanni Maria Nosseni, Carlo di Cesare del Palagio and others, *The Wettin Burial Chapel in the Choir of Freiberg Cathedral*, 1590-3.

3.2
Augustus I Elector of
Saxony, *Turned covered
beaker*, ivory, signed
'AHVCZS' (Augustus
Herzog und Churfürst
zu Sachsen), before
1586, height 17.2 cm.
Grünes Gewölbe,
Staatliche Kunst-
sammlungen Dresden
(inv. no. II. 65).

> 3.3
Jacob Zeller, *The Great
Frigate*, ivory, signed
and dated 1620,
height 51 cm. Grünes
Gewölbe, Staatliche
Kunstsammlungen
Dresden (inv. no. II. 107).

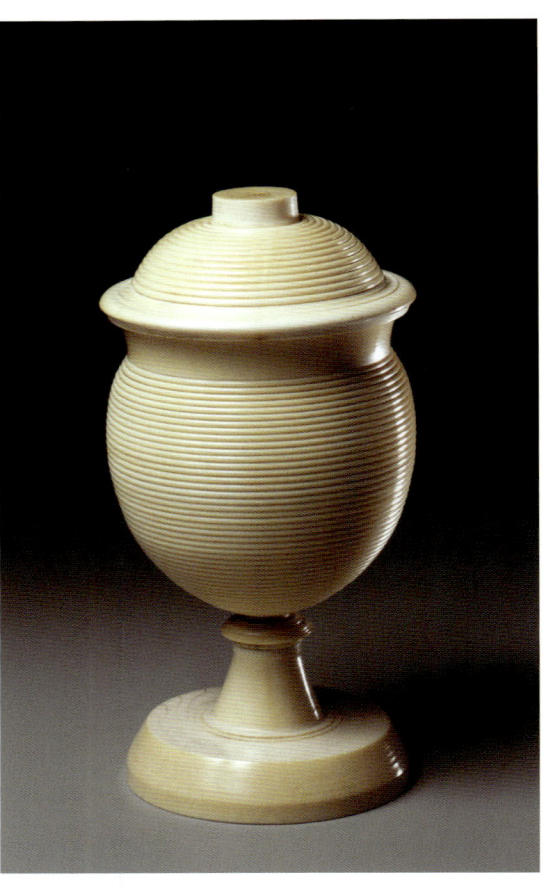

the elector's library was established at the same time, and numbered 2354 volumes by 1570.[5] Augustus's brother Maurice (1521-53; r. 1541-53), Elector of Saxony, had earlier founded the Armoury, with its choice collection of arms and armour.[6] The celebrated Grünes Gewölbe (Green Vaults), the sequence of rooms displaying ambers, ivories, bronzes, rock crystals, and many other works of art in precious materials, was constructed from 1723 onwards under Augustus the Strong, and completed in 1730.[7] It was named after the rooms' distinctive green ceilings, while its roots lay in the Treasury (*Schatzkammer*) as well as the *Kunstkammer*, assembled from the sixteenth century onwards.[8]

As in other German cities, much sculpture produced or collected in Dresden in the mid-seventeenth century was of necessity small scale because of the disruption and financial uncertainty caused by the Thirty Years' War. But even before that crisis the taste for smaller sculptures, especially ivories, was already apparent. Rulers of Saxony, including Elector Augustus in the mid-sixteenth century, his son Christian I, as well as Christian I's son Christian II (1583-1611; r. 1591-1611), even learned how to turn ivory on a lathe themselves [**3.2**].[9] In the late sixteenth and early seventeenth century a number of turners and carvers of ivory, such as Georg Wecker (active 1575-1610), Egidius Lobenigk (active c. 1584-91) and Jacob Zeller (c. 1581-1620), were appointed as artists to the Saxon court. Zeller's *Great Frigate*, a virtuoso combination of turned and carved ivory, signed and dated 1620, is a ship of state, inscribed with the names of Saxon rulers from earliest times up to Elector John George I (1585-1656; r. 1611-56), who commissioned the piece [**3.3**]. The figure of Neptune, seated on a shell chariot, surrounded by sea creatures, energetically supports the ship, while at the back a Triton, holding a plaque with the artist's name, blows on his conch. Although the ship may symbolise the unpredictability of fate as the vessel is tossed on stormy waves, the ivory also suggests (through the figure of Triton signalling the end of the storm) the ship's ultimate safe harbouring.[10] This accomplished work in ivory was perhaps inspired by the ivories being produced for the Medici court in

Moreover, the making of terracottas and stucco were skills perfected in Italy, hence Carlo's fundamental role in Saxony at that date. Over a century later, from 1703 to 1712, Balthasar Permoser was to carve marble figures for the tomb of Electress Anne Sophia of Saxony (d. 1717), the Danish mother of Augustus the Strong, and her sister Wilhelmina Ernestine of the Palatinate (d. 1706). The tomb had been made for the chapel at Schloss Lichtenburg, Prettin, Saxony, the dowager seat of the electress, but was brought to the chapel of All Saints in Freiberg Cathedral in 1811.[3]

Artistic patronage and connoisseurship at the court of Dresden in the early modern period could be said to have begun in 1560 when the *Kunstkammer* (cabinet of curiosities) was founded by Augustus, Elector of Saxony (1526-86; r. 1553-86), one of the first such princely collections in Europe, along with the collection established at Ambras Castle near Innsbruck by Ferdinand II, Archduke of Austria (1529-95; r. 1564-95), the son of Ferdinand I, Holy Roman Emperor (1503-64; r. 1556-64).[4] As well as the Dresden *Kunstkammer* founded by Augustus,

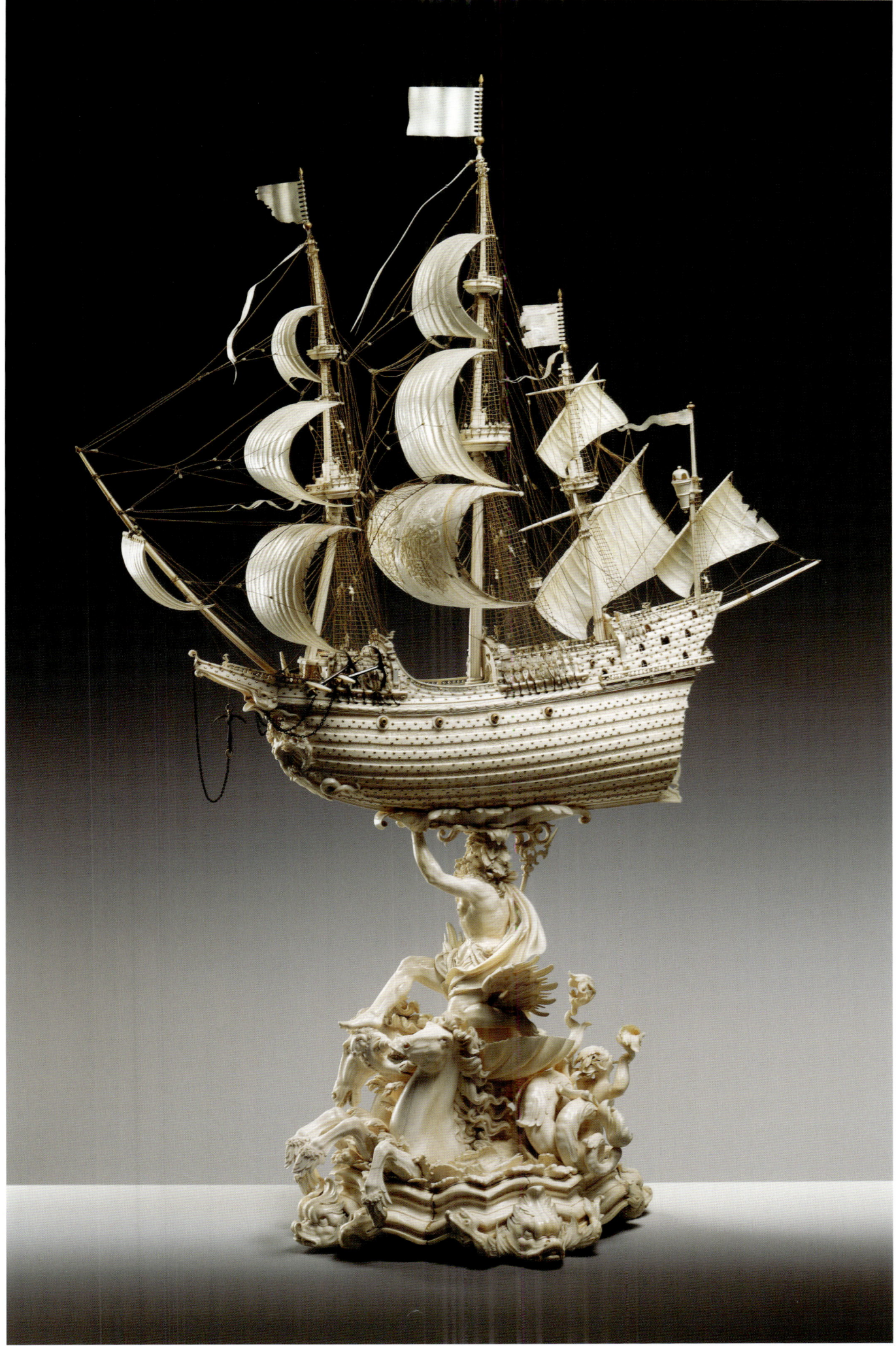

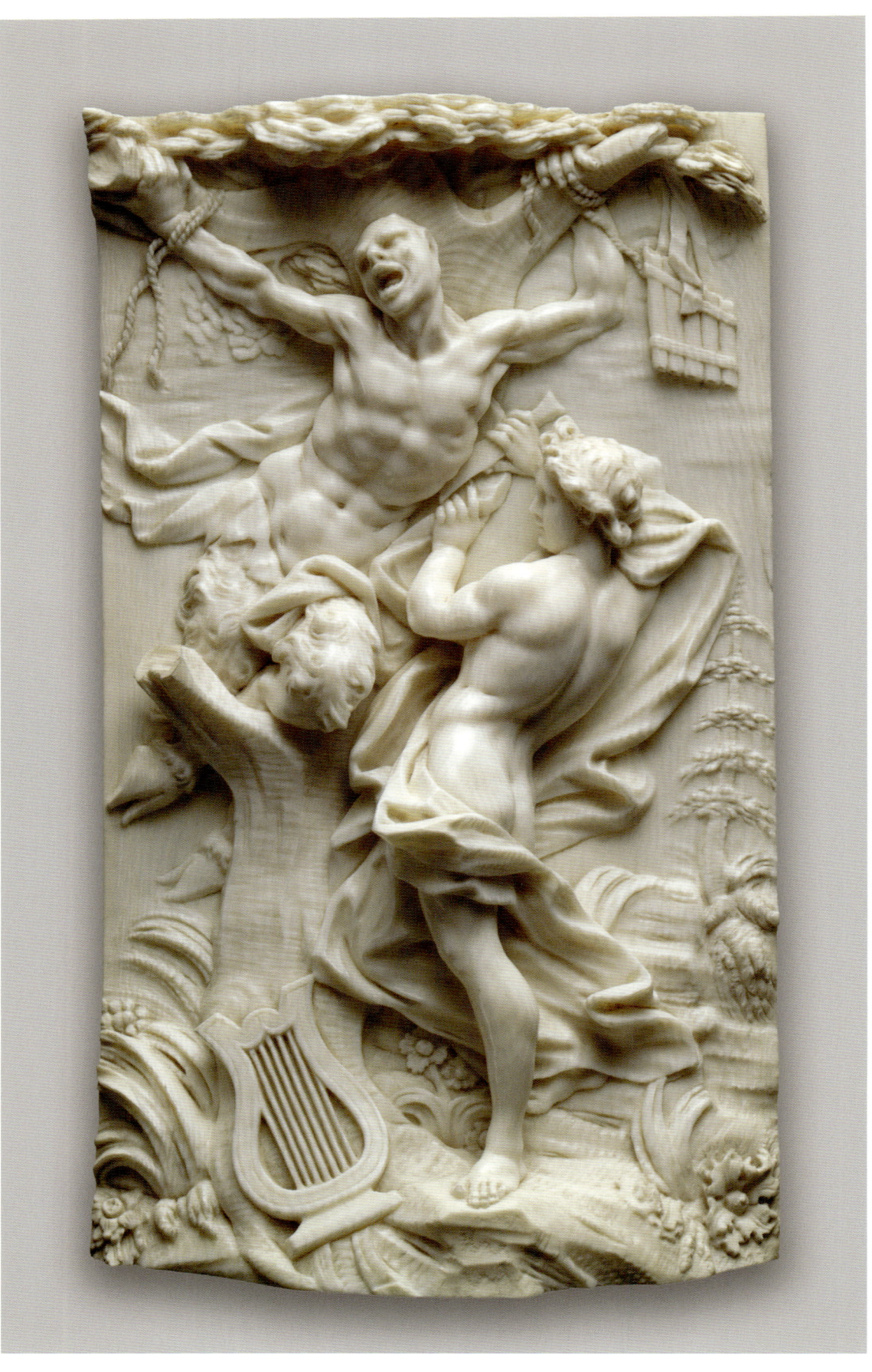

3.4
Balthasar Permoser,
Apollo Flaying Marsyas,
ivory, c. 1680, height
17.5 cm, width 10.5 cm.
Herzog Anton Ulrich-
Museum, Braunschweig
(inv. no. EL 233).

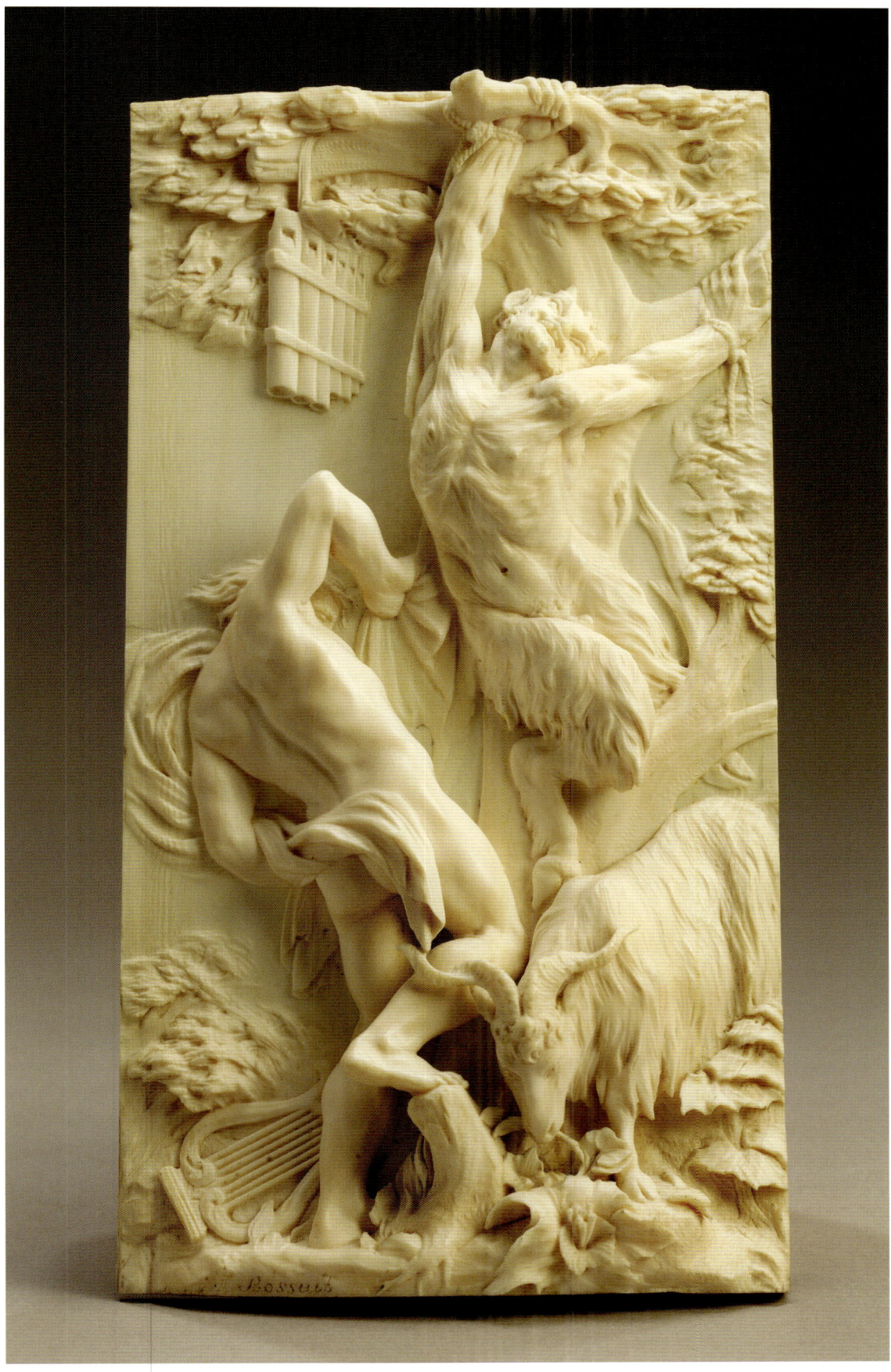

3.5
Francis van Bossuit,
Apollo Flaying Marsyas,
ivory, c. 1680, height
21.1 cm, width 11.5 cm.
Thomson Collection,
on long term loan to
the Art Gallery of
Ontario, Toronto
(inv. no. AGO ID 29173).

Florence, such as the work of the so-called Master of the Furies, who may have been active in Salzburg.[11] More probably, however, the *Frigate* is likely to be indebted to the sophisticated art at the court of Emperor Rudolph II in Prague (1552-1612; r. 1576-1612), where Zeller was known to be in 1610.[12] It was completed shortly before the artist's premature death in 1620. The *Frigate* was evidently recognized as being of the first importance, having cost the enormous sum of 3000 guilders, equivalent to approximately 1715 thalers. Whilst it is notoriously difficult to assess prices historically, and conjure up modern price equivalents, it is interesting to note that Balthasar Permoser's salary at the Dresden court in the early eighteenth century was only 200 thalers per annum, a fraction of the price of this object.[13]

The early eighteenth century was a period of intense sculptural creativity and enlightened patronage, not only of architecture and sculpture, but of ceramics and goldsmiths' work. In around 1710 the ceramicist Johann Friedrich Böttger (1682-1719) perfected the manufacture of red stoneware, known as Böttgerware, at Meissen, about 25 kilometres northwest of Dresden, shortly after he had created hard paste porcelain there, the first time this had been achieved outside China. This led to the establishment of the successful and productive porcelain factory at Meissen, where both porcelain and Böttgerware were produced.[14] By the mid-eighteenth century the factory had begun producing exceptionally fine figurative ceramics, many of which were based on models provided by leading sculptors, as will be seen below. Johann Melchior Dinglinger (1664-1731) was active as a goldsmith and jeweller at the court of Augustus the Strong from 1693 onwards, and similarly collaborated with sculptors, including Permoser, again to be seen below.[15]

Balthasar Permoser in Dresden

Balthasar Permoser was invited to work as a court artist in Dresden by John George III, Elector of Saxony (1647-91), probably through the mediation of the elector's son, Prince Frederick Augustus, later Augustus the Strong, when the prince was in Florence as the guest of

Grand Duke Cosimo III de' Medici (1642-1723) in 1689 during his Grand Tour. The elector's invitation to Permoser evidently stemmed from his wish to encourage sculpture in Saxony that reflected international, particularly Italian, currents. Indeed, Permoser's arrival in the Saxon city was to herald a new era of artistic and cultural endeavour. He remained at the Dresden court from 1690 until his death in 1732, apart from a few years in the early eighteenth century, when he was in Berlin, assisting Andreas Schlüter (c. 1659-1714) on sculpture for the royal palaces there.

Permoser had trained in Salzburg, and then Vienna, where he may have been taught by Johann Caspar Schenck (c. 1620-74), a member of a renowned family of ivory sculptors, and originally from Constance.[16] Following his training Permoser spent fourteen years in Italy, from 1675/6 to 1689, initially in Rome, where the slightly older Netherlandish sculptor Francis van Bossuit (1635-92) had been based since about 1655. The two sculptors presumably met at the Florentine Academy in Rome. Permoser may have already decided to specialise in carving ivory before he went to Italy, though Bossuit's presence could well have stimulated the German artist to concentrate on this material. A few of the two artists' ivories are of the same or similar subjects, as well as being comparable in size, suggesting they were made as complementary pieces in friendly rivalry. Probably while they were still both in Rome they carved reliefs illustrating *Apollo Flaying Marsyas*, Apollo's violent punishment of the faun Marsyas for having dared to rival the god musically by playing his pipes to compete with Apollo's playing of the lyre, a classical myth derived from Ovid [**3.4 and 3.5**].[17] The two interpretations differ in various ways: the compositions are laterally inverted, Permoser placing Apollo on the right, facing away from the viewer, while Bossuit positions the god on the left, turned slightly more towards us. Bossuit has also included the nymph Io (transformed into a heifer), more usually seen in the story of Mercury and Argus rather than that of Marsyas and Apollo.[18] But many other elements are common to the two interpretations, which are similar in size and shape: the faun's pipes hanging from a tree, Apollo's lyre, comparable background foliage, and the vivid rendering of the torso of the writhing tethered body of Marsyas. Apollo's semi-nude body is more energetically posed in Bossuit's work, while Permoser more clearly renders the muscles of the god's back as he leans on one leg to start cutting into the faun's skin. Both ivories, though cabinet-sized, are effectively monumental, showing a mastery of the material, an engagement with a classical subject, and an implicit desire to demonstrate that sculpture on a small scale in an exotic substance can equal marble or bronze. Perhaps the very subject of rivalry in the classical myth was a playful reference to the two sculptors themselves competing against each other, and implicitly with other sculptors. Both Permoser and Bossuit were Northern artists working in Rome, and this international perspective, including their mutual influence, must have been fundamental in the evolution of Permoser's style. Just as in the early seventeenth century the Netherlandish sculptors Adriaen de Vries and Hubert Gerhard were seminal figures in the production of bronzes in Bavaria, so here we may imagine that Permoser's contact with Bossuit in the Eternal City was a catalyst in the maturing of his own style. Because only one of Permoser's ivories is dated (one of his series of the *Four Seasons* of 1695), the evolution of his carving style in ivory remains uncertain.[19] Nevertheless circumstantial and documentary proof means that some of his ivories can be approximately dated, and the sequence broadly mapped, not least those he is likely to have made in Italy.[20]

By 1682, and perhaps as early as 1677, Permoser was in Florence, where he worked with Giovanni Battista Foggini (1652-1725) and at the Medici court.[21] One of the numerous ivories Permoser carved at the court can be dated from documentary evidence. This is the portrait of Princess Violante-Beatrice of Bavaria (1673-1731), the betrothed of Ferdinando de' Medici (1663-1713), Grand Prince of Tuscany, dating from 1689 [**3.6**], and evidently done shortly before the artist left Florence for Saxony.[22] The simplicity of the profile

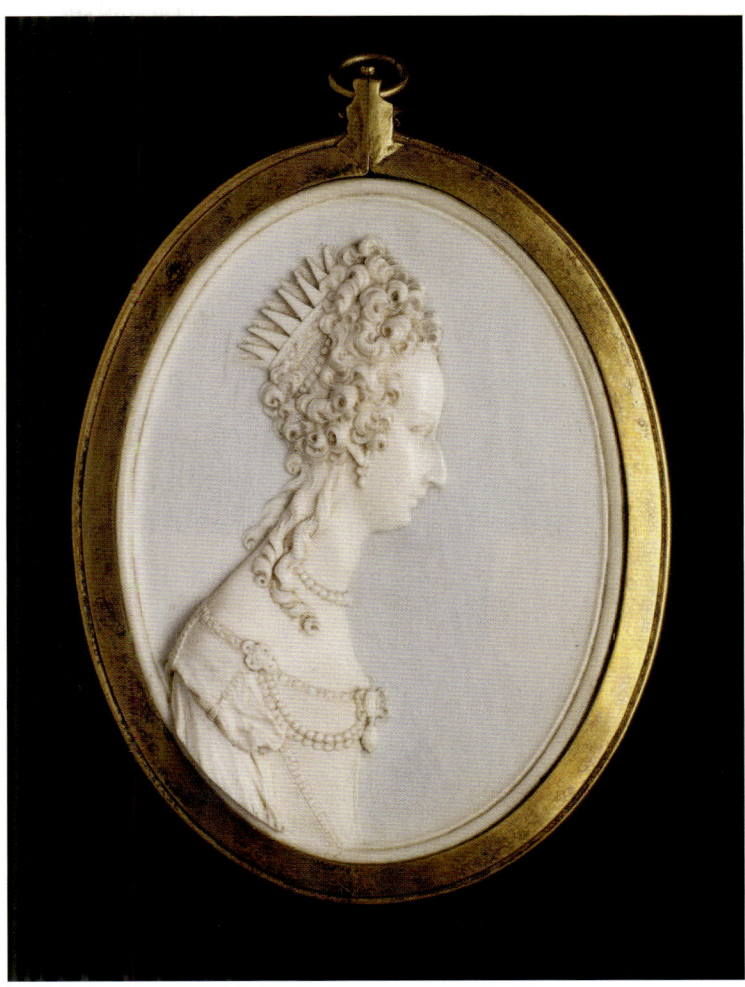

composition belies Permoser's sophisticated working of the material, and his mastery of small-scale sculpture. His handling of ivory must have appealed to the Saxon elector, surely constituting a reason for his inviting the artist to work at the Dresden court.

However Permoser did not confine his skills as a portraitist to ivory; he also worked in marble while in Tuscany, and indeed executed a portrait in that material for a German patron. This was Anthony Ulrich (1633-1714; r. 1685-1714), Duke of Brunswick-Lüneburg-Wolfenbüttel, for whom Permoser eventually made two busts: one of marble in the 1680s [**3.7**], and the other of alabaster, produced c. 1704/11 (both busts are now in the Herzog Anton Ulrich-Museum, Braunschweig). Neither the exact circumstances nor the dates of either of these commissions is certain. The marble must, however, have been commissioned when Anthony Ulrich was in Florence, though the timings of his visits to Italy are unclear.[23] Permoser portrayed the duke with

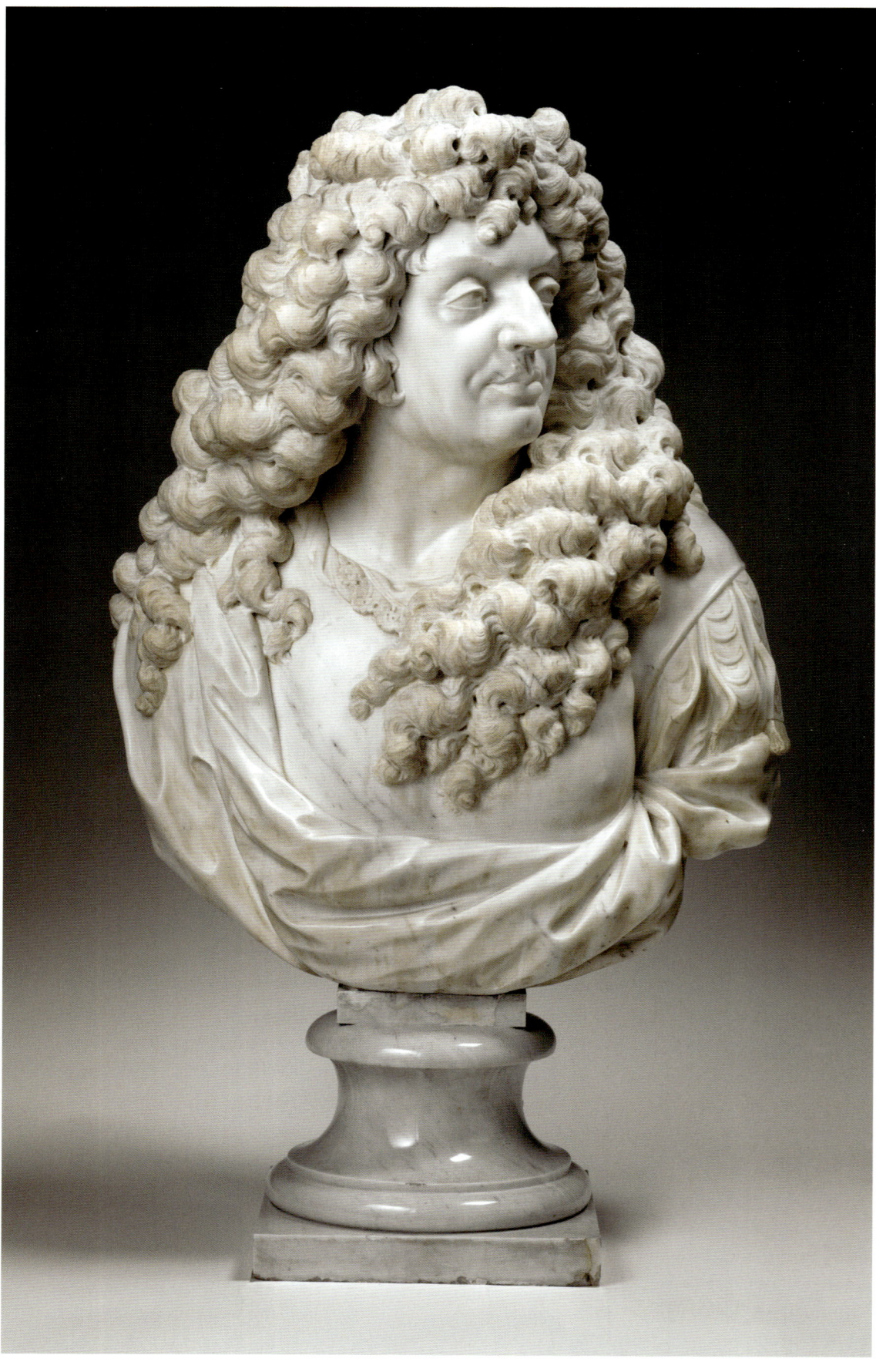

3.7
Balthasar Permoser, *Anthony Ulrich, Duke of Brunswick-Lüneburg*, marble, c. 1680/5, height 99.5 cm, with socle. Herzog Anton Ulrich-Museum, Braunschweig (inv. no. Ste 4).

his head turned to his left, wearing a long flowing wig, in the tradition of Bernini's busts, such as the *Louis XIV* of 1665 at Versailles.[24] But the flamboyance of Bernini's earlier bust is subsumed into a more subdued and controlled portrayal in Permoser's sculpture. Instead of the sun king's flamboyant windswept drapery, Anthony Ulrich wears classicising armour, glimpsed beneath his cloak. Additionally, the duke seems to be shown as a serious man of thought, a ruler who in actuality exhibited serious literary and musical interests, as well as being a collector of works of art, including outstanding ivories by Permoser himself, such as the *Four Seasons* of 1695, mentioned above [**3.8**].[25] These four statuettes, to be reproduced later in the eighteenth century as ceramic figurines at the Doccia factory near Florence, exemplify Permoser's skilful carving on a small scale (all four were made from a single tusk) and a lightness of touch. In addition to the ceramic variants, no fewer than three ivory versions of this attractive set of figures were produced by Permoser and his workshop, the only surviving other set now at the Grünes Gewölbe in Dresden.[26]

Once Permoser had arrived in Dresden he worked in partnership with other artists at the court, such as the goldsmith and jeweller Johann Melchior Dinglinger (1664-1731). The costly works of art produced as a result of their collaboration, made of ivory, enamel, precious metals and hardstones, were valued items for the elector's treasury (*Schatzkammer*). *Diana's Bath*, for example, a work comprising chalcedony, silver, steel, enamel, diamonds and pearls, was crafted by Dinglinger and his brother, the enamel painter Georg Friedrich Dinglinger (1666-1720), incorporating at its centre Permoser's ivory figures of Diana and a putto [**3.9 and 3.10**]. This precious object was recorded in the court accounts of 1704 as costing 8000 thalers, a spectacular price (as noted above, Permoser's annual salary in Dresden was 200 thalers).[27] The cost of *Diana's Bath* stemmed from the valuable materials from which it was created, as much as its artistry. But at the same time the design of the whole can be admired in its own right. The nude figure of the huntress goddess, holding a spear,

with the playful putto reaching up to her, reclines languidly in an elaborately fashioned chalcedony bath, lavishly decorated with hunting imagery, a dog sitting at one end of the vessel. Beneath the bath a stag's head gracefully supports the whole, doubtless a reference to Actaeon, transformed into a stag by Diana to punish him for spying on the goddess and her naked nymphs bathing.[28] This piece thus blends precious materials and intricate craftsmanship with mythological references, ideal feminine beauty, sensuality, and images of the chase, all features valued by aristocratic patrons. Permoser's expert carving can above all be appreciated in his creation of a miniature female nude, rivalling life-size marble statues.

During the Great Northern War at the beginning of the eighteenth century, between Russia (allied with some of the German states, including Saxony) and Sweden, the ensuing disruption in Dresden led Permoser to go to work in Berlin intermittently from around 1704 to 1709.[29] On his permanent return to Dresden in about 1710 he began carving the sandstone sculptures for the Zwinger, a palatial complex commissioned by the Elector Augustus the Strong—who was by then also King of Poland— as a grand edifice in the centre of the city [**3.11**]. While he was still in Florence, Permoser had produced architectural sculpture, including a portal for the church of SS. Michael and Gaetano, done for Prince Ferdinando de' Medici in 1683-9. He was evidently valued as an artist who could execute large-scale works as well as smaller courtly objects, and with his workshop he executed the many architectural sculptures needed for the Zwinger.[30] Just as Frederick III had elevated the status of Berlin through new architecture and urban planning, so Augustus the Strong wished to present Dresden as a great international city, its baroque architecture and sculpture worthy of comparison with Versailles or Rome. The term 'Zwinger' is normally used for the inner guard area between the outer and inner walls of a castle or fortress, although the Dresden Zwinger did not in fact form part of such a structure, since the planned fortification was never built. The architectural creation known as the Zwinger in Dresden functioned

>> 3.8
Balthasar Permoser, *The Four Seasons*, ivory, signed and dated 1695, height 22/24 cm. Herzog Anton Ulrich-Museum, Braunschweig (inv. nos. Elf 78, Elf 79, Elf 821, Elf 822).

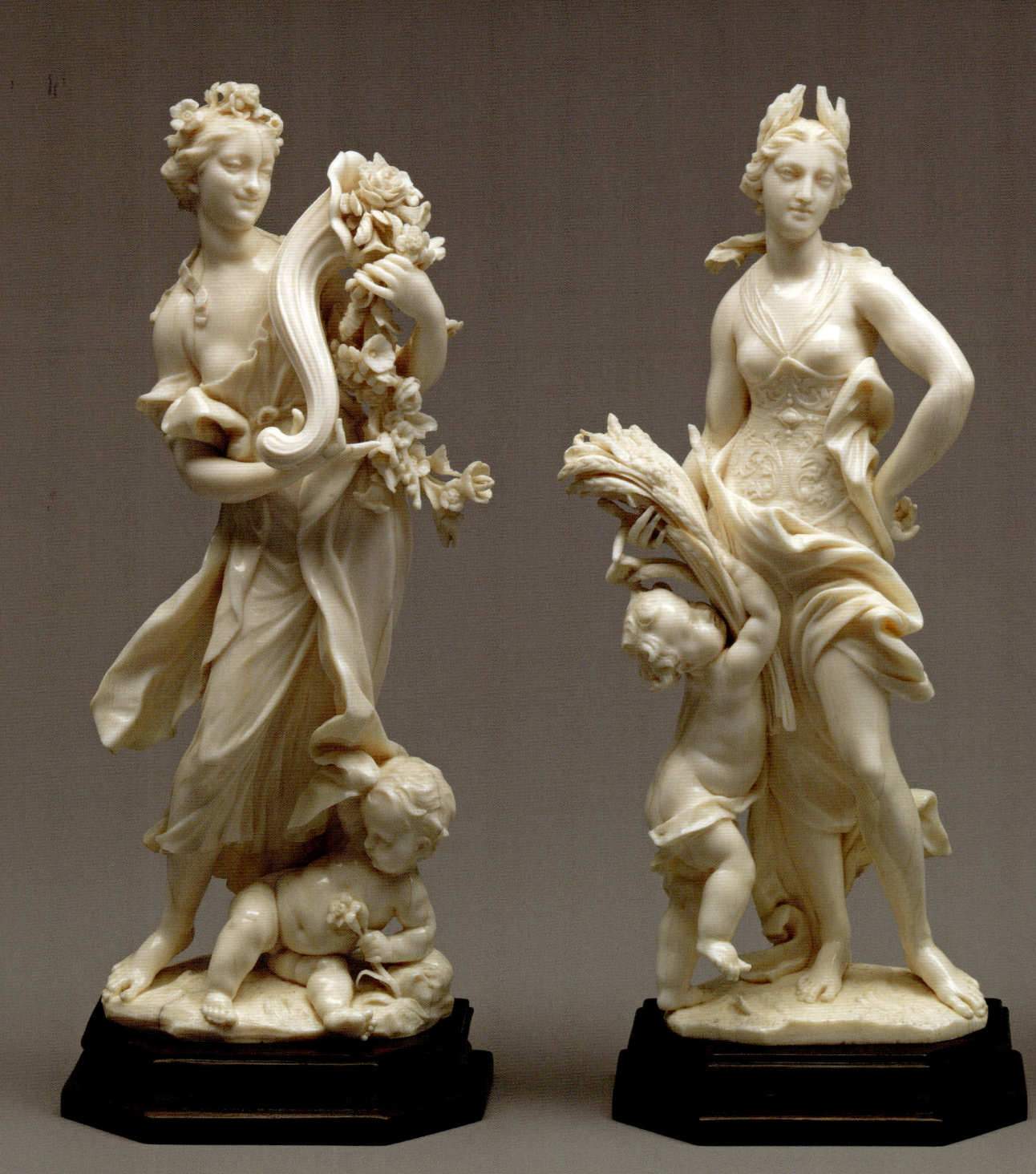

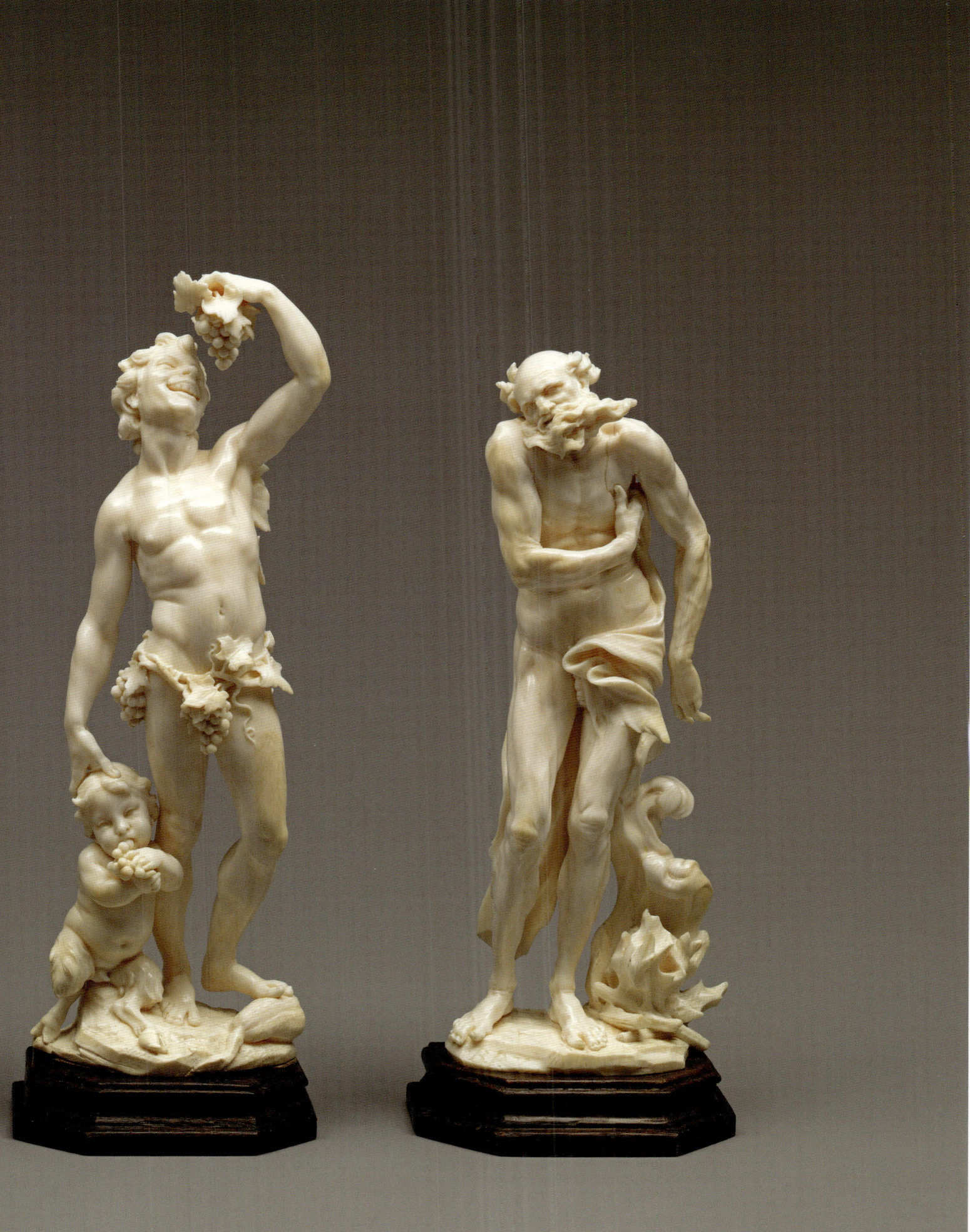

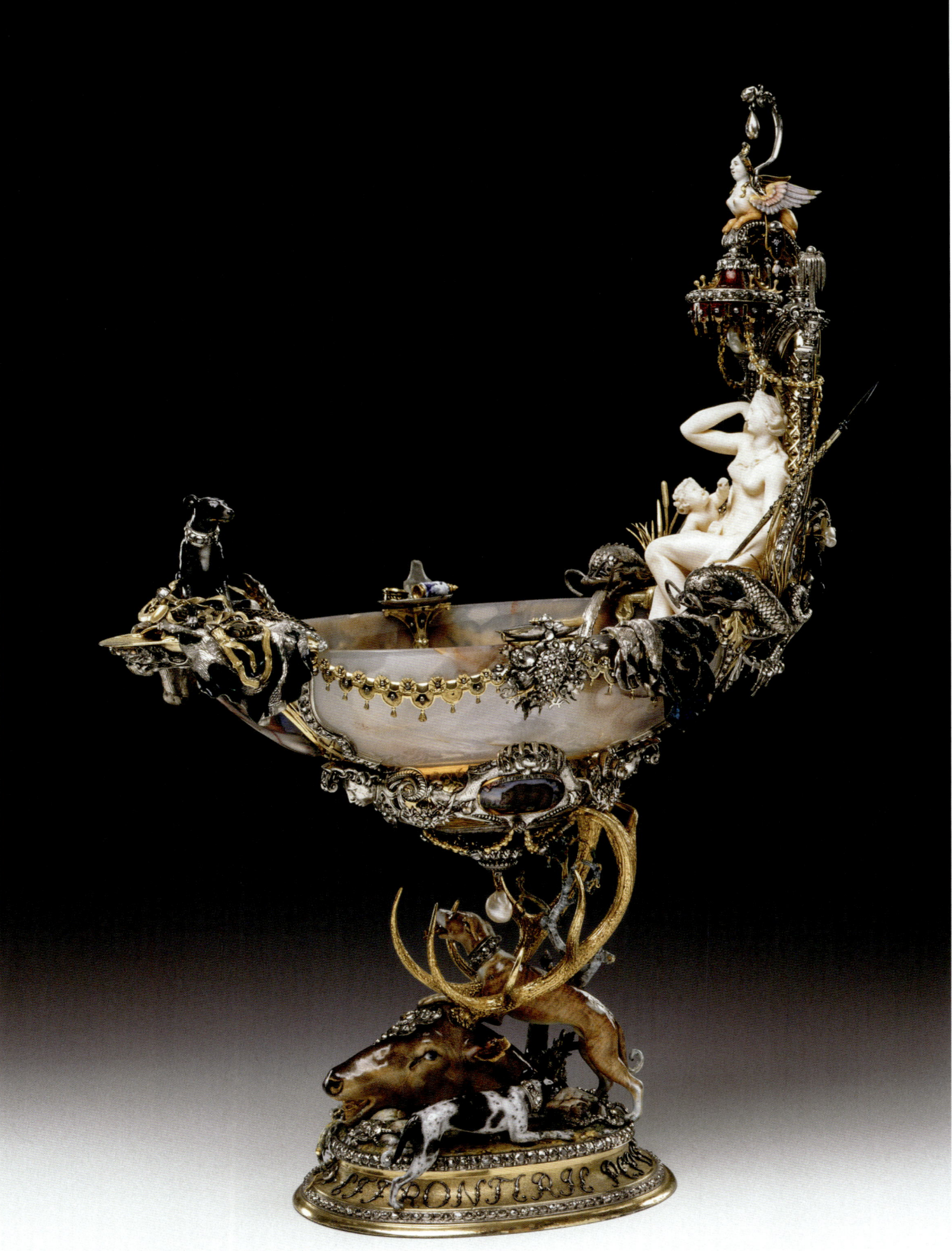

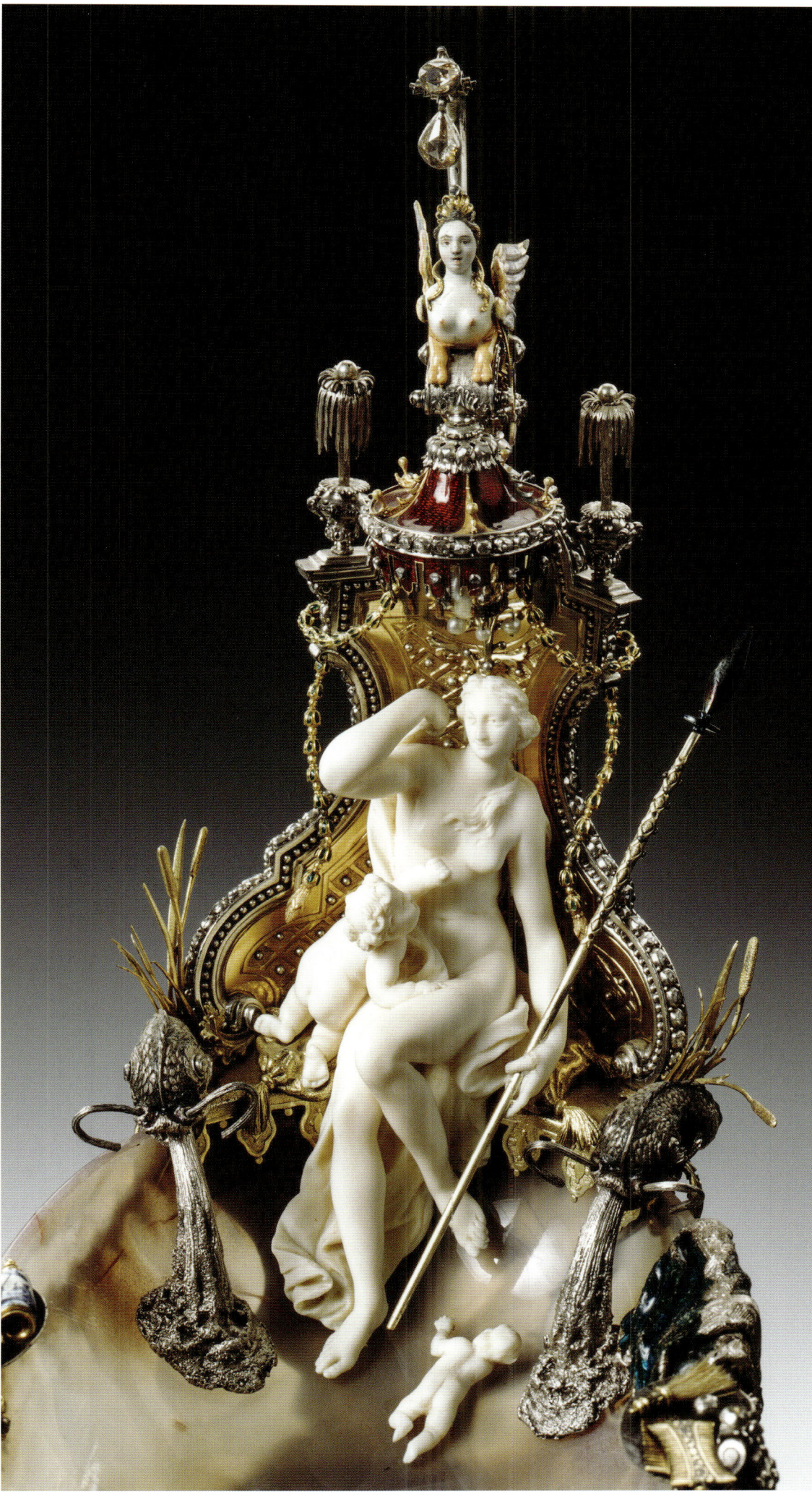

< 3.9
Johann Melchior
Dinglinger and
Balthasar Permoser,
Diana's Bath, ivory,
chalcedony, silver, steel,
enamel, diamonds and
pearls, 1704, height
38 cm. Grünes
Gewölbe, Staatliche
Kunstsammlungen
Dresden
(inv. no. VIII. 305).

3.10
Detail of Dinglinger and
Permoser, *Diana's Bath*
[3.9], ivory; Diana and
Putto by Permoser.

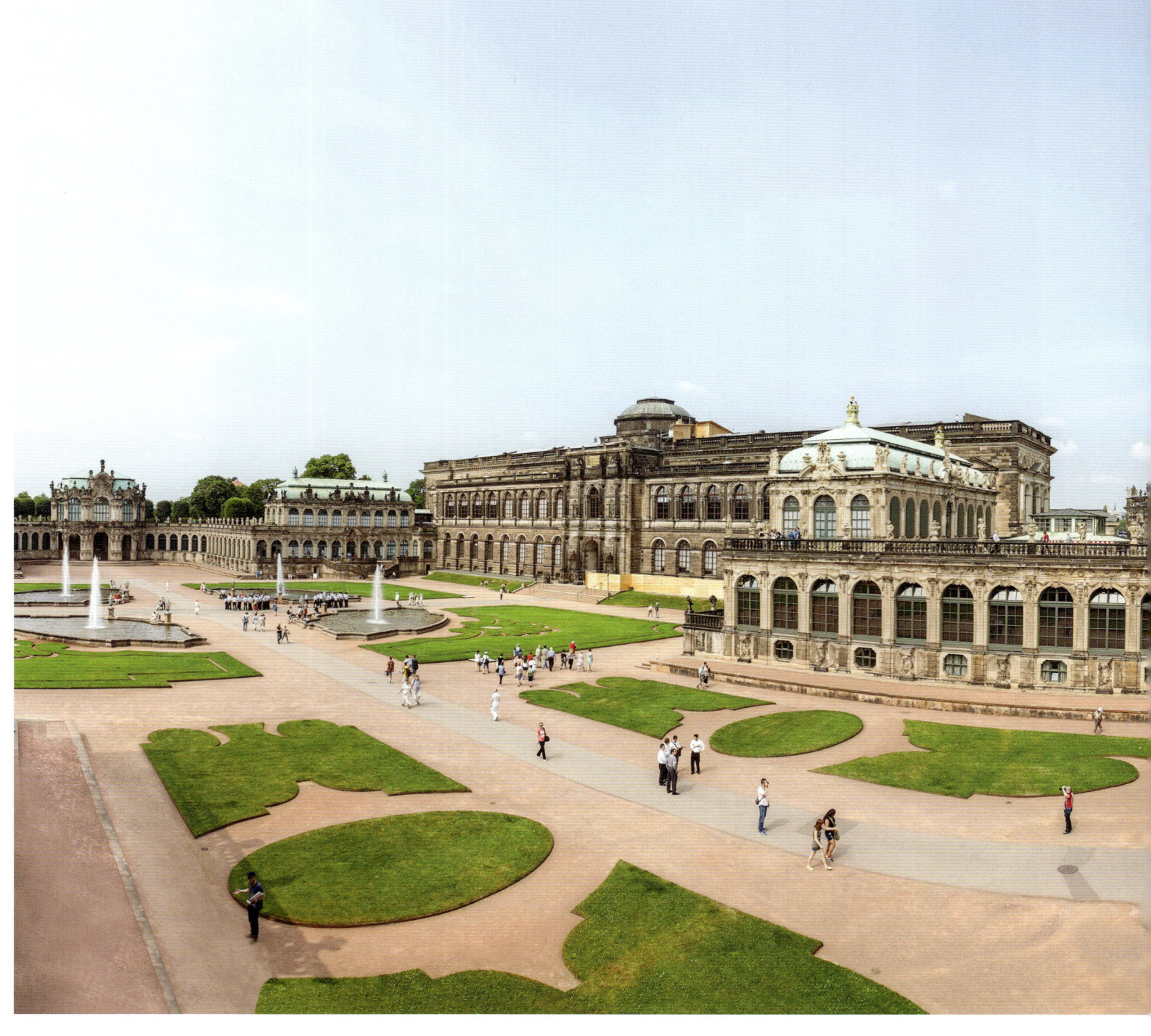

3.11
Matthäeus Daniel
Pöppelmann, Balthasar
Permoser and others,
The Zwinger, Dresden,
sandstone, 1710-18.

instead as an orangery and garden, as well as an area for festivals and receptions.

The Zwinger constitutes one of the richest assemblages of eighteenth-century sculpture anywhere, and although some features were lost or damaged in the Second World War, the surviving elements testify to the enlightened patronage of Augustus the Strong, as well as to the creative genius of the architect, Matthäeus Daniel Pöppelmann (1662-1736), and Permoser himself. Permoser worked with a team of sculptors, including Paul Egell, Paul Heermann

(1673-1732), Johann Benjamin Thomae (1682-1751), and the young French sculptor Louis François Roubiliac (1702-62), later to become one of the greatest sculptors working in eighteenth-century Britain.[31] The sculptural programme included satyr herms and heads carved as capitals on the entrance pavilion, mythological gods and goddesses in niches on the side pavilions, and nymphs for the Nymphäum. Ceres, one of the goddesses depicted, exemplifies Permoser's animated style. The sculpture was made for the *Kronentor* (the crown gate) of

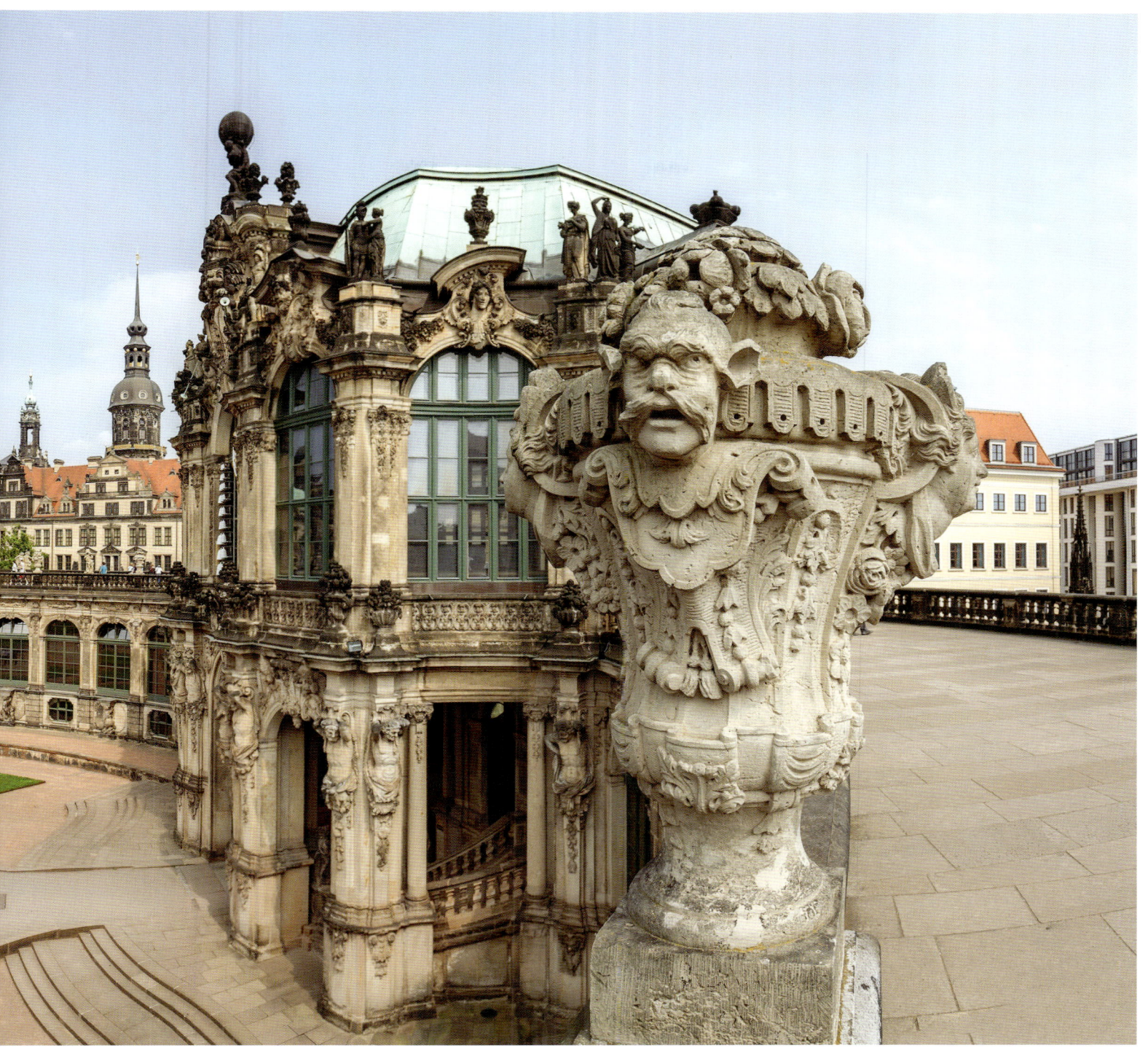

the Zwinger, and probably dates from about 1714/15 [**3.12**]. *Ceres* is from a series of four statues, the other three being Vulcan, Pomona and Bacchus.[32] The goddess of agriculture, her accompanying putto holding a scythe, stands in a contrapposto pose in a shell niche, in billowing drapery, smiling and wearing sprigs of wheat in her hair. She carries a further wreath of wheat and a wheatsheaf under her right arm, while her plinth is adorned with symbols of the harvest and plenty. Far larger than the ivories Permoser had carved for the Medici and for the courts of Braunschweig and Dresden, this statue of *Ceres*, along with the other gods and goddesses on the Zwinger—and indeed like the ivory figures carved for the courts—is a vibrant assertion of vigorous movement. The composition has a rhythmic fluidity, the putto playfully setting his right foot against the goddess's right leg, which is swathed in close-fitting wrinkled drapery while her left leg is bare. Ceres turns vividly away from the putto, looking to her left, perhaps towards her fellow gods and goddesses on the Zwinger. The movement and theatricality of this

3.12
Balthasar Permoser,
Ceres on the Kronentor,
sandstone, 1714/15.
Zwinger, Dresden.

3.13
Balthasar Permoser
with assistants, Herms
on the Wallpavilion,
sandstone, copies after
the originals of 1717-19.
Zwinger, Dresden.

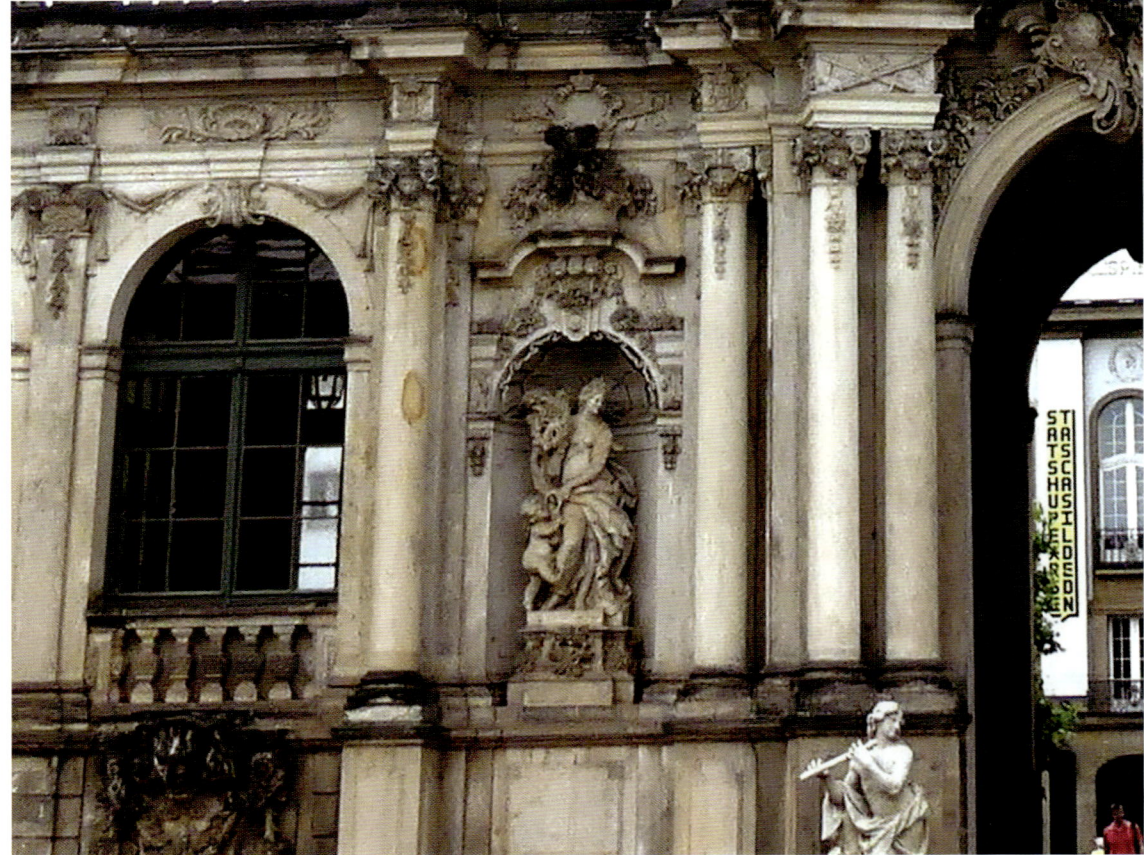

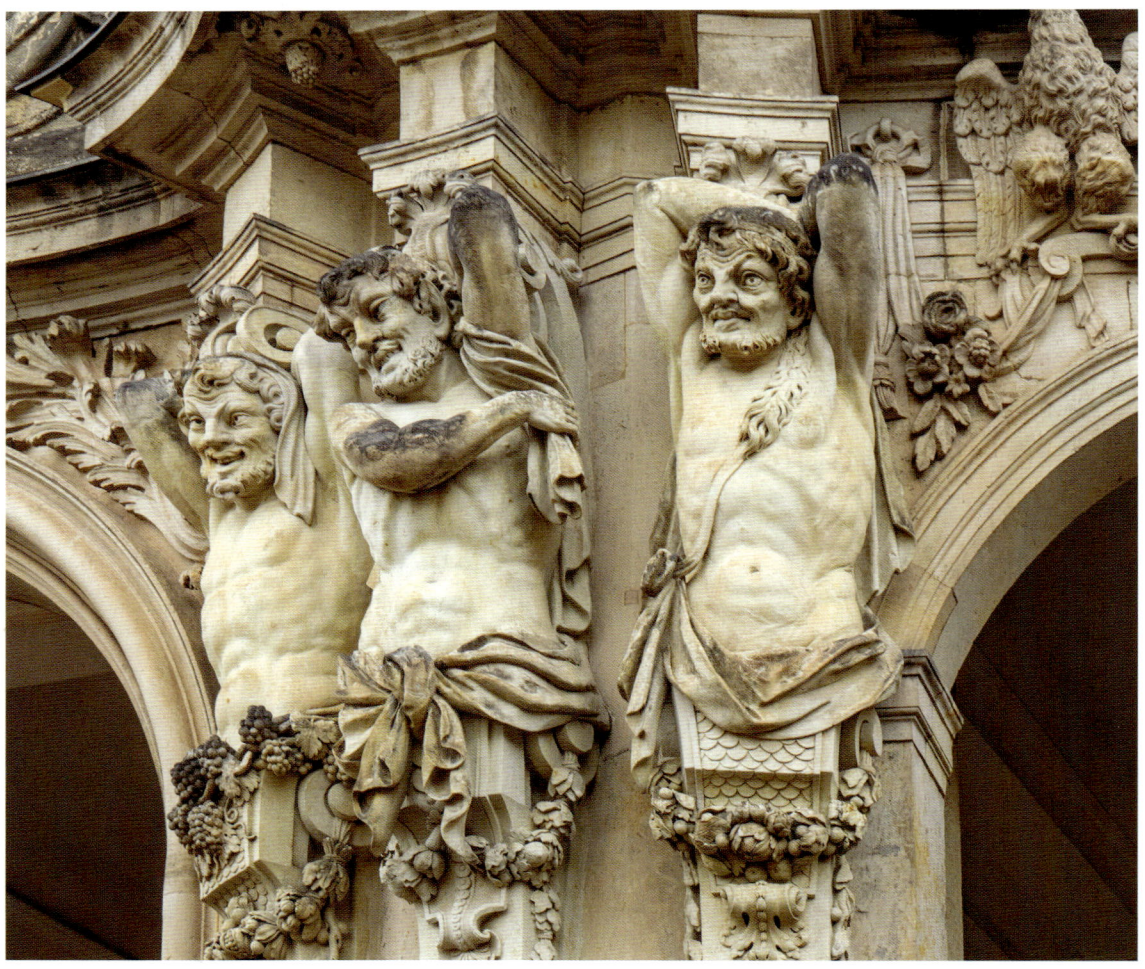

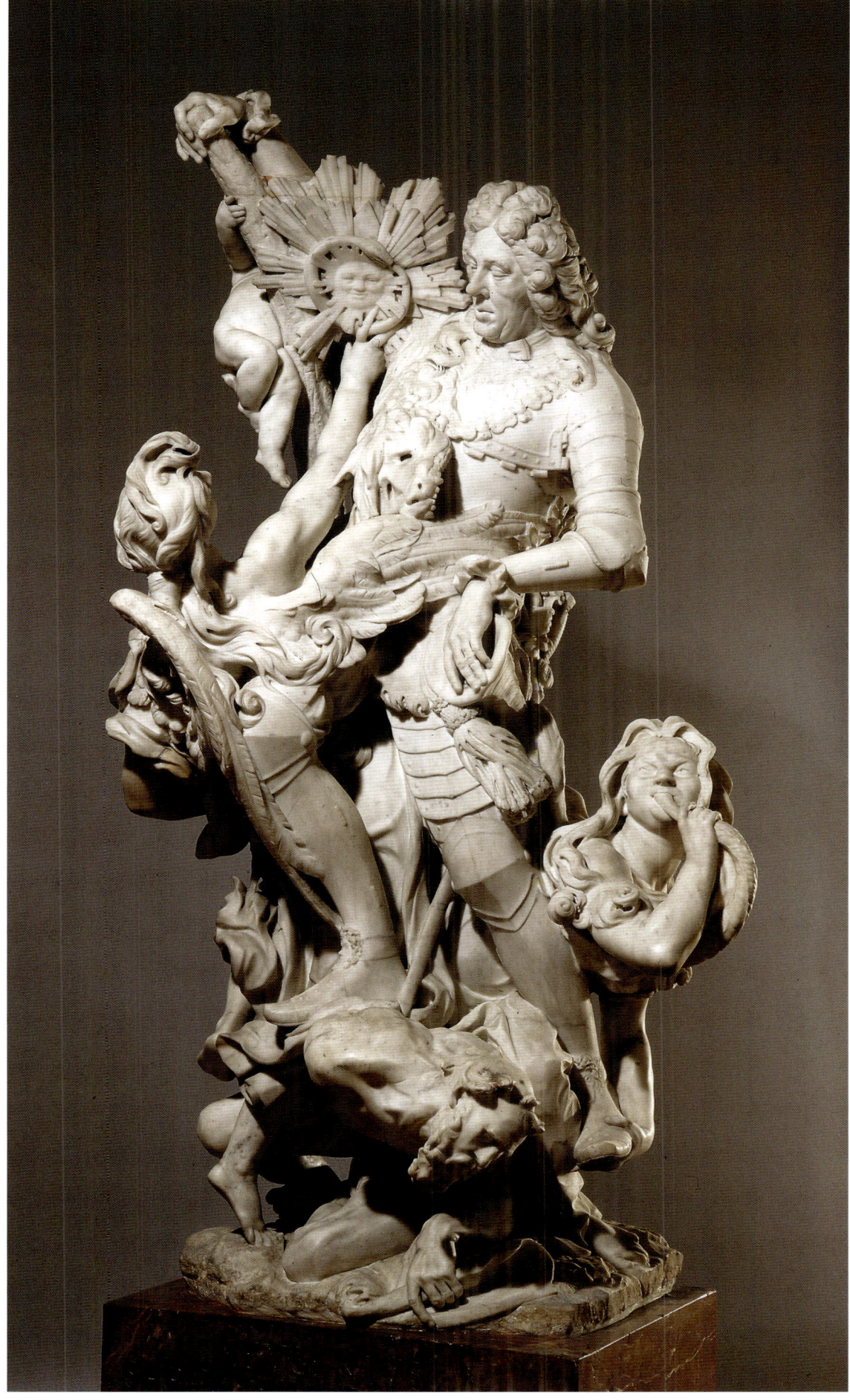

3.14
Balthasar Permoser,
*The Apotheosis of Prince
Eugene of Savoy*, marble,
1718-21, height 230 cm.
Österreichische Galer e
Belvedere, Vienna
(inv. no. 4219).

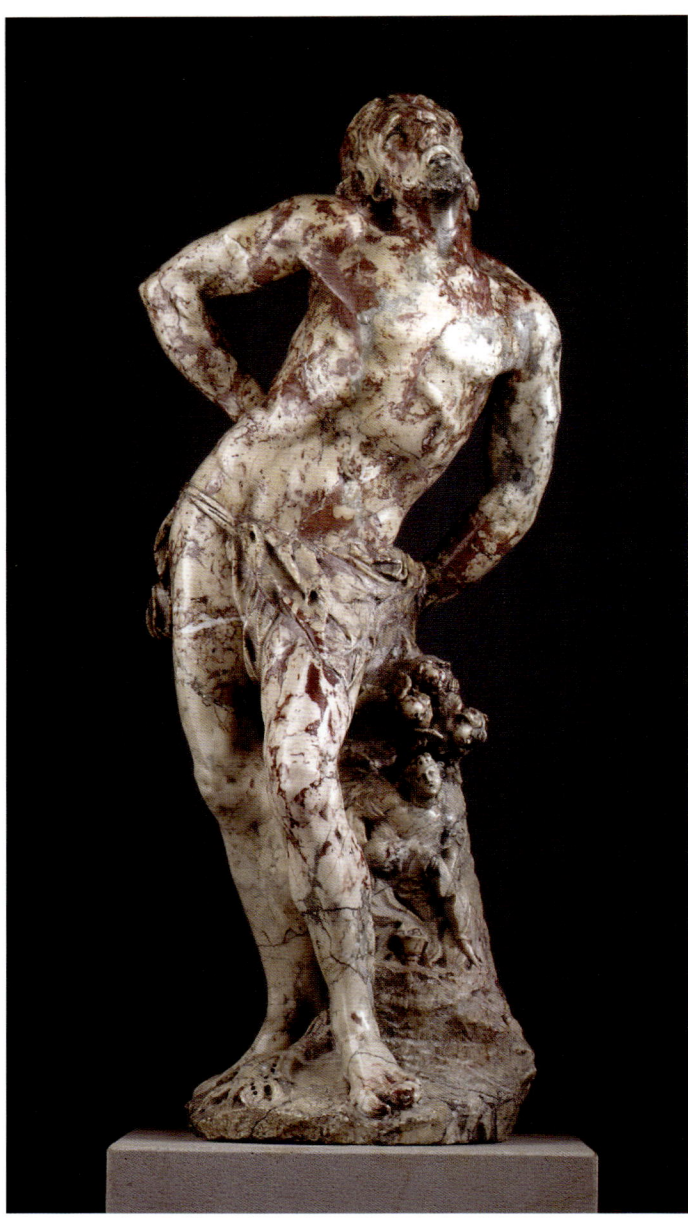

3.15
Balthasar Permoser,
Christ at the Column,
marble, 1728, height
79.5 cm. Staatliche
Kunstsammlungen,
Dresden
(inv. nr. ZV 4090).

as well as on stone sculptures. He had come to Dresden from Rome in 1701 and was thus aware of Italian artistic currents.[34]

At about the same time that he was working on the Zwinger in Dresden Permoser executed the extraordinary life-size marble figure of *The Apotheosis of Prince Eugene of Savoy* (1718-21) at the Belvedere Palace in Vienna [**3.14**]. The exact circumstances of the commission are unknown, though the Austrian architect of the Belvedere, Johann Lukas von Hildebrandt (1668-1745), may have proposed Permoser as the sculptor for this ceremonial sculpture via Pöppelmann. Prince Eugene of Savoy (1663-1736) was a military commander in the service of the Habsburg Empire, and a great patron of the arts.[35] It was clearly a commission of the first importance: Permoser was paid 600 thalers for the sculpture in 1721, a sum three times the annual salary he received at Dresden.[36] The marble, carved from one massive block, is a spiralling group of intertwined figures (there is no single viewpoint), with the armed prince at its centre, astride an allegorical figure of Fame, facing the winged figure of Victory, who holds the sun of eternal fame. The prince is surrounded by putti, one of them holding his sword, while the prince himself raises his left arm, holding a club. Beneath is a defeated bearded Turk. The spirited portrait was apparently based on a plaster cast sent from Vienna in 1720, perhaps taken from a bust of the prince, or possibly a life mask.[37] Although doubtless inspired by Italian precedents, above all Bernini and Michelangelo, Permoser's group is a unique allegorical portrayal of a leader without any close parallels, either before or since.[38]

figure typifies the emerging baroque style in Dresden.

The twelve monumental herm satyrs and the heads on the entrance pavilion (the *Wallpavilion*) of the Zwinger were carved by Permoser with the assistance of Egell and Heermann from about 1717 to 1719, although they were severely damaged in the Second World War and have now been replaced by copies, illustrated here to show their effect *in situ* [**3.13**].[33] The energetic bravura of the satyrs is comparable with Schlüter's dying warriors on the Berlin Palace of a few years earlier, which Permoser would certainly have known [**2.27 and 2.28**]. Like Permoser and Egell (whose work will be discussed below), Heermann worked in ivory

One of Permoser's last works was a figure of *Christ at the Column* in variegated coloured marble, signed and dated 1728, formerly in the chapel of the Taschenberg Palais, and since 1983 in the sculpture collection at the Albertinum in Dresden [**3.15**].[39] This is one of three variants of *Christ at the Column* by Permoser, all dating from the 1720s.[40] The marble was probably from Salzburg, and its deep red veins draws attention to this unusual material, as well as suggesting the bleeding flesh of Christ's body. In the tree trunk against which Christ stands is a small carving in high relief of the *Agony in the Garden*. At the back of the trunk above Permoser's signature and date is a carved self portrait in relief [**3.16**]. The inscription reads, 'BALTHASAR PERMOSER HATS GEMACHT IN SALLBVRG IN SEINEN 77. IHAR. 1728' (Balthasar Permoser made this in Salzburg [perhaps meaning he was originally from Salzburg, rather than having made this sculpture in that city] in his 77th year. 1728'). This self-portrait is testament to Permoser's recognition of his own achievements as an artist, and also a devotional act, his piety being recorded in stone as part of Christ's Passion.

Johann Christoph Ludwig (von) Lücke (1703–80)

One of the artists who may have trained under Permoser in Dresden (although not on the Zwinger) was the sculptor Johann Christoph Ludwig (von) Lücke, the son, or perhaps nephew, of the ivory carver Carl August Lücke the Elder (c. 1688-c. 1730). Johann Christoph Lücke was almost certainly born in Dresden, but became an itinerant artist, perhaps better described as a restless artist, working in numerous European cities (in addition to Dresden) including London, Copenhagen, Vienna, Hamburg, Bremen, Schwerin and Danzig (Gdańsk). He specialised in ivory, though he also worked in stone, clay, wax and papier maché, providing models for the Meissen and other ceramic factories. Lücke's deft and lively style is admirably seen in his small-scale sculptures. His signed and dated terracotta relief of *Poltrone* of 1729 (Museum für Kunst und Gewerbe, Hamburg) depicts a character from the commedia dell'arte, a clumsy soldier [**3.17**].[41] This was made in the year Lücke left the Meissen factory, where he had been model master for little more than a year. It is possible that this terracotta was made as a preliminary model for a ceramic commedia dell'arte figure in Böttger stoneware or porcelain. Variants of the subject are also known in other materials, including porcelain and ivory. An ivory statuette by Lücke dating from around 1730, closely related to the Hamburg relief, is in the Victoria and Albert Museum [**3.18**].[42] Carved with great finesse, the

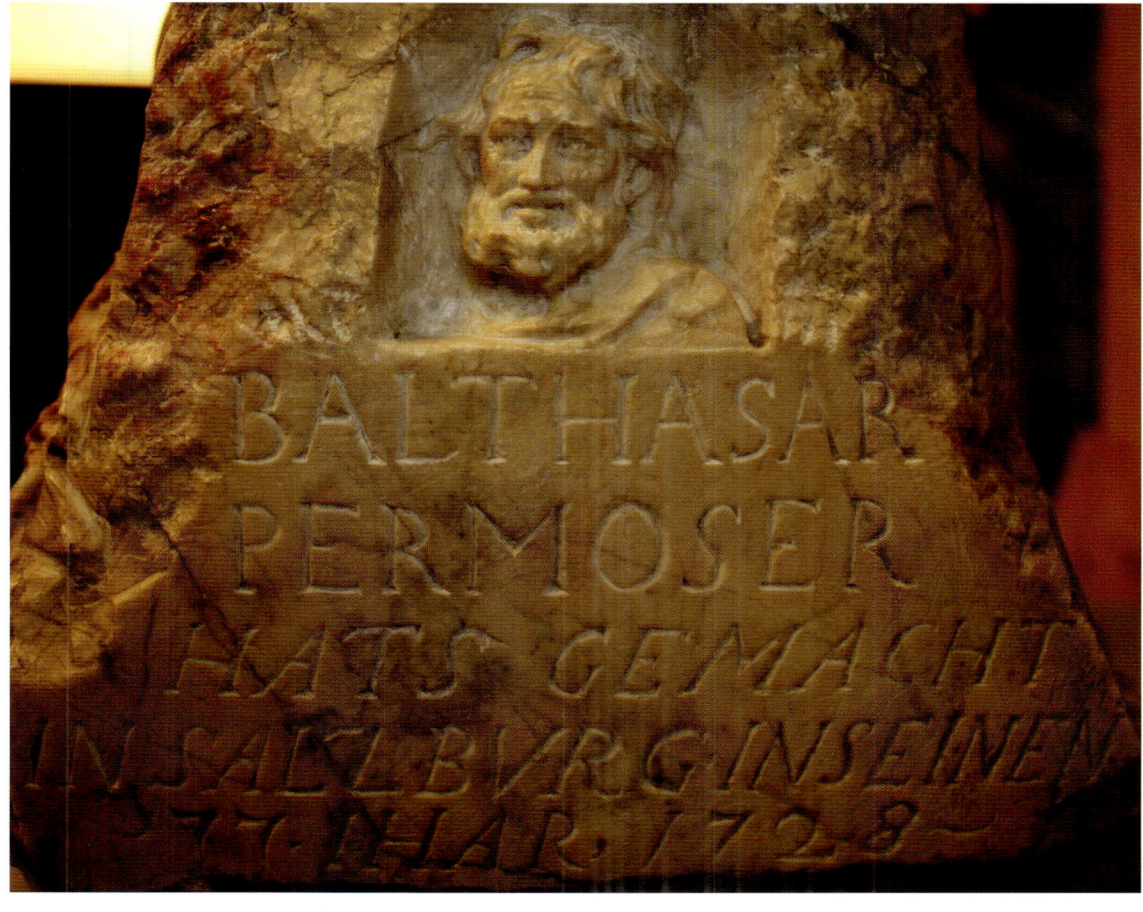

3.16
Detail of Permoser, *Christ at the Column* [3.15], Permoser's signature and self portrait.

3.17
Johann Christoph Ludwig Lücke, *Poltrone*, terracotta, monogrammed and dated 1729, height 11.4 cm, width 7.1 cm. Museum für Kunst und Gewerbe, Hamburg (inv. no. 1928. 213).

3.18
Johann Christoph Ludwig Lücke, *Poltrone*, ivory on wood socle, c. 1730, height 10.5 cm (ivory alone). Victoria and Albert Museum, London (inv. no. A. 17-1949).

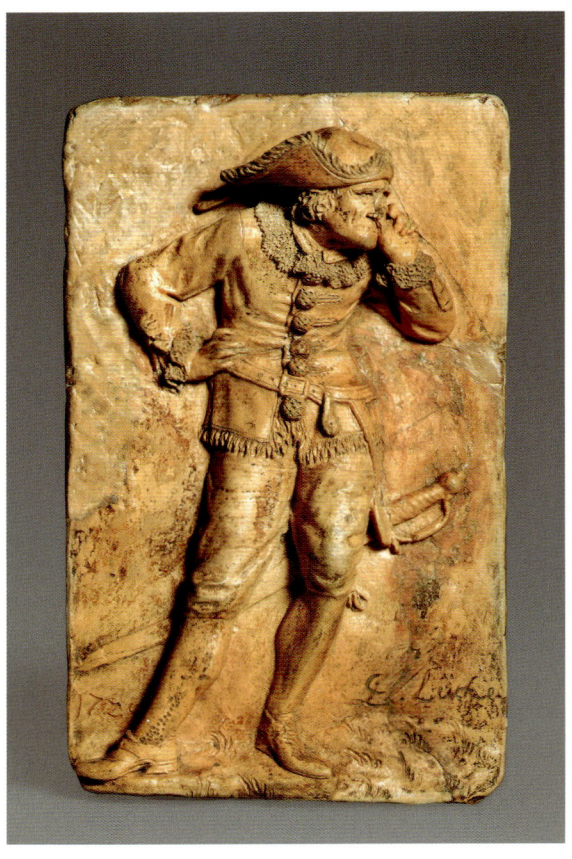
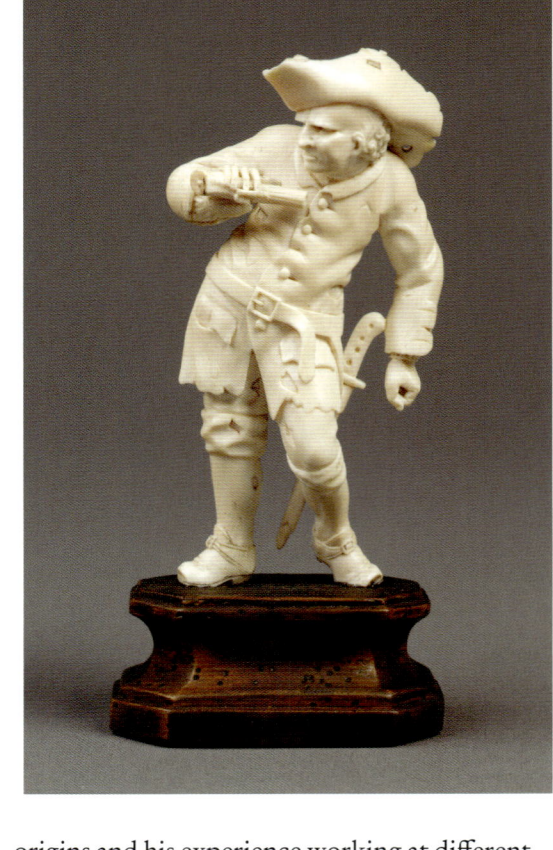

dynamic twisting pose and concentrated facial expression exude a lively energy. Lücke's younger brother, Carl August Lücke the Younger (c. 1710-after 1777), also made a pair of ivory reliefs of Poltrone and another commedia dell'arte figure, Scaramouche, in about 1745; these seem to be copies of his brother's works (Staatliche Museum, Schwerin).[43] The various extant ceramic and ivory versions of these figures indicate the taste for small-scale, finely-worked sculpture, and the fashion of reproducing popular subjects from the courtly world of Italian theatre and spectacle in a variety of luxury materials.

Lücke's ivory portrait of the British King George II (1683-1760; r. 1727-60), signed and dated 1760, shortly before the monarch died, is dexterously carved to give the appearance of a freestanding piece made in the round, rivalling marble busts, although it is in reality carved in relief (**3.19**). Lücke produced it while he was in London, apparently executing it during or after a sitting with the king. When it was exhibited at the Society of Artists in London in 1761 it was described as 'His late Majesty (George II), cut in ivory, from the life'. The sculptor's German

origins and his experience working at different German courts may have enabled him to gain access to the king. George II was not only of German birth, but was Elector of Hannover in addition to being King of Great Britain. This portrait depicts him in a full wig, wearing the Order of the Garter over his cloak, turning back towards the viewer with the hint of a smile. Lücke could give his likenesses a psychological dimension that was rarely equalled.[44]

Lücke's oeuvre epitomises important aspects of German sculpture in the mid-eighteenth century, some of which are evident in Permoser's work of the previous generation: the importance of court patronage; the value placed on small-scale sculptures, especially ivories; the existence of reproductions and variants in different materials; and the use of sculptural models for ceramics. Lücke was above all patronised by Heinrich, Count Brühl (1700-63), a powerful courtier in Dresden during the time of Augustus III (1696-1763; r. 1733/4-63) (also known as Frederick Augustus II), the son of Augustus the Strong. Many ivories by Lücke now in the Grünes Gewölbe were formerly in the Brühl collection.[45] Finally, the fact that

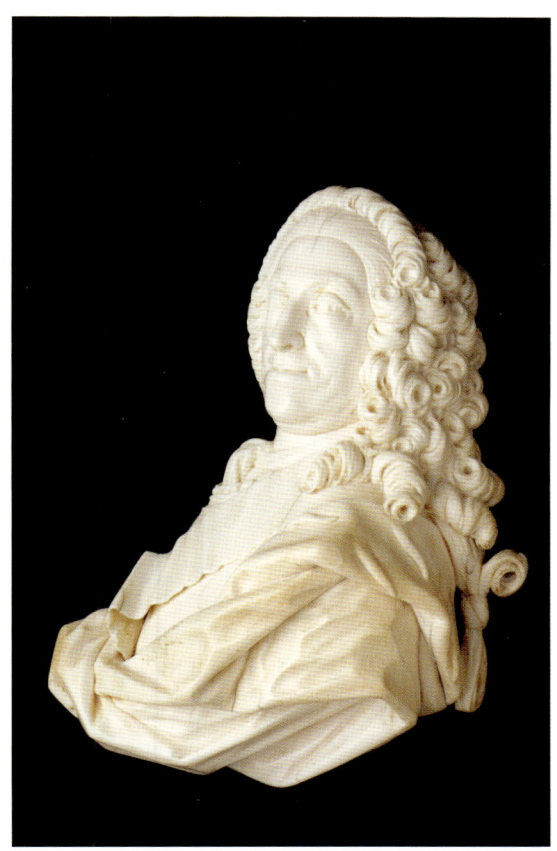

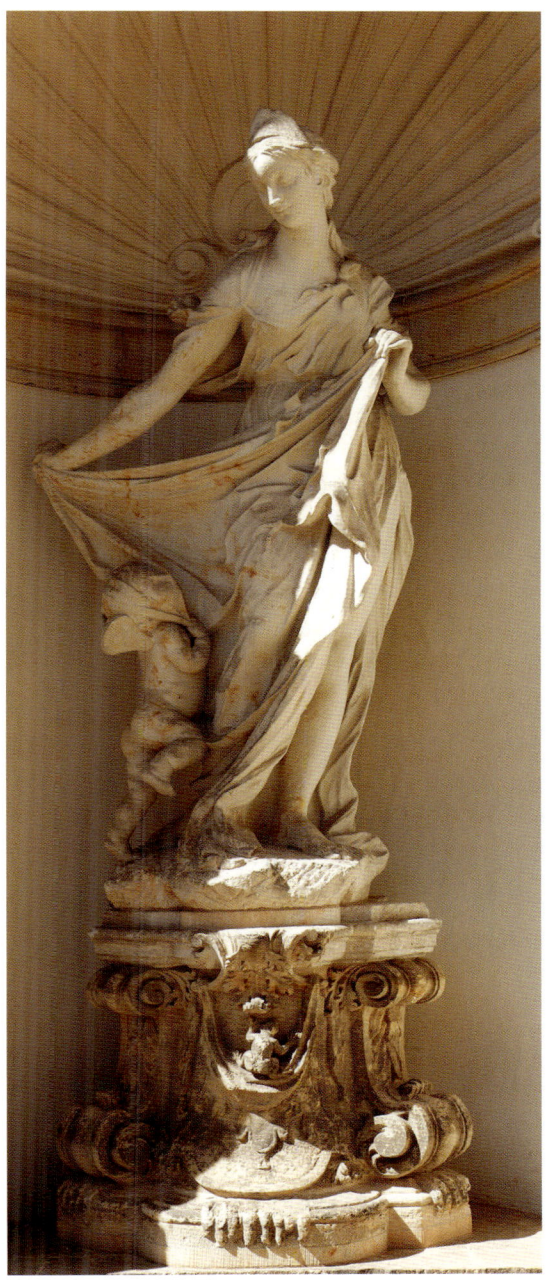

3.19
Johann Christoph
Ludwig Lücke, *King
George II*, ivory, signed
and dated 1760, height
18.7 cm, width 14 cm.
Victoria and Albert
Museum, London
(inv. no. A. 18-1932).

3.20
Paul Egell, *Nymph*,
sandstone, 1717/18,
height c. 250 cm.
The Zwinger, Dresden.

Lücke belonged to a family of sculptors can be paralleled by other artists active in Germany—and elsewhere in Europe—such as Hans Krumper, Christoph Maucher, Leonhard Kern, the Schenck family, and, as will be seen, the Asam brothers, whose work will be discussed in a later chapter.

Paul Egell: Dresden and Mannheim

As noted above, Paul Egell was one of Permoser's assistants on the Zwinger, when he would have been a young man at the start of his career. Egell's origins are uncertain; he came possibly from a Swiss family, and was probably a native of the region of Salzburg, near where Permoser had been born in 1651.[46] Egell, like Permoser, worked on large-scale architectural stone sculpture, though—like Lücke and indeed Permoser himself—he also created significant smaller works, including ivories. He was also a stuccoist of distinction, as shown by his work at Mannheim, where he was to be appointed court sculptor in 1729.[47]

Apart from collaborating on the sandstone herms of the entrance pavilion of the Zwinger [see **3.13**], Egell may have been responsible for the heads serving as capitals there, although only about eighteen of about fifty original heads survive, following damage in the Second World War.[48] The smiling, jesting faces, with their heavily lidded eyes, seem to look forward to sculpture of the later eighteenth century. Similarly, the *Playful Nymph* attributed to Egell in the Nymphäum or Nymphenbad at Dresden, dating from about the same time as the *Heads*, c. 1717/18, wears a teasing expression [**3.20**]. The Nymphäum was a grotto-like enclosure adorned with figures of nymphs, ostensibly a bathing place, with a central fountain and cascade, emulating fashionable French precedents.[49] Egell's *Nymph* seems to echo sculpture at Versailles in its playfulness and sensuality. A lock of hair is artfully tucked into her drapery over her breast. The accompanying winged putto playing hide and seek under the veil she holds out gives the sculptor the opportunity of demonstrating his virtuosity, the putto's head veiled by the seemingly translucent drapery held by the nymph. Such a skilled illusionistic device can be paralleled in seventeenth- and eighteenth-century Italian sculpture. The composition may have been made to a design by Permoser, given the years he spent working in Florence and Rome in the 1670s and 1680s.[50] However the most famous Italian practitioner of such veiled marbles, Antonio Corradini (1688-1752), was active in Rome and Naples only some years later, although he was to be employed in Dresden by Augustus the Strong in the Grosser Garten in the 1720s.[51] Egell may have gone to Rome early on in his career, although this is not documented. But any Italianate techniques and style he evinced at the Zwinger must have been imbibed at least partly via Permoser's work and teaching.

The Wittelsbachs at Düsseldorf: Gabriel Grupello (1644-1730) and Ignaz Elhafen (1658-before 1715)

After Dresden, Egell's career was spent mainly in the city of Mannheim (today in Baden-Württemberg), the seat of the Palatinate branch of the Wittelsbachs. He was appointed court sculptor there in 1721 by Charles III Philip, Elector Palatine. The Electors Palatine were a cadet branch of the Bavarian Wittelsbachs, who ruled in Munich. Their intertwined dynastic relations pre-dated the seventeenth century. In 1619, Frederick V, Elector Palatine (1596-1632; r. 1610-23), who was a Protestant, had become King of Bohemia, but was defeated the following year in the Battle of the White Mountain by the Catholic Elector of Bavaria Maximilian I (1573-1651; r. 1597-1651), a member of the Catholic Bavarian branch of the Wittelsbachs. Frederick was forced to abdicate, and the Upper Palatinate was ceded to the Bavarian Wittelsbachs in 1623. When the Thirty Years' War came to an end in 1648, an additional electorate was created for the Count

Palatine of the Rhine. This was the region over which Charles III Philip ruled in the early eighteenth century. Before looking at Egell's work in Mannheim, the patronage in Düsseldorf of his brother and predecessor as elector should be briefly examined.

Charles III Philip had inherited the princedom from his older brother, John William II (1658-1716; r. 1690-1716). During his reign, John William had moved the electoral residence from Heidelberg to Düsseldorf in Westphalia. John William's reign was also marked by abundant artistic commissions. His appointment of the Netherlandish sculptor Gabriel Grupello in 1695 led to the creation of several important sculptures, including the bronze equestrian statue of the elector of 1711 in Düsseldorf [**3.21**]. This massive, even stolid, work is in the tradition of Andreas Schlüter's great bronze of the Great Elector in Berlin of a few years prior/earlier [**see 2.29, 2.30 and 2.31**].[52] The crowned and armed ruler holding out his baton also recalls the Roman bronze monument to Marcus Aurelius in the Campidoglio in Rome, as well as Italian renaissance prototypes, in particular Donatello's *Gattamelata* of 1453 in Padua.[53] Grupello's sculpture in the Rhineland provided a valuable precedent for Egell's monumental work in Mannheim, bringing as it did an international perspective, thanks to Grupello's origins in the Netherlands.

But John William II also favoured small-scale sculpture, employing Ignaz Elhafen from 1703/4 onwards. Elhafen's ivory narrative reliefs often deliberately expose the concave form of the tusk, playing with the idea of the naturalistic representation of a mythological or religious scene, whilst at the same time drawing attention to the valuable and exotic material from which it is carved. One such example, monogrammed by the artist, and now in the Victoria and Albert Museum, depicting *The Childhood of Jupiter*, is likely to have been carved shortly before Elhafen's time in Düsseldorf, perhaps when he was in Vienna [**3.22**].[54] The composition is derived from a print after Jacob Jordaens's painting of *The Infant Jupiter fed by the Goat Amalthea* of c. 1630-35 and exemplifies Elhafen's skill in adapting the composition to the

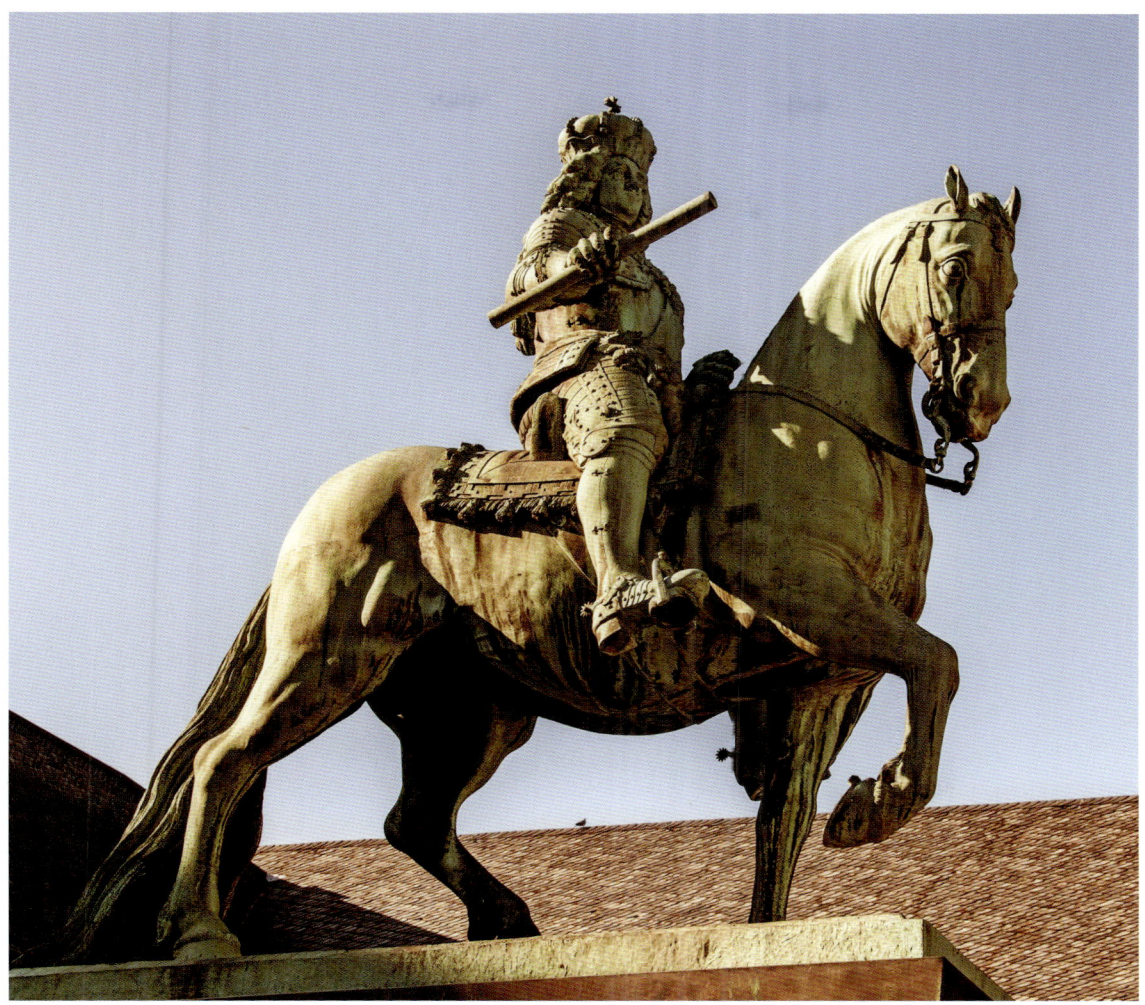

3.21
Gabriel Grupello,
*Equestrian Monument to
Elector John William*,
bronze, c. 1703-13.
Düsseldorf,
Marketplace.

horizontal format of the curved tusk. Many other ivories by Elhafen are now in the Bayerisches Nationalmuseum in Munich, having been transferred to the Bavarian court towards the end of the eighteenth century, when the Elector Palatine Charles Theodore (1724-99; r. 1777-99) became Elector of Bavaria and transferred his court from Düsseldorf and Mannheim to Munich.[55] Elector John William's patronage of the sculptor demonstrates the demand for finely-carved ivories, reflecting the wider taste for baroque ivories in Germany and Austria.

Paul Egell's Work at Mannheim

After he had inherited the throne from his older brother, Charles III Philip moved the Palatinate's capital from Düsseldorf back to Heidelberg in 1718, and then to Mannheim in 1720. As in other German states, wars had adversely affected Mannheim during the seventeenth century; the city had been largely demolished during the

Thirty Years' War. After being rebuilt in the mid-seventeenth century, it was again severely damaged by the French Army in 1689 during the Nine Years' War (1688-97), fought between Louis XIV of France (1638-1715; r. 1654-1715) and an alliance of European powers, led by Austria.

Mannheim began to be rebuilt yet again in 1698, and when it was created the capital of the Electorate of the Palatinate in 1720, Charles III Philip began construction of Mannheim Palace and the Jesuit Church. Egell was involved in both building projects. As in Berlin and Dresden, the elector wished to construct a city whose architecture and sculpture would be worthy of a great European city. In many ways the architecture and architectural sculpture of Mannheim also looked to Versailles, and Egell's indebtedness to French ornament, especially in the fine stucco reliefs (tragically destroyed in the Second World War) is evident.[56]

Egell's architectural sculpture of trophies

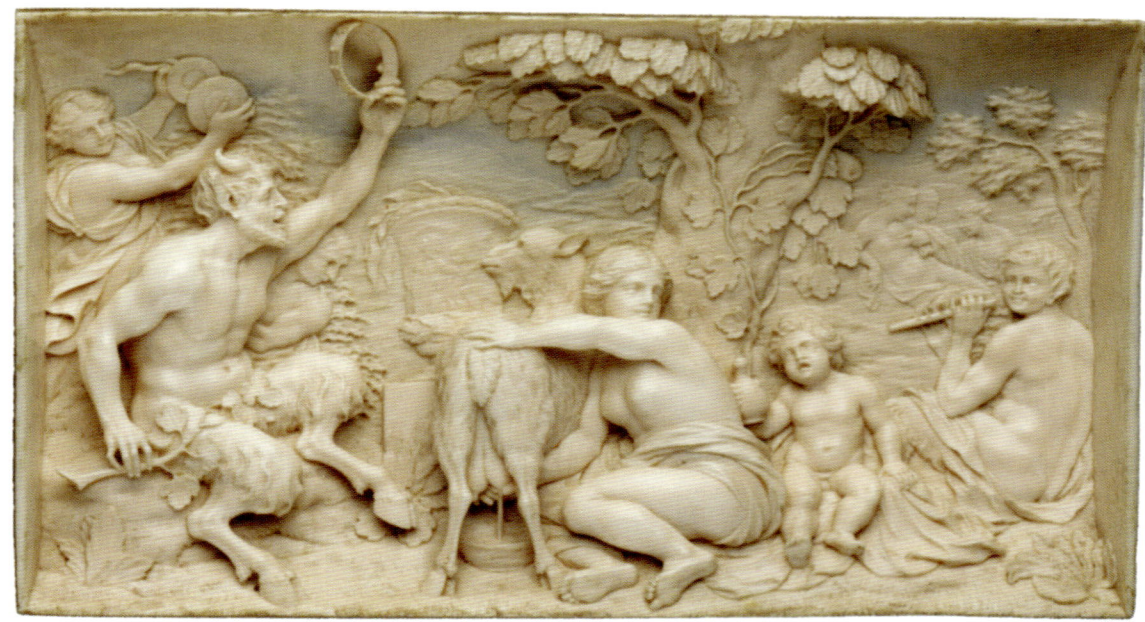

and satyr masks made for the palace at Mannheim dates from c. 1729/30 [**3.23a and b**]. Like the sculptures made for the Zwinger, they are of sandstone, and like Andreas Schlüter's helmet trophies and heads of dying warriors on the Berlin Palace [**see 2.27 and 2.28**], they are vigorously carved. The satyr masks are virtually caricatures, betraying a sense of humour and liveliness analogous to that seen in the *Playful Nymph* on the Zwinger.

Dating from the same decade, Egell's monumental sandstone pediment on the façade of the Palace Church at Mannheim of 1727-30 depicts the *Trinity* [**3.24**]. This outdoor sculpture, high above the spectator, commands our attention partly because of its swirling composition, the putti angels at the base and sides tumbling over one another beyond the confines of the architectural framework. The muscular figures of the semi-nude Christ and God the Father dominate the composition, the bearded patriarchal figure of God raising up his left hand.

Over ten years after Egell had executed the pediment for the Palace Church, he undertook the high altarpiece for the church of St Sebastian at Mannheim (1738-41/2). This was of gilded limewood, and testifies to Egell's skill in wood carving, exhibiting a rococo lightness. However

the altarpiece also typifies the hostility felt towards German baroque sculpture within Germany in the nineteenth century. It was removed by the rector from its original location in the church in 1880, because he disliked its baroque style. Then acquired by the Kunstgewerbemuseum in Berlin, the name of its creator was forgotten. Egell had become an unknown figure: the great art historian and curator Wilhelm von Bode (1845-1929) who was in charge of the sculpture collections in Berlin did not even mention him in his history of German sculpture of 1887 (*Geschichte der deutschen Plastik*). It was not until 1922 that the first scholarly monograph on Egell was published by Theodor Demmler (1879-1944), the curator who had succeeded Bode in Berlin in 1919. Under Demmler's care in 1930 the altarpiece was displayed in the newly-installed Deutsches Museum in Berlin. But in the Second World War much of the altarpiece was damaged or destroyed. The surviving elements (two panels and two cartouches, as well as two busts of St Philip Neri and St Carlo Borromeo) have recently been conserved and sensitively re-displayed at the Bode Museum in Berlin [**3.25**].[57] The altarpiece is indebted to Bernini, whose work Egell must have known through engravings. Parallels can also be made with the

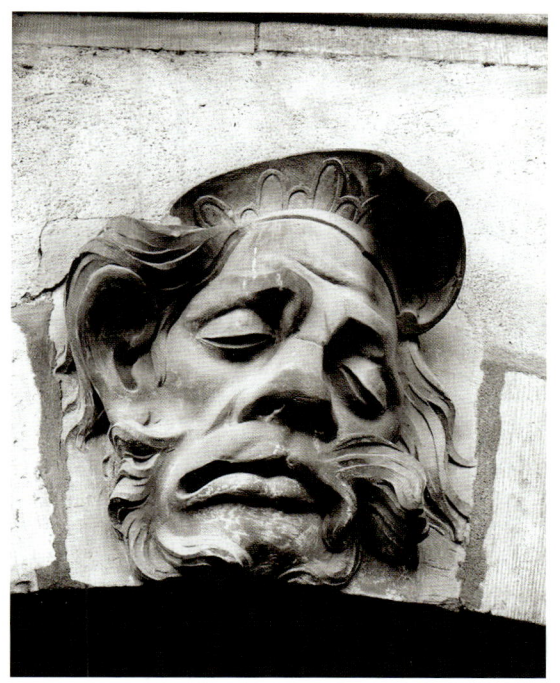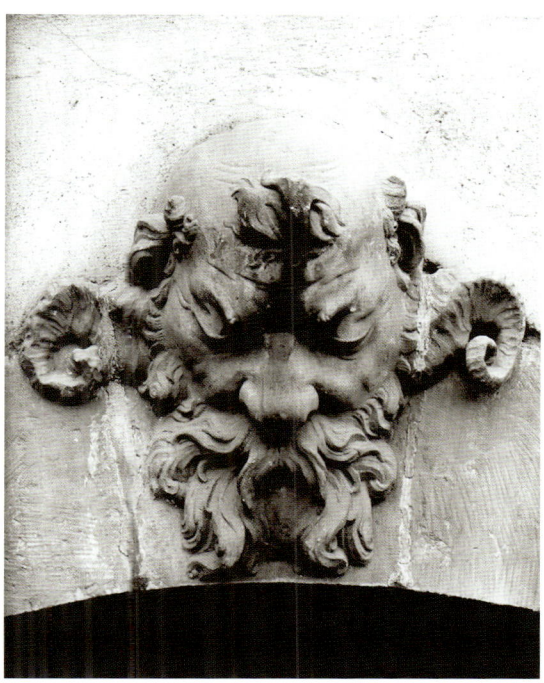

3.23a and b
Paul Egell, *Satyr Heads*,
sandstone, c. 1729/30,
height c. 70 cm.
Mannheim Palace.

3.24
Paul Egell, *The Trinity*,
sandstone, 1727-30,
height 430 cm, width
1460 cm. Church at
Mannheim Palace.

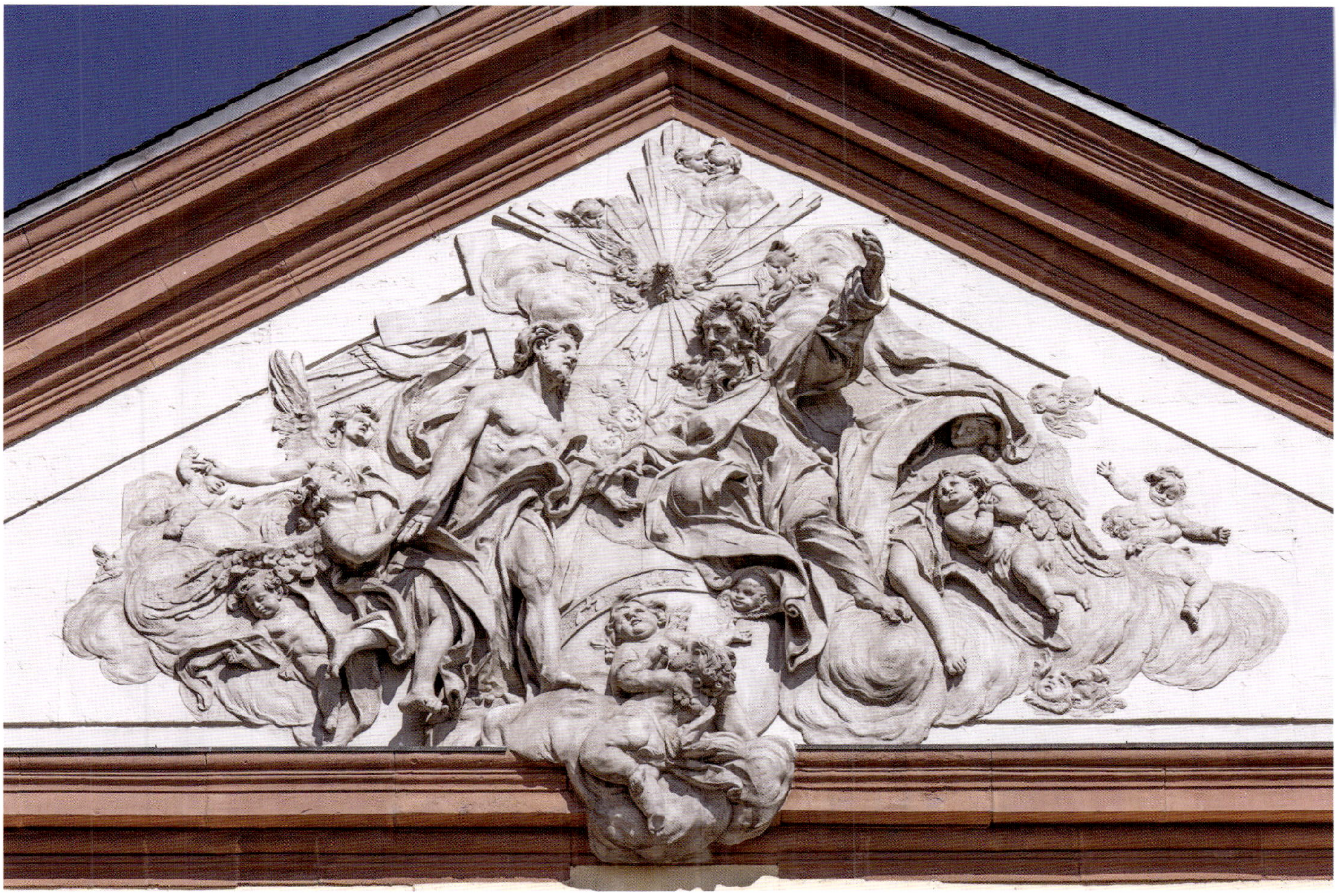

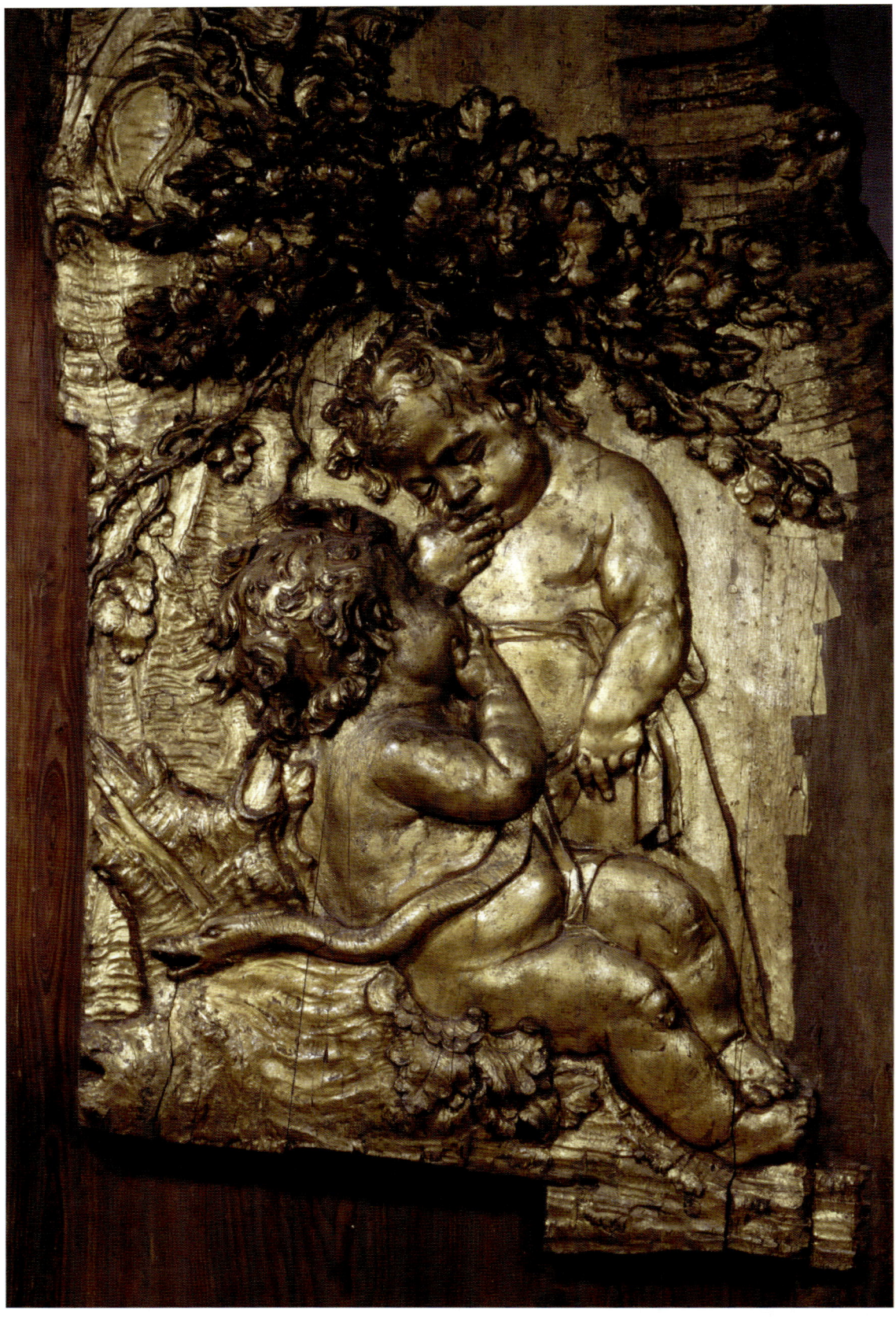

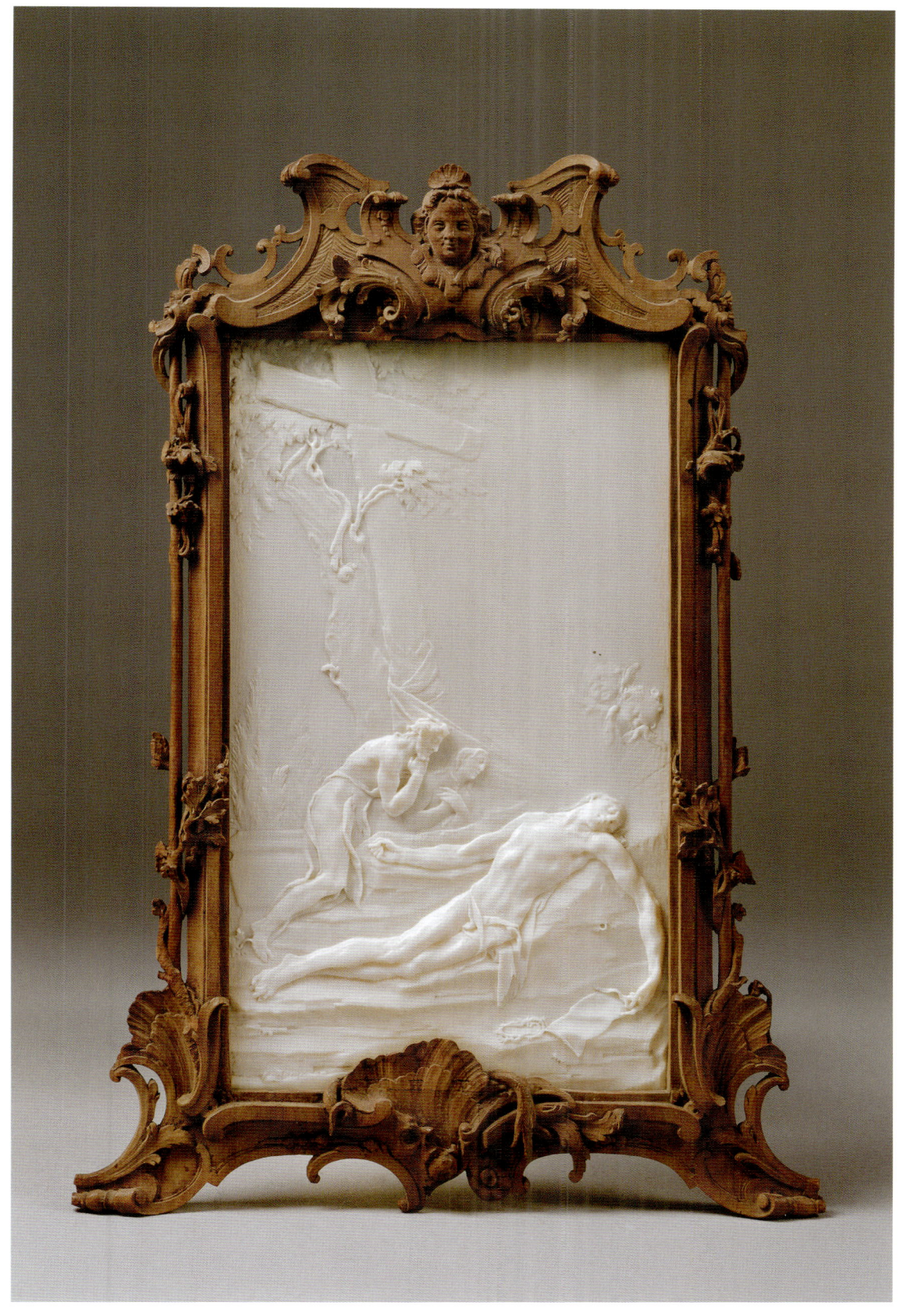

3.26
Paul Egell, *The
Lamentation, or Allegory
of the Redemption from
Sin*, ivory in pearwood
frame, c.1723-5, height
18.5 cm, width 10.8 cm
(ivory alone); height
26 cm, width 18.5 cm
(frame). Museum für
Angewandte Kunst,
Cologne (inv. no. B 73).
Copyright: Rheinisches
Bildarchiv,
rba_c003608.

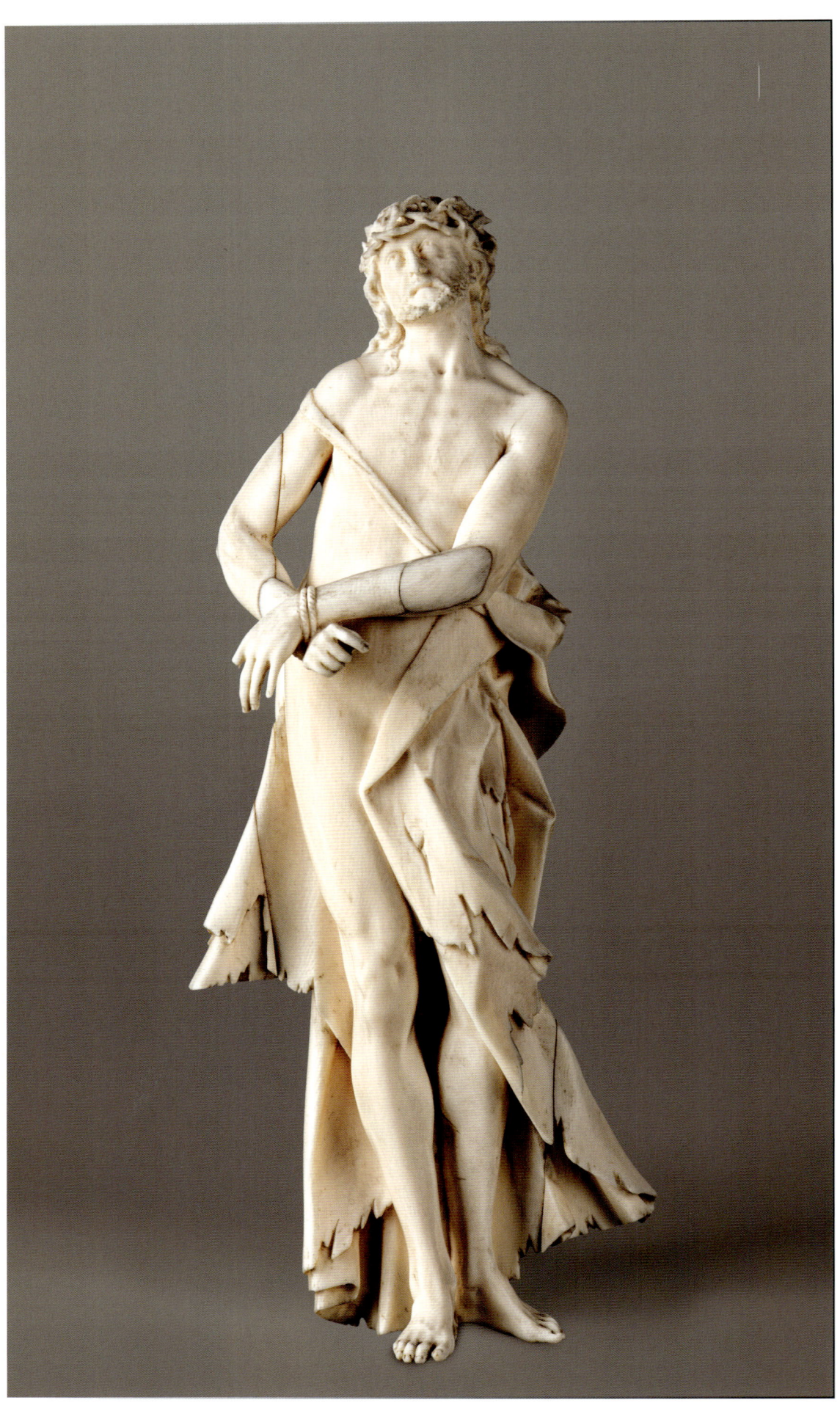

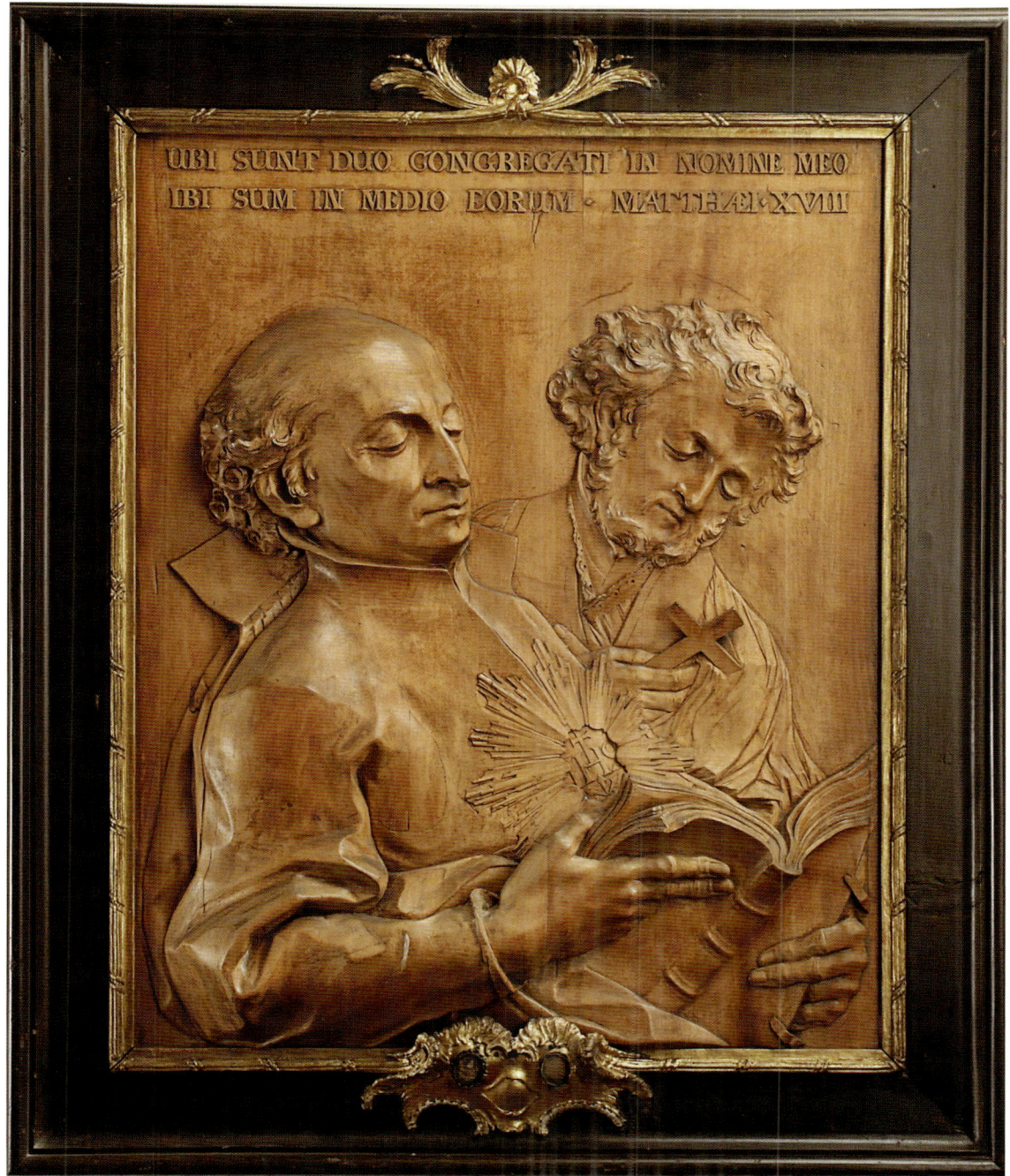

UBI SUNT DUO CONGREGATI IN NOMINE MEO
IBI SUM IN MEDIO EORUM · MATTHÆI·XVIII

3.28
Paul Egell, *St Ignatius Loyola and St Francis Xavier*, limewood, 1744, height 73.5 cm, width 59 cm (without frame). Liebieghaus Frankfurt am Main, on permanent loan from the Historisches Museum, Frankfurt am Main (inv. no. X 1902).

work of the Austrian sculptor Georg Raphael Donner (1693-1741), whose lead angels of 1733-5 for the high altarpiece of the cathedral in Bratislava are very similar in style to Egell's angels in Mannheim.[58] But much of Egell's altarpiece was highly distinctive, with leanings towards contemporary French decorative sculpture. A side panel of gilt limewood shows *Sorrowing Children (Adam and Eve after the Fall)* [**3.25**], an exceptional choice of subject. Two small children are shown as sorrowful figures, the serpent beneath them evidently an allusion

to the Fall of Man, this and their proximity to the crucifixion indicating they should be seen as Adam and Eve. This iconography is clearly at odds with the orthodox account of the Fall in Genesis, and at the same time redolent of the French rococo, with the two protagonists shown in the guise of putti, rather than as tragic adult Biblical figures.

Egell's small-scale works in wood and ivory epitomise his elegant and sophisticated style of carving. None of his ivories is documented, but a number are convincingly attributed to him for stylistic reasons. The ivory relief of *The Lamentation* or *Allegory of the Redemption from Sin* of c. 1723-5 in the Museum für Angewandte Kunst, Cologne, is a remarkable exercise in low relief carving, and again—like the relief of sorrowing children/Adam and Eve from the St Sebastian altarpiece—exceptional iconographically. The elongated body of Christ, collapsed horizontally at the front of the composition evokes the sorrows of the Passion, while the figures of Adam and Eve, redeemed by his sacrifice, kneel before his body in meditation [**3.26**].⁵⁹ The smooth bare ivory representing the open sky, filling the upper right corner, perhaps a fifth of the area of the whole, is a bold and harmonious element in the composition, adding to the contemplative mood of the scene. The relief is complemented by its contemporary carved rococo wood frame, adorned with shell motifs, rococo scrolls and foliage.

Christ as Man of Sorrows, the ivory statuette in the Museum für Kunst und Gewerbe in Hamburg, is thought to date from the 1740s [**3.27**].⁶⁰ The graceful pose and the illusionistic torn cloak around Christ's body seem to parallel the veil around the putto on the earlier *Playful Nymph* on the Zwinger [**3.20**], even though the *Christ* is of a religious subject, on a far smaller scale, and carved in a different material.

The limewood relief of the Jesuit saints *St Ignatius Loyola and St Francis Xavier* of 1744 exemplifies Egell's facility in carving wood in low relief [**3.28**].⁶¹ Originally part of a group of

sculptures commissioned by Ignatius Freiherr von Weichs and his brother Francis, a member of the ecclesiastical chapter at Hildesheim Cathedral, they were installed in the brothers' house chapel in Schloss Sarstedt in Hildesheim. Again, this relief is ascribed to Egell for stylistic reasons, partly because of the deft draughtsmanship and carving skills, seen for example in the carving of St Ignatius Loyola's slender hands and the pages of the book he holds. The faces, too, seem to bear a family resemblance to those in Egell's other works, such as the *Playful Nymph*, mentioned above.

This first half of the eighteenth century in Dresden and the Rhineland Palatinate saw the creation of sculpture of the first order, thanks in large part to Balthasar Permoser, who was without doubt a crucial influence at that time. Apart from his own genius as an artist, the years he had spent in Italy led to his importing a stylistic grandeur learnt from Rome and Florence, as well as the virtuoso skills he had perfected in carving ivories for the Medici court. This in turn meant that small-scale sculptures in this material continued to enjoy great status in Dresden, Braunschweig, Düsseldorf, Berlin and elsewhere in Germany. Like Permoser, Egell sustained a breadth of style and an ability in sculpting a range of materials (stucco, wood and stone, as well as ivory) on both a monumental and a small scale. The court patronage at Mannheim allowed him to produce architectural sculpture of superlative quality, both secular and religious.

Notes

1 For the international perspective, see *Splendor of Dresden* 1978-9, p. 15; *Barock in Dresden* 1986, p. 23 and pp. 193-5. For artistic connections with Asia, see *Goldener Drache Weisser Adler* 2008.

2 Christian I died soon after the work had commenced; his tomb was incorporated into the scheme. Diemer 2004, Vol. I, pp. 253-69. See also Koja and Kryza-Gersch 2020, cat. no. 11, p. 70 (entry by C. Kryza-Gersch).

3 Asche 1988, pp. 82-5 and pp. 159-60; see also Leibetseder 2013, p. 36.

4 For *Kunstkammer* collections, see Schlosser 1908; *Splendor of Dresden* 1978-9, pp. 17-19; MacGregor and Impey 1985.

5 Schmidt 1986, p. 191; Aurich and Kulbe 2012, p. 293.

6 Schmidt 1986, p. 191.

7 Syndram 2006, pp. 13-15.

8 Syndram 2006.

9 Kappel 2017, pp. 25-6. See also https://skd-online-collection.skd. museum/Details/Index/118475, accessed 30 September 2021.

10 Kappel 2017, p. 57 and Kappel 2021.

11 For the Master of the Furies, see *Furienmeister* 2006.

12 Kappel 2017, p. 60.

13 See Trusted 2013, p. xxxv; Leibetseder 2013, p. 27.

14 Fleming and Honour 1989, pp. 112-3 and pp. 534-7; Hildyard 1999.

15 Fleming and Honour 1989, p. 250.

16 Kappel 2001; for Schenck, see Haag 1996.

17 Asche 1978, pp. 32-3; Trusted 2014.

18 For example in Bossuit's *Mercury, Argus and Io* in the Reiner Winkler Collection, Liebieghaus, Frankfurt am Main; Asche 1978, fig. 43; Theuerkauff 1984, cat. no. 2, pp. 24-6.

19 Marth 2018, p. 20.

20 Bossuit was the first artist to be the subject of an illustrated monograph, published by Mattys Pool in Amsterdam in 1727; see Theuerkauff 1975.

21 Marth 2018, p. 20. For Permoser's time in Florence, see Schmidt 2012, pp. 203-29.

22 Schmidt 2012, pp. 215-6.

23 Asche 1978, p.150; Marth 2018, p. 50.

24 Wittkower 1999b, p. 18, fig. 22.

25 Möller 1977, p. 16; Marth 2018.

26 March 2018, p. 39. The third group, originally in the collection of Carlo Ginori (1702-57) at Doccia, is now lost. From the early nineteenth century, until they were triumphantly reunited in Braunschweig in 2016, the Braunschweig group was split between Harewood House (Yorkshire) and the Herzog Anton Ulrich-Museum.

27 Asche 1978, p. 165; Kappel and Weinhold 2007, pp. 199-200.

28 As recounted in Ovid's *Metamorphoses*, Book 3.

29 For the Northern War, see Barber 1984, pp. 120-1.

30 Asche 1978, pp. 80-1.

31 For Roubiliac, see Bindman and Baker 1995.

32 Asche 1978, pp. 172-3.

33 Asche 1978, pp. 171-2.

34 See Koja and Kryza-Gersch 2020, pp. 112-21; Trusted 2013, p. 85.

35 Asche 1978, pp. 99-102, and p. 176.

36 Leibetseder 2013, p. 27.

37 Asche 1978, p. 100.

38 See Asche 1978, pp. 102-3, for Italian comparisons.

39 Koja and Kryza-Gersch 2020 (introduction by A. Nielsen), p. 37.

40 Asche 1978, pp. 115-7 and pp. 180-2; Koja and Krza-Gersch 2020, cat. no. 38 on p. 132 (entry by A. Nielsen).

41 Theuerkauff and Möller et al. 1977, cat. no. 100, pp. 175-6.

42 Trusted 2013, pp. 95-6.

43 Möller 2000, cat. nos. 29 and 30.

44 Theuerkauff 1986, p. 194.

45 Kappel 2017, pp. 409-33.

46 Permoser was born in Kammer near Traunstein, in the region of Cheimgau, close to Salzburg. Today Kammer is in Germany, whereas Salzburg is in Austria. For Egell's

possible origins, see Leibetseder 2013; Lankheit 1988, Vol. I, p. 16.

47 Leibetseder 2013, p. 42.

48 Lankheit 1988, Vol. II, cat. no. 2, p. 284.

49 Leibetseder 2013, pp. 32-5. Two of Permoser's marble sculptures formerly in the grotto, *Apollo* (1715) and *Minerva* (1716), were moved to the sculpture collection in Dresden in 1890; Koja and Kryza-Gersch 2020, cat. no. 37 on pp. 128-31 (entry by A. Nielsen).

50 Lankheit 1988, Vol. II, cat. no. 4, p. 284. Italian precedents of baroque marble sculpture illusionistically suggesting a body beneath drapery include the *St Cecilia* by Stefano Maderno (c. 1576-1636) in Rome; see Wittkower 1999a, p. 89, fig. 94.

51 See the bust of a veiled woman in the sculpture collection at Dresden, in Koja and Kryza-Gersch 2020, cat. no. 34 on p. 122 (entry by C. Kryza-Gersch); Hodgkinson 1970. Two of Corradini's sculptures originally at Dresden are now in the Victoria and Albert Museum

52 *Europäische Barockplastik* 1971, figs. 21-24.

53 See Greenhalgh 1982, figs. 88 and 91.

54 Trusted 2013, cat. no. 7, p. 12; here an ivory in the Bayerisches Nationalmuseum, inv. no. R 4673, was erroneously noted as a variant. In fact, the BNM ivory shows a different subject, *The Childhood of Bacchus*. Many other ivories by Elhafen now at the Bayerisches Nationalmuseum came from Düsseldorf, though they may have been carved while Elhafen was still in Vienna.

55 Burk 2018, p. 224.

56 Leibetseder 2013, pp. 42-95.

57 For the altarpiece, see Lankheit 1988, Vol. II, pp. 115-23; Kammel 1998; Leibetseder 2013, pp. 112-34; Kessler 2017a. For a brief description of the surviving elements, see *Sculpture* 2008, pp. 77-8.

58 The angels are now in the Hungarian National Museum, Budapest. Kessler 2017a, p. 45 and figs. 42 and 43.

59 Volk 1982/3; Lankheit 1988, Vol. II, cat. no. 7, p. 284.

60 Theuerkauff and Möller et al. 1977, cat. no. 56, p. 105.

61 Lankheit 1988, Vol. II, cat. no. 94, p. 307. See also Kessler 2017a/b, fig. 83.

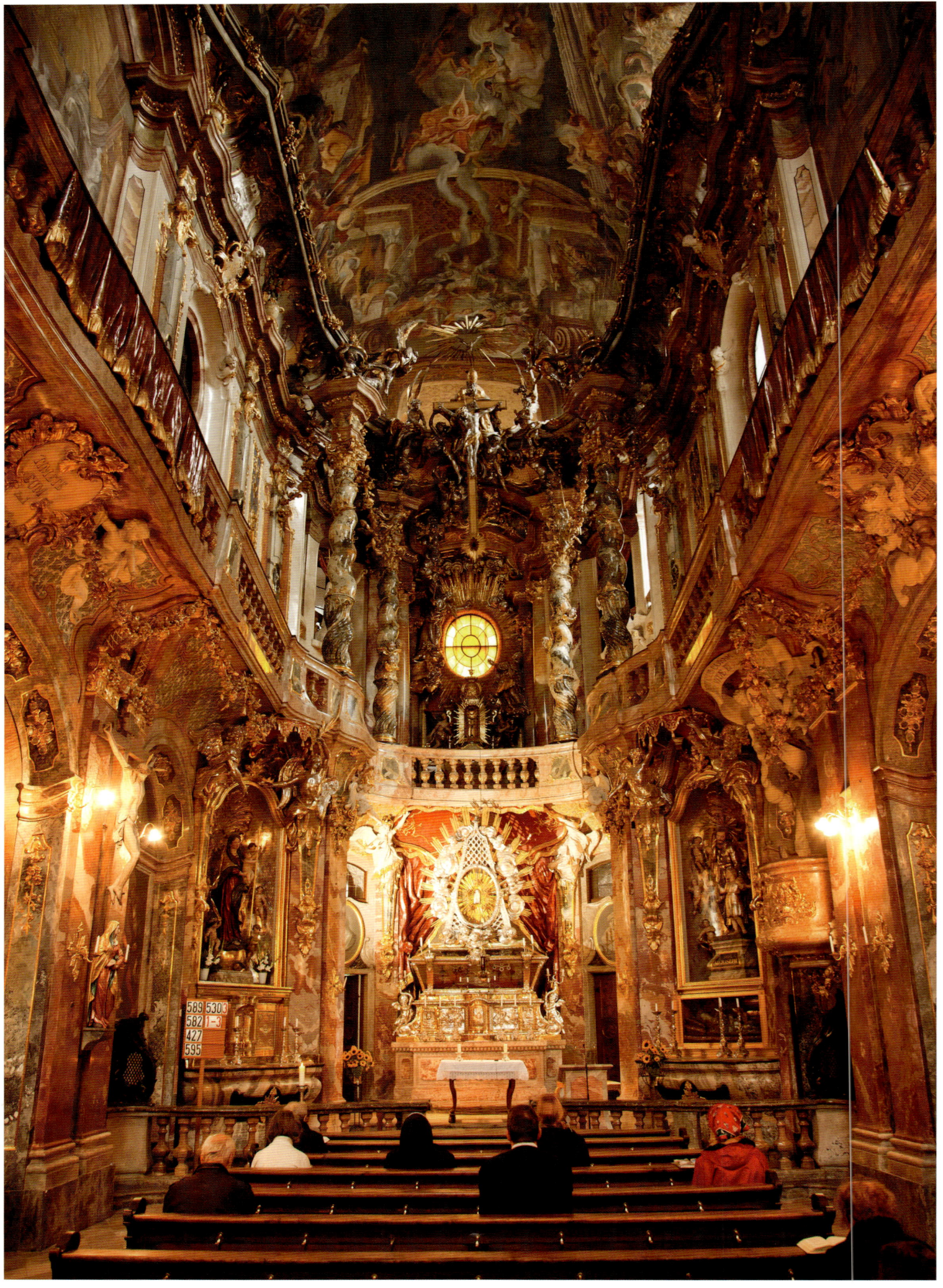

CHAPTER 4

MUNICH AND
BAVARIA IN THE
LATE SEVENTEENTH
AND FIRST HALF
OF THE EIGHTEENTH
CENTURY

Prelude: The Asams

In the centre of Munich stands the so-called Asamkirche, the church built between 1733 and 1746 for the brothers Cosmas Damian Asam (1686-1739), and Egid Quirin Asam (1692-1750). This compact church has always formed part of a busy urban street, adjacent to neighbouring buildings both commercial and residential. The external setting contrasts with the church's interior, busy in an entirely different sense: a dense treasury of baroque decoration, combining painting, sculpture and architectural design in an astonishing *Gesamtkunstwerk* (total work of art) [4.1]. The building (to be discussed in more detail later in this chapter) epitomises the Asams' revolutionary achievement as artists, and at the same time expresses the eighteenth-century Bavarian baroque, both because of its magnificence and the implicit desire of its creators to inspire devotion in the spectator. Egid Quirin's work has to be seen alongside that of his older brother, the painter Cosmas Damian, since during their lifetime the two artists collaborated closely together, and many of their commissions were jointly produced. The brothers' oeuvre from the 1720s onwards both heralds and parallels the development of some of the most important sculpture created for churches in Munich and Bavaria in the mid-third of the

eighteenth century. The Asamkirche could be said to be the triumphant culmination of their output. This chapter will focus on a few of Egid Quirin Asam's sculptures in Munich and elsewhere in Bavaria, prefaced by a brief study some of his antecedents, and closing with a review of the work of two of his contemporaries, the brothers Johann Baptist and Dominikus Zimmermann, who also collaborated together, working as painters and stuccoists in Upper and Lower Bavaria.[1] As will be seen, some of the most striking sculpture and decorative architectural work created in Bavaria (examples of which are today within the region of Baden-Württemberg) in the first half of the eighteenth century was made of stucco.[2] The use of this versatile material, usually a compound of gypsum, sometimes with other additives, affected the style and forms of much that was produced.

Balthasar Ableithner (1614-1705) and Andreas Faistenberger (1646-1735)

Both Balthasar Ableithner and Andreas Faistenberger represent a continuity of tradition in Bavarian sculpture from the seventeenth century into the eighteenth. Ableithner was Faistenberger's teacher, and Faistenberger was to teach Egid Quirin Asam. In Munich, Ableithner had himself been the pupil of Christoph Angermair (c. 1580-

4.1
Johann Michael Fischer (architect), Interior of the church of St John Nepomuk (known as the Asamkirche), Munich, 1733-46. View towards the east end.

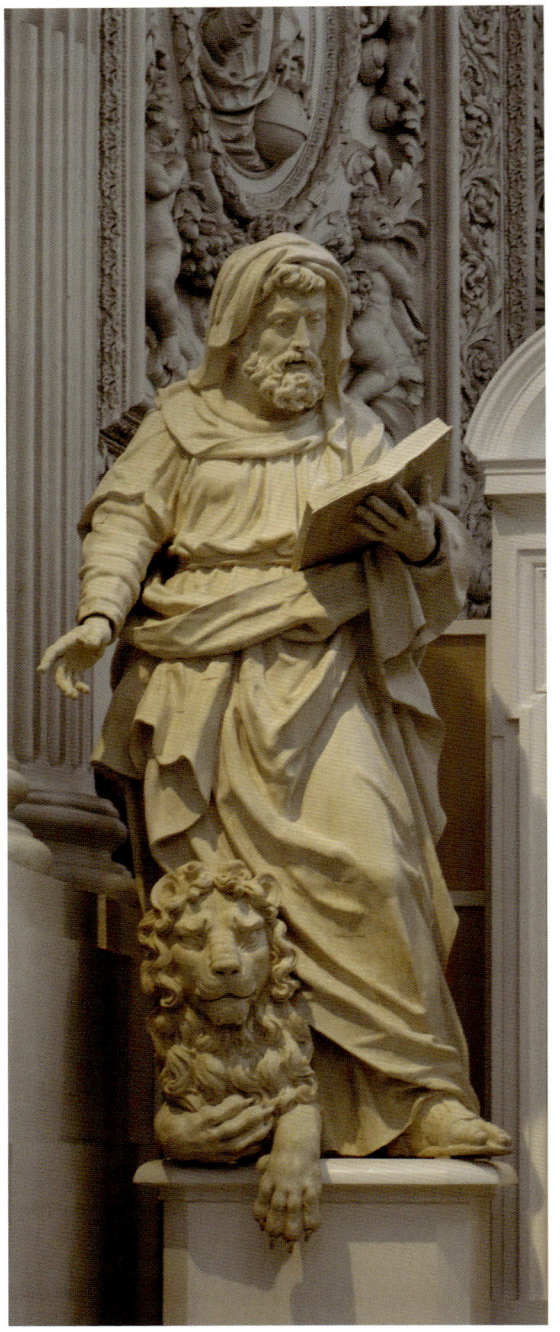

Balthasar Ableithner,
St Mark, painted wood
(the paint restored),
1670/3. Church of
St Kayetan (Theatine
church), Munich.

sixteenth-century altarpieces [see Chapter 1, 1.3]. But at the same time, he had clearly also imbibed lessons from the Italian renaissance. His over-life-size wood sculptures of the four Evangelists of 1670/3 for the chancel screen of the Theatine church of St Kajetan in Munich typify his style. Although these four statues were severely damaged, and a third was lost in the Second World War, *St Mark* survives [4.2].[3] Its graceful contrapposto pose and sense of the saint reading and speaking reflect the sculptor's Italian training, while the angular carving of the saint's hair and face, and the reclining lion at his feet are unmistakably South German. The Italianate elements evince a change of emphasis in style in Bavarian sculpture at this date, moving away from the Netherlandish currents of the early seventeenth century towards a more Roman, and at times Venetian, inflection. Sculptural links and exchanges between Germany and Venice during the seventeenth century are exemplified by the activity of various individual artists. For example, the sculptor Giovanni Giuliani (1664-1744), originally from Venice, was active in Bavaria in the early eighteenth century; Giuliani was taught by Ableithner's pupil Andreas Faistenberger. Meanwhile, Melchior Barthel (1625-72), a native of Dresden, worked in Venice from 1652 to 1670. These two artists inevitably imported stylistic features from Venice into Germany and Austria, although Barthel died soon after his return to Dresden in 1672.[4]

Andreas Faistenberger was a seminal teacher for the next generation of sculptors in Upper Bavaria and the Tyrol in the mid-eighteenth century.[5] His sculptures, commissioned by both the court and the Church, were in wood and stone (marble and alabaster), as well as ivory and boxwood, though none of his documented small-scale sculptures is known to survive. Born in the North Tyrol, he initially trained with his father Benedikt Faistenberger the Elder (1621-93). In 1665, when Andreas was in his twentieth year, he embarked on his travels as a journeyman (*Wanderschaft*), perhaps including a journey to Italy. He became a pupil of Ableithner in Munich in 1668. In around 1670 he was travelling again, possibly to Venice with Ableithner. By 1678 he was back in Munich; in 1679 he

1633), whose work was noted in Chapter 1. Ableithner also spent several years studying in Rome, and possibly Venice, from 1635 to 1642. In 1644 he was appointed sculptor to Albert VI (1584-1666), Duke of Bavaria-Leuchtenberg, working in both ivory and wood, just as his teacher Angermair had done. Ableithner's sculptures are rooted in the Weilheim school, mentioned in Chapter 1, and at the same time indirectly recall earlier German sculpture, in the same way that Hans Degler's three retables of the early seventeenth century at SS. Ulrich and Afra in Augsburg echo earlier fifteenth- and was recorded as a citizen and master sculptor there. Giovanni Giuliani, recorded as his pupil in Munich, may have accompanied him from Venice when Faistenberger returned to the city in 1678. Giuliani subsequently worked in and around Vienna, where he in turn was to motivate artists such as Johann Baptist Straub (1704-84) and Ignaz Günther (1725-75) (to be discussed in Chapter 5). Additionally, Faistenberger taught Egid Quirin Asam from 1711 to 1716, and in 1730 the ivory sculptor Simon Troger (1693-1768), another productive artistic presence in Munich in the mid-eighteenth century.[6] Towards the end of his life, in 1734, Johann Baptist Straub may have worked alongside him; Straub appears to have absorbed some stylistic traits from the older artist. Faistenberger was a *Hofbefreit* sculptor, meaning that he was free to work for the court while being regulated by the local guild. But at the same time he was not a court artist. He travelled to Cologne in 1688 to be employed by the newly-appointed Archbishop-Elector of Cologne, Joseph Clement (1671-1723), the brother of the Elector Maximilian II Emmanuel (1662-1726). Joseph Clement's youth (he was only seventeen years old) suggests that it was the elector who sent Faistenberger to Cologne to serve his younger brother. Faistenberger had returned to Munich by 1691, when he purchased a house in the city, though from 1688 onwards he signed himself as '*churcölnischer Hofbildhauer*' (court sculptor to the Prince of Cologne).

Faistenberger undertook commissions in the south of Bavaria and in the Tyrol, as well as in Munich itself. His most important (partially) surviving work is the high altarpiece made for the Bürgersaal in Munich, the meeting place of the Marian congregation, a building constructed in 1710 and consecrated in 1778. The altarpiece incorporated a large silvered and gilt wood relief of *The Annunciation* [4.3] of 1710-11; the other elements from the rest of the altarpiece were lost in the Second World War.[7] The imposing figure of the announcing angel, with massive outspread wings, as well as the demure kneeling figure of the Virgin, parallel Venetian prototypes. In particular, the elaborate lectern upon which the Virgin rests her devotional book, as well as the

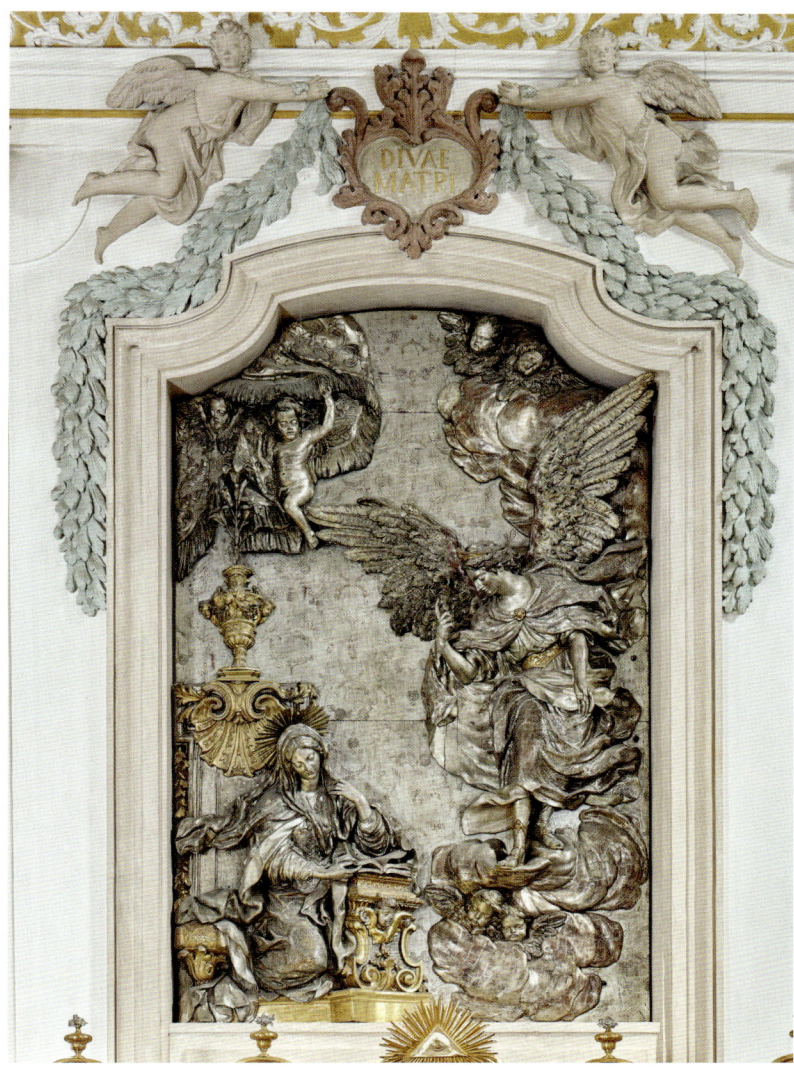

chair and urn behind her, are redolent of North Italian decorative motifs, recalling the work of the wood sculptor Andrea Brustolon (1662-1732), for example.[8] The sweep of the composition and flowing drapery are akin, too, to Italian baroque prototypes, such as the sculpture of Cosimo Fancelli (c. 1620-88) or Ercole Ferrata (1610-86) in Rome.[9]

Egid Quirin Asam (1692-1750)

As noted above, Egid Quirin Asam's sculpture cannot be easily divorced from his brother Cosmas Damian's activity as a painter and architect. The brothers were from a family of artists, and their early training was with their father, the painter Hans Georg Asam (1649-1711), and perhaps their mother, Maria Theresia Prugger, who was also a painter and daughter of the court painter Nikolaus Prugger (c. 1620-94).[10] Egid Quirin himself must have been an

4.3
Andreas Faistenberger,
The Annunciation,
silvered and gilt wood,
1710-11. Burgher's Hall
(Bürgersaal), Munich.

>> 4.4
Egid Quirin Asam,
*The Assumption of
the Virgin*, painted and
gilt stucco, 1717/23.
Benedictine Abbey
of Rohr, Bavaria.

>> 4.5
Detail of Asam,
Assumption of the Virgin
[4.4], the Virgin.

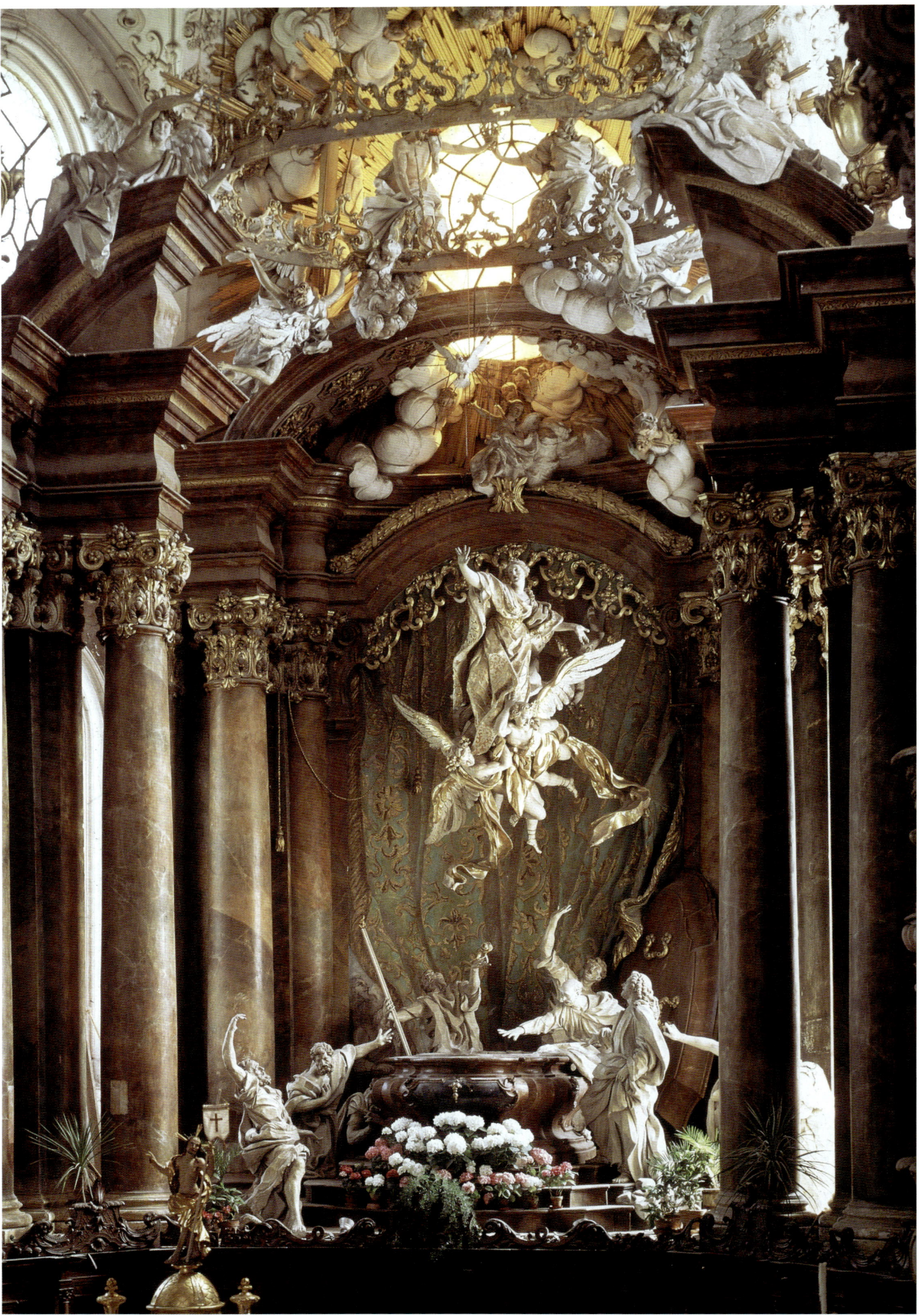

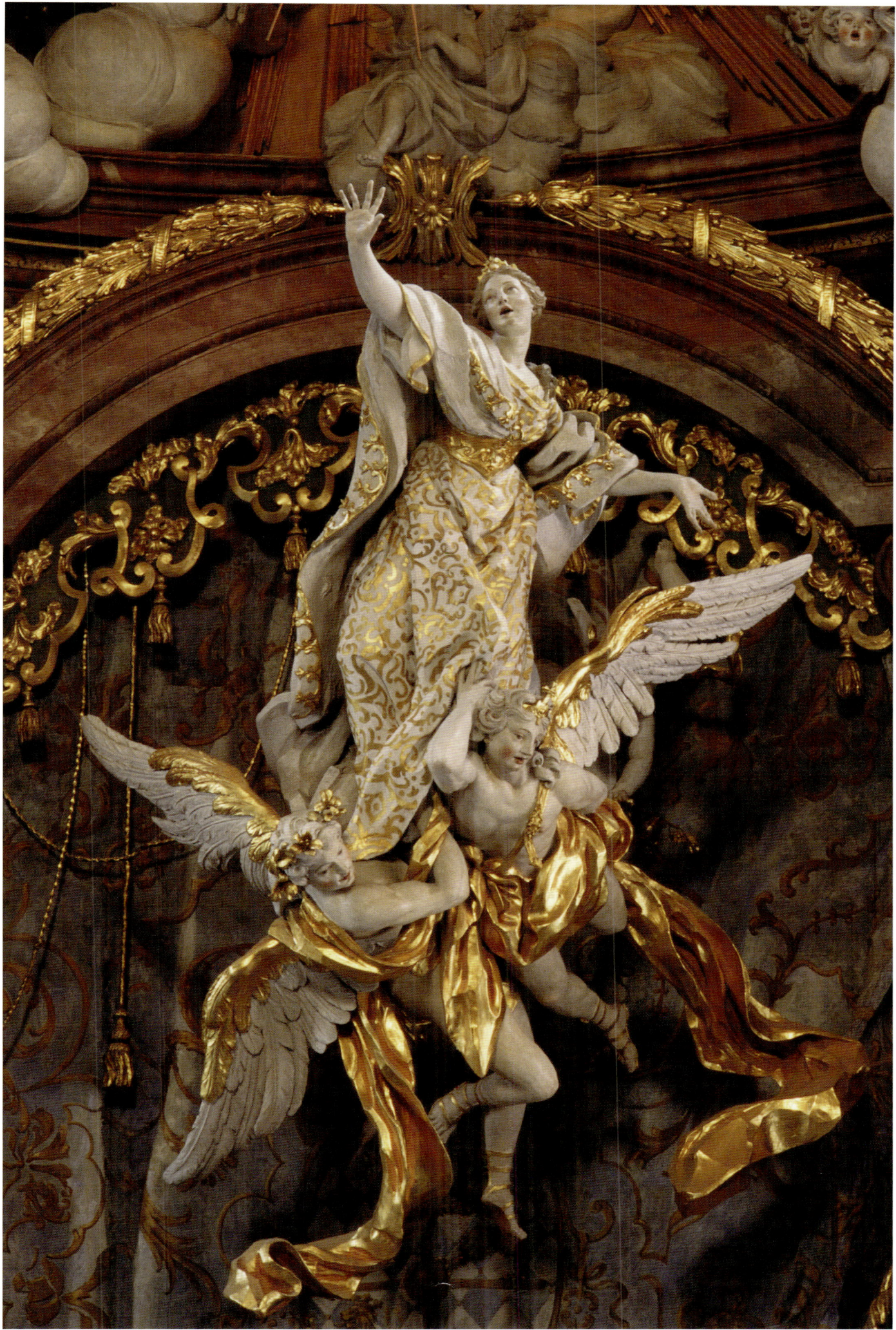

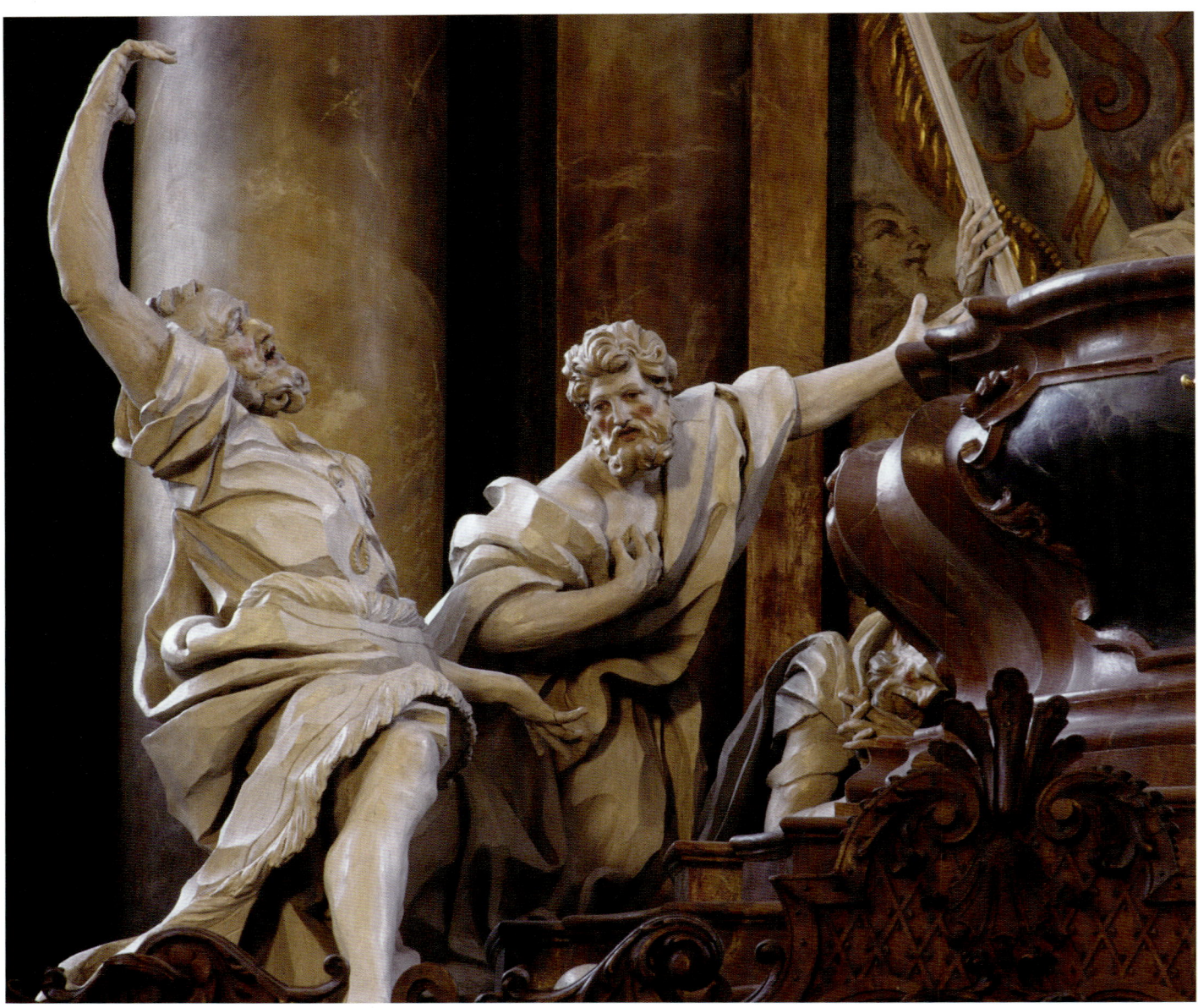

architectural designer, though the brothers commissioned the architect Johann Michael Fischer (1692-1766) to build their own church, the Asamkirche in Munich, in 1733 [4.1]. Almost all of Egid Quirin's work is in stucco, even though he had trained with Faistenberger, a wood sculptor, from 1713 to 1716. Cosmas Damian was in Rome from around 1711 to 1713; Egid Quirin's awareness of Roman baroque architecture and sculpture suggests that he may have spent time with his brother in Italy before training with Faistenberger in Munich, although no journey south of the Alps is documented for him. In 1724 he was appointed *Kammerdiener* (valet, a term used for court artist) and court stuccoist to the Prince-Bishop of Freising, Johann Franz Eckher von Kapfing und Liechteneck

(1696-1727), and in 1730 he became *Kammerdiener* at the Bavarian court.

Most of the Asams' work was for churches, whether freshly designed eighteenth-century buildings, built on the site of earlier foundations, such as those at Rohr and Weltenburg, or medieval churches given new interior decoration in the eighteenth century, such as those at Einsiedeln, Freising Cathedral and St Peter's church in Munich. Many churches in Bavaria were rebuilt or renovated in the first half of the eighteenth century, in order to repair the damage caused by the ravages of the Thirty Years' War in the previous century. But there was also an aesthetic desire to enhance and decorate ecclesiastical buildings in a contemporary mode. These so-called 'baroquised' interiors were set within earlier architectural edifices (usually medieval), but the walls and vaults of the spaces were adorned, or 're-clothed'—dressed up—with lavish eighteenth-century coloured stucco and fresco decorations.[11] The technique of stucco decoration will be discussed below.

The Asams were not the only artists who undertook this revivification of church interiors; the Zimmermanns also did so. But the Asam brothers stand apart from their contemporaries because of the overtly theatrical style of their sculpture and painting, using an idiom stemming from the Roman baroque. Moreover, Egid Quirin did not seem to directly disseminate a tradition that would be carried on after his death. Apparently he had no followers or pupils, though he certainly benefited from the help of workshop assistants on his ambitious sculpture commissions. Cosmas Damian conversely did have pupils, and his son Franz Erasmus (1720-95) became a painter. His best-known assistants were the painters Christoph Thomas Scheffler (1699-1756) and Matthäus Günther (1705-88). But his true disciple was Johann Baptist Zimmermann (1680-1758), to be discussed below.

Three newly-built churches, rather than baroquised churches, will be briefly examined here because they demonstrate most vividly the Asams' distinctive style: the churches at Rohr and Weltenburg, and the so-called Asamkirche in Munich. Egid Quirin's work as a sculptor will be the focus of discussion; Cosmas Damian's frescoes complemented his brother's stucco figures, but his paintings will not be explored in any detail. Although they were not professional architects, the Asam brothers planned the installation and context of their work within each church interior with serious deliberation in such a way as to instil a sense of wonder in the observer, creating an extraordinary atmosphere. In order to achieve such effects, they ensured their works were illuminated dramatically through strategic placing of both sculptures and windows, thereby directing the natural light and enhancing the sculptures' illusionism, whilst carefully stage-managing the viewpoints of their respective sculptures and paintings within the spaces.[12]

Egid Quirin's architectural presence can be clearly felt in the Augustinian church at Rohr (1717-25).[13] The church was designed by the architect Josef Bader (active 1695-d. 1721), but the setting and lighting of Egid Quirin's sculpture are more memorable than the building in which it is placed. The group, depicting *The Assumption of the Virgin*, of 1717/23, is at the east end, in front of the choir, lit from a lunette above [**4.4, 4.5 and 4.6**]. In the centre stands the heavy sarcophagus, raised on three steps, its lid removed, now empty of the Virgin's body, surrounded by the Apostles, wearing classical togas, though they have non-classical hairstyles. Each man is individually rendered, his face and the sweeping gestures revealing his wonderment at the miracle of the ascension of the Virgin. Their interactions indeed seem to be somewhat analogous to those of the Apostles depicted in Leonardo da Vinci's *Last Supper* in Milan of the late fifteenth century, although it is unlikely Asam was consciously quoting from that fresco.[14] Some of the Apostles look into the tomb in disbelief, some at each other, and some towards the ascending figure of the Virgin dressed in gold and white finery, a youthful beautiful figure, her arms open wide in an equally emphatic gesture. She appears to hover unsupported in the air, borne aloft by winged angels, who themselves seem to be levitating above the figures below with no visible support. They rise towards heavenly clouds and cherubim. Behind is a swathe of gilt-fringed drapery in blue and gold, forming a magnificent backdrop to the scene depicted. The over-life-size group is of stucco, the figures of the Apostles painted white, with touches of colour on their eyes, lips and cheeks, while the Virgin and angels are likewise painted white, with some polychromy highlighting their facial features, the Virgin's robe and tips of the angels' wings partly gilt, and the Virgin's falling rippling sash of gold. The group is visible from a distance as the central point as the viewer looks down the nave from the west end of the church. As will also be seen in Egid Quirin Asam's other major work, *St George* at Weltenburg, this installation was clearly planned for maximum dramatic impact. The visitor walks through the church towards the triumphant epitome of the *Assumption of the Virgin*. The

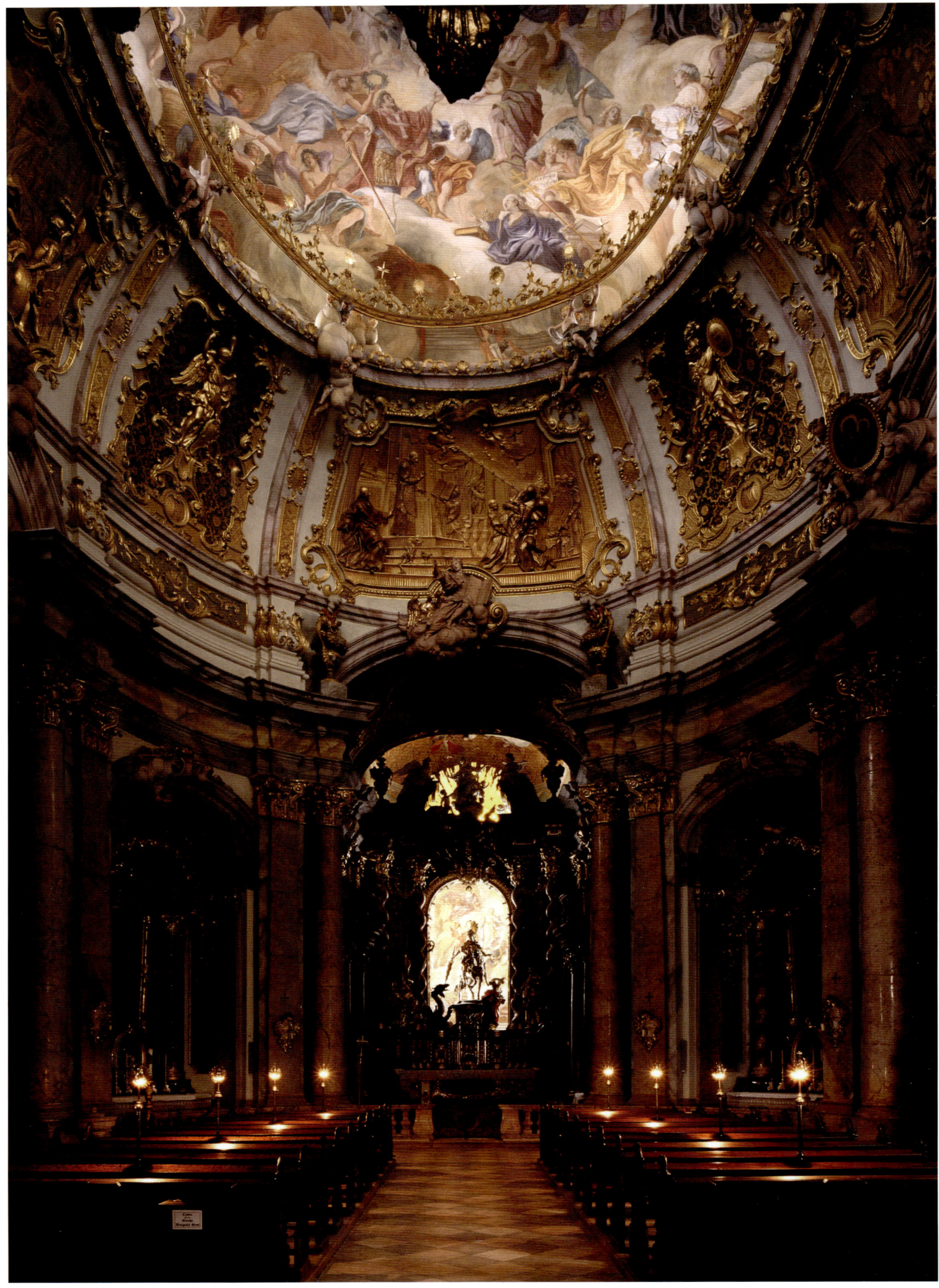

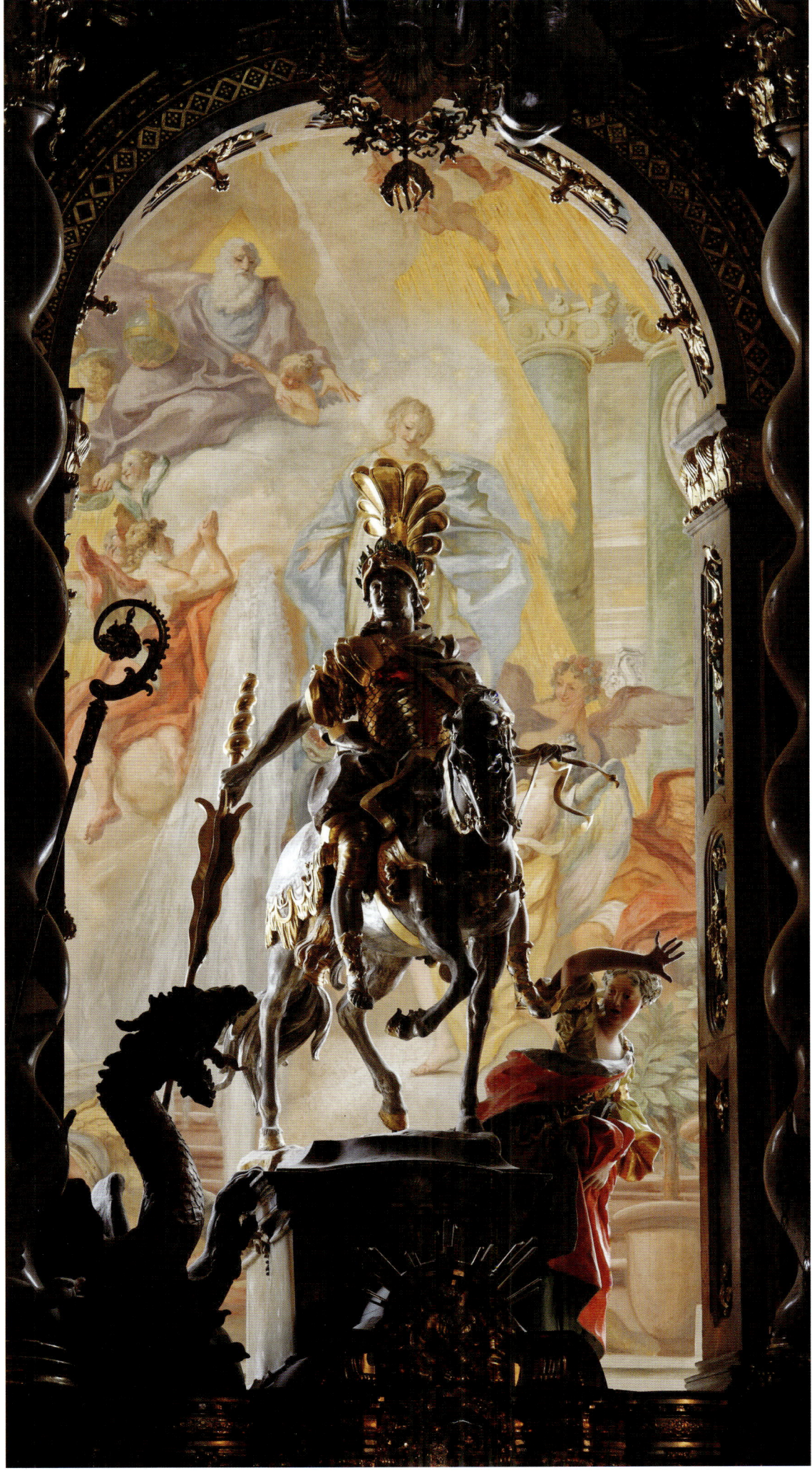

< 4.7
Egid Quirin Asam,
*St George and the
Dragon*, painted and gilt
stucco *in situ*, 1734-6.
Benedictine Abbey of
Weltenburg, Bavaria.

4.8
Egid Quirin Asam,
*St George and the
Dragon* [closer view
of 4.7].

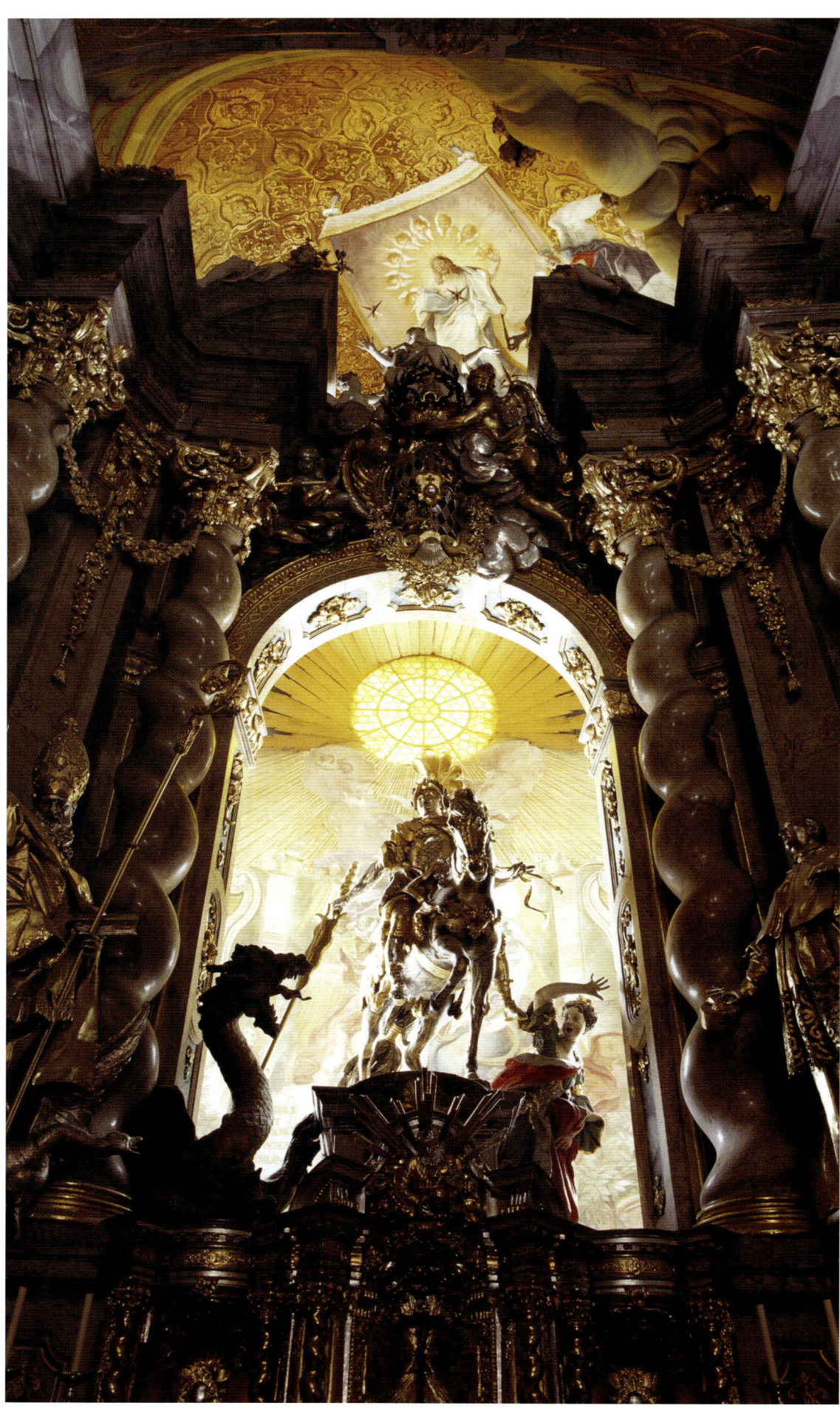

4.9
Egid Quirin Asam,
St George and the
Dragon with St Martin
and St Maurus [closer
view of 4.7].

directed lighting of the space must surely be indebted to Bernini, seen for example in his *St Teresa* in the Cornaro Chapel in S. Maria della Vittoria in Rome of 1647-52.[15] But the Asam brothers translated that Italian baroque source into a new Bavarian context. The English commentator John Bourke remarked of the *Assumption* group in the 1950s, 'The whole composition is beyond description and almost beyond praise.'[16]

Just as Egid Quirin's *Assumption of the Virgin* at Rohr forms the climax of the church at Rohr, so in the church dedicated to St George and St Martin at the Benedictine Abbey of Weltenburg does his group of *St George and the Dragon and Princess* provide the focal point within that interior [**4.7, 4.8 and 4.9**]. The church is placed high up atop an eminence above the river Danube, serving as a place of pilgrimage, both then and now. The viewer entering the church from the west end is immediately struck by the silhouetted figures under what is effectively a triumphal arch, set against the light pouring in from the window at the east end. The church was built from 1713 onwards, at the behest of the abbot Maurus

Bächl (1668-1749; r. 1713-43), the master mason/ architect being Franz Beer von Bleichten (1660-1726), based on plans by the architect Philipp Blank (d. 1720).[17] Abbot Maurus II Kammermaier (r. 1744-77), abbot Maurus Bächl's successor, helped lead the work to completion, the sculptures being undertaken by Egid Quirin from 1721 onwards. Egid Quirin's older sister Maria Salome Bornschlögl Asam (1685-1740) apparently collaborated with him.[18] Cosmas Damian was commissioned to carry out the painting of the dome and the east end of the church, assisted by his son, Franz Erasmus, who was to finish the work after his father's death. As at Rohr, the lighting is carefully controlled, daylight entering the church mainly from the windows around the central double cupola, and from the east end, behind the group of St George. The window over the door at the west end admits a limited amount of light, but essentially the visitor is drawn into the main body of the church by the illumination emanating from the central dome and from the east end. As the viewer passes under the great oval cupola, reminiscent of the Pantheon in Rome, the highly naturalistic smiling stucco figure of

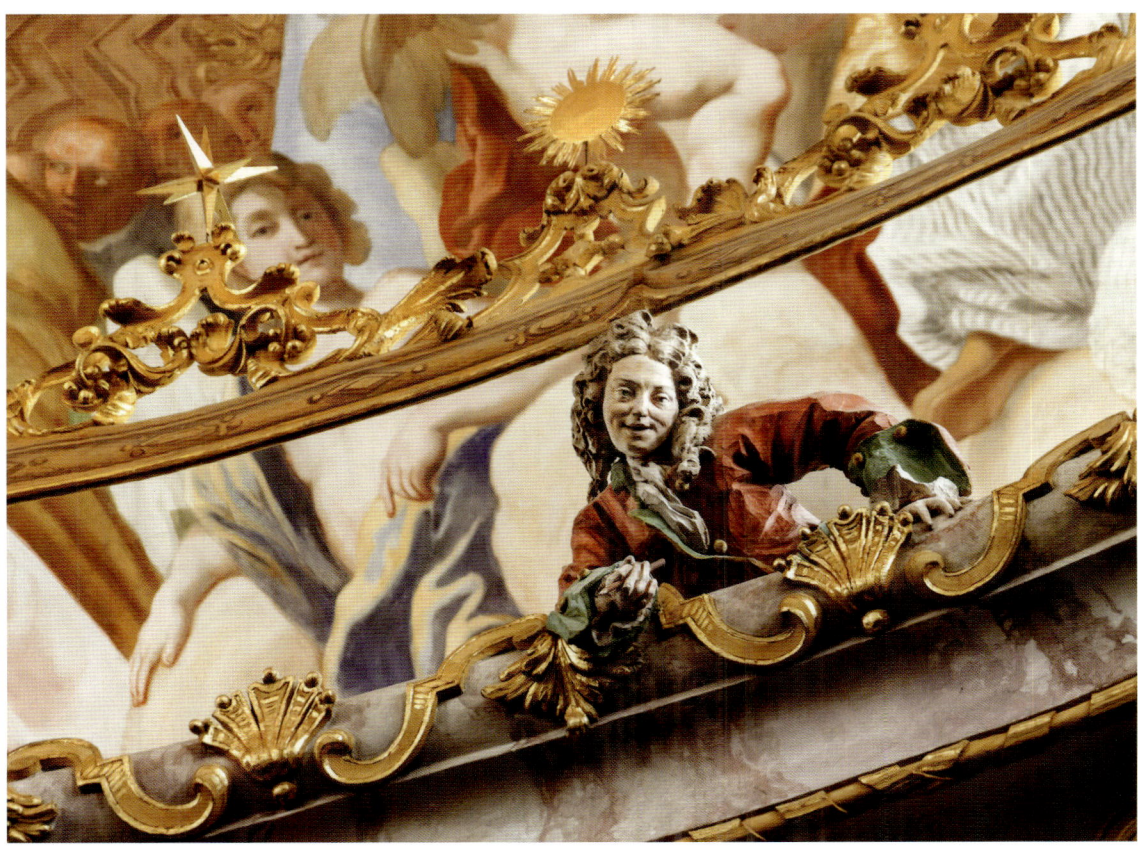

4.10
Egid Quirin Asam, *Portrait of Cosmas Damian Asam*, painted stucco, c. 1736. Benedictine Abbey of Weltenburg, Bavaria.

Cosmas Damian can be seen above, leaning over the balcony, apparently watching and welcoming those who enter below [4.10]. This lifelike figure was executed by his brother, Egid Quirin, and is placed in front of Cosmas Damian's own radiant fresco painting of *The Coronation of the Virgin and the Last Judgement* above. Other stucco reliefs and paintings adorn the walls, but the climax of the church is the *St George*.

As already mentioned, the group of *St George* was placed on the high altar at the far end of the church, clearly and overpoweringly visible from the west door, silhouetted against the light. The equestrian figure of the saint thrusts his flaming lance at the rearing dragon, the princess in swirling drapery recoiling in fear and shock, her upraised arm and expressive face not unlike the gestures of the astonished Apostles at Rohr. St George, as a Roman-Christian hero, wears a plumed helmet and classical armour; he and his finely caparisoned horse recall secular memorials to rulers, such as

Andreas Schlüter's monument to the Great Elector in Berlin of a generation before [**2.29**, **2.30** and **2.31**]. Egid Quirin's work is of stucco, though the finish of the saint's glittering armour suggests bronze, and the surface of his white steed evokes marble. This skilful illusionism epitomizes Egid Quirin's remarkable ability to imitate and recreate more solid and costly materials in plaster. Behind this monumental group is the fresco on the wall of the apse, executed by Cosmas Damian, depicting the Virgin of the Immaculate Conception crushing the serpent, with God the Father above, harmonising with the theme of the sculptures: good vanquishing evil. Above, on the triumphal arch of the altar, is the coat of arms of the Elector Maximilian II Emmanuel. The elector visited Weltenberg in 1721, at a time when he was attempting to reinstate the Wittelsbach Order of the Knights of St George, an aim eventually achieved by his son Charles Albert (1697-1745) in 1729.[19] In this way the chivalric subject of St

4.11
Egid Quirin Asam, *St Jerome*, painted stucco, c. 1735-40. Church of St John Nepomuk (known as the Asamkirche), Munich, entrance lobby.

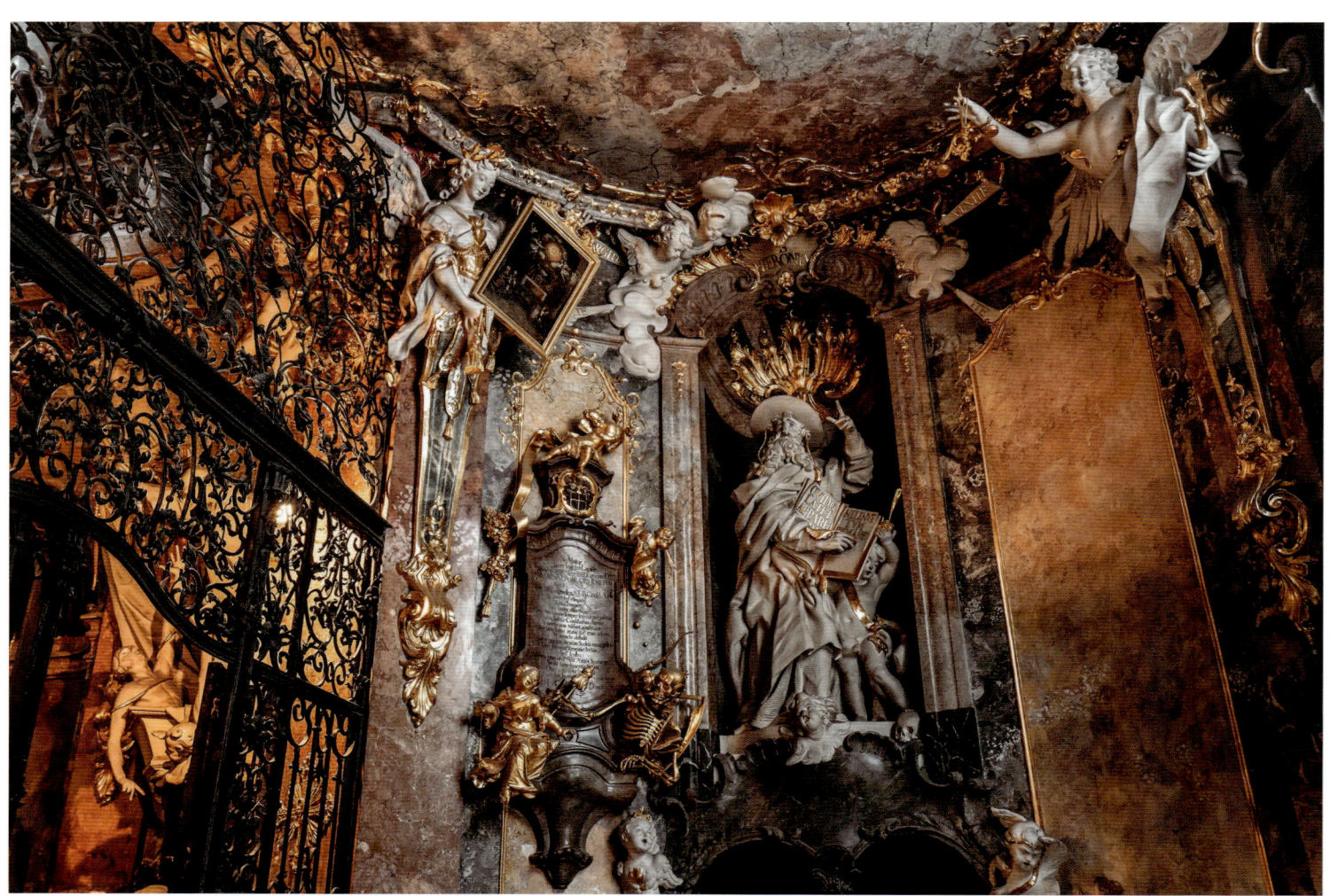

George evoked the contemporary aspirations of the secular ruler of Bavaria. The religious meaning of the whole, however, still predominates. High above the altar is Egid Quirin's stucco group of the Virgin and Child with angels, while below, flanking the *St George* group, are over-life-size figures of St Martin and St Maurus, painted white, with some polychromy highlighting their facial features. They are framed by gigantic barley-twist solomonic columns echoing those on Bernini's baldacchino in St Peter's Basilica in Rome [4.9].[20] The figure of St Martin, the other patron saint of the church, forcefully arrests the spectator, with his commanding outstretched arm, a honking goose at his side, and a putto hiding beneath his windswept robes. The effect of the whole interior, with its spectacular sculptures and paintings, is indeed a *theatrum sacrum*.

The Asams' own church, known as the Asamkirche in Munich, was an entirely new build. It is a chapel-of-ease in the parish of St Peter in Munich, dedicated to St John Nepomuk, constructed from 1733 to 1746.[21] Egid Quirin had bought three adjoining houses in a street in the centre of the city from 1729 to 1733. One provided accommodation for him (he was unmarried), as well as a workshop; one became a residence for priests, while the third was demolished so that the church, designed by the architect Johann Michael Fischer, could be erected in its stead [4.1]. Its restricted site means that it is excessively tall and narrow: 28 metres long, 19 metres high, and only 9 metres wide. These exceptional proportions inevitably affect the way in which the visitor perceives the sculptures, church furniture and frescoes. Unlike the churches at Rohr and Weltenburg, where Egid Quirin's two sculptural groups dominate and dictate our responses to the spaces, here the church truly is a total work of art: paintings, stucco and furniture complement, and at the same time merge with, the architecture. As at Weltenburg, the Asam church had strong connections to the Munich court: the Bavarian coat of arms with the imperial eagle were mounted on the organ in 1742, two days after the former Elector Charles Albert had been crowned Holy Roman Emperor, while in 1745,

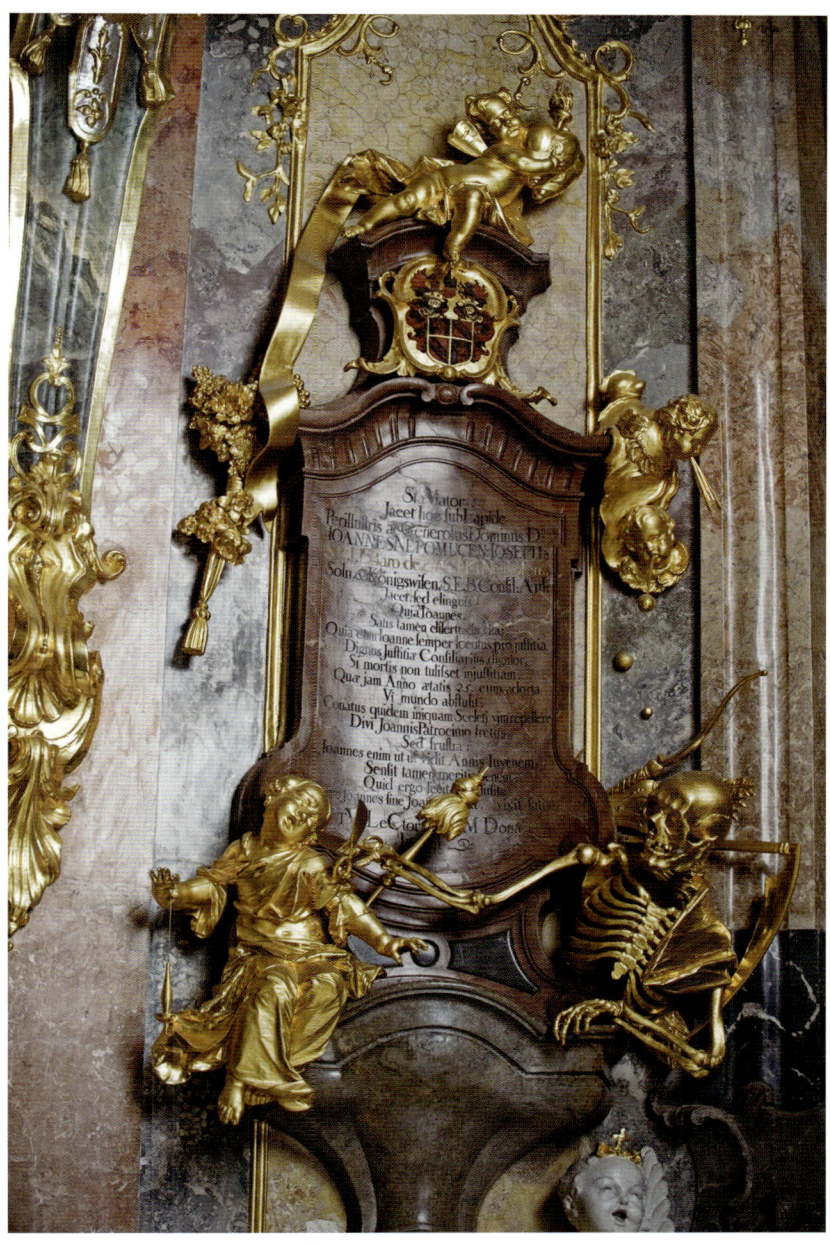

after his death, his wife, the Electress Maria Amalia (1701-57), donated the relics of St Victor to the church.[22]

The frontage of the Asamkirche is remarkable in itself. The majestic giant pilasters on the façade seem to grow out of the two clusters of boulders placed on either side of the entrance, both features (the pilasters and the boulders) seemingly at odds with the busy urban street. A stucco figure of St John Nepomuk and two angels kneel on clouds above the main door, indicating to whom the church is dedicated. The visitor enters the body of the church from the oval vestibule, or antechamber, itself elaborately adorned, furnished with two confessionals of dark wood. Egid Quirin's figures of St Jerome

4.12
Ignaz Günther, *Epitaph to Johann Nepomuk Joseph Freiherr von Zech*, gilt wood and stone, c. 1758. Entrance Lobby of the church of St John Nepomuk (known as the Asamkirche), Munich.

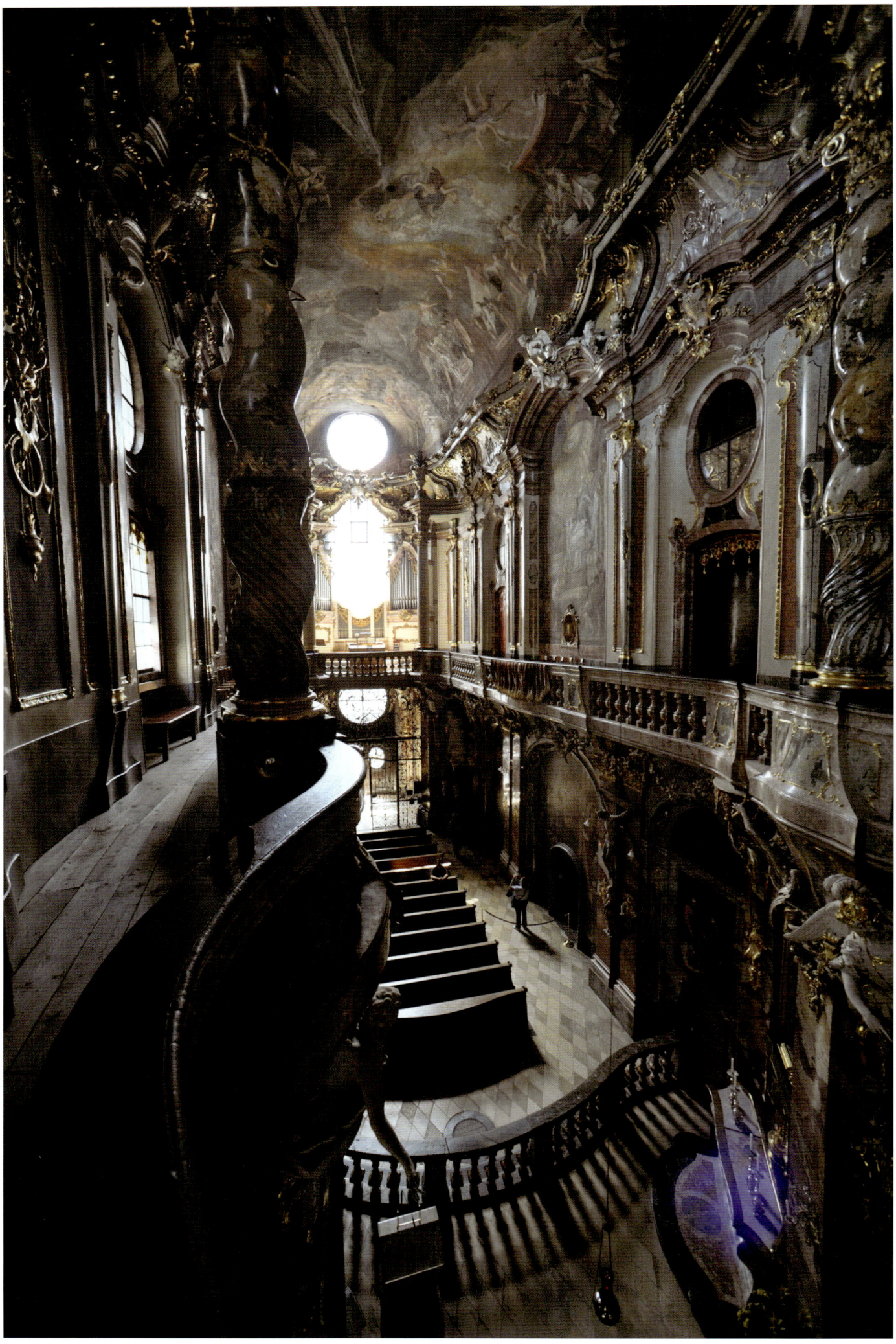

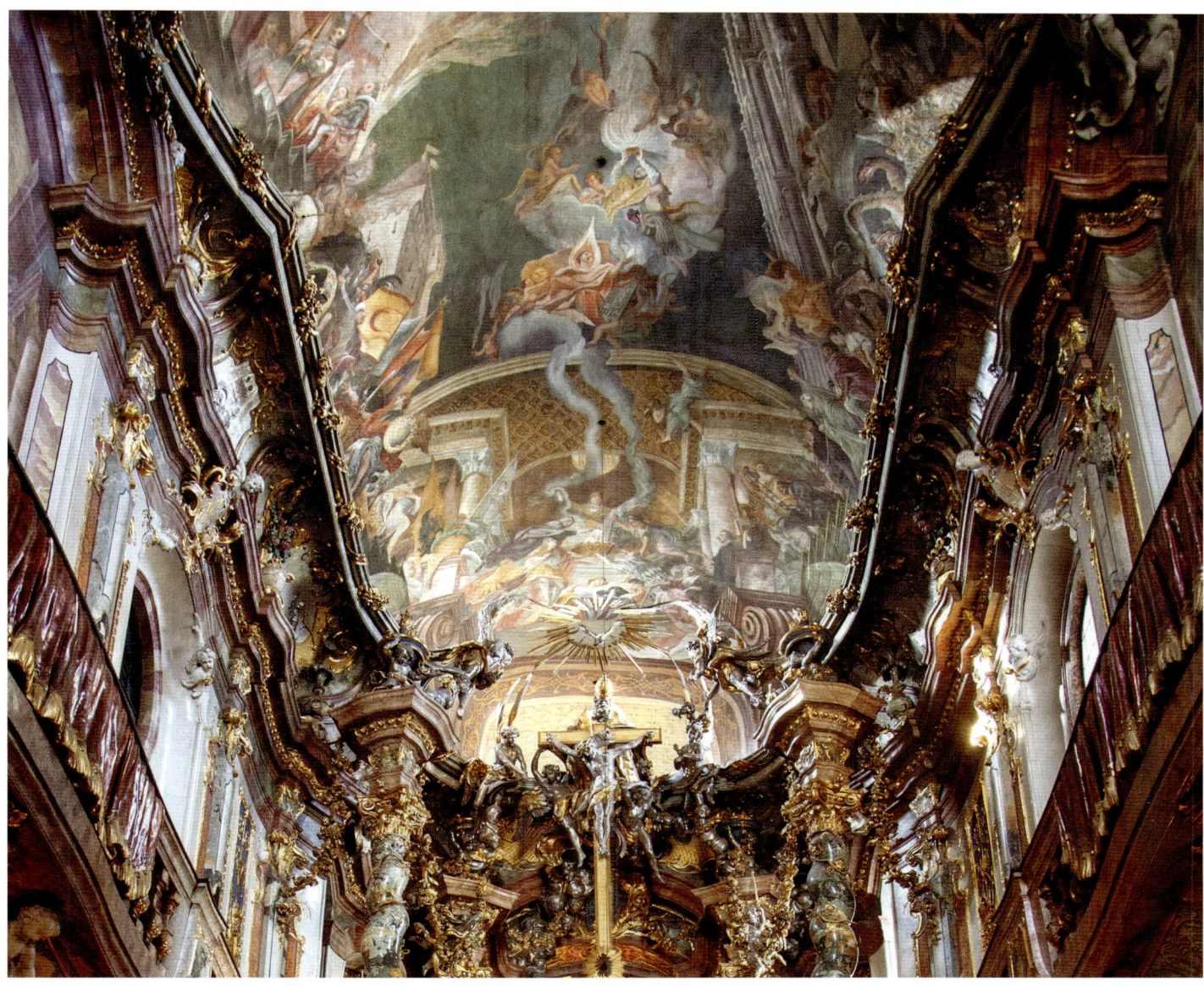

and St Peter (patron of the parish), both of white stucco with gilt highlights, stand over each one [**4.11**]. They were installed there to admonish visitors to beware the imminence of death and judgement, and to encourage the act of confession, hence the presence of the confessionals. The tomb on the wall of the antechamber by Ignaz Günther (1725-75), was installed somewhat later, in around 1758, commemorating the premature death of Johann Nepomuk Joseph Baron von Zech (1732-57).[23] Its figures of Atropos and Death underline the grim theme of mortality [**4.12**] . Günther's oeuvre is to be discussed more fully in Chapter 5.

The nave of the church is enveloped in a lush medley of decorative motifs: twisted solomonic columns, balconies draped with faux stucco hangings, stucco angels and garlands, imposing ironwork gates, a grand organ gallery at the west end, and two further confessionals with stucco figures above them [**4.13**]. The theme throughout is penance, a reminder that sinners must face the day of judgement, signifying the Asam brothers' devout personal piety. Cosmas Damian's illusionistic fresco in the vault depicts scenes from the life of the patron saint, St John Nepomuk. Above the soaring high altar is Egid Quirin's gilt and silvered stucco group of the Trinity, or Throne of Mercy, God the Father holding Christ on the crucifix beneath the holy spirit, surrounded by swooping angels [**4.14**]. The sculpture forms the culmination of the whole ensemble, and would have been seen by Egid Quirin himself as he looked down from an internal window specially inserted into his own adjoining house, so that he could gaze into the nave, a sign of his own profound spirituality.

< 4.13
Johann Michael Fischer (architect), Interior of the church of St John Nepomuk (known as the Asamkirche), Munich, 1733-46. View towards the west end.

4.14
East end of the church of St John Nepomuk (known as the Asamkirche), Munich showing Egid Quirin Asam's *The Trinity or Throne of Mercy*, gilt and silvered stucco, c. 1735-40.

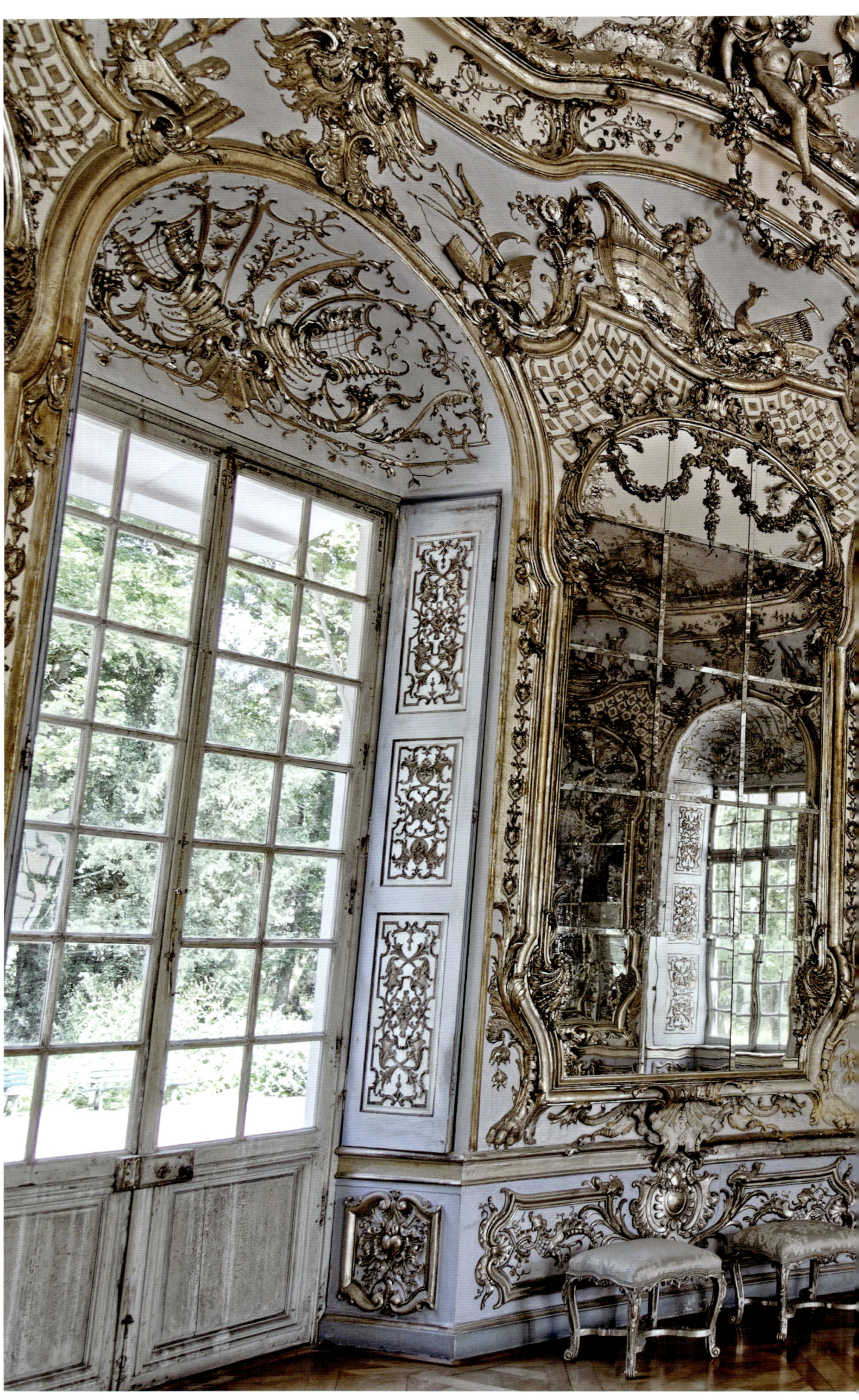

4.15
François de Cuvilliés the Elder and Johann Baptist Zimmermann, interior decoration of the Amalienburg, coloured stucco, 1734-9. Park at Nymphenburg, near Munich.

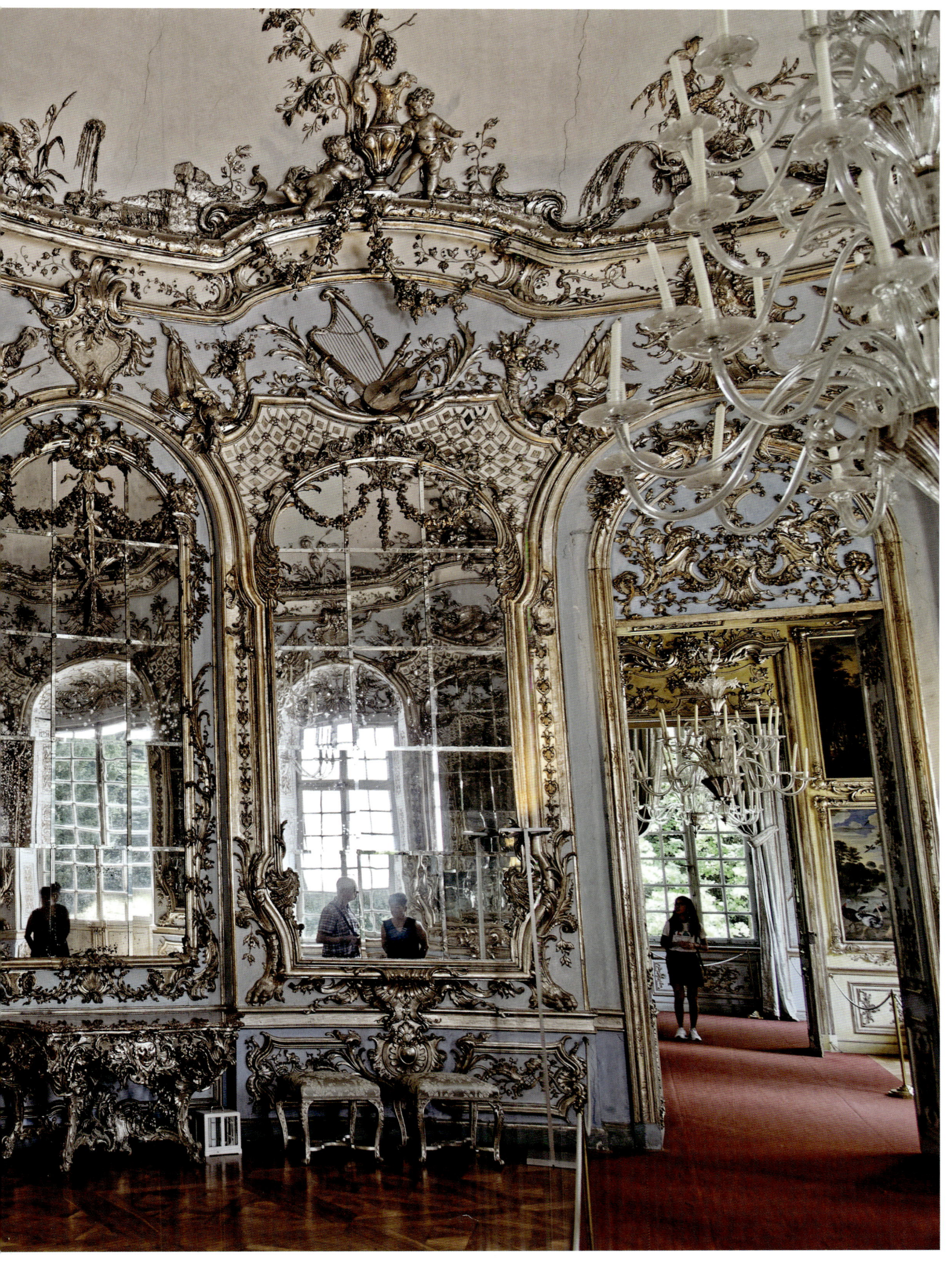

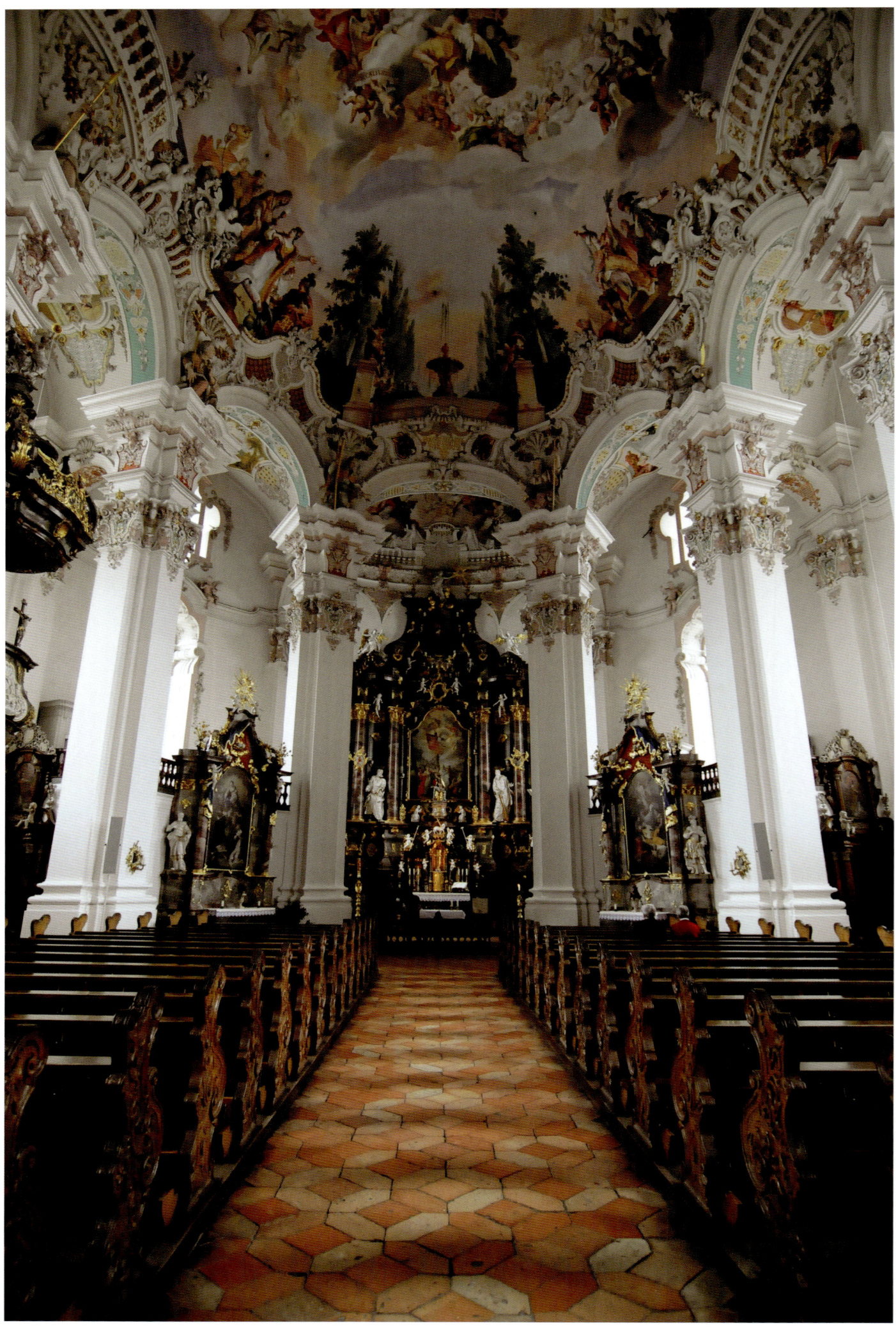

Dominikus Zimmermann (1685-1766) and Johann Baptist Zimmermann (1680-1758)

More or less contemporary with the Asam brothers, Dominikus and his brother Johann Baptist Zimmermann also worked in stucco, and additionally practised as architects. Johann Baptist was also a fresco painter, like Cosmas Damian Asam. The sons of Elias Zimmermann (1656-95), a stuccoist and stonemason from Wessobrunn, the Zimmermann brothers almost certainly trained as stuccoists in Wessobrunn, the great centre of stucco-working from the sixteenth to the eighteenth century. Dominikus undertook much work for the church, while Johann Baptist's activity was centred on the Bavarian court. Johann Baptist was appointed court stuccoist to Charles Albert, Elector of Bavaria, in around 1727, and worked with the architect Franois de Cuvilliés the Elder (1695-1768) on the stucco decorations for the *Reiche Zimmer* (the 'Rich Rooms') at the Munich Residenz (1733-7) and at Amalienburg in the park at Nymphenburg, just outside Munich (1734-9) [**4.15**].

The Zimmermann brothers worked as architects and stuccoists on two important pilgrimage churches, that at Steinhausen an der Rottum (1727-33), an independent territory in Upper Swabia (Southwest Bavaria, today part of Baden-Württemberg), and at Die Wies, Steingaden (1744-57) in Lower Bavaria. These two churches are considered to be their greatest masterpieces. Johann Baptist also undertook the fresco painting at both churches.

The church at Steinhausen, some 30 miles southwest of Ulm, was commissioned from Dominikus Zimmermann as architect in 1727 [**4.16 and 4.17**].[24] The church was newly built, and the ground plan, with a central oval rotunda, reflects Italian prototypes, such as the sixteenth-century church of the Gesù in Rome. Meanwhile the central fresco recalls Andrea Pozzo's dome painting in the Jesuit church in Vienna of 1703.[25] But in the church at Steinhausen the pastel polychromy of the architecture and stucco, fully illuminated by the daylight pouring in through multiple windows, are unmistakably South German baroque. Unlike the churches by the Asam brothers at Rohr and Weltenburg,

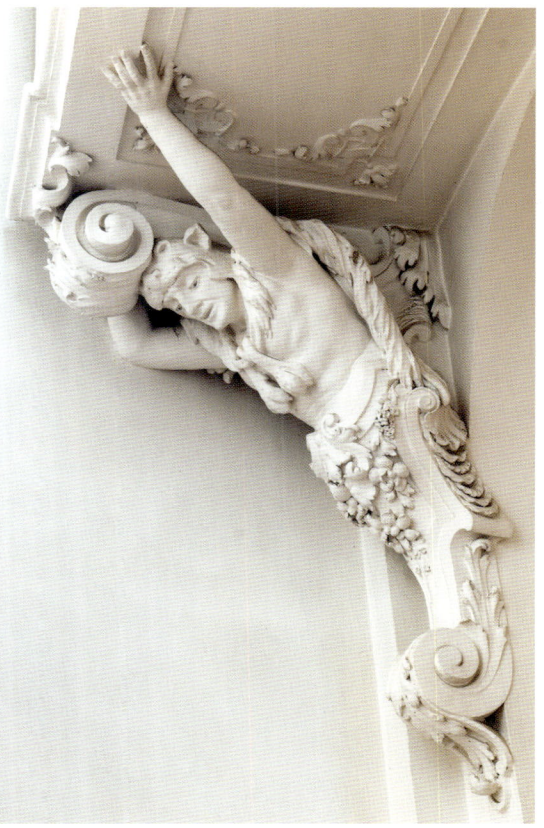

< 4.16
Dominikus and Johann Baptist Zimmermann, Interior view of the pilgrimage church of St Peter and St Paul (dedicated also to the Virgin of Sorrows), 1727-33, Steinhausen, Bavaria.

4.18
Dominikus Zimmermann, Herm under the organ loft, stucco, c. 1730-33. Church of St Peter and St Paul, Steinhausen, Bavaria.

dating from only a few years earlier, the stucco ornament at Steinhausen cannot be divorced from the architecture and frescoes; they integrally complement each other. The overall effect of the interior is not a dramatic climax at the east end: there is no theatrical placing of sculpture under directed light; we sense instead a harmonious unity of colour and forms, giving an aura of palatial grandeur.

The technique of stucco decoration to be seen at Steinhausen, and indeed elsewhere in Bavaria, was originally perfected by North Italian craftsmen such as Diego Francesco Carlone (1674-1750) and imported into Southern Germany during the eighteenth century. Numerous assistants were employed to produce these elaborate and technically demanding works. Stucco generally consists of plaster, lime and sand, mixed with water. Limewash was added to make it more malleable, and to delay hardening, while oil was added to soften the mixture.[26] The wall on which the stucco decoration was to be applied had to be prepared with two layers: the first (0.3 to 3 cm thick) consisted of sand, lime, plaster and charcoal. The second, thinner layer (0.1 to 0.6 cm thick) was composed of lime,

>> 4.17
Dominikus and Johann Baptist Zimmermann, *The Assumption of the Virgin* (detail), fresco and stucco, dated 1731. Church of St Peter and St Paul, Steinhausen, Bavaria.

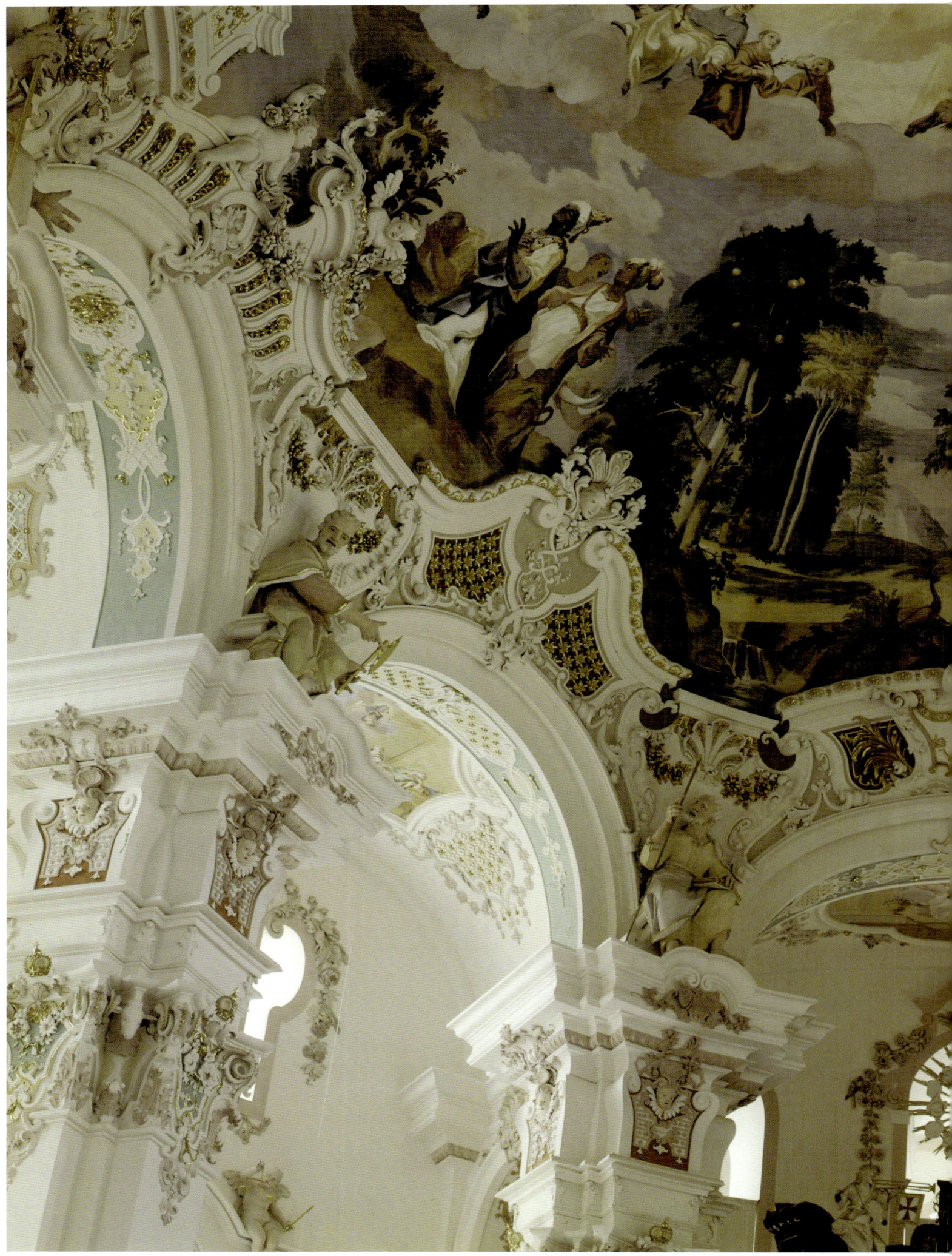

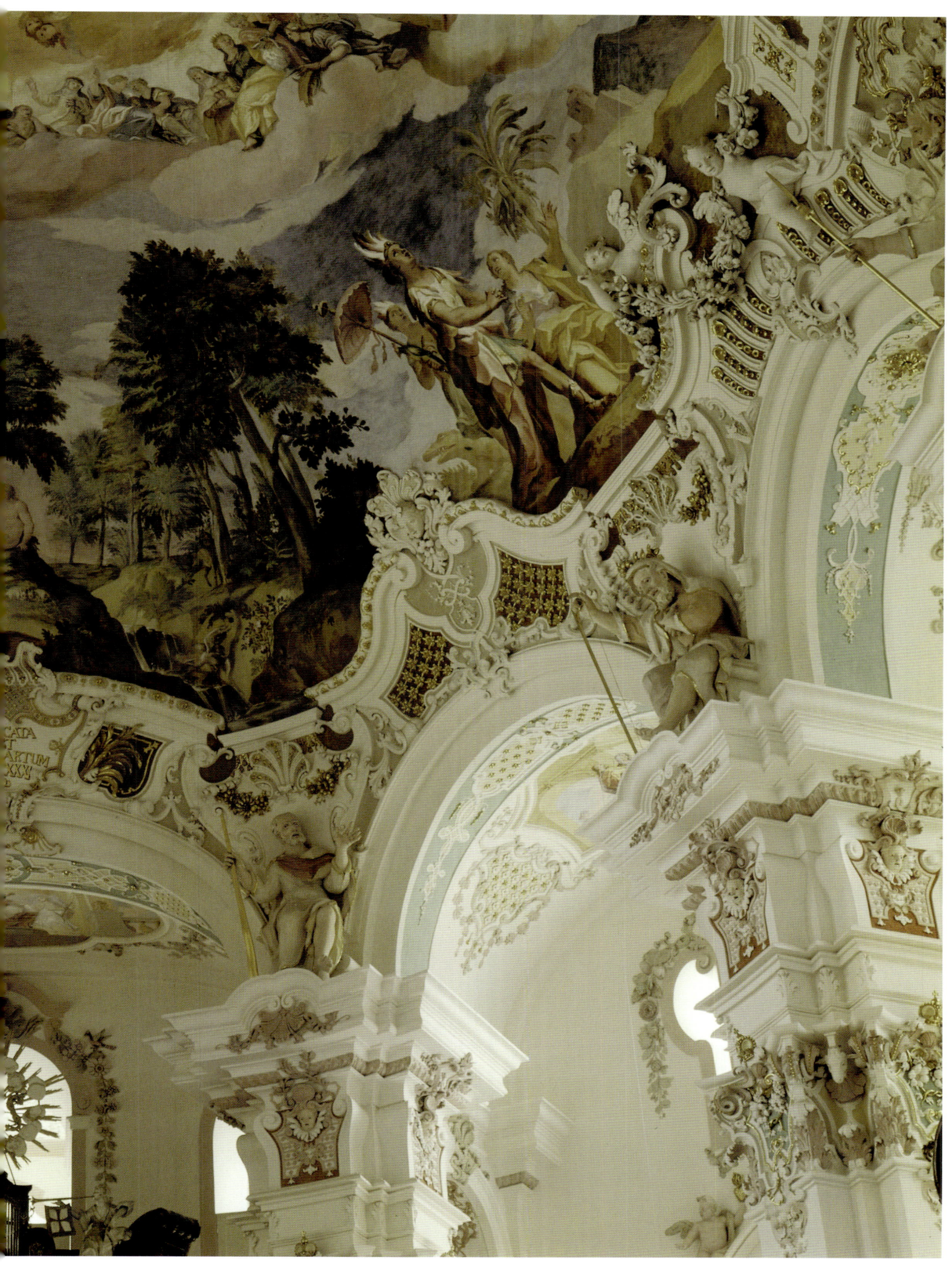

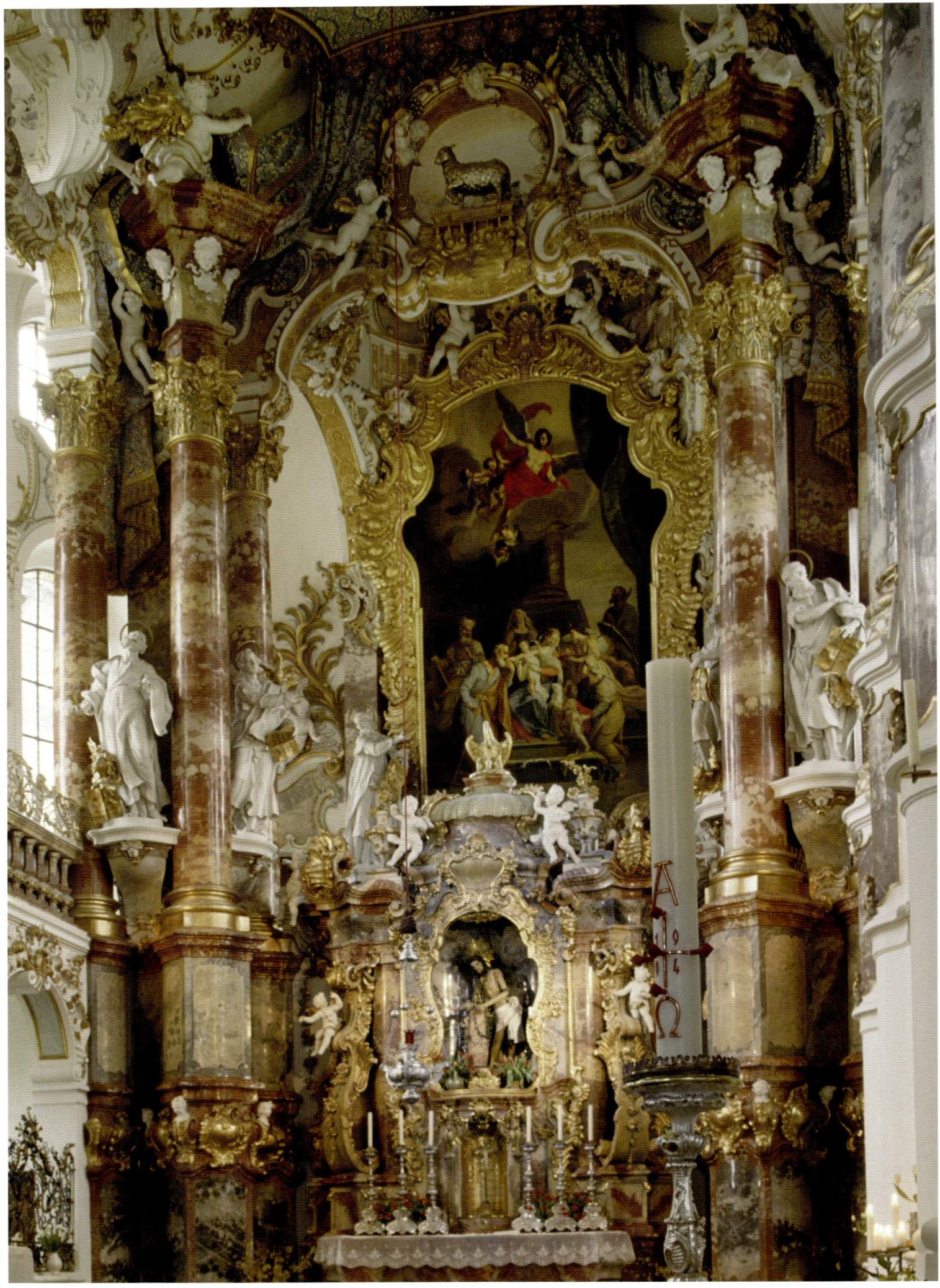

stone dust and plaster. A preliminary drawing in charcoal or red chalk would be outlined on the wall, giving the patron a last chance to request any changes in the design. Any architectural elements, such as cornices, would be put in place before decorative features. These would be supported by timbers as they were being affixed to the wall. Moulds might be used for repeated designs, such as putti. Details, such as heads, hands or feet, could be modelled or carved freehand in the stucco, using wood or metal tools, once the forms had been released from the moulds. This was often done on a work bench, before these elements were mounted on the wall. Metal armatures bolstered larger components, while wood and even reed supports were also sometimes used to strengthen smaller sections of the plaster. The stucco would then be painted.

The painting on the central dome at Steinhausen depicts the glory of the Virgin ascending to heaven, the painted imagery alluding to her immaculate conception (the fountain, the enclosed garden, or *hortus conclusus*), and at the same time suggesting the earthly beauty of landscape and natural forms [**4.17**]. Around the fresco, stucco putti cavort amongst elegant garden urns, draped in garlands. Below these figures are stucco saints, seated atop the columns. This painted composition of *The Assumption of the Virgin* dramatically contrasts with Egid Quirin Asam's earlier baroque group at Rohr [**4.4**]. The interior at Steinhausen looks forward instead to the rococo, echoing the art of the French court at Versailles.

The idea of illusionism evident in Egid Quirin Asam's work at Rohr can, however, be sensed in Dominikus Zimmermann's stucco work at Steinhausen, though Zimmermann's sculpture has an entirely different complexion. One of the stucco herms under the organ loft at Steinhausen has been published (surely incorrectly) as a stucco portrait of his brother Johann Baptist [**4.18**].[27] Its appearance is in striking contrast with Egid Quirin's mimetic portrayal of his brother Cosmas Damian in contemporary costume at Weltenburg [**4.10**]. Both figures are playful and illusionistic, but visually distinct. Zimmermann's figures are atlantes, half-figures

acting as architectural supports, and does not suggest a naturalistic likeness of a contemporary. This example is wearing an animal skin (a panther?) in the guise of a mythological being. In fact, rather than a portrait, it resembles most closely the stucco atlantes by Dominikus's brother Johann Baptist on the staircase of the Preysing Palace in Munich of c. 1724/5, or those formerly on the staircase of the Holnstein Palace (the archbishop's palace) in Munich of c. 1735-40.[28] These in turn may have inspired Johann Baptist Straub's wood Herms of 1753 in the Cuvilliés Theatre in Munich (see the next chapter [**5.9**]). The figures at Steinhausen are painted white, the arms held up as if supporting the organ in Herculean mode. Architectural ornament and sculpture are fused in these figures. The anatomy and facial features suggest living human bodies, but the sculptor is playing with our perceptions and expectations of both sculpture and architectural decoration, the contemporary and the classical intertwined. The material itself is lighthearted: stucco imitating both the human form and marble.

Like Steinhausen, Die Wies is a pilgrimage church, founded in 1743, when Dominikus Zimmermann was commissioned to build a church to house the miraculous image of the 'Scourged Saviour', a wood figure of Christ at the Column dating from 1730 [**4.19**].[29] The church at Die Wies was to be one of Dominikus's last and greatest works. It also incorporates rococo ornamentation in a way that is also seen at the Asamkirche, for example, in this respect looking forward to church decoration of the second half of the eighteenth century. Die Wies (literally The Meadow) was indeed built in the middle of a meadow, having been initially commissioned by Abbot Hyazinth Gassner of Steingaden (d. 1745), the plans subsequently being overseen by his successor Abbot Marianus II Mayer. Like the abbey at Weltenburg, its relatively distant setting, away from any urban centre, was designed to stimulate spirituality in pilgrims and visitors. Dominikus Zimmermann was a deeply pious person, like Egid Quirin Asam. In 1757 he purchased a house next to the church at Die Wies, where he was to spend the last years of his life.

The oval central vault and soaring

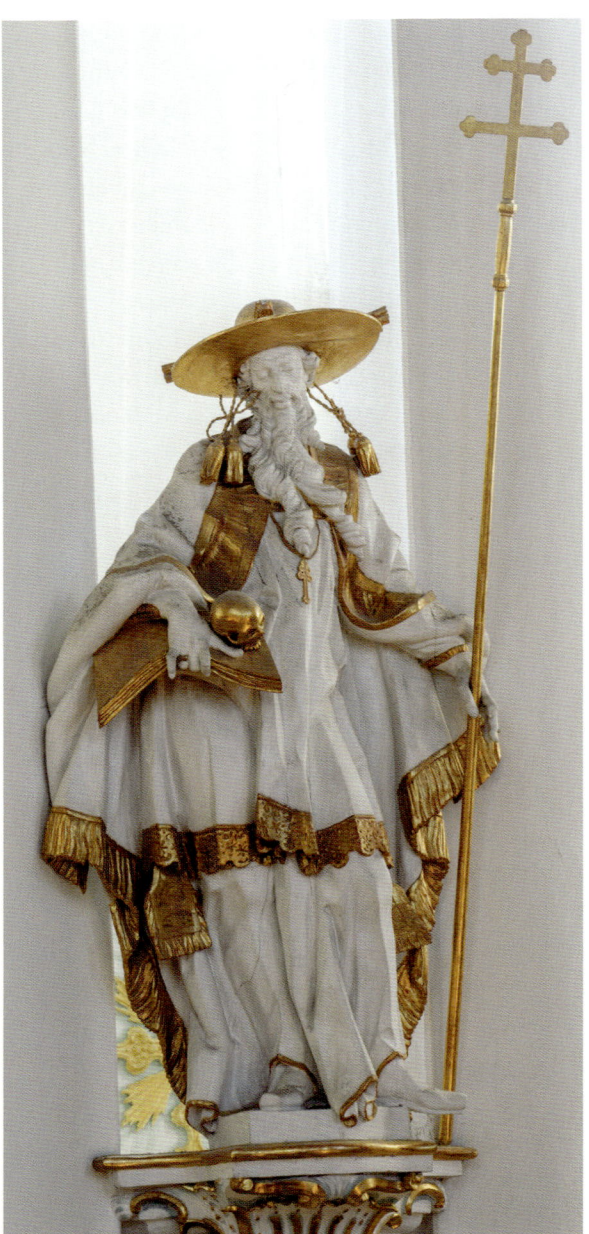

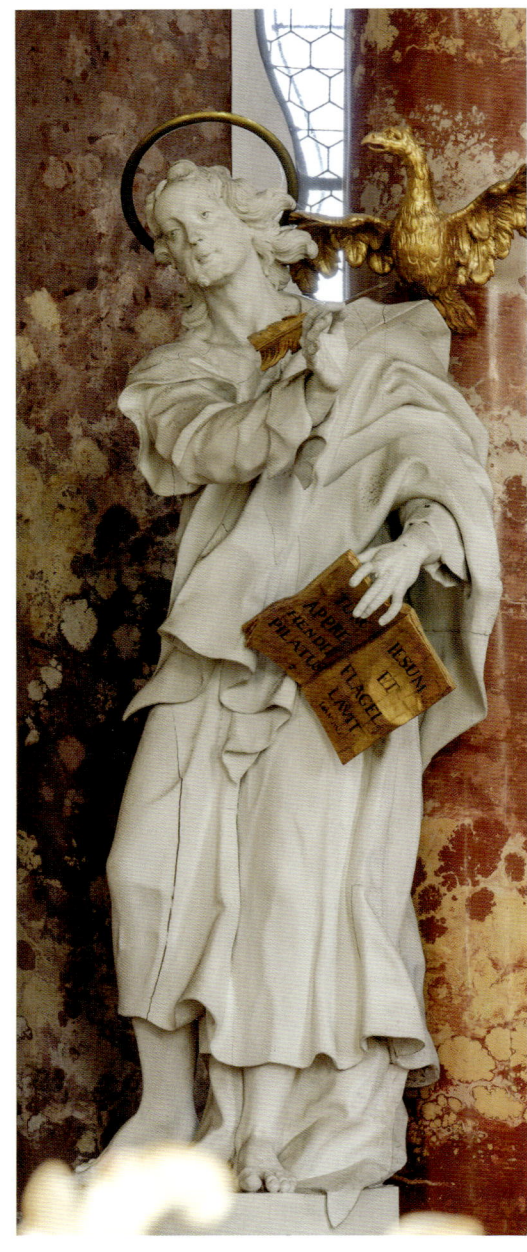

proportions of Die Wies are analogous to the interior of Steinhausen. Again, the architecture, painting and sculpture blend harmoniously together, and should be viewed as a *Gesamt-kunstwerk*. Dominikus worked at the church with his brother Johann Baptist, collaborating too with other artists, including the sculptor Anton Sturm (1690-1757) (originally from the Tyrol), based in Füssen, who produced the over-life-size wood figures of the four early Church Fathers on ornate rococo plinths from 1753 to 1756. One of these, *St Jerome*, painted white with gold highlights, stands on the south side of the nave. This figure is particularly animated, seemingly addressing the spectator

with his gestures. His contrapposto stance seems to suggest an elegant dance step, while his slender fingers gracefully and delicately clasp his book and cross [**4.20**]. The swelling forms of his fringed robe are complemented by his broad-brimmed cardinal's hat.

Dominikus's high altar is flanked by six over-life-size carved wood figures of the four Evangelists and two prophets. These are likely to be the last works by the Augsburg sculptor Aegid Verhelst the Elder (1696-1749) [**4.21**]. One of them, *St John the Evangelist*, painted white with gilded highlights, shown with his attribute of the eagle at his shoulder, exhibits particularly elongated proportions, emphasising

his imposing presence. He holds an open book of his gospel in his right hand, and a quill in his left. The inscription on the book refers to the scourging of Christ, in accord with the miraculous statue in the church.

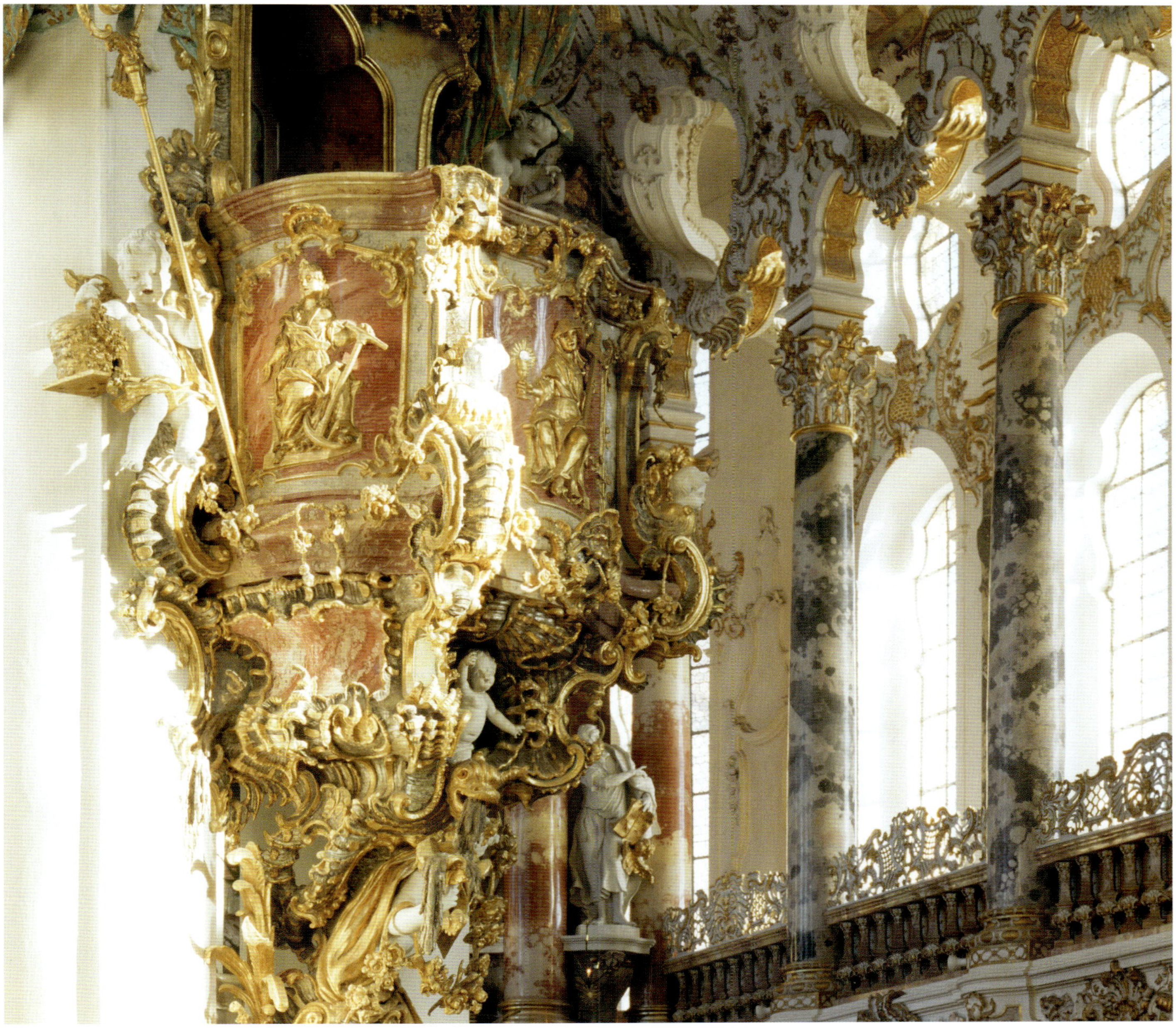

The ornate wood pulpit at the northeast corner of the nave is perhaps the other most striking sculptural ensemble in the church [4.22]. Designed by Dominikus Zimmermann, it was carved by Palier Pontian Steinhauser (1688-1755), and painted and gilded by Bernhard Ramis (d. 1759) and his son Judas Thaddäus Ramis (1734-1808).[30] This opulently encrusted structure abounds with rococo ornament, fictive drapery, decorative heads, the three cardinal virtues, and four spirited putti accompanied by symbols of the Church Fathers (a beehive for St Ambrose, the papal tiara for St Gregory, the lion's head for St Jerome, and the heart for St Augustine). The figures are painted white with gold highlights. The surfaces are highly polished, imitating stone. This richly illusionistic finish means the figures resemble carved Carrara marble, belying the fact that they are of wood and stucco. The decorative splendour of the pulpit mirrors other ecclesiastical furniture within the church, such as the abbot's gallery opposite, within the oval architectural space. The high altar, side altars and organ are further pivotal points enhancing the overall design.

4.22
Dominikus Zimmermann (designer), carving attributed to Palier Pontian Steinhauser; polychromed and gilded by Bernhard Ramis and Judas Thaddäus Ramis, Pulpit, wood, c. 1750-54. Church of Die Wies, Steingaden.

Such congruity was clearly intended both by Zimmermann and the abbots who commissioned the building and its profuse decoration.

The works commissioned from the Asam brothers and the Zimmermann brothers reveal the immense wealth of the Church, as well as the sincere piety of many in Bavaria and South Germany, including the artists themselves. The first half of the eighteenth century saw a large number of churches and monasteries being built and decorated. Sculpture was fundamental to the adornment of these buildings, and the employment of stucco meant that many sculptures could be produced and installed in a relatively short time, and at relatively low cost. The sculptors who specialized in stucco benefited from this surge of patronage. The decorative and figurative style of their work, though ultimately deriving from Italian traditions of plasterwork south of the Alps, evolved into a distinctive school of German baroque sculpture, exemplified by the greatest works of Egid Quirin Asam and Dominikus Zimmermann. This school was ultimately theatrical and illusionistic, its works emotive and powerful visualizations of the pious feelings of artists and patrons alike.

Notes

1 As noted in the introduction, in the eighteenth century Upper Bavaria was centred on Munich and areas and towns along the upper reaches of the river Danube, including Freising and Rohr. Lower Bavaria was located in the east of the country, and bordered the Upper Palatinate in the north, South Bohemia (today the Czech Republic) in the northeast, Upper Austria (Innviertel, Mühlviertel) in the southeast, and Upper Bavaria in the southwest. See Volk 1981, pp. 40-41; https://en.wikipedia.org/wiki/Upper_Bavaria; https://en.wikipedia.org/wiki/Lower_Bavaria.

2 See Bauer-Empel 2007.

3 The figure of *St John* also survives in the church.

4 For Barthel, see Kappel 2017, pp. 104-8. The Tyrolean sculptor Paul Strudel (1648-1708) studied in Venice before going to Vienna in 1684.

5 Rösner 1988.

6 For Troger, see Trusted 2013, pp. 101-4.

7 Brinckmann n.d. [1930?], pp. 354-5.

8 Fleming and Honour 1989, pp. 134-5.

9 For Fancelli, see Montagu 1989, pp. 78-82, for instance Fancelli's bronze relief of *The Trinity* in S. Maria della Pace in Rome. For Ferrata, see his stucco relief *Attributes of Alexis* in S. Agnese, Rome; Montagu 1989, fig. 112.

10 See Hahn 2007, pp. 9-13.

11 See Steiner 2007.

12 See Bourke 1962, p. 93.

13 It is now Benedictine; see Coburger 2011, pp. 226-7; Zeschick 2015; Rupprecht 1987, pp. 104-14. For an architectural discussion of the church, see Lieb 1953, pp. 33-8 and p. 160.

14 For Leonardo's mural, see Kemp 2011, p. 26.

15 Wittkower 1999b, p. 13.

16 Bourke 1962, p. 95.

17 Lieb 1953, pp. 38-46 and pp. 160-1; Bourke 1962, pp. 95-7; Rupprecht 1987, pp. 88-100; Coburger 2011, pp. 223-5; Altmann 2015.

18 Altmann 2016, p. 14.

19 Altmann 2016, p. 18.

20 Wittkower 1999b, p. 16. So-called Solomonic columns were thought to derive from Solomon's temple; see Fleming, Honour and Pevsner 1977, p. 268.

21 Bauer and Dischinger 2019; Steiner 2010.

22 Steiner 2010, p. 11.

23 Woeckel 1975, pp. 246-51; Statnik 2019, pp. 135-6 and fig. 152 on p. 135.

24 For the church, see Urban 2015; Bauer and Bauer 1985, pp. 54-7 and 176-86, and https://www.sueddeutscher-barock.ch/In-Werke/s-z/Steinhausen.html, accessed 23 August 2020.

25 Urban 2015, p. 4.

26 The technique of stucco is admirably described in Bauer-Empel 2007. This paragraph is a summary of her essay. It is based on a study of the stucco by Egid Quirin Asam at Freising, and must also apply to stucco work elsewhere. See also Krummholz 2012 and Rinn 2012, with further references.

27 Urban 2015, p. 3.

28 See Thon 1977, figs. 73, 75-6 on p. 40; Volk 1984, figs. 52 and 53 on p. 44. Conversely, the painting of a man leading a horse reputed to be a likeness of Dominikus Zimmermann in a fresco by his brother Johann Baptist at Steinhausen can more convincingly be claimed as a portrait; see Lampl 1987, fig. 1 on p. 10.

29 Kirchmeir and Hasenmuller n.d. [1991?], pp. 4-7. For the church, see Bauer and Bauer 1985, pp. 230-49.

30 See https://www.sueddeutscher-barock.ch/In-Werke/s-z/Wies.html, accessed 23 August 2020.

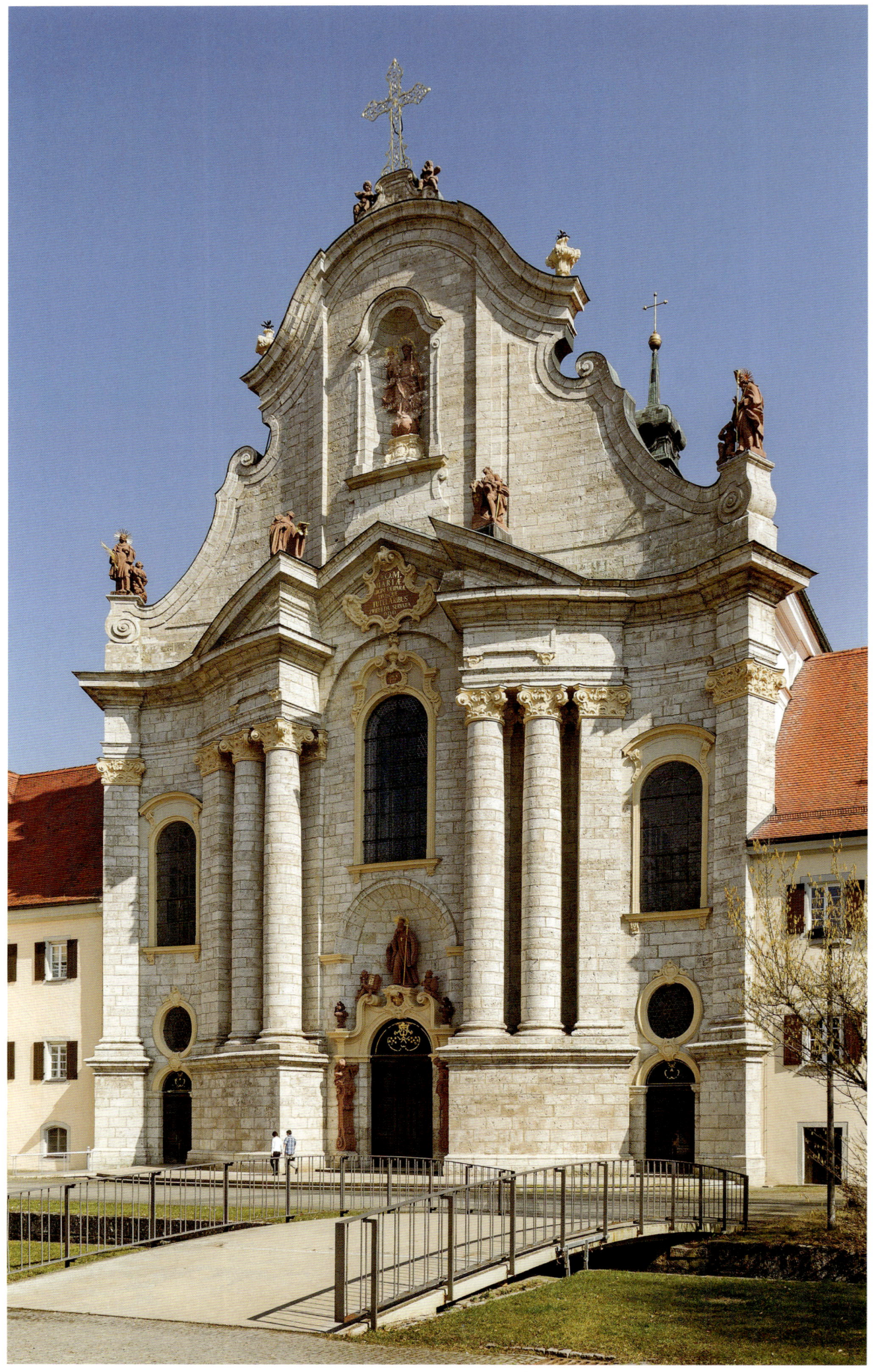

CHAPTER 5

THE MID-EIGHTEENTH CENTURY IN BAVARIA

Both wood sculpture and stucco work flourished in Bavaria in the mid-eighteenth century, in secular and ecclesiastical spheres alike. The return of Maximilian II Emmanuel (1662-1726), the Elector of Bavaria, to Munich from his exile in France in 1714, as well as the continuing desire to rebuild churches and monasteries that had been affected by the violence of the Thirty Years' War, led to numerous commissions for both palace and church. Max Emmanuel brought with him artists from France to work at the court, such as François de Cuvilliés the Elder (1695-1768) and Guillielmus (Wilhelm) de Grof (1676-1742). Those artists introduced architectural and decorative styles and forms from the court in France that were to inspire sculptors working in Bavaria in the ensuing decades. This chapter will examine the work of some of the Bavarian sculptors working in the mid-eighteenth century, including Johann Joseph Christian (1706-77), Johann Michael Feichtmayr (1709/10-72), Joseph Joachim Dietrich (1690-1753) and Johann Baptist Straub (1704-84), culminating in Ignaz Günther (1725-75). Another underlying subject of this chapter is that of surviving models and drawings for sculptures, and their sometimes complex relationships with the finished works.[1]

Johann Joseph Christian and Johann Michael Feichtmayr: Zwiefalten and Ottobeuren

Johann Joseph Christian produced both stone and wood sculptures for the churches of Zwiefalten and Ottobeuren respectively from 1744 onwards. He had trained with Johann Eucharius Hermann (1666-1727) in Biberach an der Riss in Bavaria (Upper Swabia; today Baden-Württemberg), and after Hermann's death established a workshop nearby in Riedlingen in 1728. Primarily a wood carver, he also worked in stone and stucco. His work cannot be separated from either the architecture created by Johann Michael Fischer (1692-1766) or the stucco work produced by Johann Michael Feichtmayr for these churches, the architecture and sculptural decoration enhancing each other in multifarious ways.

The former Benedictine abbey and church of Our Lady at Zwiefalten, Upper Swabia, southwest of Ulm, was mainly designed by Fischer from 1741 to 1753, replacing an earlier medieval church. The architecture both externally and internally acts as a foil to the sculpture and decorative features of the church. Fischer's baroque façade [5.1] is complemented by Christian's statues of saints standing within the niches silhouetted against the skyline and the architecture (1750-53).[2] In the interior, the mass of sculpture and stucco produced by both Christian and Feichtmayr from 1744 to 1755

5.1
West front of the church of Our Lady at Zwiefalten, Baden-Württemberg, 1750-3, designed by Johann Michael Fischer, sculpture by Johann Joseph Christian.

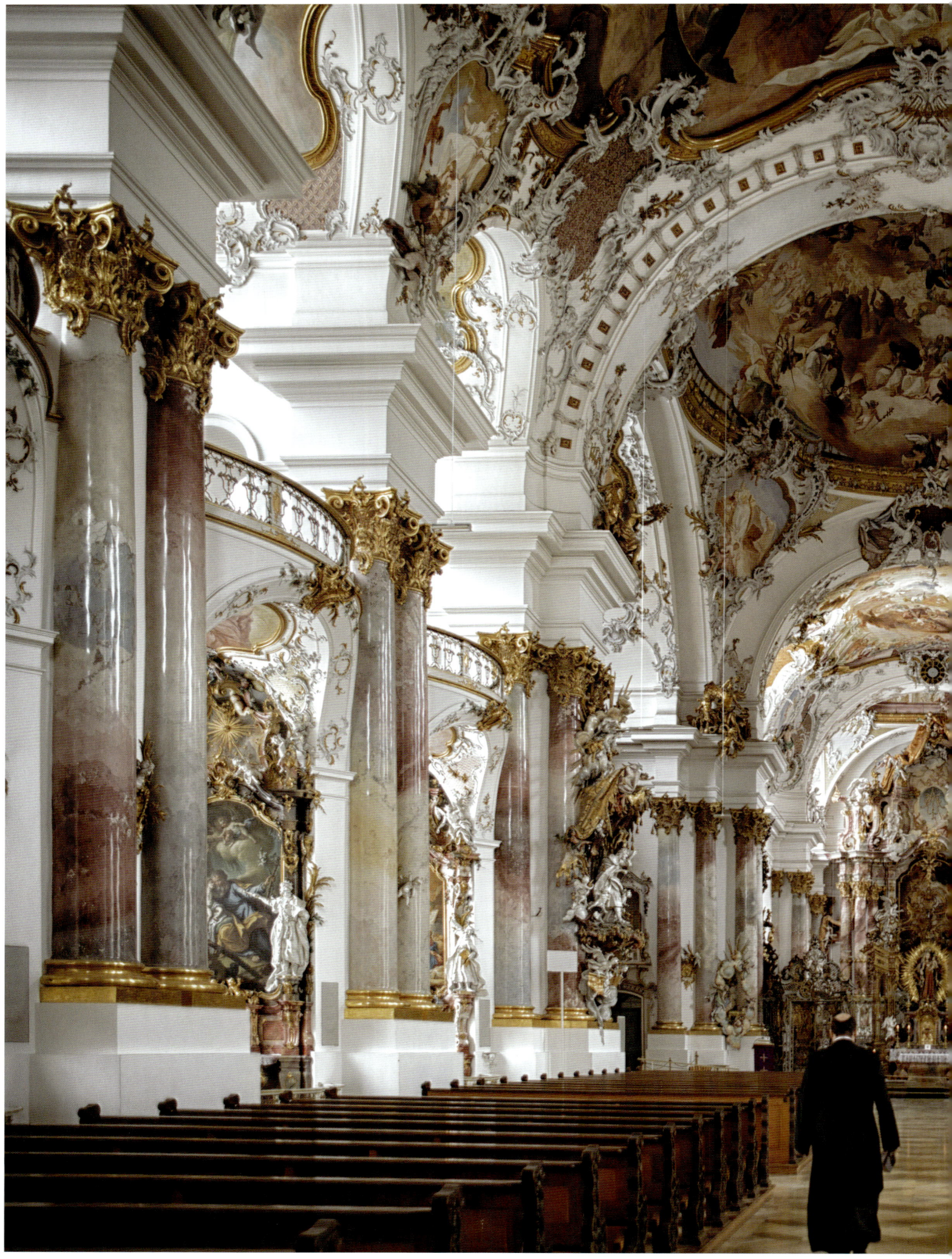

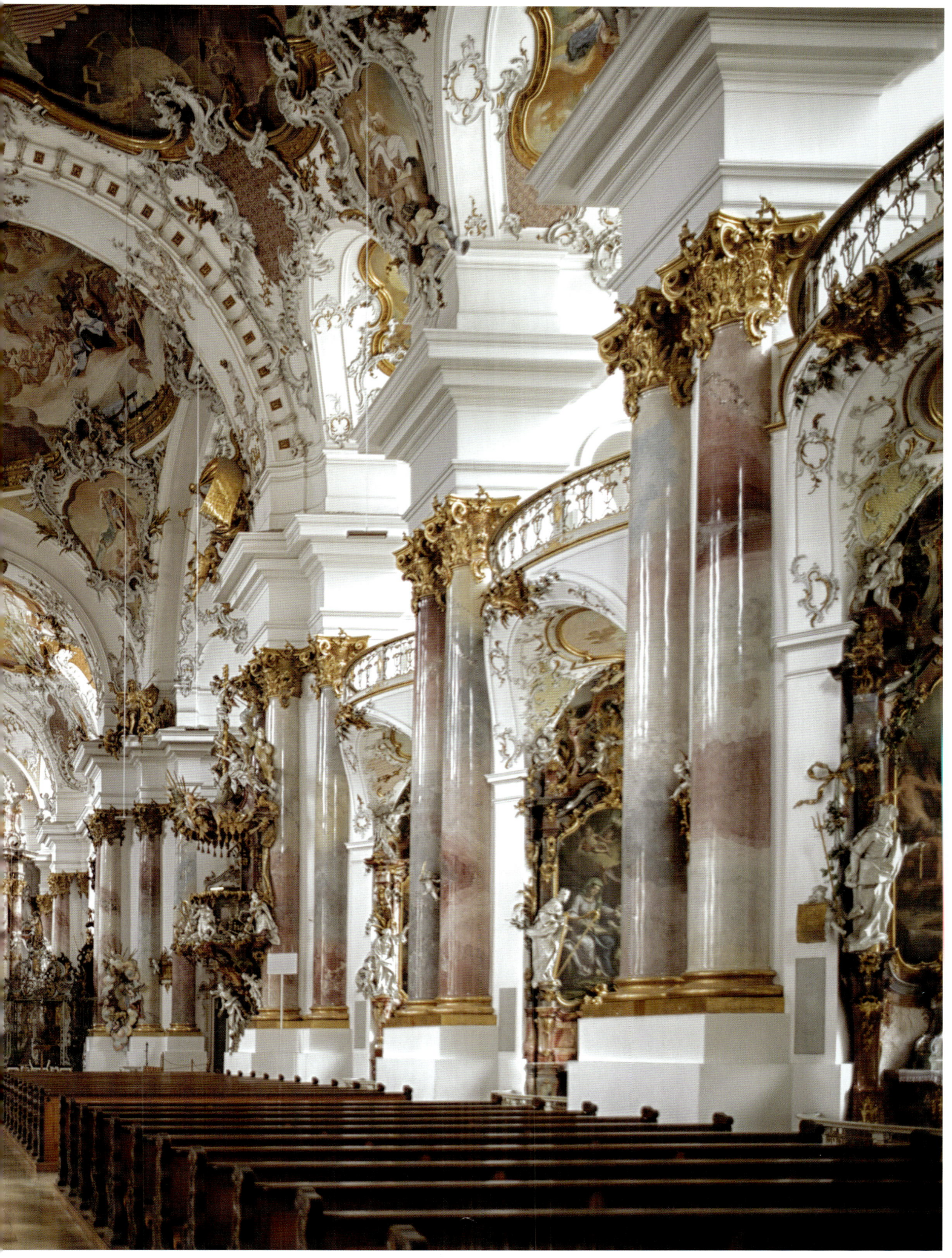

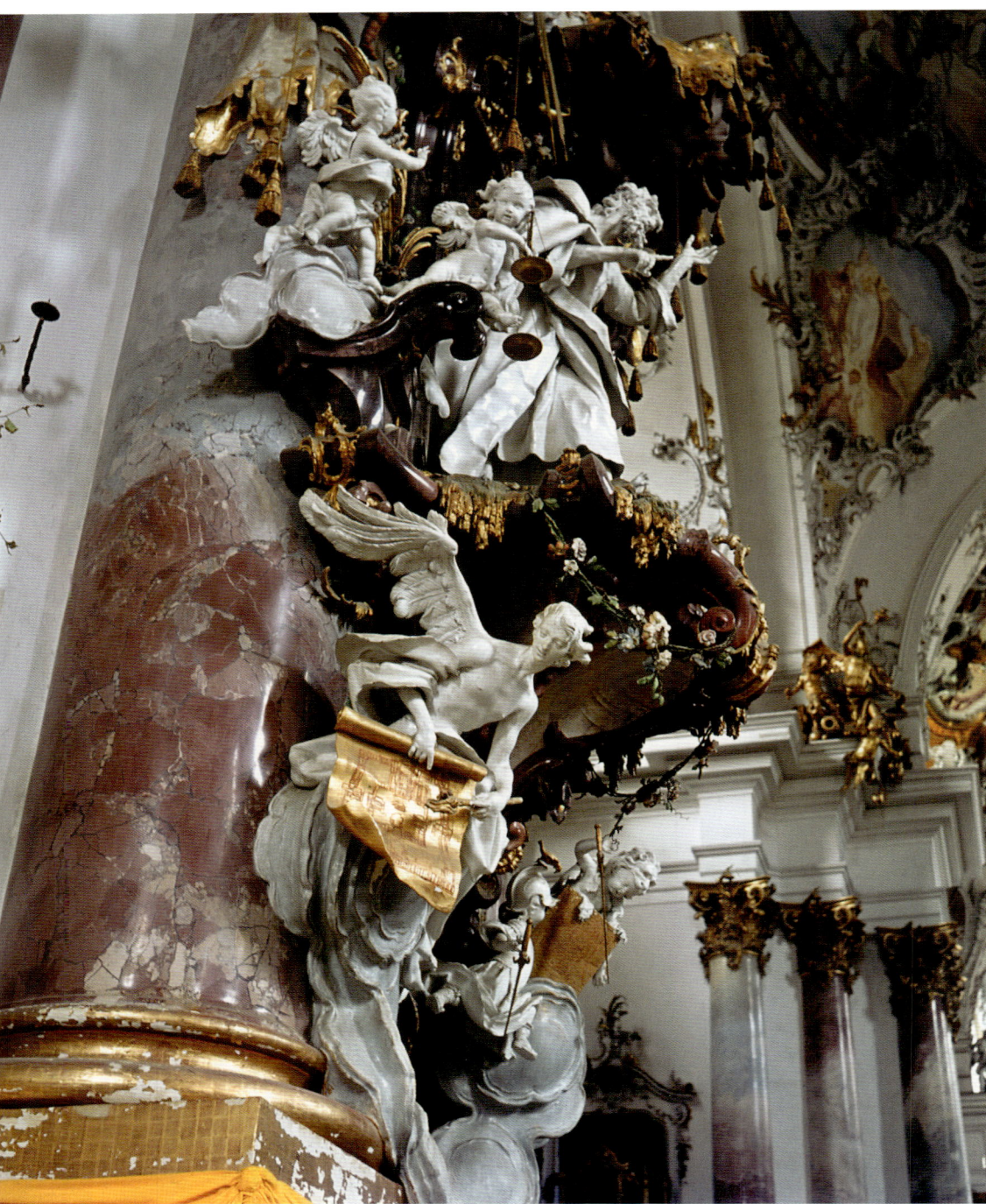

<< 5.2
Interior of the church of Our Lady at Zwiefalten, Baden-Württemberg, c. 1747-73, designed by Johann Michael Fischer, sculpture by Johann Joseph Christian, stucco by Johann Michael Feichtmayr.

5.3
Johann Joseph Christian and Johann Michael Feichtmayr, *Ezekiel with God the Father and Angels,* painted and gilt wood and stucco, c. 1749-67, pulpit on the north pillar at the east end of the nave. Church of Our Lady at Zwiefalten, Baden-Württemberg.

adorns the long and expansive nave, endowing it with what might be metaphorically termed a series of visual vibrations [5.2]. The stuccoist Feichtmayr had initially trained in Augsburg under the stonemason J. Paulus from 1722 to 1725, while working with his brothers on the stucco work at the former Dominican church in Augsburg. The most impressive sculptural work at Zwiefalten is Christian and Feichtmayr's ensemble of the over-life-size white and gold statue of the prophet Ezekiel, carved in wood, with numerous surrounding stucco angels and decorative work, placed beneath the smaller figure of God the Father hovering above, the

angelic figures and clouds spilling onto the surrounding rococo architecture [5.3]. The prophet is enveloped in copious drapery, stepping forward in sandalled feet, whilst dramatically pointing and gesticulating [5.4]. His commanding pose and sweeping forms indicate that by the mid-eighteenth century Bernini's earlier sculptures at St Peter's had become fundamental precedents for South German baroque sculpture.[3] The Italian stuccoist Diego Francesco Carlone (1674-1750), active in Bavaria as well as Austria, was a fundamentally important conduit for this Berniniesque style.[4]

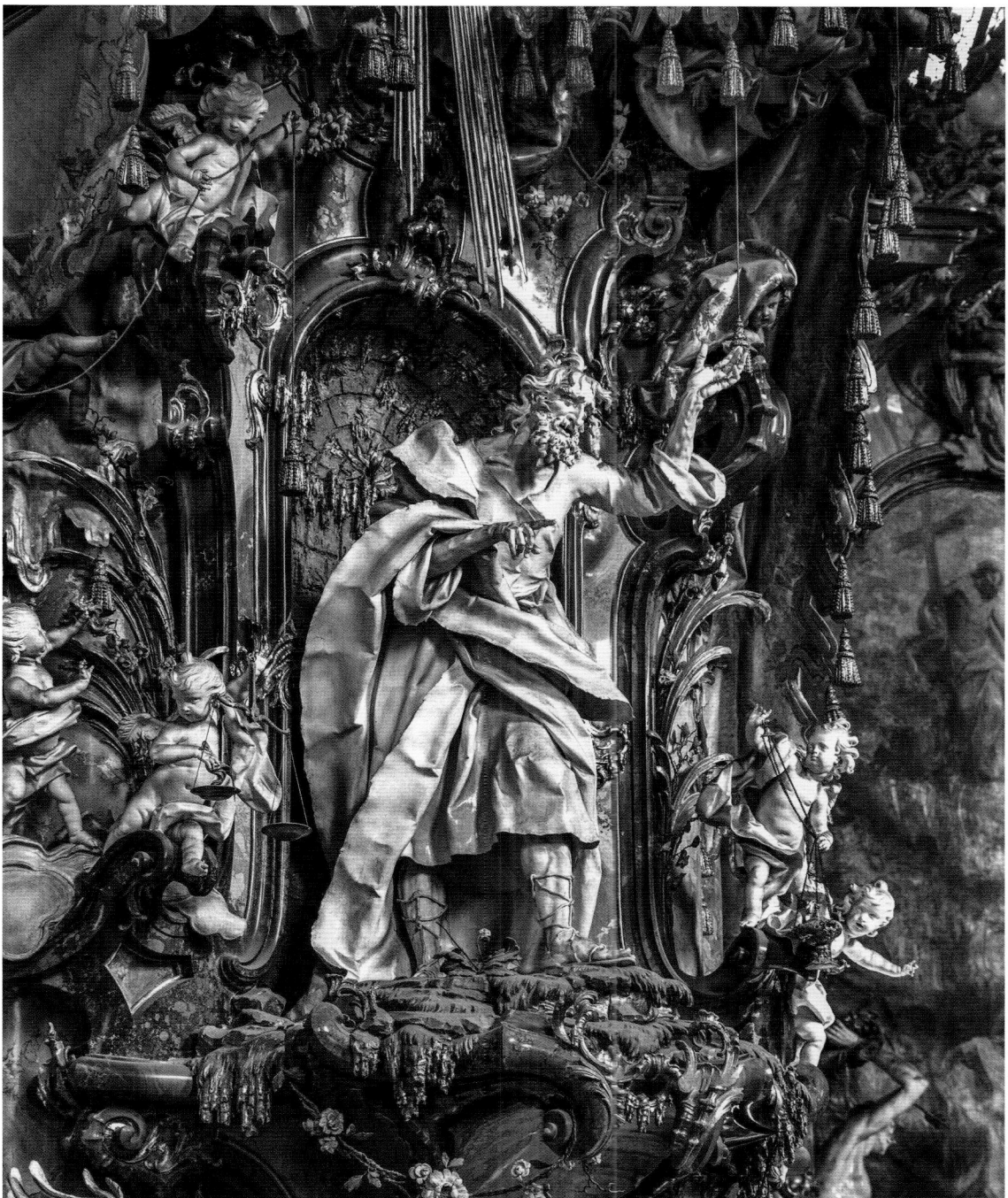

5.4
Detail of the prophet
Ezekiel on the north
pillar at Zwiefalten
[5.3].

The rebuilding of the Benedictine abbey of Ottobeuren, also in Swabia, dedicated to St Alexander and St Theodore, was planned from 1711 onwards. Like Zwiefalten, the church was designed by Fischer, who commenced work on it in 1748. The sculpture and stucco were likewise undertaken by Christian and Feichtmayr once again, their activity there dating from 1755-64 and 1756-67 respectively.[5] The interior blends the mass of sculpted wood figures and decorative stucco work into a complex architectural space of frescoed domes, ornate wood choirstalls and organ loft, amidst tall, coloured scagliola columns and pilasters [5.5].[6] The baptismal font carved by Christian, incorporating stucco by Feichtmayr, soars above the west side of the nave, like the earlier figure of Ezekiel at Zwiefalten. It depicts *The Baptism*, the figures of Christ and St John the Baptist surrounded by angels, with God the Father and the Holy Spirit above [5.6]. The font is complemented by the equally effervescent pulpit opposite, depicting *The Transfiguration* above, with God the Father and an abundance of angels amidst clouds [5.7]. The sculptures form part of a complex artistic whole. The church also incorporates other separate figures of saints and prophets, and decorative reliquary caskets containing the

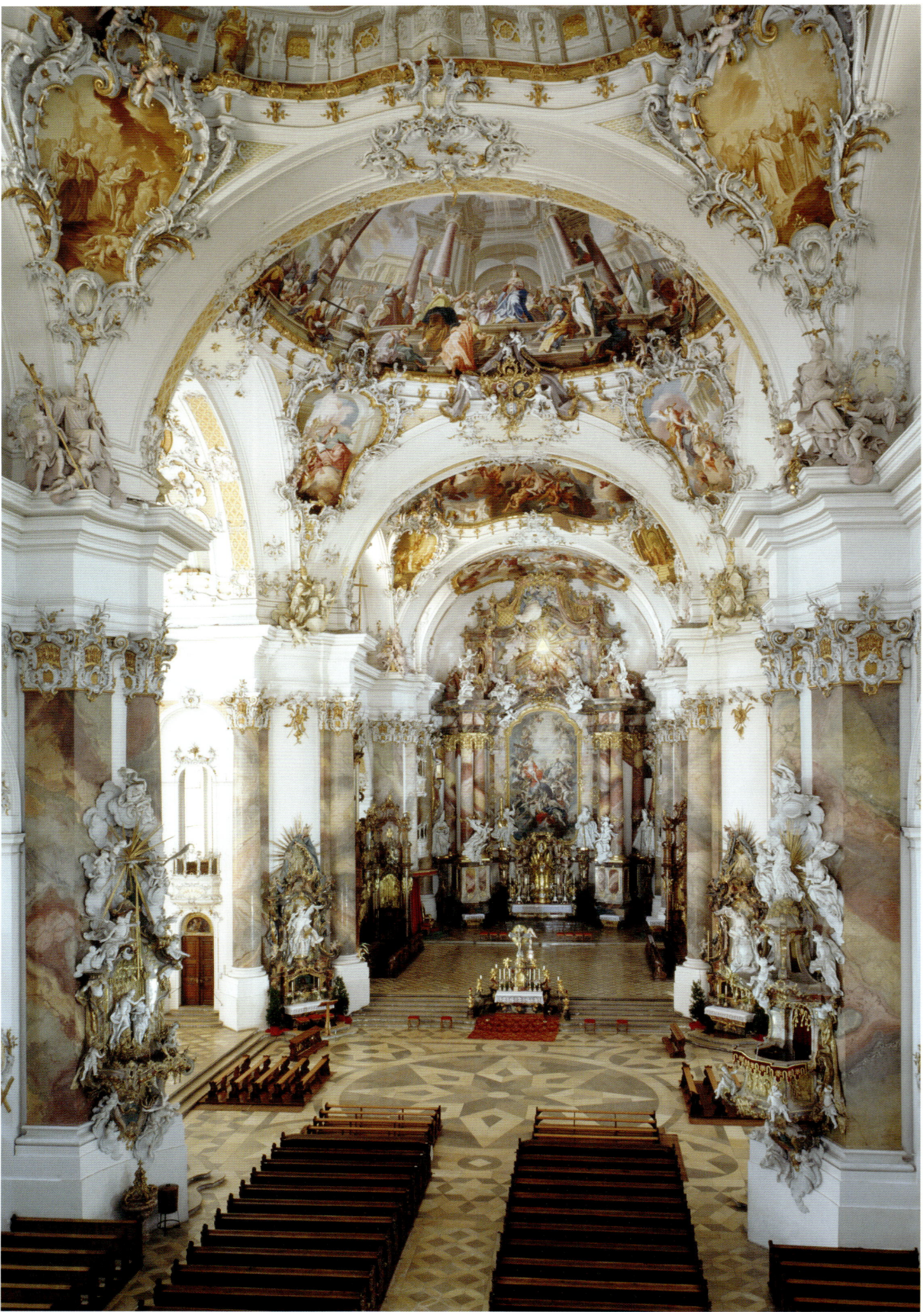

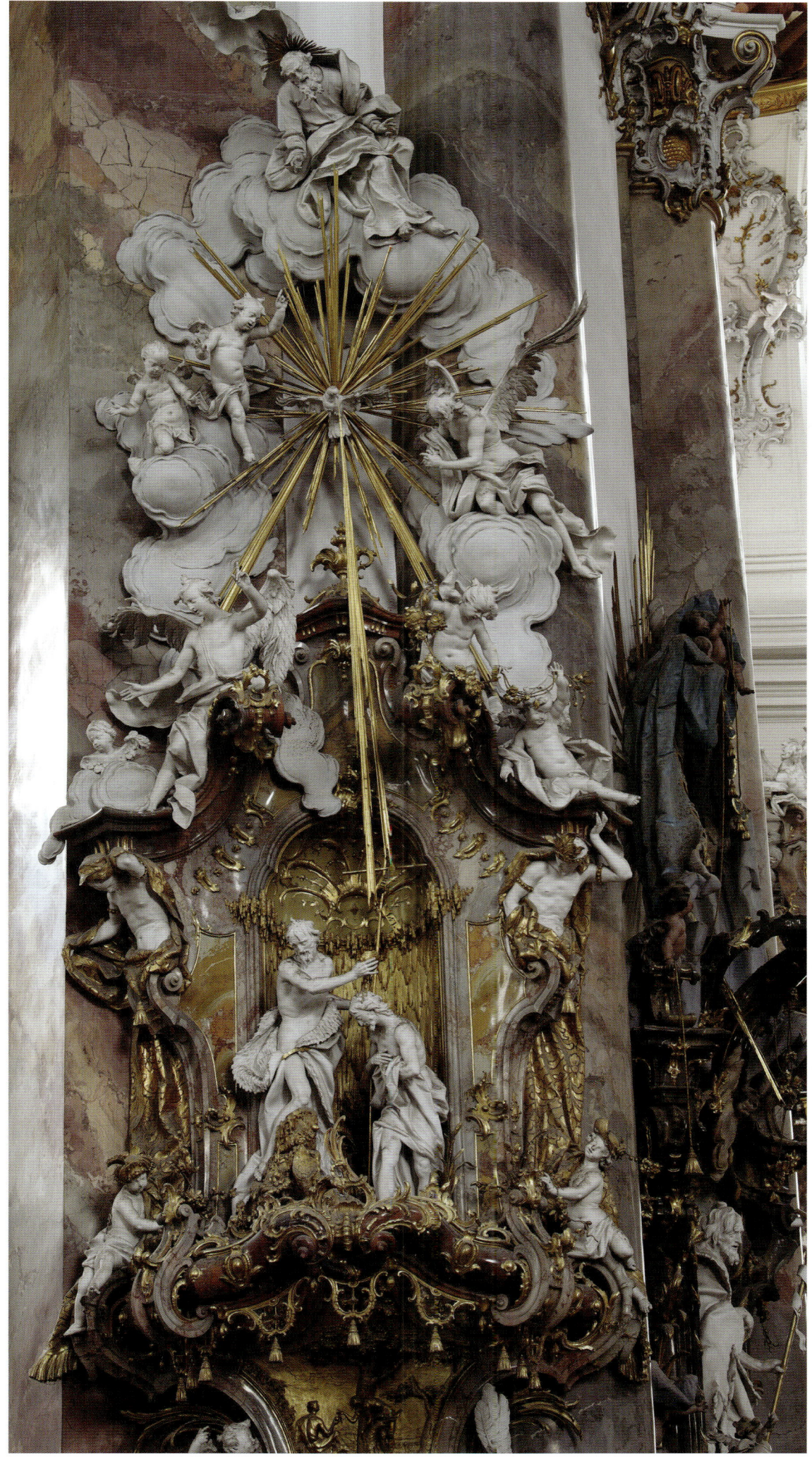

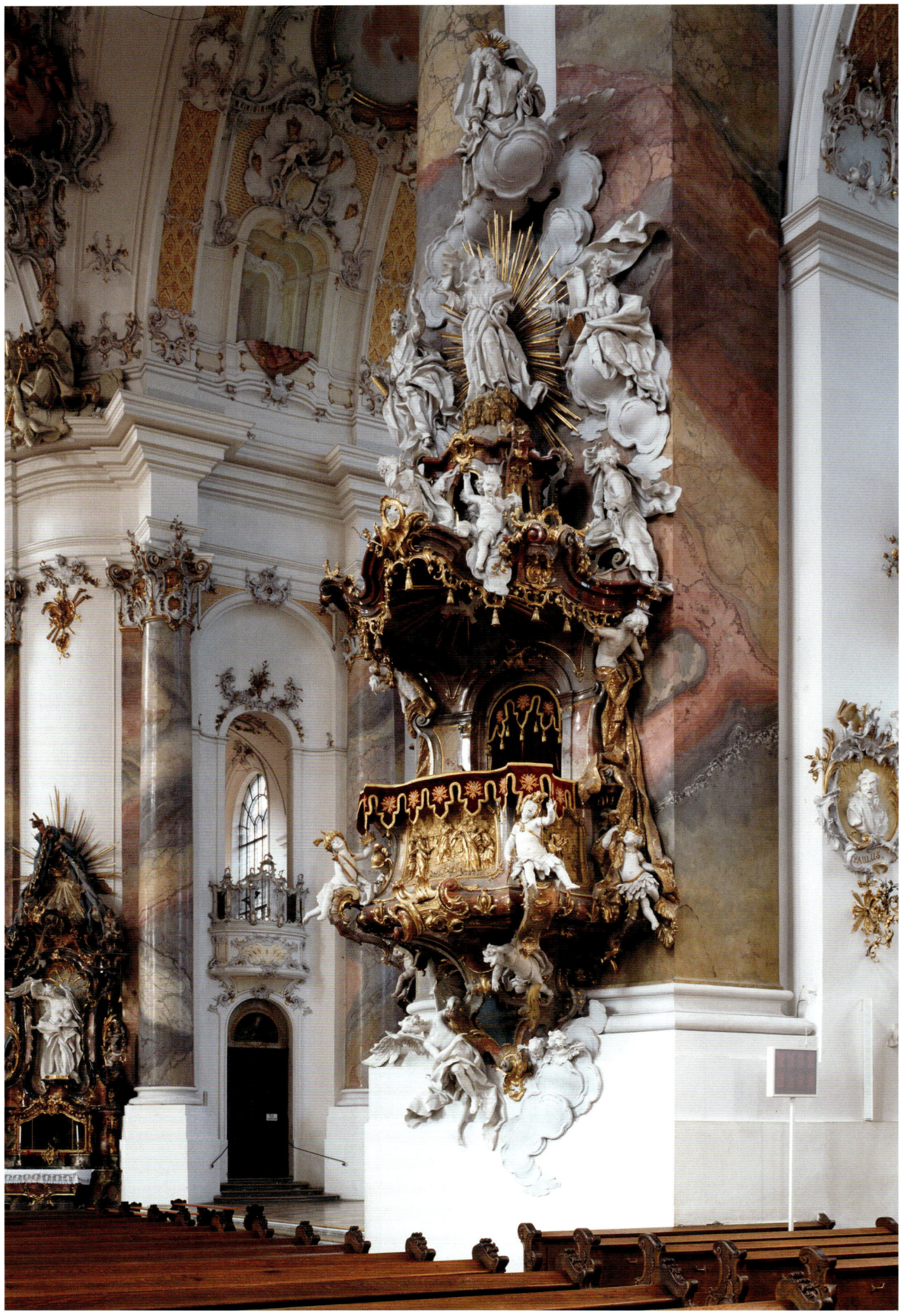

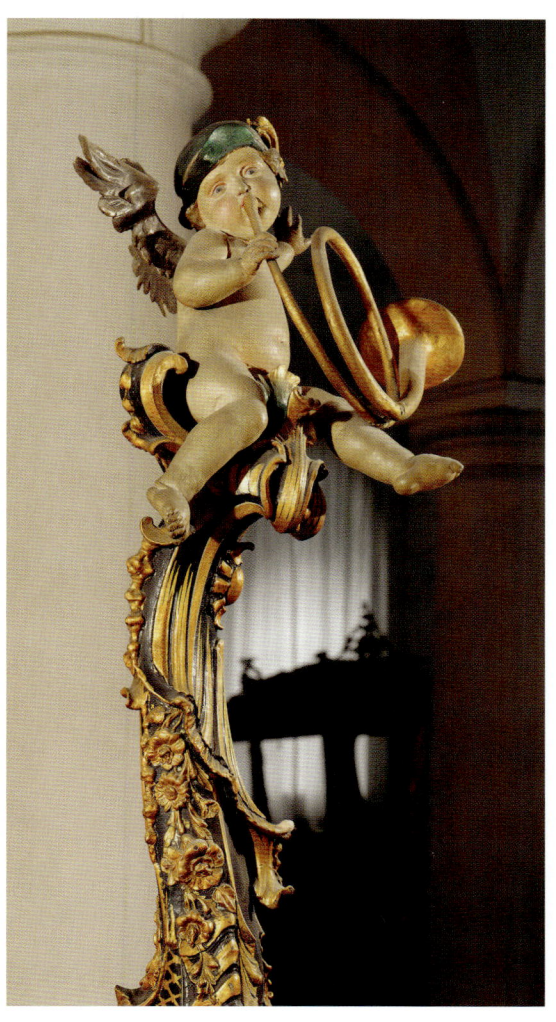

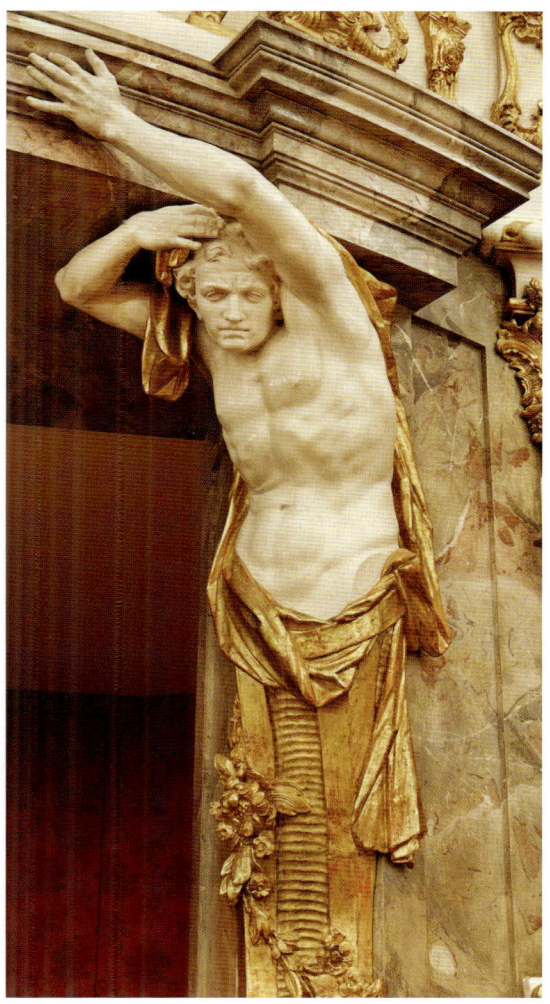

< 5.7
Johann Joseph
Christian and Johann
Michael Feichtmayr,
Pulpit with *The
Transfiguration*, painted
and gilt wood and
stucco, c. 1756-66.
West side of the nave of
the Benedictine abbey
at Ottobeuren, Bavaria.

5.8
Johann Baptist Straub.
Diana Sleigh (detail of
putto blowing a horn),
painted wood, c. 1737-
45. Stables (Marstall)
Museum, Schloss
Nymphenburg.

5.9
Johann Baptist Straub
(attributed), *Atlante
(Herm)*, painted and gilt
wood, 1753, under the
Elector's Box. Residenz
Theatre (Cuvilliés
Theatre), Munich.

relics and remains of the two saints to whom the church is dedicated, located elsewhere in the nave and crossing.[7]

Johann Baptist Straub; Joseph Joachim Dietrich

Johann Baptist Straub, a contemporary of Christian and Feichtmayr and arguably the finest wood sculptor of his generation, was the teacher of Ignaz Günther (whose work will be discussed later in this chapter), even though he outlived Günther because of his younger contemporary's premature death. He also taught Christian Jorhan the Elder (1727-1804), Roman Anton Boos (1733-1810) and his nephew Franz Xaver Messerschmidt (1736-83).

Straub came from a family of wood carvers, and after initially training with his father, Johann Georg Straub the Elder (1674-1755), went to Munich in about 1721, where he studied under the court sculptor Gabriel Luidl (1688-1741). There he would have seen the works of another

court sculptor, Guillielmus de Grof, and the sculpture of Aegid Verhelst the Elder (1696-1749), as well as that of Egid Quirin Asam (1692-1750), whose work was discussed in the previous chapter, and who can be seen as one of Straub's precursors.[8] But it was almost certainly Straub's subsequent stay in Vienna from 1726 to 1734 that crucially helped shape his development as a sculptor. There he undertook his first independent work, carving pews and other sculpture for the Augustinian church of the Black Robed Spaniards (the Schwarzspanier-kirche). His return to Munich in 1734 was apparently at the suggestion of the sculptor Andreas Faistenberger (1646-1735), with whom he probably worked, but who was to die the following year. In 1737 Straub was appointed court sculptor by the Elector of Bavaria, Charles Albert (1697-1745), for whom he made numerous secular pieces. He designed and carved sleighs for the elector and undertook decorative carving for the Residenz at Munich, notably

>> 5.10
François de Cuvilliés the
Elder (designer), carved
by Johann Joachim
Dietrich, *High Altar-
piece*, painted and gilt
wood, c. 1738. Church
of the Assumption of
the Virgin, Diessen am
Ammersee.

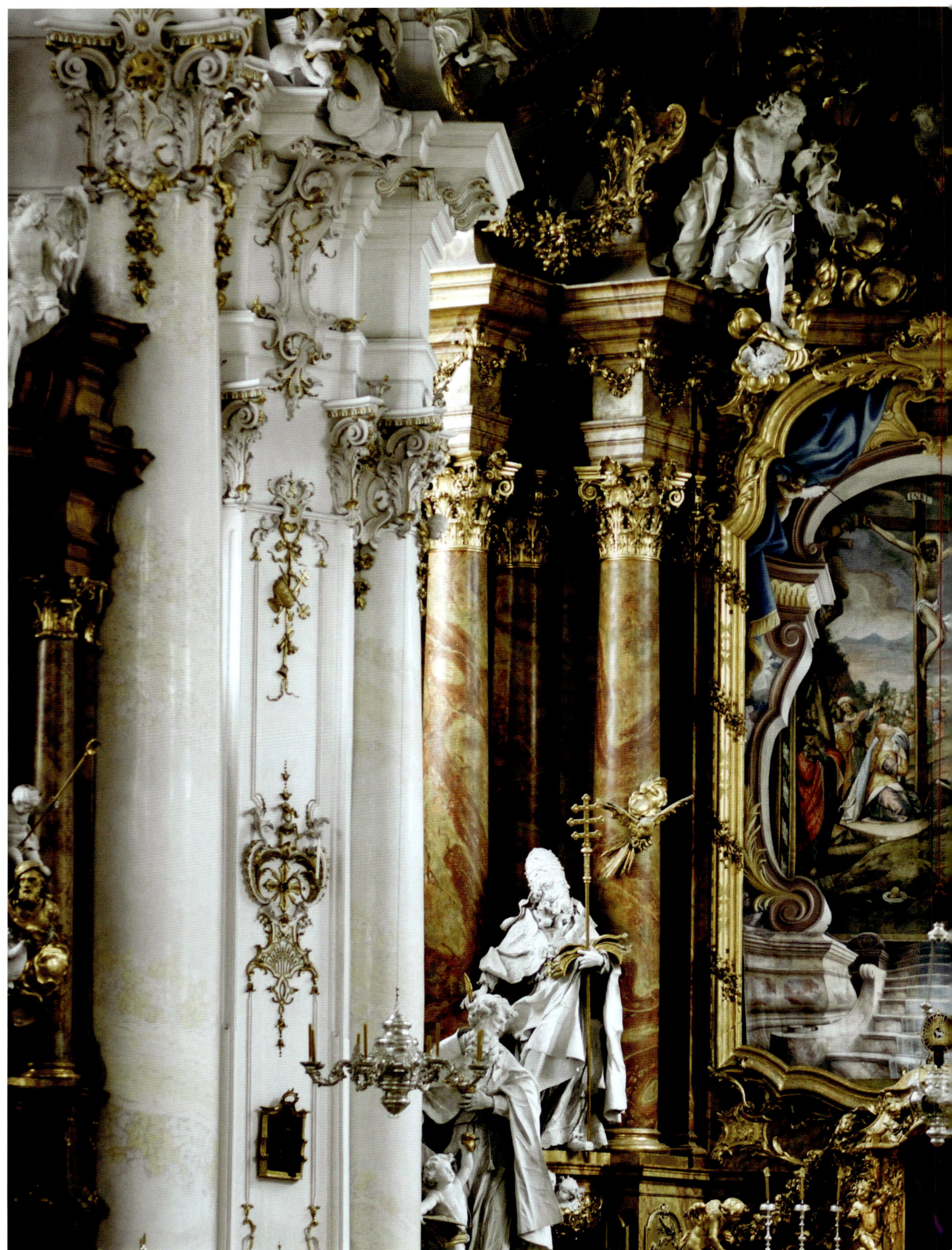

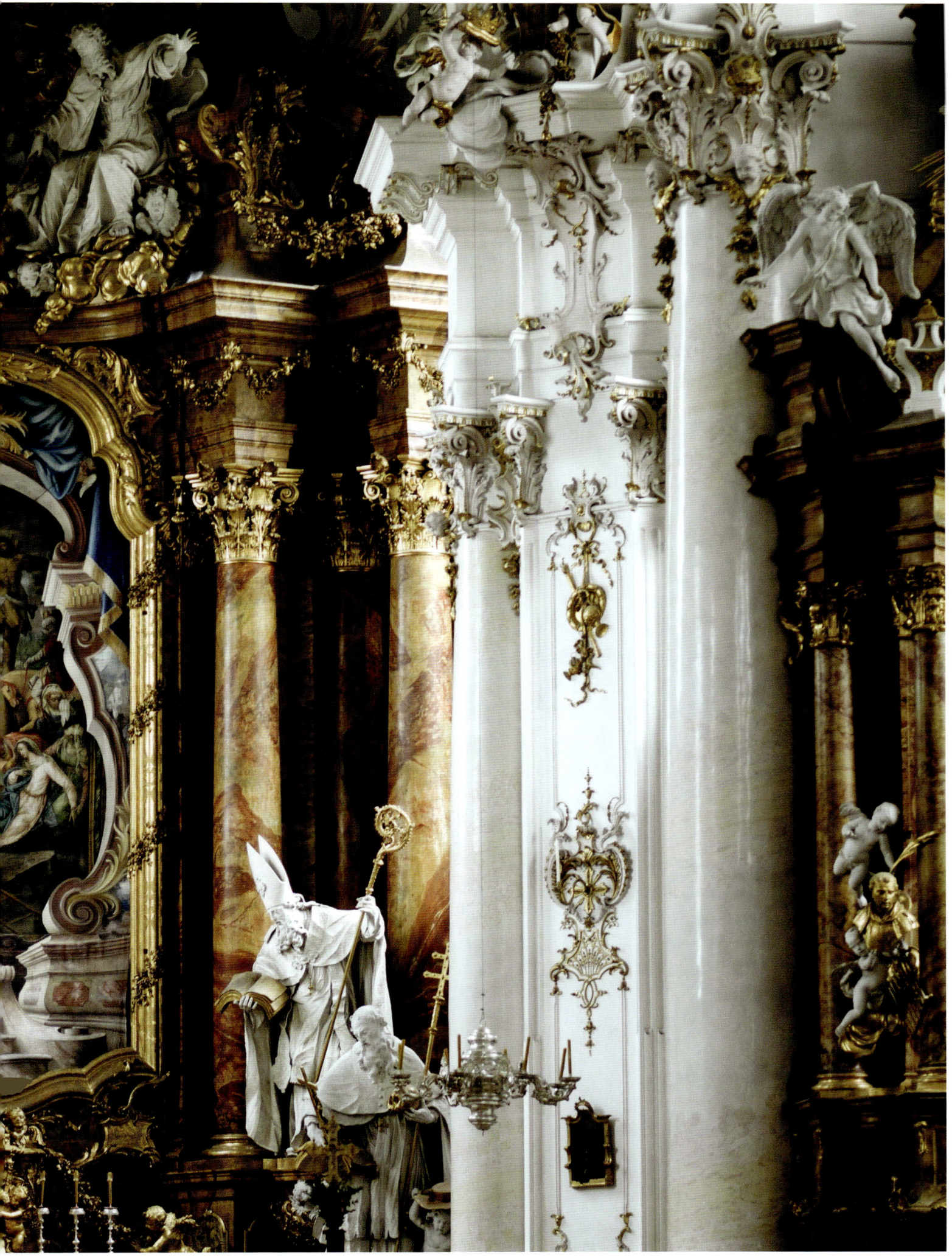

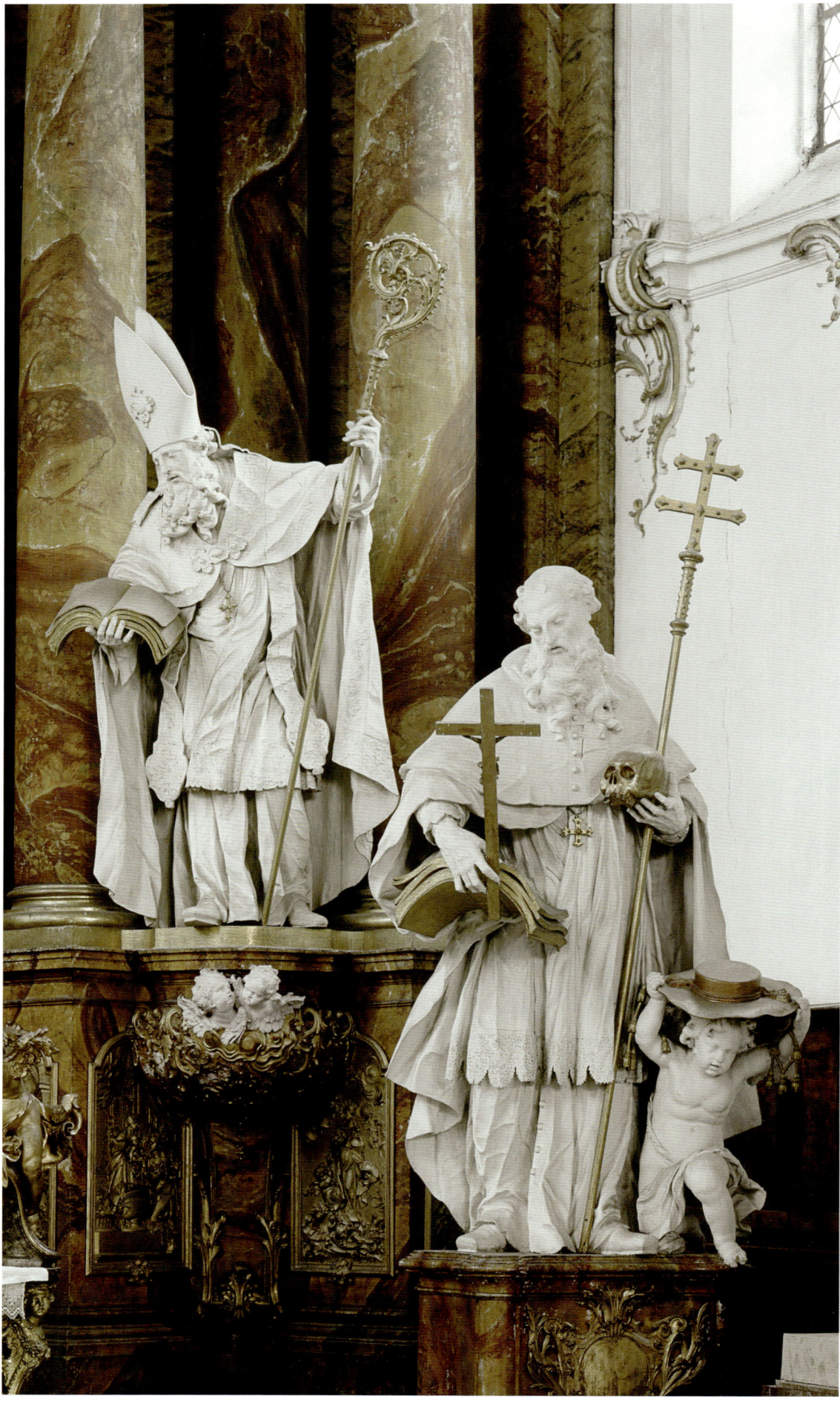

5.11
Joseph Joachim Dietrich, St Ambrosius and *St Jerome*, painted and gilt wood, c. 1738. High Altarpiece, church of the Assumption of the Virgin, Diessen am Ammersee [detail of 5.10].

> 5.12
Johann Baptist Straub, Altarpiece dedicated to *St Sebastian*, with painting by Giovanni Battista Tiepolo, dated 1739. Frame and figures of St Thomas and St Matthew painted and gilt wood. Church of the Assumption of the Virgin, Diessen am Ammersee.

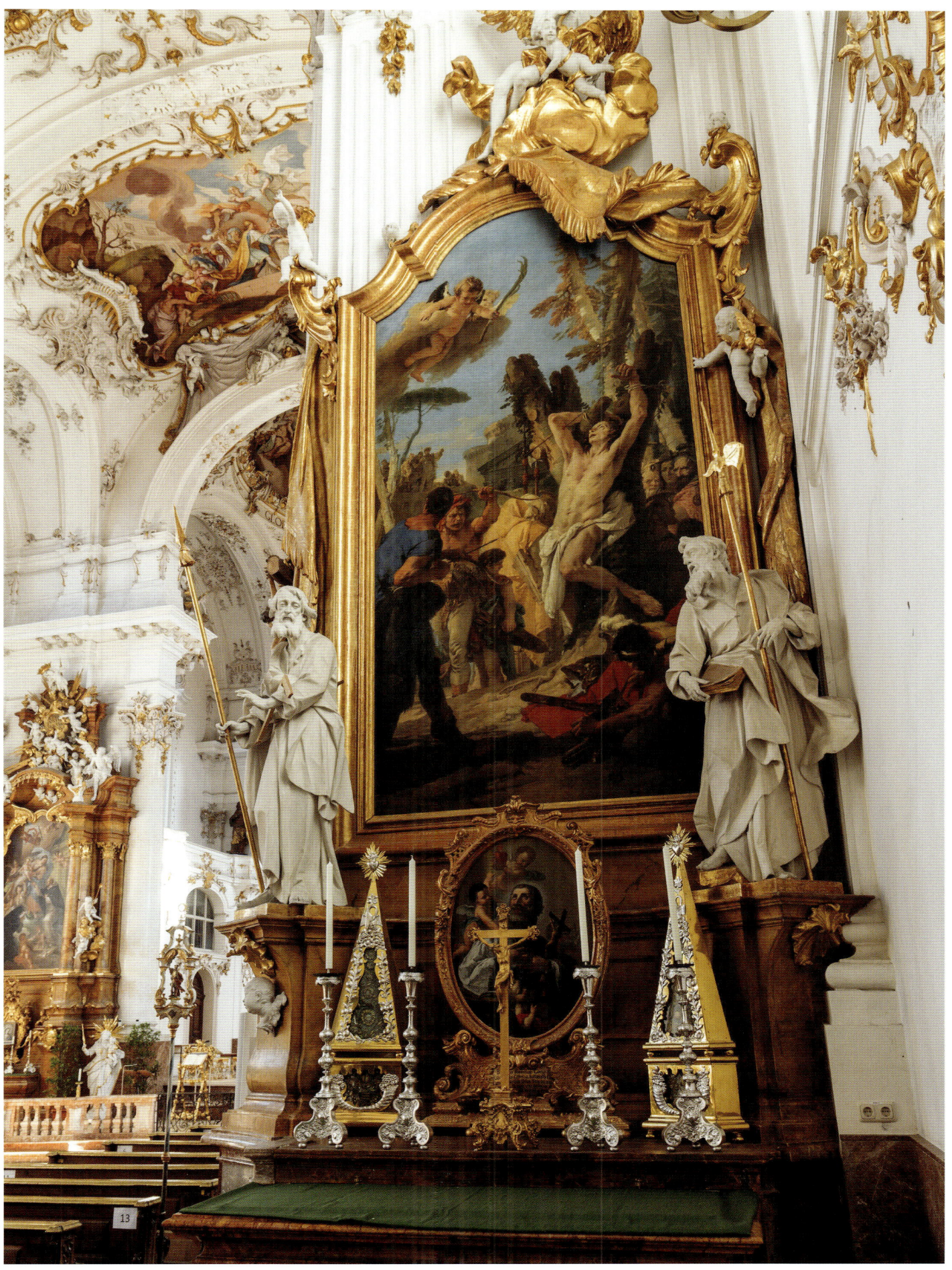

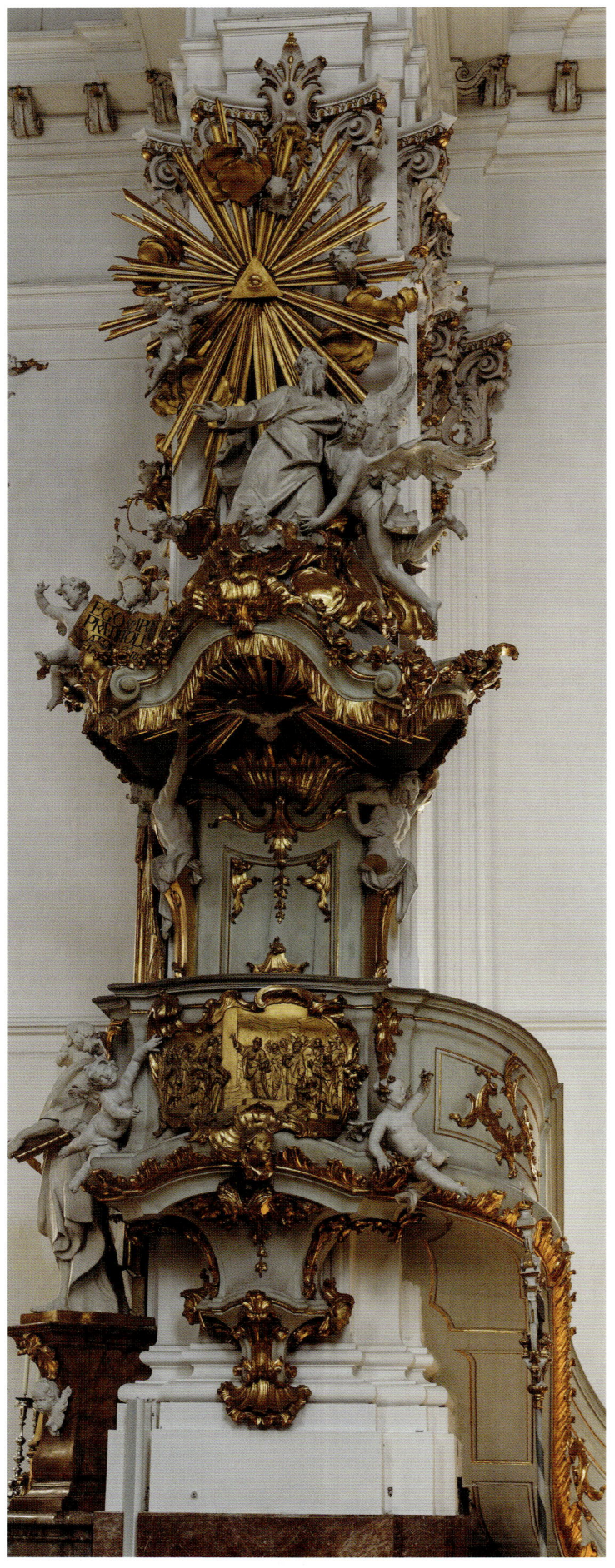

for the court theatre designed by François de Cuvilliés the Elder (1695-1768) [**5.8 and 5.9**]. Straub's *Herm* of 1753 at the Cuvilliés theatre recalls Johann Baptist Zimmermann's slightly earlier stucco *Herm* at the Palais Holnstein (the archbishop's palace) of c. 1735-40, as well as Zimmermann's figure under the organ loft at Steinhausen [**see 4.18 in the previous chapter**]. Clearly the classicizing visual language of the French court was being emulated and echoed in such decorative architectural details for Bavarian rulers.

From 1738 to 1740 Straub worked at the former Augustinian church dedicated to the Assumption of the Virgin at Diessen am Ammer-see. Again, as at Zwiefalten and Ottobeuren, the architect was Johann Michael Fischer, who designed the church from 1732 onwards, while the high altarpiece was conceived by François de Cuvilliés the Elder and carved by Joseph Joachim Dietrich [**5.10**].[9] Dietrich's figures in white and gold represent the four Church Fathers, and amply suggest ultimately Italianate roots with their sweeps of drapery and gesture, as well as hinting at French rococo humour, seen for instance in the putto trying on St Jerome's cardinal's hat, while the saint contemplatively holds a skull in his left hand as he solemnly reads his book [**5.11**]. The church at Diessen, like those at Zwiefalten and Ottobeuren, is a *Gesamtkunstwerk*, a complete work of art, the architecture, paintings and sculpture informing each other in a unified whole. Straub executed numeroussculpturesforDiessen,includingtwoside-altarpieces, the pulpit, two tabernacles, and the organ case. The side-altarpiece dedicated to St Sebastian, with a magnificent painting of the saint's martyrdom by Giovanni Battista Tiepolo (1696-1770) as its central feature, is flanked by Straub's full-size figures of two Apostles, St Thomas and St Matthew [**5.12**]. Straub's idiosyncratic contribution to the design is the exuberant carved gilt wood frame with illusionistic drapery and soaring winged putti-angels. Again, the mischievousness of the work looks forward to the rococo.

Straub's pulpit in the same church is likewise a vivid piece of church furniture, harmoniously blending in with Fischer's

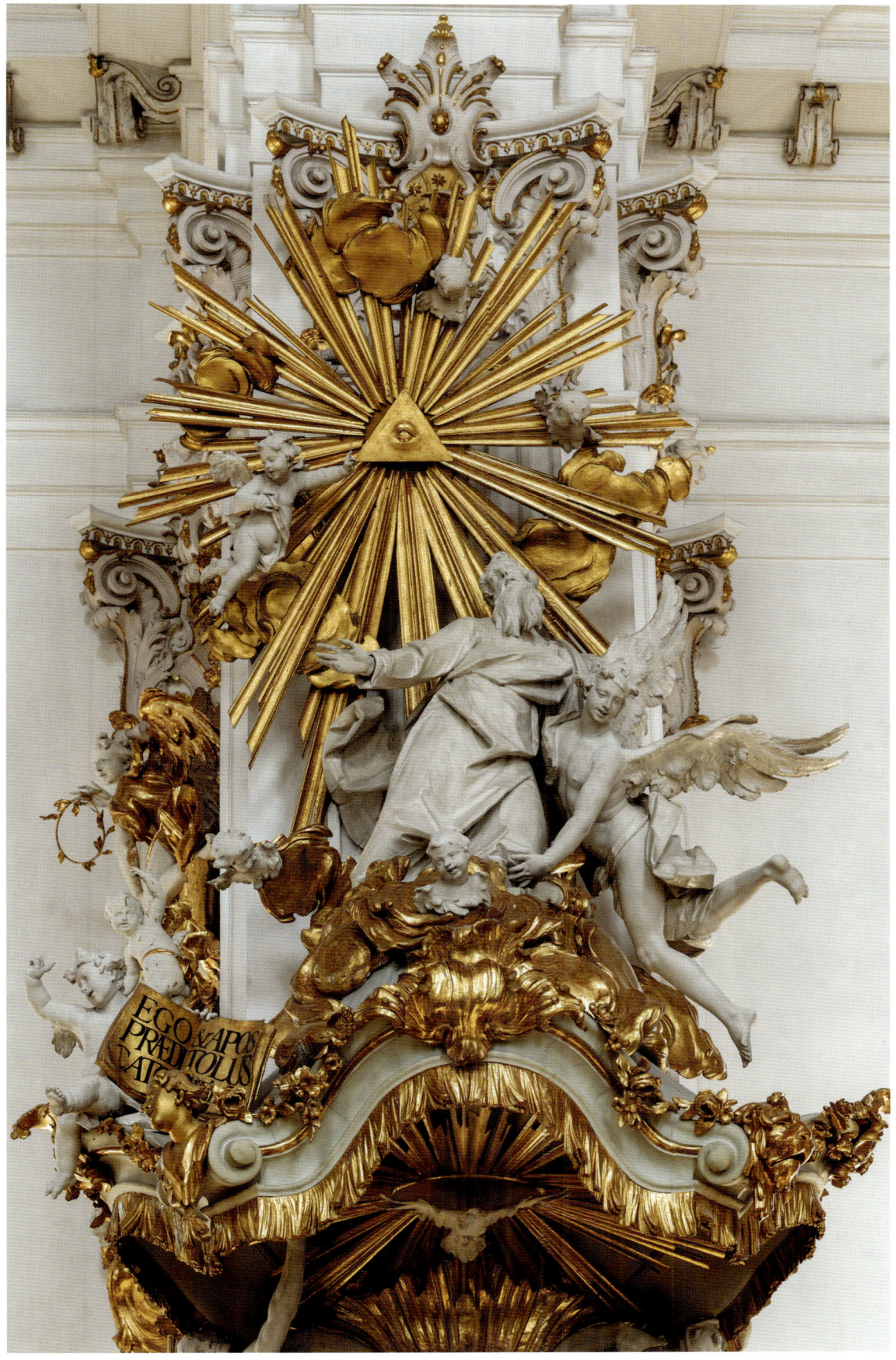

< 5.13
Johann Baptist Straub, *Pulpit*, painted and gilt wood, c. 1738-40. Church of the Assumption of the Virgin, Diessen am Ammersee.

5.13a
Johann Baptist Straub, *St Paul* at the apex of the pulpit [detail of 5.13].

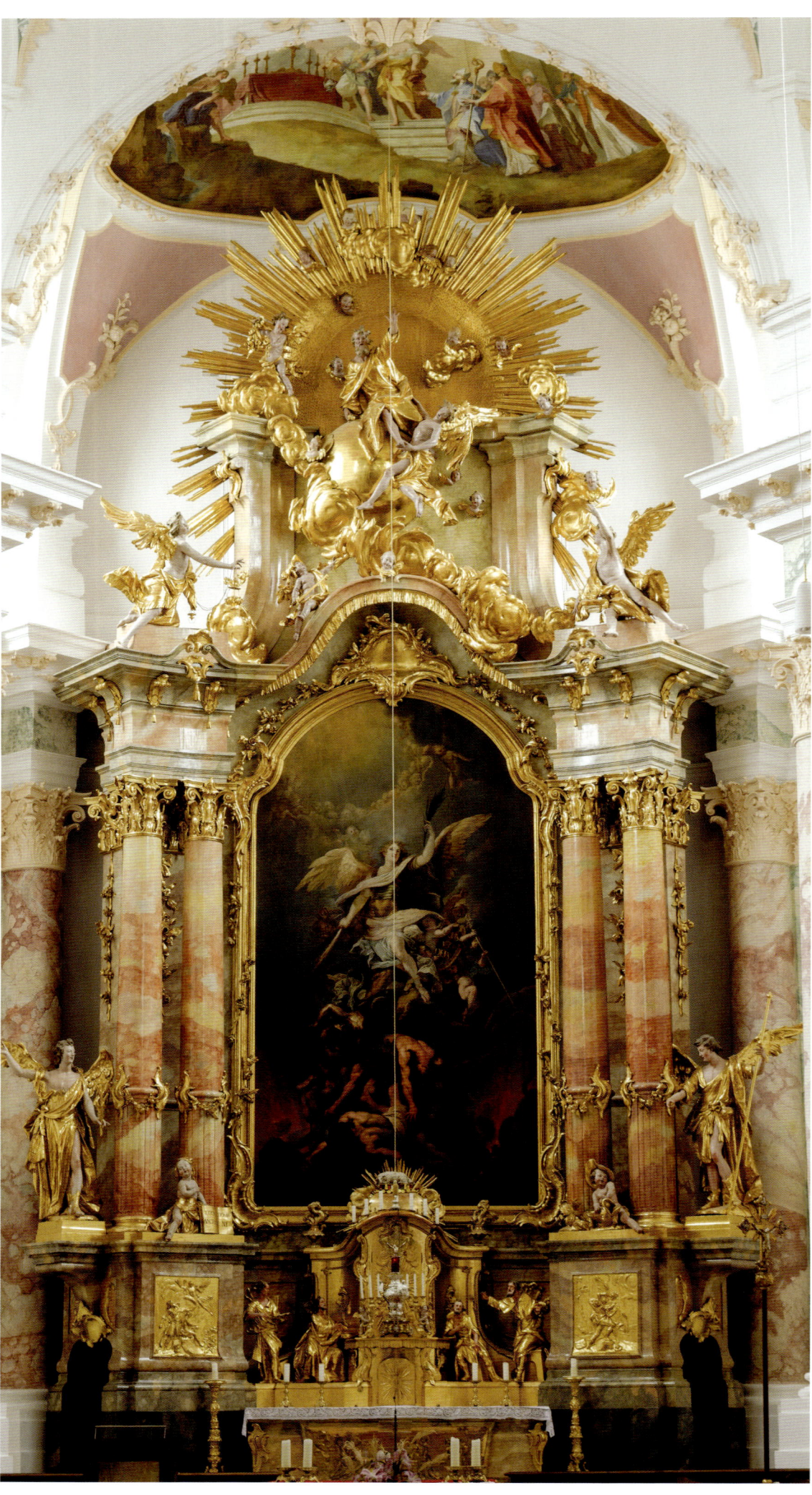

5.14
Johann Baptist Straub,
High Altar with *God the
Father on the Globe*,
painted and gilt wood,
c. 1767. Church of
St Michael,
Berg am Laim.

> 5.15
Johann Baptist Straub,
*God the Father on the
Globe* [detail of 5.14].

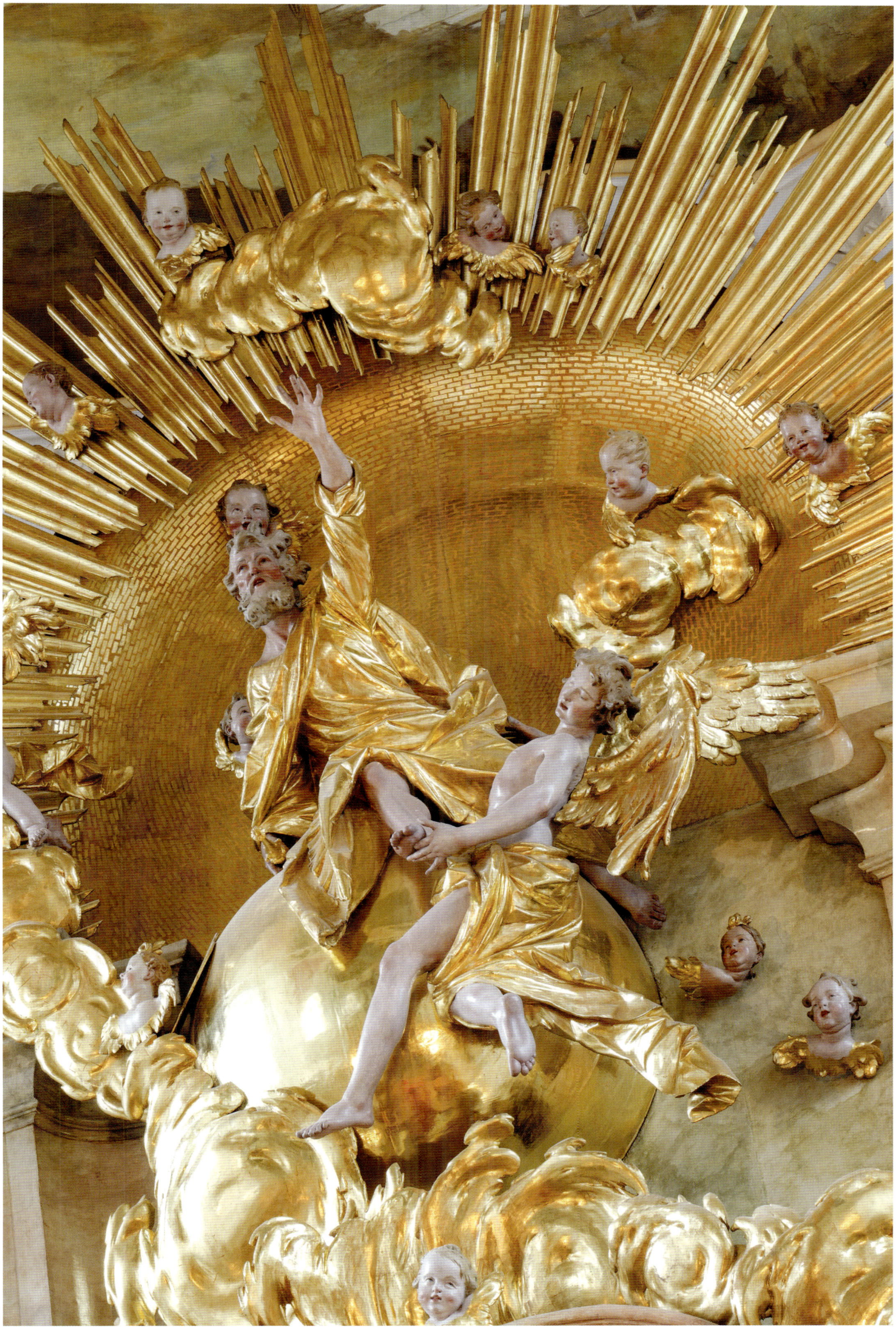

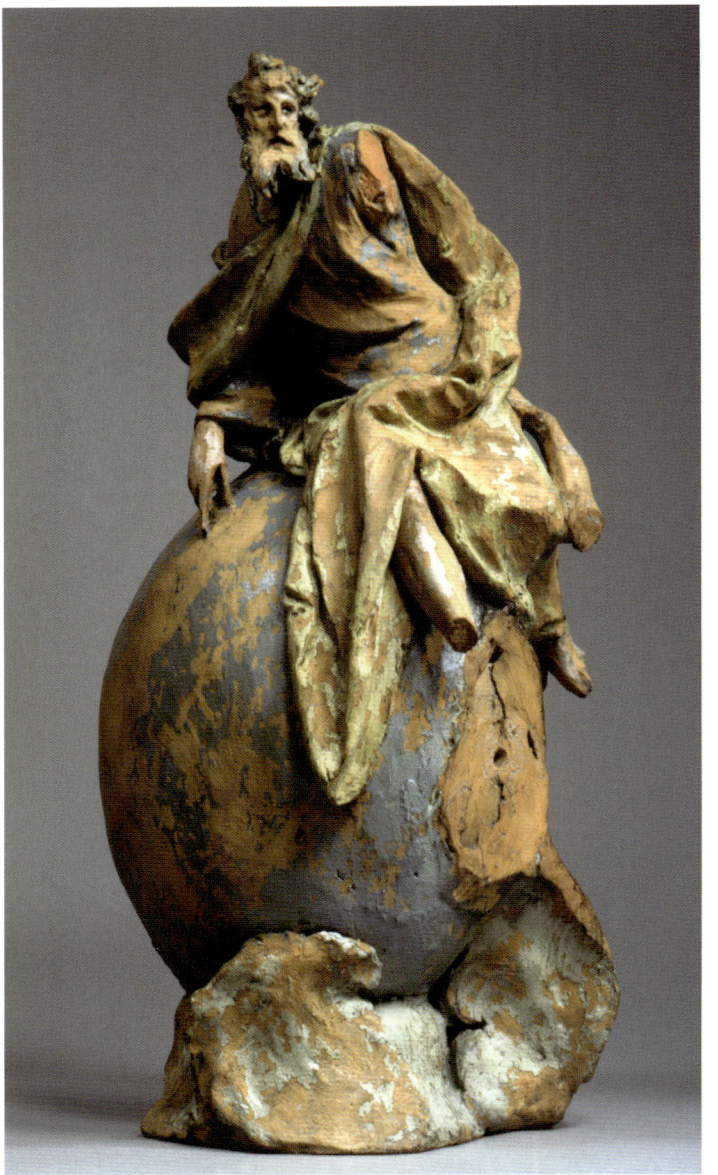

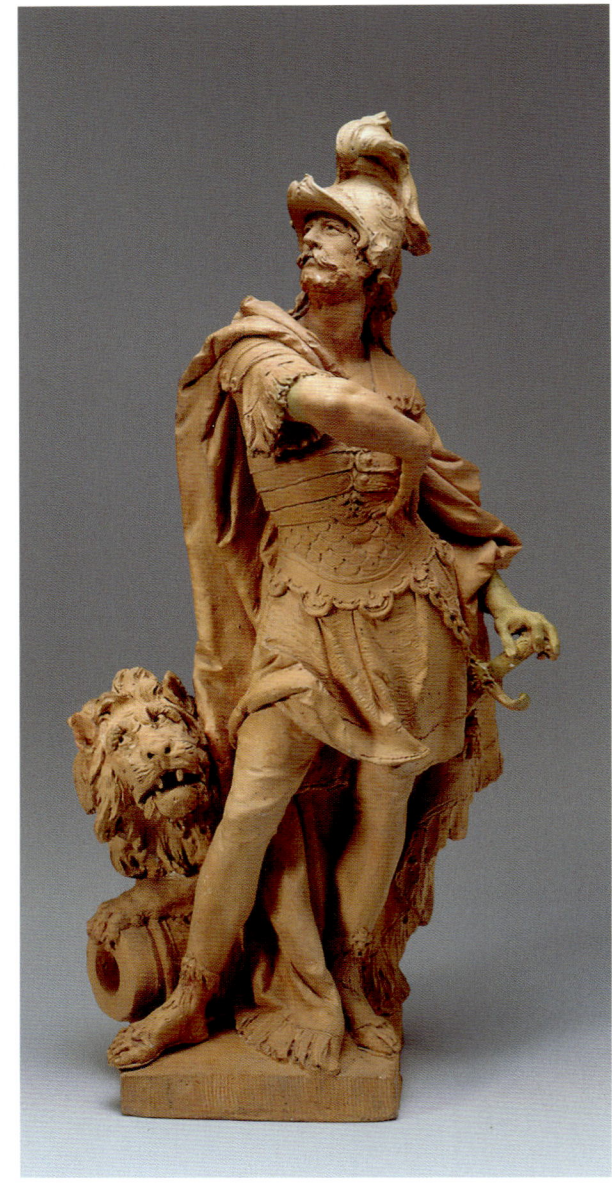

5.16
Johann Baptist Straub,
*God the Father on the
Globe*, painted
terracotta, c. 1760/5,
height 29.5 cm. Bode
Museum, Berlin
(inv. no. 7068).

5.17
Johann Baptist Straub,
Mars, terracotta,
c. 1772, height 45.3 cm.
Bayerisches National-
museum, Munich
(inv. no. R 7817).

architecture [**5.13 and 5.13a**]. Crowning the sounding board is the dramatic figure of St Paul kneeling on clouds, accompanied by an angel, under the eye of God at the centre of a dazzling aureole. A putto-angel beneath holds a book inscribed with the words 'EGO/ PRAEDI/CATOR/ & APOS/TOLUS/ 1. TIM.2.' (Where-unto I am appointed a preacher and an Apostle. St Paul First Epistle to Timothy, Chapter 2). Two herms support the sounding board, and on the body of the pulpit two gilt wood reliefs in elaborate frames depict *The Conversion of St Paul on the Road to Damascus* and *St Paul Preaching*. Overall, the pulpit seems to embody the movement and almost the instability of the late baroque/early rococo style, with figures leaning diagonally, wavy borders and fringed edgings, and with plentiful

amounts of gold, setting off the white structure and figures.[10]

Straub's sculptures for the church of St Michael, Berg am Laim, a suburb of Munich, were produced over a long period, from 1742 to 1767.[11] There he executed the high altarpiece, six side-altarpieces and two single figures of Christ and the Virgin, as well as stone sculptures for the façade that no longer survive. Johann Michael Fischer was again the architect, commencing work in 1738, the building being consecrated in 1744. The church was built for the Wittelsbach Prince-Archbishop of Cologne, Clement August (1700-61), one of the sons of Elector Maximilian Emmanuel. The foundation was a collegiate church for the Brotherhood of St Michael the Archangel, the fresco in the vault of the nave depicting the *Vision of St Michael* by Johann Baptist Zimmermann (1680-1758), who also executed the stucco work in the church. Straub's reputation is sometimes said to have suffered from the fact that he never produced a major work, but rather sculptures that were assimilated into larger ensembles. His strength can be seen in his individual sculptures and groups gracing, even amplifying, the churches for which he worked, rather than in isolated figures. The latter can only be fully seen and understood in context, and would surely lose some of their impact were they to be re-located in a museum. Berg am Laim resoundingly demonstrates this notion of Straub's output. His high altarpiece is the culminating feature of the interior, triumphantly enriching Fischer's architecture [**5.14**]. The dominating figure of God the Father sits asymmetrically on a globe, his left arm upraised, a supportive angel leaning backwards below him [**5.15**]. Above this group a glory like a giant halo surrounds the figures, peopled with cherubim and smaller angels, while clouds tumble down below the globe. Straub's preparatory terracotta model for the figure of God the Father on the globe survives, albeit in damaged form, at the Bode Museum, Berlin [**5.16**].¹² The terracotta (height 29.5 cm) is much smaller than the finished life-size wood carving at Berg am Laim, and the upraised left arm and right foot are now missing. But because of these losses and the intimate size of the piece, it can be seen and appreciated as a working model, part of Straub's creative process, the tool marks still visible in the modelling of the clay.

Straub's secular work comprised a series of over-life-size wood statues of Roman gods and goddesses made for Count Maximilian Emmanuel von Törring-Jettenbach (1715-73) for his palace in Munich (today the site of shops) in 1772. The palace was rebuilt in the nineteenth century and then badly damaged during the Second World War. The statues are now all in the Bayerisches Nationalmuseum in Munich.¹³ Some of Straub's terracotta models for the statues, also in the Bayerisches Nationalmuseum, are both monumental, despite their relatively modest size, and imbued with movement. His figure of *Mars* fuses these qualities: whilst being

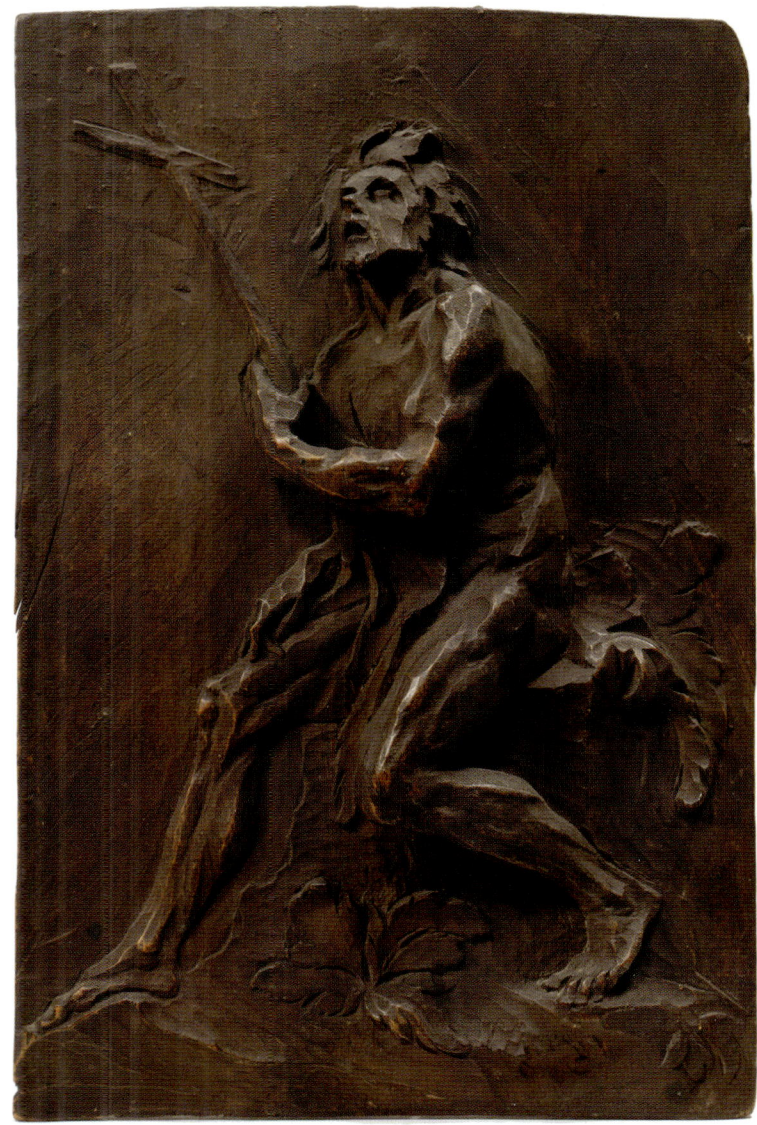

a rococo statuette it also suggests the full-size statue for which it was a preparatory study and exudes the classical language that Straub would have learnt in Vienna [**5.17**].¹⁴ The bearded Roman god of war is dressed in classical armour, his left hand on his sword, the roaring lion (omitted in the final statue) and cannon at his feet symbolizing war-like valour. The twisting contrapposto of the pose paradoxically combines energetic movement and calm classical nobility. The statuette is highly finished, implying it was a presentation model, rather than a bozzetto for use in the workshop. As mentioned above, sculptors' models can have different functions and purposes, depending on their role in the creative and commissioning process.

5.18
Ignaz Günther (after Paul Egell), *St John the Baptist*, limewood relief, signed and dated 1751, height 16.8 cm. Bayerisches Nationalmuseum, Munich (inv.no. 20/16).

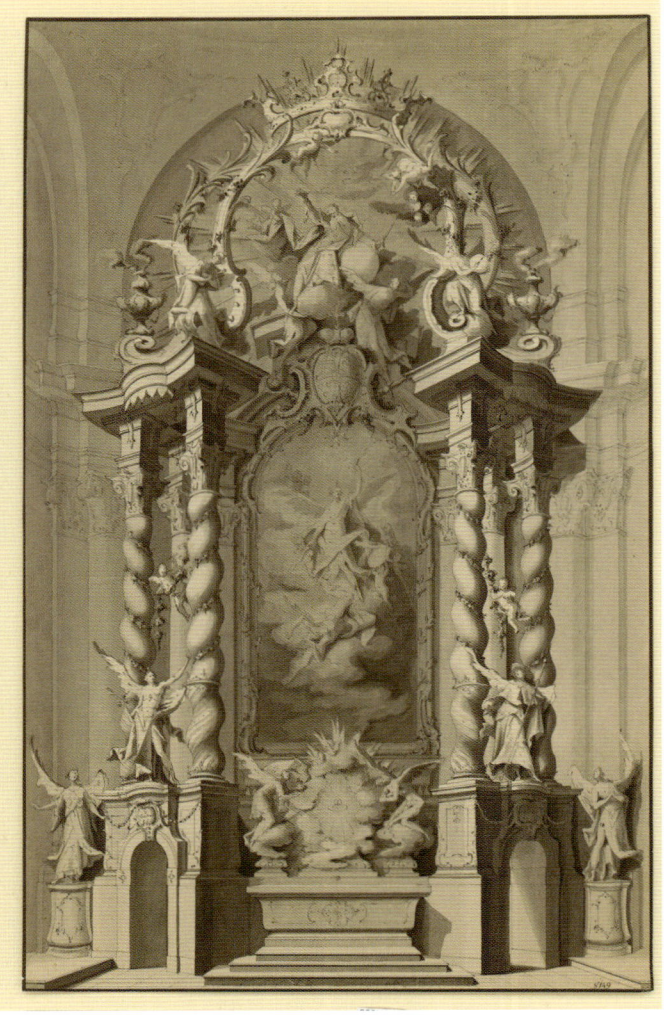

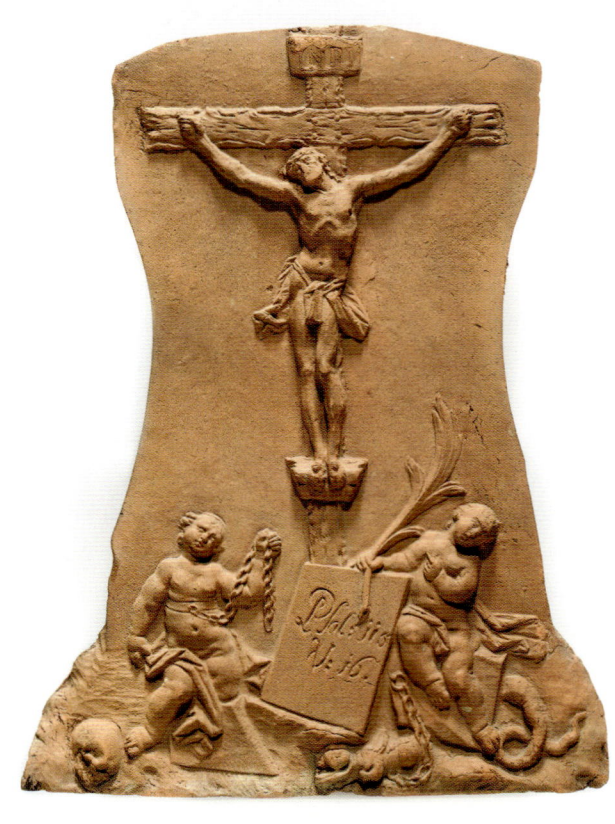

Franz Ignaz Günther

Franz Ignaz Günther (known as Ignaz Günther) was the leading sculptor in Bavaria in the mid-eighteenth century, and despite his relatively early death at the age of fifty, he produced numerous significant and seminal works, in many ways defining and shaping South German rococo sculpture.[15] Having initially trained under his father, he studied under Johann Baptist Straub in Munich from 1743 to 1750. His travels as a journeyman (his *Wanderschaft*) took him to Salzburg, Vienna and Mannheim, where he was to study with Paul Egell from 1751 to 1752. A small limewood relief (height 16.5 cm) by Günther, dating from 1751, was made after a now lost work by Egell. Depicting the seated St John the Baptist, it is now in the Bayerisches National-museum [**5.18**].[16] This model was presumably in part a homage to the older artist, and its purpose must have been primarily for study and training,

rather than a preparatory work for a finished piece.

In 1753 Günther enrolled at the Academy of Fine Arts in Vienna, setting up his own workshop in Munich in 1754; he remained there until his death in 1775. In 1737 he was appointed *Hofbefreit* sculptor by the Elector of Bavaria, Charles Albert, meaning that he was free of guild rules, and was allowed to employ more than the two apprentices allowed by the guild, although he was not paid a salary by the court. This was in contrast to Straub, who became court sculptor in the same year, and did receive a salary. Günther was conversely never appointed as court sculptor, despite his request for such an appointment in 1773. He produced sculptures for numerous Bavarian churches, such as that of Die Wies and the Asamkirche in Munich (both discussed in Chapter 4). A drawing by Günther signed and dated 1760 has been identified as an

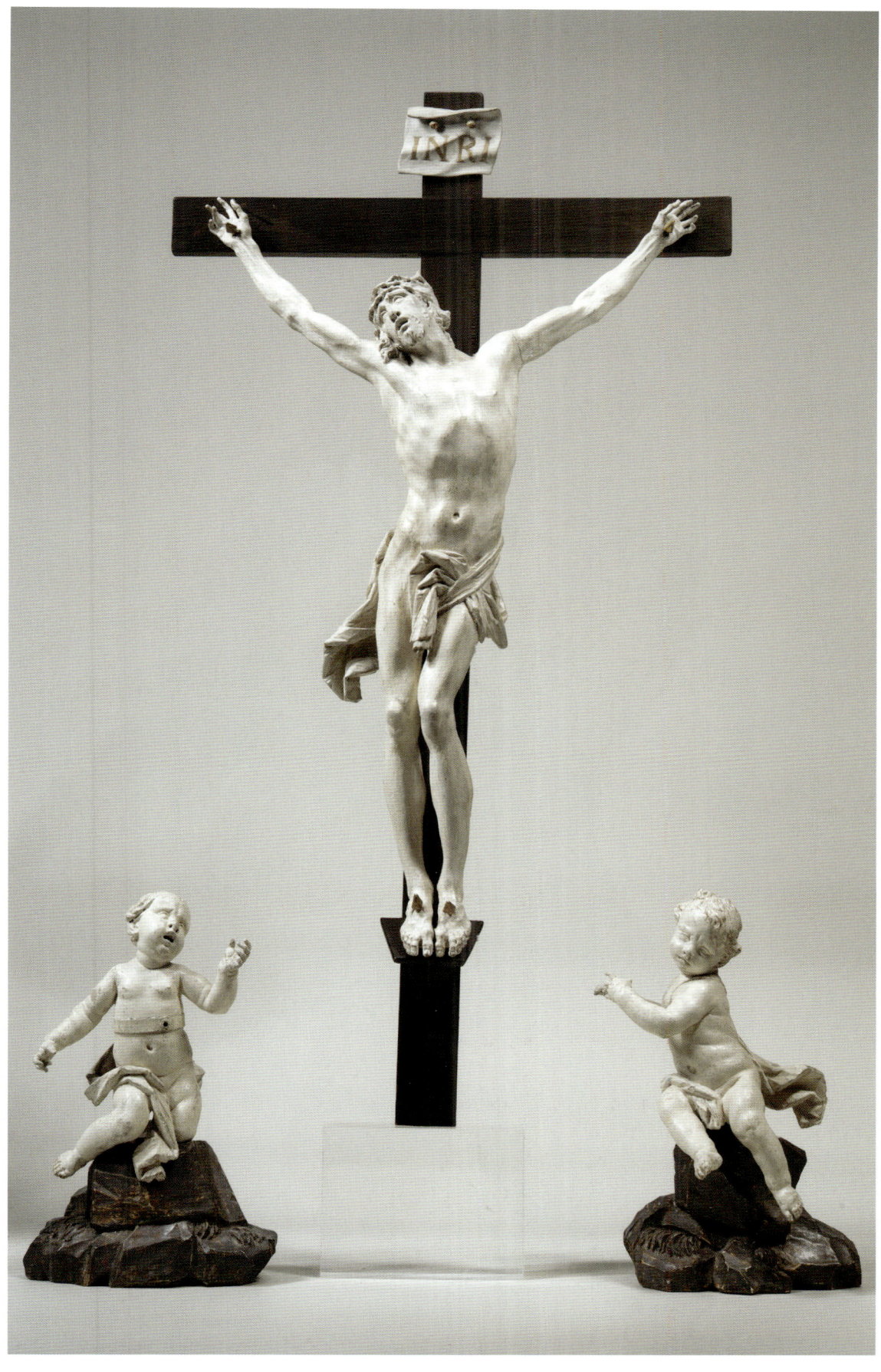

5.21
Ignaz Günther,
*Crucifixion with Two
Mourning Putti,* painted
wood, before 1770.
Bayerisches National-
museum, Munich
(inv. no. 2017/118.1-2).

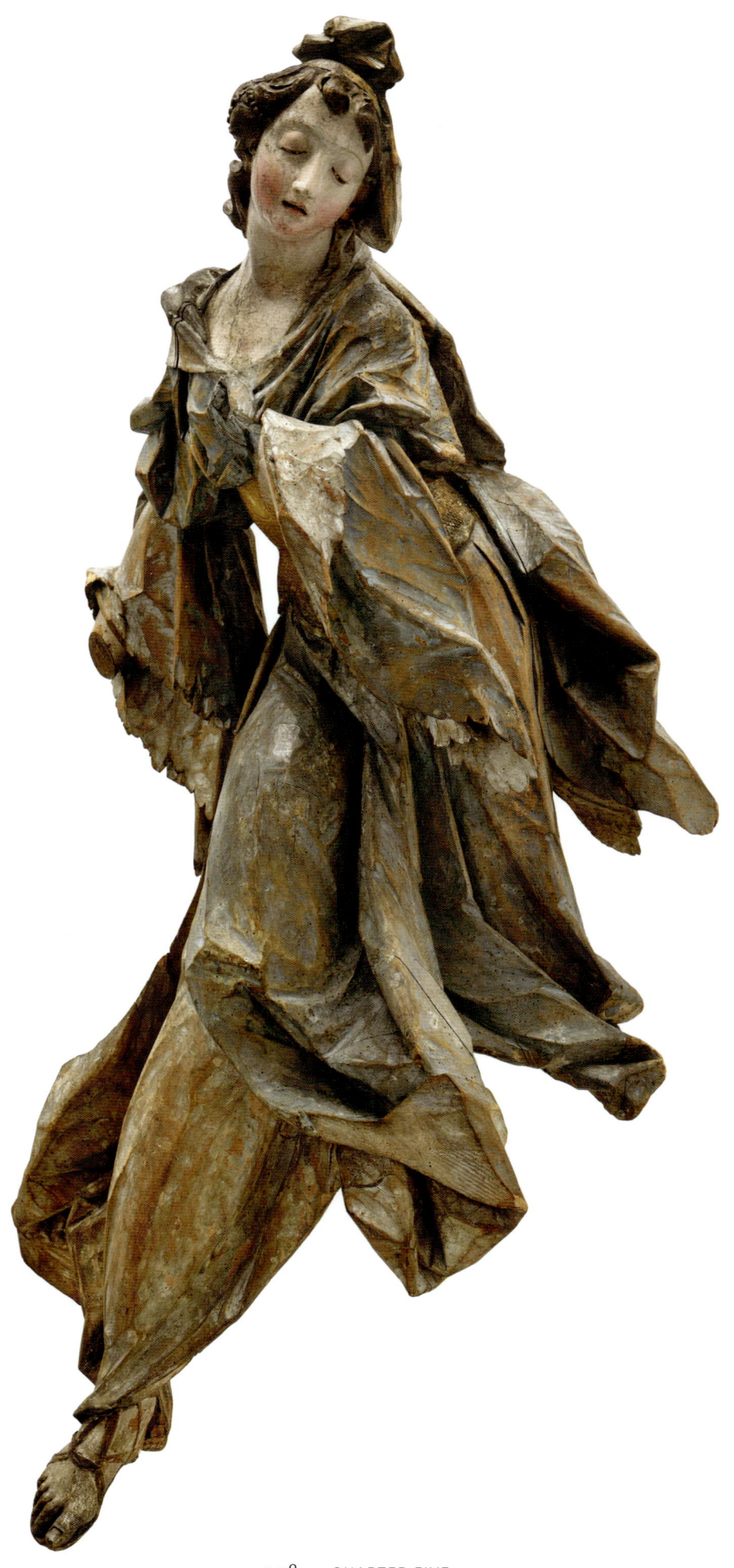

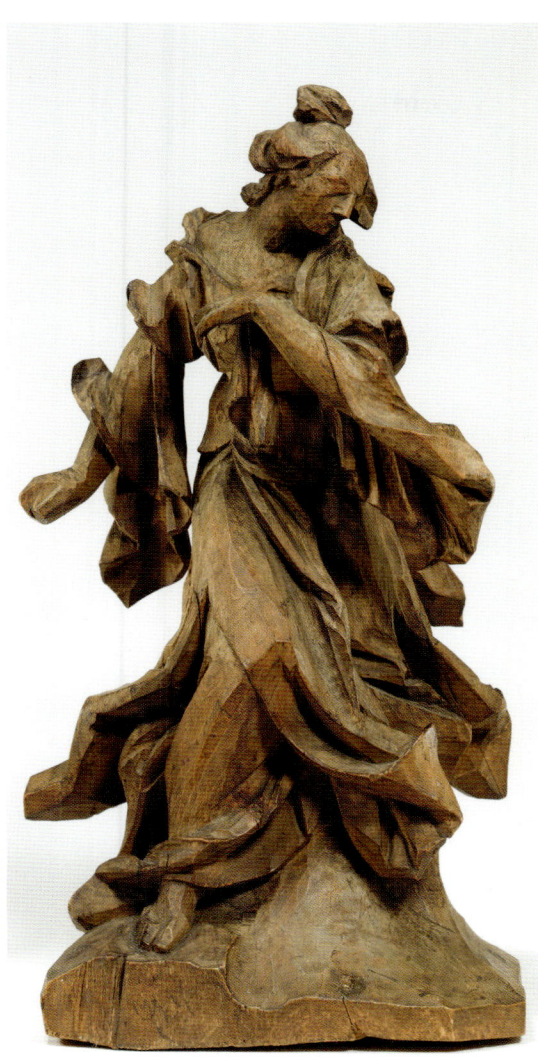

5.23
Ignaz Günther, *Model for Starnberg Female Saint*, limewood, 1755, height 20.9 cm. Bayerisches National-museum, Munich (inv. no. H 724).

carved wood model made by the artist, in this case Günther. Wax would have been poured into this clay negative. The resulting wax relief could then be applied to the model for the bell in order for it to be cast in metal. 5.20 is a terracotta squeeze from the negative clay model, possibly made at the bell foundry, rather than by Günther or one of his assistants. It may have been used as a master model for subsequent reliefs. Such models must have existed in numerous bell foundries in Munich; they depended upon Günther's original designs, but were surely produced by others. A small painted wood crucifixion group by Günther recently acquired by the Bayerisches Nationalmuseum must have been the modello used as the starting point for the reliefs [5.21].[19]

Some of Günther's preliminary models in wood for his large-scale sculptures also survive. One such is an extraordinary limewood bozzetto, just over 20 cm high, for one of the so-called Starnberg female saints that the artist produced for a now-lost altarpiece at Starnberg in around 1755, now in the Bayerisches Nationalmuseum [5.23].[20] The angular carving of the raw wood and the vibrant twisting pose of the figure, seemingly in motion even as she stands, evince Günther's distinctive power, albeit on a small scale. The larger figure for which this was a model [5.22] is signed and dated on the back 'F. j. Gindter / fecit. 1755'.

Günther's Sculpture at Rott am Inn

Günther's work at the Benedictine abbey at Rott am Inn in Upper Bavaria was carried out in 1761/2.[21] The church, dedicated to St Marinus and St Anianus, was built between 1759 and 1763 at the instigation of the abbot, Benedikt II Lutz (1720-77). The architect was once more Johann Michael Fischer, and the interior was adorned with stucco work by Jakob Rauch (1718-85) and frescoes by Matthäus Günther (1705-88) (a pupil of Cosmas Damian Asam). The frescoes include a magnificent image of the glory of the Benedic-tine Order painted on the central dome [5.24 and 5.25]. Ignaz Günther's sculptures for the church, carried out from 1760 to 1762, are to be seen throughout the interior, like the paintings and stucco, suffusing and enhancing the archi-

alternative design for Straub's high altarpiece of the church of St Michael at Berg am Laim [5.14], indicating that the younger artist was compet-ing with Straub at that time, although he did not win the commission [5.19]. Straub's own drawing for the high altarpiece as executed also survives.[17]

In addition to his drawings, several extant small terracotta reliefs by Günther for ornamen-tation on church bells demonstrate his varied output, and the relationship of modelled sculp-ture (clay) to metalwork, in this case bronze casting. A terracotta squeeze from one such model depicts a crucifix with two sorrowing putti holding broken chains, a martyr's palm, a skull and a serpent with a tablet inscribed with a Biblical reference from the Book of Psalms [5.20].[18] In order to decorate the cast bronze bells with such designs, a negative model in clay would have been cast from the original

>> 5.24
Johann Michael Fischer, Interior of the Benedic-tine church of Rott am Inn, Bavaria, with stucco work by Jakob Rauch, 1759 onwards.

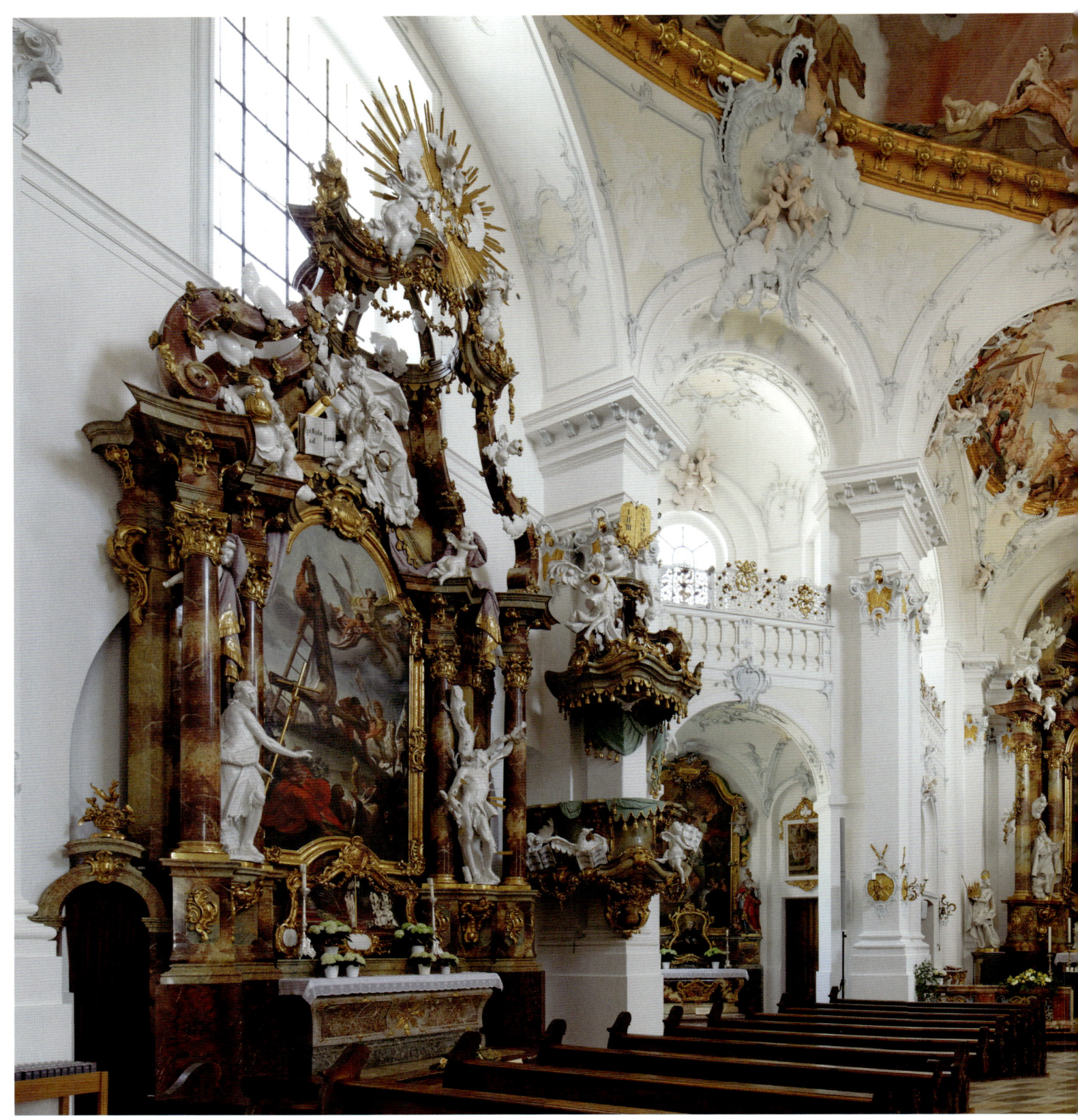

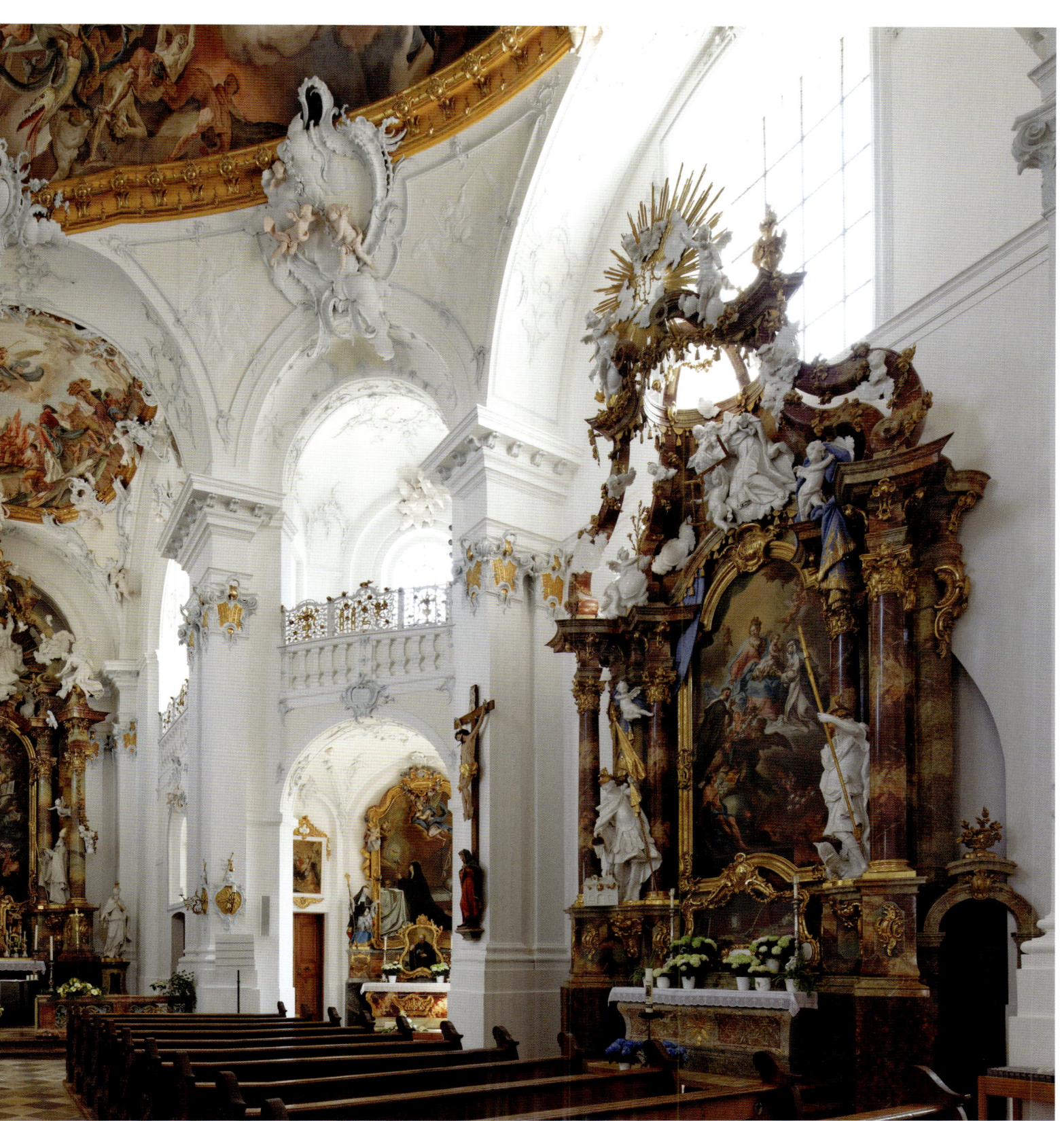

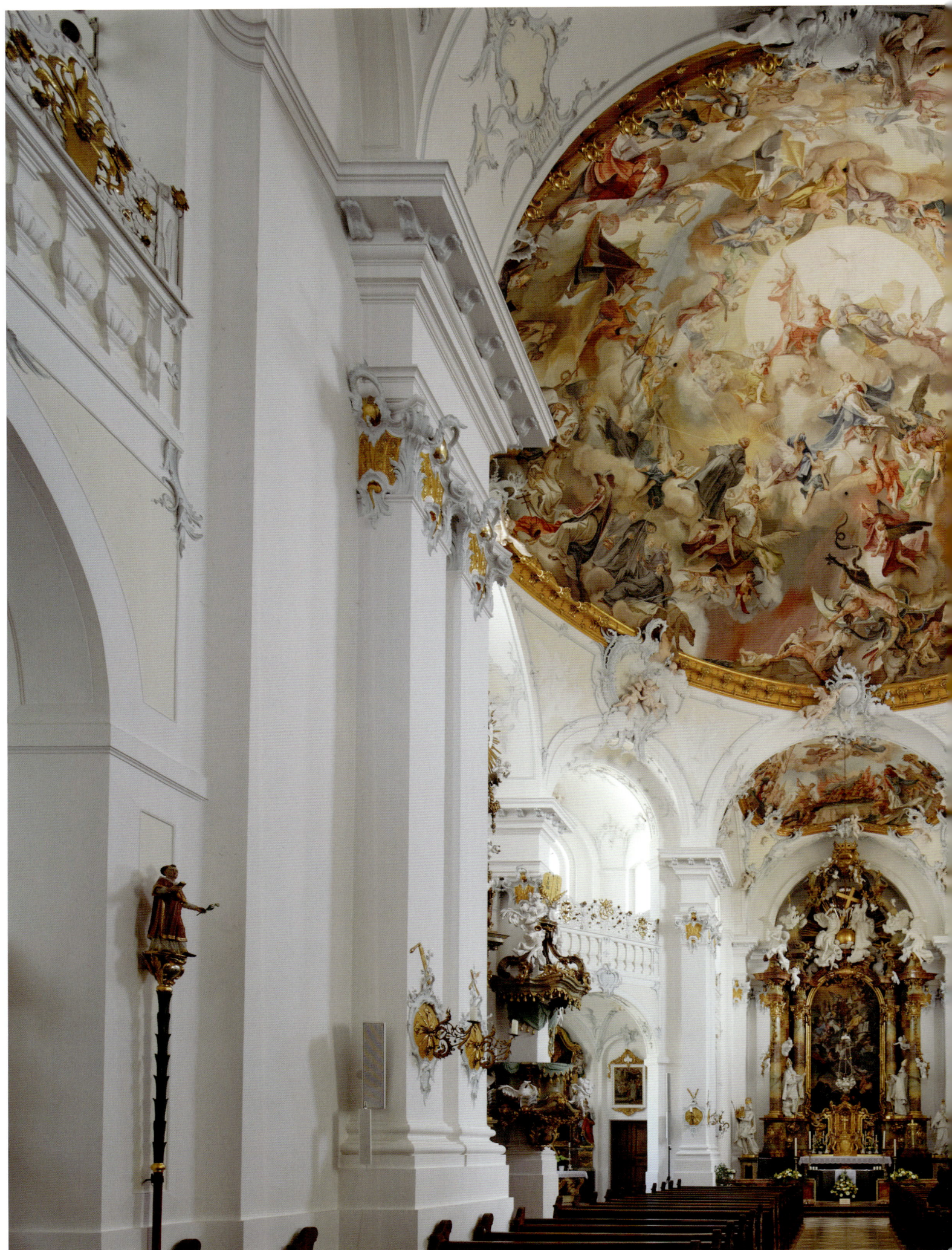

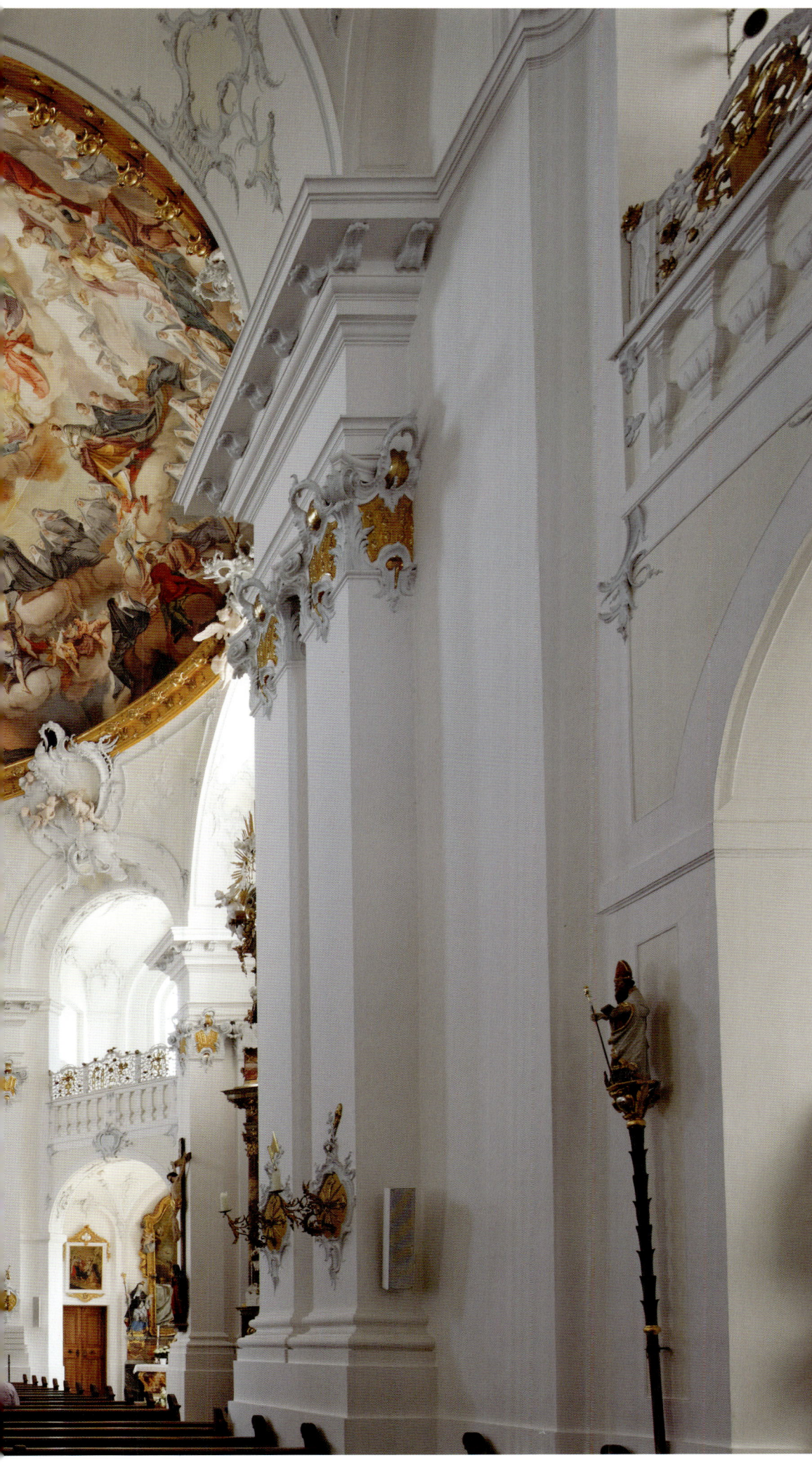

5.25
Matthäus Günther,
The Glory of the
Benedictine Order on
the central dome of the
church of Rott am Inn,
fresco, c. 1765-7.
Benedictine church of
Rott am Inn, Bavaria.

>> 5.26
Interior of the
Benedictine church
at Rott am Inn,
c. 1761-5. Benedictine
church of Rott am Inn,
Bavaria.

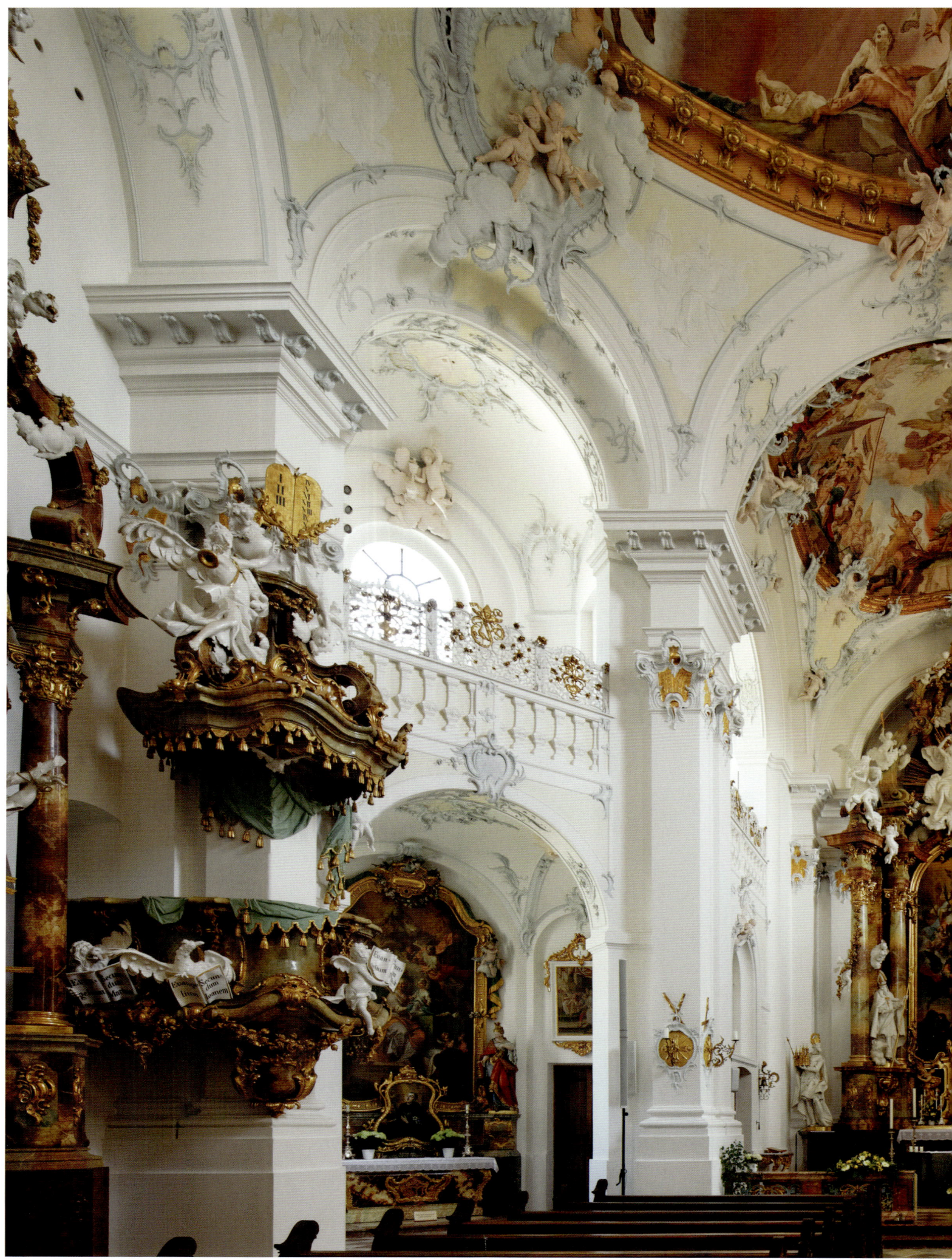

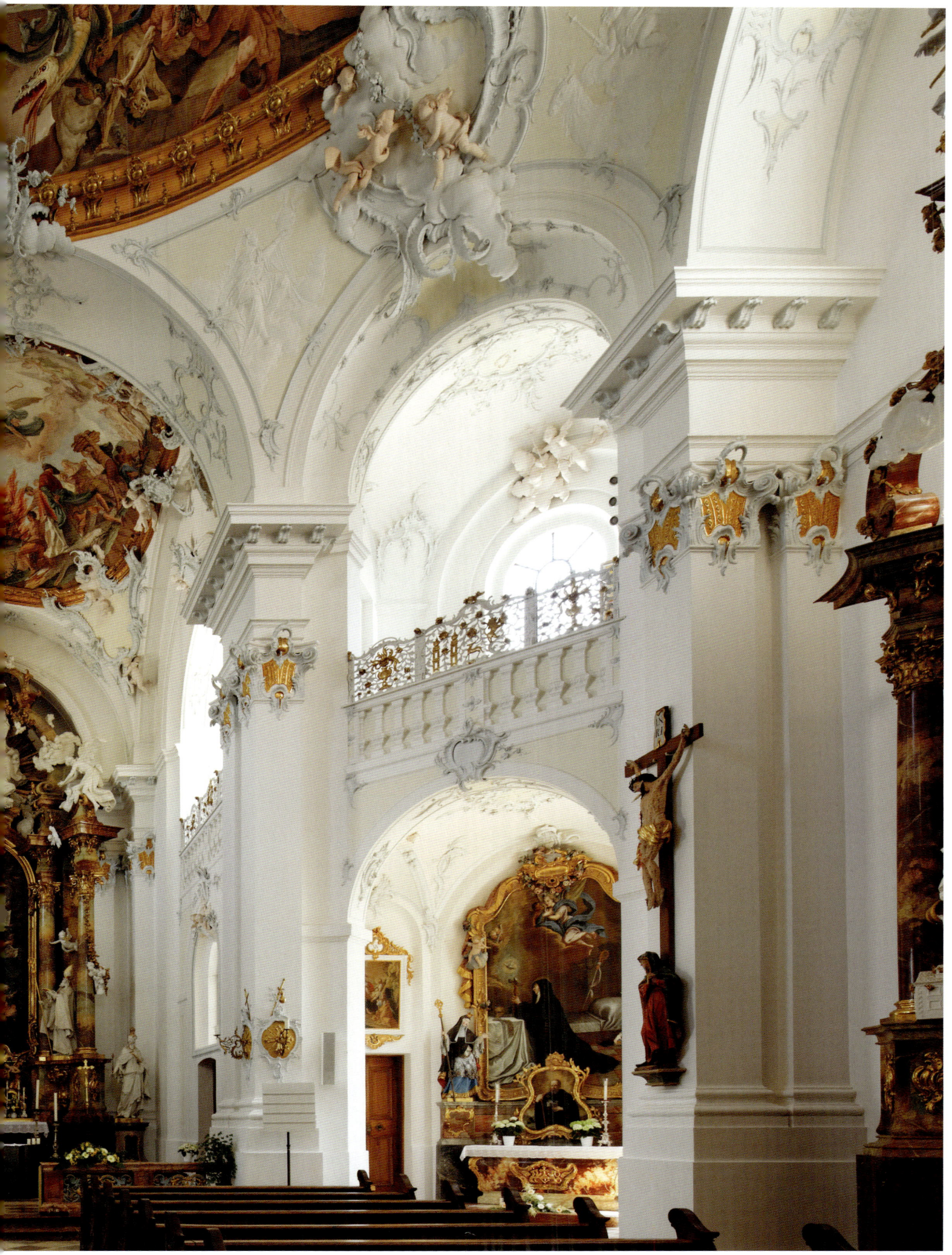

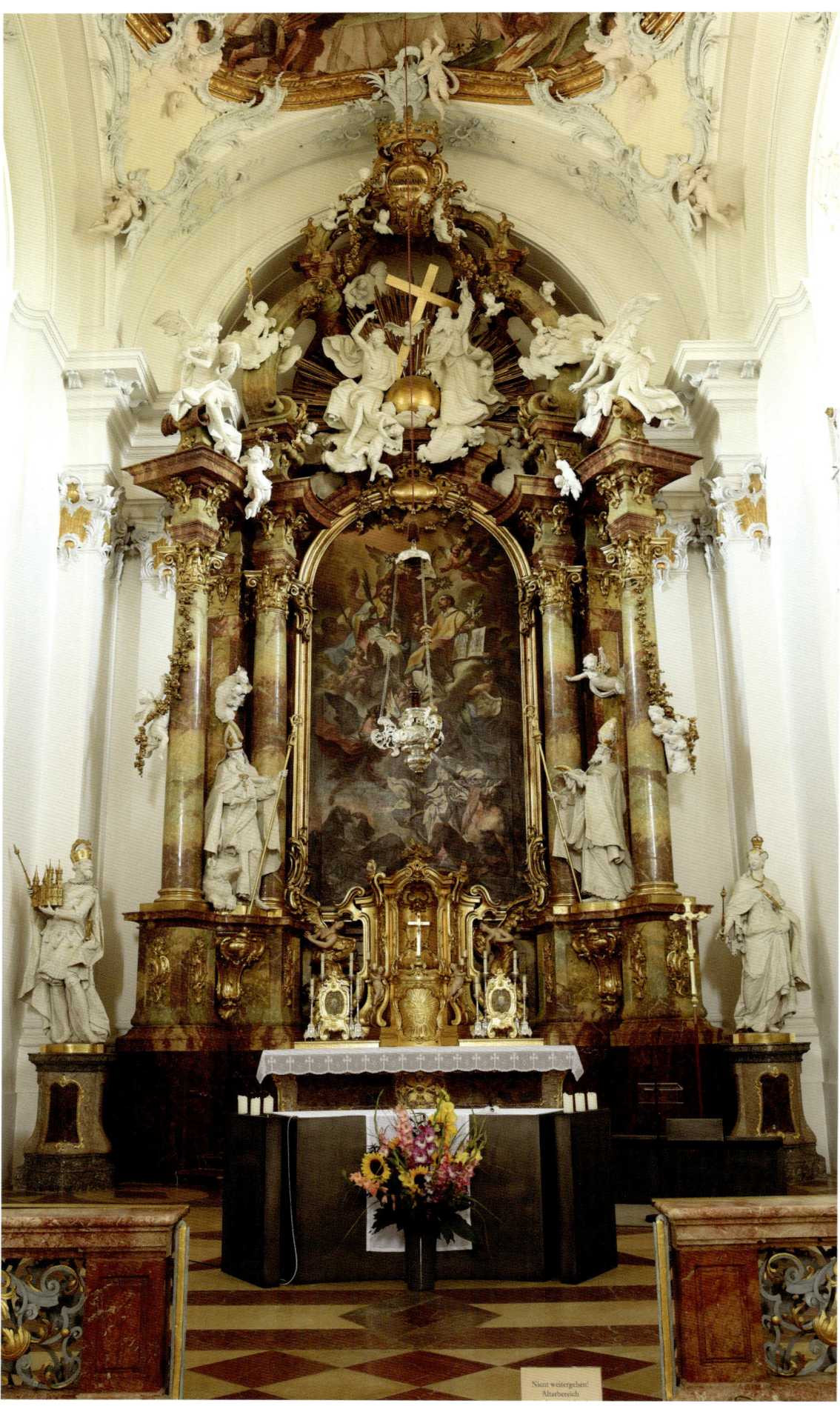

5.27
Ignaz Günther, High
Altarpiece, painted and
gilt wood and marble
columns, c. 1761-2.
Benedictine church of
Rott am Inn, Bavaria.

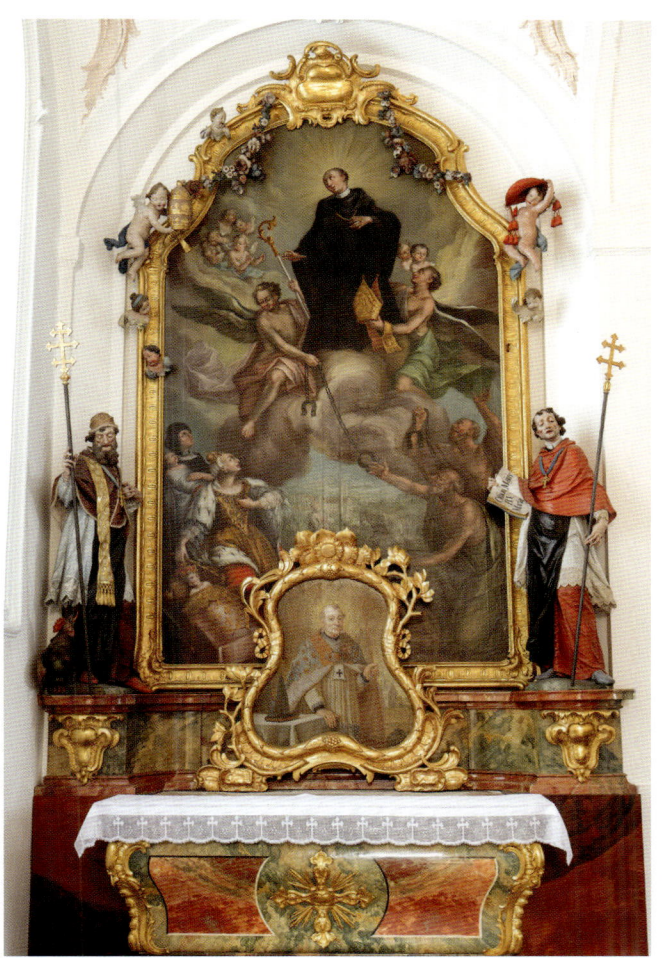
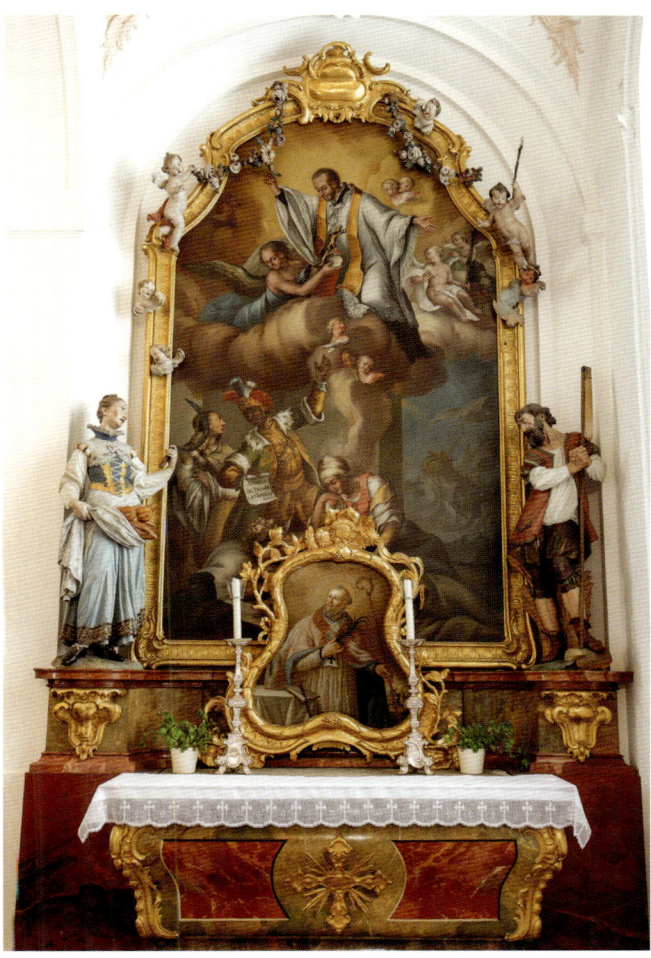

tectural whole. He executed the high altarpiece [**5.26 and 5.27**], as well as the side altars dedicated to St Leonard and St Francis Xavier respectively, with paintings by Franz-Anton Höttinger [**5.28 and 5.29**]. His pupil Joseph Götsch (1728-93) assisted him in the wood carving and was responsible for the pulpit [**5.30**], as well as the small heads on the confessionals, including a disturbing skull representing Death.

The form of the imposing high altarpiece at Rott am Inn [**5.27**] seems to be a precursor of Straub's slightly later one at Berg am Laim of c. 1767 [**5.14**], for which indeed Günther was to submit a design, as noted above. This resemblance between the two works indicates the stylistic proximity of the two sculptors. The Rott am Inn high altarpiece is also reminiscent of that at Diessen by François de Cuvilliés the Elder and Joseph Joachim Dietrich [**5.10**]. The group of the Trinity crowning the Rott am Inn retable is encircled by angels and cherubim. Meanwhile, standing at the foot of the altar are two pairs of saints: the figures of St Corbinian

and St Ulrich, and the Holy Roman Emperor St Henry II and his empress, St Cunigunde [**5.31**]. All the figures are painted white with gold highlights, imitating the marble of Bernini, their bright surfaces also seeming to ape the glossiness of contemporary porcelain as much as Carrara marble. The saints frame the central painting of *The Assumption of the Virgin*, an appropriate triumphant focus for Fischer's church. The figure of the pious empress, St Cunigunde, stands on the south side of the high altarpiece, her swinging pose mirroring that of her consort Emperor Henry on the north side. She holds a sceptre, the gesture balancing her contrapposto, while her crown suggests that her imperial status is only slightly inferior to the glory of the high altar.

The figures of saints on the side-altars at Rott am Inn flanking the central paintings are polychromed, positioned on either side of the paintings in the same way that the white and gilt figures are placed at the sides of the high altarpiece. The central painting on the St Leonard

5.28
Franz-Anton Höttinger and Ignaz Günther, *Side-altarpiece dedicated to St Leonard*, paint on canvas and gilt wood frame and painted wood figures, c. 1762. Benedictine church of Rott am Inn, Bavaria.

5.29
Franz-Anton Höttinger and Ignaz Günther, *Side-altarpiece dedicated to St Francis Xavier*, paint on canvas with gilt wood frame and painted wood figures, c. 1762. Benedictine church of Rott am Inn, Bavaria.

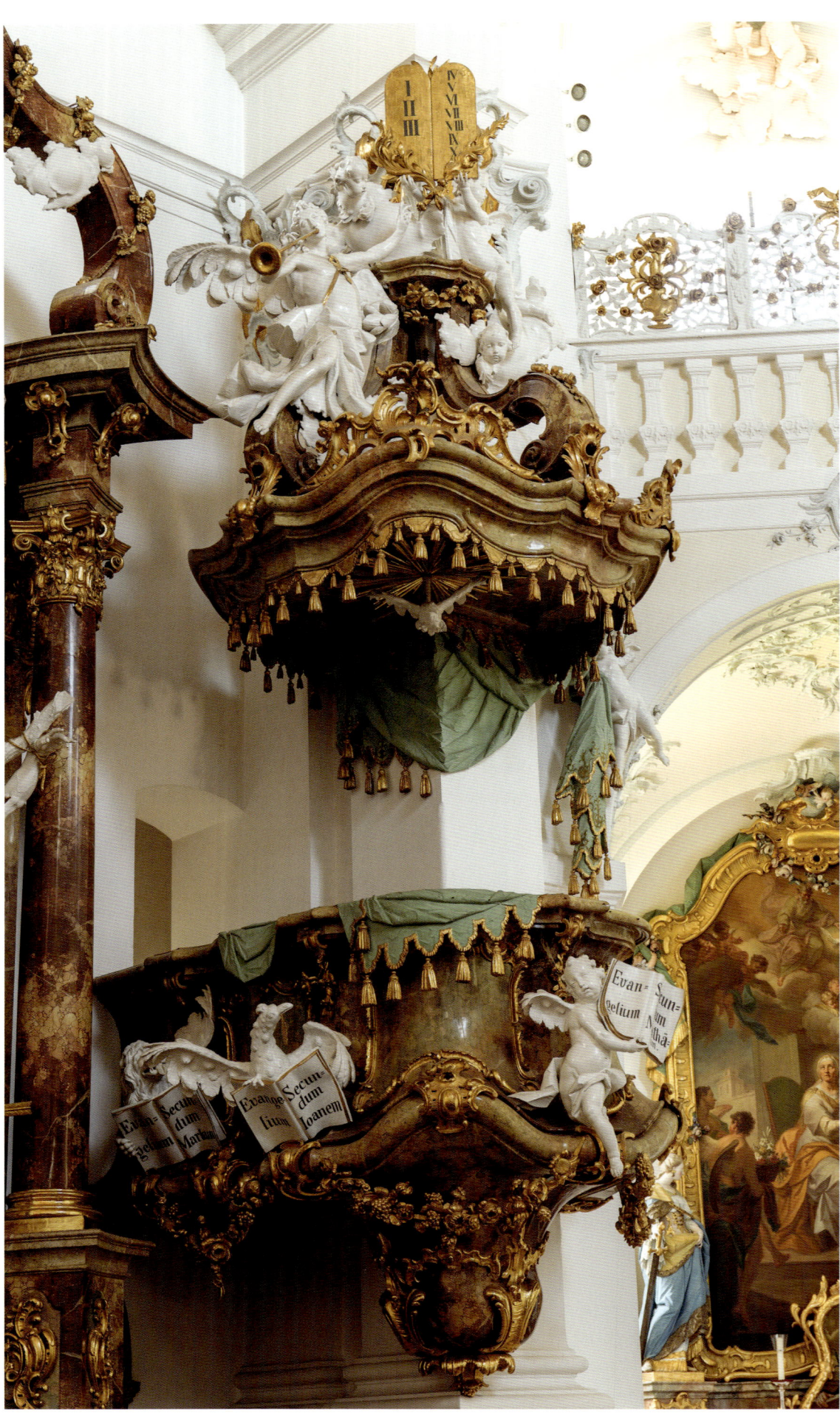

5.30
Joseph Götsch, *Pulpit
with the Giving of the
Law on Sinai*, wood,
c. 1762. Benedictine
church of Rott am Inn,
Bavaria.

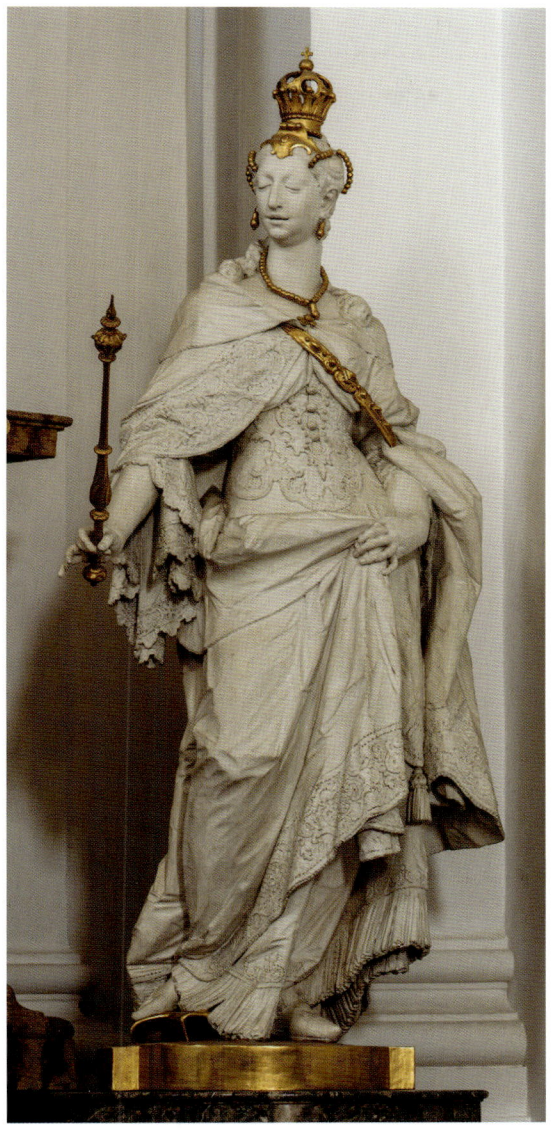

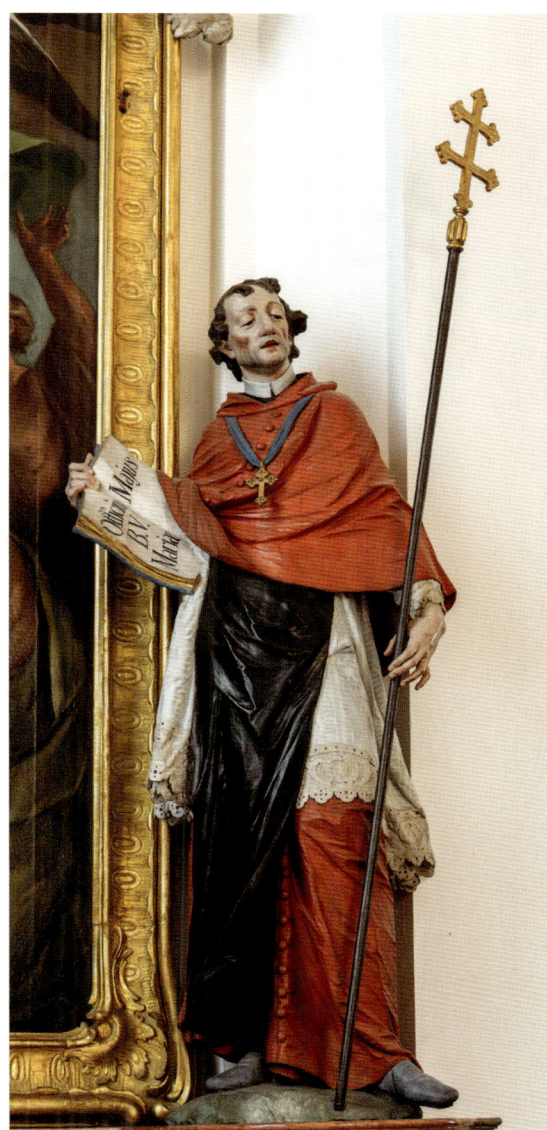

5.31
Ignaz Günther, Empress
St Cunigunde on the
High Altarpiece, painted
and gilt wood, c. 1761-2.
Benedictine church of
Rott am Inn, Bavaria.

5.32
Ignaz Günther, St Peter
Damian, on the side-
altarpiece dedicated
to St Leonard, painted
wood, c. 1761-2.
Benedictine church of
Rott am Inn, Bavaria.

side-altarpiece on the north side of the nave is the *Apotheosis of St Leonard*, with statues of Pope Leo IV and St Peter Damian on either side of the picture. Like the figures of the empress and emperor on the high altarpiece, here that of *St Peter Damian* [**5.32**] symmetrically echoes the corresponding figure of Pope Leo IV. The brilliant red, white and black of St Peter's vestments attest to the saint's almost regal presence, while his turned face and twisting pose, his left foot extended from beneath his robes, half suggest he is dancing. He is not wearing his cardinal's hat because a putto several feet above him, perched on the frame of the picture, is frolicking with it, the tassels dangling down on either side [**5.33**]. Such a playful detail recalls the putto on Dietrich's altarpiece at Diessen [**5.10**]. The solemnity of the saint is lightly

mocked, although perhaps Günther's motivation in giving the putto this role was rather to indicate the joys of Christianity. A matching putto on the other side holds the papal tiara high above the figure of Pope Leo IV. Günther's presentation drawing shows both men wearing their respective headgear, suggesting these details were later modifications [**5.34**].

The altarpiece on the opposite (south) side of the nave from the St Leonard altar is dedicated to St Francis Xavier, and in contrast to the almost aristocratic St Leonard altarpiece it is flanked by two rustic saints: the Austrian St Notburga [**5.35**] and St Isidore of Seville, the farmer saint [**5.36**]. Both are dressed in peasant costume, St Notburga holding a scythe and half a dozen loaves in her apron, while St Isidore stands with sheaves of corn and his staff. Despite their dress

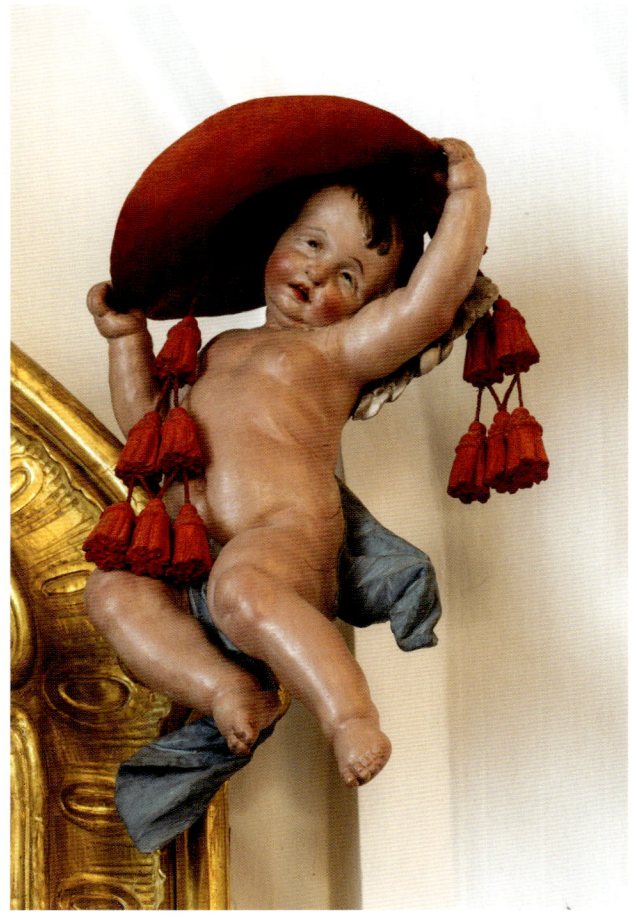

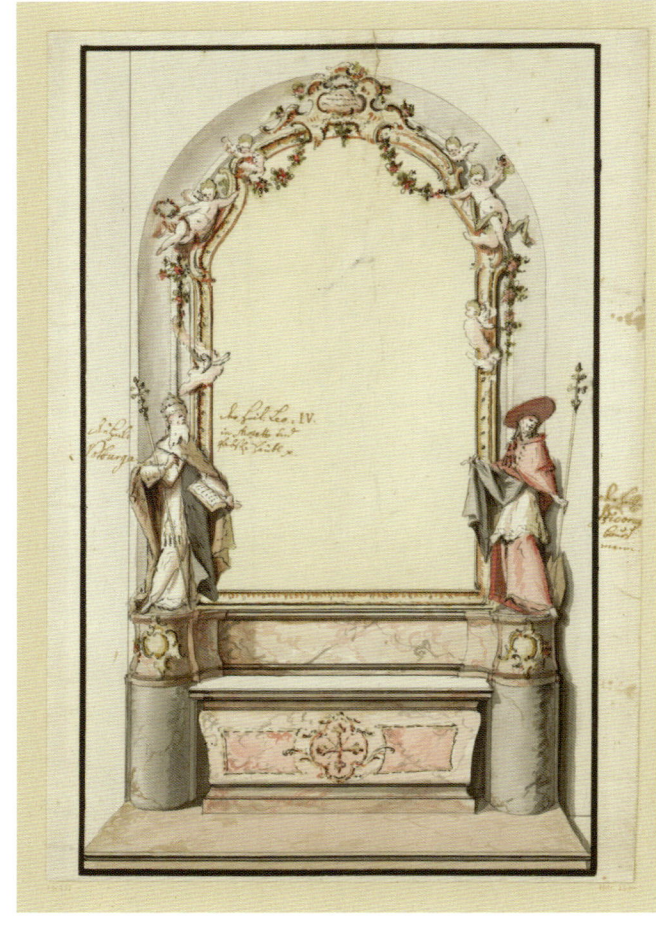

5.33
Ignaz Günther, *Putto Playing with Cardinal's Hat, on the side-altar-*piece dedicated to St Leonard, painted wood, c. 1761-2. Benedictine church of Rott am Inn, Bavaria.

5.34
Ignaz Günther, Presentation drawing for the side-altarpiece dedicated to St Leonard at Rott am Inn, watercolour, c. 1761, height 24.2 cm, width 22.6 cm.

intimating their lack of worldly power, their poses and facial expressions imply nobility and sanctity.

Günther's *Guardian Angel*, and Sculptures at Weyarn and Nenningen

Günther's *Guardian Angel* in Munich was originally a processional sculpture, made for the city's Carmelite monastery of St Nicholas [**5.37**]. It is signed and dated 16 July 1763 on a piece of paper found in the base relatively recently, in 1994. Now in the Bürgersaal church in Munich, the group was acquired by the Marian congregation there after the secularization of abbeys and monasteries in Bavaria in 1810.[22] A preparatory wash drawing for the sculpture, signed and dated 1763, is extant in the Staatliche Graphische Sammlung, Munich, showing the group as it would have been displayed on an altar, under a canopy; the drawing exhibits various differences from the finished wood group, evident in the poses and costumes of both figures.[23] It was apparently commissioned by Father Lucas, the

Carmelite prior of the monastery. Perhaps the wash drawing was a presentation sketch for this patron, and his response dictated the changes in the final group. The sculpture as executed depicts the elongated and elegant figure of the angel with expansive fluttering wings, crushing the serpent beneath his feet, his slim proportions contrasting with the chubby boy wearing a woven headband and smock, holding the angel's hand and stepping forward, while lifting up the hem of his garment as if to avoid a muddy puddle. The sculpture is reminiscent of a depiction of *Tobias and the Angel*, although the child is not here carrying a fish.[24] The guardian angel's oval face with its heavy eyelids and sickle-shaped eyes has been compared with the facial features of the earlier bronze angel of c. 1595 by Hubert Gerhard on the tomb of Duke William V in St Michael's church in Munich [**for which see Chapter 1**].[25] Günther must certainly have been aware of Netherlandish precedents for the facial features, and could have drawn on Gerhard's work as a prototype.

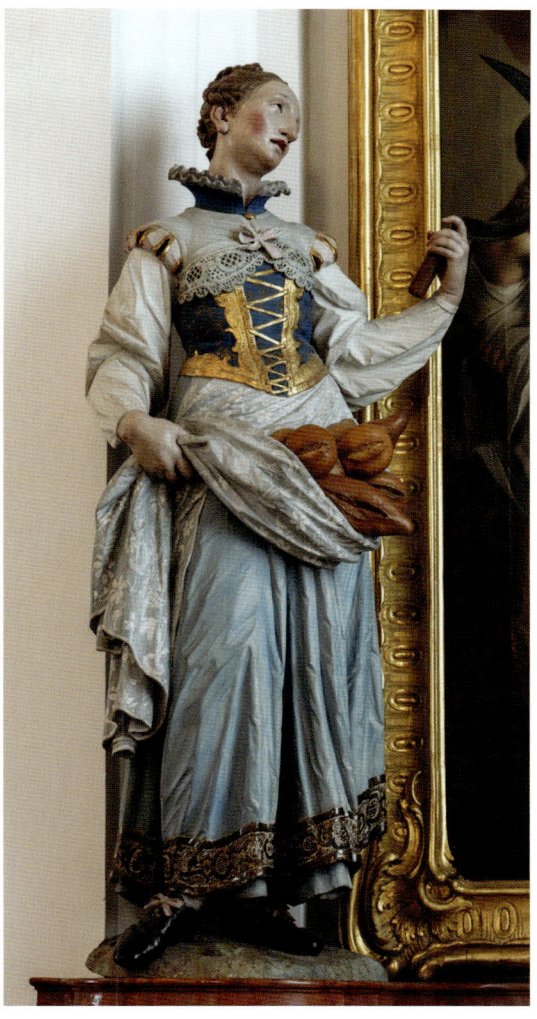

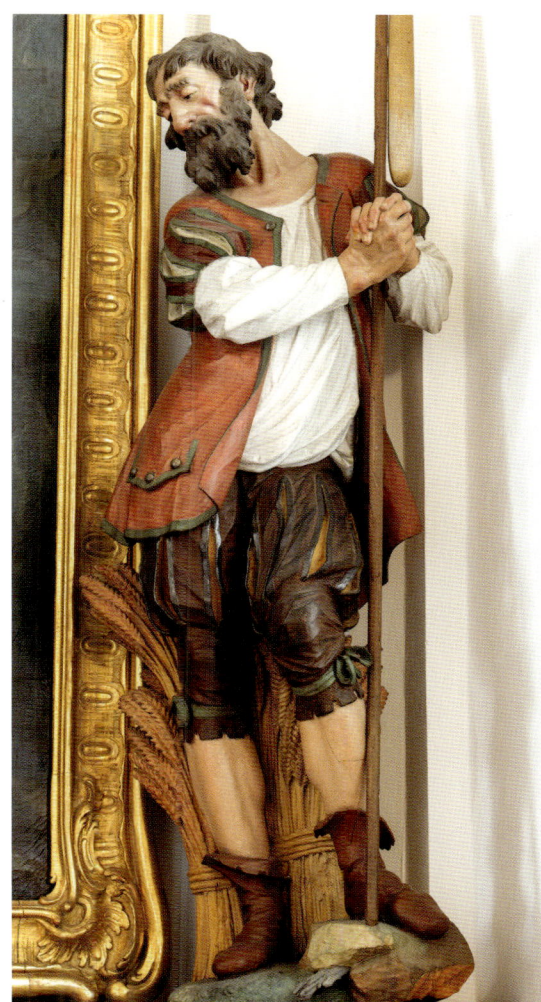

5.35
Ignaz Günther,
St Notburga, on the
altarpiece dedicated
to St Francis Xavier,
painted wood, c. 1761-2.
Benedictine church of
Rott am Inn, Bavaria.

5.36
Ignaz Günther,
St Isidore, on the
altarpiece dedicated
to St Francis Xavier,
painted wood, c. 1761-2.
Benedictine church of
Rott am Inn, Bavaria.

Two more processional sculptures by
Günther are in the parish church of St Peter
and St Paul at Weyarn (formerly an Augustinian foundation): *The Annunciation* [**5.38**] and
The Pietà [**5.39**].[26] Both date from 1764 and
were made for the Confraternity of the Rosary
at Weyarn. Each of these two groups expresses
Günther's sophisticated yet simple style. In
both cases the protagonists communicate with
each other emotively: Gabriel's upraised arm
in *The Annunciation* hails the Virgin, pointing
upwards to the Holy Spirit hovering above.
The youthful Virgin half-kneels meekly over
her lectern, overawed by the message the angel
brings. In the group of *The Pietà*, the Virgin as
mother of Christ—a dagger of agony piercing
her breast with sorrow—leans her head
sideways towards Christ's outstretched body,
his long limbs forming a sinuous convex curve
at the base of the pyramidal composition.
A putto at Christ's feet sorrowfully contem-
plates his winding sheet, exhibiting pathos
and tenderness. Both groups are coloured

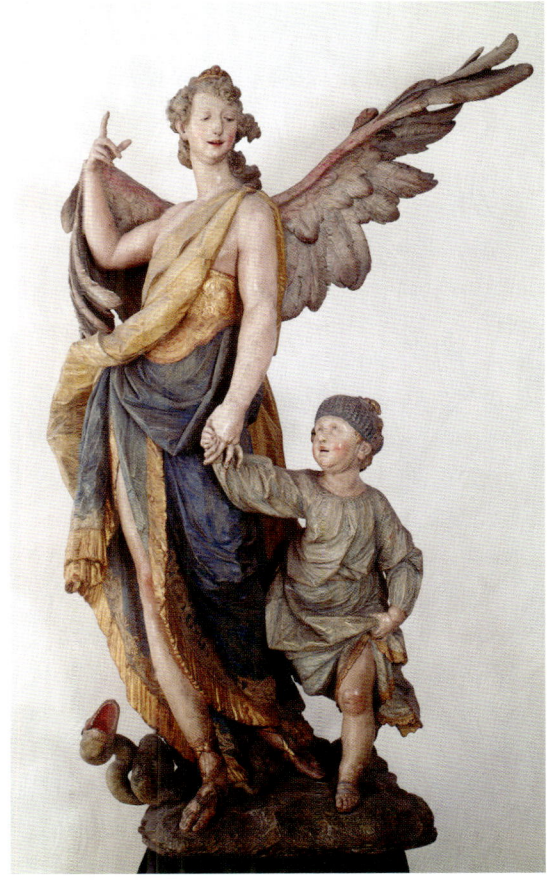

5.37
Ignaz Günther,
Guardian Angel, painted
wood, signed and dated
1763. Burghers' Hall
(Bürgersaal), Munich.

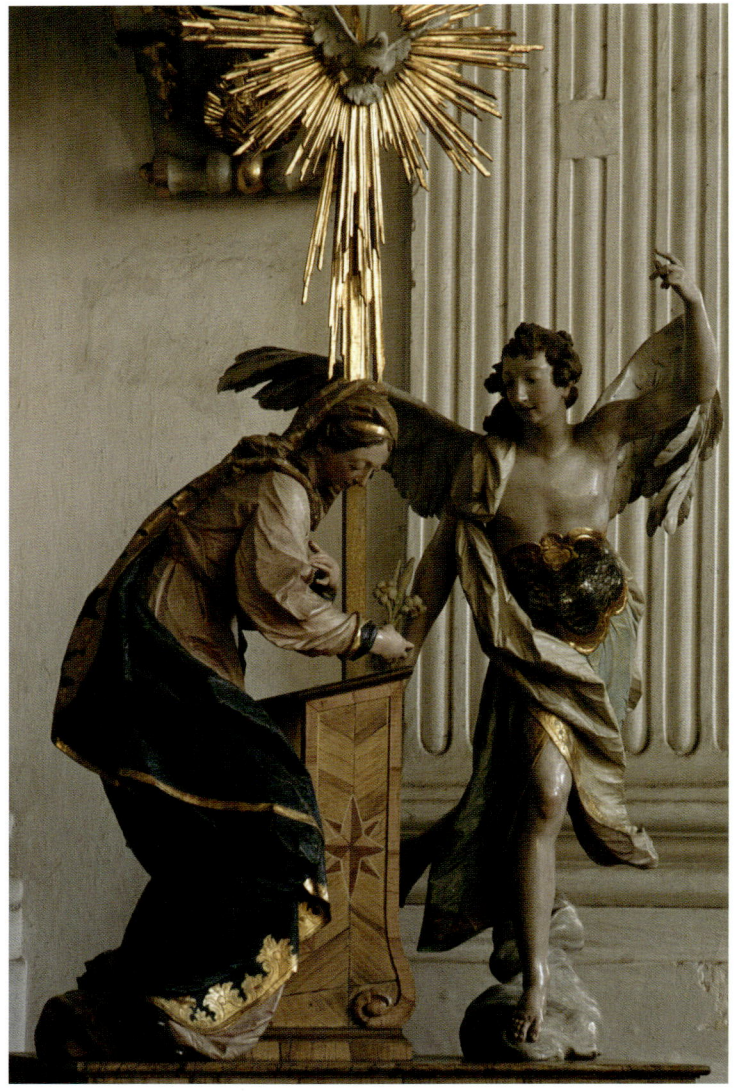

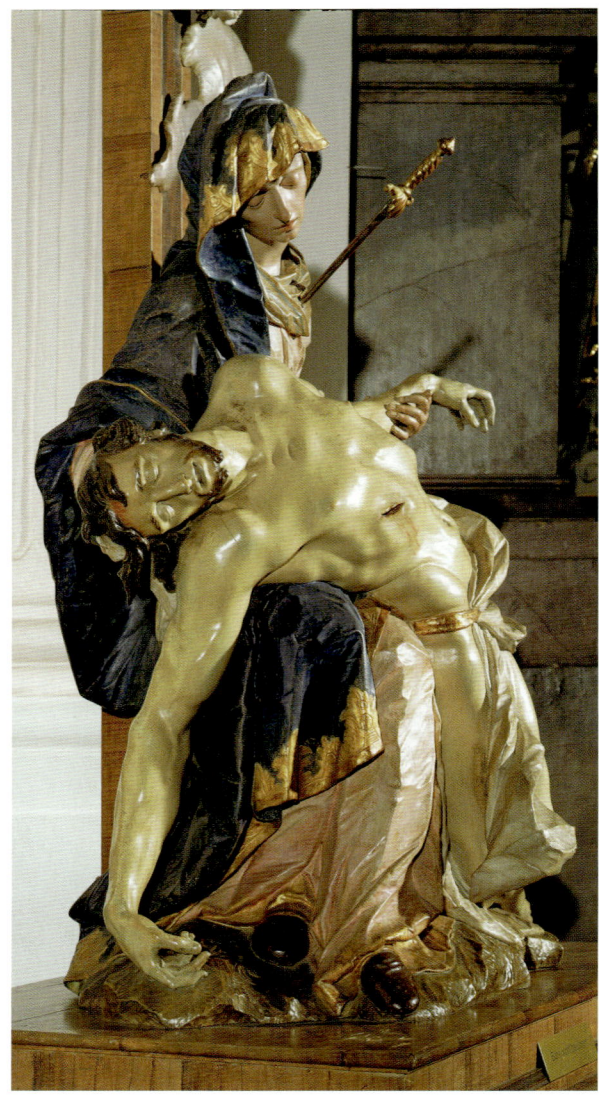

naturalistically, as would have been fitting for sculptures to be carried in procession. Like the *Guardian Angel*, but unlike much of the other sculpture discussed in this chapter, neither work forms part of an integrated architectural whole. Although housed in the church, their primary location was the streets through which they were to be processed.

Günther's final known work was another *Pietà*, created in 1774, just before his premature death. It was made for the cemetery chapel at Nenningen, Bavaria (today in Baden-Württemberg) [**5.40**]. Two reduced unpainted wood versions of the group survive, one in the Bayerisches Nationalmuseum in Munich and the other in the Landesmuseum Württemberg in Stuttgart. Both show Christ's legs lying more horizontally, flattening the composition. The one in Munich shows traces of colour, suggesting it was once

painted [**5.41**]. The status of these two smaller versions, and their relationship to the finished group, remains uncertain, partly because the carving of both is sufficiently highly finished to suggest they are unlikely to be working models from Günther's workshop.[27] Perhaps one of them was a presentation model to be shown to the patrons, although that remains unclear. Like the *Pietà* at Weyarn of ten years before, the finished group at Nenningen is polychromed, while being more vertical in form. As at Weyarn, the long pale form of Christ's corpse dominates, supported by his mother, who is here swathed in voluminous drapery. The group appears yet more bleak than Günther's earlier rendering of a *Vesperbild* at Weyarn, perhaps because, unlike that group, it lacks a child seated at one side.[28] And possibly this intense melancholy seems more apparent because it is known as Günther's

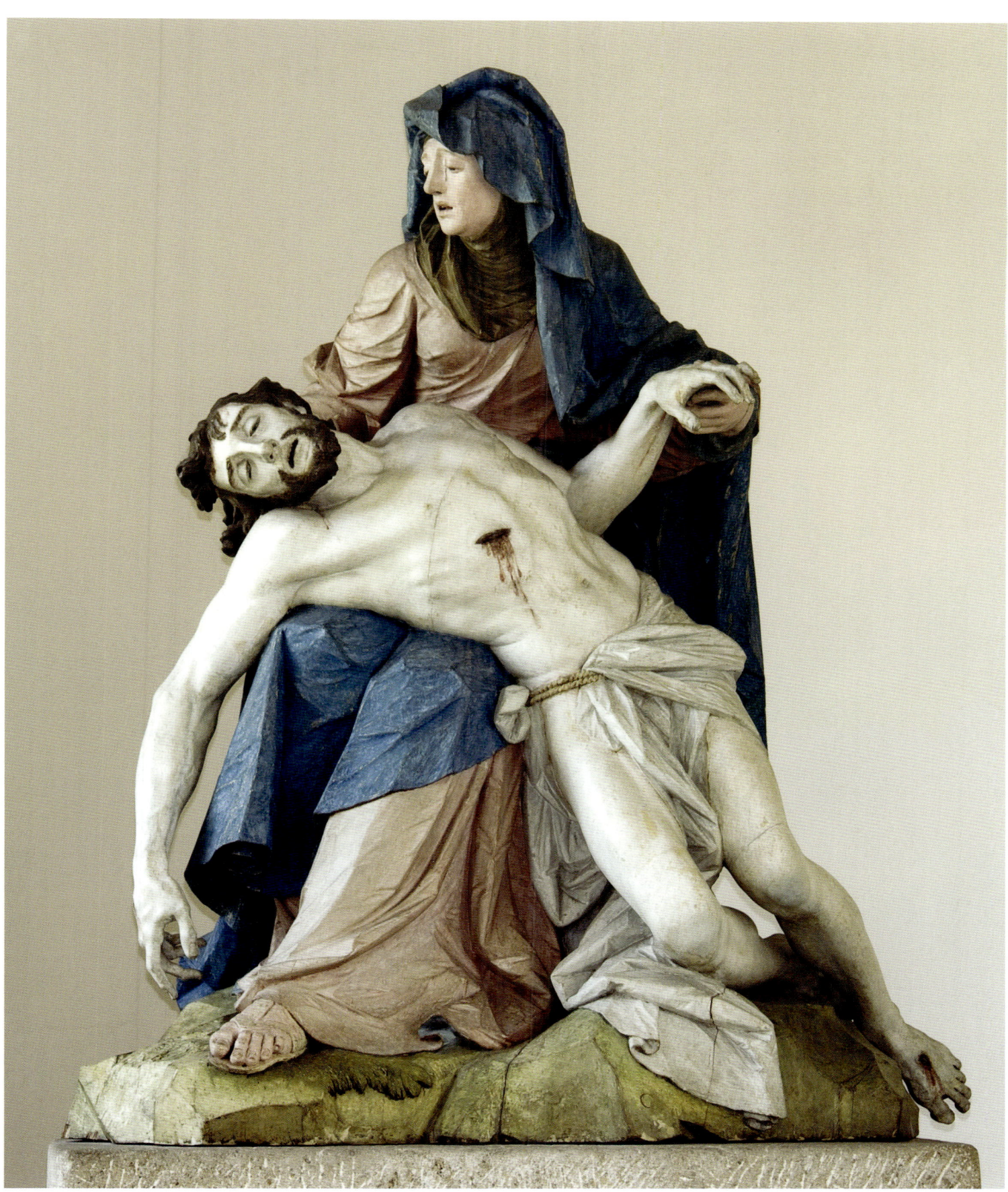

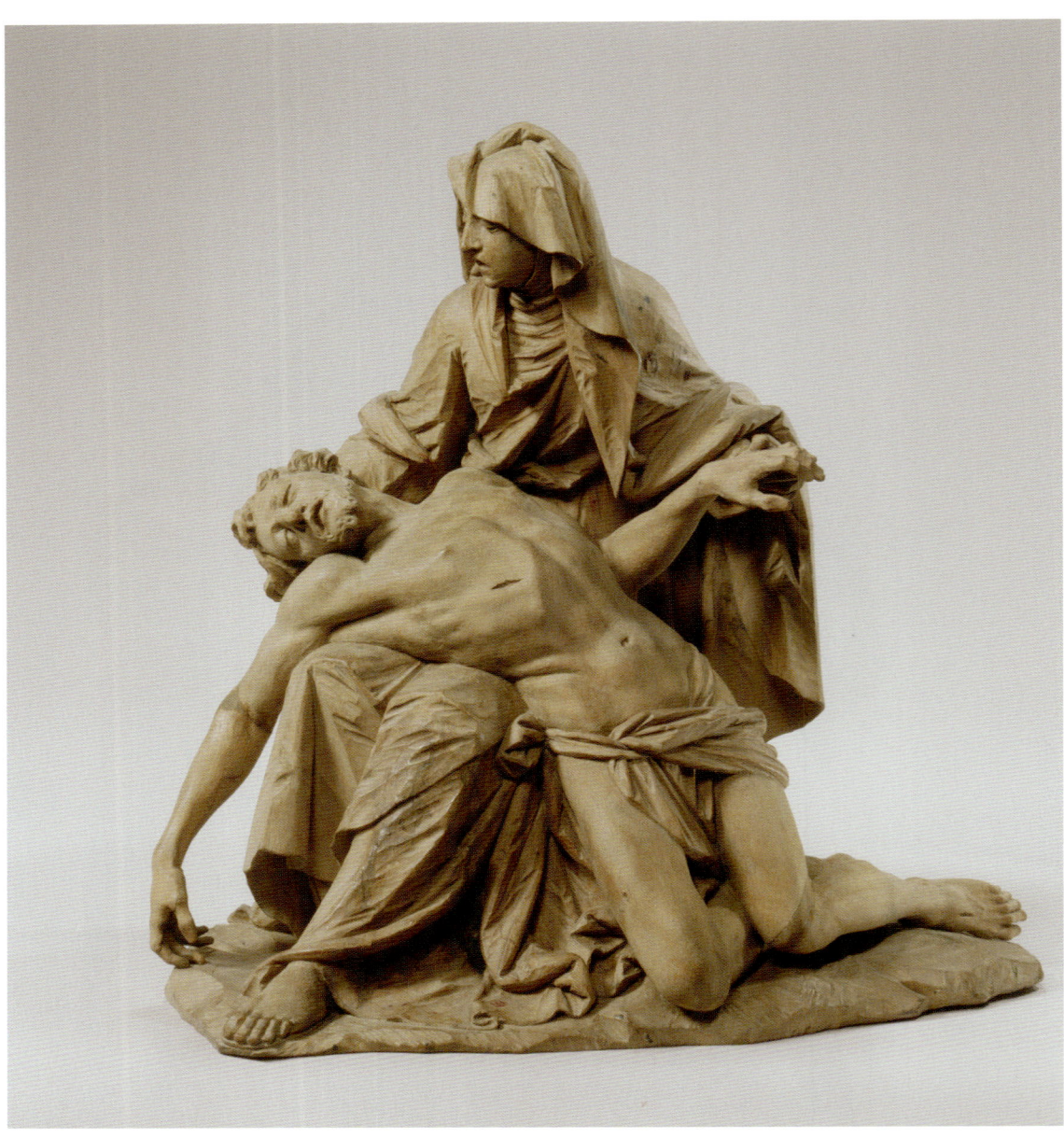

last work, seeming to foreshadow the sculptor's own death.

The sculpture produced by Günther, Straub and their contemporaries in mid-eighteenth-century Bavaria typifies the blossoming of the German baroque. Perhaps most important of all are the ways in which many of the figures and altarpieces commissioned for ecclesiastical contexts formed an indissoluble whole with the architecture, as well as other works of art, including church furniture, such as pulpits and

organ lofts, decorative stucco work and painting. Additionally, during this period the baroque style seems to merge with what can be termed rococo: asymmetry; extreme poses, gestures and facial expressions; slender human forms; frequently non-naturalistic colouring; and harmonies of white and gold that mirror contemporary porcelain. This will be considered further in the following chapter.

Notes

1. Modelli and sketches of the eighteenth century are illuminatingly discussed in *Bayerische Rokokoplastik* 1985, an exhibition catalogue of many models from the collections of the Bayerisches Nationalmuseum, a publication to which this chapter is greatly indebted. See also Volk and Seling 1986.

2. For the church, see Lieb 1953, pp. 73-9, 162-3; Bourke 1962, pp. 80-81; Pechloff and Schirmer 2012; https://www.sueddeutscher-barock.ch/index.html, accessed 29 August 2020.

3. See for example Bernini's *St Longinus* of 1629-38; Wittkower 1999b, fig. 5 on p. 7.

4. See Decker 1943, pp. 47-9; Feulner and Müller 1953, p. 578.

5. For the church, see Lieb 1953, pp. 81-9 and 163-4; Bourke 1962, pp. 81-2; Prusinovsky 2019; https://www.sueddeutscher-barock.ch/In-Werke/h-r/Ottobeuren_Kirche.html, accessed 31 August 2020.

6. The frescoes were painted from 1756 to 1764 by the brothers Johann Jakob Zeiller (1708-1783) and Franz Anton Zeiller (1716-94).

7. Prusinovsky 2019, especially pp. 16-17.

8. For Guillielmus de Grof, see Saur 1992-2019, Vol. 62, pp. 493-4.

9. For the church, see Lieb 1953, pp. 61-7 and 149; Bourke 1962, pp. 76-8; Volk 1984, pp. 186-7; Schnell 2016.

10. The herms supporting the pulpit can be compared with the slightly earlier herms by Dominikus Zimmermann of c. 1730-3 supporting the organ loft at Steinhausen; see Fig. 4.18.

11. For the church, see Lieb 1953, p. 162; Bourke 1962, pp. 78-9; Volk 1984, pp. 199-200; Heisig 2018.

12. Volk 1984, fig. 169; *Bayerische Rokokoplastik* 1985, cat. no. 175, pp. 158-9; *Sculpture* 2008, cat. no. 93 on pp. 80-1.

13. That of Minerva and another female allegory were formerly in the vestibule of the main post office in Munich. See *Bayerische Rokokoplastik* 1985, p. 141.

14. The damaged wood figure for which this is a model is on long-term loan to the Bayerisches Nationalmuseum (inv. no. L 46/91), as mentioned above; *Bayerisches Rokokoplastik* 1985, cat. no. 156, p. 143.

15. For Günther, see Woeckel 1975; Volk 1991; Hertel 2011; Statnik 2019.

16. *Bayerische Rokokoplastik* 1985, cat. no. 18, p. 45.

17. For both drawings, see *Bayerische Rokokoplastik* 1985, cat. nos. 172 and 173, pp. 155-8. See also Woeckel 1975, pp. 309-14; Statnik 2019, pp. 145-9 and fig. 157 on p. 145.

18. *Bayerische Rokokoplastik* 1985, cat. no. 75, p. 80 (Bayerisches Nationalmuseum, inv. no. 13/262). I am most grateful to Jens Burk for his helpful comments on the production of the bell reliefs.

19. Bayerisches Nationalmuseum, inv. no. 2017/118.1-2.

20. See Diederen and Kürzeder 2014, cat. nos. 74 and 75 on pp. 286-7; Statnik 2019, pp. 114-15, and *Bayerisches Rokokoplastik* 1985, cat. nos. 47 and 48 on p. 59. Another closely similar bozzetto is in the Metropolitan Museum of Art, New York, acquired in 2008; see https://www.metmuseum.org/art/collection/search/236118, accessed 21 March 2021.

21. For Günther's work at Rott am Inn, see Statnik 2019, pp. 179-219. For the church, see Lieb 1953, pp. 89-94; Bourke 1962, pp. 82-4; and Heisig 2015.

22. See Statnik 2019, pp. 308-12, for a full account of the sculpture.

23. Inv. no. 32082; Woeckel 1975, cat. no. 61, pp. 381-9. *Bayerische Rokokoplastik* 1985, cat. no. 223, pp. 184-5.

24. For the story of Tobias and the Angel, from the Old Testament Apocrypha, see Hall 1979, pp. 304-5.

25. Statnik 2019, p. 311.

26. For the church, see Oberberger 2005. For Günther's works there, see Statnik 2019, pp. 314-19.

27. *Bayerische Rokokoplastik* 1985, cat. nos. 244 and 245, pp. 205-6.

28. For Günther's Kircheiselfing *Pietà*, see Volk 1984, pp. 68-71.

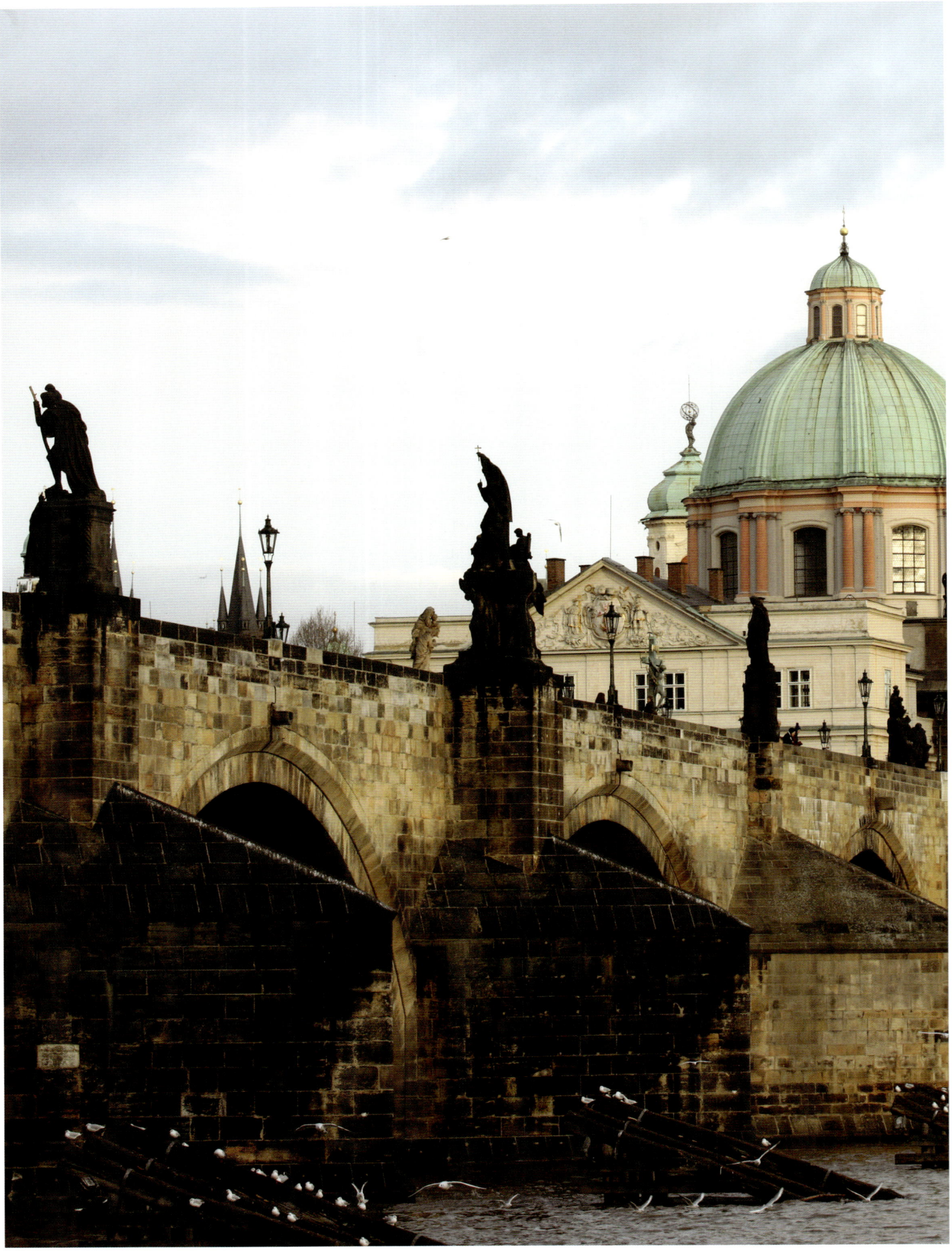

CHAPTER 6

SCULPTURE IN PRAGUE C.1650-1750

During the baroque period numerous important sculptures, both religious and secular, were produced by German and Austrian sculptors who had settled in Bohemia (now the Czech Republic), particularly the city of Prague. Although this book centres on German baroque sculpture, Bohemia is the subject of the present chapter, both because of that country's importance in the history of baroque sculpture and because of its inseparable links with those sculptors.

The kingdom of Bohemia prospered in the late seventeenth and early eighteenth centuries, when the patronage of both the Church and the aristocracy attracted numerous sculptors from elsewhere, notably from Bavaria and the Tyrol, as noted above. Since 1526, Bohemia, as well as Moravia to the east, had formed part of the Habsburg Empire. Emperor Rudolph II (1552-1612) had ruled from his court in Prague, but in 1612 his successor Matthias (1577-1619), who had ascended the throne of Bohemia in 1611, moved the capital to Vienna, partly to avoid pressure from the Bohemian Estates, who were pressing for more political and religious autonomy from the (Catholic) Habsburgs. The Bohemian Estates represented the different estates, or legal orders, of Bohemia, and at that date were dominated by the Czech nobility.[1] In 1609 Rudolph II had issued a Letter of Majesty guaranteeing religious liberties in Bohemia, which was predominantly Protestant, and creating a Protestant State Church, run by the Bohemian Estates. But Matthias, a fervent Catholic, wished to assert centralised control over the kingdom. Dissension erupted when the Bohemian Estates chose the Protestant Frederick V of the Palatinate (1596-1632) to reign over the kingdom in 1619, after Matthias's death. Frederick's reign was however to last only a year, hence his sobriquet, the Winter King. At the Battle of the White Mountain in November 1620 he was defeated by the armies led by Matthias's successor, the Habsburg Emperor Ferdinand II (1578-1637) and the German Catholic League, the battle being an early struggle in the long series of conflicts between Catholics and Protestants during the Thirty Years' War (1618-48). Following this clash, virtually the entire kingdom of Bohemia reverted to Ferdinand II, to be ruled from Vienna.[2] The rule of the Habsburgs during the baroque period led not only to an influx of Austrian and German artists, but to a renewed patriotic identity for Bohemian art and culture, perhaps somewhat paradoxically, given the existence of two distinct ethnic and linguistic groups in the country: Czechs and Germans. Much of the sculpture produced was rooted in Germanic techniques and tendencies, while at the same time expressing a vernacular energy

6.1
The Charles Bridge, Prague, stone, built 1357 onwards.

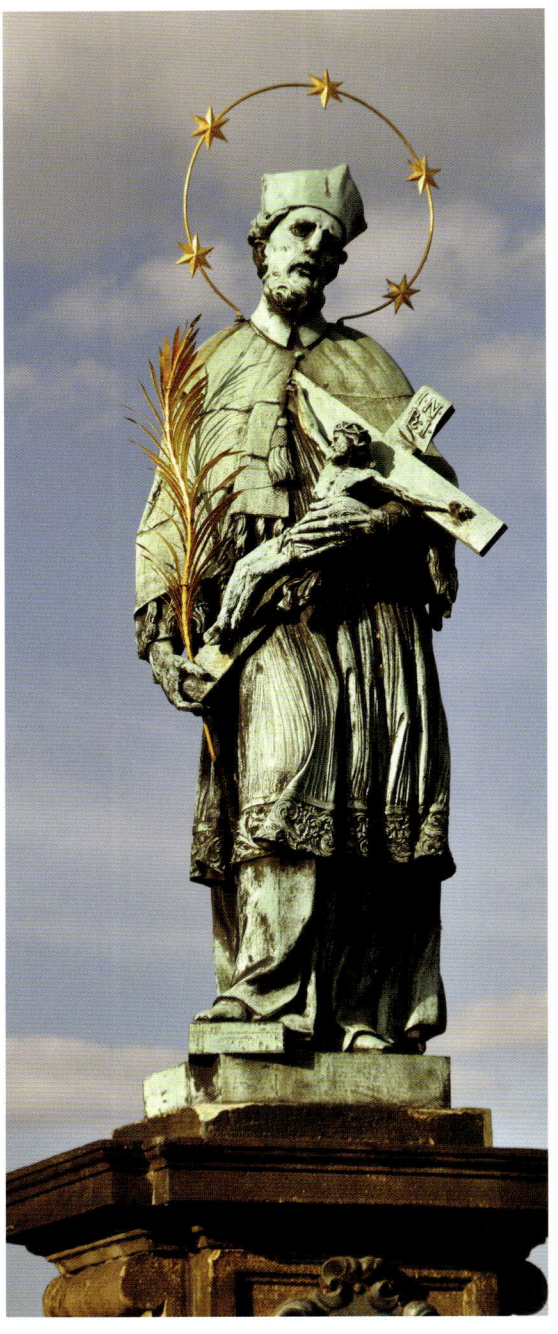

6.2
Matthias Rauchmiller,
Jan Brokoff and
Hieronymus Herold,
St John Nepomuk,
bronze, 1683. Charles
Bridge, Prague.

peculiar to Bohemia. The materials used, notably the local sandstone, embody this distinctive style. Rather than attempt to describe the breadth of sculpture produced across Bohemia at this time, this chapter will concentrate on the greatest sculptors active mainly in Prague: Jan Brokoff and his son Ferdinand Maximilian Brokoff, and Matthias Bernhard Braun. The first section deals with the Charles Bridge in Prague.

The Charles Bridge, Prague

In many ways the sculptures made for the Charles Bridge in Prague epitomise Bohemian

sculpture and its baroque identity, even though German and Austrian artists were frequently inextricably involved in their production. The bridge, in the centre of the city, between the west and east banks of the river Vltava (Moldau in German), connects the Malá Strana ('Little Side') of Prague with the Old Town on the east side of the bridge. It is a memorial to Charles IV (1316-78; r. 1347-78), the first king of Bohemia to become Holy Roman Emperor, although its name, the Charles Bridge, was in fact only bestowed on it in 1870 [**6.1**].[3] The foundation stone of the present bridge, replacing earlier constructions, was laid during Charles IV's reign in 1357. The bridge was in use by the 1380s, though work continued on it and the tower on the side of the Old Town until the early fifteenth century.[4] Until the late seventeenth century sculpted calvaries and painted panels had been set up on the bridge, though some of these had been lost during the Thirty Years' War, when the Swedish army invaded Prague in 1648. The thirty sculpted groups commissioned to replace them from the late seventeenth century onwards constitute a gallery of Bohemian baroque and later statuary; a few will be discussed here. The concept of a bridge decorated with statuary must have been inspired by Italian prototypes, most notably the Ponte Sant'Angelo in Rome, adorned with figures of angels from Gian Lorenzo Bernini's workshop in the mid-seventeenth century.[5] The majority were carved in local sandstone, and many became weathered, or were damaged through intermittent flooding over the centuries. For those reasons a number are no longer *in situ* but have been removed to the Lapidarium in Prague, substituted by copies on the bridge.[6]

The first major work to be set up on the Charles Bridge was not in fact of sandstone, but of bronze. The figure of St John Nepomuk (c. 1345-93) was installed in 1683 [**6.2**]. Because it is of a more durable material than the stone used for subsequent sculptures, the original still stands in place. It is the combined work of three practitioners: Matthias Rauchmiller (whose work was also discussed in Chapter 2), Jan Brokoff and Wolfgang Hieronymus Herold. The initial terracotta modello for the figure was produced by Rauchmiller (1645-86) in Vienna in 1681, and is now in the National Gallery, Prague [**6.3**].[7] The Prague sculptor Jan Brokoff (1652-1718) carved the full-size wood model from this bozzetto, and this wood figure is now in the church of St John Nepomuk of the Rock in Prague.[8] Brokoff's model was cast in bronze in 1683 by Wolfgang Hieronymus Herold (1627-93), a bell-founder in Nuremberg. The statue was made to commemorate the supposed 300th anniversary of John Nepomuk's death in 1383 (in fact he had been killed in 1393). The location of the statue was highly appropriate, since Nepomuk had been thrown from the Charles Bridge into the river Vltava at the behest of Wenceslaus IV of Bohemia, apparently for thwarting the king's plan to seize property from a monastery in Kladrau (although according to a later legend he was said to have been executed for having refused to betray the queen's confession to the king, as depicted on one of the reliefs on the pediment of the statue).[9] Nepomuk was to be canonised in 1729, when he became the patron saint of Bohemia. The appearance and pose of the bronze figure on the Charles Bridge became the prototype for numerous later representations of him as a saint throughout the eighteenth century. The bearded Nepomuk stands with a meek and saddened facial expression, contrapposto, wearing his vestments and biretta, and carrying a martyr's palm and crucifix. The balanced, if stiff, pose echoes that of François Du Quesnoy's *St Susanna* of 1629-33 at S. Maria di Loreto in Rome.[10] On the pediment two bronze reliefs depict *The Confession of the Queen* and *St John Nepomuk's Fall from the Bridge* [**6.4**].[11] Between these figurative scenes is a votive inscription, set under the coat of arms of the patron of the statue, Matthias Freiherr von Wunschwitz. The large dog and armed warrior in the foreground of the scene of the *Confession* is a symbolic reference to King Wencelaus's cruelty, whilst Nepomuk's fall from the bridge forms the background to a rendition of *The Massacre of the Innocents*, the act of another tyrannical king, Herod. The style of the reliefs is somewhat archaic, recalling Italian renaissance bronze reliefs of the quattrocento.[12] This monumental ensemble is thus a fusion of German,

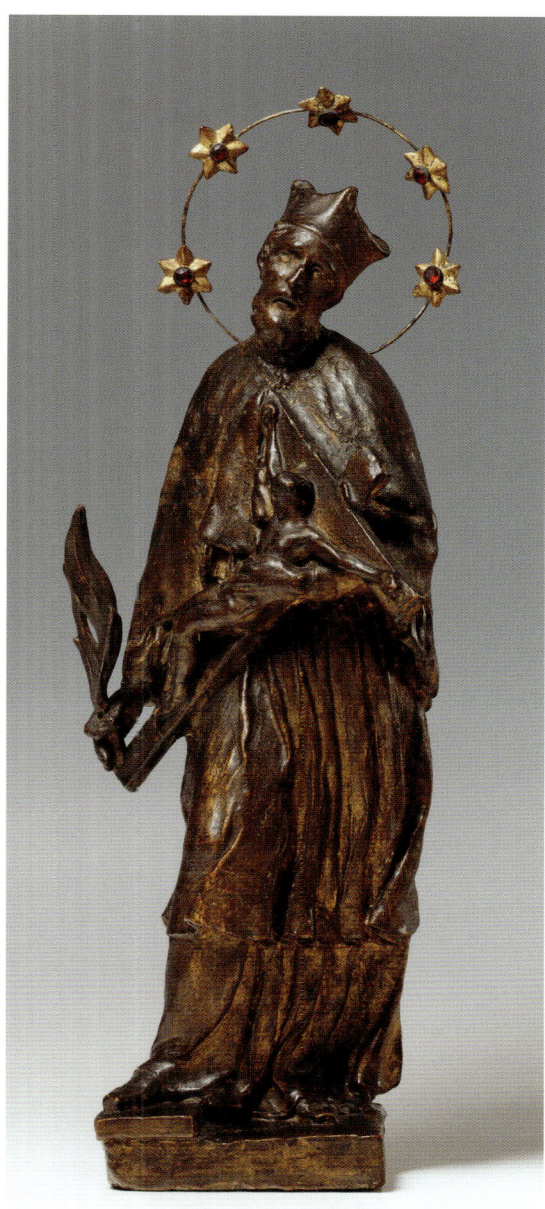

6.3
Matthias Rauchmiller, *St John Nepomuk*, terracotta with traces of gilding, the martyr's palm of wood and later metal halo, height 41 cm. Later inscription on the back, dating from c. 1740: 'Matthias Rauchmiller fec. Viennae ao. 1681'. National Gallery, Prague (inv. no. P 613).

Austrian and Bohemian artistry, albeit with Italianate roots, the figure itself symbolising the patriotism and pride of the city of Prague.

Jan Brokoff, the maker of the wood model of Nepomuk, was originally from the Spiš (Zips) region in Upper Hungary, today the Slovak Republic. He had subsequently moved to Bohemia in 1675 and settled in Prague by 1692. His son Ferdinand Maximilian (1688-1731) was born in West Bohemia at Červený Hrádek (Castle Rothenhaus) u Chomutova (near Komotau) during Jan Brokoff's artistic sojourn there. Jan Brokoff initially trained his son, who was also to study under the sculptor brothers Peter (1660-1714) and Paul Strudel (1648-1708) at the Academy of Fine Arts in Vienna in the early

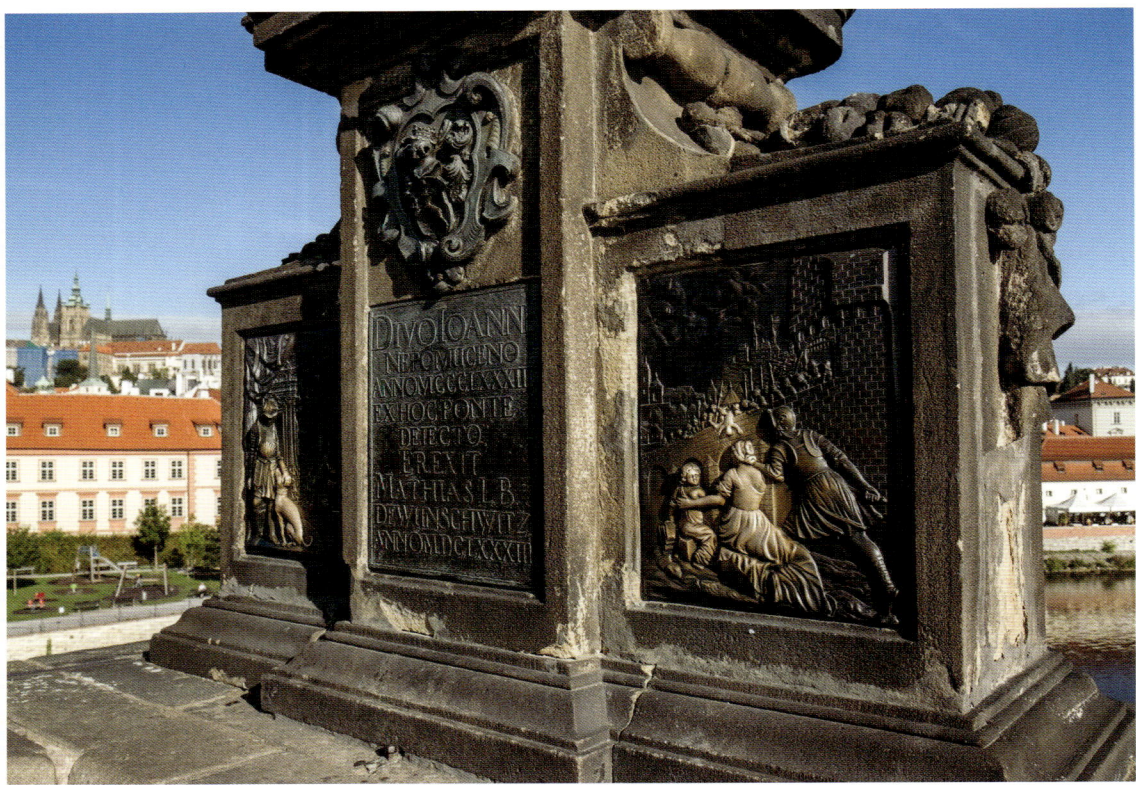

years of the eighteenth century. Ferdinand became a more fluent and accomplished artist than his father, partly because of this training in the Habsburg capital. Father and son collaborated on a number of sandstone sculptures for the Charles Bridge, including *The Baptism of Christ* (1706; now in the Lapidarium, Prague) [6.5]. In this group the figure of Christ is considerably more accomplished than that of the Baptist and must have been carved by Ferdinand.

The fluency of carving and complex composition of the figures comprising the group of the Jesuit saint *St Francis Borgia* with accompanying angels (1710) [6.6] similarly suggest that Ferdinand Brokoff was responsible for its execution, even though it is signed at the feet by his father Jan, as head of the workshop.[13] The elaborate plinth with its ornamental volutes and scrolls elegantly harmonise with the swing of the figures above. The location of the group enhances its impact: it is both set on a commanding eminence on the bridge, with the broad vista of the river and city behind, and is at the same time visually accessible for viewers. The sculpture can therefore be seen clearly and appreciated in what is both a fitting and visually powerful setting.

Ferdinand Maximilian Brokoff was again probably solely responsible for *St John of Matha, St Felix of Valois and St Ivan* (1714) [6.7], although this group too is signed in Latin with his father's name.[14] The sculpture was commissioned by Franz Josef, Count of Thuringia (1686-1720), Governor of Bohemia, to commemorate the ending of the attack of plague, and to celebrate peace with the French in his own homeland (Klösterle in Austria), as noted on the base of the plinth.[15] The three saints are set upon a rocky eminence of roughly-hewn stone blocks in a dramatic grouping above a prison, St Felix freeing a manacled prisoner while St John holds up the chains and St Ivan stands in meditation. Half-figures of three other chained prisoners are to be seen bewailing their fate from behind metal bars below. The oval cartouche beneath the saints depicts other manacled prisoners in low relief. The most striking single figure of the whole ensemble is the pensive, corpulent Turk at the foot of the main group, guarding the prison, a sabre tucked into his belt and a scourge held behind his back. His lively hound crouches on the other side of the composition [6.8]. St John of Matha (1160-1213) and St Felix of Valois (1127-1212) were the founders of the Order

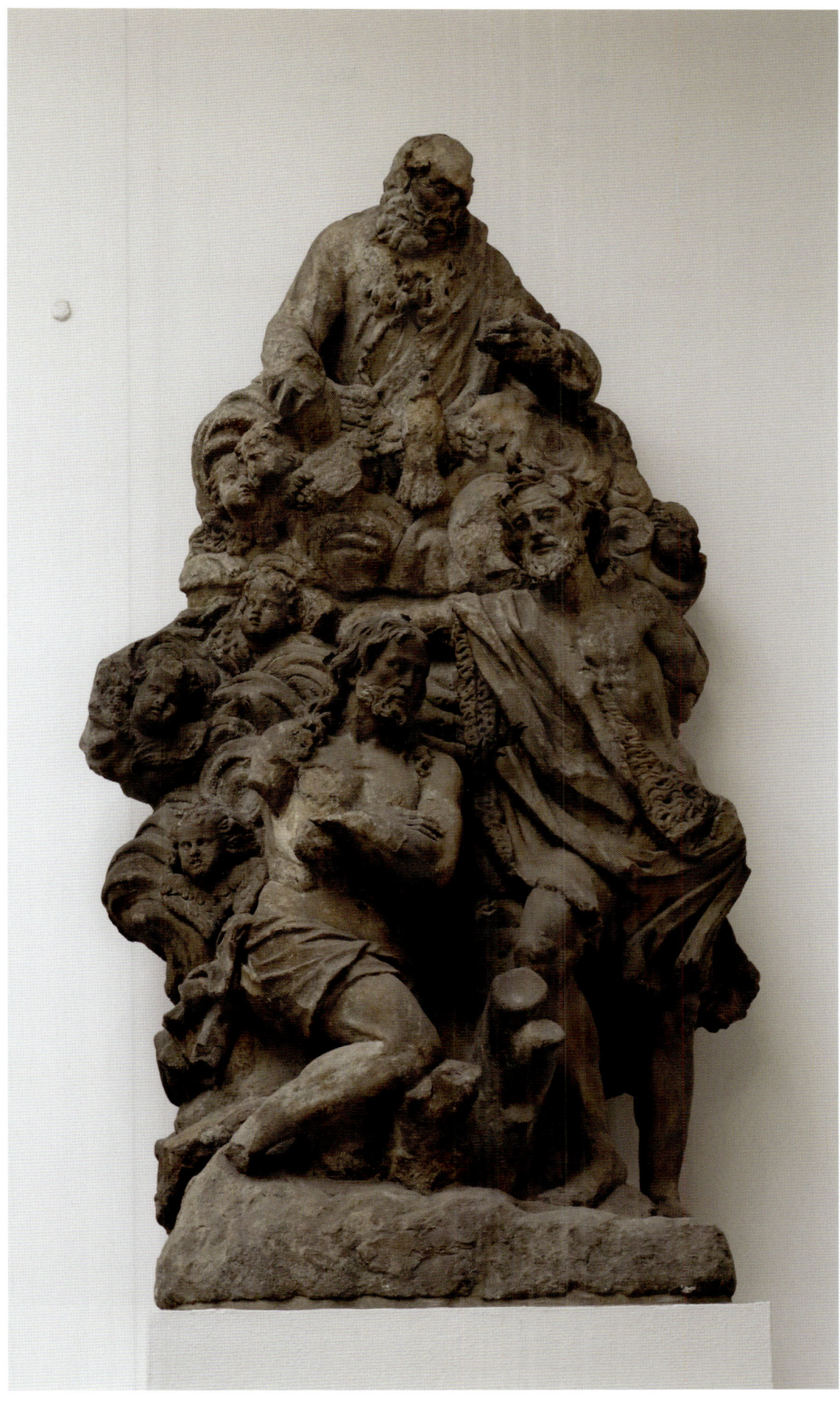

6.5
Jan and Ferdinand
Maximilian Brokoff,
The Baptism of Christ,
sandstone, 1706.
Lapidarium, Prague
(formerly Charles
Bridge, Prague).
(inv. no. H2-38135).

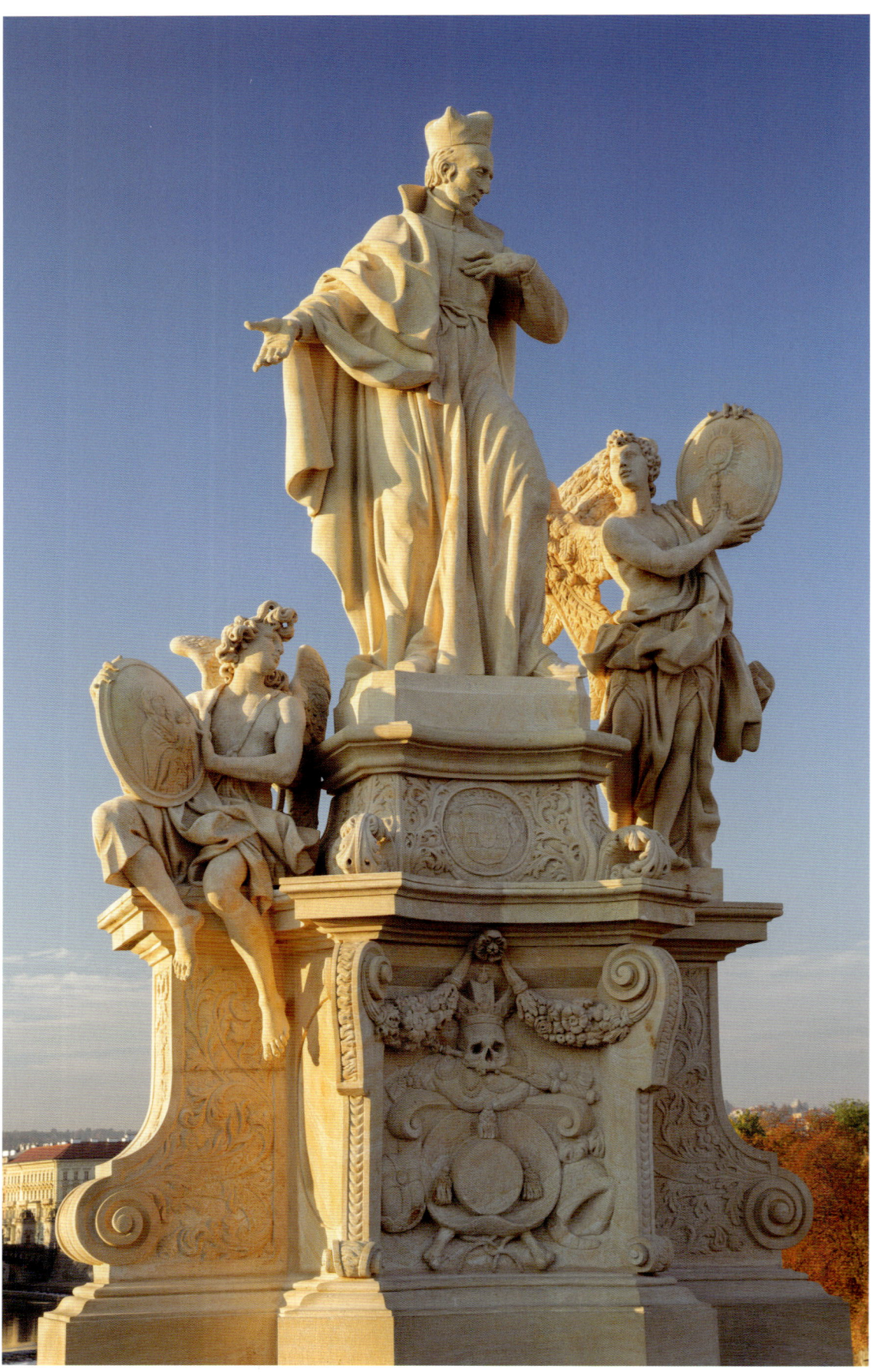

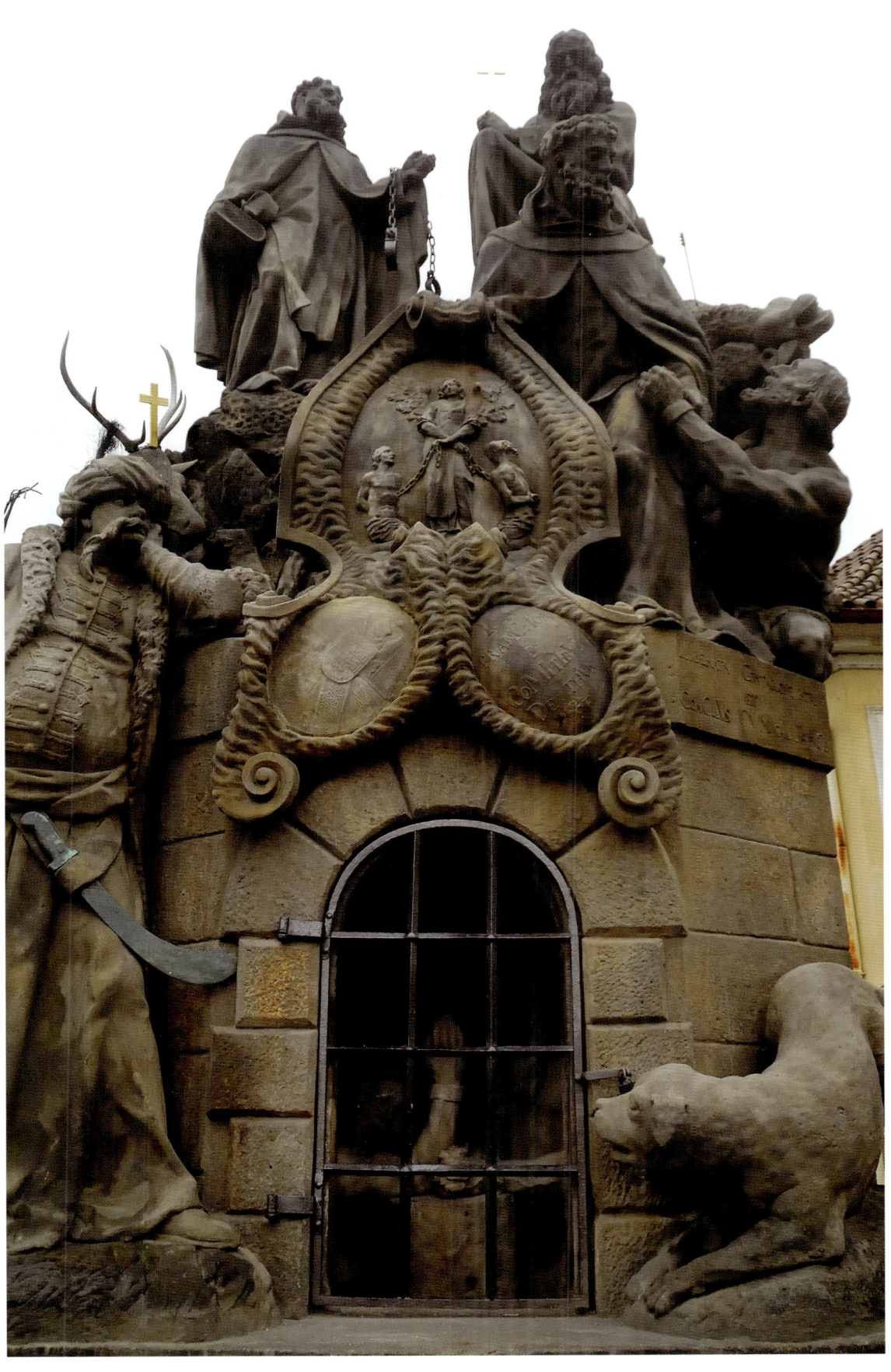

6.7
Ferdinand Maximilian
Brokoff, *St John of
Matha*, *St Felix of Valois
and St Evan*, sandstone,
1714. Charles Bridge,
Prague.

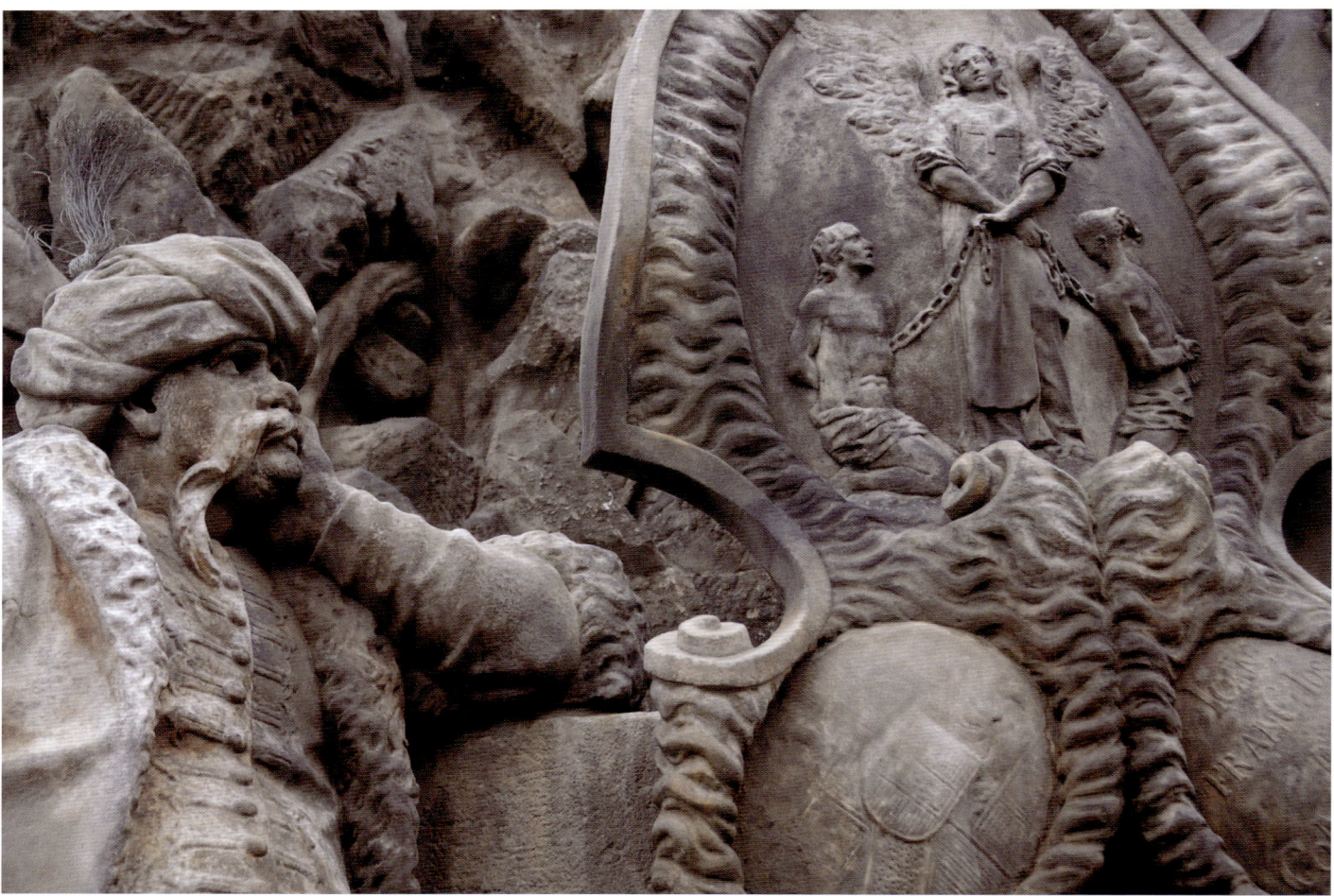

of Trinitarians, who freed Christians from captivity in Turkish prisons. St Ivan, a ninth-century hermit, was the patron saint of Slavs; the stag standing on the left of the group with a crucifix between its antlers is his attribute. The solidity of the rounded bodies, as well as the complex yet harmonious composition, is typical of Ferdinand Brokoff's assured work.

From 1707 to 1714 five other sandstone groups for the bridge were produced by the Brokoff workshop, who executed more sculptures for it than any other individual workshop, contributing to its justified reputation as a monumental manifestation of baroque art.[16]

Apart from the Brokoff workshop, the other major sculptor whose work was commissioned for the Charles Bridge was Matthias Bernhard Braun (1684-1738), although he only executed two such groups.[17] Like Jan Brokoff, Braun was a native of Austria, having been born near Innsbruck, and probably trained with the sculptor Andreas Tamasch (1639-97) at Stams in the Imst district of the Tyrol. He worked with

the sculptor Michael Bernhard Mandl (1660-1711) in Salzburg, and is likely to have travelled to Italy, probably Venice, Verona and Rome, in his youth. Additionally, he was in Dresden from 1704 to 1709, when he probably worked under Balthasar Permoser.[18] But he was primarily active in Prague and elsewhere in Bohemia. In 1630 he settled in Prague, where he established a large workshop. *The Vision of St Luitgarde (or Lutgardis)*, his first independent work, was commissioned for the Charles Bridge by the abbot of the Cistercian cloister at Plasy in Bohemia, Eugen Tyttl (1666-1738) in 1710 [**6.9**].[19] St Luitgarde (1182-1246) was a blind Cistercian nun in the Netherlands who experienced a mystical vision of Christ on the cross, the scene depicted in Braun's sculptural group. The saint turns upward to Christ's face, touching his left leg, while he bends towards her, placing his right arm on her shoulder. On Christ's left, balancing the figure of the saint, cherubim and putti-angels hover. The bulky cross from which Christ half-descends is set on a rocky eminence. A devotional

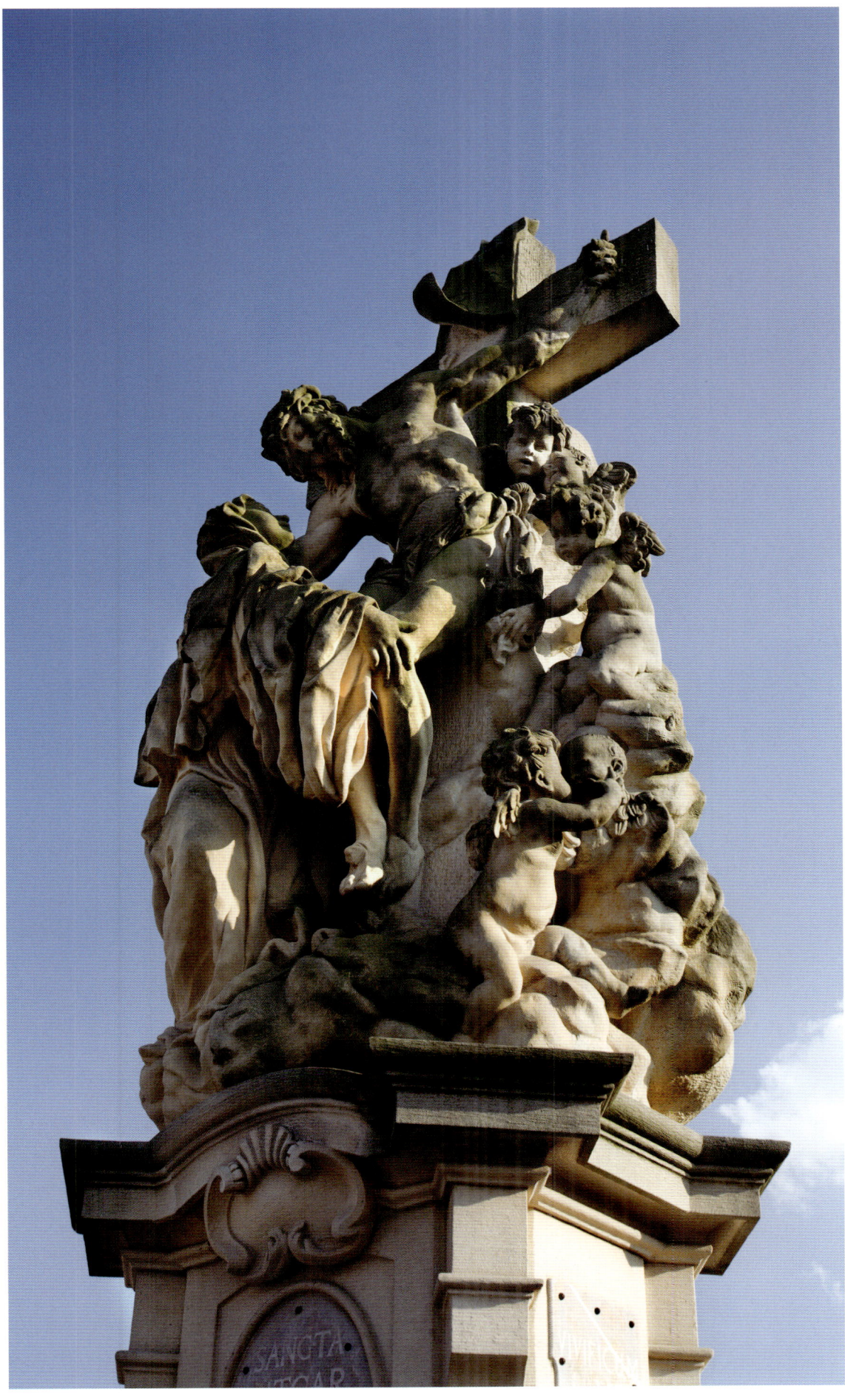

6.9
Matthias Bernhard
Braun, *The Vision of
St Luitgarde*, sandstone,
dated 1710 (Christ's left
hand and the top of
the cross are later
replacements; the
originals are now in the
Lapidarium, Prague).
Charles Bridge, Prague.

6.10
Matthias Bernhard
Braun, *The Vision of
St Luitgarde*, gilt
limewood modello, after
1710, height 68 cm.
National Gallery, Prague
(inv. no. P 3244).

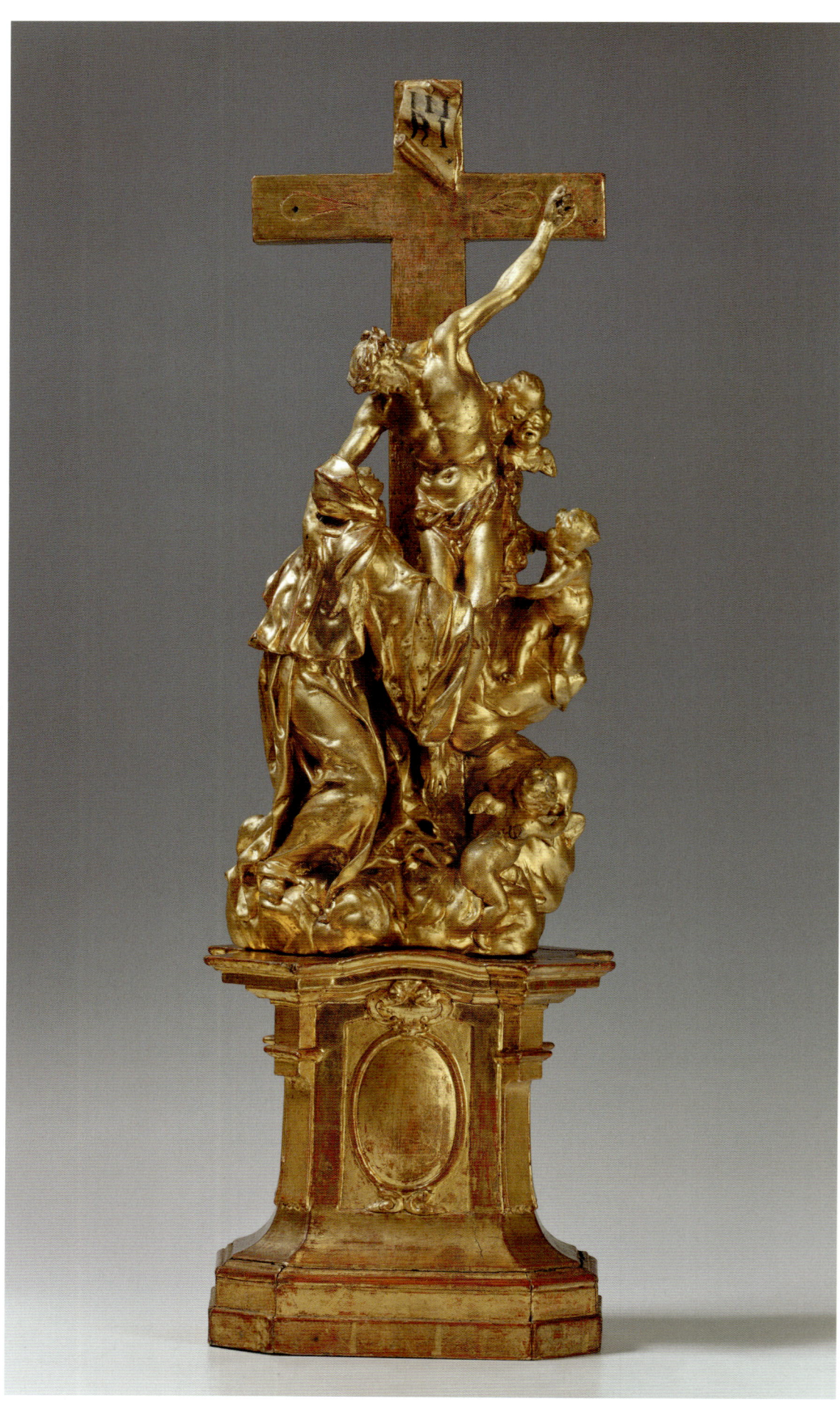

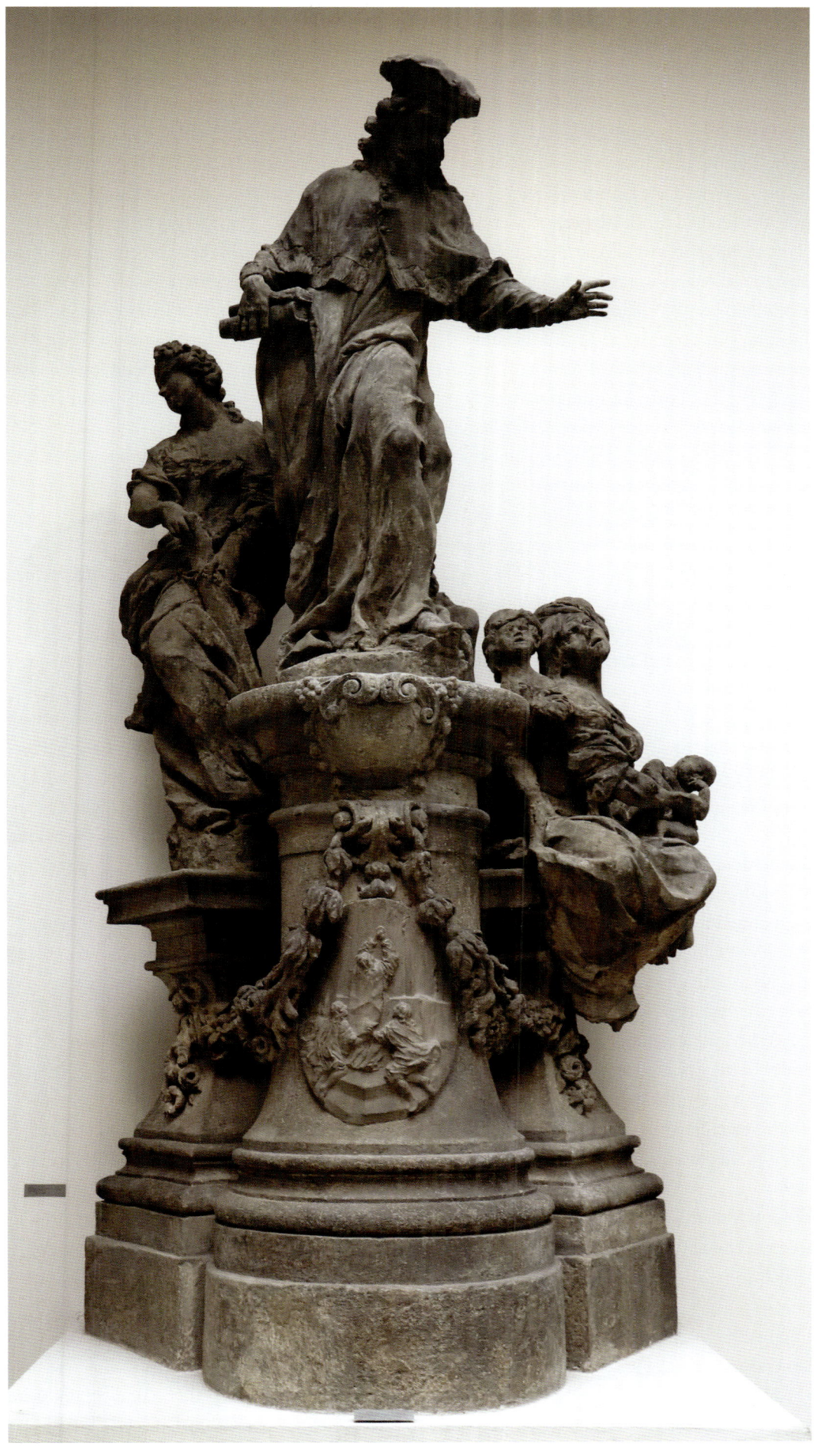

6.11
Matthias Bernhard
Braun, *Ivo of Chartres*,
sandstone, 1711.
Lapidarium, Prague
(formerly Charles
Bridge, Prague).
(inv. no. H2-38134).

inscription in Latin is inscribed in an oval cartouche on the plinth below.[20] The group was probably designed by the painter Peter Brandel (or Brandl) (1660/8-1739), who is known to have worked at Plasy in western Bohemia. A gilt limewood group, a reduced version of the stone sculpture, is now in the National Gallery, Prague. Its detailed finish suggests it was made after the stone group was completed, to be presented to the abbot, rather than as a preliminary modello [6.10].[21] The baroque confidence of the composition of *St Luitgarde* indicates Braun's and perhaps Brandel's ultimate indebtedness to Gian Lorenzo Bernini, possibly via engraved sources.[22] The expression of spiritual feeling and the sense of communication between the crucified Christ and the saint are unparalleled in Bohemian or indeed German sculpture before this date, and can only be compared with Bernini's *Ecstasy of St Teresa* in Rome of 1647-52.[23] Braun's animated, restless style of carving and his ability to convey the sense of pathos as seen here contrast with, and at the same time complement, the complex monumentality evident in Ferdinand Brokoff's imposing stone groups.

The second group Braun produced for the Charles Bridge, and indeed only his second work made in Prague, was that of *Ivo of Chartres*, dating from 1711 and displayed in the Lapidarium of the National Museum in Prague (replaced by a copy on the bridge in 1908) [6.11].[24] This group was commissioned by the Faculty of Law at the University of Prague. Ivo of Chartres (c. 1040-1115) (who in actuality may not have been canonised) was the patron saint of jurists, and is shown here in academic robes as the legal defender of the poor, gesturing towards the mother with her child and supplicant elderly man at his feet. The blindfolded allegorical figure of Justice stands behind the main group.[25]

Ferdinand Maximilian Brokoff

Other than the sculptures he produced for the Charles Bridge, Ferdinand Brokoff executed numerous sculptures over the brief course of his life (he died prematurely in 1731). He was commissioned to make architectural sculptures for the Morzin Palace in 1714 (today the Romanian Embassy), a building designed by Jan Blažej Santini-Aichel (1677-1723) in the Malá Strana district of Prague. These sculptures comprise a pair of atlantes, each one positioned on either side of the coat of arms of the Morzin family set onto the façade [6.12 and 6.13], as well as allegorical busts of *Day* and *Night*, and figures of the *Four Seasons* on the attic storey of the building.[26] The two gigantic sandstone atlantes were almost certainly inspired by the four caryatid figures made by Melchior Barthel (1625-72) for the tomb of Doge Giovanni Pesaro in the basilica of S. Maria Gloriosa dei Frari in Venice of 1655-60.[27] But although Italo-German prototypes may lie behind the Prague atlantes, Brokoff has infused them with an extraordinary force undeniably Bohemian and baroque. Even more than in the groups he carved for the Charles Bridge these massive bodies are permeated with a flamboyant power. The atlantes are semi-nude with curly hair and African faces. They wear short feather-like coverings around their hips, similarly feathered armlets, and buskins on their feet, nods towards antique classical armour, while they are also partly swathed in heavy folds of drapery around and behind their legs. The chains running across their chests suggest they are captives, while their frowning facial expressions convey both the strain of supporting the weight of the balcony above them and their anger and frustration as bound prisoners.

In 1714, the same year in which Brokoff was commissioned to work on the Morzin Palace, he was given the task of carving the tomb of Count Johann Wenzel Wratislaw von Mitrowitz (Jan Václav Vratislav z Mitrovic) (c. 1670-1712), Chancellor of Bohemia. The tomb was designed in Vienna by the architect Johann Bernhard Fischer von Erlach (1656-1723) and erected in the church of St James the Greater in Prague two years later in 1716 [6.14]. See also frontispiece.[28] The count, wearing armour, reclines on his sarcophagus, supported by an allegorical figure of Renown, who holds a laurel wreath aloft, while a winged figure representing Fame, holding a trumpet, writes an inscription recording the count's achievements as Chancellor of Bohemia on the pyramid behind. Seated below on the left is the kneeling figure of Contemplation, mourning his loss, and on the other side the winged figure of Time, turning to one side, appears to support the pyramid with his right hand [**6.14 and frontispiece**]. The marble figures on the tomb are coated in gesso, a rare sculptural practice, thereby softening the surfaces.[29] The count's coat of arms in bronze are set onto the centre of the sarcophagus. The tomb is reminiscent not only of the papal tombs by Bernini in Rome, but the tomb of the Viscount of Turenne (1676-80) at Les Invalides in Paris by Jean-Baptiste Tuby (1635-1700) and Gaspard Marsy (1624/5-81).[30] It foreshadows too the great tomb of the Duke of Argyll in Westminster Abbey of a generation later (1745-9) by Louis François Roubiliac (1702-62), and must have been seen at the time as a seminal European work.[31] While Fischer von Erlach was responsible for the architectonic design, Brokoff's carving of the figures endows the whole with monumental strength. The powerfully sculpted body of the figure of Time, notably the twisting torso and muscular arms and legs, paradoxically rich in both vibrant movement and solidity, recalls the vigorous atlantes on the façade of the Morzin Palace.

Brokoff's sculpture, as demonstrated by these few selected examples of his work, can be seen to be both rooted in European sculpture (Vienna, Rome and Paris) and simultaneously embedded in the city of Prague, exuding a potency and even virility that is distinctively Bohemian, even while his oeuvre can be paralleled with the German or Austrian baroque.

Matthias Bernhard Braun and Johann Georg (Jan Jiří) Bendl

Like Brokoff, Braun was a leading sculptor in Bohemia in the first half of the eighteenth century. Because he lived a few years longer than his (slightly younger) contemporary, his output is greater, though only a few of his major works will be discussed here.[32] In addition to the groups on the Charles Bridge, Braun produced sculptures for churches and some exceptional works for his most important patron, Count Franz Anton Sporck (1662-1738).

Soon after he had executed the group of St Luitgarde for the Charles Bridge, Braun

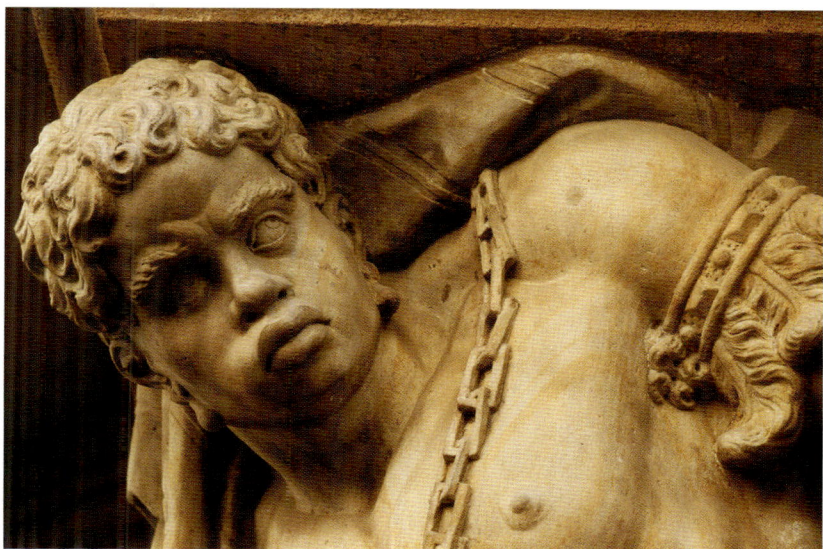

carved the limewood figure of *St Jude (Judas Thaddäus)* in about 1712 [**6.15**].[33] The sculpture was originally made for the church of St Mary of the Pond in the Old Town of Prague, where the sculptor was commissioned to make a number of works. After the demolition of the church in 1788 they were moved to the Jesuit College of Prague in the Clementinum area of the city, the complex of buildings originally owned by the Jesuits until their suppression in 1773. By 1918 the *St Jude* was the only one of the ensemble from the church of St Mary to survive; it then entered the collections of the National Gallery of Prague. The figure is carved in limewood with a white gesso finish. The saint depicted is an anguished and at the same time inspired man, his right hand grasping his attributes, a club and a book, his left arm raised as he looks upwards. His craggy face, curly hair and beard parallel the angular drapery of his robes. His demeanour echoes that of Bernini's *St Longinus* at St Peter's of 1629-33, although Braun's figure is fiercely energetic in comparison with the fluent, almost classical statue in Rome.[34] This is partly because of the material: the carved wood is sharper and more organic than the marble favoured in Italy, or even the sandstone Braun employed for his statues on the Charles Bridge. He would have been trained in carving wood in his homeland of the Tyrol, and the vibrancy of this figure testifies to his technical skill. A chalky gesso finish to the surface was chosen, rather than polychromy, possibly to suggest stone rather than wood, just

6.13
Ferdinand Maximilian Brokoff, *Head of Atlante* [detail of 6.12].

>> 6.12
Ferdinand Maximilian Brokoff, *Atlantes*, sandstone, signed and dated 1714. Morzin Palace, Prague.

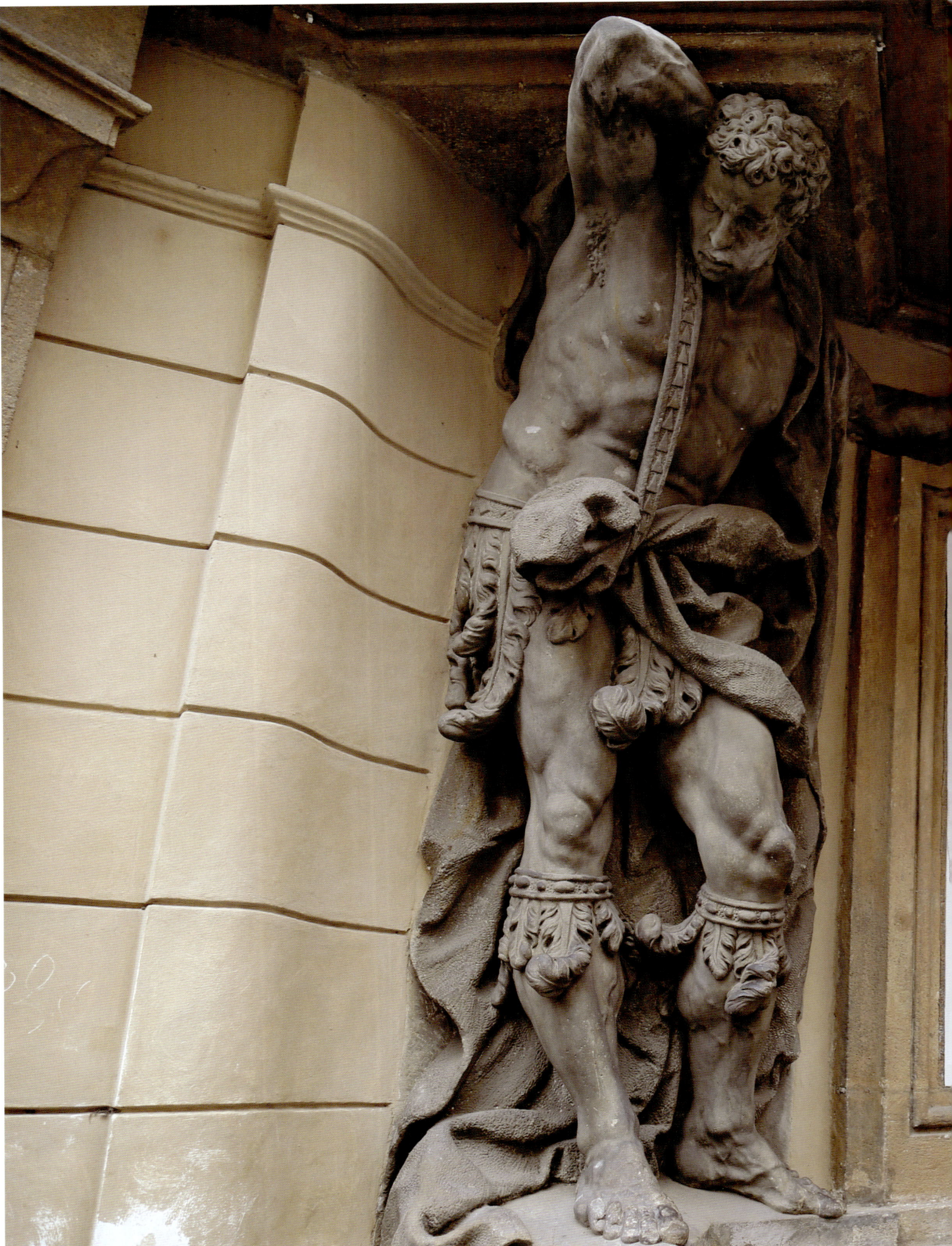

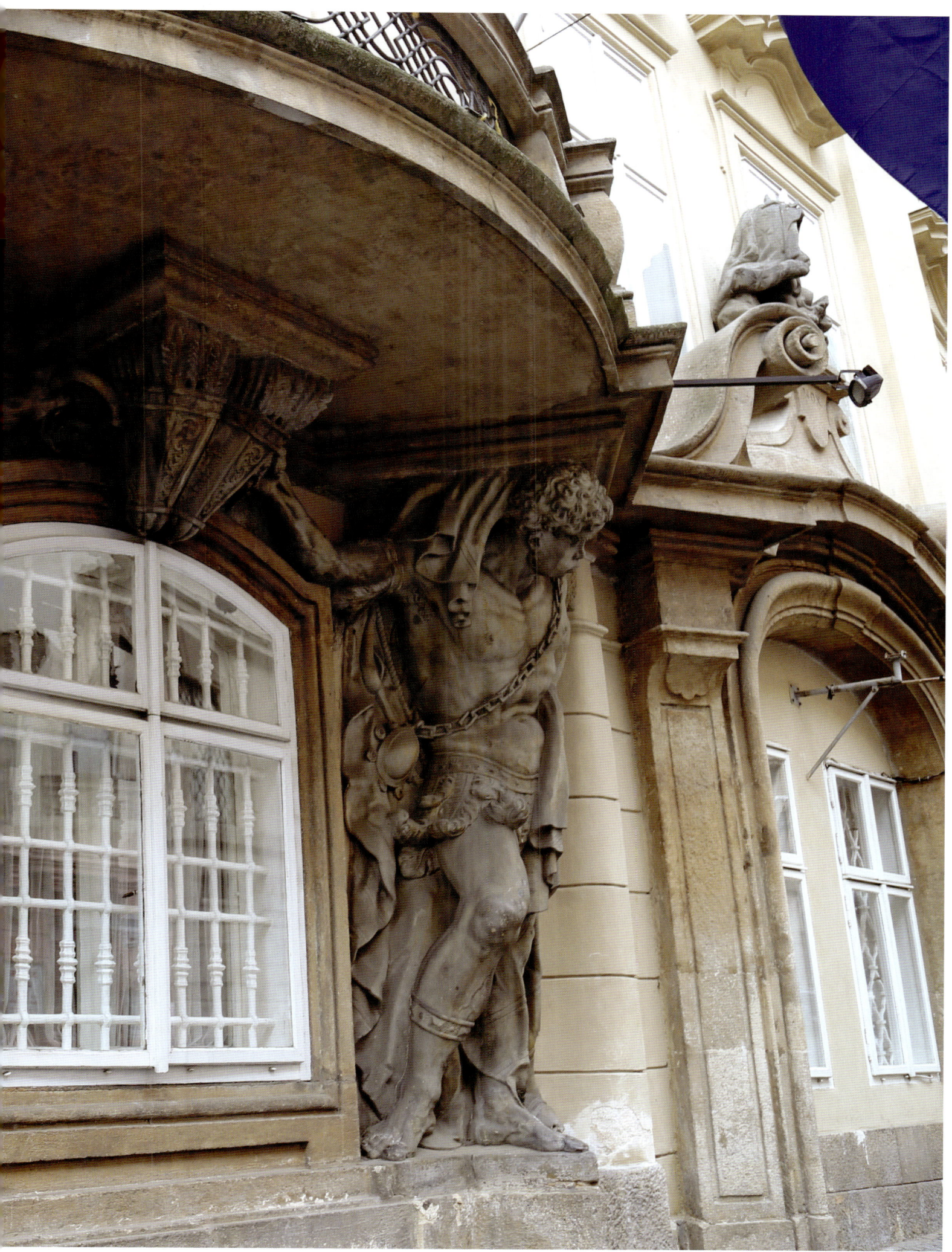

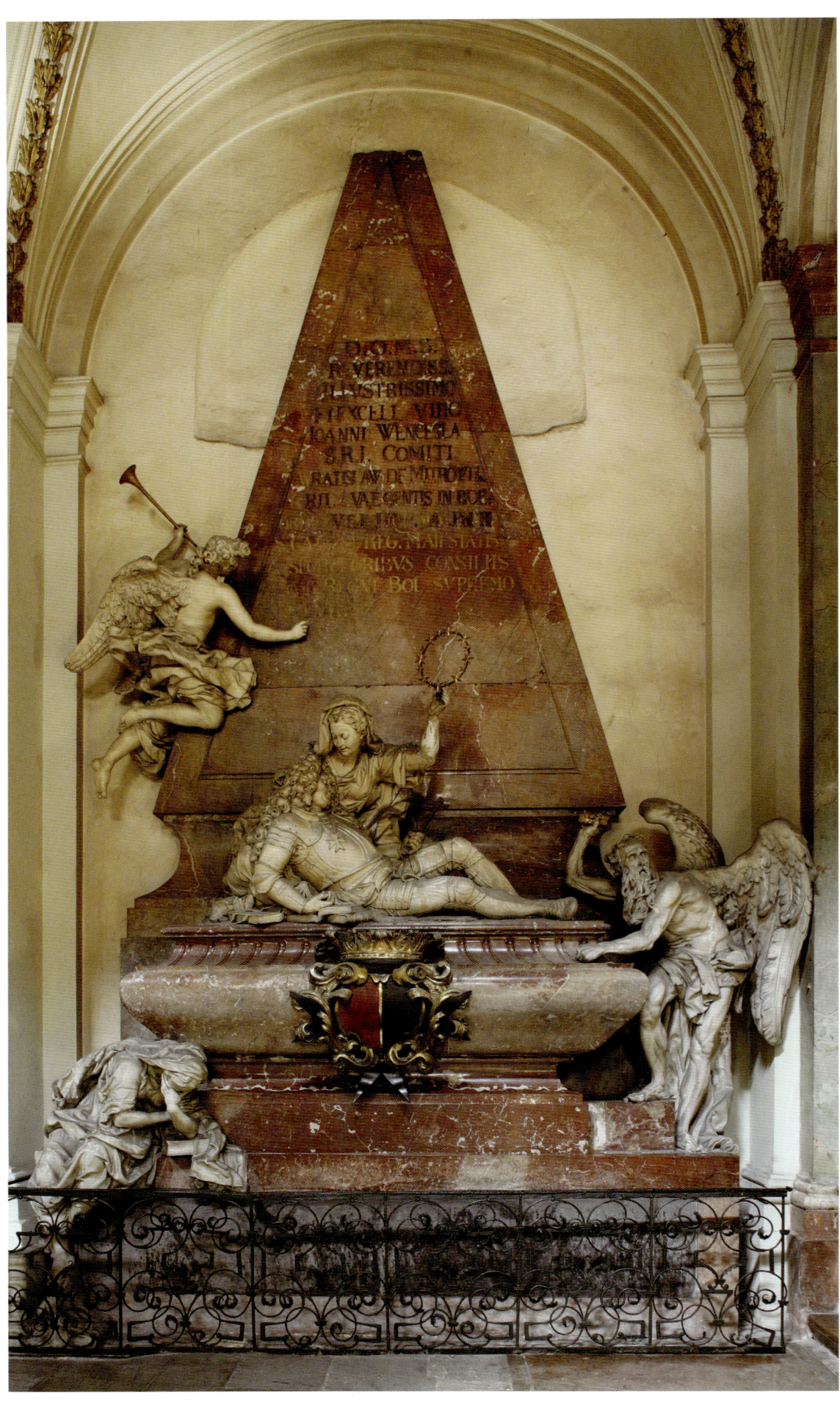

6.14
Johann Bernhard
Fischer von Erlach and
Ferdinand Maximilian
Brokoff, *Tomb of Count
Johann Wenzel
Wratislaw von Mitrowitz*,
marble and limestone,
signed and dated 1716.
Church of St James the
Greater, Prague.

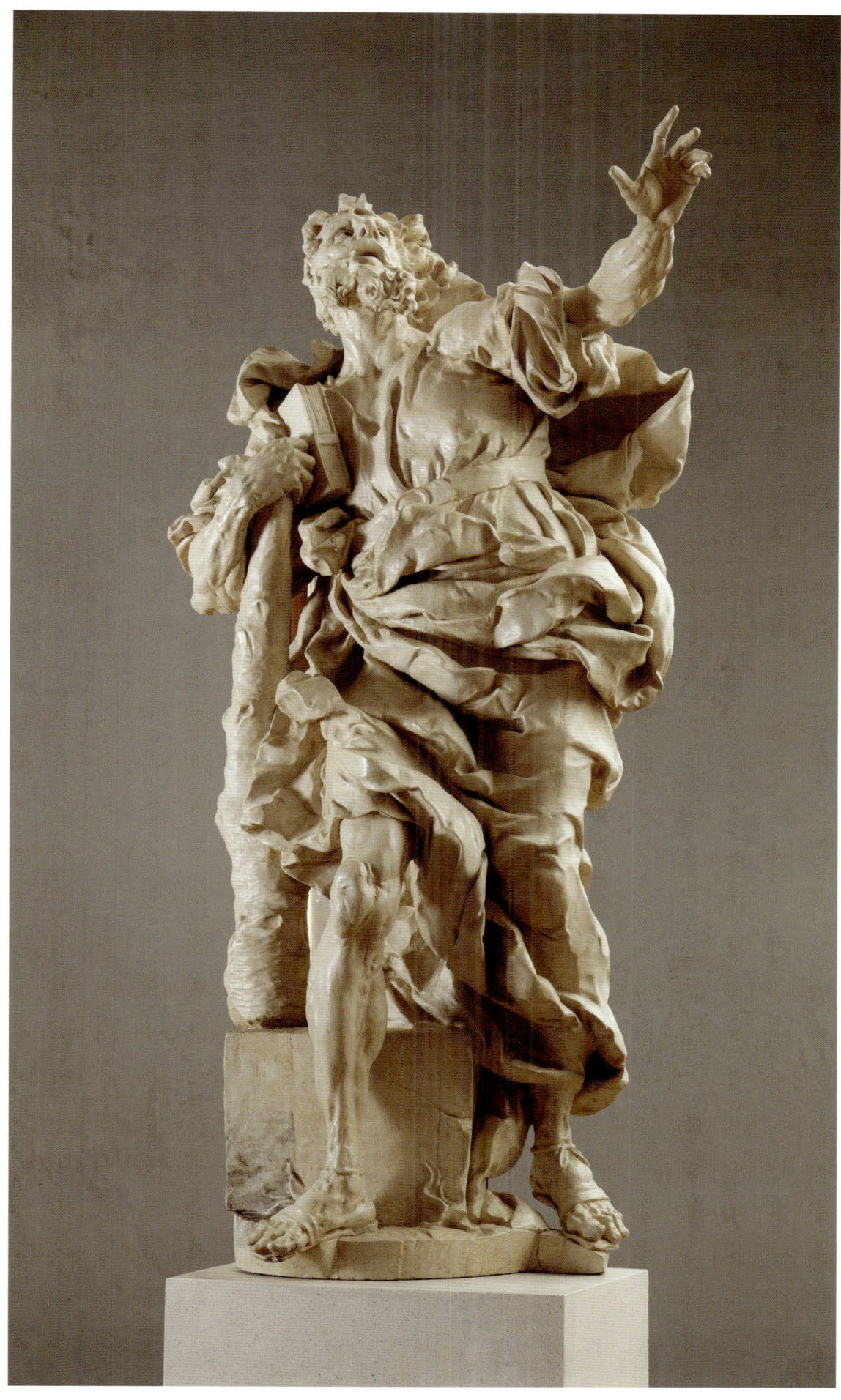

6.15
Matthias Bernhard
Braun, *St Jude (Judas
Thaddäus)*, limewood
with gesso finish,
c. 1712, height 192 cm.
National Gallery, Prague
(inv. no. P 4260).

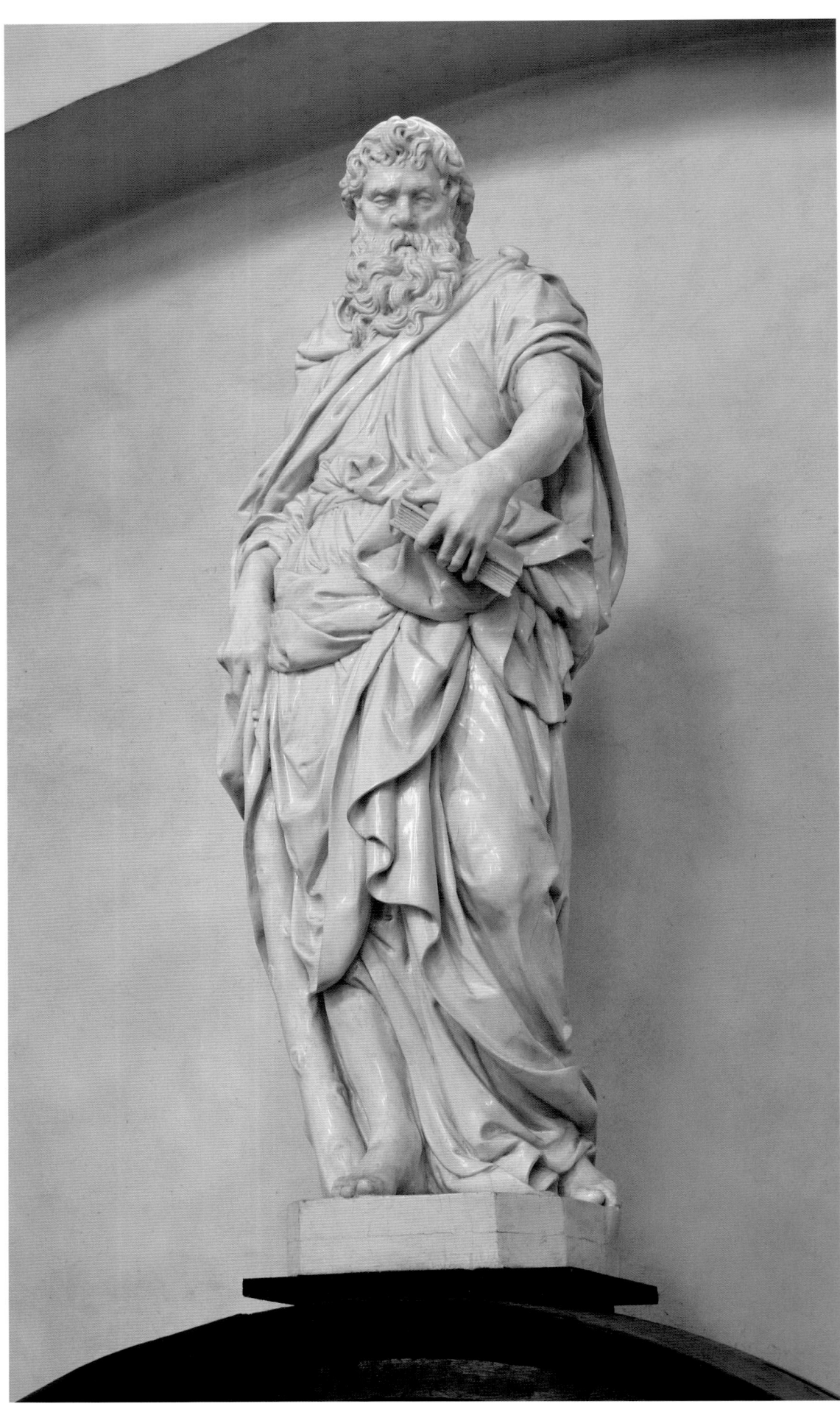

6.16
Johann Georg Bendl,
St Jude, limewood
painted white, 1673–5,
figure surmounting
confessional at the
church of St Salvador,
Prague.

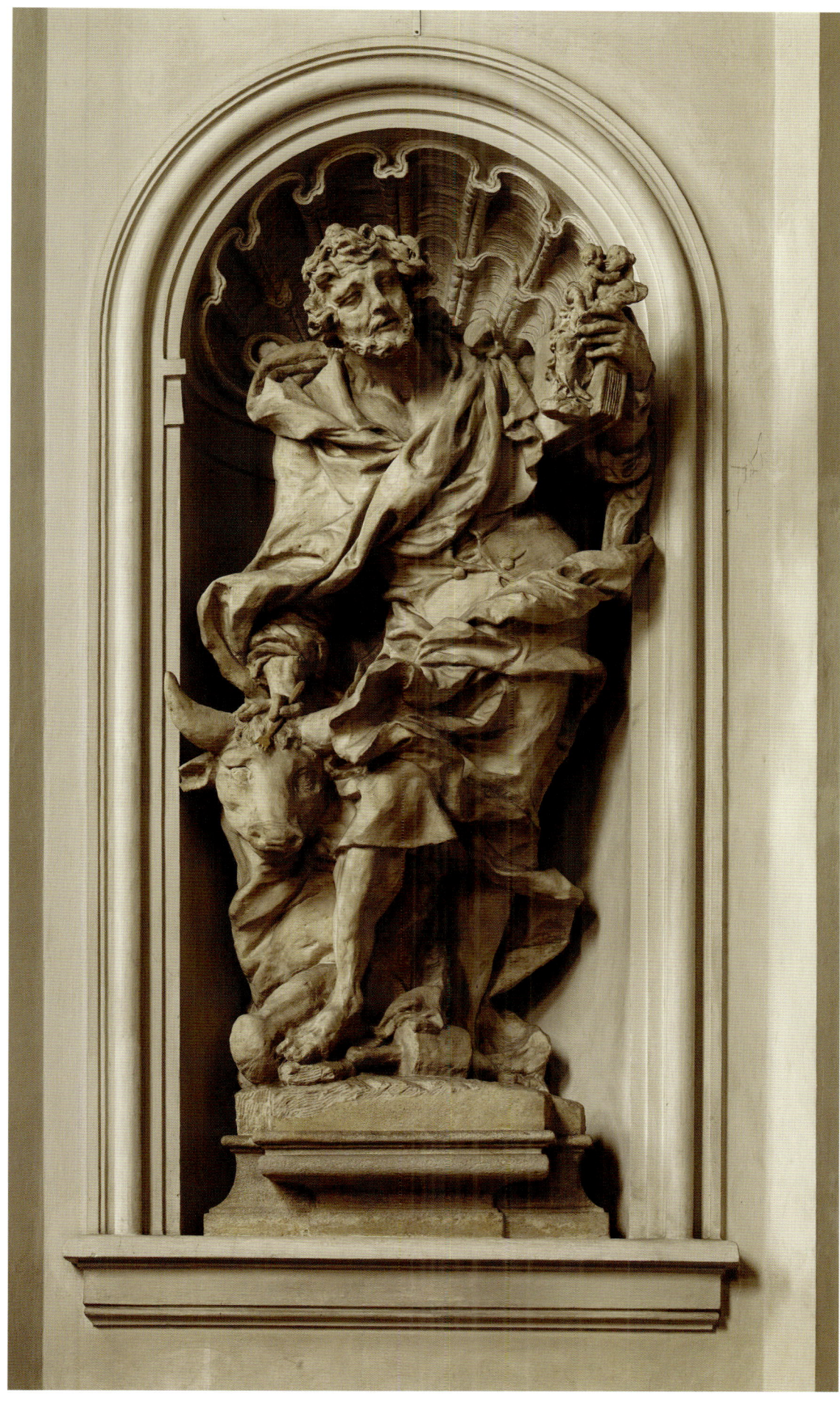

6.17
Matthias Bernhard
Braun, *St Luke*, stone
painted white, after
1715. Church of
St Clement, Prague.

6.19
Matthias Bernhard
Braun, *Envy*, sandstone,
c. 1719. Hospital at Kuks.

as the slightly later white stucco statues by Egid Quirin Asam at Rohr (see Chapter 4) or the wood figures painted white by Ignaz Günther at Rott am Inn (see Chapter 5) were to suggest stone or porcelain. Braun's figure also recalls the rendering of the same subject by Johann Georg (Jan Jiří Bendl) (b. before 1620-80), a highly productive sculptor active in Prague in the previous century. Bendl's *St Jude*, likewise a wood figure painted white, was carved to surmount a confessional at the church of St Salvator in Prague in 1673-5 [6.16].[35] This monumental, heavily draped bearded figure, severe in expression, is unmistakably Northern European, despite its classicizing style and indebtedness to the work of Michelangelo.

From about 1715 to 1718 Braun executed numerous sculptures for the Jesuit church of St Clement (now the Cathedral of St Clement) in Prague, located within the Clementinum.[36] Some of these were stone statues painted white to resemble marble, while others were carved in wood. The stone sculptures included the *Four Church Fathers* and the *Four Evangelists*. One of the Evangelists, *St Luke*, like the figure of *St Jude* discussed above and indeed like Braun's other statues made for the church of St Clement, is vivacious, imbued with movement, crisply carved swirling drapery and windswept hair [6.17].[37] The momentum of the figure is partly due to the exaggerated contrapposto pose and swing of the body seeming to burst out of the confines of its shell niche. As the patron saint of artists, the Evangelist holds in his left hand a small group of the *Virgin and Child*, and in his right hand a modelling tool. His attribute, the bull, lies behind him, the block from which it is carved literally supporting the main figure and the horns compositionally strengthening the whole, the clearly defined forms complementing the mass of the saint's drapery.

As noted above, Braun's leading patron was Count Franz Anton Sporck, who was not only a wealthy landowner and Governor of Bohemia from 1691 to c. 1710, but additionally a writer and musicologist. The count commissioned a number of exceptional sculptures, notably the life-size sandstone figures of *Virtues*

and Vices in about 1718-19 for the spa hospital at Kuks [6.18 and 6.19].[38] He had established a complex of buildings on his estate at Kuks, about 130 kilometres northeast of Prague, around a spa that he created from the local mineral springs. Braun produced twelve *Virtues* and twelve *Vices* to stand on the terrace outside the hospital, while nearby figures of *Angels* stand outside the church. Some of the *Virtues* and *Vices* were subsequently repositioned (including *Envy*, discussed below), and one of the *Vices* no longer survives, but in essence the series remains *in situ*, although the originals are now displayed indoors. The sandstone was quarried locally, and thus the figures convey a strong localised identity. One of the figures outside the church, the statue of *Religion*, is illustrated in the 1718 edition of *Uralter Kukus-Brunn*, a book on the 'ancient' spa at Kuks by Carl Valentin Kirchmeyer, first published in 1696.[39] The date of publication of 1718 gives an *ante quem* for the creation of the statue of *Religion*. Conversely, the other sculptures at Kuks are not mentioned in the publication, implying they must have been made later, although almost certainly soon after 1718. All the sculptures are now seriously weathered and partly restored, since they were exposed to the elements for three centuries and have been conserved at different times during the nineteenth and twentieth centuries. Nevertheless, their potency indubitably remains.[40] The *Virtues and Vices* are based on engravings by Martin Engelbrecht (1684-1756), published in Augsburg c. 1710-15.[41] Although the Kuks sculptures are derived from these Bavarian engravings, Braun and his workshop translated the decorative two-dimensional print sources into powerful, energetic figures in the round. *Envy* from the series of *Vices* exemplifies his sculptural prowess [6.19]. The very pose of this allegorical figure suggests distress, as he leans over uncomfortably to his right, holding up a hand to his face, the drapery billowing out behind. An angry barking dog with arched back at his feet appears to empathise with his agony, threatening to maul any intruder. The bitterness of feeling exuded by this sculpture typifies many of Braun's works, while the surface of the grainy sandstone, admittedly much eroded today (and hence

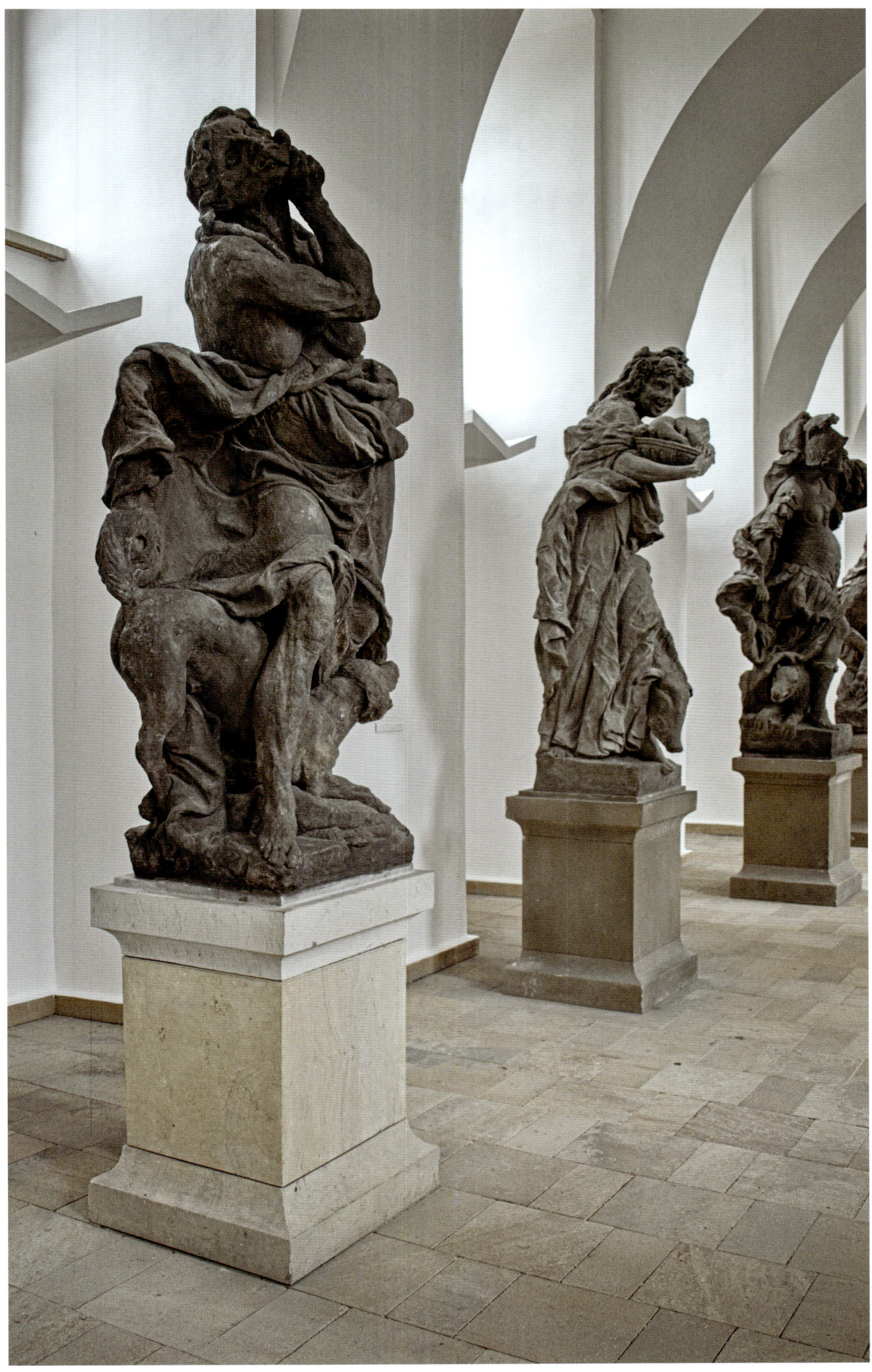

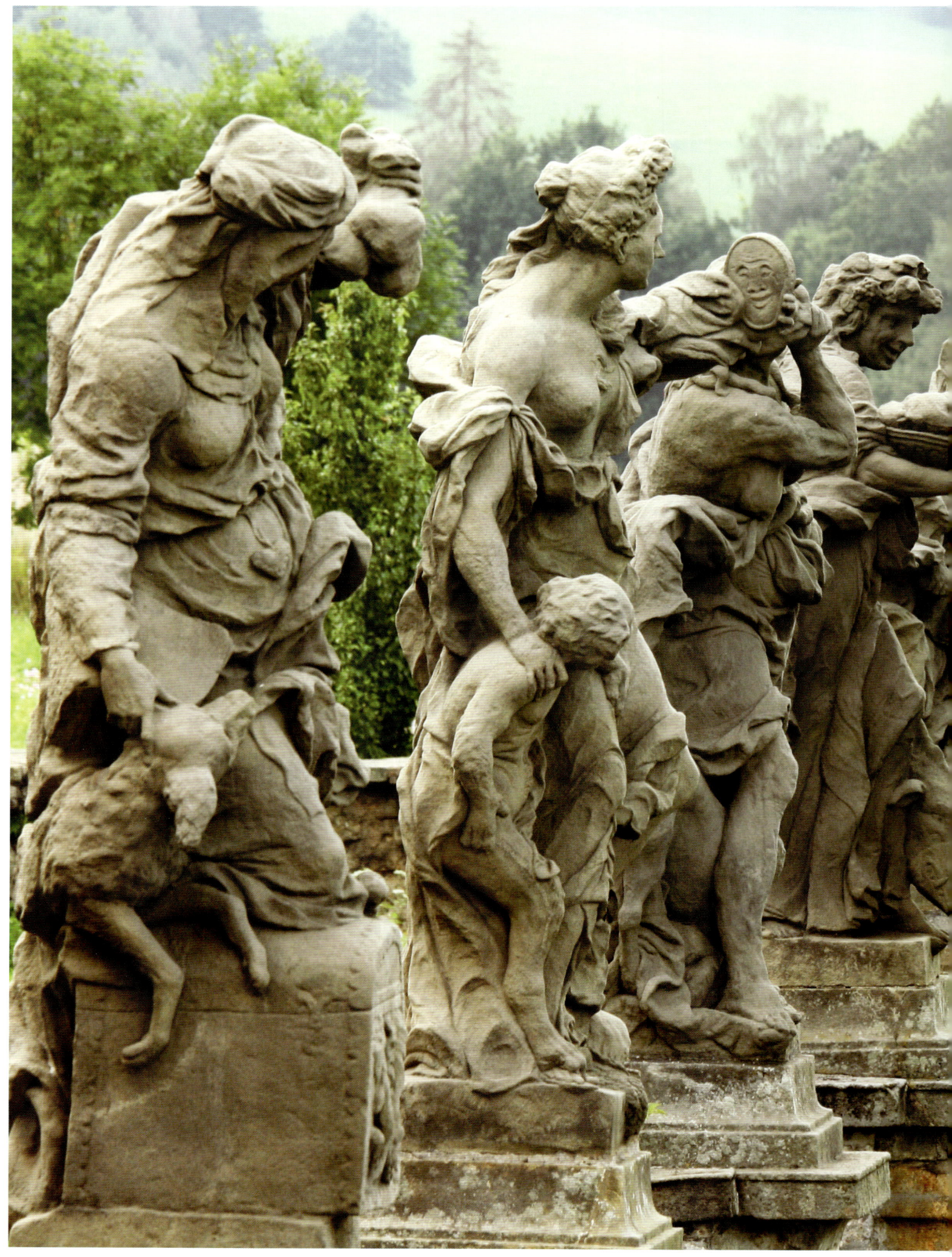

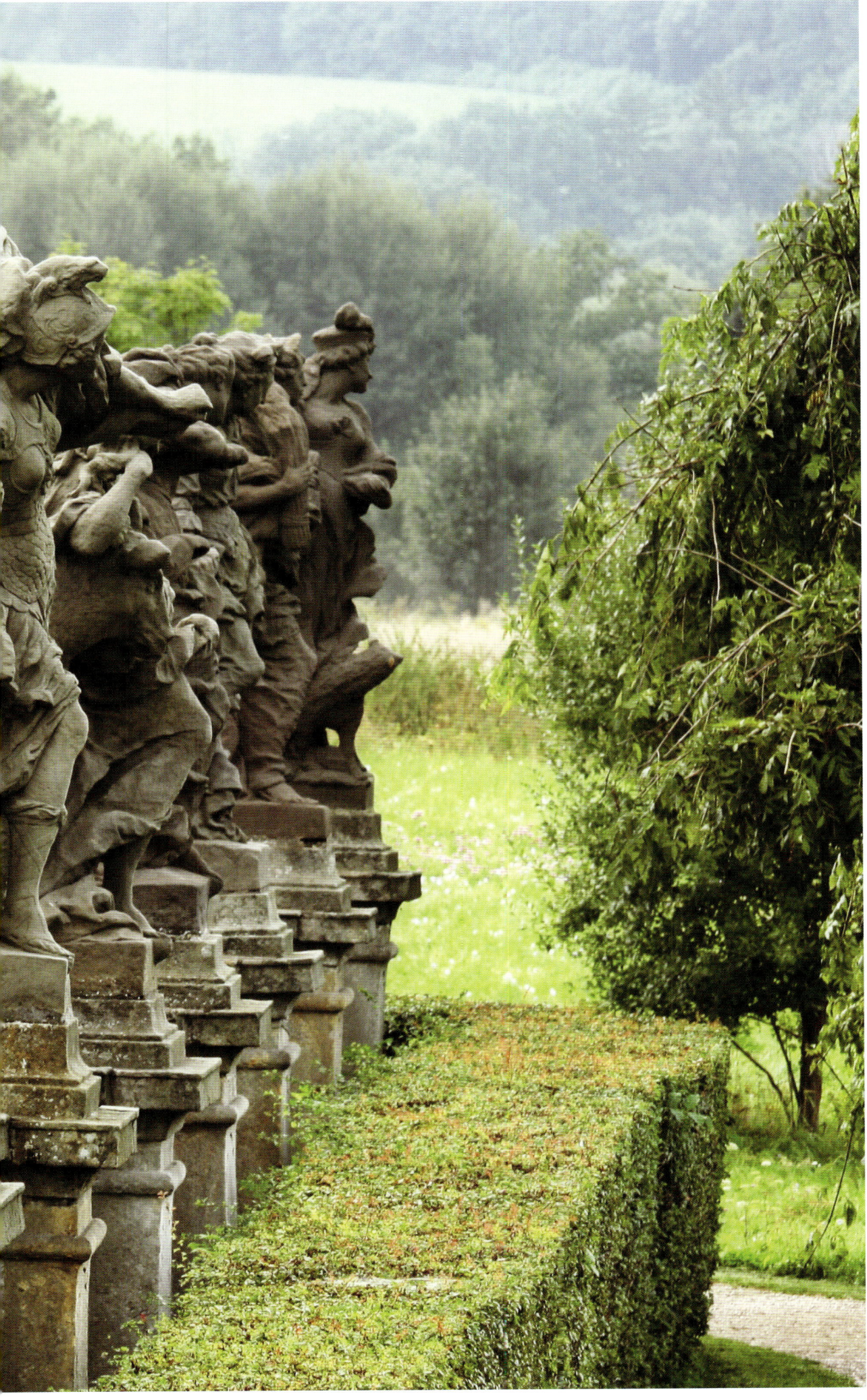

6.18
Copies made 1980-88 of Matthias Bernhard Braun, *Figures of Virtues and Vices*, after the sandstone origirals of c.1719. Hospital at Kuks.

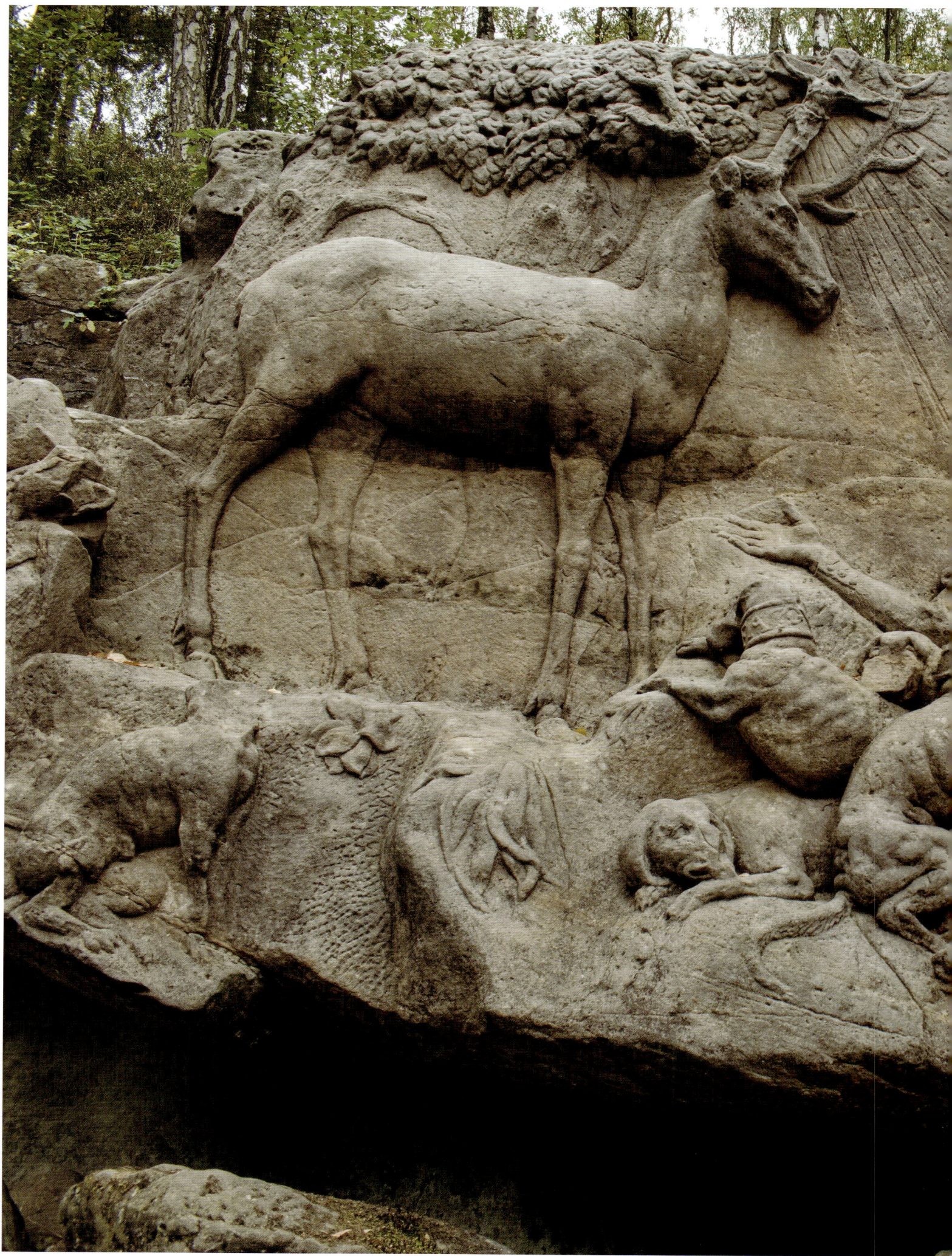

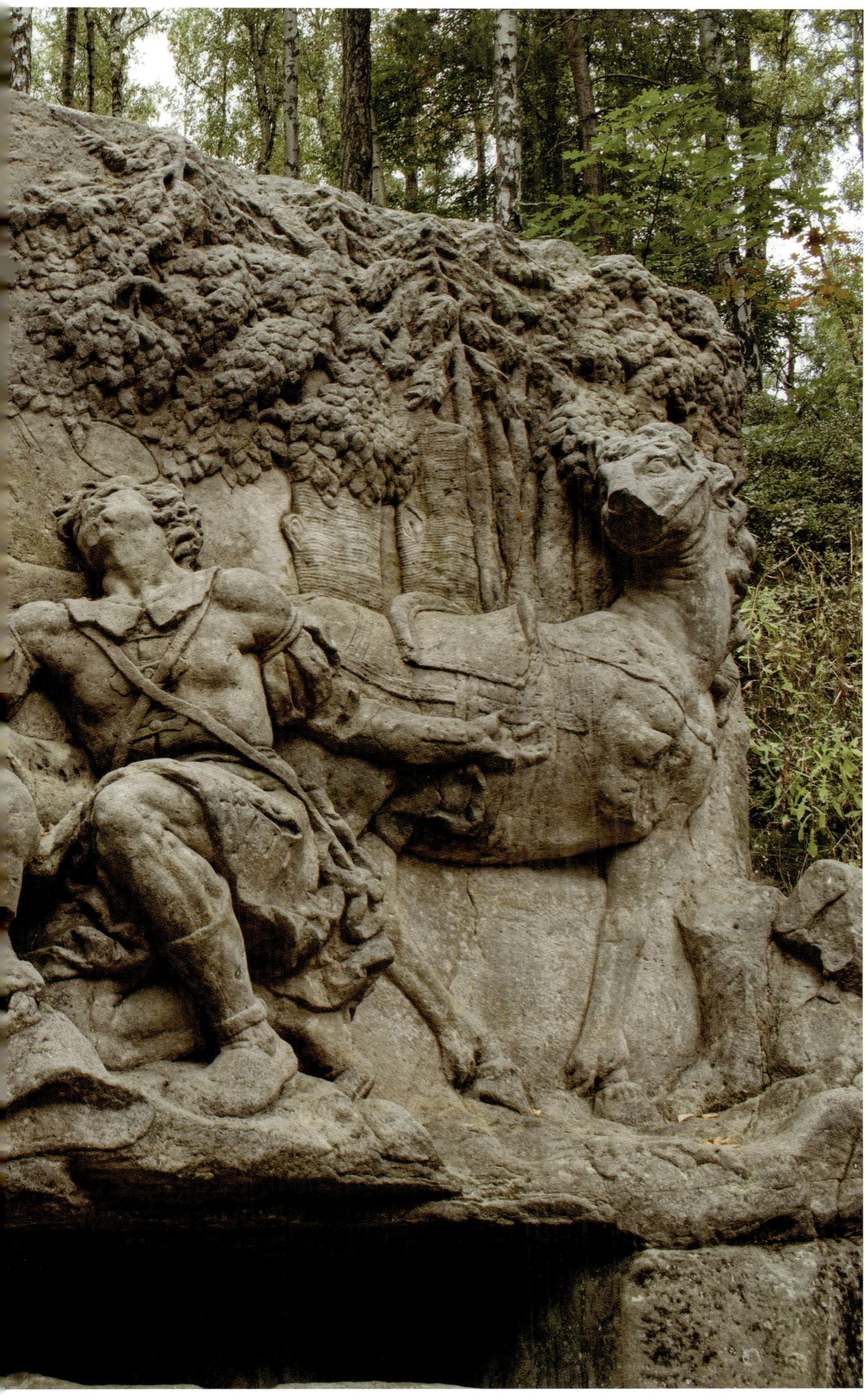

6.20
Matthias Bernhard
Braun, *St Hubert*,
sandstone, 1726.
Bethlehem Wood near
Kuks.

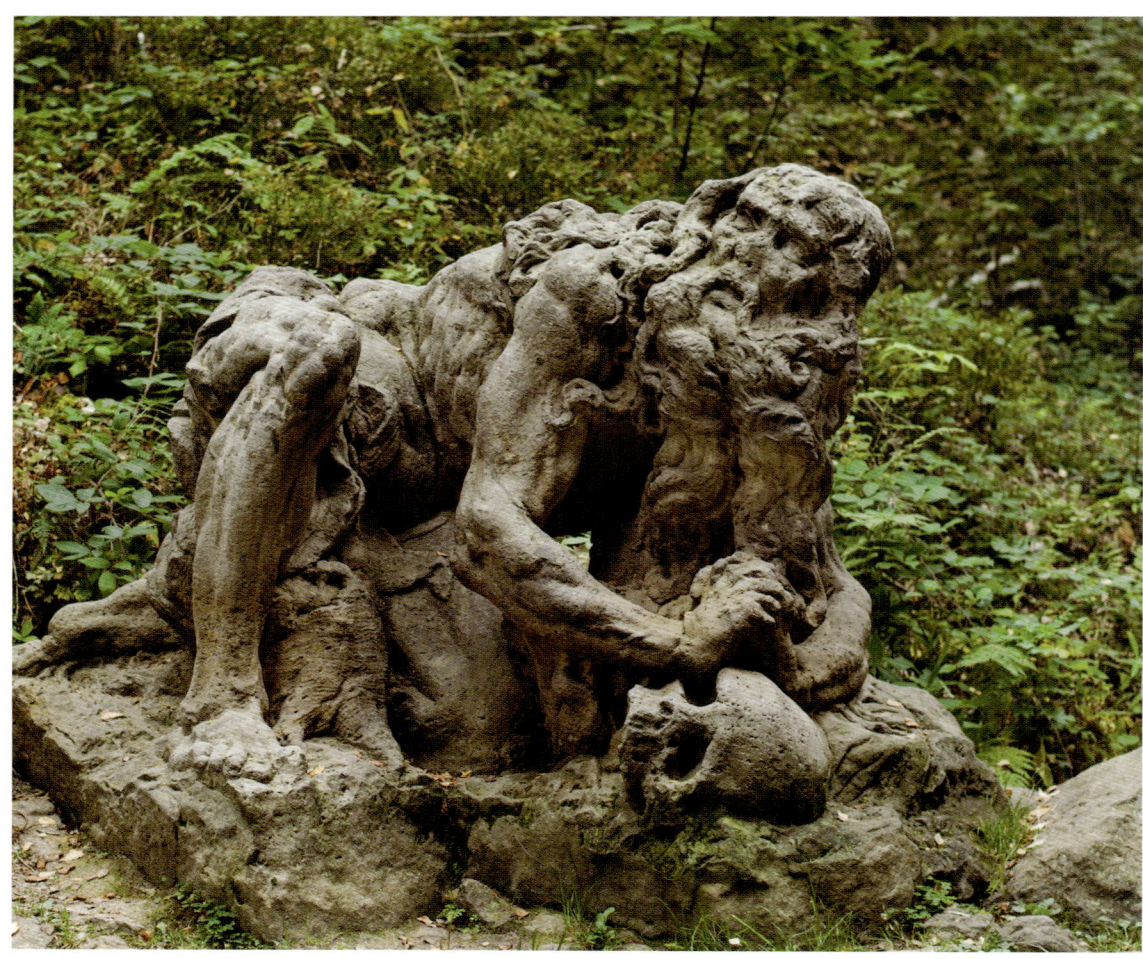

6.21
Matthias Bernhard
Braun, *St Onuphrius*,
sandstone, 1726.
Bethlehem Wood
near Kuks.

6.22
Matthias Bernhard
Braun, *St Garin*,
sandstone, 1726.
Bethlehem Wood
near Kuks.

> 6.23
Matthias Bernhard
Braun, *Tomb of Anna
Miselius*, sandstone,
c. 1722-3. Cemetery at
Jaroměř.

> 6.24
Matthias Bernhard
Braun, *Tomb of Anna
Miselius*, view of
inscription.

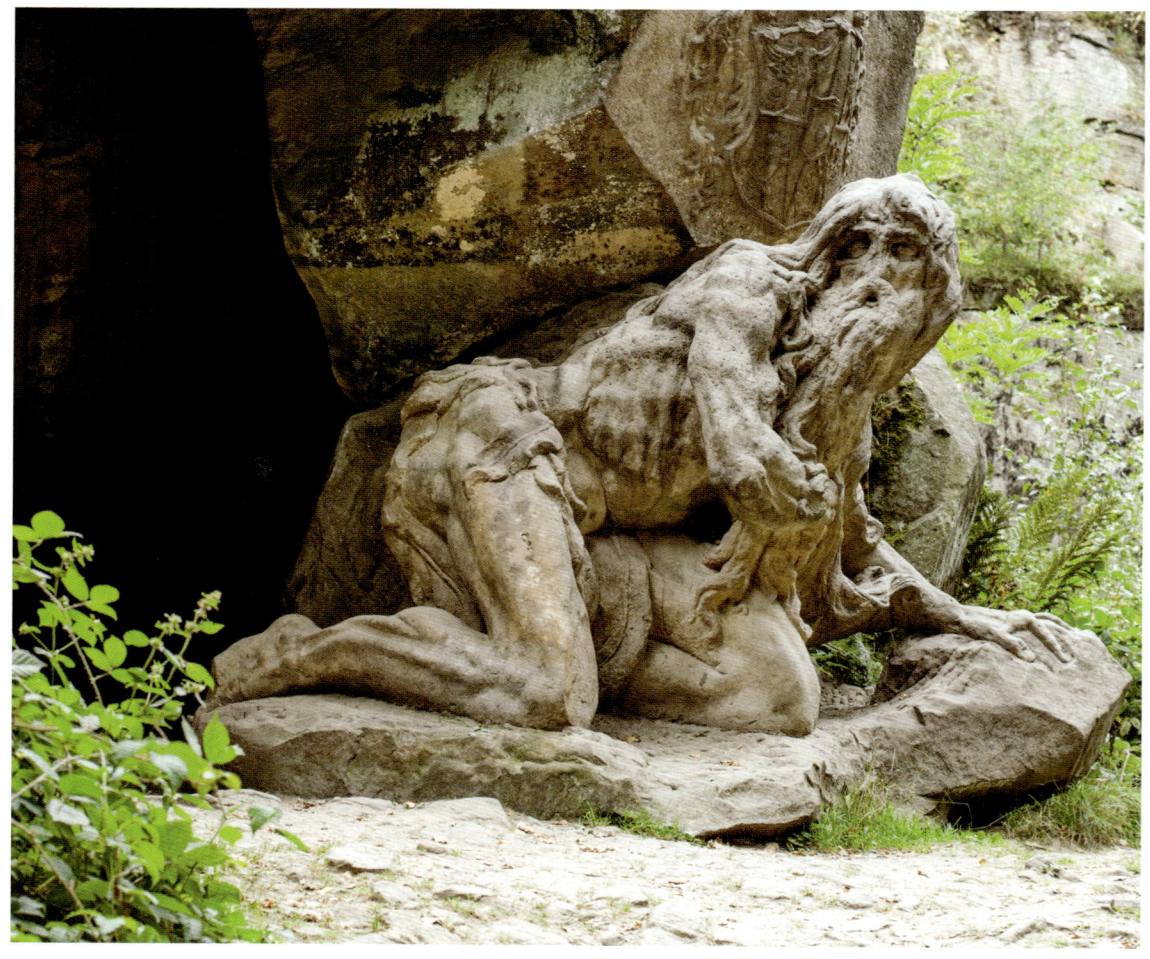

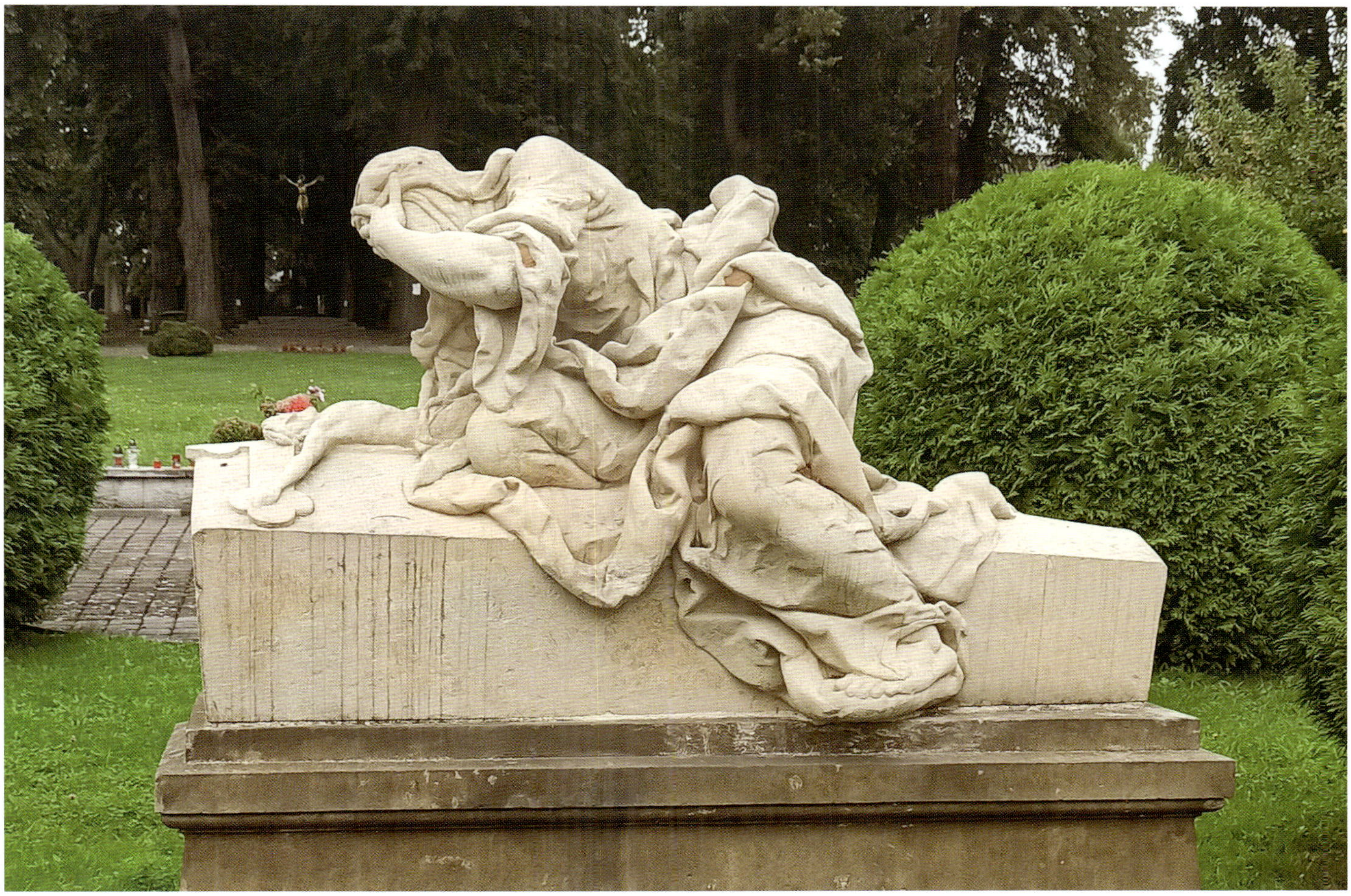

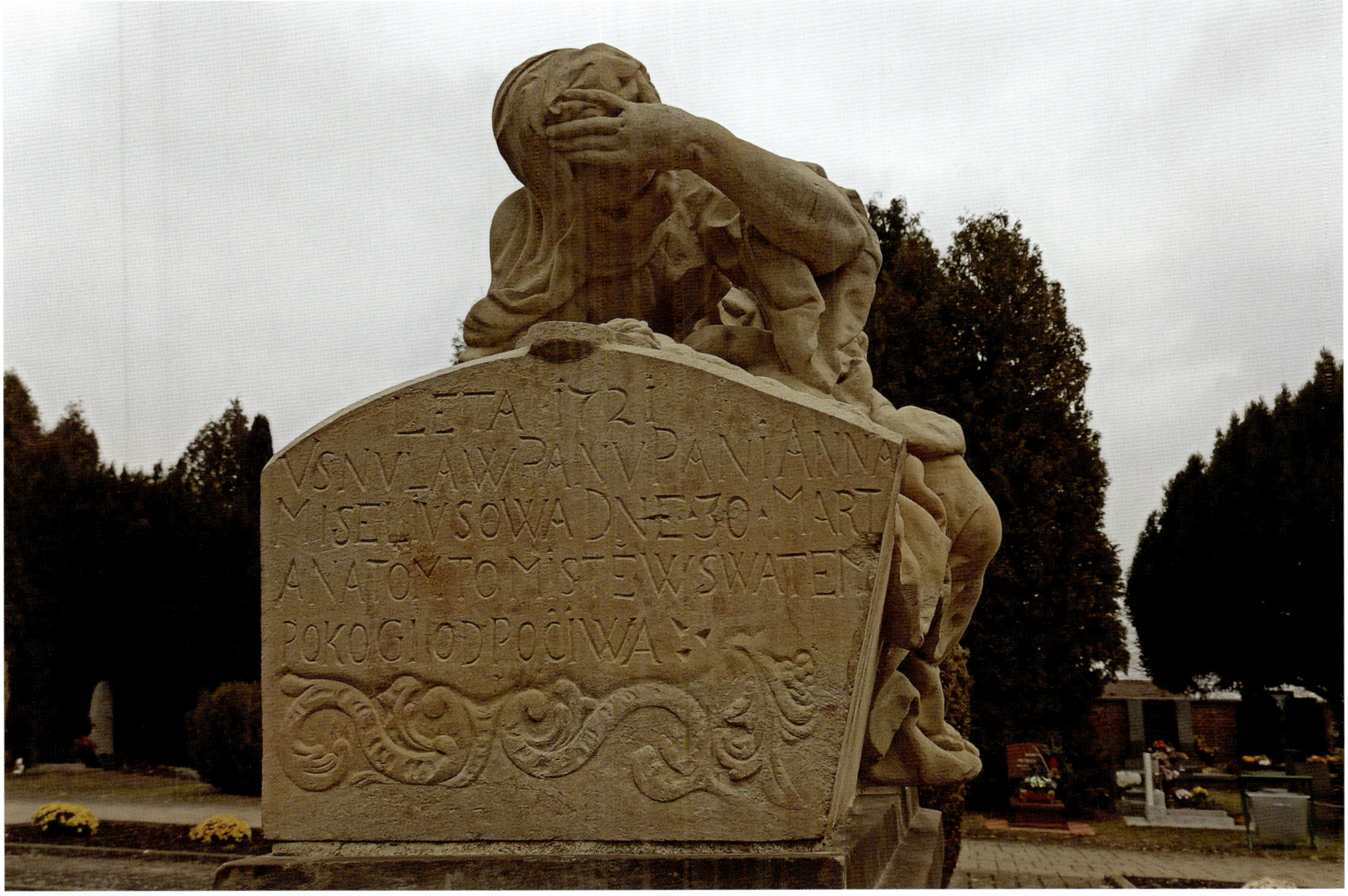

today displayed indoors), must surely always have intensified this rawness.

Braun continued to work for Count Sporck through the 1720s and 1730s, his most remarkable commission being the series of reliefs and figures hewn from the rocks in the woodland on the count's estate, Neuwald bei Schurz (Žírec), 3 kilometres northwest of Kuks, an area now known as the Bethlehem wood.[42] The count desired Biblical sculptures and sculptures of saints and hermits to be carved out of the local sandstone in the woods. He had purchased the land in 1717, and in 1718 planned to build hermitages dedicated to St Anthony and St Paul, and a relief depicting *St Hubert's Vision of the Stag* along an avenue that would lead to the Jesuits' sanctuary; the hermitages do not survive, although the relief of St Hubert is still extant [**6.20**]. Hewn out of the rock, its environment is highly appropriate for the saint who experienced a vision of Christ on the Cross on the antlers of a stag whilst out hunting in the woods.[43] The sculptures and hermitages that Braun's workshop carried out for Count Sporck in the Bethlehem wood effectively formed a religious equivalent to the garden and grotto statues seen in sixteenth-century Italy, such as Giambologna's *Appenine* of 1580 made for the garden of the Villa of Pratolino in Tuscany, or the same sculptor's *Fountain of Ocean* of 1570-75 in the Boboli Gardens in Florence.[44] The count's commission for the Bethlehem wood sparked disputes with the Jesuits, who owned the bordering land that was worked by a tenant farmer. The debate dragged on over six years, causing interruptions and delays to the commission, Braun having to stop work from 1729 to 1731.[45] The forms of his sculptures were partly determined by the rocks from which they were carved, as seen in the relief of *St Hubert*; the energetic, raw marks of the tools on the mineral surface of the stone are clearly visible. The two hermits *St Onuphrius* and *St Garin (Juan Garino)* both date from 1726, near the start of the project. They are each depicted as rough, hairy, over-life-size figures [**6.21 and 6.22**], demonstrating Count Sporck's profound fascination with the history of hermits and hermitages. St Onuphrius was a hermit and ascetic of the

fourth or fifth century who lived in the Egyptian desert, venerated in both the Eastern Church and Southern Germany.[46] The sculpture emerges out of the ground, from the rock from which it is carved at the side of an avenue of trees, the figure placed a few feet away from another of *St John the Baptist*. The other hermit depicted, St Garin, was a Spanish hermit who lived on Montserrat in Catalonia, condemning himself to crawl on all-fours and live like a beast to atone for his assassination of Count Winifrid's daughter.[47] The sculptor renders him as a bearded hirsute figure crawling out of his cave. Behind, the count's coat of arms is carved in relief on the rock, while a bird is depicted perched nearby, a harmonious integration of the sculpted forms with their surrounding natural environment. Both the hermits' long flowing beards and turned heads must have been in part inspired by Michelangelo's *Moses* on the tomb of Pope Julius II in the church of S. Pietro in Vincoli in Rome, completed in 1545, in addition to Giambologna's garden sculptures, as noted above.

Some years before his work at the Bethlehem wood Braun carried out what was effectively a private commission. This chapter fittingly ends with this contemplative and personal sculpture, even though this work was produced a few years earlier than those discussed above. Soon after Braun's mother-in-law Anna Miselius died in 1721, he carved her memorial [**6.23 and 6.24**].[48] Unlike the rest of his oeuvre, this tomb was made for a member of his family, a woman who was an ordinary citizen rather than an aristocrat or wealthy patron. It was originally located near the church of St James in Jaroměř, where Anna Miselius had lived, a small town not far from Kuks. In 1888 it was moved to the town cemetery. An inscription written in Czech at one end of the tomb chest above a decorative band carved in relief states that Anna Miselius was laid to rest on 30 March 1721. A heavily draped female figure representing Contemplation sorrowfully leans, half-reclining, over a crucifix carved integrally into the lid of the simple oblong sarcophagus. Her left hand supports her head in a pose redolent of mourning. As has been pointed out, the figure of Contemplation on Brokoff's tomb in the church of St James commemorating Count Wratislaw von Mitrow-itz of 1716 [**6.14**] is closely analogous to this figure and must surely have served as an inspira-tion for Braun.

Braun's output was extensive; he ran a highly productive workshop, employing his nephew Antonin, who took over the workshop after his death. Like his near contemporary

Brokoff, he clearly helped create and define baroque sculpture in Bohemia in the first half of the eighteenth century. Links with Bavaria and Vienna are undeniable, yet at the same time the remarkable works created by both sculptors for Prague and elsewhere in Bohemia are powerfully distinctive, a confluence of vernacular Bohemian, Germanic and Italianate sources.

Notes

1 Petráň 1998. For patronage and art in Moravia during and after the Thirty Years' War, see Kroupa 1998.
2 Petráň 1998 and Chaline 1998.
3 For the history and names of the bridge and its predecessors, see Novotny and Poche 1947, pp. 7-41. See also Gajdošová 2015 for the medieval history of the bridge.
4 Novotny and Poche 1947, pp. 34-6.
5 Wittkower 1999b, p. 9.
6 Fajt and Sršeň 1993.
7 Neumann 1970, pp. 159-60; Birke 1981, cat. no. 7 on p. 72; https://www.deutsche-biographie.de/sfz30225.html, accessed 16 January 2021.
8 Neumann 1970, p. 159.
9 https://www.christianiconography.info/johnNepomuk.html, accessed 16 January 2021. The supposed confession of the queen is depicted in a relief on the pediment, on which see below.
10 Wittkower 1999b, pp. 95-7.
11 The lighter areas of the bronze reliefs reflect the visitors who have touched them for good luck.
12 For example Lorenzo Ghiberti's *Gates of Paradise* on the Baptistery in Florence of 1425-52; see Motture 2019, plate 3.8.
13 Novotny and Poche 1947, p. 72; Neumann 1970, p. 160.
14 Neumann 1970, p. 164.
15 Neumann 1970, p. 164.
16 *St Barbara, St Margaret and St Eliza-beth* (1707); *St Gaetano* (1709); *St Adalbert* (1709); *St Ignatius Loyola* (1714); and *St Guy* (1714); see Novotny and Poche 1947.

17 A third group from Braun's work-shop, dating from c. 1720, depicts St Ludmila and her grandson St Wenceslas. This group, now on the Charles Bridge, was originally placed elsewhere and only moved to the bridge after 1784. See Novotny and Poche 1947, figs. 15 and 15a on pp. 65 and 67; and pp. 122-4.
18 Poche and Kořán 2003, p. 25.
19 Neumann 1970, pp. 169-70; Poche and Kořán 2003, pp. 40-1. Plasy is about 100 kilometres west of Prague.
20 'VIVIFICUM LATUS EXUGIT COR MUTUANS CORDE' (The live side released the heart that he freely gave for another heart). This is a refer-ence to Christ exchanging his heart for Luitgarde's, according to her mystical vision.
21 Braun's terracotta modello for the group is in the collection of the Turmmuseum, Oetz in the Tyrol; see https://sbirky.ngprague.cz/en/dielo/CZE:NG.F_3244. Poche and Kořán 2003, fig. 016 on p. 37.
22 Neumann 1970, p. 170.
23 Wittkower 1999b, p. 13 and fig. 16.
24 Neumann 1970, p. 169; Poche and Kořán 2003, p. 41.
25 The group may be based on a design by Peter Brandel originally intended for Brokoff's group of St Xavier; Neumann 1970, p. 169.
26 Neumann 1970, p. 166.
27 Neumann 1970, p. 165.
28 Neumann 1970, pp. 166-7.
29 Neumann 1970, p. 167.
30 Neumann 1970, p. 167.
31 Bindman and Baker 1995, p. 289.
32 Poche and Kořán 2003 is the standard monograph on Braun.

33 Neumann 1970, pp. 170-171; Poche and Kořán 2003, p. 46.
34 Wittkower 1999b, p. 7.
35 Neumann 1970, p. 151. See also Stech 1959, p. 11.
36 Neumann 1970, pp. 173-5; Poche and Kořán 2003, pp. 46-56.
37 Neumann 1970, p. 174.
38 Neumann 1970, pp. 177-80; Poche and Kořán 2003, pp. 93-131. For Sporck, see *Neue Deutsche Biographie* n.d., https://www.deutsche-biogra-phie.de/sfz80808.html, accessed 29 January 2021.
39 *Uralter Kukus Brunn*, Prague, 1696. The second edition was published in 1718; Neumann 1970, p. 177; see https://archiwum.allegro.pl/oferta/kirchmeyer-uralter-kukus-brunn-praha-1696-i8031020649.html, accessed 29 January 2021.
40 Modern copies produced 1980-88 are to be seen in the original loca-tions outside, while the eighteenth-century figures are displayed in-doors [6.18 and 6.19]. Protective measures are currently in place to help decrease further erosion; see https://en.wikipedia.org/wiki/Kuks, accessed 29 January 2021.
41 Neumann 1970, p. 178.
42 Neumann 1970, pp. 181-3; Poche and Kořán 2003, pp. 180-95.
43 Poche and Kořán 2003, pp. 184-6.
44 Avery 1987, pp. 221-3 and p. 217.
45 Neumann 1970, p. 182; Poche and Kořán 2003, pp. 181-2.
46 https://en.wikipedia.org/wiki/Onuphrius, accessed 30 January 2021.
47 Neumann 1970, p. 183.
48 Neumann 1970, p. 180; Poche and Kořán 2003, pp. 165-7; note 257 on p. 321.

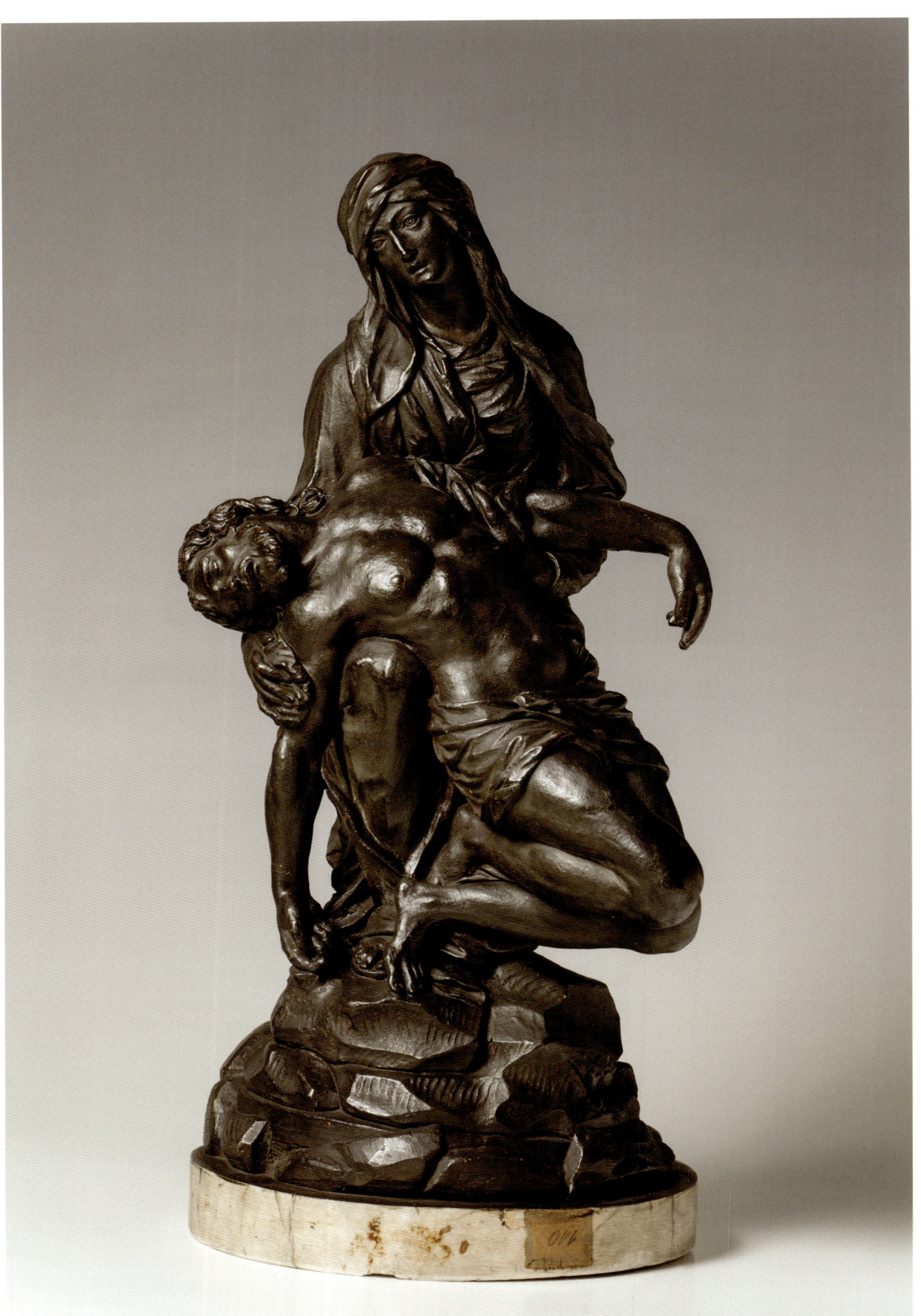

CHAPTER 7

SCULPTURE IN VIENNA, GURK, WÜRZBURG AND TRIER. CERAMICS.

As the capital of the Habsburg Empire, Vienna was a major centre for art and culture with close cultural links with Prague. Its Academy of Fine Arts was founded by Peter Strudel (1660-1714) in 1692, and although it closed at Strudel's death in 1714 it was to re-open in 1725. Vienna thus attracted many sculptors from elsewhere who trained in the city during the eighteenth century. As noted in Chapter 6, these included the Prague sculptor Ferdinand Maximilian Brokoff in the first decade of the eighteenth century. Later Johann Baptist Straub and Ignaz Günther, active mainly in Bavaria, were to train in Vienna, as mentioned in Chapter 5.

The first part of this chapter will discuss Georg Raphael Donner's sculpture in Vienna, Bratislava and Gurk. The next section will discuss the sculptural porcelain figures modelled by Johann Gottlieb Kirchner and Johann Joachim Kändler at Meissen, and by Franz Anton Bustelli at Nymphenburg. Finally, the extraordinary garden sculpture in Würzburg executed by Ferdinand Tietz, who had worked alongside Matthias Braun in Prague, will be considered.

Georg Raphael Donner (1693-1741)

Donner became one of the leading sculptors in Austria in the first half of the eighteenth century. A sculptor and medallist, he was born at Essling near Vienna, the son of a carpenter. He was probably taught by the sculptor Johann Franz Prenner in Vienna and by the Venetian sculptor Giovanni Giuliani in Heiligenkreuz, 25 kilometres southeast of Vienna. Through Giuliani, Donner came to know bronzes in the Liechtenstein Collection by François Du Quesnoy (1597-1643), Giambologna (1529-1608), Adriaen de Vries and others. Donner mistakenly thought the bronze statuettes by Du Quesnoy were antique, this misconception possibly inspiring him to emulate them.[1] In 1713 he studied the art of lead casting and medal-making under the Swedish court medallist Benedikt (Bengt) Richter (1670-1735). Before 1715 Donner went to Munich, where he is thought to have studied further the technique of lead casting with the court sculptor Guillielmus de Grof. He visited Dresden in 1720, where he would have become acquainted with Balthasar Permoser's work. These artistic models, both past and contemporary, as well as the techniques of lead casting and the striking of medals, were formative influences on Donner's future work.[2]

Donner's earliest known sculpture dates from 1721. This is a terracotta group of *The Pietà*, now in the National Gallery of Prague [7.1].[3] The Italianate roots of this piece are evident, though it is uncertain if Donner travelled to Italy. Reminiscences of sixteenth-century Florentine or Roman sculpture, for example the

7.1
Georg Raphael Donner, *The Pietà*, terracotta painted black, signed and dated 1721, height 36 cm. National Gallery, Prague (inv. no. P 5189).

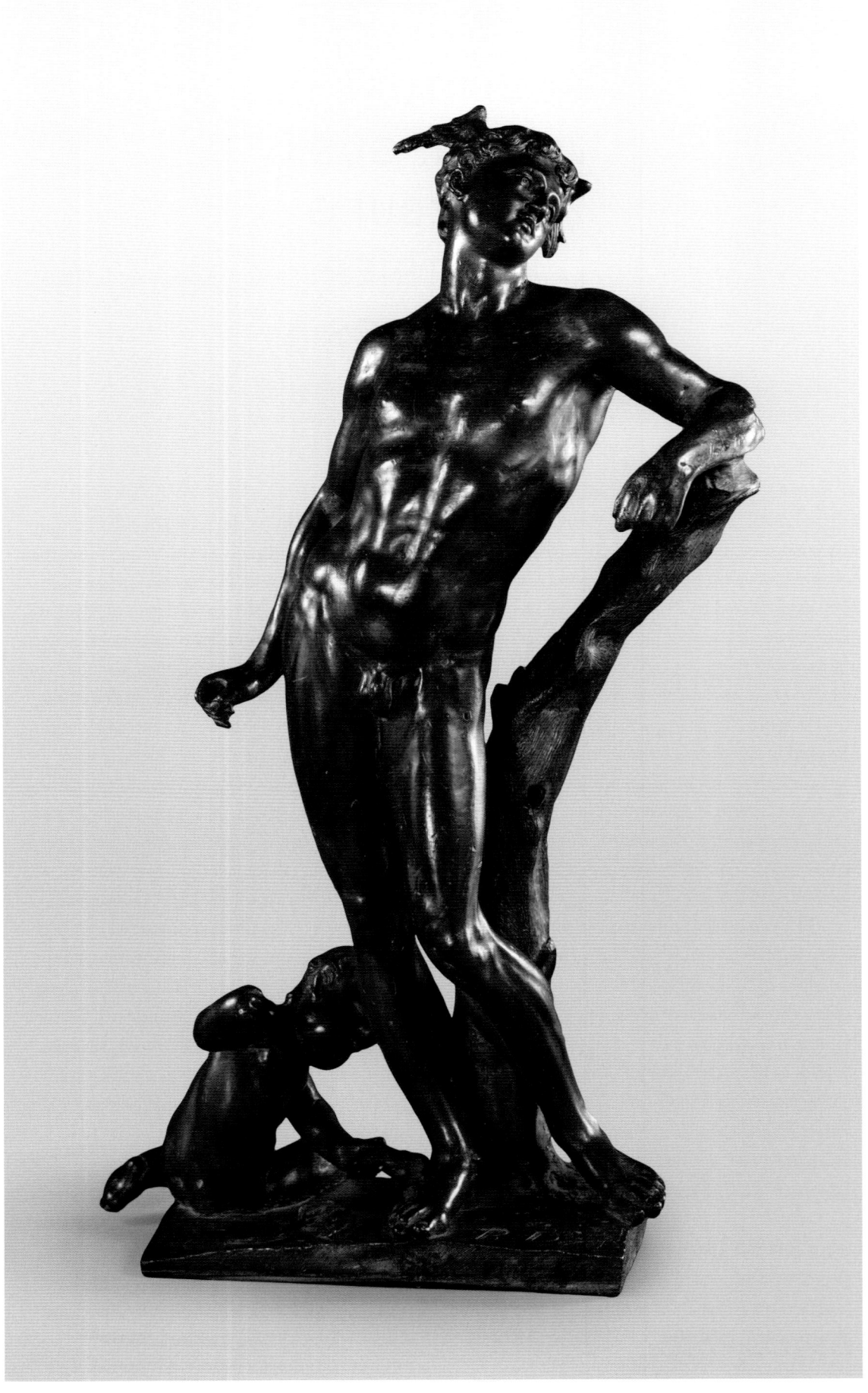

7.2
Georg Raphael Donner,
Mercury and Cupid,
lead, monogrammed
'R.D.', height 44.5 cm.
Abbey Museum,
Klosterneuburg
(inv. no. KG 176).

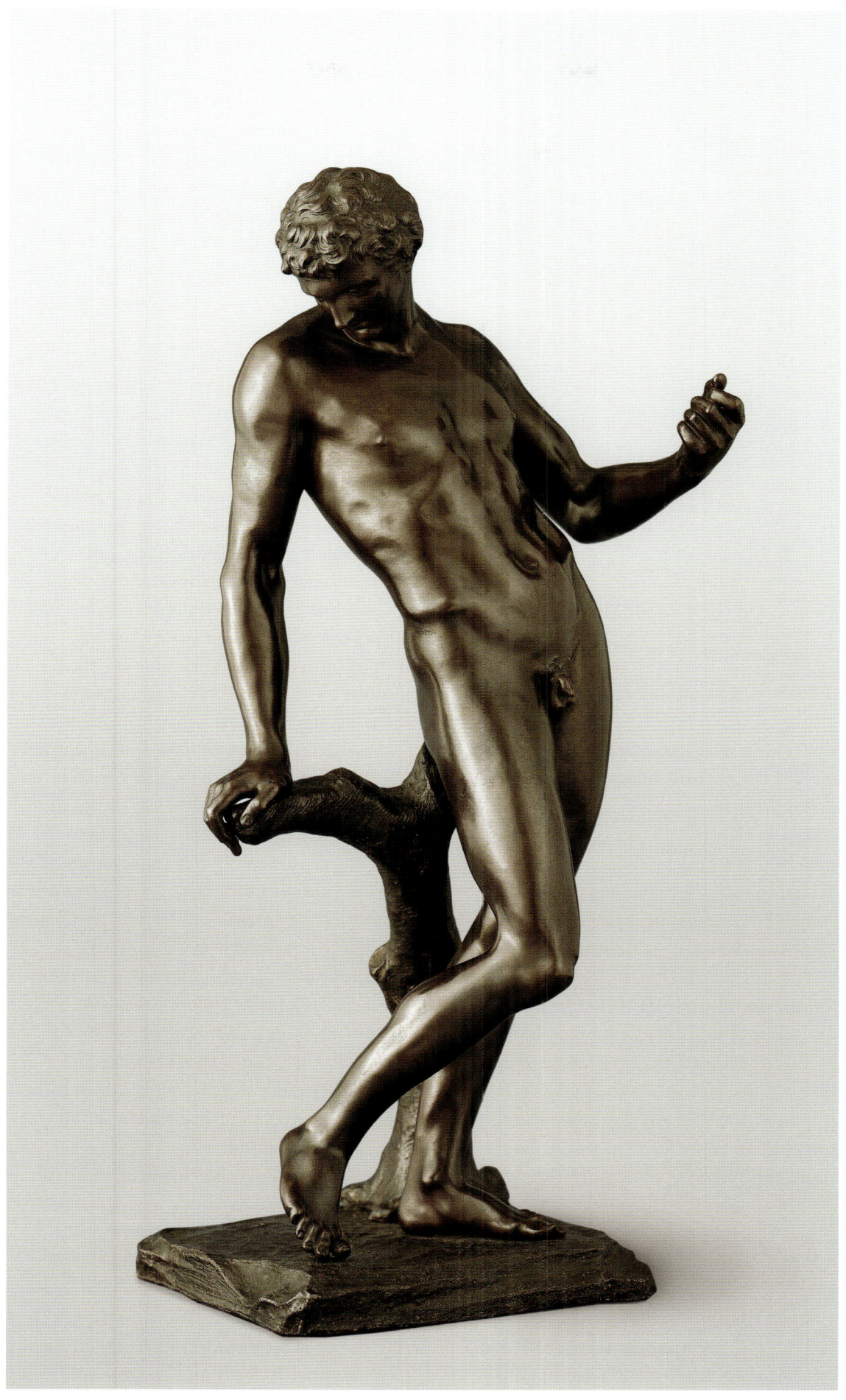

7.3
François Du Quesnoy,
Mercury, bronze,
1629/30. Schloss
Vaduz, Liechtenstein
Collection
(inv. no. SK 611).

7.4
Georg Raphael Donner,
Paris, marble, signed
and dated 1726. Schloss
Mirabell, Salzburg.

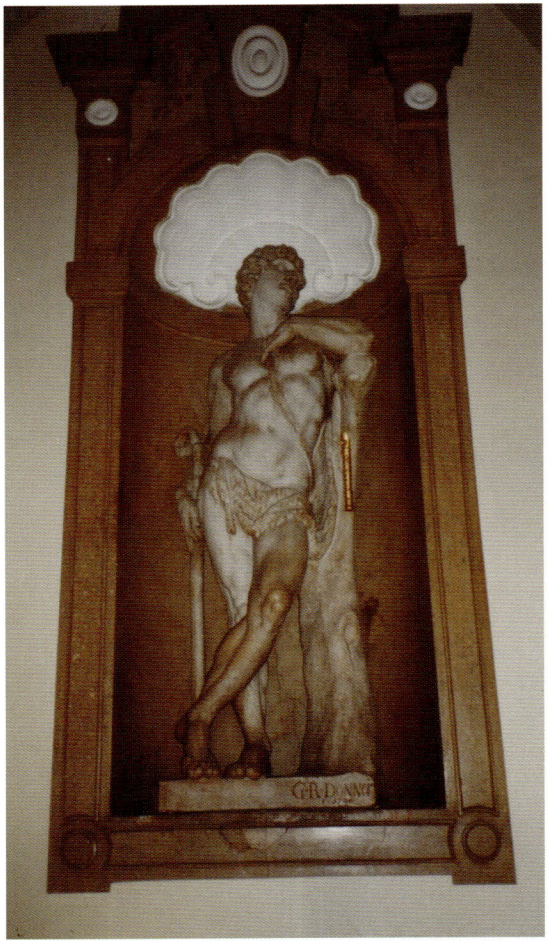

ankle. Mercury must have originally held a caduceus, now missing, in his right hand. As noted above, through Giuliani Donner would have known of François Du Quesnoy's bronzes in the Liechtenstein Collection. These were reductions of full-size marbles in Rome, and considered antique in Donner's day, even though they only dated back just under a century. Du Quesnoy's *Apollo and Cupid* (1635/40) and his *Mercury* (c. 1629/30) (**7.3**) must have been fundamental prototypes for Donner's own *Mercury*. He would also almost certainly have known Adrian de Vries's *Mercury* fountain in Augsburg of 1599, probably via the engraving by Wolfgang Kilian (1581-1662) dating from 1614.[5] Donner's lead statuette is indebted to the elegance of Du Quesnoy's figures. But he also made significant adaptations to the composition, notably in the turn of the putto, and the way in which the putto's left leg overhangs the socle, just as Mercury's left foot similarly extends beyond the integral base of the sculpture. These minor changes endow the figure with a turning, serpentine form and a more complex open outline, a spiralling sense of movement, in spite of its languorous form.

Although Donner's small-scale sculptures are central to his work, he was also a skilled sculptor of larger sculpture. He travelled to Salzburg in 1725, and there, in addition to working as a die-cutter at the mint, he produced for the ruling Prince-Bishop, Count Franz Anton Count Harrach (1665-1727), eleven over-life-size marble figures for niches on the staircase at Mirabell Palace (Schloss Mirabell) in Salzburg (1725-7), designed by Johann Lukas von Hildebrandt (1668-1745) [**7.4**]. Donner's figure of *Paris* is the only one to have been identified. The other statues, likewise mythological heroes, were damaged in a fire in 1818 and their present restored state may not reflect their original appearance.[6] The thickset figure of the Trojan hero rests elegantly against a supportive tree trunk. The contrapposto of the semi-nude youth, his left leg crossed in front of his right, and his left hand resting on his shoulder strap, suggests suitably classical roots, as does the mythological subject, and the fact that the figure is of marble. But the stumpy proportions are at

work of Michelangelo, may derive from print sources, or from his teacher Giuliani's work, as well as the Italianate bronzes Donner had studied in the Liechtenstein Collection. His mastery of composition is evident in the controlled pyramidal form of the whole, the languid semi-nude body of Christ drooping heavily to one side. The purpose of the terracotta is unknown: it may have been a modello for a lost larger work, though it is relatively highly finished. It entered the Prague National Gallery in 1948, having been previously in the collection of Count Waldstein. Although the feeling expressed in the group epitomizes the baroque, the simple columnar composition can be seen as a precursor of classicism.

In about 1725/6 Donner produced a lead group of *Mercury and Cupid*, now in the Abbey Museum (Stiftsmuseum) at Klosterneuburg, just outside Vienna [**7.2**].[4] The messenger god, wearing only a winged helmet, leans his left arm gracefully against a tree trunk, whilst Cupid, kneeling at his feet, is about to affix a wing to his

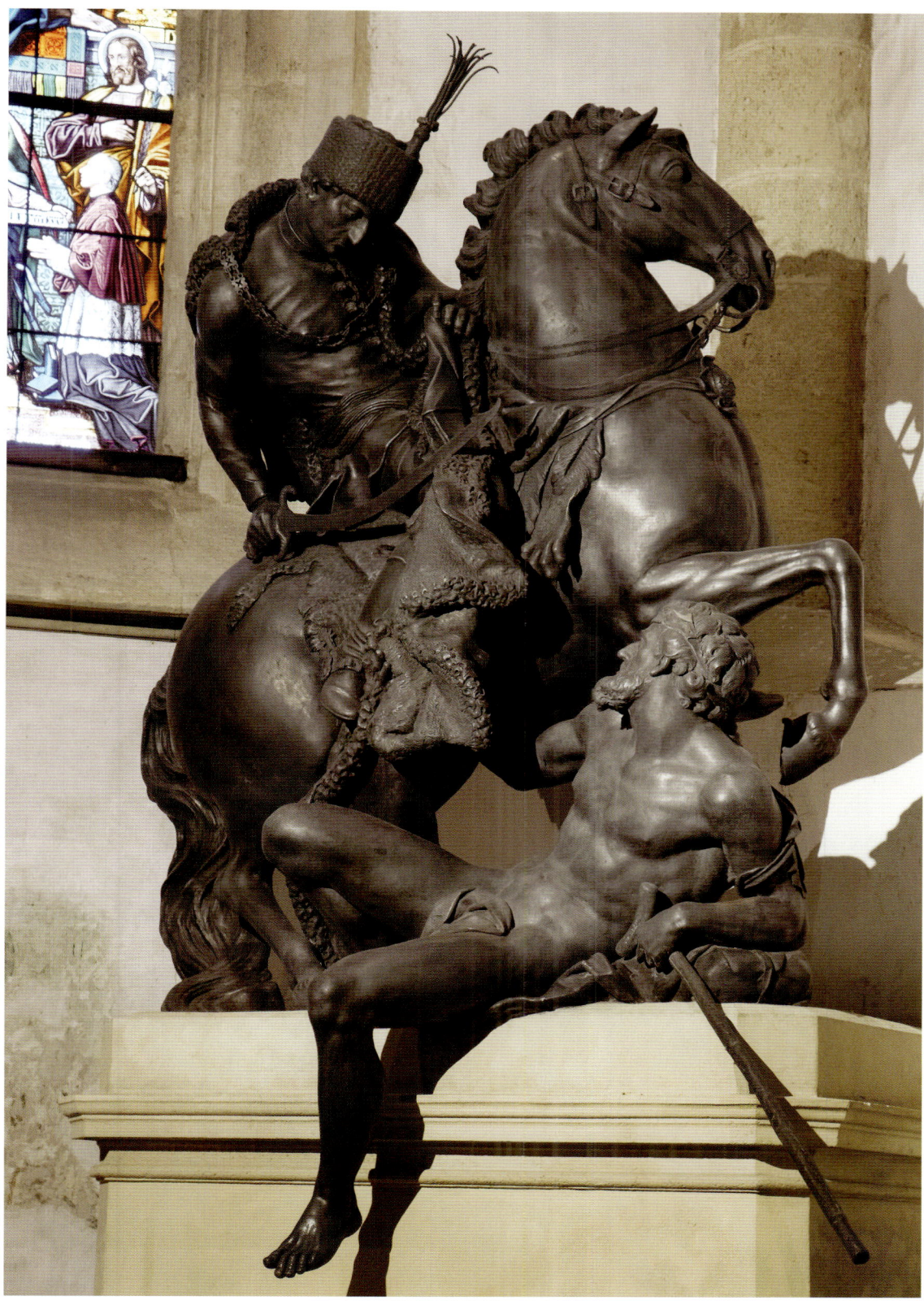

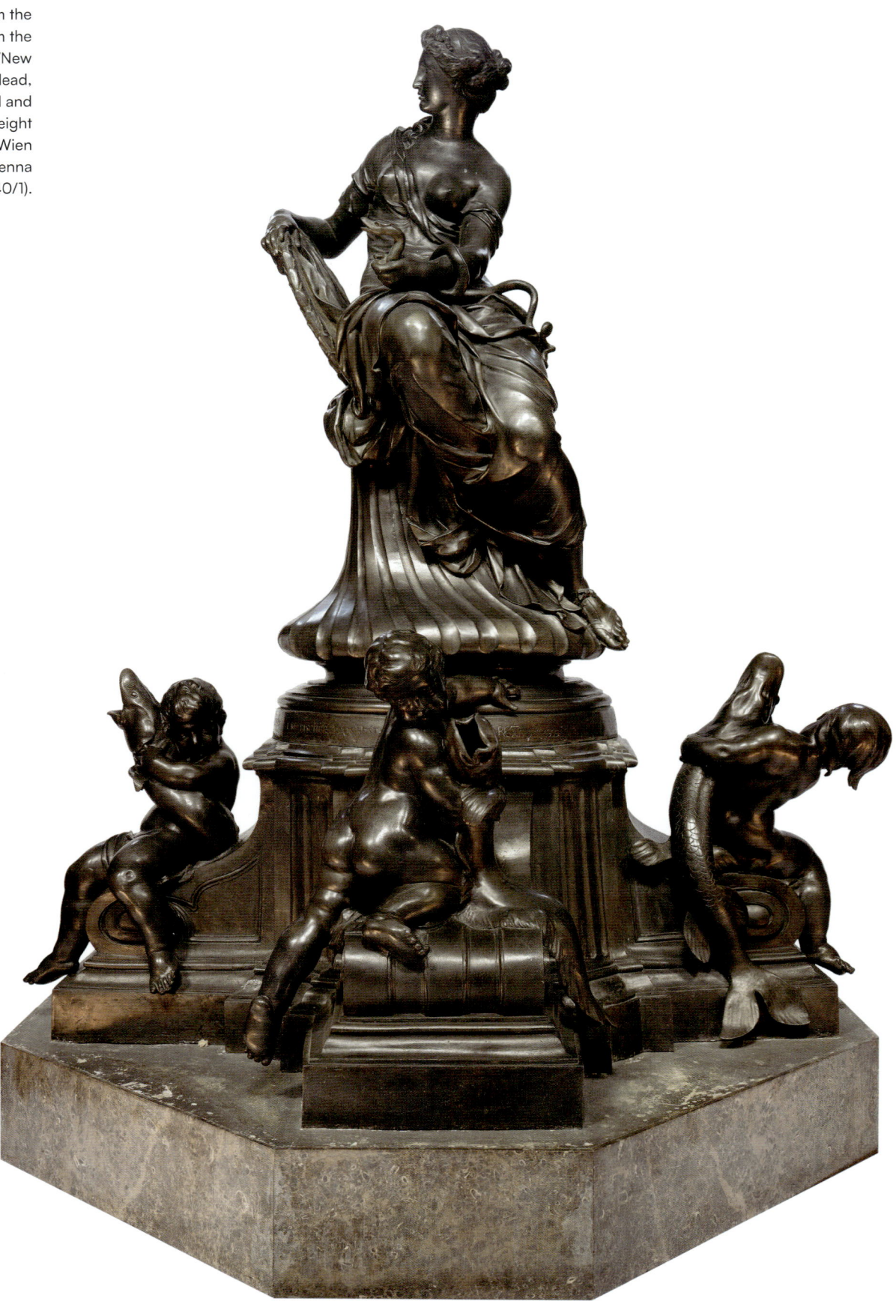

7.6
Georg Raphael Donner, *Providentia* (from the fountain formerly in the Flour Market/New Market, Vienna), lead, 1737-9 (signed and dated 1738), height 337 cm. Wien Museum, Vienna (inv. no. 145040/1).

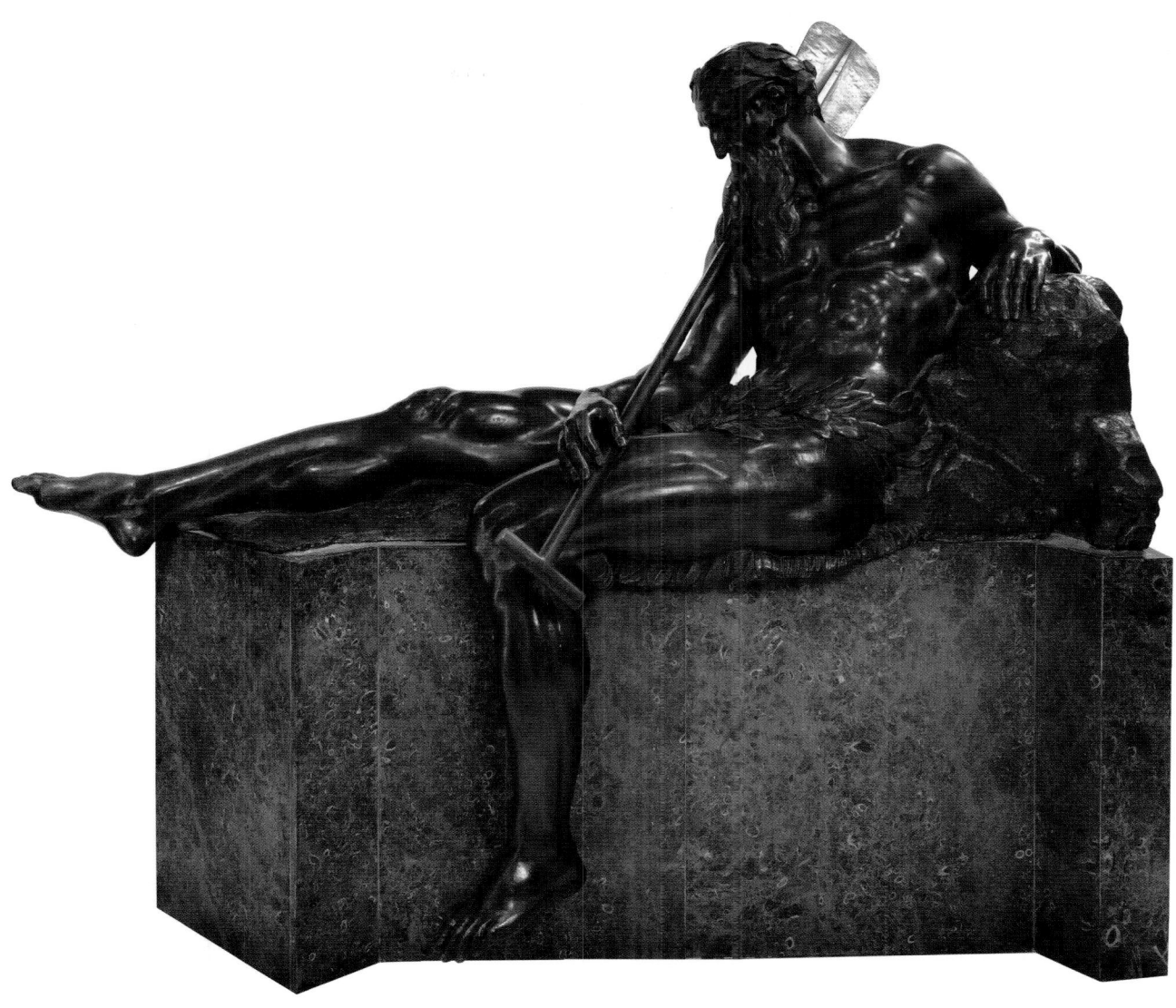

7.7
Georg Raphael Donner,
The River Enns, lead,
1739, height 207 cm,
width 235 cm. Wien
Museum, Vienna
(inv. no. 145040/6).

the same time redolent of Donner's Northern European origins. This is a resolutely baroque statue, rather than a proto-neoclassical sculpture.

Archbishop Harrach died in 1727, and his successor was not as keen a patron of the arts. Donner therefore left Salzburg, returning to Vienna in 1728, where he encountered Emmerich (Imre) Count Esterházy, Archbishop of Estzergom (Hungary) (1663-1745), Prince Primate of Hungary. The archbishop's residences were in Bratislava (Slovakia), 80 kilometres east of Vienna. After Estzergom had been occupied by the Turks in 1543, the seat of the archbishopric was moved from Estzergom to Tyrnau (Slovakia). But the archbishops resided in Bratislava, at that time capital of Hungary, just under 50 kilometres southwest of Tyrnau. In the autumn of 1729 Donner travelled to Bratislava (then known by its German name Pressburg), where he entered the service of the archbishop; he remained there until 1739.

In 1733-5 Donner executed a high altarpiece for the cathedral in Bratislava, with a powerful equestrian group in lead of *St Martin and the Beggar* at its centre [7.5].[7] The high altarpiece was unfortunately dismantled in the nineteenth century; some elements are now displayed in the Hungarian National Museum in Budapest.[8] But the group of *St Martin* remains in the nave of the cathedral. The fourth-century saint had been born in Central Europe in an area that had become Hungarian territory, and was regarded as a national saint.[9] In Donner's group St Martin is dressed in Hungarian national costume, wearing a fur-lined cloak and distinctive

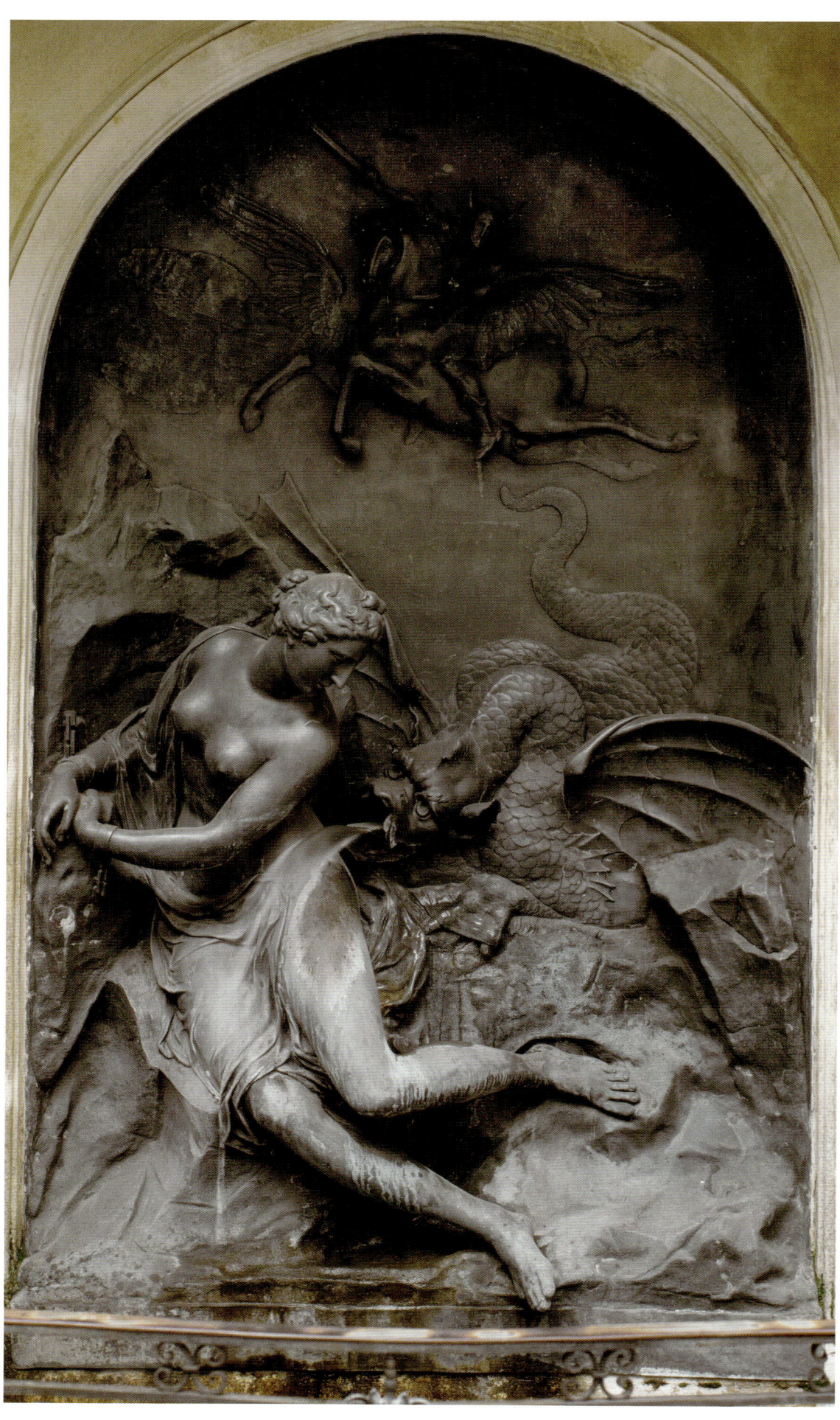

7.8
Georg Raphael Donner,
Perseus and Andromeda,
lead, 1740/1. Old Town
Hall, Vienna.

hat with a crest of feathers. He rides a rearing horse, caparisoned with a fur saddle cloth. Although he is represented mercifully cutting his cloak in two to share with the unclad beggar, the group's dramatic composition and the rider's own vigorous pose suggest rather a victorious conqueror. The saint's facial features are those of Emmerich Esterházy, emphasizing the archbishop's patronage of the group and his identification with the national saint. The bearded beggar, portrayed as a reclining nude, wearing a headband and a wisp of drapery over his thighs, his crutch diagonally overhanging the plinth, resembles a defeated antique hero, passively accepting the saint's gift of apparel. Whilst the group is therefore ostensibly religious in subject matter, it is also reminiscent of great secular monuments in public spaces. The fact that St Martin is a portrait of the archbishop only seems to support this impression: the group aims to be both spiritual and theatrical.

Donner had produced works for clients in Vienna from 1734 onwards, and by 1739 he had returned to Vienna. His major work there, conceivably the most significant of his career, is the lead fountain he made for the Flour Market, the *Mehlmarktbrunnen* (later the New Market), with a figure of *Providentia* at the centre, surrounded by four allegorical river figures (the originals were replaced by bronze replicas in the nineteenth century and are now in the Wien Museum, Vienna) [7.6].[10] *Providentia* (or *Prudence*) is portrayed as a seated female figure, barebreasted, wearing loose classicizing drapery. She holds a serpent in her left hand, whilst her right hand rests on a large medallion wreathed in laurel showing the double-headed Janus in relief, looking to both the past and the future, iconographical features suitable for Prudence, derived from the engravings of Cesare Ripa.[11] Below the ornate curved plinth on which Providentia is seated, four twisting putti clasp unruly fish. The four reclining male figures, allegories of the rivers of Austria, were originally placed at the corners of the basin of the fountain. *Providentia* dominated the fountain, which was placed in the centre of the marketplace.[12] Once more Donner seems to be drawing on Italian precedents: this central turning figure echoes art of the cinquecento, for example Michelangelo's seated Sybils in the frescoes of the Sistine Chapel ceiling of 1508-12, as well as the same artist's marble statue of Giuliano de' Medici of 1526-34 in the Medici Chapel at S. Lorenzo in Florence.[13] *Providentia* also recalls Giambologna's refined bronze statuettes of female figures, such as *Venus Drying Herself* of c. 1565.[14] The figure of the River Enns, one of the four rivers, is personified as an old man, leaning against rocks, seemingly exhausted, wearing a laurel wreath around his head, a propping a paddle over his shoulder [7.7]. His elderly tired body with sagging flesh contrasts with the lithe figure of the beggar in the group of *St Martin* at Bratislava of two years prior [7.5]. The figure of the River Enns must also be indebted to Michelangelo's sculpture in the Medici Chapel, notably his *Evening*, as well as French prototypes, such as the marble *Rivers* by Antoine Coysevox (1640-1720) of 1705 at the château of Versailles.[15] Donner's travels to both France and Italy remain uncertain, though likely. These probable prototypes for his Flour Market fountain figures suggest he may have known such works at first hand.

Donner also produced a wall fountain for Vienna in 1739, placed in the inner courtyard of the former town hall (Altes Rathaus). This depicts *Perseus and Andromeda* in relief [7.8]. The dragon about to devour Andromeda spouts water from its mouth. Its tail snakes out behind in low relief, in contrast to the high relief form of Andromeda, twisting away from her attacker in a serpentine form recalling once more the proportions and poses of Giambologna's female nudes. The composition was in part derived from a print after the ceiling fresco by Annibale Carracci (1550-1609) of the same subject (1597) in the Palazzo Farnese in Rome, hence the sculpture's strongly Italianate quality.[16] Above, the distant form of Perseus, astride the winged Pegasus, is both dramatically and subtly conveyed, rendered almost entirely in low relief. The figure of Andromeda symbolised the liberation of Vienna from the threat of Turkish invasion, and so Donner's work, commissioned by the town council of Vienna, is not simply a mythological scene but imbued with civic and political overtones.[17]

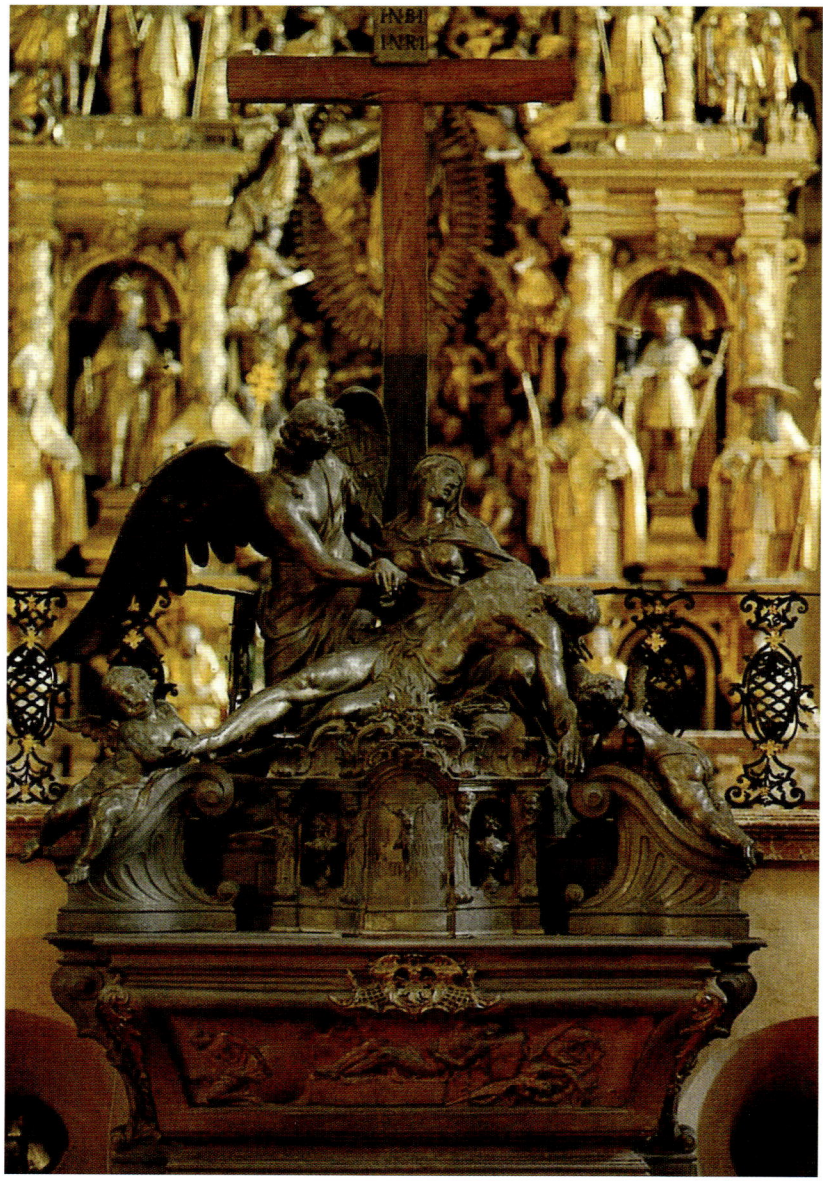

altar, a pyramidal composition created by the angel and Virgin's turning head. The muscular anatomy of Christ's nude body is once again potently rendered, recalling both Italian and French models, such as the marble *Pietà* of 1723 by Nicolas Coustou (1658-1733) in the church of Notre Dame, Paris.[19] The composition of Donner's monumental lead group, whose softly modelled surfaces reflect the nature of the material, seems to resonate with the small terracotta modello of twenty years before, the sculptor's first known work: both exhibit the same preoccupation with a careful delineation of anatomy combined with profound emotion.

Figurative Ceramics at Meissen: Johann Gottlieb Kirchner and Johann Joachim Kändler

Although this survey of German baroque sculpture concentrates on sculpture in stone, terracotta, ivory, bronze and lead, a vital facet of baroque and rococo art is the extraordinary ceramic sculpture produced in the mid-eighteenth century by Johann Gottlieb Kirchner (1706-after 1737) and Johann Joachim Kändler (1706-75) at Meissen in Saxony (just over 20 kilometres northwest of Dresden), and by Franz Anton Bustelli (active 1754-d. 1763) at Nymphenburg in Bavaria, 5 kilometres northwest of Munich, to be discussed below. Other key centres producing ceramics in Germany during the eighteenth century include Fürstenberg an der Havel (Mecklenberg), Vienna, Berlin and Höchst, but this brief excursus into German baroque porcelain will focus only on some of the more sculptural ceramics produced at Meissen and Nymphenburg.

European porcelain originated with the discoveries made by Johann Friedrich Böttger (1682-1719), a chemist and alchemist. Porcelain vessels had been known in the West from Chinese exports for several centuries, but the recipe for manufacturing these luxury ceramics was still a secret. The Elector of Saxony, Augustus II (the Strong), King of Poland (1670-1733), was keen to learn how porcelain could be manufactured in Europe, and specifically in Dresden. He succeeded in capturing Böttger when he fled to Dresden from Prussia, and

The freestanding *Pietà* of 1741 for the high altar of the cathedral at Gurk (just over 200 kilometres southwest of Vienna) is Donner's last known work [**7.9 and 7.10**].[18] It was commissioned by the provost of the cathedral, Franz Otto Kochler von Jochenstein, who had met Donner in Vienna in 1737, and who had also requested a pulpit for the cathedral from him, a pulpit that was executed by his assistants. The *Pietà* conversely reveals the hand of Donner himself; it is a fittingly elegiac work by an artist who died prematurely. The sorrowing Virgin supports the dead Christ on her lap above the tabernacle, herself supported by an attendant angel. Two smaller angels mourn on either side, reclining on scrolled plinths. The elongated body of Christ stretches diagonally across the

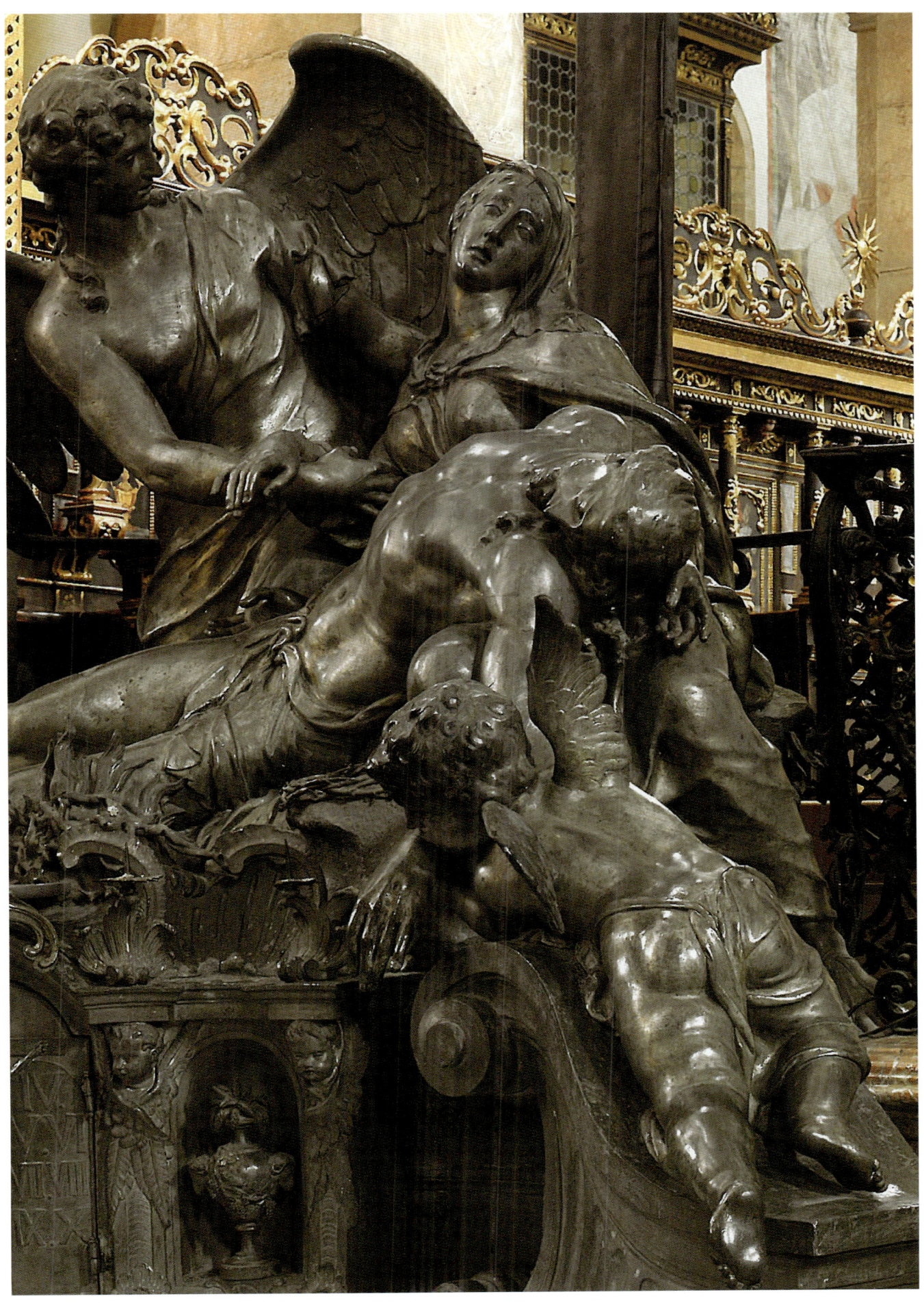

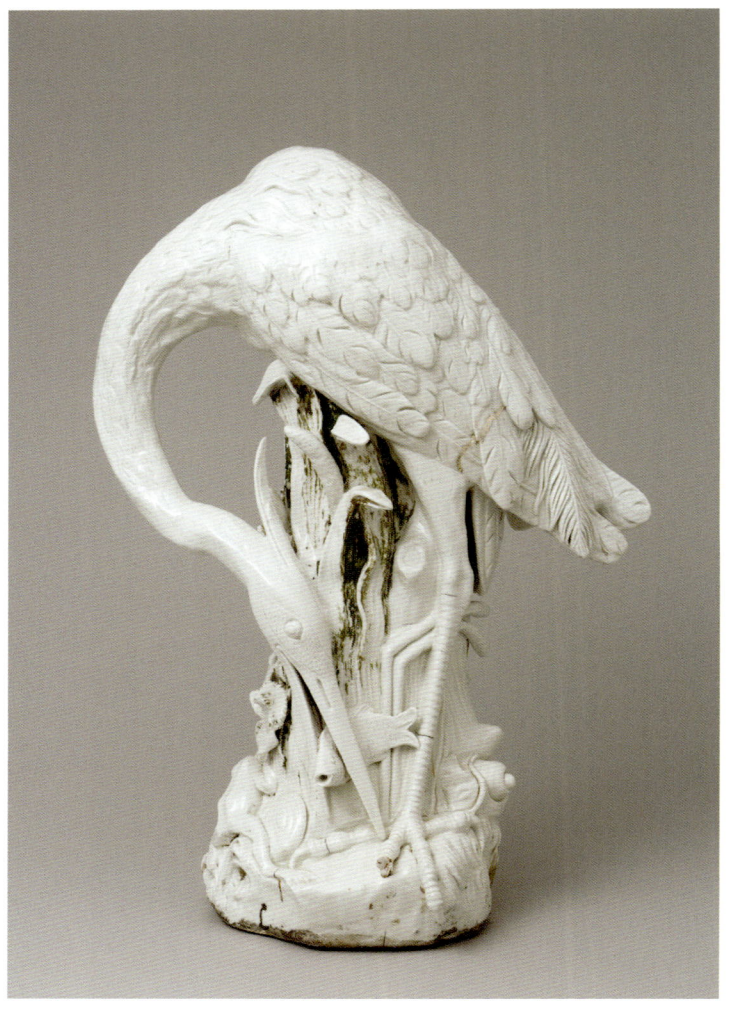

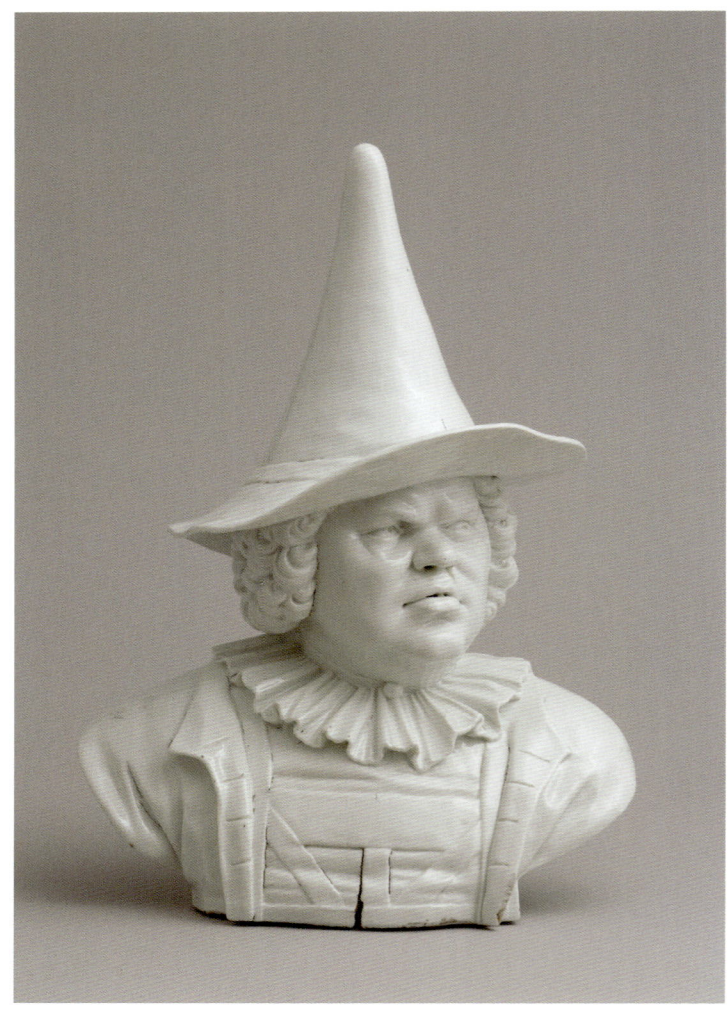

7.11
Johann Joachim Kändler, *Heron with Small Carp in its Beak*, Meissen porcelain, 1731, height 62.9 cm. Staatliche Kunstsammlungen Dresden (inv. no. PE 685).

7.12
Johann Gottlieb Kirchner, *Bust of the Court Jester Joseph Fröhlich*, Meissen porcelain, c. 1730-3, height 53 cm. Staatliche Kunstsammlungen Dresden (inv. no. PE 247).

initially made him practise as an alchemist, rather than employing him to discover the recipe for porcelain. But the alchemical experiments were doomed to failure, and Böttger, along with the physicist Ehrenfried Walter Count von Tschirnhaus (1651-1708), turned his attention elsewhere. By 1708 the two men had successfully produced a porcellaneous red stoneware, sometimes now called Böttgerware. Böttger continued working on perfecting the production of porcelain after Tschirnhaus's death. In 1709, after finding the correct china clay, kaolin, he was able to manufacture hard paste white porcelain, with the addition of feldspar (a crystalline mineral). He became the first director of the Meissen factory, founded in 1710, producing porcelain wares in imitation of silver vessels.

The flowering of figurative ceramics in Meissen came about a few years after Böttger's pioneering discoveries thanks to two artists, Johann Gottlieb Kirchner and Johann Joachim Kändler, and their patron, Augustus the Strong.

The elector was determined to amass an unrivalled collection of porcelain, both Oriental and European, and to display it appropriately he purchased and subsequently renovated the Dutch House, a grand edifice on the banks of the Elbe in Dresden Neustadt in 1717. He renamed this building the Japanese Palace. In addition to ceramics from China and Japan, the elector commissioned a vast collection of porcelain animals, birds and human figures, to be manufactured at Meissen. After Augustus the Strong's death in 1733 his son Augustus III (1696-1763) continued the tradition of commissioning and displaying ceramics, but in a more limited fashion. Plans for further building work at the Japanese Palace were halted, and some ceramic pieces were put into storage and later dispersed.[20]

Kirchner's appointment as modeller at the Meissen factory by Augustus the Strong in 1726 initiated the start of the tradition of sculptural porcelain at Meissen. Kirchner was tasked with producing large ceramic animals for the elector, to be displayed in the Japanese Palace, as a vast

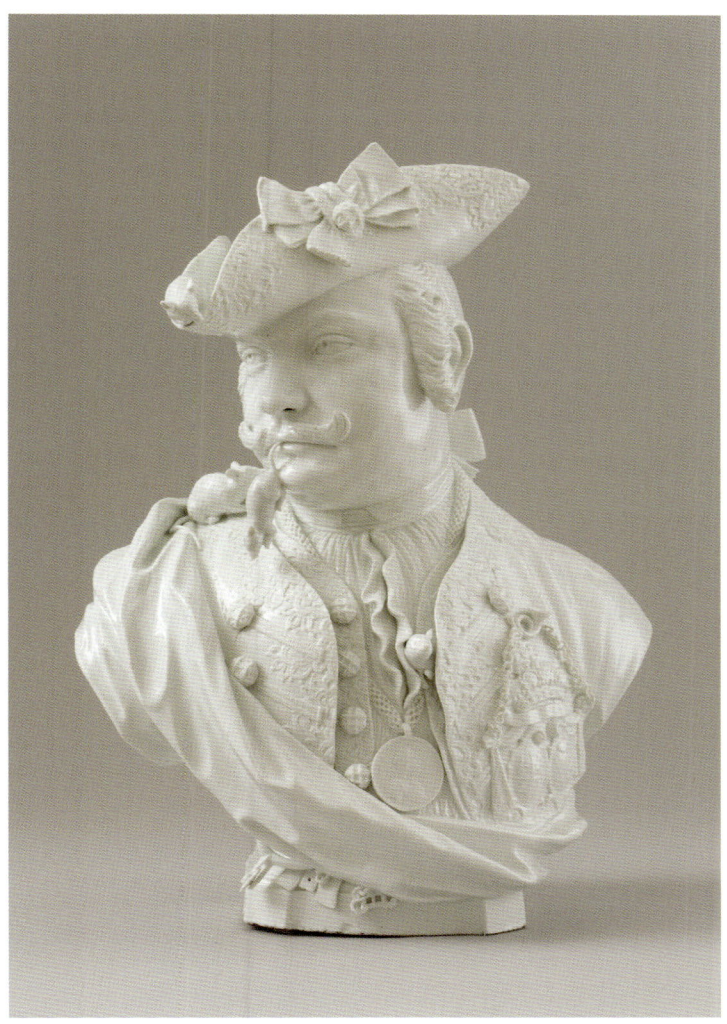

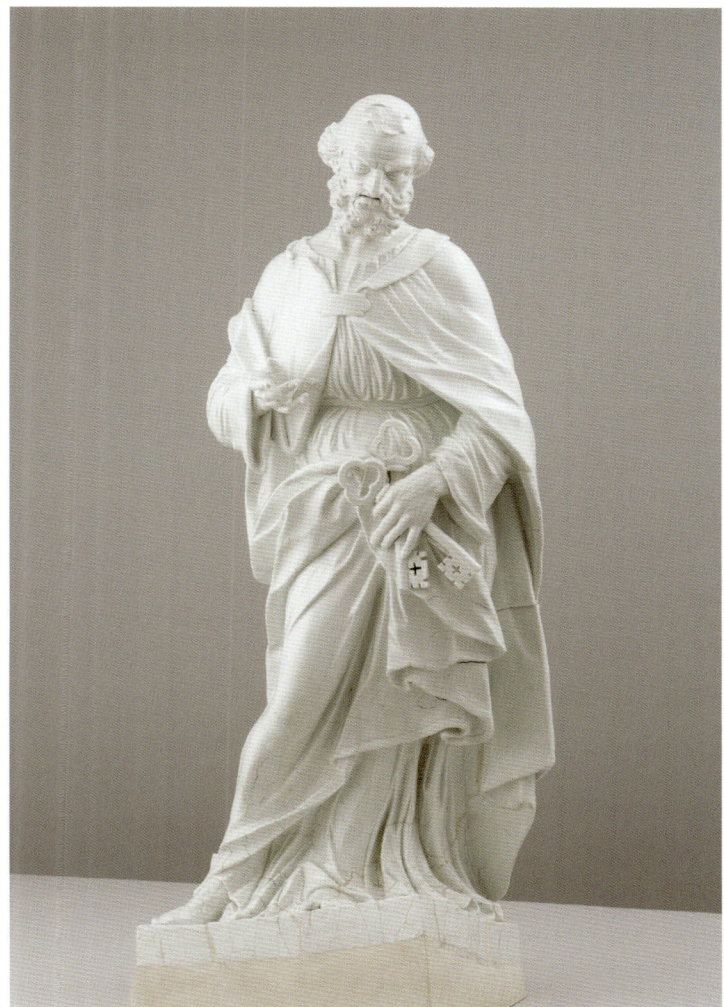

ceramic zoo. Kirchner's role at the factory signalled Augustus's desire to produce monumental figures in porcelain, but the technical challenges of firing such large pieces were immense. Defeated by these, Kirchner resigned in 1729. He moved to Weimar to become a court sculptor. However only a few months later, in May 1730, he returned to Meissen at the request of the factory's Board of Directors, and at his own wish. Johann Joachim Kändler was hired as a modeller the following year, and tensions apparently arose between the two men. In 1732 Kirchner tendered his resignation once more, leaving Meissen for good in 1733. Kändler was established as the chief modeller at the factory from then until the end of his life, undertaking a wide range of figurative ceramics.[21]

The many animals and birds in porcelain made by Kirchner and Kändler respectively for the Meissen factory are analogous to renaissance bronzes: they were produced in a reproductive material, fired clay—rather than cast bronze—and are at the same time extraordinary and sometimes unique works of art, made for a courtly patron. The *Heron with Small Carp in its Beak* made by Kändler in 1731 exemplifies the high quality artistically of the large group of ceramic animals fashioned to adorn the Japanese Palace [**7.11**].[22] This engaging work is of a scale comparable with monumental sculpture, a life-size rendition of the wading bird. The graceful curve of the bird's neck is naturalistically observed, based on sketches that the artist could have made from herons kept at the court. At the same time, it is a finely judged dynamic sculptural composition, indicating Kändler's earlier training under Johann Benjamin Thomae (1682-1751), who had himself worked alongside Balthasar Permoser in Dresden.

Apart from such numerous large-scale animals and birds produced by both Kirchner and Kändler for the elector's porcelain menagerie, the two artists also produced portrait busts, again in the tradition of sculpture. Kirchner's likeness of the court jester Joseph Fröhlich (1694-1757) was made in about 1730 [**7.12**].[23]

7.13
Johann Joachim Kändler, *Bust of the Court Jester Gottfried Schmiedel*, Meissen porcelain, 1739, height 48.5 cm. Staatliche Kunstsammlungen Dresden (inv. no. PE 248).

7.14
Johann Joachim Kändler, *St Peter* (part of the altar garniture made for the Japanese Palace, Dresden), Meissen porcelain, 1731, height 115.7 cm. Staatliche Kunstsammlungen Dresden (inv. no. PE 498).

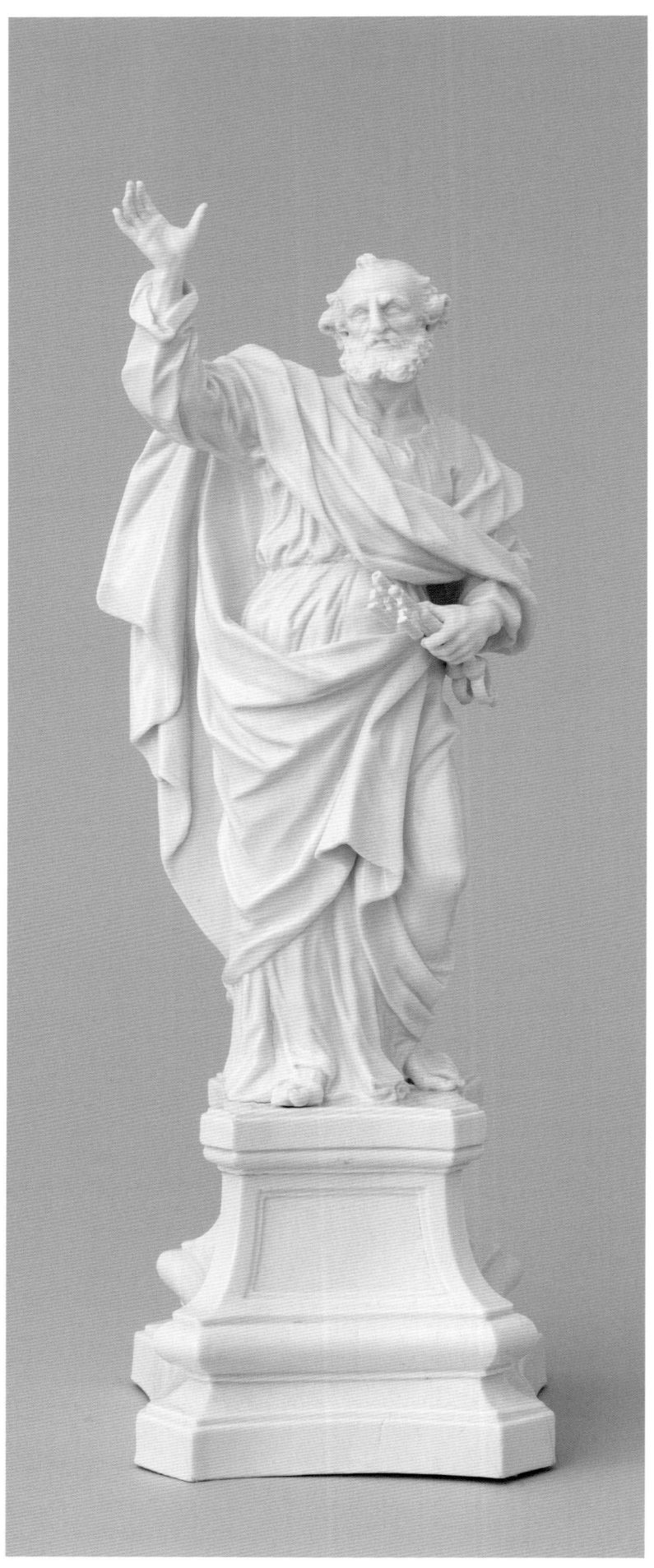

The jester wears a tall conical Tyrolean hat, and his facial expression, as if he is in the act of speaking, suggests the jester's freedom to be caustically impudent even towards the monarch himself. The monochromatic life-size ceramic bust apes a marble likeness. A professional entertainer at the Saxon court is thus given the same status and grandeur as a duke or a count, the material of the piece paralleling the noble substance of marble.

Nearly a decade later Kändler's bust of another court jester, Gottfried Junge (1700-56), known as 'Baron Schmiedel', of 1739, also life size, complements Kirchner's earlier portrait [7.13]. Schmiedel was nicknamed 'courier of the chamber' (*Kammer Courier*) and is here dressed as an official postman from Langensalza (Thuringia).[24] Hanging over his left breast is a small shield inscribed with the arms of the King of Poland and Elector of Saxony, and a post horn suspended from two chains. But most remarkable are the mice running over him, including one whose tail is in his mouth. These are apparently facetious references to Schmiedel's fear of mice. Like Kirchner's rendition of Fröhlich, this finely executed porcelain bust imitating marble is both lively and yet replete with indications of the sitter's character, in this case a certain pensive melancholy visible in his face.

Kändler undertook numerous commissions of religious subjects in porcelain from the 1730s onwards. Augustus the Strong commissioned him to make a set of twelve 'just under life-size' Apostles for the chapel at the Japanese Palace in 1731. These exceptionally large figures were technically difficult to fire in the kiln, because of their scale. Only *St Peter* was successfully produced, although this figure too shows evidence of damage and repairs to the socle and the right hand [7.14].[25] The saint, just over 115 cm high, stands in contrapposto, carrying the keys in his left hand. The monochromatic porcelain once more echoes marble, and the pose is clearly based on Italianate models.

From 1737 to 1740 Augustus the Strong's son Augustus III commissioned Kändler to produce two further series of Apostles as altar-piece garnitures, though somewhat smaller than the figures intended by his father for the

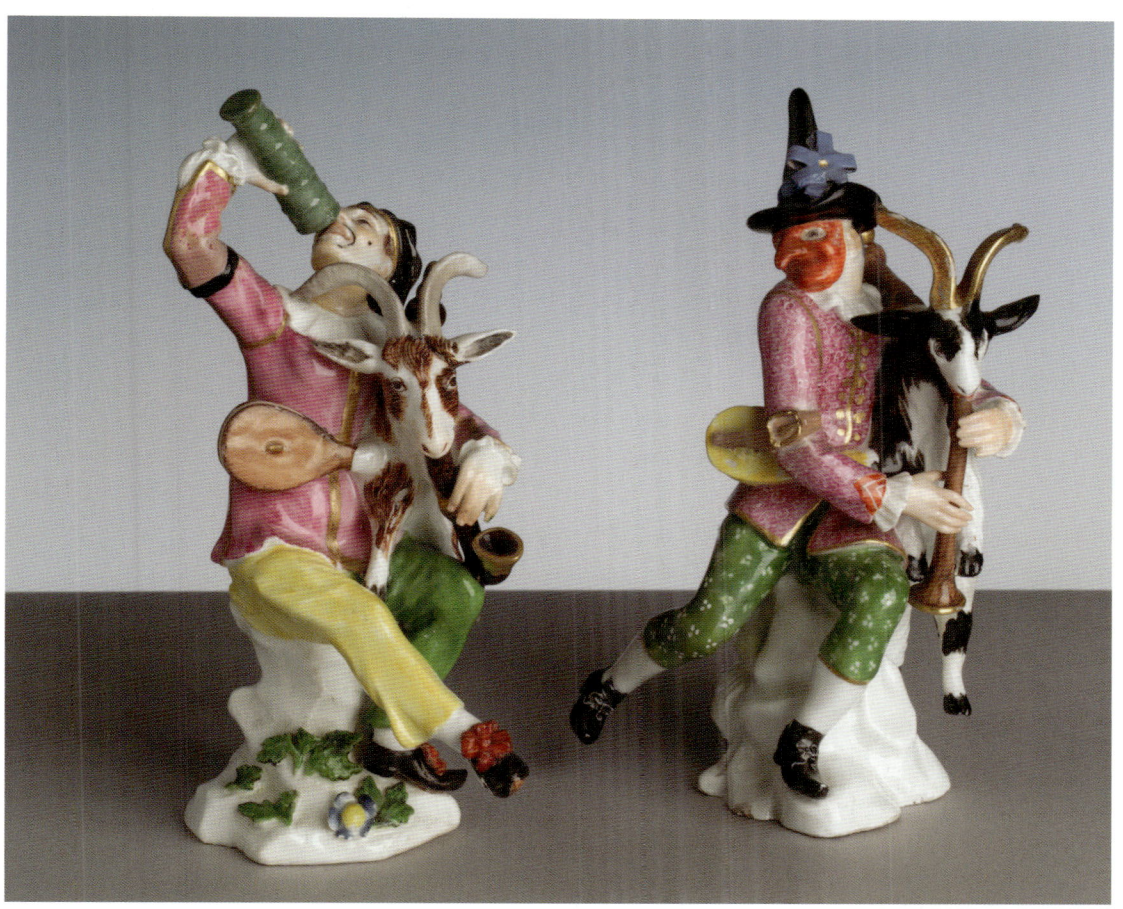

< 7.15
Johann Joachim Kändler, *St Peter* (part of the altar garniture made for Cardinal Albani), Meissen porcelain, 1737, height 48.4 cm. Staatliche Kunstsammlungen Dresden (inv. no. PE 131).

7.16
Johann Joachim Kändler, *Harlequin with Ram-Piper* (height 14.2 cm) and *Harlequin with a Goat as Bagpipes* (height 15 cm), Meissen porcelain, c. 1740. Staatliche Kunstsammlungen Dresden (inv. nos. PE 114 and PE 118).

Japanese Palace. One set was a gift for his mother-in-law, the widow of the Habsburg Emperor Joseph I, Wilhelmina Amalia von Braunschweig-Lüneburg (1673-1742) in Vienna, while another was made for Cardinal Annibale Albani (1682-1751) in Rome.[26] These statuettes were directly based on Italian prototypes, taken from engravings after the colossal marble statues installed from 1704 to 1718 at the church of St John Lateran in Rome, carved by Camillo Rusconi (1658-1728), Pierre-Étienne Monnot (1657-1733), Pierre Le Gros (1666-1719) and others.[27] A few of the Meissen figures made for Vienna and Rome respectively survive, as well as contemporary and later variants, but the complete sets have been dispersed. The *St Peter* from the garniture made for Cardinal Albani derives from Monnot's marble of 1713 in Rome [7.15].[28] Although under half the size of the example made a few years earlier, the pose is significantly more dramatic. The saint holds up his right hand, his mouth open as if preaching, his dynamic stance suggesting he is in the act of stepping forward.

The many small genre groups and figures from the commedia dell'arte were a critical part of the production at the Meissen factory, and certainly relate closely to small-scale sculpture. As noted in Chapter 3, the sculptor Johann Christoph Ludwig Lücke (1703-80) produced models for the Meissen factory. Unlike the large busts and animals and sets of religious figures made at the factory, the commedia dell'arte figures also indicate that a middle-class market was eager to acquire and display luxury porcelain, on a scale more affordable than the large pieces made for the elector. Kändler's animated commedia dell'arte figurines made in the 1730s and 1740s express his inventiveness and humour. For example, the *Harlequin with Ram-Piper* shows a masked harlequin holding a ram that appears to blow on a pipe held by the jesting performer [7.16].[29] The twisting figure, one leg stretched out behind him over the base, his smiling masked face, as well as the bright pink, green and orange glazes, epitomise both the vivacity and comedy of the piece.

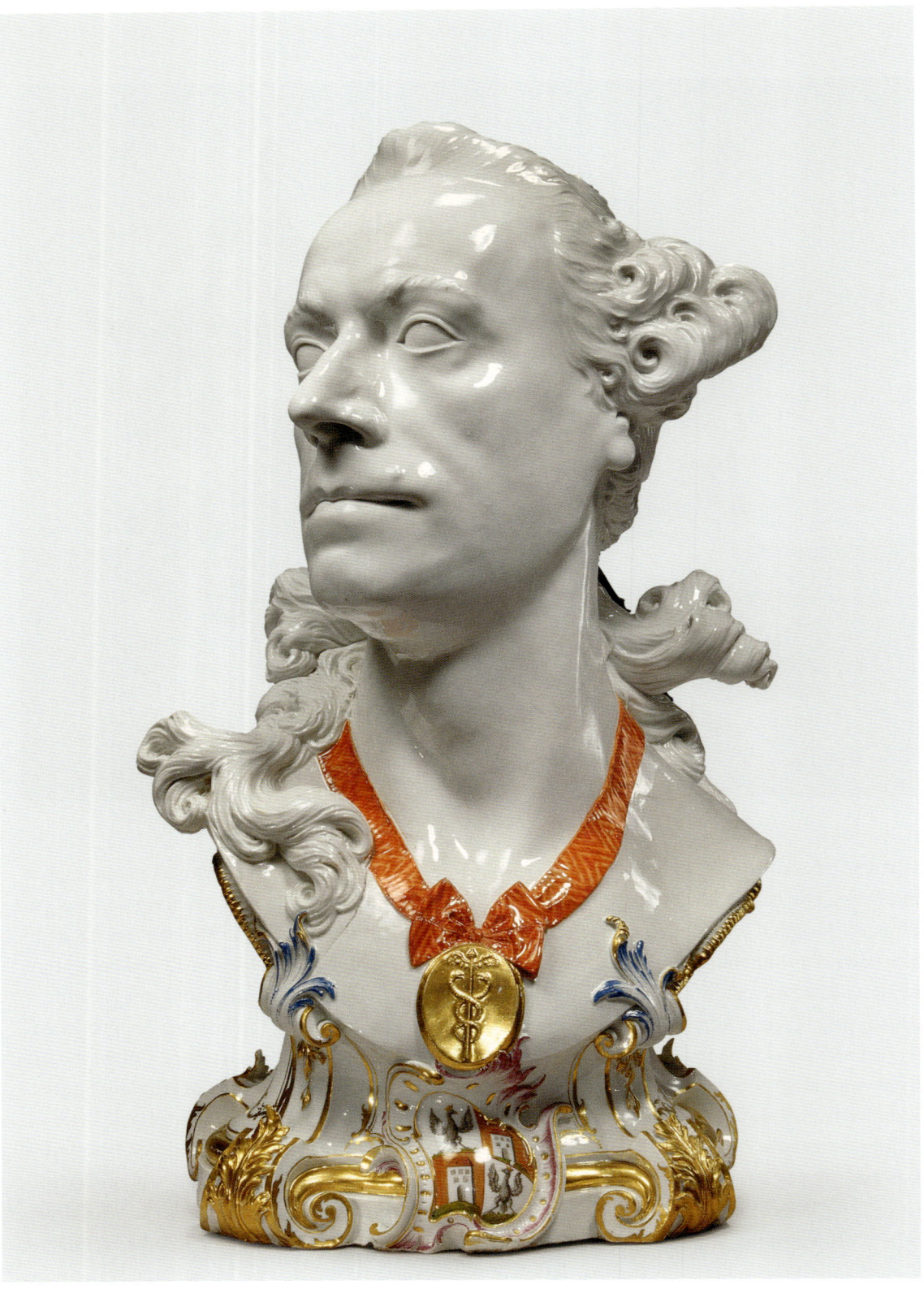

7.17
Franz Anton Bustelli,
*Count Sigismund von
Haimhausen*, Nymphen-
burg porcelain partly
coloured and gilt,
c. 1761, height 45 cm.
Bayerisches National-
museum, Munich
(inv. no. Ker 4369).

Nymphenburg: Franz Anton Bustelli

The porcelain factory at Nymphenburg, just outside Munich, was transferred there in 1761, a generation after that at Meissen.[30] Its predecessor was the manufactory at the castle of Neudeck in der Au, also near Munich, set up by the Elector Maximilian III Joseph (1727-77) in 1747. Maximilian had married Maria Anna Sophia of Saxony (1728-97), the granddaughter of Augustus the Strong; this dynastic connection with Saxony may have partly led to a porcelain manufactory being established in Bavaria. But it was not until 1754 that porcelain was produced successfully at Neudeck, after Count Sigismund von Haimhausen (1708-93) was appointed director of the factory, with the help of Joseph Ringler (1730-1804), the Viennese arcanist (one who knew the secrets of manufacturing

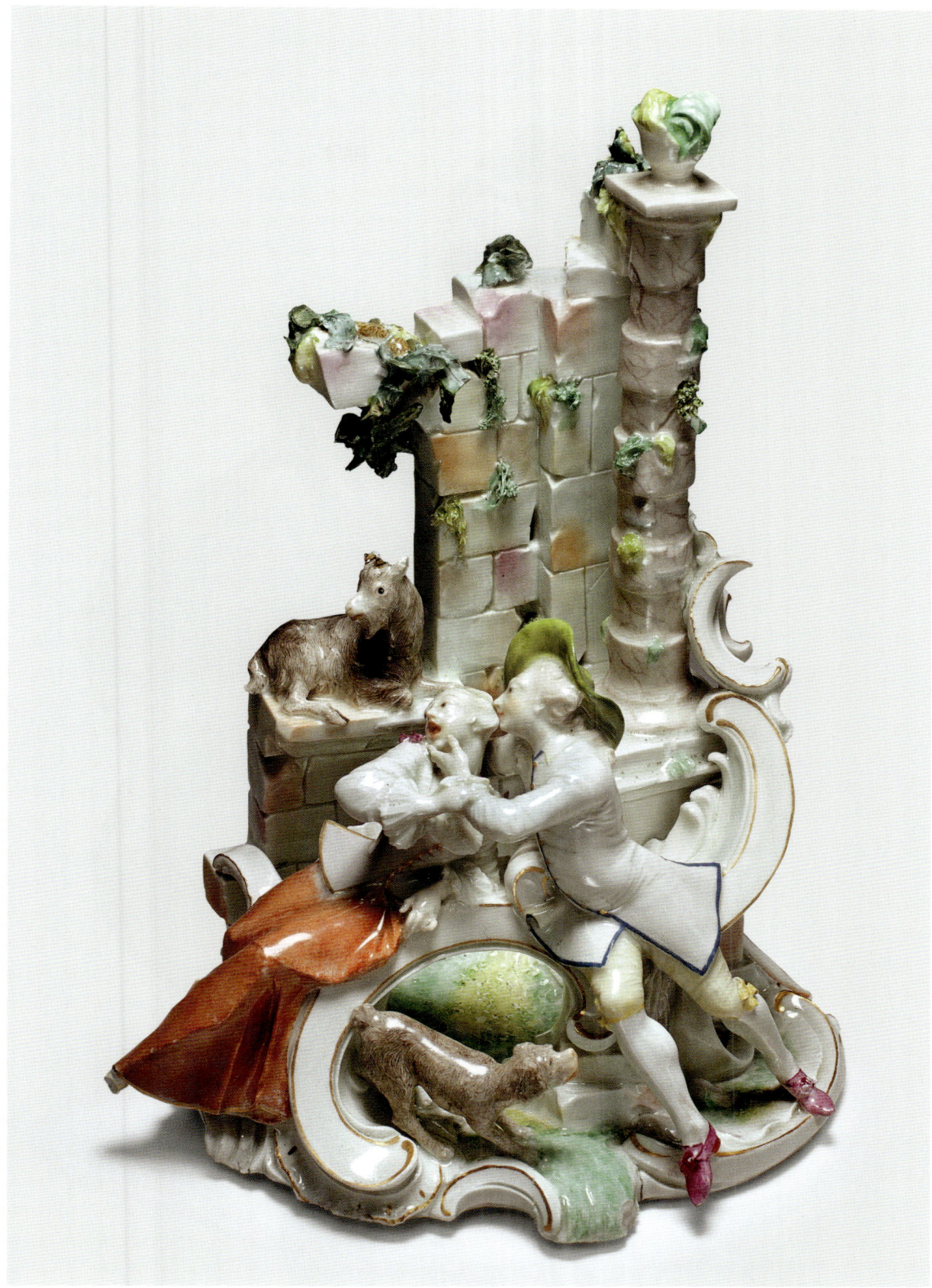

7.18
Franz Anton Bustelli,
*Courting Couple among
the Ruins*, Nymphen-
burg porcelain partly
coloured, c. 1760,
height 26.4 cm.
Bayerisches National-
museum, Munich
(inv. no. Ker 4205).

porcelain), whom Haimhausen hired in 1754.[31] The count had invested in the porcelain factory during the 1750s and had additionally acquired expertise in mining and manufacturing through extensive travels in Europe. He had been made Master of the Mint in Munich in 1751, in addition to serving as General Director of Mines. He was later to become the first president of the Bavarian Academy of Sciences in 1759/61. In 1761 the Electoral Porcelain Factory moved from Neudeck to Nymphenburg, where it flourished and expanded with Haimhausen in charge as the director.

The principal modeller at Neudeck, and subsequently at Nymphenburg, was Franz Anton Bustelli (d. 1763), whose family were located in Locarno in the Ticino region (now Switzerland). Bustelli was first recorded at

7.19
Ferdinand Tietz, *Mars*,
sandstone, c. 1747-53,
height 198 cm.
Badisches Landes-
museum Karlsruhe
(inv. no. 65/33).

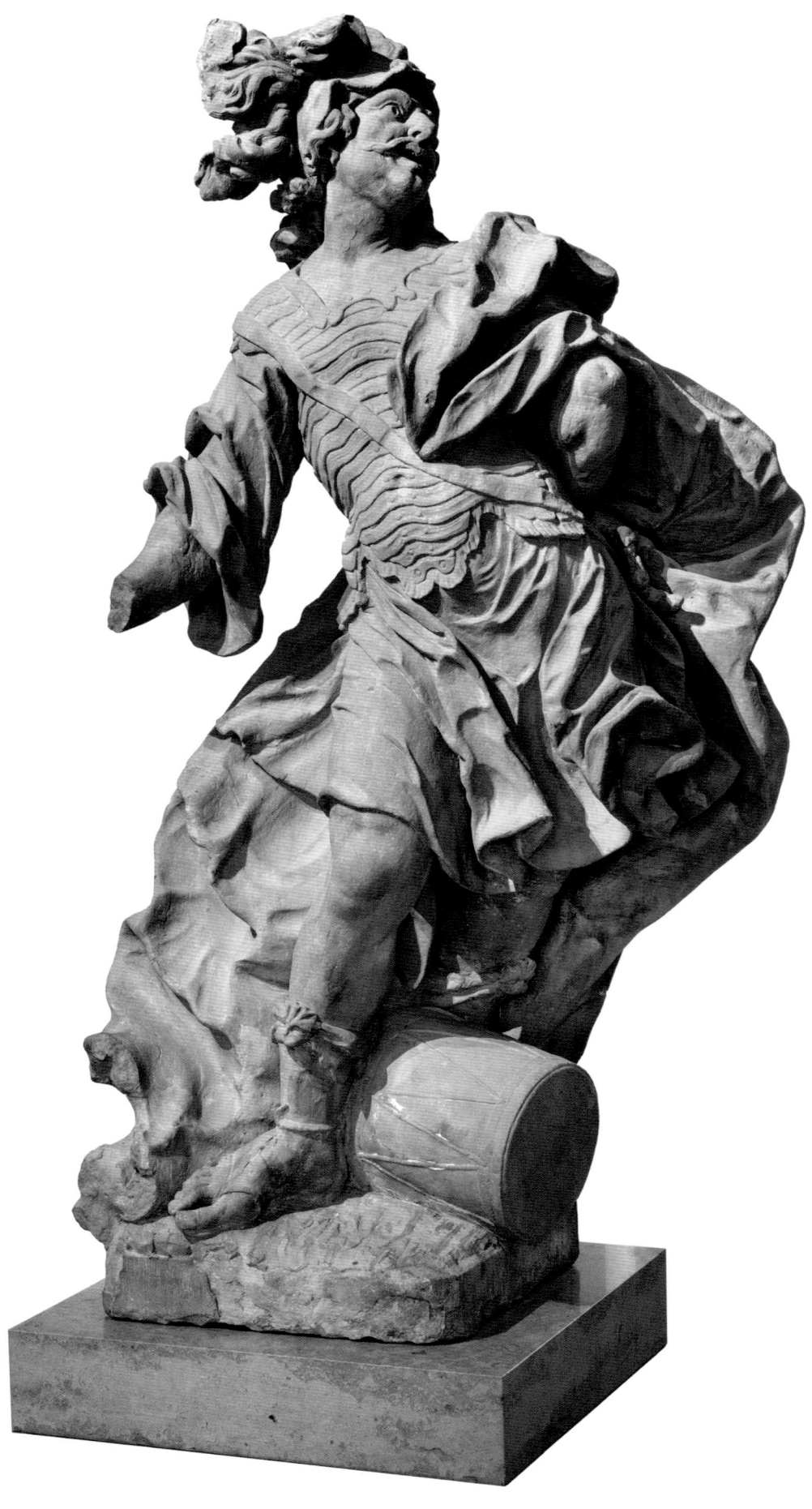

Neudeck in 1754, before the factory moved to Nymphenburg. Again, the porcelain figures produced by Bustelli parallel eighteenth-century Bavarian sculpture. His ceramic figurines are stylistically analogous to the rococo sculpture produced by sculptors such as Johann Baptist Straub and Ignaz Günther, and he may well have trained as a sculptor, although nothing is known of his early life. Like Böttger before him, he was clearly fascinated by the science of ceramic manufacture. He was named in contemporary sources as an 'arcanista', one who knew the secrets of porcelain, and at his death he owned 31 books on chemistry, in addition to 288 engravings that were almost certainly employed as sources for some of his figure groups.[32]

Bustelli's porcelain works, like those by Kirchner and Kändler, could be said to challenge the perceived higher status of stone sculpture. His bust of Haimhausen, of about 1761, mimics Carrara marble, though the bright colours and gilding of the red ribbon and gold medal, as well as the elaborate socle, with its coat of arms and rococo flourishes, also recall the polychromed and gilt wood sculpture in Bavarian churches [7.17].[33] Haimhausen proudly sports the medal awarded to him by the elector in reward for his service to the Bavarian state, its central position and gilding emphasizing and defining his highly respected official role. Bustelli's likeness seems to express the count's thoughtful character, seen in his facial expression and the turn of his head, analogous to the subtle features seen in the slightly earlier marble portraits executed in London by the ceramicist's older contemporary Louis François Roubiliac (1702-62). Apart from the bust indicating the intellectual, perhaps also the spiritual character, of the subject, the surface of the porcelain paradoxically suggests the very texture of his skin and hair.[34] A similarly sensitive rendering of surfaces can be seen in Roubiliac's carved marble portraits made a generation before. Such a comparison is nevertheless purely visual and does not imply that Bustelli was directly inspired by Roubiliac, who had worked in Britain since the early 1730s, although it should be noted that the Frenchman had trained in Dresden with Permoser in the 1720s. The implied resemblances indicate rather that

Bustelli was working in the tradition of European marble portraiture, and that porcelain (associated with mass production) seems to be competing with the noble material of marble. Moreover, Bustelli's bust of Haimhausen appears to be a unique survivor, rather than being one of several versions. Paradoxically, then, the ceramic bust, made in a medium that invites multiples, is in fact the sole version, contrasting with some eighteenth-century marble portraits, which we merely perceive as unique. Yet such a perception can itself be mistaken, since some marbles, though carved rather than cast from a mould, could be, and sometimes were, produced in more than one version.[35]

Bustelli is most renowned for his small genre groups, along with figures from the commedia dell'arte. Just as at Meissen, such figures became immensely popular during the eighteenth century and appealed to the middle-class market. They were luxury items, but within the means of the prosperous bourgeoisie.[36] Bustelli's compositions do not seem to derive from print sources but were rather his own inventions. His *Courting Couple in the Ruins* of about 1760 illustrates his ability to create a complex composition and suggest a delicate drama, a human comedy [7.18].[37] The lovers are posed diagonally with genre details such as a goat and a dog in a fanciful rococo setting backed by ruins. The woman twists agitatedly away from her ardent lover, her mouth agape in an unsettling manner. But perhaps this is not intended as a scene of violence but playfulness, the youth seducing rather than seizing her. The classical architecture is adorned with plants growing out of the crevices, while the curlicue ornament at the base undermines any idea that this is a real genre scene. Although on a small scale (height 26.5 cm), the group invites comparison with larger pieces in other media, such as cabinet paintings.

Ferdinand Tietz

Possibly because Tietz was almost certainly not trained academically he developed an idiosyncratic, occasionally humorous, sculptural style. Perhaps more than any of the other sculptors discussed in this book his work could be

>> 7.20
Balthasar Neumann with sculpture by Ferdinand Tietz, The High Altar of the church of St Paulinus, Trier, painted limewood and stucco, c. 1755-60.

>> 7.21
Ferdinand Tietz, *The Virgin of the Immaculate Conception* from the High Altar of the church of St Paulinus, Trier, painted limewood and stucco, c. 1755-60 [detail of 7.20].

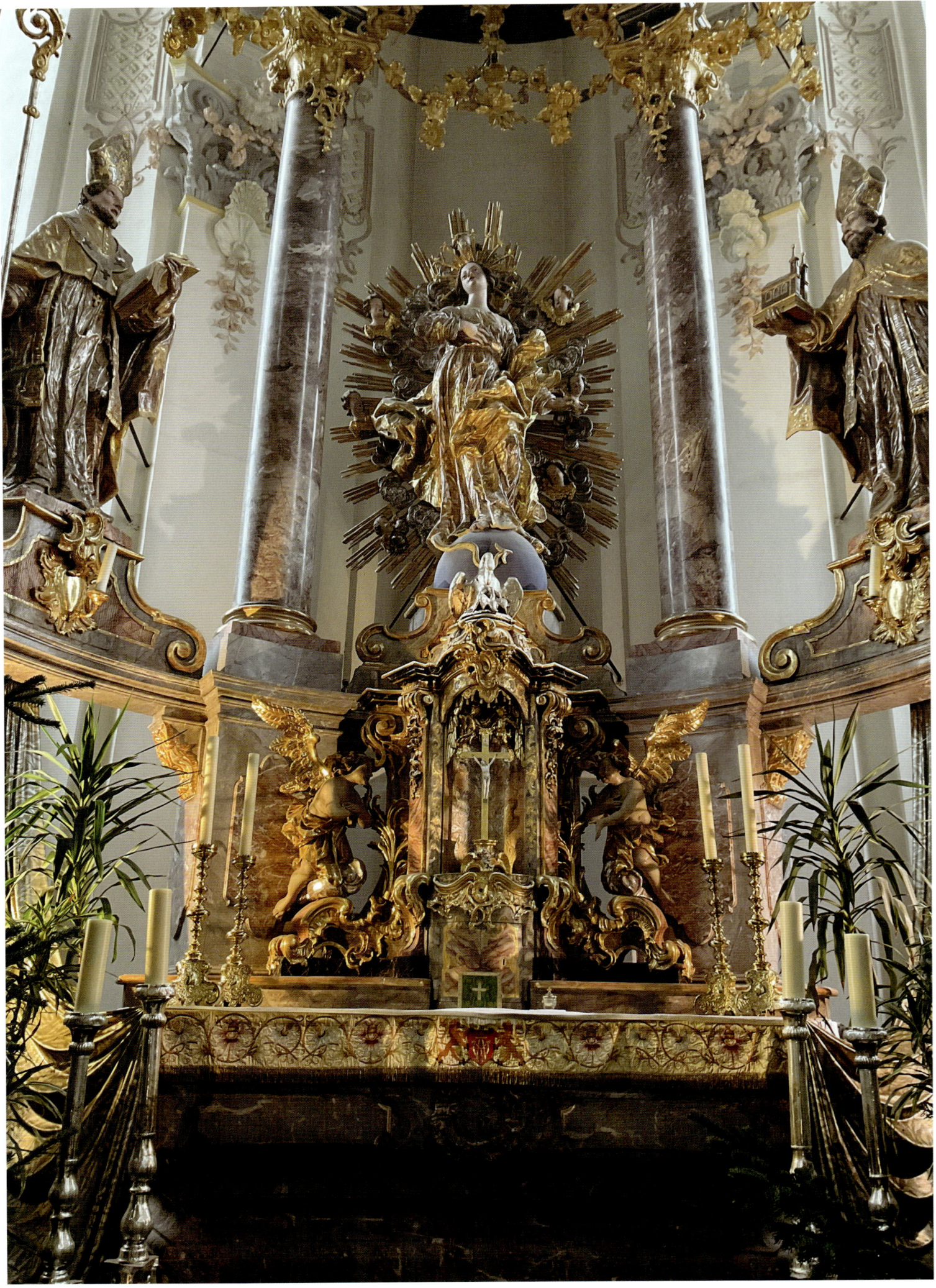

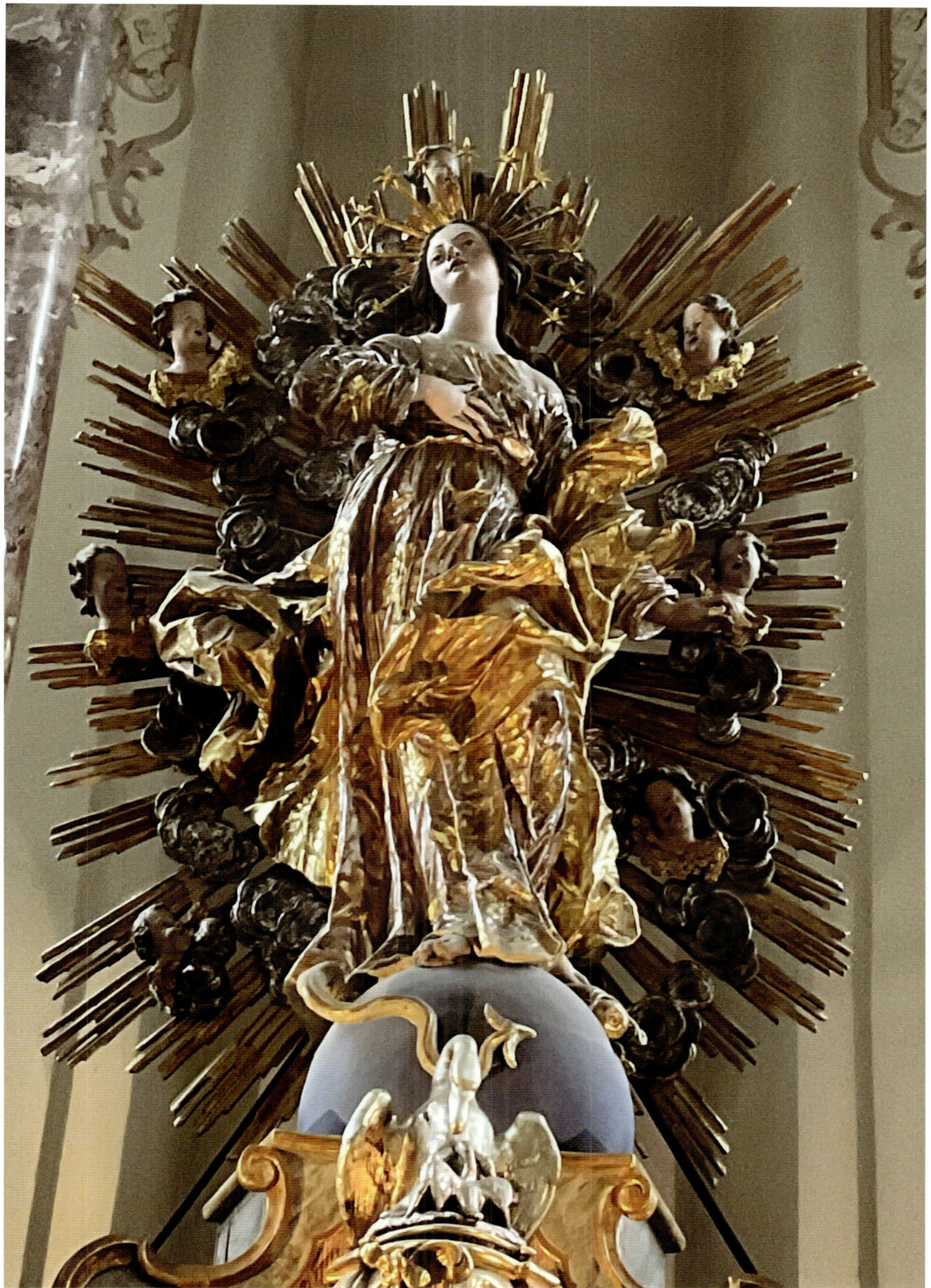

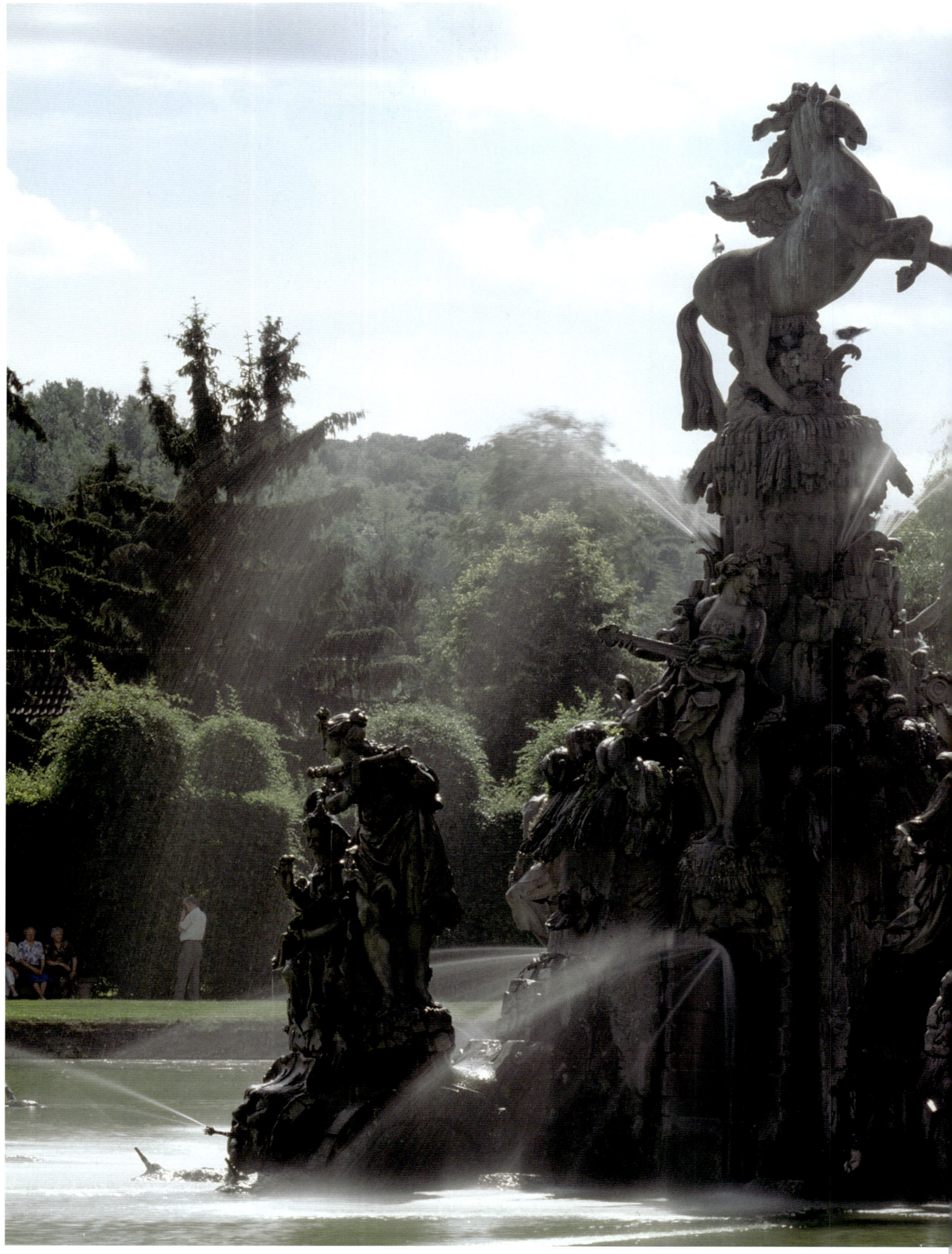

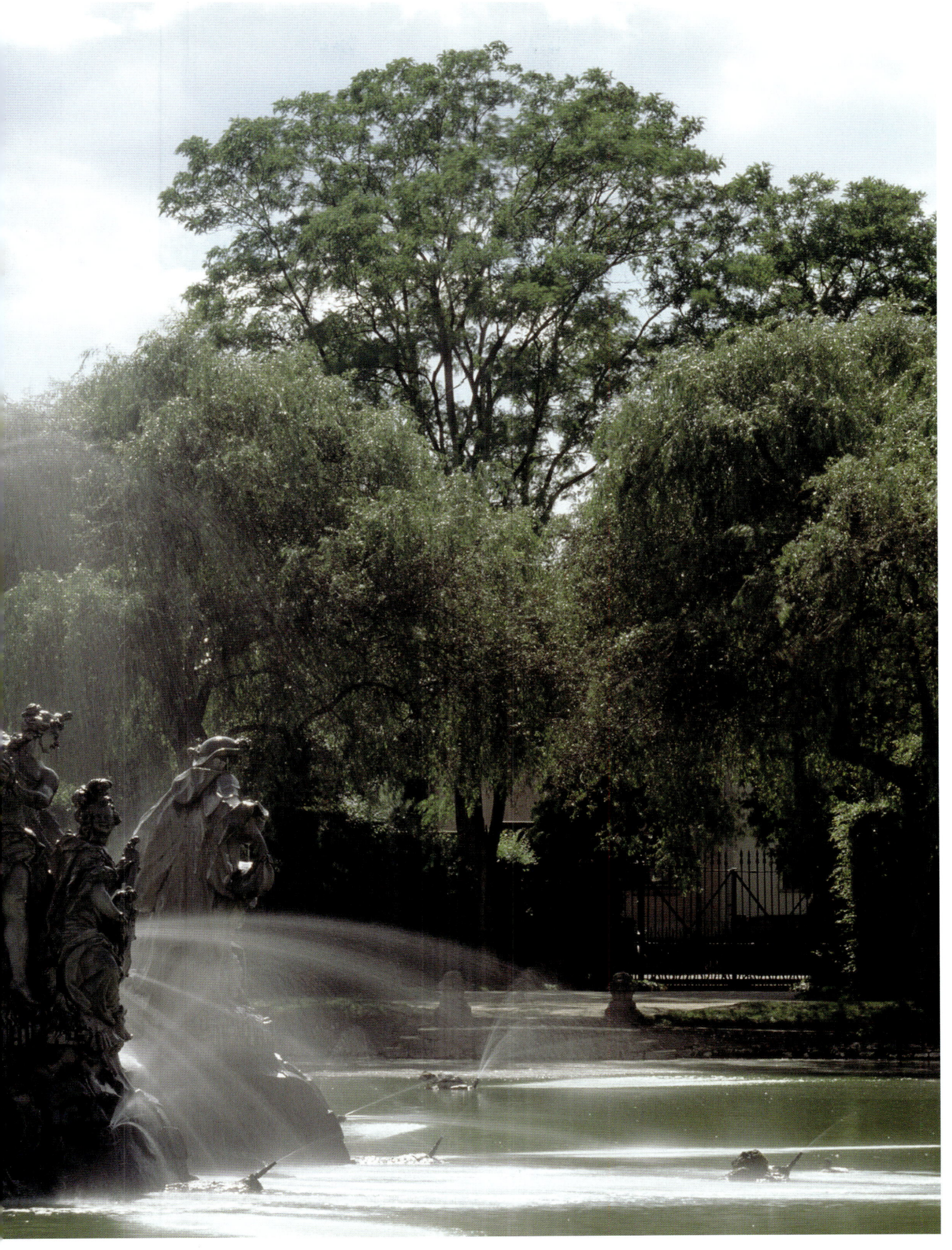

described as rococo, rather than baroque. He seems to have looked to France for inspiration as much as Italy, as seen in the prints after statues at Versailles used as sources for a number of his garden sculptures (see below). He worked in both wood and stone, executing garden sculptures and decorative architectural sculpture, as well as devotional figures and altarpieces, receiving a wealth of prestigious court commissions for different aristocratic and ecclesiastical patrons in Franconia. Born probably in the region of Komotau (Chomutov) in Bohemia, he was the son of a sculptor, Johann Adam Dietz (1671-1742), and trained in his father's workshop. Subsequently he worked in Prague under Matthias Bernhard Braun, for whom see Chapter 6. Apart from Braun he may well have been aware of the work of Ottavio Mosto (1659-1701) in Prague and Salzburg, and that of Lorenzo Mattielli (1687-1748) in Vienna.[38] Tietz is first recorded in 1736 assisting on the programme of architectural sculpture for the Residenz at Würzburg under the court sculptor Jakob von der Auwera (1672-1760); the city of Würzburg was to be one of the chief centres for his work. His first independent sculpture dates from 1740: the coat of arms of Friedrich Karl von Schönborn-Buchheim (1674-1746; Prince-Bishop of Würzburg, 1729-46) for the gable of Schloss Werneck, the summer residence of the Prince-Bishops of Würzburg.[39]

From 1747 to 1753 Tietz executed the first series of sandstone garden sculptures of classical gods and mythological figures at Schloss Seehof, a few kilometres northeast of Bamberg, near Memmelsdorf, and the summer residence of the Prince-Bishops of Bamberg. Johann Philipp Anton von Franckenstein (1695-1753; Prince-Bishop of Bamberg, 1746-53) appointed Tietz to be court sculptor there in 1748. The Seehof sculptures were dispersed in the twentieth century, and those that survive are weathered and damaged. The original layout of the gardens has been largely lost, although some plinths remain in place, and some sculptures have been replaced by copies.[40] A number were based on French engravings, notably by Simon Thomassin (1655-1733) after statues at Versailles. Although Tietz adapted them for his own

purposes—hence his sandstone figures cannot be confused with French court sculptures—their rococo lightness surely derives ultimately from fashionable French culture. A few of Tietz's dispersed figures are now in museum collections; one of these is *Mars* [7.19]. Although it is no longer at Seehof, its history as a sculpture intended for a landscaped park is readily apparent: the rough, weathered sandstone and the pose of the figure, visually responding to its now lost pendant, point to its original context. The god of war is depicted dramatically, standing astride a military drum, wearing classical armour and a billowing cloak. He sports generous moustaches and flowing hair under an elaborate helmet. His mouth is half open as if shouting, and his eyes wildly alert. His right hand (now broken) must have once held a weapon. Tietz's energetic diagonal composition complements the bold working of the rough sandstone: turning to his left, the god would have served as a pendant to an answering figure in the Seehof Park.[41]

Tietz was to execute a second series of sculptures for Seehof during the reign of Adam Friedrich von Sensheim (1708-79; Prince-Bishop of Würzburg, 1755-79; Prince-Bishop of Bamberg, 1757-79). This second programme of works (1761-3) included mythological figures, benches and decorative stonework, though many are now lost or destroyed. The central feature was a monumental *Cascade* incorporating the Months of the Year and other allegorical figures.[42]

In 1753, after the death of his patron at Bamberg, Johann Philipp Anton von Franckenstein, Tietz was summoned to Trier by the Archbishop-Elector Franz Georg von Schönborn (1682-1756; Archbishop-Elector of Trier, 1729-56), a younger brother of Friedrich Karl von Schönborn-Buchheim. Here Tietz was again appointed court sculptor in 1754. His most important commission was the sculptural decoration of the church of St Paulinus in Trier.[43] The archbishop paid for the church to be rebuilt after the former building had been destroyed by French troops in 1674. Construction had commenced in 1734, the new church being designed by the architect Johann Balthasar Neumann (c. 1687-1753). In 1755 Tietz was

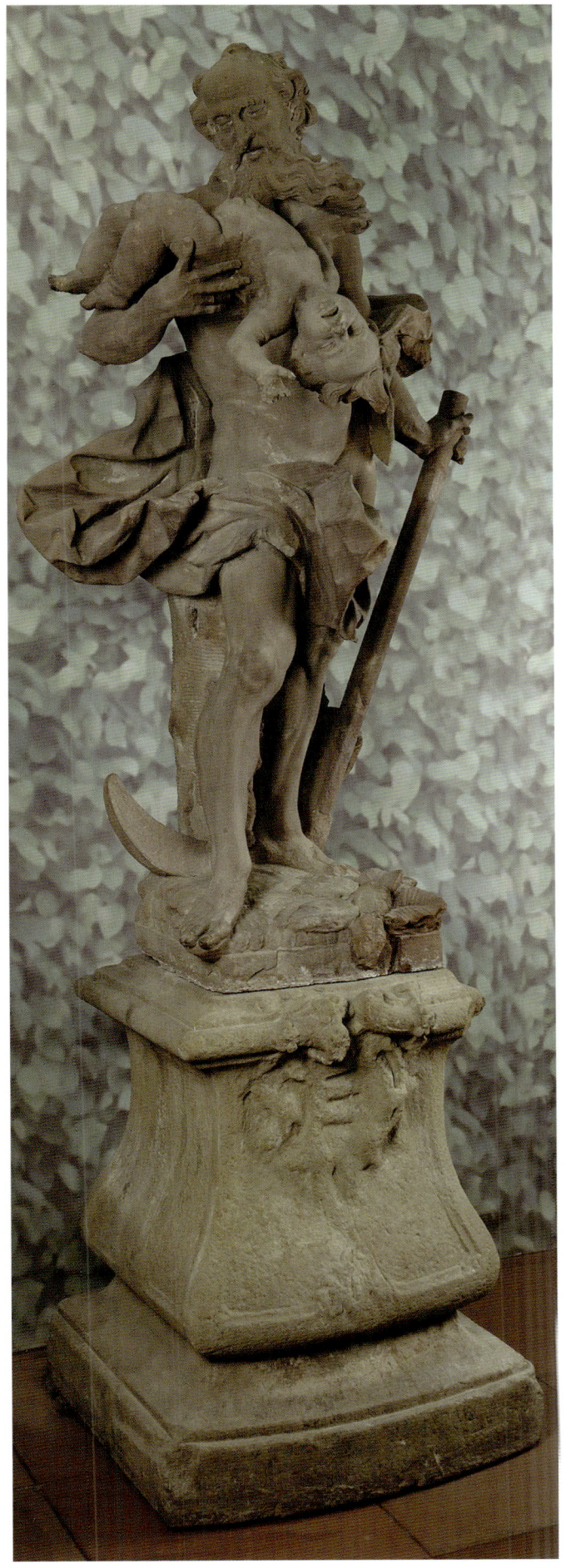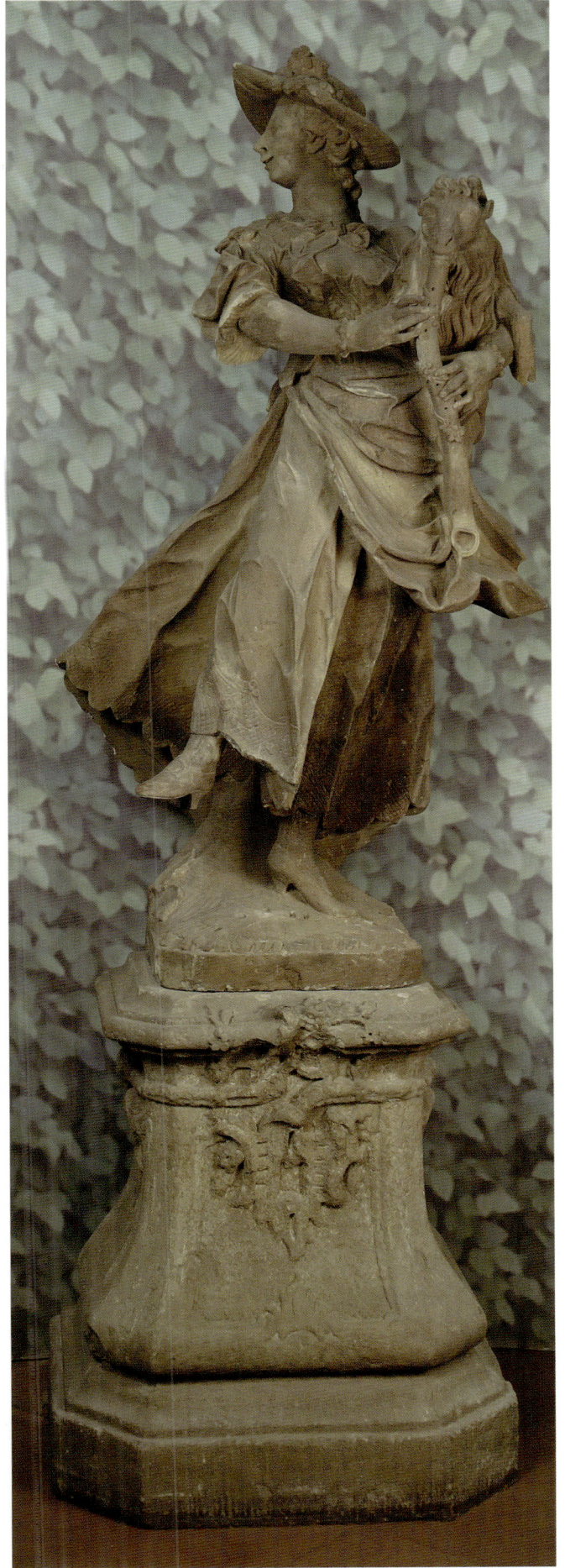

251 — SCULPTURE IN VIENNA, GURK, WÜRZBURG AND TRIER. CERAMICS.

commissioned to produce sculptures for the high altar, which was likewise designed by Neumann. Tietz also carried out the choirstalls, altarpieces for the main church and further altarpieces and figures for the crypt; work was completed in 1760. The high altarpiece is a resplendent array of life-size figures grouped around the central *Virgin of the Immaculate Conception* under a baldacchino prominently displaying the arms of the archbishop [**7.20 and 7.21**]. Around the Virgin is an aureole of sun rays, stars, cherubim and clouds; she stands victorious over a globe encircled by the serpent. The contrapposto pose and crumpled drapery lend the figure movement and vivacity; her youthful smiling face looks downwards, her graceful left hand held to her breast suggesting her empathy with the worshipper.[44]

In 1763-8 Tietz carved a range of sandstone figures for the park at Veitshöchheim, the summer palace of the Prince-Bishops of Würzburg.[45] Tietz collaborated once more with Balthasar Neumann, who was in charge of the landscape design of the park. Many of these outdoor sculptures were subsequently lost or damaged, and in 1927 most were taken from Veitshöchheim to the Mainfränkisches Museum in Würzburg, where they can be cared for, studied and enjoyed, although inevitably lacking their original context. One element that however remains in place in the garden is the monumental *Parnassus* fountain, completed in 1766, an assembly of over-life-size gods and mythological figures surmounted by the winged horse Pegasus [**7.22**].[46]

From the vast assemblage of mythological figures originally at Veitshöchheim one of the most striking is that of *Saturn*, or *Time* [**7.23**].[47] The bearded god stands holding his baby in his right arm and his scythe in his left, personifying the destructive force of time, devouring his own children. The melancholic semi-nude figure

standing contrapposto, with flowing drapery around his hip and left arm, must be indebted to Italian precedents, notably Gian Lorenzo Bernini (1598-1680).

But the gardens at Veitshöchheim also comprised a range of contemporary rustic figures, personifying pleasure. The pose and expression of a female bagpipe player, one of the many Veitshöchheim garden figures of dancers and musicians produced by Tietz, provides a contrast to the *Saturn* [**7.24**].[48] The joyful twirling figure lifts up her right foot in dance, turning her head and simultaneously playing her bagpipes. Her facial features, a pointed nose, small smiling mouth and incipient double chin, are typical of Tietz's garden figures, and oddly attractive. Indeed, they recall some of the contemporary figures by Ignaz Günther [**see for example 5.31**, *Empress St Cunigunde* at Rott am Inn]. The figure wears a lace-trimmed dress and a broad-brimmed hat adorned with a flower. The bagpipes themselves incorporate an animal, almost satyr-like, head. The mood of the whole is playful and pastoral, befitting the park at Veithochsheim, echoing Versailles rather than Rome.

Tietz's work throughout his life can be seen to be indissolubly linked with architecture and gardens, the taste of his court and ecclesiastical patrons, and the sophisticated international taste of the time, particularly France and Italy. The original contexts of many of his sculptures, notably at Veitshöchheim, lent them a further dimension, a sense of actual figures peopling a park, whilst their rough sandstone carving and natural stone colouring (as opposed to polychromy imitating flesh) emphasized their artifice as works of art. Tietz's sculptures can thus be seen as exemplifying three-dimensional baroque and rococo art in Germany at this time, exuding skilful illusionism and vivacity, and at the same time artifice and artfulness.

Notes

1 See *Georg Raphael Donner* 1993, cat. no. 256, pp. 256-9.

2 Donner's medals are not discussed here, but his 1727 medal of Elector Charles Albert of Bavaria, for example, can be found in *Georg Raphael Donner* 1993, cat. no. 197 on pp. 632-3.

3 Inv. no. P 5189. *Georg Raphael Donner* 1993, pp. 34-5, note 37 on p. 78, and fig. 16 on p. 30. See also https://sbirky.ngprague.cz/dielo/CZE:NG.P_5189, accessed 5 March 2021.

4 *Georg Raphael Donner* 1993, cat. no. 19 on pp. 256-9.

5 *Welt im Umbruch* 1980, cat. no. 216, illustrated on p. 264.

6 *Georg Raphael Donner* 1993, p. 36. Another of the marble figures may represent Aeneas.

7 *Georg Raphael Donner* 1993, pp. 54-5.

8 *Georg Raphael Donner* 1993, pp. 100-7.

9 For St Martin of Tours, see https://www.britannica.com/biography/Saint-Martin-of-Tours, accessed 6 March 2021.

10 *Georg Raphael Donner* 1993, p. 61, pp. 93-9 and pp. 366-391.

11 *Georg Raphael Donner* 1993, p. 369.

12 *Georg Raphael Donner* 1993, fig. 42 on p. 99.

13 *Georg Raphael Donner* 1993, p. 369.

14 Kunsthistorisches Museum, Vienna; see Avery 1987, fig. 134 on p. 134.

15 *Georg Raphael Donner* 1993, p. 381.

16 *Georg Raphael Donner* 1993, p. 74; see https://www.lookandlearn.com/history-images/preview/YW/YW036/YW036103V_Perseus-and-Andromeda.jpg, accessed 7 March 2021.

17 *Georg Raphael Donner* 1993, p. 74. In fact, it is placed beneath a balcony where town officials made civic pronouncements. I am most grateful to Konrad Schlegel for this information.

18 *Georg Raphael Donner* 1993, p. 74.

19 *Georg Raphael Donner* 1993, p. 76; see https://it.wikipedia.org/wiki/File:Paris_Notre-Dame_cathedral_statue_Pieta_by_Nicolas_Coustou_altar.jpg, accessed 7 March 2021.

20 For the Japanese Palace and the history of the display of porcelain in Dresden, see Pietsch et al. 2006, pp. 5-8.

21 Pietsch et al. 2006, and Pietsch 2006.

22 Pietsch 2006, cat. no. 179 on p. 128. Variant models of the heron also exist; see Pietsch 2006, pp. 128-9.

23 Pietsch 2006, cat. no. 2 on pp. 10-11. For other full-length portrayals of Fröhlich in the form of ceramic statuettes after models by Kändler, see Pietsch 2006, pp. 11-14.

24 https://skd-online-collection.skd.museum/Details/Index/115712, accessed 14 May 2021. Pietsch 2006, cat. no. 3 on p. 11.

25 Pietsch 2006, cat. no. 126 on p. 90; Pietsch et al. 2006, p. 100.

26 Rasmussen 1977, p. 536; Pietsch 2006, p. 99.

27 https://en.wikipedia.org/wiki/Archbasilica_of_Saint_John_Lateran#Statues_of_the_Apostles, accessed 17 May 2021.

28 Pietsch 2006, cat. no. 135 on p. 100.

29 Pietsch 2006, cat. no. 90 on p. 65.

30 For the manufacture of porcelain at Nymphenburg, see Rückert 1963 and Bacci 1966.

31 Rückert 1963, p. 7; *Neue Deutsche Biographie* n.d.; https://www.deutsche-biographie.de/sfz25494.html, accessed 1 June 2021.

32 Rückert 1963, p. 25.

33 Eikelmann 2004, pp. 496-7.

34 For example, see Roubiliac's bust of Alexander Pope (1688-1744) dating from 1741 at the Yale Center for British Art; Baker 2014, fig. 287.

35 Roubiliac's portrait of Pope cited above was indeed produced in several versions.

36 Rückert 1963, p. 33.

37 The foot of the lady is broken. I am most grateful to Katharina Hantschmann for sending me information on this group. Eikelmann 2004, pp. 453-4; Rückert 1963, fig. 13.

38 Lindemann 1989, pp. 72-5.

39 Lindemann 1989, pp. 11 and 316; fig. 86 on p. 85.

40 The sandstone figure of *Minerva* from Schloss Seehof is in the Germanisches Nationalmuseum, Nuremberg; Maué 1997-2005, Vol. 1, cat. no. 47 on pp. 134-8. *Chronos* is the National Gallery of Ireland, Dublin; *Orpheus* is in the Cleveland Museum of Art; *Actaeon* is in the Liebieghaus, Frankfurt; see Lindemann 1989, pp. 320-3.

41 Lindemann 1989, fig. 11 on p. 27 and cat. no. 7.1.2 on p. 320. A drawing of the figure *in situ* in 1900 by Fritz Bayerlein shows the full unbroken cloak, although the right hand was broken even then; Lindemann 1989, fig. 12 on p. 28.

42 Lindemann 1989, pp. 346-60.

43 Lindemann 1989, pp. 133-56 and pp. 329-30.

44 The angle of the Virgin's head was evidently altered at some point before 1938; she would apparently have been looking upwards, rather than down towards the spectator; Lindemann 1989, p. 133.

45 Lindemann 1989, pp. 247-302 and pp. 361-72.

46 Lindemann 1989, pp. 252-61, and cat. 18.1 on p. 362.

47 Lindemann 1989, cat. 18.7.6 on p. 353 and fig. 226 on p. 250.

48 Lindemann 1989, cat. 18.13.1 on p. 368 and fig. 259 on p. 279.

BIOGRAPHICAL
LIST OF ARTISTS

Balthasar Ableithner (Ableitner) (1614-1705)

He trained with Christoph Angermair in Munich, 1627-33, and was an important early practitioner of the baroque in Germany. He was in Rome, and perhaps Venice, in 1635-42. From 1644 he was court sculptor at Munich for Duke Albert VI (1584-1666), and he continued to work at court in the following years. From 1652/3 onwards he was appointed sculptor to Duke Albert's nephew, Elector Ferdinand Maria of Bavaria (1636-79). He then worked for Maximilian Philip, Duke of Bavaria-Leuchtenberg (1638-1705) from 1676 to 1680. He executed portrait busts of the ducal family, as well as carving ivories. He produced wood sculptures of the four Evangelists for the chancel screen of the Theatine church of St Cajetan in Munich in 1670/73 (one was severely damaged and another destroyed in the Second World War). Andreas Faistenberger and Giovanni Giuliani trained with him until c. 1690. (Feulner 1922, p. v; Saur 1992-2019, Vol. 1, pp. 145-6; *Neue Deutsche Biographie* n.d.)

Christoph Angermair (c. 1580-1633)

Born in Weilheim, the son of a goldsmith, he specialised in ivory and wood sculptures. He trained under Hans Degler in Weilheim and undertook travels (his *Wanderschaft*) to Munich in 1604-5, and to Innsbruck in 1606, where he carved an ivory Christ child, perhaps for the Archduchess Anna Katherina Gonzaga (1566-1621), the widow of Archduke Ferdinand II of Tyrol (1529-95), who was the founder of the *Kunst-* *kammer* collection at Schloss Ambras. He was appointed court artist in Munich by Duke Maximilian I, Elector of Bavaria (1573-1651; Duke 1597-1651) from 1613 onwards, specialising in ivory and wood. He may have taught the elector to turn ivory. Angermair was a member of the so-called Weilheim school, along with Hans Degler, as well as Hans Krumper, Bartholomäus Steinle and Georg Petel. Through Degler he would have known the court sculptors Hans Reichle, Hubert Gerhard and Krumper, and he perhaps worked in Gerhard's studio. He worked with the merchant and art collector Philipp Hainhofer (1578-1647) in Augsburg in 1611-12 on the production of a chess set in ivory and serpentine, commissioned by Duke Philipp II of Pomerania-Stettin (1573-1618) (individual pieces are now in the collections of the Kunstgewerbe Museum, Berlin; the Herzog Anton Ulrich-Museum, Braunschweig; and St Petersburg). His workshop also produced wood sculptures for altarpieces, leading to friction with the Munich sculptors' guild, of which he was forced to become a member. In 1622 he became master of the guild and was thus exceptional in his status as both an artist employed by the court and a guild master. His fine ivory relief of *The Temptation of Christ*, signed and dated 1616, is at the British Museum, London. But his most famous work, of great virtuosity, is the coin cabinet of 1618-24, commissioned by Duke Maximilian I (Bayerisches National Museum, Munich). He also made fountain figures for the city of Munich (1628 and 1629). His court appointment was terminated in 1631, perhaps because of the disruptions caused by the Thirty Years' War. The troops of Gustav Adolphus of Sweden occupied Munich for three weeks in 1632, when the elector and his family fled to Salzburg with some of their works of art. Angermair's last known work is the ivory skeleton dated 1632 (Grünes Gewölbe, Dresden). He was the teacher of both Petel and Balthasar Ableithner. (Grünwald 1975; Saur 1992-2019, Vol. 3, pp. 253-4)

Egid (Aegid) Quirin Asam (1692-1750)

A sculptor and architect, he was born in Tegernsee in Bavaria into a family of artists. He trained under his father Georg (Hans Georg) Asam (1649-1711), a painter at the Benedictine monastery in Tegernsee, and worked closely with his brother Cosmas Damian Asam (1686-1739), who was a painter and architect. Egid Quirin was also assisted by his sister Maria Salome Bornschlögl Asam (1685-1740). Cosmas Damian was in Rome from around 1711 to 1713, winning first prize in painting at the Accademia di San Luca in 1713. Egid Quirin's presence in Rome is not recorded, although his awareness of Roman baroque architecture and sculpture suggests that he may have been with his brother in the Eternal City. From 1713 to 1716 he trained with Andreas Faistenberger in Munich. In 1724 he was appointed *Kammerdiener* (valet/court artist) and court stuccoist to the Prince-Bishop of Freising, Johann Franz Eckher von Kapfing und Liechteneck (1696-1727), and in 1730 he became *Kammerdiener* at the Bavarian court. He bought three houses in the centre of Munich 1729-33, and along with Cosmas Damian he began building a church there, known as the Asamkirche, living in an adjoining house that he built on the same site. The church is dedicated to St John Nepomuk, and was designed by the architect Johann Michael Fischer (1692-1766). The Asam brothers worked in numerous Benedictine abbeys, including Freising and Weltenburg, as well as Augustinian monasteries, such as Rohr, and at the Jesuit foundation in Mannheim. Controlling and directing lighting was fundamental to the brothers' conception of sculpture and architecture. As well as the undeniable theatrical power to be seen in their work, Egid Asam's sculptures and his brother Cosmas Damian's paintings express their deep piety. (Rupprecht 1985; Hojer 1986; *Asam in Freising* 2007; Coburger 2011; Steiner 2010; Altmann 2016; *Neue Deutsche Biographie* n.d.; Saur 1992-2019, Vol. 5, pp. 371-3)

Jacob Auer (1645-1706)

An Austrian sculptor, he trained under Michael Lechleitner (c. 1611-69) in the Tyrol. Auer worked in wood and rhinoceros horn, as well as ivory. Additionally he carved a marble portal for the Benedictine monastery at Lambach (1681-93), and other full-scale stone figures, such as those at St Florian bei Linz. In 1685 he may have carved some of the reliefs on the Plague Column in Vienna, designed by Matthias Rauchmiller. Generally, however, he seems to have worked on small-scale sculpture. One of his masterpieces is the ivory group of *Apollo and Daphne* in the Kunsthistorisches Museum, Vienna of c. 1688/90. (Theuerkauff 1994, pp. 23-5; Trusted 2013, p. 9)

Johann Wolfgang van/von der Auwera (1708-1756)

Trained by his father Jakob (1672-1760), he was the most important sculptor of his family. He trained at the Academy of Fine Arts in Vienna 1730-37, where he met Johann Baptist Straub, later travelling to the Rhineland and the Netherlands with Johann Balthasar Neumann (c. 1687-1753), the architect of the Würzburg Residenz. Van der Auwera oversaw the interior stucco decoration (figures and ornamental sculptures) at the Residenz from 1738 onwards. Along with the stuccoist Antonio Giuseppe Bossi, he was responsible for 'Würzburg rococo'. Johann Peter Wagner was an assistant in his workshop at Würzburg, and he also taught the sculptor (not the architect) Johann Michael Fischer (1717-1801). (*Neue Deutsche Biographie* n.d.; Saur 1992-2019, Vol. 5, pp. 697-8)

Melchior Barthel (1625-1672)

Born in Dresden, he trained initially with his father, the sculptor Hieronymus Barthel, until 1645 when he studied under Johann Böhm (1600-67) in Schneeberg, Saxony. He travelled in Regensburg, Passau and Ulm (his *Wanderschaft*), and then spent two years in Rome. From 1652 onwards he worked in Venice, producing figures for tombs, including that of Doge Giovanni Pesaro in the Frari of 1655-60. In 1670 he returned to Dresden where he was appointed to the Saxon court by Elector Johann Georg II (1613-80). His most important surviving works at Dresden are his ivory sculptures in the Grünes Gewölbe. (*Neue Deutsche Biographie* n.d.; Kappel 2017, pp. 104-8, 586)

Ehrgott Bernhard Bendl (c. 1660-1738)

Originally from South Tyrol, he undertook travels as a journeyman (his *Wanderschaft*) in 1678-84, visiting Prague, Vienna, Rome and Paris. He was possibly related to the sculptors Johann Georg Bendl, active in Prague, and Ignaz Bendl (d. c. 1730), active in Vienna. From 1684 to 1687 he was in the workshop of the sculptor Johann Jakob Rill (active c. 1686-99) at Augsburg, becoming an independent master in 1687. Inspired by sculpture in Vienna and by the Italian high baroque, he made models for goldsmiths, as well as carving ivories. From 1733 to 1738 he worked at the cloister church of Diessen am Ammersee. (Saur 1992-2019, Vol. 8, pp. 630-2)

Johann Georg Bendl (Jan Jiří Bendl) (b. before 1620-1680)

He was the first major baroque sculptor in Bohemia, producing numerous sculptures for the churches of Prague. The son of the Prague sculptor Georg Bendl (c. 1570-1656), he is first recorded in Prague in 1630. One of his earliest surviving works is the stucco decoration of the dome of the Jesuit church of St Salvator in Prague, 1648-9. He subsequently sculpted sandstone statues of saints for the church, and a wood figure of St Jude for one of the confessionals (1673-5). In 1650 he was commissioned by Ferdinand III, Holy Roman Emperor, to produce a sculpture of the Immaculate Conception to commemorate the Peace of Westphalia ending the Thirty Years' War in 1648. His monumental Marian Column (1650) on the Old Town Square in Prague (destroyed in 1918) was a seminal work. Fragments of it are extant in the Lapidarium in Prague. In 1662 he sculpted the statue of St Wenceslaus in the old deanery of the St Vitus Cathedral at Prague Castle. In

1670 he sculpted the *Hercules and Cerberus* fountain for the imperial garden in the Belvedere of the same castle. He sculpted a statue of a saint for the high altar of St Stephen's Church in 1678. His last known works are two statues of St Wenceslaus (1676-8), one on a column near the Charles Bridge and an equestrian statue on Wenceslas Square. Some of his works are now in the collections of the National Gallery Prague. (Stech 1959; Neumann 1970)

Roman Anton Boos (1733-1810)

He trained with Anton Sturm (1690-1757) at Füssen until Sturm's death in 1757. From 1760 onwards he worked under Johann Baptist Straub in Munich, and his second marriage was to Straub's daughter. He attended the Academy of Fine Arts in Vienna in 1763, where he studied under Jacob Schletterer (1699-1774), and was then at the Academy in Augsburg, where he was employed in the workshop of Ignaz Wilhelm Verhelst (1729-92). He returned to Munich in 1765. In 1766 he made over-life-size figures for 78/*the abbey at Fürstenfeld. He co-founded a drawing school in Munich with Thomas Christian Winck (1738-97) and Franz Xaver Feichtmayr the Younger (1735-1803). His most important works were the four colossal marble figures for the façade of the Theatine church of St Cajetan in Munich, after designs by Ignaz Günther, in 1768. He became official court sculptor to Elector Maximilian III Joseph (1727-77) in Munich in 1775, supplying nine statues for the Schloss Park at Nymphenburg from 1775 to 1790 (following Charles de Grof's death) after models by Günther, de Grof and Johann Baptist Hagenauer. His marble self-portrait dates from c. 1790 (Bayerisches National Museum, Munich). His work generally depends on antique prototypes. (Diederen and Kürzeder 2014, pp. 371-91; Saur 1992-2019, Vol. 12, pp. 641-2)

Antonio Giuseppe Bossi (1699-1764)

A stuccoist from Lombardy, he was a fundamental influence on the development of the rococo in South Germany through his introduction of Italian styles and forms. He worked at the abbey of Ottobeuren from 1719 to 1729, and thereafter in Mainz, before going to Würzburg in 1734, where he carried out his most important work, effectively creating along with Johann Balthasar Neumann and Johann Wolfgang von der Auwera the 'Würzburg rococo'. In addition to his work at the Residenz he undertook stucco work for numerous churches in Würzburg and Franconia. (Volk 1981; *Neue Deutsche Biographie* n.d.)

Johann Friedrich Böttger (1682-1719)

The discoverer of European porcelain, he was a chemist and alchemist originally from Prussia. At the age of fourteen, Böttger started his apprenticeship with the chemist Friedrich Zorn in Berlin and soon gained a reputation as a skilled manufacturer of gold. This caused such a stir that Elector Frederick III (1657-1713), King in Prussia, became aware of him, wanting to hold him captive in order to make use of his apparent miraculous abilities. Böttger however managed to escape to Wittenberg in February 1701. Augustus the Strong, King of Poland (1696-1763), also hoped to promote the manufacture of gold. He succeeded in bringing Böttger to Dresden, where he was temporarily imprisoned in the Königstein fortress, employed as a laboratory assistant to the physicist Ehrenfried Walter Count von Tschirnhaus (1651-1708). The two men were commissioned to investigate how base metals could be converted into gold. Having fruitlessly spent some years practising alchemy, they embarked instead on trying to determine how porcelain could be manufactured. Porcelain vessels were known in the West from Chinese exports, but the recipe for manufacturing these luxury ceramics was still a secret. By 1708 Böttger and Tschirnhaus had successfully produced a porcellaneous red stoneware. Böttger continued the experiments after Tschirnhaus's death, and, after finding the correct china clay, kaolin, was able to manufacture hard paste white porcelain with the addition of feldspar in 1709. This heralded the highly successful production of porcelainin Meissen, which was to continue throughout the eighteenth century and beyond. Böttger became the first director of the Meissen factory in 1710, producing porcelain wares in imitation of silver. Porcelain factories were later established at Vienna in 1720, Höchst in 1740, Fürstenberg in 1744, Nymphenburg near Munich in 1747, and Berlin in 1751. (Fleming and Honour 1989, pp. 112-13; Röbbig 2008; *Neue Deutsche Biographie* n.d.)

Matthias Bernhard Braun (1684-1738)

He was born near Innsbruck, and probably trained with the sculptor Andreas Tamasch (1639-97) at Stams in the Imst district of the Tyrol. He is likely to have travelled to Italy in his youth (probably Venice, Verona and Rome), and subsequently worked with Michael Bernhard Mandl (1660-1711) in Salzburg. But he was primarily active in Prague and elsewhere in Bohemia. He had probably settled in Prague by 1710. His expressive baroque style was redolent of the cinquecento of Michelangelo (1475-1564), and of the baroque sculpture of Gian Lorenzo Bernini (1598-1680), Giusto (Josse) Le Corte (1627-79) and Filippo Parodi (1630-1702). Braun's lively and emotive sculptural style dominated baroque sculpture in Bohemia, both contrasting with and complementing the work of his great contemporary, Ferdinand Brokoff. *The Vision of St Luitgarde* (1710), his first independent work, was executed for the Charles Bridge, commissioned by Eugen Tyttl, Abbot of the Cistercian Convent at Plasy, West Bohemia. This was followed shortly afterwards by the figure of *St Ivo* (1711; formerly on the bridge, now in the Lapidarium in Prague). His limewood figure of *St Judas Thaddäus* (c. 1712; now in the National Gallery Prague), made for the church of St Mary of the Pond in the Old Town of Prague, was subsequently moved to the Clementinum, the Jesuit complex in the city, after the church was demolished. In 1715 Braun was commissioned to carve a series of sandstone figures of Apostles and Church Fathers for the church of St Clement (now the Orthodox Cathedral of St Clement) in the same complex. Count Franz Anton Sporck (1662-1738) was Braun's most important patron and commissioned numerous sculptures, including the sandstone statues of *Virtues and Vices* (1719-20) at the Kuks Hospital, and possibly the marble monument to Charles VI at Hlavenec (1720). He produced a fine tomb to his mother-in-law Anna Muselius now in the cemetery at Jaroměř soon after her death in 1721. Braun's sandstone memorial monument to Count Sporck of 1733 is in the garden of the château at Valeč (Waltsch) and was inspired by Balthasar Permoser's monument to Prince Eugene of Savoy in Vienna of 1718-21, which Braun could have seen in 1727. Among Braun's most striking works is the series of monumental sculptures carved from the rocks in the wooded area at Neuwald near Žírec (Schurz), now known as the Bethlehem wood, for Count Sporck, a few kilometres northwest of Kuks, from 1717 onwards. Some of the sculptor's terracotta models are in the National Gallery, Prague. (Blažíček 1968; Neumann 1970; Saur 1992-2019, Vol. 14, pp. 7-9; Poche and Kořán 2003,; *Neue Deutsche Biographie* n.d.)

(Johann) Jan Brokoff (Brokof) (1652-1718) and Ferdinand Maximilian Brokoff (Brokof) (1688-1731)

Jan Brokoff was originally from the Spiš (Zips) region in Upper Hungary, today the Slovak Republic, and had moved to Bohemia in 1675 and settled in Prague by 1692. He trained as a wood carver in the workshop of his father, a sculptor. His son Ferdinand Maximilian was born in 1688 in West Bohemia at Červený Hrádek (Castle Rothenhaus) u Chomutova (near Komotau) during Jan Brokoff's artistic sojourn there. He initially trained with his father Jan in Prague, and then (before 1708) with Peter and Paul Strudel at the Academy of Fine Arts in Vienna. Ferdinand Maximilian was more accomplished than his father, collaborating with him on groups of *The Baptism of Christ* and *St Caetan* (Gaetano) in 1709, and *St Francis Xavier* in 1711 for the Charles Bridge in Prague. In 1714 he executed architectural sculptures for the exterior of the Morzin Palace in Prague, and from 1714-16 carved the monument to Count Johann Wenzel Wratislaw von Mitrowitz designed by the architect Johann Bernhard Fischer von Erlach for the minorite church of St James the Greater in Prague. Brokoff was also active in Silesia (Wrocław). Like the work of his contemporary, Matthias Bernhard Braun, his sculpture exercised a seminal influence in Bohemia. He died prematurely of tuberculosis in Prague. (Blažíček 1968; Neumann 1970; Saur 1992-2019, Vol. 14, pp. 344-5; *Neue Deutsche Biographie* n.d)

Franz Anton Bustelli (d. 1763)

A modeller for the porcelain factory at Neudeck and then at Nymphenburg outside Munich, little is known of Bustelli's life. His name suggests that he was born in Locarno in the Ticino region where many members of a vast Bustelli family are recorded. But the modeller must have grown up in a German-speaking area as he later wrote in German, rather than Latin. He was first recorded at Neudeck in 1754. The style of his lively ceramic figures parallels the rococo sculpture produced by eighteenth-century Bavarian sculptors such as Johann Baptist Straub or Ignaz Günther. He specialised in figures from the commedia dell'arte, as well as genre scenes. One of his masterpieces however is his life-size bust of Count Sigismund von Haimhausen (1708-1793), the director of the Nymphenburg porcelain manufactory, dating from 1761 (Bayerisches National Museum, Munich). (Rückert 1963; Bacci 1966; Volk 1981; Eikelmann 2004)

Carlo di Cesare [Cesari] del Palagio [Pallago] (1538-98/1600)

He was a sculptor, stuccoist and bronze-caster, born in Florence, but spending most of his career at the courts of German princes. In his youth he assisted Giorgio Vasari (1511-74) and Giambologna (1529-1608) at the Medici court in Florence. From 1569 to 1573 he worked for Hans Fugger (1531-98) in Augsburg, making sculptural decorations in stucco and terracotta for his house as part of the decorative scheme designed by Friedrich Sustris (c. 1540-99). In 1573 he was employed by the Crown Prince of Bavaria, later Duke William V (1548-1626; r. 1579-97), who wanted his castle, Burg Trausnitz in Landshut, to emulate Hans Fugger's house. From 1574 Carlo divided his time between Munich, where he produced marble busts for the Antiquarium in the Residenz, and Landshut, where he worked on the stucco decoration (destroyed in 1961) in Burg Trausnitz, and on bronze figures for a fountain there. Between 1579 and 1581 he was in Florence, and from 1581 he again worked for the Fuggers. With Hubert Gerhard he created twelve over-life-size figures of famous men and women for Hans Fugger at Kirchheim an der Mindel (1578-83). In 1588 he returned briefly to Florence, but was engaged later that year to work for Christian I, Elector of Saxony (1560-91; r. 1586-91) on sculpture for the choir of Freiberg Cathedral, Saxony, which was being transformed into a burial chapel for the Wettin dynasty (1590-93) by the architect and sculptor Giovanni Maria Nosseni (1554-1620). Five life-size portrait figures in bronze of the electors and their consorts kneel in adoration, while additional bronze, terracotta and stucco figures adorn the chapel. Carlo began working with Gerhard on the tomb for Duke William V in 1592, intended for the church of St Michael, Munich, though the installation was never completed. In 1597 he returned to Italy, dying soon afterwards. (Diemer 1988; Diemer 2004)

Diego Francesco Carlone (1674-1750)

An important Italian stuccoist active in Austria and Bavaria, he probably trained in the workshop of his father in Scaria in Lombardy. In 1701 he inherited the workshop, which he ran until 1720. He probably travelled north to Bavaria in 1695 and was there again from 1714 onwards. He was active in Passau Cathedral and at Weingarten, an important precursor of his pupil Joseph Anton Feuchtmayer. His distinctive forms, profuse fleshy leaves and acanthus, seen for example in his stucco work at Weingarten, influenced other artists in Bavaria, such as Johann Baptist and Dominikus Zimmermann. (Decker 1943, pp. 47-9; Saur 1992-2019, Vol. 16, pp. 436-7; Rinn 2012; *Neue Deutsche Biographie* n.d.)

Johann Joseph Christian (1706-1777)

Having trained with Johann Eucharius Hermann (1666-1727) in Biberach an der Riss in Bavaria (Upper Swabia), he established a workshop nearby in Riedlingen in 1728, after Hermann's death. He was primarily a wood carver, but also produced sculpture in stone and stucco. He worked primarily for the Church, for example at the abbey church in Zwiefalten, under the architect Johann Michael Fischer (1692-1766), and alongside the stuccoist Johann Michael Feichtmayr the Younger (1709-1772) from 1744 to 1755. He collaborated with both artists once more some years later at the abbey church of Ottobeuren from 1755 to 1764. His Bernini-esque style of carving was also influenced by the stucco work of Diego Francesco Carlone. (Woeckel 1958; Huber 1960; Saur 1992-2019, Vol. 19, pp. 40-41; *Neue Deutsche Biographie* n.d.)

François de Cuvilliés the Elder (1695-1768)

Born in Soignes, Hainaut in the Southern Netherlands, he was an architect who spent most of his career in Bavaria. He had a seminal influence on contemporary and later German architects and sculptors, such as Johann Michael Fischer (1692-1766), Johann Baptist Straub, Ignaz Günther and Roman Anton Boos. In fact, Cuvilliés was originally appointed as a court dwarf in 1708 by Elector Maximilian II Emmanuel (1662-1726) when he was living in Brussels, due to Cuvilliés's diminutive stature. But Max Emmanuel recognized his abilities and encouraged his education under the architect Joseph Effner (1687-1745), before sending him to study in Paris (1720-24), where he trained in the studio of Jean-François Blondel (1683-1756). Cuvilliés worked at the Residenz in Munich, in particular on the theatre, now known as the Cuvilliés theatre (1751-5), though his masterpiece is generally thought to be the Amalienburg in the park at Nymphenburg with its lively rococo decoration (1734-9), on which he worked with the stuccoist Johann Baptist Zimmermann. (Volk 1981; *Neue Deutsche Biographie* n.d.)

Hans Degler (1564/5-1635)

One of the most important of the so-called Weilheim school of sculptors, along with Christoph Angermair, Hans Krumper and Georg Petel, he was born perhaps in Munich. He worked with Adam Krumper, father of Hans, from 1590 to 1595 for the Munich court, and married Adam Krumper's daughter in 1590, taking over his father-in-law's workshop in Weilheim after his death. A new generation of sculptors trained in his workshop, including Angermair and Hans Jakob Zürn. He was active in Augsburg, producing altarpieces for the church of SS. Ulrich and Afra, with his brother-in-law Hans Krumper. Sculptors in Weilheim had no guild of their own, being allied with the Munich sculptors' and craftworkers' guild, until in 1616/17 a dispute broke out, which was heard before the town council. Degler had questioned the credentials of two sculptors in Weilheim: Melchior Bendl from Waldsee, and a local sculptor, Philipp Dirr (c. 1582-1633). As a result of this disagreement, sculptors in Weilheim were required to be members of the guild of cabinetmakers, painters, glassworkers, coopers and turners in Weilheim. Degler was a councillor at Weilheim from 1607 to 1628, later dying of the plague there under financial difficulties. (Zohner 1977; Saur 1992-2019, Vol. 25, pp. 229-30)

Joseph Deutschmann (Teutschmann) (1717-1787)

He was born in Imst, Tyrol, training under Balthasar Jais (1694-1757). He undertook travels (*Wanderschaft*) as a journeyman 1734-8, and perhaps went to Prague, where Matthias Braun was active. He possibly worked in Johann Baptist Straub's workshop in Munich. His sculptures were of wood, stone and ivory. He worked under Joseph Matthias Götz (1696-1760) at St Nicholas, Passau, in 1740-42 and became sculptor for the church after Götz's death in 1760. Deutschmann was thus at work in Passau for over forty years, from 1742 to 1787, the last sculptor to be appointed by the church. (Vogl 1989; Trusted 2013, p. 79)

Joseph Joachim Dietrich (1690-1753)

The son of a cabinetmaker, he trained as a sculptor, travelling to Prague and Italy during his *Wanderschaft* as a journeyman. He settled near Munich in about 1720, working with the court joiner Johann Pichler. He produced figurative sculpture in wood for both the court and the church, for example the high altarpiece at Diessen am Ammersee of c. 1738, designed by François de Cuvilliés, and was appointed court sculptor in 1736. As a collaborator with Cuvilliés he received many commissions for the Residenz in Munich, including the theatre at the Residenz and the pavilion at Amalienberg. (Volk 1981, pp. 33-4; Schnell 2016)

Johann Christian Döbel (1640-1713)

A sculptor from east Prussia active in Berlin at the Brandenburg court who executed a marble statue of Elector Frederick III (1657-1713) in c. 1691/8. Only the marble head survives (Akademie der Künste, Berlin, Kunstsammlung), though a plaster bozzetto is extant (Kunstgewerbemuseum, Berlin). (*Andreas Schlüter* 2014, pp. 115-17)

Georg Raphael Donner (1693-1741)

The sculptor and medallist Donner specialised in lead and bronze, though he also executed important works in marble. He produced both large- and small-scale sculptures, his style epitomising a transition between the baroque and classicism. He was born at Essling near Vienna, the son of a carpenter, and was probably taught by the sculptor Johann Franz Prenner in Vienna and by the Venetian sculptor Giovanni Giuliani in Heiligenkreuz. In 1713 he probably studied the art of lead casting and medal-making under the Swedish court medallist Benedikt (Bengt) Richter (1670-1735). Donner's younger brother Matthäus (1704-56) worked with him as an assistant from an unknown date after 1714 until 1730. Through Giuliani Donner came to know bronzes in the Liechtenstein Collection by François Du Quesnoy (1597-1643) (which he mistakenly thought to be antique), Giambologna (1529-1608), Adriaen de Vries and others. Before 1715 he travelled to Munich, where he learnt the technique of lead casting with the court sculptor Guillielmus de Grof. In 1720 he visited Dresden, where he saw Balthasar Permoser's work. He travelled to Salzburg in 1725, and there worked as a die-cutter at the mint of the Prince-Bishop, Franz Anton Count Harrach (1665-1727). He produced over-life-size marble figures for the staircase at Mirabell Palace (Schloss Mirabell), Salzburg (1725-7). After Harrach's death in 1727 Donner returned to Vienna, where he encountered Prince Emmerich Count Esterházy, Archbishop of Estzergom (c. 1663-1745), who became his new patron, and whose residence was in Bratislava (Pressburg). Donner went to Bratislava to work for the count in the autumn of 1729, remaining there until 1739. His large-scale sculptures of the kneeling archbishop, a pair of monumental bronze candelabra and two angels for the chapel of St Johannes Elemosynarius (St John the Merciful) in Bratislava Cathedral were completed by 1734. He executed a high altarpiece for the cathedral in 1733-5, with a central equestrian group in lead of *St Martin and the Beggar*. The high altarpiece was dismantled in the nineteenth century and is now partly displayed in the Hungarian National Museum in Budapest, although the group of *St Martin* remains in the cathedral. Donner had produced works for clients in Vienna from 1734 onwards, and by 1739 he was based once more in Vienna. His most important work there is the lead fountain he made for the Flour Market, the Mehlmarktbrunnen, with a figure of *Providentia* at the centre surrounded by allegorical river figures (the originals were replaced by bronze replicas in the nineteenth century and are now in the Österreichische Galerie, Vienna). His marble group of the *Apotheosis of Emperor Charles VI* dates from 1737-9 (Österreichische Galerie, Vienna). He also produced a lead wall fountain depicting in relief *Perseus and Andromeda*, placed in front of the town hall of Vienna (1740/41), and a freestanding *Pietà* for the cathedral at Gurk in 1741, his last known work. Although Donner himself did not have an appointment at the Academy of Fine Arts in Vienna, his students successfully competed in competitions run by the Academy, which had re-opened in 1725. His brother Matthaeus took over his workshop and used his terracotta models to teach Academy students from 1743 onwards. (Feulner and Müller 1953, pp. 556-63; Saur 1992-2019, Vol. 28, pp. 570-2; *Aspekte der Stilbildung* 1993; *Georg Raphael Donner* 1993; *Neue Deutsche Biographie* n.d.)

(Johann) Paul Egell (1691-1752)

He was a sculptor, stuccoist and draughtsman, born in the region of Salzburg, from a family of possibly Swiss origins. Perhaps the pupil of Balthasar Esterbauer, he collaborated on the decorative sculpture for the cloisters at Banz. From 1717 to 1719/20 he worked with Balthasar Permoser on the Zwinger pavilion in Dresden, probably carving capitals and a *Playful Nymph and Putto* for the Nymphenbad there. At the Dresden court he executed small-scale ivories, sometimes working alongside jewellers, such as Johann Heinrich Köhler (1669-1736). He also worked for the cathedral prelate Ernst Friedrich Freiherr von Twickel on the limewood and alabaster altarpiece at Hildesheim Cathedral (1729-31), now partly destroyed. He became court sculptor to Charles III Philip, Elector Palatine (1661-1742) in Mannheim in 1729. In about 1731 he carved the marble figure of *Apollo Lykeios* (Bruchsal Palace). He undertook the high altarpiece for the church of St Sebastian at Mannheim (1738-41/2). Because it was out of kilter with contemporary taste, by 1880 the altarpiece had been removed from the church and transferred to the Berlin museums. It was severely damaged in the Second World War, but the surviving elements are now displayed in the Bode Museum. Egell may have visited Rome and Florence in his youth, where he could have studied the works of Gian Lorenzo Bernini (1598-1680), although such a journey is not documented. He could also have known of Bernini's work indirectly, through for example Permoser. Egell's fine stucco reliefs and his decorative scheme for Mannheim Palace were largely destroyed in the Second World War. He also undertook other commissions in Mannheim: his sandstone sculptures of the Cardinal Virtues of 1750 are on the façade of the Jesuit church of St John Nepomuk. His pearwood statuette of *St Francis Borgia* (1750/1), thought to be a preliminary model for a figure for a side altar inside that church, is at the Victoria and Albert Museum, London. Other pearwood bozzetti for figures made for the balustrade of the Mannheim Palace are in the Louvre and elsewhere. His limewood relief of the Jesuit saints Ignatius Loyola and Francis Xavier, dating from 1744, is in the Historisches Museum, Frankfurt am Main. He also worked in ivory; his framed relief of *Christ as Man of Sorrows* of c. 1725 is in the Kunsthistorisches Museum, Vienna. As well as being the teacher of Ignaz Günther and the ceramic modeller Johann Joachim Kändler, he was a seminal influence on numerous other Bavarian artists, including Egid Quirin Asam, Georg Raphael Donner and Joseph Anton Feuchtmayer. (Feulner 1929, pp. 95-9; Lankheit 1988; Kammel 1998; Leibetseder 2013; Lindemann 2017; Kessler 2017b; Kappel 2017, pp. 151-3 and 255-6; Saur 1992-2019, Vol. 32, pp. 301-3; Statnik 2019, pp. 48-63; *Neue Deutsche Biographie* n.d.)

Ignaz Elhafen (1658-before 1715)

He trained in Innsbruck, and then travelled to Italy, probably between 1675 and 1678. Subsequently he worked in Vienna, and then in Düsseldorf, where he was based at the court of Elector John William II (1658-1716; r. 1690-1716) from 1703/4 onwards. Elhafen specialised in ivory, many based on engraved sources, and also produced small-scale reliefs in wood. (Theuerkauff 1968; Trusted 2013, pp. 11-13)

Andreas Faistenberger (1646-1735)

Born in north Tyrol, he initially trained with his father Benedikt Faistenberger the Elder (1621-93). From 1665 onwards he embarked on his travels (*Wanderschaft*) as a journeyman, perhaps including a trip to Italy. He became a pupil of Balthasar Ableithner in Munich in 1668. In around 1670 he was travelling again, perhaps to Venice with Ableithner. By 1678 he was back in Munich, where he taught Giovanni Giuliani in the 1680s, and later Egid Quirin Asam from 1711 to 1716, as well as the ivory sculptor Simon Troger (1693-1768) in around 1730. Johann Baptist Straub perhaps worked with him at the end of Faistenberger's life from c. 1734 onwards. Like Ignaz Günther, Faistenberger became a *Hofbefreit* sculptor, meaning that he was free to work for the court while being regulated by the local guild, but at the same time he was not a court artist. In 1688 he went to Cologne to be employed by the young newly-appointed Archbishop of Cologne, Joseph Clement(1671-1723), probably sent by Clement's brother, Elector Maximilian II Emmanuel (1662-1726). Faistenberger's sculptures, commissioned by both the court and the church, were in wood and stone (marble and alabaster), as well as ivory and boxwood, though none of his documented small-scale sculptures is known to survive. His pulpit and the group of *Abraham and Isaac* are in the Theatine church of St Cajetan, Munich. His large gilt wood relief of *The Annunciation* is in the Bürgersaal, Munich (1709/10) (the former high altar was destroyed in the Second World War). Other sculptures are in St Michael, Berg am Laim. (Rösner 1988; *Neue Deutsche Biographie* n.d.)

Johann Michael Feichtmayr (1709/10-72)

A stuccoist and sculptor, he initially trained in Augsburg under the stonemason J. Paulus from 1722 to 1725, while working with his brothers on the stucco work at the former Dominican church in Augsburg. He became one of the leading practitioners of stucco work in the mid-eighteenth century, mainly active in Swabia and Upper Austria. His work includes the stucco at Diessen am Ammersee (1738/9); Zwiefalten (1747-58); Ottobeuren (1754 and 1756/64); the Käppele at Würzburg (c. 1752); and the church of Vierzehnheiligen (1763-71). (*Neue Deutsche Biographie* n.d.)

Joseph Anton Feuchtmayer (1696-1770)

He was a member of the famous Feuchtmayer family of stuccoists, part of the so-called Wessobrunn school, a term first used in 1888. He studied sculpture in Augsburg in 1715, and worked at Weingarten in 1718, where he would have known Diego Francesco Carlone's works. After the death of his father Franz Joseph in 1718, Joseph Anton took over his workshop at Mimmenhausen. He became house sculptor for the monastery at Salem in the same year, his first commission being the organ case for Salem Münster. He was active working in numerous baroque monastic churches in Swabia, producing stucco work for Bachhaupten and Salem from 1726 onwards. His most famous sculpture is the *Honigschlecker* (honey-eater) at Birnau. (Knapp 1996)

Johann Bernhard Fischer von Erlach (1656-1723)

An Austrian architect, sculptor and architectural historian, his architectural designs and publications had a seminal impact on the art and culture of the Habsburg Empire. His book, *A Plan of Civil and Historical Architecture* (1721), was one of the first comparative studies of international architecture. Born in Graz, he received his early training in the workshop of his father, Johann Baptist Fischer, who contributed to the interior sculptural decorations of the Landhaus and Eggenberg Palace in Graz. From 1671 to 1687 Fischer studied and worked in Italy, joining the workshop of his compatriot Johann Paul Schor (1615-1674) and studying under Gian Lorenzo Bernini (1598-1680). On his return to Austria in 1687, he was appointed court architect, and was to serve under three successive Habsburg Emperors, being elevated to the nobility by Emperor Joseph I (1678-1711) as Fischer von Erlach in 1696. His many influential buildings included palaces, churches and libraries in Vienna, Salzburg, Prague and Wrocław. (Aurenhammer 1973; Dotson 2012)

Hubert Gerhard (c. 1550-1620)

Born in 's-Hertogenbosch, he may have left the Netherlands in order to escape the religious conflicts and iconoclasm of 1566-7. He is recorded in Florence, working in the circle of Giambologna (1529-1608), almost certainly befriending Adriaen de Vries and Carlo di Cesare del Palagio, with whom he often worked subsequently. He returned north in 1581. In Augsburg he was commissioned to produce the *Augustus* fountain by the city council (1589-94). These were later to be complemented by De Vries's *Mercury* and *Hercules and Hydra* fountains (1597 and 1602, respectively) in the Maximilianstrasse. His gilt bronze memorial to Christoph Fugger (d. 1579), commissioned by Hans Fugger (1531-98) and executed in collaboration with Carlo di Cesare del Palagio, dates from 1581-4. It was originally in the church of St Magdalena in Augsburg (now Victoria and Albert Museum, London). When the Italo-Dutch artist Friedrich Sustris (c. 1540-99) became the artistic superintendent for Duke William V, known as William the Pious (1548-1626), he lured Gerhard to Munich, where the sculptor resided from 1584 to 1597. Gerhard produced a fountain for Duke Ferdinand of Bavaria (1550-1608), the younger brother of Duke William, 1584/7 (Residenz, Munich). His monumental bronze *St Michael*, over four metres high, was made for the façade of the Jesuit church of St Michael (the *Michaelskirche*) in Munich in 1588, and he started work on the tomb for William V (never to be completed) in the same church in about 1593, again with Carlo di Cesare del Palagio. Many of the figures intended for the tomb were re-displayed elsewhere, although the angel made for the tomb by Gerhard is still in the church, along with the crucifixion group by Giambologna and Hans Reichle. Two of Gerhard's lions made for the tomb stand in front of the Residenz, while two knights also for the tomb now form part of Hans Krumper's monument to Louis of Bavaria (1282-1347) in the church of Our Lady (the *Frauenkirche*). Gerhard's figure of the Virgin for William V's tomb was actually installed on the high altar of the *Frauenkirche* in 1603, and later crowned the Marian Column (*Mariensäule*) in Munich, erected in 1638. He had made a series of over-life-size terracotta statues of Apostles to line the choir of the *Michaelskirche* in the 1580s. They were destroyed when the tower collapsed in 1590. He then made replacement terracotta Apostles and prophets for the choir, and terracotta angels for the nave in the 1590s. His bronze fountain of *Mars and Venus* (the colossal group completed in 1590; the fountain dating from 1595) was commissioned by Hans Fugger for his palace (Schloss) at Kirchheim, Swabia (the central colossal group from the fountain is now in the Bayerisches Nationalmuseum, Munich). After Duke William's abdication in 1597, from 1599 until 1613 Gerhard was at Mergentheim, the residence of the Teutonic Order, working for the younger brother of Emperor Rudolph II, Maximilian III,

Archduke of Austria (1558-1618; r. 1612-18), who was Grand Master of the Order. Gerhard took on as an apprentice Caspar Gras (1584-1674), who was to go to Innsbruck with him in 1602. He was commissioned to make small-scale bronzes by both Archduke Maximilian and Emperor Rudolph, including an equestrian portrait and mythological statuettes, in addition to producing Maximilian's tomb in St Jacob's church in Innsbruck. In 1613 Gerhard returned to Munich, where he remained until his death seven years later. Along with the sculpture by his contemporary and rival Adriaen de Vries, his work is the most representative of late mannerism in Germany, reflecting his Netherlandish roots and his Italian training, heralding the German baroque. In Munich his legacy can be seen in the work of his pupil Hans Krumper. (Saur 1992-2019, Vol. 52, pp. 110-12; Diemer 1988; Diemer 2004; *Bella Figura* 2015)

Giovanni Giuliani (1664-1744)

Born in Venice, he probably studied under Giuseppe Mazza (1653-1741) in Bologna. He may have trained under Giusto (Josse) le Court (1627-1749) in Venice until 1679. As a journeyman he undertook travels (*Wanderschaft*) in Lower (South) Bavaria and Upper Austria, perhaps including Salzburg. He was in Munich in 1680-90, where he worked under Andreas Faistenberger in 1687-89/90. He settled in Vienna in 1690, benefiting from the reconstruction of the city after the siege of Vienna by the Turks in 1683. In 1697 he was appointed court sculptor by Franz Anton, Prince of Liechtenstein (1656-1721). Having worked for the Cistercian abbey of Heiligenkreuz near Vienna in 1694, he became a lay brother at the abbey in 1711, due to his financial difficulties. There he devoted himself almost exclusively to commissions for the abbey. He taught Georg Raphael Donner. (Saur 1992-2019, Vol. 55, pp. 409-12)

Justus Glesker (1610/23-1678)

The son of a sculptor, he travelled in Italy and the Netherlands before settling in Frankfurt in 1646. He was commissioned to make large gilt wood crucifixion figures and other large wood figures for Bamberg Cathedral in 1648-53. He subsequently lived and worked in Frankfurt am Main. He almost certainly executed ivories as well as large-scale sculptures, though none is signed. (Trusted 2013, p. 14; *Neue Deutsche Biographie* n.d.)

Joseph Götsch (1728-93)

He was an Austrian sculptor in wood, born in Langenfeld in the Tyrol. The son of a carpenter, he probably trained first with his father and then with Johann Reindl in Stems. From 1753 to 1758 he ran his own workshop at Oetzal in the Tyrol. He worked at the Benedictine abbey church at Rott am Inn in 1762-6, where his work shows the influence of Iganz Günther, notably in the dramatic heads of Death, Heaven and Hell on the confessionals. He also worked for churches in Munich and Chiemse, his sculptures recalling not only Günther but Johann Baptist Straub, in a style that was at the same time a transition from the rococo to the neo-classical. (Unger 1972; Saur 1992-2019, Vol. 57, pp. 81-2; Statnik 2019, pp. 203-17)

Joseph Matthias Götz (1696-1760)

From 1713 onwards Götz travelled as a journeyman (his *Wanderschaft*), probably in Würzburg and Regensburg, as well as Passau. He worked in Reichersberg, Passau and Aldersbach, carving altarpieces, pulpits and organ cases. He was influenced by the work of Matthias Steinl and Lorenzo Mattielli in Vienna. Due to economic difficulties, suffered as a result of the War of Austrian Succession in 1741, he sold his workshop to his former pupil Joseph Deutschmann. (Volk 1981; Saur 1992-2019, Vol. 57, pp. 108-10)

Charles de Grof (Groff) (1712/13-74)

The son and pupil of Guillielmus (Wilhelm) de Grof, he came with his father to Munich from Paris in 1716. In 1738 he went to the Academy of Fine Arts in Vienna, and in 1739 to Venice, and probably Rome. After his father's death in 1742 he worked in Strassbourg, Paris and Rouen. In 1749 he returned to Munich, where he was appointed court sculptor by Elector Maximilian III Joseph (1727-77) in 1751. He was in contact with the courts of Würzburg (1755) and Bayreuth (1756), helping to found art academies in Strassbourg and Bayreuth. (Saur 1992-2019, Vol. 62, p. 495)

Guillielmus (Wilhelm) de Grof (Groff) (1676-1742)

A Flemish sculptor and draughtsman born in Antwerp, he was active in France and Germany. In 1700 he went to Paris, where he trained as a founder and sculptor in metal. In 1708 he was employed by the French court, there coming into contact with the exiled Elector of Bavaria, Maximilian II Emmanuel (1662-1726). He was appointed Bavarian court sculptor by the elector in 1716, a position he retained until his death. He worked

in marble, bronze and lead, and produced garden sculptures for the Nymphenburg and Schleissheim. His masterpiece is the silver votive statue of the young Elector Maximilian III Joseph (1727-77) of 1737 in Altötting. (Saur 1992-2019, Vol. 62, pp. 493-4)

Johann Wilhelm Gröninger (1675/6-1724)

He was born and died in Münster, the son of Johann Mauritz Gröninger (d. 1707/8). After travelling (his *Wanderschaft*), he joined his father's workshop, before establishing his own. He specialised in funeral monuments, including that of Elector Frederick Christian von Plettenberg (c. 1709) and the cathedral provost Ferdinand von Plettenburg (d. 1712), both in the cathedral at Münster, Westphalia. From 1718 onwards he executed garden sculptures and portrait busts for Schloss Nordkirchen in Westphalia. (*Europäische Barockplastik* 1971, pp. 224-9)

Gabriel Grupello (1644-1730)

The son of an Italian cavalry captain and his Flemish wife, Grupello trained in Antwerp under Artus Quellinus. He may have assisted Quellinus in the sculptural work for the Amsterdam Royal Palace, and his work suggests the influence of Peter Paul Rubens (1577-1640). He was then at Paris and Versailles, where he was in contact with his compatriots Gérard van Opstal (1594/7-1668) and Martin Desjardins (1637-94). He learned the art of bronze casting with the founder Johan Larson (c.1625/30-64) in The Hague. In 1671 he opened a workshop in Brussels. He enjoyed the patronage of Charles II of Spain (1661-1700), William II of Orange (1626-50), and Frederick III Elector of Brandenburg (1657-1713). In 1695 he was appointed official court sculptor by John William II, Elector Palatine (1658-1716), and moved to Düsseldorf. He worked in marble and bronze, as well as ivory. His equestrian statue of John William in Düsseldorf dates from 1711 and is in the same tradition as Andreas Schlüter's monument to the Great Elector in Berlin of a few years earlier. Perhaps Grupello's most important work was the fountain, known as the Grupello Pyramid, designed for Düsseldorf, and now in Mannheim. (*Europäische Barockplastik* 1971).

(Johann) Meinrad Guggenbichler (1649-1723)

Born in Einsiedeln, he was active in Austria, but initially trained in Dillingen an der Donau, in Swabia (Bavaria) in the workshop of his father Georg, and perhaps also trained with his brother Johann Michael Guggenbichler (1639-81/2). He travelled as a journeyman to Italy. His first independent work of 1675 was the high altarpiece in the church of Strasswalchen in the district of Salzburg. His style, both dramatic and decorative, with lively putti, strongly recalls that of Thomas Schwanthaler, made for the monastery of St Florian, Linz. Guggenbichler produced altarpieces and individual sculptures for altarpieces in Mondsee, east of Salzburg, and elsewhere in Upper Austria, including the church at Oberhofen (1709-12) and the collegiate church of Salzburg (1720-22). His large output, indebted to the help of many assistants, comprises numerous repetitions. (Decker 1949; Saur 1992-2019, Vol. 65, pp. 72-4).

Ignaz Günther (1725-75)

He initially trained under his father Johann Georg Günther the Elder in Altmannstein, where he was born. He then studied in Munich from 1743 to 1750 under Johann Baptist Straub, with whom he was in competition as a carver of altarpieces, as indicated by a dated drawing of 1760 related to Straub's high altarpiece at Berg am Laim, produced by Günther presumably in the hope of being awarded the commission. Günther's travels as a journeyman (his *Wanderschaft*) took him to Salzburg, Vienna, and then Mannheim, where he worked under Paul Egell in 1751-2, a decisive period, leading Günther to adopt his own distinctive style. In 1753 he enrolled at the Academy of Fine Arts in Vienna, where he won the annual students' prize. A leading sculptor of his generation, he was able to express a range of facial expressions in his sculptures, and with distinctive stylistic features, such as the sickle-shaped eyes, elongated figures and swirling drapery. Partly inspired by Gian Lorenzo Bernini (1598-1680), he was a scholarly artist, owning a substantial library. Many of his own drawings survive, illuminating and complementing his work as a sculptor. He made terracotta models for ornamentation on bronze bells (some models now in the Bayerisches National Museum, Munich). In addition, some of his preliminary wood models for sculpture survive, such as a bozzetto for one of the so-called Starnberg saints of 1754/5 (Bayerisches National Museum). In 1752/3 he executed the figure of the Virgin of the Immaculate Conception for the high altarpiece of the parish church of Kopřivná (Geppersdorf) in Bohemia (now the Czech Republic). He set up his own workshop in Munich

in 1754, where he remained until his premature death. Die Wies, the Bavarian church built by the architect and stuccoist Dominikus Zimmermann (1745-54) was adorned with sculptures by Günther, as well as paintings and stucco ornament by Dominikus's brother, Johann Baptist Zimmermann. The fame of Die Wies led to Günther's own renown. In 1757 he was appointed *hofbefreit* sculptor by the Elector of Bavaria, Charles Albert (1697-1745). The title *hofbefreit* meant he was free of guild rules and was allowed to employ more than the two apprentices allowed by the guild, although he was not paid a salary by the court. He was never indeed appointed as court sculptor, despite his request for such an appointment in 1773. He worked at the Benedictine abbey church at Rott am Inn from 1761-2 and was to produce processional groups of the *Annunciation* and the *Pietà* for the church of St Peter and St Paul at Weyarn in 1763. His *Guardian Angel* was originally a processional sculpture commissioned by the prior of the Carmelite monastery of St Nicholas in Munich, signed and dated 1763 on a piece of paper recently found in the base. The group was acquired by the Marian congregation of the Bürgersaal in Munich after secularization in 1810. His *Christ at the Column* is at the Detroit Institute of Arts, signed and dated 1754. He executed the Starnberg high altar, c. 1765-8, and the Freising-Neustift high altar, 1765. Günther carried out allegorical reliefs as architectural sculpture for the Schloss at Sünching (1761/2), and shortly before he died he designed garden statuary for the Schloss at Nymphenburg, the finished stone sculptures being eventually carved by Roman Anton Boos. One of Günther's last works is his great Nenningen *Pietà* of 1774. (Woeckel 1975; Volk 1991; Hertel 2011; Statnik 2019)

Johann Baptist Hagenauer (1732-1810)

Hagenauer was a native of Salzburg. With the support of the Prince-Archbishop of Salzburg, Sigismund Graf Schrattenbach (1698-1771), and his own uncle, Johann Lorenz von Hagenauer (1712-92), he studied at the Vienna Academy of Fine Arts from 1754 onwards, training in the use of plaster, bronze and lead. He went on from there to the Accademia Clementina in Bologna, and also studied in Florence and Rome in 1762-64. Returning to Salzburg in 1764, he was appointed court sculptor (*Hofstatuarius*). From 1771 he worked for both the Munich and Viennese courts; in 1774 he was appointed director of the sculpture

class at the Academy in Vienna, succeeding Messerschmidt in this post. He executed sculpture for the park at Schönbrunn Palace with Johann Wilhelm Beyer (1725-96) in 1774-9. Like Donner, Hagenauer represented the transition from baroque to classicism, while also heralding the rococo. (Saur 1992-2019, Vol. 67, pp. 438-40)

Paul Heermann (1673-1732)

He was a leading sculptor in Dresden in the first third of the eighteenth century. He worked with his uncle Johann Georg Heermann at Schloss Troja in Prague in his youth, and subsequently travelled to Rome in about 1700, settling in Dresden in 1701/2. He worked in ivory and provided models for Meissen porcelain. His large-scale sculptures include his work at the Zwinger in Dresden (1710-18), where he worked alongside Balthasar Permoser; his marble bust of *August the Strong* of c. 1718 (Albertinum, Dresden); and marble busts of the Four Seasons of c. 1720 (also Albertinum, Dresden). (Trusted 2013, p. 85; *Neue Deutsche Biographie* n.d.; Koja and Kryza-Gersch 2020, pp. 112-21)

Christian Jorhan the Elder (1727-1804)

A sculptor, draughtsman and printmaker active primarily in Landshut in Lower (South) Bavaria, he trained initially under his father Wenzeslaus (d. 1752), who probably came from Bohemia. His sculptural style was profoundly influenced by Johann Baptist Straub, with whom he studied in Munich in about 1744, probably alongside his near-contemporary Ignaz Günther. After travelling in Riedlingen and Salzburg (his *Wanderschaft*), he studied at the Augsburg Academy for three years, before settling in Landshut in 1755. Like Straub and Günther, his work typifies rococo sculpture in Bavaria. (Volk 1981, p. 41; *Neue Deutsche Biographie* n.d.)

Johann Joachim Kändler (1706-75)

A sculptor and porcelain modeller, he was born in the Saxon village of Fischbach, and was apprenticed to a sandstone sculptor from Zeitz, Johann Christoph Feige the Elder (b. 1689) in Dresden. Kändler continued training as a journeyman from 1723 onwards under the sculptor Johann Benjamin Thomae (1682-1751), an assistant of Balthasar Permoser. In 1723 Kändler worked alongside Thomae on the decoration of the Green Vaults. Kändler was appointed as a sculptor at the Saxon court in 1730, and in June 1731 he was employed as a modeller at the Meissen porcelain factory, founded in 1710, after Johann Friedrich Böttger had discovered the secret of the manufacture of hard paste porcelain. Initially Kändler assisted the modeller Johann Gottlieb Kirchner, but he was to become head of the sculpture department at the factory in 1733, following the departure of Kirchner, with whom he may have had a dispute. In 1740 Kändler was additionally appointed teacher at the Meissen drawing school. None of his documented wood carving survives, although some sandstone sculptures have been preserved in the Meissen Museum, and in some local churches. Despite significant successes at the Meissen factory, notably in the creation of the large figures of animals by Johann Gottlieb Kirchner, it was not until Kändler's appointment in 1731 that the art of modelling in porcelain truly flourished. Kändler was tasked with continuing the series of large animals that Kirchner had begun for Augustus the Strong, and that were technically difficult to produce because of their size. Kändler created unique, richly animated works. Not only did he devise new spouts, handles and terrine feet in ingenious animal and plant forms, but he decorated the flat surfaces of his ceramic creations with delicate reliefs. He also created lively freestanding statuettes and groups, including commedia dell'arte figures and courtly scenes. His most notable works are the Sulkowski service of 1735/7 and the Swan Service of 1737/41. (Gröger 1956; Bursche 1980; Pietsch 2006; Röbbig 2008; Kappel 2018, pp. 30-4; *Neue Deutsche Biographie* n.d.)

Leonhard Kern (1588-1662)

He worked in a variety of materials, including alabaster, wood and bronze, as well as ivory. Born in Forchtenberg, Baden-Württemberg, the son of the sculptor Michael Kern the Elder, he trained initially with his older brother Michael Kern the Younger (1580-1649). He was in Italy from 1609 to 1613/14, spending time in Rome and Florence and also visiting North Africa and Slovenia. On his return to Germany he worked with his brother Michael, before going to Heidelberg, where he was employed by Frederick V Count Palatinate (1596-1632), the Protestant 'Winter King'. From Heidelberg he carried out commissions for Nuremberg, including stone sculptures for the pediments of antique rulers for the portals of Nuremberg town hall. Because of the upheavals caused by the Thirty Years' War, and Frederick V's departure for Prague in 1619 to become King of Bohemia (and shortly to be defeated at the Battle of

the White Mountain in 1620), Kern left Heidelberg, settling in Schwäbisch Hall in 1620. In 1648 he visited Cleve, one of the seats of the Elector of Brandenburg, Frederick William (1620-88), and was appointed court sculptor for one year. The ivories he carved for the elector include a portrait of the elector's infant son, Kurprinz William Henry von Brandenburg (1648-49), who died as a young child (destroyed in 1945). His ivory group of *Adam and Eve* (nude portraits of the elector and his consort Louise Henrietta) stands out as a particularly fine example of his work (Bode Museum, Berlin). (Grünenwald 1969; Siebenmorgen 1988 and 1990; Maué 1997-2005, Vol. 1/2, pp. 35-7; Trusted 2013, p. 31; Laue and Spenlé 2016; *Leonhard Kern* 2021)

Johann Gottlieb Kirchner (1706-after 1737)

He was taught sculpture by his brother Christian Kirchner (1691-1732), who was an assistant of Balthasar Permoser in Dresden. On 23 April 1726 he was appointed as a modeller at the Meissen porcelain factory, a date that could be said to mark the birth of European figurative porcelain. He had great difficulty, however, overcoming the technical difficulties caused by the material in terms of shape and firing. He resigned from the factory in 1729 and went to Weimar, where he became a court sculptor. But he returned to Meissen in May 1730 at the request of the factory's Board of Directors, and at his own wish. Nevertheless, when Johann Joachim Kändler was hired as a modeller the following year, tensions arose between the two men. In 1732 Kirchner tendered his resignation once more, leaving in 1733. He may have subsequently worked as a sculptor and painter in Berlin, as well as undertaking architectural sculpture in Dresden in 1737. His porcelain bust of one of the court jesters, *Joseph Frölich*, of c. 1730 demonstrates his sculptural abilities, as do his large ceramic birds and animals (Staatliche Kunstsammlungen Dresden). (Fleming and Honour 1989, p. 446; Bursche 1980; Pietsch 2006; Röbbig 2008; Kappel 2018, pp. 29-30; *Neue Deutsche Biographie* n.d.)

Hans Krumper (Krumpper) (c. 1570-1634)

An architect, sculptor, stuccoist and painter, he was the son of the Weilheim sculptor and cabinetmaker Adam Krumper (1542/3-1624/5), and the brother-in-law of Hans Degler. Like Degler, Georg Petel and Christoph Angermair, he is of the so-called Weil-

heim school. From 1584 to 1590 he trained under Hubert Gerhard in Munich, and undertook a year's travel in Italy, though no details of this trip are known. Following this apprenticeship he worked with his father for Duke William V (1548-1626; abdicated 1597) in 1590 at the Munich court, and had contact with the *Kunstintendant* (art director) Friedrich Sustris (c. 1540-99), later marrying Sustris's daughter. Employed by Duke (later Elector) Maximilian I (1573-1651) at Munich from 1609 to 1632, his most celebrated work is perhaps the bronze *Patrona Boiariæ* made in 1615, and the four bronze *Virtues* for the façade of the Residenz, Munich (1614-16). His bronze tomb of Louis IV, Emperor of Bavaria (1282-1347; r. 1314-47) of 1619-21, including the over-life-size figures of Duke William IV of Bavaria (1493-1550; r. 1508-50) and his son Duke Albert V (1528-79; r. 1550-79) (the great-grandfather and grandfather respectively of Maximilian), was made for the Frauenkirche in Munich. It is a seminal seventeenth-century monumental bronze ensemble for Bavarian sculpture. As a stuccoist Krumper was also responsible for the interior stucco and grotesque decorations of Maximilian's Residenz, and additionally he supplied designs and models for goldsmiths. (Feulner 1926, pp. 26-7; Feuchtmayr, in Thieme-Becker; Saur 1992-2019, Vol. 82, pp. 96-8; Diemer 1980; *Neue Deutsche Biographie* n.d.)

Adam Lenckhardt (1610-61)

He was active mainly in Vienna, though born in Würzburg, where he trained initially with his father, Nikolaus Lenckhardt. He subsequently travelled to Italy and elsewhere from 1632 onwards. In 1638 he settled in Vienna, and from 1642 to 1660 was employed by Elector Charles Eusebius von Liechtenstein (1611-84) as his official court sculptor (*Kammerbildhauer*). He specialised in small-scale sculpture and ivory. His ivory sculptures rank high among the ivory masterpieces produced in Vienna at that time. (Baumstark and Volk 1995; Trusted 2013, p. 36)

Gottfried Christian Leygebe (1630-83)

Born at Freystadt, Schlesien, he was a die-cutter, medallist and sculptor. In 1645 he went to Nuremberg to train with the armourer Albrecht Liechtmann. He specialised in engraving on iron, making contact with Georg Pfründt (1603-63), an expert in metalworking. Appointed to the Brandenburg court in 1668 as sculptor, die-cutter and medallist, he moved to Berlin, where he executed portraits in clay and wax, medals, decorative motifs for cannons, and a games board in silver and gold. He produced commemorative coins and a bronze relief of Elector Frederick William (1620-1688) in 1671, as well as the small equestrian figure in iron of the elector as St George, now in the Bode Museum, Berlin. (Nagler 1872-85, Vol. VIII, pp. 343-4; Hildebrand and Theuerkauff 1981, pp. 14 and 136-7; *Neue Deutsche Biographie* n.d.)

Johann Christoph Ludwig (von) Lücke (1703-80)

The son, or perhaps the nephew, of Carl August Lücke the Elder (c. 1688-c. 1730), Lücke may have trained under Balthasar Permoser in Dresden, working there as well as in Hamburg, Bremen, London (1726 and 1757-60), the Netherlands and France. He was the first *Modellmeister* (master modeller) in Vienna in 1750-1. He is also recorded in Copenhagen in 1752, and in Schwerin from 1742 onwards, and again in Dresden, before settling in Danzig (Gdańsk) until his death in 1780. He specialised in ivory sculpture, though he also provided models for the Meissen porcelain factory, and for those at Vienna and Fürstenberg, as well as for the faience factory at Hamburg. He also produced a pair of monumental sandstone lions for the park of the Schloss at Ahrensburg, Hamburg in 1765. (Theuerkauff and Möller 1977, pp. 175-6; Theuerkauff 1986, pp. 193-204; Trusted 2013, pp. 95-100; Kappel 2017, pp. 409-33; Kappel 2018, pp. 28-9; *Neue Deutsche Biographie* n.d.)

Lorenzo Mattielli (1687-1748)

Born in Vicenza, he trained under Orazio Marinali (1643-1720). From 1711 he worked at the court of Vienna, under the protection of Wilhelmina Amalia von Braunschweig-Lüneburg (1673-1742), consort of Emperor Joseph I (1678-1711). He was named court sculptor to Joseph's successor and brother Emperor Charles VI (1685-1740) in 1714. In 1738 he was summoned to Dresden by Elector Frederick Augustus III (1696-1763), King of Poland (known as Augustus the Strong), and in 1739 was appointed the first royal court sculptor. He produced seventy-eight over-life-size sandstone statues for the Hofkirche (Court Church), Dresden. He also executed sculpture for the baroque garden of the Brühl-Marcolini Palace, at Friedrichstadt, Dresden, producing the Neptune Fountain there in 1741-6. (Grove Art Online)

Christoph Maucher (1642-1706/7)

A leading sculptor in ivory and amber in the late seventeenth century from Schwäbisch Gmünd, Maucher also produced sculpture in stone, and was at the court of Charles Eusebius von Liechtenstein (1611-84) for nine months in 1667. He settled in Danzig (Gdańsk) in 1670, where he probably worked with the amber sculptor Nikolaus Turow on the great amber throne, made as a diplomatic gift to be presented to the Holy Roman Emperor Leopold I (1640-1711) by Frederick William the Great Elector of Brandenburg (1620-88). Maucher was permitted by the city of Danzig to work as a sculptor in 1684, despite objections from the amber guild, since he was not a guild member. But he had clearly acquired an international reputation, epitomised by his monumental ivory sculpture of the Apotheosis of Leopold I (Kunsthistorisches Museum, Vienna). Amber sculptures by him are housed in the Victoria and Albert Museum, London, and the Bode Museum, Berlin. His younger brother Johann Michael Maucher (1645-1701) was also active as an ivory sculptor. (Hildebrand and Thuerkauff 1981, pp. 196-8; Trusted 1984; Trusted 1985, pp. 59-63; Ehmer 1992)

Franz Xaver Messerschmidt (1736-83)

He was the nephew of Johann Baptist Straub, and trained with him from 1746 onwards in Munich, and then under another uncle, Philipp Jakob Straub (1706-74), in Graz. In 1755 he enrolled as a student in the Academy of Fine Arts in Vienna. After training as a wood carver, he also learnt the techniques of stone carving and working in metal. He made numerous official portraits. In 1765 he travelled to London and Rome. He was appointed professor of sculpture at the Academy in Vienna but retired when he fell mentally ill in 1774. From 1777 onwards he was in Pressburg, producing his character heads. (Saur 1992-2019, Vol. 89, pp. 201-4; *Messerschmidt* 2001)

Balthasar Permoser (1651-1732)

Born in Kammer bei Otting, Salzburg (now part of the Bavarian town of Traunstein), he was one of the greatest German baroque sculptors, producing both large- and small-scale pieces. He trained with Wolfgang Weissenkirchner the Younger (1639-1703) in Salzburg from at least 1667, and perhaps as early as 1663. From c. 1671 he was in Vienna, where he trained with Tobias Kracker (active 1650-91). In Vienna he almost certainly learnt ivory carving, probably with Johann Caspar Schenck (c. 1620-

74). He may also have known the work of another ivory sculptor, Balthasar Griessmann (1620-1706), who was active in both Salzburg and Vienna in the 1660s. In 1675/6 Permoser went to Italy, where he initially worked in Rome, and where he executed several/various ivory carvings, some apparently made in friendly rivalry with the Netherlandish ivory sculptor Francis van Bossuit (1635-92). The two Northern artists would also have come into contact with the Italian sculptors Giovanni Battista Foggini (1652-1725) and Carlo Marcellini (c. 1644-1713) at the Florentine Academy in Rome. By 1682, and possibly by 1677, Permoser was in Florence, where he joined Foggini's studio. In Florence Permoser produced ivories for Ferdinando de' Medici (1663-1713), Grand Prince of Tuscany. He also created stone sculptures for the portal of the church of St Michael and Gaetano in Florence (1683-9), and a marble bust of Anthony Ulrich, Duke of Braunschweig-Lüneburg (1633-1714; r. 1685-1714). He was called to Dresden by John George III, Elector of Saxony (1647-91; r. 1680-91), probably through the mediation of the elector's son, Prince Frederick Augustus, later Augustus II the Strong, King of Poland (1670-1733; r. 1697-1733), when the prince was on his Grand Tour in Italy in 1689. Permoser continued to work in ivory when he settled in Dresden, executing the *Four Seasons* in 1695, the only signed and dated ivories known by him, acquired by Louis Rudolph, Duke of Braunschweig-Lüneburg (1671-1735) when he was visiting Dresden, and now in the Herzog Anton Ulrich-Museum, Braunschweig. Two other ivory versions of Permoser's *Seasons* are known, while a third once in Doccia is now lost. Ceramic variants of the series were manufactured at the Ginori factory in Doccia in c. 1770. Similarly, porcelain versions of Permoser's later ivory group of *Hercules and Omphale* of c. 1700 were produced at the Fürstenberg factory in Brandenburg in 1773. In 1697 Permoser was to return to Italy, and stayed for a year in Salzburg en route, sculpting stone atlantes for a doorway. He probably worked with Andreas Schlüter at the Berlin Palace (Schloss) and at the Charlottenburg Palace, Berlin, c. 1704-9. This was during the Great Northern War between Sweden and other European powers, causing disruption in Saxony and forcing Permoser to absent himself from Dresden. By 1709, however, he had returned to the Saxon court, where his most important sculptures are the monumental marble figures he carved for the

Zwinger, the structure designed by the architect Matthäeus Daniel Pöppelmann (1662-1736) in 1710-18. Permoser's assistants on that project included Paul Egell, Paul Heermann and Johann Benjamin Thomae (1682-1751). He also undertook marble figures for the tomb of Electress Anne Sophia of Saxony (d. 1717) and Wilhelmina Ernestine of the Palatinate (d. 1706) in the cathedral at Freiberg (1703/12), complementing the earlier bronzes in the cathedral by Carlo di Cesare del Palagio. Permoser's marble *Apotheosis of Prince Eugene of Savoy* (1663-1736) dates from 1718-21 (Belvedere, Vienna), while the pulpit and figures of the Church Fathers he made for the Catholic court church (*Hofkirche*), Dresden, were produced in 1725. His marble *Christ at the Column* of 1728 incorporates a signed and dated self-portrait at the back, which depicts the artist at the age of seventy-seven (formerly Taschenbergpalais, now Staatliche Kunstsammlungen, Dresden). At the end of his life, he produced a sandstone crucifix group for his own tomb (1730/31) (chapel of the Catholic churchyard, Dresden). In addition, Permoser produced models for the court goldsmith and jeweller Johann Melchior Dinglinger (1664-1731), as well as for the Meissen porcelain factory. He was a seminal influence on later work of the eighteenth century. One of the pupils of Permoser's assistant Paul Egell was Johann Joachim Kändler (1706-75), a leading modeller at the Meissen factory. Permoser could thus perhaps be said to be the grandfather of some of the finest Meissen models. (Asche 1978; Kappel 2001; Schmidt 2012, pp. 203-29; Trusted 2013, pp. 42-4; Kappel 2001; Kappel 2017, pp. 214-17 and 218-20; *Neue Deutsche Biographie* n.d.)

Georg Petel (1601/2-35)
Regarded by his patrons as the most outstanding ivory carver of all time, he was born in Weilheim, Bavaria, the son of a cabinetmaker and sculptor, Clemens Petel (c. 1560-1612), and is considered to be a member of the so-called Weilheim school of sculptors, along with Hans Degler, Hans Krumper and Christoph Angermair. He worked mainly in wood and ivory, though he also produced some important bronzes. Initially he trained in Weilheim, probably under Bartholomäus Steinle, and then almost certainly as an ivory carver under Angermair in Munich, probably while Angermair was working on the ivory coin cabinet for the court. At the start of the Thirty Years' War in 1618 he became an itinerant craftsman, travelling to the

Netherlands and elsewhere, and meeting Peter Paul Rubens (1577-1640) in Antwerp 1620/1. He later went to Paris and Rome. There he met Anthony van Dyck (1599-1641) and François Du Quesnoy (1597-1643). He was in Genoa 1622-4, returning to Antwerp in 1624, visiting Rubens again. He settled in Augsburg in late 1624, remaining there for the rest of his life, apart from occasional trips to the Southern Netherlands. He died prematurely, probably of the plague. (Feuchtmayer and Schädler 1973; Schädler 1985; Krempel and Söding 2009)

(Johann) Matthias (Mathias) Rauchmiller (Rauchmüller) (1645-86)
A painter, sculptor and ivory carver, he was born at Radolfzell, near Lake Constance, and perhaps trained in the Schenck workshop. In his youth he may have travelled to the Netherlands, where he would have seen the work of Peter Paul Rubens (1577-1640). He could perhaps have assisted in the workshop of Lucas Faydherbe (1617-97) in Mechelen, or in the Quellinus workshop in Amsterdam. In about 1675 he was commissioned to make a marble tomb for Charles Heinrich von Metternich-Winneburg (1622-79), who was elected as Archbishop-Elector of Mainz in 1679, but who died before he could be consecrated. This tomb, in the Liebfrauenkirche, Trier, was one of the first funerary monuments to be made after the Thirty Years' War with a recumbent figure (earlier tombs showed the deceased kneeling). From 1675 onwards Rauchmiller executed the frescoes for the cathedral in Vienna and was appointed *hofbefreiter Maler* (court painter, though without receiving a salary). The ivory tankard depicting *The Rape of the Sabines*, signed and dated 1676 and now in the Liechtenstein Collection, is his masterpiece. His four alabaster statues of the Legnica/Liegnitz family are in the Piastów Chapel in the church of St John the Baptist, Legnica (formerly Liegnitz), Silesia, which he also painted with frescoes (1677-9). The contemporary alabaster tomb commemorating Adam Caspar von Arzat (d. 1676) was installed in the church of Mary Magdalene, Wrocław in 1679. The Plague Column in Vienna was based on Rauchmiller's designs of 1679, to be completed after his death by the architect Johann Bernard Fischer von Erlach and other artists in 1694, perhaps including Jacob Auer. Rauchmiller's clay model for St John Nepomuk for the Charles Bridge, Prague, dates from 1681 (National Gallery, Prague). The sculpture, executed in wood by Johann (Jan)

Brokoff and subsequently cast in bronze by Hieronymus Herold, a bell-maker of Nuremberg, was installed in 1683. The iconography of Nepomuk represented by that figure inspired numerous later sculptures. (Novotny and Poche 1947; Saur 1992-2019, Vol. 97, pp. 537-8; Birke 1981; *Neue Deutsche Biographie* n.d.)

Hans Reichle (c.1565/70-1634)
Born in Schongau in the south of Bavaria, the son of a sculptor and joiner, he trained in Munich, later working with the court sculptor Hubert Gerhard in 1586, producing bronze and terracotta sculptures for the Munich court. In 1588, Duke William V of Bavaria (1548-1626; abdicated 1597) sent him to acquire further training in Florence, where he remained for seven years. He was to join the workshop of Giambologna (1529-1608), later working on the equestrian monument to Cosimo I de' Medici (1591-3), becoming proficient in the art of bronze casting, as well as producing ephemeral decorative sculptures for the court. He returned to Munich in 1594/5, his earliest known independent work there being the bronze Magdalene at the foot of the crucifix by Giambologna, made in 1595 to the design of Friedrich Sustris (c. 1540-99). This was originally intended for the unfinished tomb of William V in the church of St Michael (*Michaelskirche*) in Munich, and is still in the church, although other elements of the tomb have been dispersed. The crucifix was designated as an epitaph for Duchess Renata of Lorraine (1544-1602), consort of William V. From 1596 to 1601, and again in 1607, he worked in Brixen for Prince-Bishop Andreas of Austria (1558-1600) (cardinal and son of the Habsburg Archduke Ferdinand of Austria, later Holy Roman Emperor), and for his successor, on forty-four terracotta figures of the prince-bishops' antecedents for the courtyard of the Residenz. He accompanied Cardinal Andreas on a journey to Rome in 1600, but on the cardinal's sudden death Reichle returned to Florence to work on a bronze relief for the doors of Pisa Cathedral. In 1602 he went to Augsburg, producing monumental bronzes, including the great figure of St Michael on the façade of the Armoury (1603/6), and the crucifixion group in the church of SS. Ulrich and Afra (1605), inspired by the earlier crucifixion in St Michael's church. He also produced a series of thirty-two over-life-size terracotta figures of saints and prophets for the choir and transepts of SS. Ulrich and Afra (mostly destroyed in 1873 when the church was renovated; fragmentary heads are in the Maximilian

Museum, Augsburg). Reichle settled in Brixen in 1607, where he spent the rest of his life, active primarily as a building engineer. (Feulner 1926, pp. 30-2; Saur 1992-2019, Vol. 98, pp. 140-2; Diemer 2006; Diemer 2012; *Bella Figura* 2015; *Neue Deutsche Biographie* n.d.)

Christoph Rodt (c. 1578-1634)

He was based in Neuburg an der Kammel, west of Munich, the son and grandson of cabinetmakers. He trained and later briefly worked with his father, Hans. He was also probably apprenticed to Hans Degler in Weilheim, before embarking on his journeyman travels (*Wanderschaft*), perhaps around Lake Constance, which must have taken place at some time between 1592 and 1601. Having established his own workshop at Neuburg an der Kammel, he worked there until 1627 and then for the rest of his life at Großkötz, only 15 kilometres away. His masterpiece, and his earliest known work, is the vast polychromed and gilt wood altarpiece of 1604 at the church of St Martin, Illertissen, about 30 kilometres from Neuburg an der Kammel. He also executed other altarpieces in Swabia, from which in some cases only the figures are extant; these include the retables at Schwabmünchen (c. 1620), Gundelfingen (1623/5), and the monastic church at Roggenburg (1628). He executed a *Deposition* for the parish church of Neuburg an der Kammel, and single devotional figures of the Virgin and Child and large crucifixes for other churches. He may already have been ill in the late 1620s, before dying relatively young in 1634. (Hartmetz 2019)

Christoph Daniel Schenck (1633-91)

He was born and died in Constance. His work includes life-size altar figures, as well as small-scale ivories and boxwoods. He probably trained under his father, Johann Christoph Schenck (1612-after 1656). The high altar in the former monastery church at Kreuzlingen, executed in 1650-3, is the first real evidence of his work. The expressive gestures and narrow parallel folds of drapery recall fifteenth- and early sixteenth-century sculptures and panel paintings. One of his relatives was Johann Caspar Schenck (c. 1620-74), who probably taught ivory carving to Balthasar Permoser in Vienna (Haag 1996)

Andreas Schlüter (c. 1659-1714)

He was probably born in Danzig, the son of a sculptor, and was active as a sculptor and architect. His early works were executed in Poland, where he went in 1681, working in Warsaw and elsewhere, employed by the King of Poland, Johann III Sobieski (1629-96). Elector Frederick William III of Brandenburg (later King Frederick I) (1657-1713) called Schlüter to the court in 1694, and before he started serious work in the Prussian city the elector sent him to the Netherlands, France and perhaps Italy to study and purchase plaster casts of antique sculptures for the newly founded Academy of Arts in Berlin (1695-6). In 1695 he was commissioned to make sandstone sculptures of heads of dying warriors for the arches of the Berlin Armoury (*Zeughaus*), a building begun by the architect Johann Arnold Nering (1659-95). Plaster aftercasts of the clay models for these are in the Academy of Arts, Berlin (on loan to the Bode Museum). His great equestrian bronze statue of the Great Elector, cast by the founder Johann Jacobi (1661-1726), dates from 1696 onwards. This was originally placed on the Lange Brücke leading to the Berlin Palace (Schloss). It is now to be seen in the court of honour in front of Charlottenburg Palace. His life-size bronze statue of Frederick III was cast by Jacobi in 1698 (the original is lost, though two aftercasts of 1972 survive). In 1699 he designed the façade of the Berlin Palace, partly destroyed in the Second World War, and demolished in 1950. From c. 1704-9 he may have been assisted at the Berlin Palace and at Charlottenburg by Balthasar Permoser. The memorial he designed commemorating the court goldsmith Daniel Männlich and his wife, of 1699/1700, is in the church of St Nicholas, Berlin, while the Italianate pulpit he made for the church of St Mary, Berlin, dates from 1703. Schlüter was appointed Rector of the Academy of Arts in 1698, retaining this post until 1713. The bronze tin sarcophagi he designed for King Frederick I (1713) and his consort Sophie Charlotte of Hanover (1668-1705) (1705) were installed in Berlin Cathedral. On the death of the king in 1713 Schlüter went to Moscow to enter the service of Czar Peter the Great (1672-1725), but he was to die there shortly after his arrival in 1714. Schlüter was one of the most important sculptors of the North German Baroque, and one of the inventors of a unified, stately architecture previously unknown in Prussia. (Ladendorf 1937; Kühn 1977; *Andreas Schlüter* 2014; Kessler 2014c)

Thomas Schwanthaler (1634-1707)

He was a Bavarian/Austrian sculptor, working in stone and wood, and one of the best known of the Schwanthaler dynasty of sculptors, active particularly in Ried in Upper Austria. He probably trained with his father Hans (d. 1656), and in Martin Zürn's workshop in Braunau until 1656, when he inherited his father's shop. In 1660/1 he produced his first independent work, figures for the altarpiece in the parish church of Eitzing. In 1661 he undertook the high altarpiece for the church at Ried. He was highly productive, making many altarpieces for churches in the Inn valley. In later years he and his workshop also produced stone tombs. In addition, he carved small-scale sculptures in wood and ivory. His sculpture is redolent of the Roman baroque, in particular the work of both Gian Lorenzo Bernini (1598-1680) and François Du Quesnoy (1597-1643). Four of his sons became sculptors. (*Schwanthaler* 1974)

Georg Schweigger (1613-90)

Schweigger was a sculptor and medallist based in Nuremberg, working in wood, stone, terracotta and bronze, including fine medallic portraits of Lutheran Reformers. He executed Kelheim stone reliefs of the life of St John the Baptist in the Habsburg imperial collections in Vienna and at Schloss Ambras in the 1640s. His international reputation was noted by the contemporary writer and artist Joachim von Sandrart (1606-68). Schweigger's monumental bronze Neptune fountain made for the Hauptmarkt in Nuremberg in 1652/60 is now in the Peterhof in St Petersburg (a cast is in Nuremberg), while his Kelheim stone relief of *The Birth and Naming of St John the Baptist* (after Albrecht Dürer) of 1642 is in the British Museum, London. (Hildebrand and Thuerkauff 1981, pp. 138-41; *Dürers Verwandlung* 1981, pp. 125-30 and pp. 326-53; *Neue Deutsche Biographie* n.d.)

Matthias Steinl (c. 1644-1727)

He was a wide-ranging Austrian artist, active as a sculptor, painter, architect and designer. He probably came from the area around Salzburg, though he may have trained in the Netherlands and Prague. He worked in Silesia (now Poland), producing polychromed wood sculptures for the Cistercian abbey of Leubus (Lubiąż) (1676-80). In 1682 he moved to Breslau (Wrocław), carving sculptures for the high altar of the Heinrichau Abbey (Henryków). He was appointed court ivory carver (*Kammerbeinstecher*) by Emperor Leopold I (1640-1711) at Vienna in 1688, retaining that post until his death in 1727. For the imperial court he carved the *Allegory of the Elements of Water and Air* from a walrus tusk, c. 1688-90, and three monumental ivory equestrian statues of Emperor

Leopold I (1690/3), King Joseph I (dated 1693) and Emperor Charles VI (1711/12) (Kunsthistorisches Museum, Vienna). His numerous marble sculptures are at Klosterneuburg, as well as a pulpit for the Dominican church, Vienna; two altars for St Stephen's Cathedral, Vienna, of 1700 and 1708; and the pulpit, side altars, pews and confessionals for St Peter's church, Vienna, of 1716 and 1726. He also designed monstrances for Klosterneuburg (1710-14) and Herzogenburg (1722). (Pühringer-Zwanowetz 1966; Trusted 2013, p. 47)

Bartholomäus Steinle (c. 1580-1628)

A Weilheim sculptor who specialised in polychromed wood altarpieces, he was probably taught by Hans Degler, before undertaking travels (*Wanderschaft*) in Constance and Switzerland, settling in Weilheim in 1605. He assisted Degler on the altarpieces at SS. Ulrich and Afra in Augsburg (1604-7), as well as working for the court in Munich. His workshop produced various polychromed wood retables and some stucco work in and around Weilheim, including at Polling, Rottenbuch and Wessobrunn, though not all his altarpieces survive in their entirety. His style partly recalls the late gothic of German sculptors such as Hans Leinberger (c. 1475/80-after 1531), and partly the Italian high renaissance, as seen in the work of Carlo di Cesare del Palagio, whose terracotta figures of 1582 were in the church of SS. Ulrich and Afra. Steinle's most important extant work is the twelve-meter-high altarpiece of 1609-11 at the abbey of Stams in the Tyrol, depicting the Tree of Jesse. He was almost certainly Georg Petel's first teacher, having been appointed one of his two guardians on the death of Petel's father in 1612. He was a town councillor in Weilheim from 1624 to 1628, dying prematurely, probably of the plague. (Sauermost 1988, pp. 93-103; Zohner 1993)

Johann Baptist Straub (1704-84)

Born in Wiesensteig, Baden-Württemberg, he came from a family of wood carvers. Both his grandfather and father were cabinetmakers, but his father, Johann Georg Straub the Elder (1674-1755), was also a sculptor, who initially taught Johann Baptist and three of his brothers, all of whom became sculptors. In about 1721 he went to train in Munich under the court sculptor Gabriel Luidl (1688-1741), who was originally from Antwerp. There he would have seen the works of another court sculptor, Guillielmus de Grof (1676-1742), and

the sculpture of Aegid Verhelst the Elder (1696-1749), as well as the work of Egid Quirin Asam (1692-1750), who can be seen as a precursor. Through De Grof, Straub learnt the art of lead casting. From 1726 to 1734 he was in Vienna, working for Abbot Anton Vogl von Krallern (1666-1751) and carrying out his first independent sculpture, pews and the pulpit for the church of the *Schwarzspanierkloster* (the Abbey of the Black Robed Spaniards). In Vienna he came into contact with the court architect Joseph Bernhard Fischer von Erlach and the Italian designer Giuseppe Galli Bibiena (1696-1757), as well as Lorenzo Mattielli. Andreas Faistenberger invited him to return to Munich in 1734 but was to die the following year. In 1737 Straub was appointed court sculptor by the Elector of Bavaria, Charles Albert (1697-1745). His first known independent commission was the high altarpiece at Au in 1735. He worked with various architects, including Fischer von Erlach, François de Cuvilliés the Elder and Johann Michael Fischer (1692-1766). As the teacher of Ignaz Günther, Christian Jorhan the Elder (1727-1804), his nephew Franz Xaver Messerschmidt, and Roman Anton Boos, he has been called the 'father of Bavarian rococo sculpture'. In addition to secular decorative sculpture in Munich, he produced funerary monuments and numerous figures and reliefs for altarpieces. Many preliminary drawings for his works also survive, including designs for altarpieces, vases and fantastical scrollwork. His wood figures generally have relatively simple surface finishes, painted white with gold edging, but his figurative style is more naturalistic than Günther's. His major works are in the churches at Andechs, Berg am Laim, Diessen am Ammersee, Fürstenzell (the tabernacle on the high altar), in the Residenz at Munich (the Cuvilliés theatre), and at Nymphenburg (the Diana and Hercules sleighs in the Marstall Museum). (Steiner 1974; Volk 1984; *Neue Deutsche Biographie* n.d.)

Anton Sturm (1690-1757)

A Tyrolean sculptor, he was apprenticed to the sculptor Johann Paul Tschiderer in Donauwörth from 1705 to 1709. He worked in both stucco and wood, completing work in Füssen (1715-25) and Ottobeuren (1722-5) as well as elsewhere in Bavaria, notably alongside the Zimmermann brothers at the church of Die Wies, where he completed figures of the four early Church Fathers in wood. His small wood group of *The Death of St Benedict* is in the collection of the Bayerisches National Museum in

Munich (*Anton Sturm* 1990; Kirchmeir and Hasenmuller n.d. [1991?]; personal communication Jens Burk, Munich)

Paul Strudel (1648-1708)

A sculptor, architect and painter, he was born in the village of Cles in the Tyrol. He studied first with his father, and later in Venice with the painter Johann Carl Loth (1632-98), and the Flemish sculptor Giusto (Josse) le Corte (1627-79). He was also inspired by the work of Gian Lorenzo Bernini (1598-1680) and Alessandro Algardi (1598-1654). In 1684 he arrived in Vienna, where he made three statues for Johann Adam I Andreas, Prince of Liechtenstein (1657/62-1712). He directed the iconography and manufacture of the sculpture for the eighteen-metre-high Vienna Plague Column (1686-93) for Emperor Leopold I (1640-1705). In 1686 he was employed as court painter at the Hofburg in Vienna, mostly working with his younger brother, the painter and sculptor Peter Strudel (1660-1714). He was commissioned to carve seven marble busts of the imperial family by Leopold in 1695 (Kunsthistorisches Museum, Vienna). In 1696 he was appointed court sculptor by Leopold I, and was charged to produce thirty-one life-size marble figures for the ancestor gallery of the Habsburgs (the Hof Bibliothek). By the time of his death he had delivered sixteen of these figures; the remainder were made by his brother Peter. Peter established the Academy of Fine Arts in Vienna in 1688, which temporarily closed at his death in 1714, and was reopened in 1725. Like Peter, and a third brother, Dominik, also a painter (1667-1715), Paul was given an imperial baronetcy for service to the imperial house as artist and engineer. (Barber 1984; Koller 1993; Grove Art Online; *Neue Deutsche Biographie* n.d.)

Ferdinand Tietz (Dietz) (1708-77)

Born probably in the region of Komotau (Chomutov) in Bohemia, he was the son of a sculptor, Johann Adam Dietz (1671-1742). He trained in his father's workshop, and subsequently with Matthias Bernhard Braun in Prague, and in Würzburg under the architect Johann Balthasar Neumann (1687-1753). He was employed by all the royal courts of Franconia. He executed a first series of garden sculptures at Schloss Seehof, near Bamberg (1747-52) for the Prince-Bishop of Bamberg, Johann Philipp Anton von Franckenstein (1695-1753), becoming court sculptor in 1748. In 1754 he was summoned by Prince-Bishop Franz Georg von Schönborn (1682-1756) to

Trier, where he was again appointed court sculptor. Here he created the most extensive of his architectural decorations for Neumann's Schloß Schönbornlust (now destroyed). Towards the end of his stay at Bamberg he executed sculptures for the façade and the magnificent staircase of the prince-bishop's Residenz. Returning to Bamberg, he decorated the gardens of the Residenz, and produced a gilded equestrian monument for the Seesbrücke bridge in Bamberg. Renovations in the gardens of Seehof (Nuremberg) led to commissions for numerous individual sculptures, including a tall, standing *Athena*. His sculptures for the parish church of St Paulinus at Trier (designed by Johann Balthasar Neumann) from 1755 to 1760, include a magnificent figure of the *Virgin of the Immaculate Conception*. From 1761 to 1763 Tietz executed a second series of sandstone sculptures for Seehof during the reign of Adam Friedrich von Sensheim (1708-79; Prince-Bishop of Würzburg, 1755-79; Prince-Bishop of Bamberg, 1757-79), including mythological figures, benches and decorative stonework; many are now lost or destroyed, although the monumental *Cascade* remains. From 1765 to 1768 he carved a range of sandstone figures of gods and goddesses, including a Mount Parnassus, for the garden of Veitshöchheim, the summer palace of the Würzburg prince-bishops. In 1927 many of the weathered originals were taken to the Mainfränkisches Museum in Würzburg to be replaced by copies in the garden. Some of Tietz's limewood bozzetti are in the Germanisches Nationalmuseum in Nuremberg; others are in The Metropolitan Museum of Art, New York. His polychromed limewood model for the element of *Water*, made for Seehof, is in the Museum für Kunst und Gewerbe, Hamburg. He was inspired above all by French print sources, notably the engravings by Simon Thomassin (1655-1733) after the figures at Versailles. His playful compositions and idiosyncratic decorative style epitomise rococo sculpture. (Lindemann 1989; Maué 1997-2005, Vol. 1, pp. 134-47; *Neue Deutsche Biographie* n.d.)

Simon Troger (1693-1768)

Troger's early training is unknown, though he may have studied in Italy. In 1723-5 he worked with Nikolaus Moll (1676-1754) in Innsbruck. By 1726 he was in Munich, working alongside Andreas Faistenberger in about 1730. He then opened his own workshop in the city, and was much patronized by the Elector of Bavaria, Maximilian III Joseph (1727-77; r. 1745-77). His groups of figures,

often depicting a biblical narrative or genre scenes, distinctively combine wood and ivory, frequently with inset glass eyes and sometimes with applied metal details. (Trusted 2013, pp. 101-4; *Neue Deutsche Biographie* n.d.)

Aegid (Egid) Verhelst the Elder (1696-1749)

A sculptor and stuccoist, working predominantly in wood but also in marble, stucco, lead and ivory, he trained in Antwerp, probably with his father Gillis Verhelst, and was in Munich from 1718 onwards. There he worked with his compatriot Guilliemus de Grof, as well as at the monastic church at Ettal in Bavaria intermittently from 1726 to 1736. He moved to Augsburg in 1738, collaborating with various goldsmiths, for whom he provided models. He completed four side altars and other sculptures for the abbey church at Diessen am Amersee in 1738-40, the pulpit of the abbey church at Ochsenhausen in 1741, as well as figures of the four Evangelists and two prophets at the church of Die Wies in Bavaria towards the end of his life. He taught his sons Ignaz Wilhelm (1729-92) and Placidus (1727-78?). (Grove Art Online)

Giuseppe Volpini (1670-1729)

Volpini was probably born in Milan. In 1704 he became the court sculptor in Ansbach, and in 1711 went to Munich, where he was to be appointed court sculptor in 1715. In 1728, Elector Charles Albert (1697-1745) named him Court-Inspector of Antiquities, with the task of restoring antique sculptures at the Residenz, as well as installing sculpture and stuccos in the elector's palaces and gardens. Many of his sculptures are in the gardens at Nymphenburg. (Feulner 1926, p. 4; Grove Art Online)

Adriaen de Vries (c. 1556-1626)

Born in the Hague, he was a truly international artist, renowned for his bronzes, made in the tradition of Giambologna (1529-1608). He was recorded in Giambologna's workshop in Florence in 1581. Subsequently he was in Milan working with Pompeo Leoni (1533-1608) on bronzes for the high altarpiece of San Lorenzo at the Escorial in Spain. He was briefly employed in Turin, and then worked for Emperor Rudolph II (1552-1612) in Prague from 1589 to 1594. His monumental bronze group of *Mercury and Psyche* made for the emperor dates from 1593 (Louvre, Paris). He then went to Rome from 1595 to 1602, providing models for the bronze *Mercury* and *Hercules and Hydra* fountains in 1596 for

Augsburg. In 1603 he returned to Prague, where he made two bronze portraits of Emperor Rudolph, a bust of 1603 (Kunsthistorisches Museum, Vienna), and a relief of 1609 (Victoria and Albert Museum, London). His bronze figure of the *Seated Christ* of 1607 (Liechtenstein Collection) was made for Prince Charles I of Liechtenstein (1569-1627). His great marble and bronze Resurrection group of 1618-20, commemorating Prince Ernst of Holstein-Schaumburg (1569-1622), is in the St Martini-Kirche, Stadthagen, Lower Saxony. He also executed important bronzes for the gardens of Wallenstein (now Waldštejn) Palace in Prague in 1623-6 for Albert von Wallenstein (1583-1634). These were plundered by the Swedish army towards the end of the Thirty Years' War in 1648, and are now in the Nationalmuseum, Stockholm (Larsson 1967; *Adriaen de Vries* 1999; Grove Art Online)

Johann Peter Wagner (1730-1809)

Taught by his father, Johann Thomas Wagner (b. 1691), he worked in wood and stone, including marble and alabaster, using clay bozzetti. He travelled as a journeyman (his *Wanderschaft*) during 1747, when he went to Vienna and Mannheim, where he worked under Paul Egell or his son Augustin (1730-86). He became assistant to Johann Wolfgang von der Auwera in Würzburg, and married Von der Auwera's widow in 1756, inheriting the workshop, along with his brother-in-law, Lukas von der Auwera (1710-66), Johann Wolfgang's son. From 1763 to 1766 he carved figures for the Four Ears (*Vieröhren*) Fountain in Würzburg, collaborating with Lukas von der Auwera. He produced fourteen groups of figures of the Stations of the Cross for the approach to the pilgrimage church of the Visitation (*Mariae Heimsuchung*), known as the Käppele, in Würzburg, completed in 1775. He had become court sculptor to Adam Frederick von Seinsheim, Prince-Bishop of Würzburg (1708-79) in 1771, carrying out extensive decorative sculptural work for the interior of the Residenz at Würzburg. His large and prolific workshop also produced sculptures for numerous churches in Franconia. (Trenschel 1969; Trenschel 1980a; Trenschel 1980b; *Neue Deutsche Biographie* n.d.)

Weilheim School

Weilheim, in the Pfaffenwinkel area of Upper Bavaria, is a small town located southwest of Munich and Augsburg. Various important sculptors were natives or settled in Weilheim from approximately 1590 to 1630, a period of fertile creative activity that was only curbed by the Thirty Years' War. Christoph Angermair, Hans Degler, Bartholomäus Steinle, Hans Krumper and Georg Petel are all members of the so-called Weilheim school. (Sauermost 1988)

Wessobrunn (Wessobrunner) School

The so-called Wessobrunn school of stucco workers, a term first coined in 1888, takes its name from the Wessobrunn Benedictine abbey in Bavaria, and surrounding villages. Over six hundred stuccoists from this region were active from the late seventeenth to the late eighteenth century. In the mid-eighteenth century the Zimmermann brothers, as well as the Feichtmayr and Feuchtmayer families, were amongst the dominant artists in this field. (Schnell 1972; Goldner and Bahnmüller 1992)

Jacob Zeller (c. 1581-1620)

He was an ivory turner and carver born in Essing near Regensburg, the son of the ivory turner Pancraz Zeller (active 1583-93), who was active in Colditz (between Freiberg and Leipzig in Saxony) and employed by Augustus, Elector of Saxony (1526-86; r. 1553-86) and his son Christian I (1560-91; r. 1586-91), though he does not seem to have been based in Dresden itself. Pancraz's son Jacob was in Dresden by 1611 at the latest, when he arrived in the city from Prague, and was appointed court ivory turner, with his own workshop in the Dresden palace. Among his numerous ivory pieces for the Dresden *Kunstkammer* (later exhibited in the Grünes Gewölbe) were virtuoso goblets and the so-called *Great Frigate* made for Johann Georg I, signed and dated 1620. (Kappel 2017, pp. 53-61; Tarnai and Weber 2017)

Dominikus Zimmermann (1685-1766) and Johann Baptist Zimmermann (1680-1758)

Born near Wessobrunn, the two brothers were both architects and stuccoists; Johann Baptist was also a fresco painter. The sons of Elias Zimmermann (1656-95), a stuccoist and stonemason from Wessobrunn, they almost certainly trained as stuccoists in Wessobrunn. Dominikus tended to work for the Church, while Johann Baptist carried out more commissions for the Bavarian court. From 1720 to 1726 Johann Baptist worked with the architect Joseph Effner (1687-1745) on stucco decorations for the staircase at the palace of Schleissheim, a favoured project of Elector Max Emmanuel (1662-1726). Johann Baptist obtained the protection of the Bavarian court (*Hofschutz*) in 1724, meaning that he did not have to abide by guild rules. In around 1727 he was appointed court stuccoist to Max Emmanuel's son, later Emperor Charles VII (1697-1745), and worked on stucco decoration of the Amalienburg designed by François de Cuvilliés the Elder (1734-9). Two of the brothers' greatest joint achievements were the architecture and stucco work they undertook at the pilgrimage churches at Steinhausen (1727-33) and Die Wies (1744-57). (Thon 1977; Bauer and Bauer 1985; Lampl 1987; *Neue Deutsche Biographie* n.d.)

Zürn Family (Sixteenth-Seventeenth Centuries)

The sculptor Hans Zürn the Elder (c. 1555-after 1631) had six sons who became artists. Jörg Zürn of Überlingen (1583/4-1635/8) produced the imposing high altarpiece at Überlingen Minster in 1613-16. Martin Zürn (1585/90-after 1645) and his younger brothers Michael (c. 1590-after 1651), Hans Jakob and David settled in the Inn valley in eastern Bavaria and Upper Austria. They are chiefly known for the altarpieces they produced in that region. Their style straddles the gothic and the baroque. (Zoege von Manteuffel 1998)

LIST OF RULERS
AND PATRONS

House of Griffins

Philip II Duke of Pomerania-Stettin (1573-1618; r. 1606-18).

House of Guelph (Braunschweig-Lüneburg)

Anthony Ulrich (1633-1714; r. 1685-1714) Duke of Brunswick-Lüneburg and ruling Prince of Brunswick-Wolfenbüttel from 1685 until 1704 jointly with his elder brother Rudolph August, and solely from 1704 until his death. The father of August William.

August William (1662-1731; r. 1714-31) Duke of Brunswick-Lüneburg. The son of Anthony Ulrich.

Rudolph August (1627-1704; r. 1685-1704) Duke of Brunswick-Lüneburg and ruling Prince of Brunswick-Wolfenbüttel from 1685 until 1704 jointly with his younger brother Anthony Ulrich.

House of Habsburg (Vienna and Prague)

Andrew of Austria (1558-1600; r. 1589-1600) Margrave of Burgau; Cardinal and Prince-Bishop of Constance and Brixen. The son of Ferdinand II Archduke of Austria.

Charles V (1500-58; r. 1519-58) Holy Roman Emperor and Archduke of Austria from 1519; King of Spain from 1516, and Lord of the Netherlands as titular Duke of Burgundy from 1506. The older brother of Ferdinand I. Charles VI Holy Roman Emperor, King of Hungary (1685-1740; r. 1711-40). The

son of Leopold I and younger brother of Joseph I.

Ferdinand I Holy Roman Emperor (1503-64; r. 1556-64) Holy Roman Emperor from 1556, King of Bohemia and Royal Hungary from 1526, and King of Croatia from 1527 until his death in 1564. The younger brother of Charles V, Holy Roman Emperor, and father of Ferdinand II, Archduke of Austria.

Ferdinand II Archduke of Austria and Imperial Count of Tyrol (1529-95; r. 1564-95). The son of Ferdinand I and uncle of Rudolph II; the father of Andrew of Austria.

Ferdinand II Holy Roman Emperor (1578-1637; r. as Holy Roman Emperor (1619-37), King of Bohemia (1617-19, 1620-37), and King of Hungary and Croatia (1618-37). He succeeded his childless cousin Matthias as Holy Roman Emperor and was the father of Emperor Ferdinand III.

Ferdinand III Holy Roman Emperor (1608-57; r. 1637-57). The son of Emperor Ferdinand II and older brother of Leopold Wilhelm Archduke of Austria.

Joseph I Holy Roman Emperor, King of Hungary (1678-1711; r. 1705-11). The son of Leopold I, and older brother of Charles VI. Married to Wilhelmina Amalia von Braunschweig-Lüneburg, and father of Maria Josepha, who married Augustus III Elector of Saxony.

Leopold I Holy Roman Emperor, King of Hungary (1640-1705; r. 1658-1705). The father of Joseph I and Charles VI. Leopold Wilhelm Archduke of Austria

(1614-62). The younger brother of Emperor Ferdinand III.

Maximilian II Holy Roman Emperor (1527-76; r. 1564-76), King of Bohemia and elected King of Germany (King of the Romans) 1562; King of Hungary and Croatia in 1563. The son of Ferdinand I and father of Rudolph II.

Matthias Holy Roman Emperor (1557-1619). Holy Roman Emperor 1612-19, Archduke of Austria 1608-19, King of Hungary and Croatia 1608-18 and King of Bohemia 1611-17. He was the brother of Emperor Rudolph II, whom he succeeded as Emperor; and the cousin of Emperor Ferdinand II, who succeeded him as emperor.

Maximilian III Archduke of Austria (1558-1616; r. 1612-16). The younger brother of Emperor Rudolph II.

Rudolph II, Holy Roman Emperor (1552-1612; r. 1576-1612), King of Hungary and Croatia (as Rudolph I, 1572-1608); King of Bohemia (1575-1608/11). The son of Maximilian II.

House of Hohenzollern (Prussia)

Frederick William (1620-88; r. 1640-88) Margrave and Prince-Elector of Brandenburg and Duke of Prussia, known as the Great Elector. The son of George William, and father of Frederick III.

Frederick III (1657-1713; r. 1688-1713) Margrave and Prince-Elector of Brandenburg and Duke of Prussia; from 1701 King in Prussia. The son of Frederick William.

George William (1595-1640; r. 1619-40), Margrave and Prince-Elector of Brandenburg and Duke of Prussia. The father of Frederick William, the Great Elector, and the son of John Sigismund.

Joachim II Hector (1505-71; r. 1535-71) Margrave and Prince-Elector of Brandenburg. The father of John George.

Joachim Frederick (1546-1608; r. 1598-1608) Margrave and Prince-Elector of Brandenburg. The son of John George and father of John Sigismund.

John George (1525-98; r. 1571-98) Margrave and Prince-Elector of Brandenburg. The son of Joachim II Hector and father of Joachim Frederick.

John Sigismund (1572-1619; r. 1608-19) Margrave and Prince-Elector of Brandenburg, and Duke of Prussia through his marriage to Duchess Anna, the eldest daughter of Duke Albert Frederick of Prussia, who died without sons. Their marriage resulted in the creation of Brandenburg-Prussia. John Sigismund was the son of Joachim II and father of George William.

House of Liechtenstein

Anton Florian (1656-1721; r. 1718-21) Prince of Liechtenstein. The father of Joseph Johann Adam, Prince of Liechtenstein.

Charles Eusebius Prince of Liechtenstein (1611-84). The son of Charles I (1569-1627) Prince of Liechtenstein, who was the founder of the princely family of Liechtenstein.

Joseph Johann Adam (1690-1732; r. 1721-32) Prince of Liechtenstein. The son of Anton Florian.

House of Schönborn

Franz Georg von Schönborn (1682-1756). Archbishop-Elector of Trier 1729-56; Prince-Bishop of Worms and Prince-Provost of Ellwangen 1732-56. The younger brother of Friedrich Karl von Schönborn-Buchheim.

Friedrich Karl von Schönborn-Buchheim (1674-1746). Prince-Bishop of Würzburg and Bamberg 1729. *Reichsvizekanzler* (Vice-Chancellor) of the Holy Roman Empire 1705-34. The elder brother of Franz Georg von Schönborn.

House of Sobieski (Poland)

John Sobieski III (1629-96; r. 1674-96) King of Poland, Grand Duke of Lithuania.

House of Wettin (Albertine line) (Saxony)

August Prince-Elector of Saxony (1526-86; r. 1553-86). The younger brother of Maurice, his predecessor as Prince-Elector, and father of Christian I.

August II the Strong (1670-1733; r. 1697-1733), also known in Saxony as Frederick August I, Prince-Elector of Saxony, Imperial Vicar and elected King of Poland and Grand Duke of Lithuania 1697-1706 and 1709-33. The son of John George III and younger brother of John George IV (his predecessor as Prince-Elector); and the father of August III (Frederick August II).

August III (1696-1763; r. 1733/4-63) Prince-Elector of Saxony 1733-63, where he was known as Frederick August II; Grand Duke of Lithuania 1734-63. Elected king of Poland 1733, subsequently banishing the former Polish king Stanisław I (1677-1766). The son of August II the Strong. Married to Maria Josepha, daughter of Joseph I, Holy Roman Emperor. The father of Frederick Christian (1722-63; r. 1763) Prince-Elector of Saxony.

Christian I Prince-Elector of Saxony (1560-91; r. 1586-91). The son of August, Prince-Elector of Saxony and father of John George I and Christian II.

Christian II Prince-Elector of Saxony (1583-1611; r. 1591-1611). The son of Christian I and older brother of John George I, who succeeded him as Prince-Elector.

Frederick August III Prince-Elector of Saxony (1750-1827; r. 1763-1827) Prince-Elector of Saxony 1763-1806, and known as Frederick August I King of Saxony 1806-27; Duke of Warsaw 1807-13.

Frederick Christian (1722-63; r. 1763) Prince-Elector of Saxony. The son of Frederick August II (August III) and father of Frederick August I Prince-Elector of Saxony (known as Frederick August III).

John George I Prince-Elector of Saxony (1585-1656; r. 1611-56). The son of Christian I and younger brother of Christian II, his predecessor as Prince-Elector.

John George II Prince-Elector of Saxony (1613-80; r. 1656-80). The son of John George I and father of John George III.

John George III Prince-Elector of Saxony (1647-91; r. 1680-91). The son of John George II, and father of John George IV and August II the Strong.

John George IV Prince-Elector of Saxony (1668-94; r. 1691-4). The son of John George III and older brother of Frederick August, known as August II the Strong.

Maurice Duke and later Prince-Elector of Saxony (1521-53; r. 1541-53). The elder brother of August, Prince-Elector of Saxony, who succeeded him.

House of Wittelsbach (Bavaria and the Palatinate)

Albert V, Duke of Bavaria (1528-79; r. 1550-79). The grandfather of Maximilian I and the father of William V.

Albert VI, Duke of Bavaria-Leuchtenberg (1584-1666). The son of William V and grandson of Albert V. The brother of Maximilian I, and uncle of Ferdinand Maria.

Charles III Philip Prince-Elector Palatine, Count of Palatinate-Neuburg, and Duke of Jülich and Berg; until 1728 Count of Megen (1661-1742; r. 1716-42). The younger brother of John William, Prince-Elector Palatine.

Charles Albert Prince-Elector of Bavaria (1697-1745; r. 1726-45); Archduke of Austria 1740-45; King of Bohemia (as Charles III) 1741-3; Holy Roman Emperor (as Charles VII) 1742-5. The son of Maximilian II Emmanuel, father of Maximilian III Joseph, and older brother of Clement August and John Theodore.

Clement August Archbishop-Elector of Cologne (1700-61; r. 1723-61). The son of Maximilian II Emmanuel, nephew of Joseph Clement, and brother of John Theodore and Charles Albert (Emperor Charles VII).

Ferdinand Maria (1636-79; r. 1651-79) Prince-Elector of Bavaria. The son of Maximilian I, husband of Henriette Adelaide, and father of Maximilian II Emmanuel and Joseph Clement.

Frederick V, Prince-Elector Palatine (1596-1632; r. 1610-23) King of Bohemia 1619-20. Known as the Winter King.

Henrietta Adelaide (1636-76) Princess-Electress of Bavaria, the wife of Ferdinand Maria (m. 1650) and mother of Maximilian II Emmanuel and Joseph Clement.

John Theodore of Bavaria, Cardinal (1703-63; r. 1721-63) Prince-Bishop of Regensburg 1721, Prince-Bishop of Freising 1723 (confirmed by the Pope 1726), Cardinal-Priest 1743; Prince-Bishop of Liège 1744. The son of Maximilian II Emmanuel, and younger brother of Clement August and Charles Albert (Emperor Charles VII).

John William II (1658-1716; r. 1690-1716) Prince-Elector Palatine, Duke of Neuburg, Duke of Jülich and Berg (1679-1716), Duke of Upper Palatinate and Cham (1707-14), Count of Megen (1697-1716). Married Anna Maria Luisa de' Medici (1667-1743; m. 1689), daughter of Cosimo III de' Medici, Grand Duke of Tuscany (1642-1713; r. 1670-1723), and the last scion of that house. John William II was the elder brother of Charles III Philip Prince-Elector Palatine, who succeeded him.

Joseph Clement (1671-1723) Co-Prince-Bishop of Regensburg 1683 and Prince-Bishop of Freising 1684; Archbishop and Prince-Elector of Cologne 1688; also bishop of Hildesheim and Liège. The brother of Maximilian II Emmanuel, uncle of Clement August, and son of Ferdinand Maria and Henrietta Adelaide.

Louis of Bavaria, Duke of Upper Bavaria (1282-1347; r. 1294/1301), Margrave of Brandenburg until 1323; Count Palatine until 1329; Duke of Lower Bavaria 1340-7. Holy Roman Emperor 1328-47.

Maximilian I Duke of Bavaria (1573-1651; r. 1597-1651). The son of William V and father of Ferdinand Maria.

Maximilian II Emmanuel (Max Emmanuel) Prince-Elector of Bavaria (1662-1726; r. 1679-1726). The son of Ferdinand Maria and Henriette Adelaide, and father of Charles Albert (Emperor Charles VII) and Clement August. The brother of Joseph Clement.

Maximilian III Joseph Prince-Elector of Bavaria (1727-77; r. 1745-77). The son of Charles Albert (Emperor Charles VII), and the husband of Maria Anna Sophia of Saxony (1728-97), the daughter of Augustus III and granddaughter of Augustus II the Strong.

William V (William the Pious) Duke of Bavaria (1548-1626; r. 1579-97). The son of Albert V and father of Maximilian I.

House of Medici (Florence)

Cosimo III de' Medici, Grand Duke of Tuscany (1642-1713; r. 1670-1723).

Ferdinando de' Medici, Grand Duke of Tuscany (1549-1609; r. 1587-1609).

Ferdinando de' Medici, Grand Duke of Tuscany (1663-1713)

Prince-Bishops of Salzburg

Sigismund Graf Schrattenbach (1698-1771; r. 1753-71) Prince-Archbishop of Salzburg.

Wolf Dietrich von Raitenau (1559-1617; r. 1587-1612) Prince-Archbishop of Salzburg.

BIBLIOGRAPHY

Adriaen de Vries 1999: *Adriaen de Vries, 1556-1626* (exh. cat.), ed. F. Scholten, Rijksmuseum, Amsterdam and J. Paul Getty Museum, Los Angeles, 1999

Albrecht 2014: D. Albrecht, *Maximilian von Bayern 1673-1651*, Berlin, 2014

Altmann 2016: L. Altmann (tr. J. Swann), *Benedictine Abbey Weltenburg on the Danube*, Regensburg, 2016

Andreas Schlüter 2014: *Andreas Schlüter und das Barocke Berlin* (exh. cat.), ed. H.-U. Kessler, Skulpturensammlung, Museum für Byzantinische Kunst, Staatliche Museen zu Berlin, 2014

Anton Sturm 1990: *Anton Sturm. 1690-1757. Bildbauer und Bürger in Füssen* (exh. cat.), Museum der Stadt Füssen, Füssen, 1990

Asam in Freising 2007: *Asam in Freising* (exh. cat.), Diocesan Museum Freising, 2007

Aspekte der Stilbildung 1993: *Aspekte der Stilbildung bei Georg Raphael Donner (1693-1741) Eine Kabinett-Ausstellung* (H.C. Beck, P.C. Bol and M. Bückling) (exh. cat.), Liebieghaus. Museum Alter Plastik, Frankfurt am Main, 1993

Augsburger Barock 1968: *Augsburger Barock* (exh. cat.), ed. C. Thon, Augsburger Rathaus and Holbeinhaus, International Council of Museums, Augsburg, 1968

Aurenhammer 1973: H. Aurenhammer, *J.B. Fischer von Erlach*, Cambridge, MA, 1973

Aurich and Kulbe 2012: F. Aurich and N. Kulbe, 'Geordnetes Wissen. Die Bücher in der Kunstkammer am Dresdner Hof', in Syndram and Minning 2012, pp. 292-329

Avery 1987: C. Avery, *Giambologna. The Complete Sculpture*, Oxford, 1987

Avery and Radcliffe 1978: C. Avery and A. Radcliffe (eds.), *Giambologna (1529-1608). Sculptor to the Medici* (exh. cat.), Arts Council of Great Britain, London, 1978

Bacci 1966: M. Bacci, *Bustelli (I Maestri della Scultura)*, Milan, 1966

Bailey 2003: G.A. Bailey, *Between Renaissance and Baroque: Jesuit Art in Rome, 1565-1610*, Toronto, 2003

Bailey 2014: G.A. Bailey, *The Spiritual Rococo. Décor and Divinity from the Salons of Paris to the Missions of Patagonia*, Farnham, 2014

Baker 1998: M. Baker, 'Limewood, Chiromancy and Narratives of Making. Writing about the Materials and Processes of Sculpture', *Art History*, Vol. 21, no. 4, December 1998, pp. 498-530

Baker 2014: M. Baker, *The Marble Index. Roubiliac and Sculptural Portraiture in Eighteenth-Century Britain*, New Haven, 2014

Bange 1930: E.F. Bange, *Die Bildwerke in Holz, Stein und Ton. Kleinplastik. Die Bildwerke des Deutschen Museums Staatliche Museen zu Berlin IV*, Berlin, 1930

Barber 1984: P.M. Barber, 'Art and Diplomacy: The Background to Peter Strudel's Drawing of Time Revealing Truth and Confounding Fraudulence', *Journal of the Warburg and Courtauld Institutes*, Vol. 47, 1984, pp. 119-35

Barock in Dresden 1986: *Barock in Dresden. Kunst und Kunstsammlungen unter der Regierung des Kurfürsten Friedrich August I. von Sachsen und Königs August II. von Polen genannt August der Starke 1694-1733, und*

des Kurfürsten Friedrich August II. von Sachsen und Königs August III. von Polen 1733-1763 (exh. cat.), Staatliche Kunstsammlungen Dresden, Kulturstiftung Ruhr, Leipzig, 1986

Barocke Bauwerke n.d.: *Barocke Bauwerke im Süddeutschen und Schweizerischen Raum, Ihre Baurherren und Meister*, https://www.sueddeutscher-barock.ch/ (accessed during 2020 and 2021)

Bauer 1962: H. Bauer, *Rocaille*, Berlin, 1962

Bauer and Bauer 1985: H. Bauer and A. Bauer (with photographs by W.-C. von der Mülbe), *Johann Baptist und Dominikus Zimmermann. Entstehung und Vollendung des bayerischen Rokoko*, Regensburg, 1985

Bauer and Dischinger 2019: R. Bauer and G. Dischinger (tr. B. McNeil), *The Asam Church of St. John Nepomucene*, Regensburg, 2019 [1st ed. 1981]

Bauer and Rupprecht 1976: H. Bauer and B. Rupprecht, *Corpus der barocken Deckenmalerei*, Munich, 1976

Bauer-Empel 2007: R. Bauer-Empel, '"AEGIDIUS ASAM – Ein Meister in der Stuckador-Arbeit". Zur Technik von Stuck und Stuckmarmor im Freisinger Dom', in *Asam in Freising* 2007, pp. 81-90

Barock in Baden-Württemberg 1981: *Barock in Baden-Württemberg. Vom Ende des Dreissigjährigen Krieg bis zur Französichen Revolution* (exh. cat.) (2 vols.), Badisches Landesmuseum Karlsruhe, Bruchsal, 1981

Baumstark and Volk 1995: R. Baumstark and P. Volk (eds.), *Apoll schindet Marsyas. Über das Schreckliche in der Kunst. Adam Lenckhardts Elfenbeingruppe* (exh. cat.), Bayerisches Nationalmuseum, Munich, 1995

Baxandall 1981: M. Baxandall, *The Lime-wood Sculptors of Renaissance Germany*, New Haven, 1981

Bayerische Rokokoplastik 1985: *Bayerische Rokokoplastik. Vom Entwurf zur Aus-führung* (exh. cat.), Bayerisches National-museum, Munich, 1985

Bayern. Kunst und Kultur 1972: *Bayern. Kunst und Kultur* (exh. cat.), Stadt-museum, Munich, 1972

Beck and Schulze 1989: H. Beck and S. Schulze (eds.), *Antikenrezeption im Hochbarock*, Berlin, 1989

Bedürftig 2006: F. Bedürftig, *Der Dreissig-jährige Krieg. Ein Lexikon*, Darmstadt, 2006

Beier and Wahnschaffe 2009: B. Beier and J. Wahnschaffe (eds) *Die Chronik der Deutschen*, New York, 2009.

Bella Figura 2015: *Bella Figura: Europäische Bronzekunst in Süddeutschland um 1600* (exh. cat.), ed. R. Eikelmann, with contributions by J.L. Burk, D. Diemer, C. Quaeitzsch, S. Wölfle and D. Zikos, Bayerisches Nationalmuseum, Munich, 2015

Bernstein für Thron und Altar 2005: *Bernstein für Thron und Altar. Das Gold des Meeres in fürstlichen Kunst- und Schatzkammern* (exh. cat.), ed. W. Seipel, Kunsthistorisches Museum, Vienna, 2005

Beyer and Mielke 1961: G. Beyer and G. Mielke (tr. L. Jaeck), *Baroque Archi-tecture in Germany*, Leipzig, 1961

Biermann 1914: G. Biermann, *Deutsches Barock und Rokoko, herausgegeben in An-schluss an die Jahrhundert-Ausstellung Deutscher Kunst 1650-1800. Darmstadt 1914* (exh. cat.) (2 vols.), Leipzig, 1914

Bindman and Baker 1995: D. Bindman and M. Baker, *Roubiliac and the Eigh-teenth-Century Monument. Sculpture as Theatre*, New Haven, 1995

Birke 1981: V. Birke, *Mathias Rauchmiller. Leben und Werk*, Friburg, 1981

Blažíček 1968: O.J. Blažíček (tr. S. Kadečka), *Baroque Art in Bohemia*, Feltham, 1968

Bode 1886: W. von Bode, *Geschichte der deutschen Plastik*, Berlin, 1886

Bourke 1962: J. Bourke, *Baroque Churches of Central Europe*, London, 1962 [2nd revised ed.]

Breuer 1995: D. Breuer (ed.), *Religion und Religiosität im Zeitalter des Barock* (2 vols.), Wiesbaden, 1995

Brinckmann 1924: A.E. Brinckmann, *Barock-Bozzetti. Deutsche Bildhauer German Sculptors (Barock-Bozzetti IV)*, Frankfurt am Main, 1924

Brinckmann 1927: A.E. Brinckmann, 'Barock und Rokoko in Süddeutschland', *Historisches Zeitschrift*, Vol. 136, 1927, pp. 253-65

Brinckmann n.d. [1930?]: A.E. Brinck-mann, *Barockskulptur. Entwicklungs-geschichte der Skulptur in den romanischen und germanischen Länddern seit Michelan-gelo bis zum Beginn des 18. Jahrhunderts*, Potsdam [1917], n.d. [1930?]

Brucher 1994: G. Brucher (ed)., *Die Kunst des Barock in Österreich*, Salzburg, 1994

Bruhn 1981: T.P. Bruhn, *Hans Reichle (1565/70-1642). A Reassessment of his Sculp-ture*, Unpublished PhD dissertation, University of Pennsylvania, 1981

Brulliot 1832: F. Brulliot, *Dictionnaire des monogrammes usw.*, Munich, 1832

Burk 2018: J.L. Burk, 'The Display of Baroque Ivories in the Bayerisches Nationalmuseum from the Foundation of the Museum in 1855 to the Present (2018)', *Curator. The Museum Journal*, Vol. 61, no. 1, January 2018, pp. 223-45

Bursche 1980: S. Bursche, *Meissen. Stein-zug und Porzellan des 18. Jahrhunderts. Kunstgewerbemuseum Berlin*, Berlin, 1980

Bushart and Rupprecht 1986: B. Bushart and B. Rupprecht (eds.), *Cosmas Damian Asam (1686-1739). Leben und Werk* (exh. cat.), Kloster Aldersbach Lower Bavaria, Munich, 1986

Bussmann and Schilling 1998: K. Bussmann and H. Schilling (eds.), *1648. War and Peace in Europe* (exh. cat.) (3 vols.), Westfälisches Landesmuseum für Kunst und Kulturgeschichte Münster, 1998

Casey and Lucey 2012: C. Casey and C. Lucey (eds.), *Decorative Plasterwork in Ireland and Europe*, Dublin, 2012

Chaline 1998: O. Chaline, 'The Battle of the White Mountain', in Bussmann and Schilling 1998, Vol. I, pp. 95-101

Chipps Smith 1994: J. Chipps Smith, *German Sculpture of the Later Renaissance c.1520-1580. Art in an Age of Uncertainty*, Princeton, 1994

Chipps Smith 2002: J. Chipps Smith, *Sensuous Worship. Jesuits and the Art of the Early Catholic Reformation in Germany*, Princeton, 2002

Chipps Smith 2014: J. Chipps Smith, 'Sculpting Sacred Theatre. Hans Degler and the Basilica of St Ulrich and St Afra in Augsburg', in K. Friedrich (ed.), *Der Erschliessung des Raumes: Konstruktion, Imagination und Darstellung von Räumen und Grenzen im Barockzeitalter* (2 vols.) (Wolfenbütteler Arbeiten zur Barock-forschung, ed. Herzog August Biblio-thek, 51), Wiesbaden, 2014, Vol. 1, pp. 207-28

Coburger 2011: U. Coburger, *Von Ausschweifungen und Hirngespinsten. Das Ornament und das Ornamentale im Werk von Egid Quirin Asams (!692-1750)*, Göttingen, 2011

Corpis 2010: D.J. Corpis, 'Losing One's Place: Memory, History and Space in Post-Reformation Germany', in L. Tatlock (ed.), *Enduring Loss in Early Modern Germany. Cross Disciplinary Perspectives*, Leiden and Boston, 2010, pp. 326-67

Davidson 2007: P. Davidson, *The Universal Baroque*, Manchester, 2007

Decker 1943: H. Decker, *Barockplastik in den Alpenländern*, Vienna, 1943

Decker 1949: H. Decker, *Meinrad Guggenbichler*, Vienna, 1949

Demmler 1923-30: T. Demmler (ed.), *Die Bildwerke des Deutschen Museums* (4 vols.), Berlin, 1923-30

Diafane Passioni 2013: *Diafane Passioni. Avori barocchi dale corti europee* (exh. cat.), eds. E.D. Schmidt and M. Sframelli, Palazzo Pitti, Museo degli Argenti, Florence, 2013

Diederen and Kürzeder 2014: R. Diederen and C. Kürzeder (eds.), *Mit Leib und Seele. Münchner Rokoko von Asam bis Günther* (exh. cat.), Kunsthalle der Hypo-Kulturstiftung, Munich, 2014

Diemer 1980a: D. Diemer, 'Hans Krumper', *Wittelsbach und Bayern*, 1980, pp. 279-311

Diemer 1980b: D. Diemer, 'Quellen und Untersuchungen zum Stiftergrab Herzog Wilhelms V. von Bayern under der Renata von Lothringen in der Münchner Michaelskirche', in Glaser 1980, pp. 7-33

Diemer 1988: D. Diemer, 'Hubert Gerhard und Carlo Pallago als Terra-kottaplastiker', *Jahrbuch des Zentralinsti-tuts für Kunstgeschichte*, Vol. 4, 1988, pp. 19-141

Diemer 2004: D. Diemer, *Hubert Gerhard und Carlo di Cesare del Palagio. Bronze-plastiker der Spätrenaissance* (2 vols.), Berlin, 2004

Diemer 2006: D. Diemer, 'Hans Reichle: ein Modello für die Augsburger Zeughausgruppe und Werkstattfragen', *Münchner Jahrbuch der bildenden Kunst*, 3rd series, Vol. LVII, 2006, pp. 31-56

Diemer 2012: D. Diemer, 'Hans Reichles Werke für St Ulrich und Afra', *Jahrbuch des Vereins für Augsburger Bistumsgeschichte*, Vol. 46, 2012, pp. 21-76.

Diemer 2015: D. Diemer, 'Die Grosse Zeit der Münchner und Augsburger Bronzeplastik um 1600', in *Bella Figura* 2015, pp. 19-49

Diemer et al. 2008: P. Diemer, D. Diemer, L. Seelig, P. Volk, B. Volk-Knüttel et al., *Die Münchner Kunstkammer* (3 vols.), Munich, 2008

Dilly 1988: H. Dilly, *Deutsche Kunsthistoriker 1933-1945*, Munich, 1988

Dotson 2012: E.G. Dotson, *J. B. Fischer Von Erlach: Architecture as Theater in the Baroque Era*, New Haven, 2012

Dürers Verwandlung 1981: *Dürers Verwandlung in der Skulptur zwischen Renaissance und Barock* (exh. cat.), eds. H. Beck and B. Decker, Liebieghaus Museum alter Plastik, Frankfurt am Main, 1981

Durian-Ress 2017: S. Durian-Ress, *Christian Wenzinger*, Munich, 2017

Ehmer 1992: A. Ehmer, *Die Maucher. Eine Kunsthandwerkerfamilie des 17. Jahrhunderts aus Schwäbisch Gmünd. Herausgegeben vom Stadtarchiv Schwäbisch Gmünd*, Schwäbisch Gmünd, 1992

Eikelmann 2004: R. Eikelmann (ed.), *Franz Anton Bustelli: Nymphenburger Porzellanfiguren des Rokoko: Das Gesamtwerk* (exh. cat.), Bayerisches Nationalmuseum, Munich, 2004

Eindeutig bis Zweifelhaft 2017: *Eindeutig bis Zweifelhaft. Skulpturen und ihre Geschichten* (exh.cat.), Liebieghaus, Frankfurt, 2017

Elias Holl 1985: *Elias Holl und das Augsburger Rathaus* (exh. cat.), Augsburg, Stadtarchiv, ed. W. Baer, H.-W. Kruft, B. Roeck, Regensburg, 1985

Engelberg 2016: M. Engelberg, 'Baroque in West Germany', *Journal of Art Historiography*, Vol. 15, 2016, pp. 1-21

Europäische Barockplastik 1971: *Europäische Barockplastik am Niederrhein. Gabriel Grupello und seine Zeit* (exh. cat.), Kunstmuseum, Düsseldorf, 1971

Europäisches Rokoko 1958: *Europäisches Rokoko. Kunst und Kultur des 18. Jahrhunderts* (exh.cat.), Munich Residenz, 1958

Fajt and Sršeň 1993: J. Fajt and L. Sršeň, *Das Lapidarium des Nationalmuseums Prag. Führer durch die ständige Sammlung der Böhmische Bildwerke aus Stein vom 11.-19. Jahrhundert*, Prague, 1993

Falcke 2006: J. Falcke, *Studien zum diplomatischen Geschenkwesen am brandenburgisch-preussischen Hof im 17. Und 18. Jahrhundert (Quellen und Forschungen zur Brandenburgischen und Preussischen Geschichte*, Vol. 31), Berlin, 2006

Felder 1988: P. Felder, *Barockplastik der Schweiz (Beiträge zur Kunstgeschichte der Schweiz 6. Gesellschaft für Schweizerische Kunstgeschichte)*, Bern, 1988

Feuchtmayr and Schädler 1973: K. Feuchtmayr and A. Schädler, with contributions by N. Lieb and T. Müller, *Georg Petel 1601/2-1634*, Berlin, 1973

Feulner 1922: A. Feulner, *Münchner Barockskulptur*, Munich, 1922

Feulner 1926: A. Feulner, *Die Deutsche Plastik des Siebzehnten. Jahrhunderts*, Florence and Munich, 1926

Feulner 1929: A. Feulner, *Skulptur und Malerei des Achtzehnten. Jahrhunderts in Deutschland*, Wildmark-Potsdam, 1929

Feulner and Müller 1953: A. Feulner and T. Müller, *Geschichte der Deutschen Plastik*, Munich, 1953

Fischer 1986: F. Fischer, *Der Meister des Buxheimer Hochaltars. Ein Beitrag zur süddeutschen Skulptur der ersten Hälfte des 17. Jahrhunderts*, Berlin, 1986

Fischer 2004: F. Fischer, *Grosse Kunst in Kleinem Format*, Stuttgart, 2004

Fleming, Honour and Pevsner 1977: J. Fleming, H. Honour and N. Pevsner, *The Penguin Dictionary of Architecture*, Harmondsworth, 1977

Fleming and Honour 1989: J. Fleming and H. Honour, *The Penguin Dictionary of Decorative Arts* (New Edition), London, 1989

Forster 2001: M.R. Forster, *Catholic Revival in the Age of the Baroque. Religious Identity in Southwest Germany 1550-1750*, Cambridge, 2001

Furienmeister 2006: *Der Furienmeister* (exh. cat.), eds. H. Beck, P.C. Bol M. Bückling and M. Hollein, Liebieghaus, Frankfurt am Main, Petersberg, 2006

Gajdošová 2015: J. Gajdošová, *The Charles Bridge. Ceremony and Propaganda in Medieval Prague*, Unpublished PhD dissertation, University of London, 2015

Georg Raphael Donner 1993: *Georg Raphael Donner (1693-1741)* (exh.cat.), Österreichische Galerie, Vienna, 1993

Glaser 1980: H. Glaser (ed.), *Quellen und Studien zur Kunstpolitik der Wittelsbacher vom 16. Bis zum 18. Jahrhundert*, Munich, 1980

Glaser and Werner 1998: H. Glaser and E.A. Werner, 'The Victorious Virgin: The Religious Patronage of Maximilian I of Bavaria', in Bussmann and Schelling 1998, Vol. II, pp. 141-51

Goldener Drache Weisser Adler 2008: *Goldener Drache Weisser Adler. Kunst im Dienste der Macht am Kaiserhof von China und am sächsisch-polnischen Hof (1644-1795)*, ed. C. Bischoff (exh. cat.), Staatliche Kunstsammlungen Dresden, Munich, 2008

Goldner et al. 1992: J. Goldner, L. Bahnmüller and W. Bahnmüller, *Wessobrunner Stukkatorenschule. Kleine Pannonia Reihe 209*, Freilassing, 1992

Greenhalgh 1982: M. Greenhalgh, *Donatello and his Sources*, London, 1982

Gröger 1956: H. Gröger, *Johann Joachim Kaendler. Der Meister des Porzellans*, Hanau am Main, 1956

Grove Art Online: Grove Art Online, https://www.oxfordartonline.com/groveart/ (accessed during 2020 and 2021)

Grünenwald 1969: E. Grünenwald, *Leonhard Kern. Ein Bildhauer des Barock*, Schwäbisch Hall, 1969

Grünwald 1975: M.D. Grünwald, *Christoph Angermair. Studien zu Leben und Werk des Elenbeinschnitzers und Bildhauers*, Munich, 1975

Guinomet 2014: C. Guinomet, 'Die Kanzel in der Berliner Marienkirche', in *Andreas Schlüter* 2014, pp. 344-57

Gurlitt 1889: C. Gurlitt, *Das Barock- und Rokoko-Ornament Deutschlands*, Berlin, 1889

Haag 1996: S. Haag, 'Johann Caspar Schenck (um 1620-1674). "Cammerdrechsler von Ynsprug" und "Cammerpainstecher" am Hof Leopolds I. in Wien', in J. Thorbecke, *Christoph Daniel Schenck 1633-1691* (exh. cat.), Sigmaringen, 1996, pp. 93-106

Haag 2007a: S. Haag, *Kaiserliches Elfenbein. Matthias Steinl (1643/44-1727) in der Kunstkammer des Kunsthistorischen Museums*, ed. W. Seipel, Vienna, 2007

Haag 2007b: S. Haag, *Meisterwerke der Elfenbeinkunst*, Vienna, 2007

Häberlein and Burkhardt 2002:
M. Häberlein and J. Burkhardt (eds.), *Die Welser: Neue Forschungen Zur Geschichte Und Kultur des Oberdeutschen Handelshauses (Colloquia Augustana)*, Berlin, 2002

Haberstock 2016: E. Haberstock, *Der Augsburger Stadtwerkmeister Elias Holl (1573-1646): Werkverzeichnis (Beiträge zur Geschichte der Stadt Augsburg, Vol. 7)*, Petersberg, 2016

Hahn 2007: S. Hahn, 'Die Familie Asam', in *Asam in Freising* 2007, pp. 9-13

Halbertsma 1992: M. Halbertsma, *Wilhelm Pinder und die deutsche Kunstgeschichte*, Worms, 1992

Hall 1979: J. Hall, *Dictionary of Subjects and Symbols in Art* (revised ed.), New York, 1979

Hannesen 2014: H.G. Hannesen, 'Andreas Schlüter und die Akademie der Künste', in *Andreas Schlüter* 2014, pp. 118-22

Hansmann 2000: W. Hansmann, *Zauber des Barock und Rokoko*, Cologne, 2000

Harding 1972: A. Harding, *German Sculpture in New England Museums*, Boston, 1972

Harries 1983: K. Harries, *The Bavarian Rococo Church. Between Faith and Aestheticism*, New Haven, 1983

Hartmetz 2019: G. Hartmetz, *Christoph Rodt. Bildhauer zwischen Renaissance und Barock*, Weissenhorn, 2019

Haskell and Penny 1982: F. Haskell and N. Penny, *Taste and the Antique. The Lure of Classical Sculpture 1500-1900*, New Haven, 1982

Hauttmann 1921: M. Hauttmann, *Geschichte der kirchlichen Baukunst in Bayern, Schwaben und Franken 1550-1780* (3 vols.), Munich, 1921

Hawes 2018: J. Hawes, *The Shortest History of Germany*, Yowlestone House, 2018

Heal 2011: B. Heal, 'Mary, "Triumphant over Demons and also Heretics". Religious Symbols and Confessional Uniformity in Catholic Germany', in H. Louthan, G.B. Cohen and F.A.J. Szabo (eds.), *Diversity and Dissent. Negotiating Religious Differences in Central Europe, 1500-1800*, Oxford and New York, 2011, pp. 153-72

Heal 2017: B. Heal, *A Magnificent Faith. Art and Identity in Lutheran Germany*, Oxford, 2017

Hegemann 1958: H.W. Hegemann, *Deutsches Rokoko. Die Blauen Bücher*, Königstein im Taunus, [1942] 1958

Heisig 2015: A. Heisig, *Rott am Inn*, Rott am Inn, 2015

Heisig 2018: A. Heisig, *St. Michael in München Berg am Laim*, Lindenberg, 2018

Hempel 1965: E. Hempel, *Baroque Art and Architecture in Central Europe: Germany, Austria, Switzerland, Hungary, Czechoslovakia, Poland (The Pelican History of Art)*, Harmondsworth, 1965

Hertel 2011: C. Hertel, *Pygmalion in Bavaria. The Sculptor Ignaz Günther and Eighteenth-Century Art Theory*, University Park, PA, 2011

Hildebrand and Theuerkauff 1981: J. Hildebrand and C. Theuerkauff, *Die Brandenburgisch-Preussische Kunstkammer. Eine Auswahl aus den alten Beständen*, Berlin, 1981

Hildyard 1999: R. Hildyard, *European Ceramics*, London, 1999

Hinterkeuser 2014: G. Hinterkeuser, 'Andreas Schlüters Skulpturenprogramm für das Berliner Schloss', in *Andreas Schlüter* 2014, pp. 286-327

Hitchcock 1968: H.-R. Hitchcock, *Rococo Architecture in Southern Germany*, London, 1968

Hladík 2016: T. Hladík, *Die Bildhauer Werkstatt der Barockzeit in Mitteleuropa. Von Entwurf zur Ausführung*, Prague, 2016

Hodgkinson 1970: T. Hodgkinson, *Two Garden Sculptures by Antonio Corradini*, London, 1970

Hojer 1986: G. Hojer, *Cosmas Damian und Egid Quirin Asam. Ein Führer durch ihren Kunstwerken*, Munich, 1986

Huber 1960: R. Huber, *Joseph Christian. Der Bildhauer des schwäbischen Rokoko*, Tübingen, 1960

Husslein-Arco et al. 2016: A. Husslein-Arco, M. Hohn and G. Lechner (eds.), *Himmlisch! Der Barockbildhauer Johann Georg Pinsel* (exh. cat.), Belvedere Winterpalais, Vienna, 2016

Jacob 1976: S. Jacob, *Europäische Kleinplastik aus dem Herzog-Anton-Ulrich-Museum Braunschweig* (exh. cat.), St Annen-Museum, Lübeck, Osnabrück, 1976

Jahn 1990: W. Jahn, *Stukkaturen des Rokoko. Bayreuther Hofkünstler in Markgräflichen Schlössern und in Würzburg, Eichstätt, Ansbach, Ottobeuren*, Sigmaringen, 1990

Jászai 1979: G. Jászai, *Barockskulptur im Westfälischen Landesmuseum für Kunst und Kulturgeschichte Münster*, Münster, 1979

Justi 1943: C. Justi, *Winckelmann und seine Zeitgenossen*, [Bonn, 1866], introduction L. Curtius, Leipzig, 1943

Kahsnitz and Volk 1998: R. Kahsnitz and P. Volk (eds.), *Skulptur in Süddeutschland 1400-1770. Festschrift für Alfred Schädler*, Munich, 1998

Kammel 1998: F.M. Kammel, 'Vermischte Notizien zum Mannheimer Hochaltar von Paul Egell. Von Entdeckungen im Archiv und Funden im Depot', in R. Kahsnitz and P. Volk (eds.), *Die Skulptur in Süddeutschland 1400-1770. Festschrift für Alfred Schädler*, Munich, 1998, pp. 309-22

Kappel 2001: J. Kappel, *"Hier wird allzeit bleiben in Gunst und Hochachtung seine Kunst". Zum 350. Geburtstag Balthasar Permoser (Dresdener Kunstblätter, 6)*, Dresden, 2001

Kappel 2017: J. Kappel, *Elfenbeinkunst im Grünen Gewölbe zu Dresden. Geschichte einer Sammlung. Wissenschaftlicher Bestandskatalog – Statuetten, Figurengruppenj, Reliefs, Gefässe, Varia*, Dresden, 2017

Kappel 2018: J. Kappel, *Augen-Blicke: Barocke Elfenbeinkunst in Dialog der Kunste*, Dresden, 2018

Kappel 2021: J. Kappel, 'Unwägbarkeiten des Herrscherglücks: Die Elfenbeinfregatte von Jacob Zeller. Eine ikonografische Betrachtung', in T. Jürjens and D. Syndram (eds.), *Bellum und Artes. Sachsen und Mitteleuropa im Dreissigjährigen Krieg* (exh. cat.), Staatlichen Kunstsammlungen Dresden, Residenzschloss Dresden, Dresden, 2021, pp. 42-51

Kappel and Weinhold 2007: J. Kappel and U. Weinhold, *The New Grünes Gewölbe. Guide to the Permanent Exhibition*, Berlin and Munich, 2007

Kaufmann 1998: T. DaCosta Kaufmann, 'War and Peace, Art and Destruction, Myth and Reality: Considerations on the Thirty Years' War in Relation to Art in (Central) Europe', in Bussmann and Schilling 1998, Vol. II, pp. 163-72

Kaufmann 2004: T. DaCosta Kaufmann, *Towards a Geography of Art*, Chicago, 2004

Keller 2014: F.-E. Keller, 'Die Schlusssteine der Bögen am Erdgeschloss des Zeughauses', in *Andreas Schlüter* 2014, pp. 136-67

Kemp 2011: M. Kemp, *Leonardo. Revised Edition*, Oxford, 2011

Kessler 2014a: H.-U. Kessler, 'Johann Jacobi und der Bronzeguss', in *Andreas Schlüter* 2014, pp. 208-21

Kessler 2014b: H.-U. Kessler, 'Das Reiterdenkmal des Grossen Kurfürsten', in *Andreas Schlüter* 2014, pp. 222-35

Kessler 2014c: H.-U. Kessler et al., *Schlüter in Berlin. Stadtführer. A City Guide*, Berlin, 2014

Kessler 2017a: H.-U. Kessler, 'Paul Egell und die Berliner Museen', *Patrimonia*, Vol. 264, 2017, pp. 27-65

Kessler 2017b: H.-U. Kessler, 'Kurze Lebensbeschreibung des Johann Paul Egell', *Patrimonia*, Vol. 264, 2017, pp. 67-123

Kirchmeir and Hasenmuller n.d. [1991?]: G. Kirchmeir and M. Hasenmuller (tr. B. Schmid-Burleson and C.-P. Schmid), *The Wies. Pilgrimmage Church of the 'Scourged Saviour'*, Lechbruck, n.d. [1991?]

Kluger 2014: M. Kluger, *The Fugger Dynasty in Augsburg. Merchants, Mining Entrepreneurs, Bankers and Benefactors*, Augsburg, 2014

Knapp 1996: U. Knapp, *Joseph Anton Feuchtmayer (1696-1770)*, Constance, 1996

Knauer 1998: M. Knauer, 'War as Memento Mori. The function and significance of the series of engravings in the Thirty Years' War', in Bussmann and Schilling 1998, Vol. II, pp. 509-15

Knox 1965: B. Knox, *The Architecture of Prague and Bohemia*, London, 1965

Koller 1993: M. Koller, *Die Brüder Strudel. Hofkünstler und Gründer der Wiener Kunstakademie*, Innsbruck, 1993

Koja and Kryza-Gersch 2020: S. Koja and C. Kryza-Gersch (eds.), *Meisterwerke der Renaissance und des Barock. Skulpturensammlung Dresden*, Dresden, 2020

Krapf 1998: M. Krapf, *Triumph der Phantasie. Barocke Modelle von Hildebrandt bis Mollinarolo* (exh. cat.), Galerie Belvedere, Vienna, 1998

Krempel and Söding 2009: L. Krempel and U. Söding (eds.), *Georg Petel. Neue Forschungen*, Munich, 2009

Kroupa 1998: J. Kroupa, 'Art, Patronage and Society in Moravia 1620-1650', in Bussmann and Schilling 1998, Vol. II, pp. 253-61

Krummholz 2012: M. Krummholz, 'Baroque stucco in Bohemia and Moravia' in Casey and Lucey 2012, pp. 93-110

Kühn 1977: M. Kühn, 'Andreas Schlüter als Bildhauer', in Rasmussen 1977, pp. 105-83

Kuhn 1965: C.L. Kuhn, *German and Netherlandish Sculpture 1280-1800. The Harvard Collections*, Cambridge, MA, 1965

Ladendorf 1937: H. Ladendorf, *Andreas Schlüter*, Berlin, 1937

Lampl 1987: S. Lampl, *Dominikus Zimmermann*, Regensburg, 1987

Langer 1998: H. Langer, 'The Royal Swedish War in Germany', in Bussmann and Schilling 1998, Vol. I, pp. 187-96

Lankheit 1962: K. Lankheit, *Die Florentinische Barockplastik. Kunst am Hofe der Letzten Medici 1670-1743*, Munich, 1962

Lankheit 1988: K. Lankheit, *Der Kurpfälzische Hofbildhauer Paul Egell* (2 vols.), Munich, 1988

Larsson 1967: L. Larsson, *Adriaen de Vries*, Vienna and Munich, 1967

Laue and Spenlé 2016: G. Laue and V. Spenlé, *Leonhard Kern. Der Deutsche Giambologna. The German Giambologna*, Munich, 2016

Lehner 2018: U. Lehner, *The Catholic Enlightenment*, New York, 2018

Leibetseder 2013: S.M. Leibetseder, *Johann Paul Egell (1691-1752). Der kurpfälzische Hofbildhauer und die Hofkunst seiner Zeit. Skulptur – Ornament – Relief*, Petersberg, 2013

Leonhard Kern 2021: *Leonhard Kern und Europa. Die Kaiserliche Schatzkammer Wien in Dialog mit der Sammlung Würth* (exh. cat.), Kunsthalle, Schwäbisch Hall, 2021

Lieb 1953: N. Lieb, *Barockkirchen zwischen Donau und Alpen*, Munich, 1953

Lieb 1982: N. Lieb, *Johann Michael Fischer. Baumeister und Raumschöpfer im Späten Barock Süddeutschlands*, Regensburg, 1982

Lieb 1984: N. Lieb, *Augsburg St. Ulrich und Afra*, Munich, 1984

Liechtenstein 1985: *Liechtenstein. The Princely Collections* (exh. cat.), Metropolitan Museum of Art, New York, 1985

Lindemann 1989: B.W. Lindemann, *Ferdinand Tietz 1708-1777. Studien zu Werk, Stil und Ikonographie*, Weissenhorn, 1989

Lindemann 2014: B.W. Lindemann, 'Die Prunksärge für Sophie Charlotte und Friedrich I', in *Andreas Schlüter* 2014, pp. 400-415

Lindemann 2017: B.W. Lindemann, 'Die Hl. Familie von Johann Paul Egell', *Patrimonia*, Vol. 264, 2017, pp. 7-25

Lipowsky 1810: F.J. Lipowsky, *Baierisches Künstlerlexikon*, Munich, 1810

Loers 1976: V. Loers, *Rokokoplastik und Dekorationssysteme: Aspekte der Süddeutschen Kunst und des ästhetischen Bewusstseins im 18. Jahrhundert*, Regensburg, 1976

MacGregor and Impey 1985: A. MacGregor and O. Impey (eds.), *The Origins of Museums. The Cabinet of Curiosities in Sixteenth- and Seventeenth-Century Europe*, Oxford, 1985

Marth 2018: R. Marth, *Die Vier Jahreszeiten von Balthasar Permoser in Braunschweig 1695 – 1806 – 2016*, Kulturstiftung der Länder and Herzog Anton Ulrich-Museum Braunschweig, *Patrimonia*, Vol. 265, Berlin, 2018

Maué 1997-2005: C. Maué, *Die Bildwerke des 17. und 18. Jahrhunderts im Germanischen Nationalmuseum* (2 vols.), Vol. 1: *Franken*, Mainz, 1997; Vol. 2 (with K. Telp and G. Weiner): *Bayern, Österreich, Italien, Spanien*, Mainz, 2005

Messerschmidt 2001: *Franz Xaver Messerschmidt 1736-1783* (exh. cat.), eds. G. Scherf, A. Boström, M.-C. Lambotte, M. Pötzl-Malikova, Musée du Louvre, Paris, 2001

Möller 1977: L.L. Möller, 'Einige fürstliche Kunstförder des 17. und frühen 18. Jahrhunderts im nördlichen Deutschland', in Rasmussen 1977, pp. 9-61

Möller 2000: K.A. Möller, *Elfenbein. Kunstwerk des Barock*, Schwerin, 2000

Montagu 1989: J. Montagu, *Roman Baroque Sculpture. The Industry of Art*, New Haven, 1989

Motture 2019: P. Motture, *The Culture of Bronze. Making and Meaning in Italian Renaissance Sculpture*, London. 2019

Mülbe 1991: W.-C. von der Mülbe, *Ignaz Günther. Vollendung des Rokoko*, Regensburg, 1991

Müller 1959: T. Müller, *Die Bildwerke in Holz, Ton und Stein von der Mitte des XV. bis gegen Mitte des XVI. Jahrhunderts. Kataloge des Bayerisches Nationals Museums*, Munich, 1959

Nagler 1872-85: G.K. Nagler, *Neues allgemeines Künstler-Lexikon* (25 vols.), [Munich, 1835] Leipzig, 1872-85

Neue Deutsche Biographie n.d.: *Neue Deutsche Biographie (NDB)*, http://www.ndb.badw-muenchen.de/ (accessed during 2020 and 2021)

Neumann 1970: J. Neumann (tr. H. Gaertner), *Das Böhmische Barock*, Prague, 1970

Novotny and Poche 1947: K. Novotny and E. Poche (with photographs by J. Ehm), *The Charles Bridge of Prague*, Prague, 1947

Oberberger 2005: E. Oberberger, *Weyarn Stiftskirche*, Regensburg, 2005
Oxford English Dictionary 1972: *Oxford English Dictionary* (Compact Edition) (2 vols.), Oxford, 1972

Park 1992: W. Park, *The Idea of Rococo*, Newark, 1992

Parker 1985: G. Parker, *The Thirty Years' War*, London, 1985

Pechloff 2005: U. Pechloff (with photographs by G. Peda), *Münster Zwiefalten*, Passau, 2005

Penny 1992: N. Penny, *Catalogue of European Sculpture in the Ashmolean Museum, 1540 to the Present Day* (3 vols.), Oxford, 1992

Petráň 1998: J. Petráň, 'The Beginnings of the War in Bohemia', in Bussmann and Schilling 1998, Vol. I, pp. 85-93

Pevsner 1990: N. Pevsner, *Leipziger Barock. Die Baukunst der Barockzeit in Leipzig*, [Dresden, 1928] Leipzig, 1990

Pfister 2013: P. Pfister (ed.), *Fürstenfeld. Ehemaliges Zisterzienkloster*, Regensburg, 2013

Pietsch 2006: U. Pietsch, with contributions by D. Antonin, *Die Figürliche Meissner Porzellanplastik von Gottlieb Kirchner und Johann Joachim Kändler. Bestandskatalog der Porzellan Sammlung. Staatliche Kunstsammlungen Dresden*, Munich, 2006

Pietsch et al. 2006: U. Pietsch, A. Loesch and E. Ströber, *China – Japan – Meissen. Die Porzellansammlung zu Dresden*, Dresden, 2006

Pinder n.d. [1912]: W. Pinder, *Deutscher Barock. Die großen Baumeister des 18. Jahrhunderts. Die Blauen Bücher*, Königstein im Taunus/Leipzig, n.d. [1912]

Pinsel 2012: *Johann Georg Pinsel. Un Sculpteur baroque en Ukraine au XVIIIe siècle* (exh. cat.), eds. J.K. Ostrowski and G. Scherf, Musée du Louvre, Paris, 2012

Poche and Kořán 2003: E. Poche and I. Kořán, *Matthias Bernhard Braun. Der Meister des Böhmischen Barock und seine Werkstatt* (ed. H. Jäger), Innsbruck, 2003

Prag 1988: *Prag um 1600: Kunst und Kultur am Hofe Rudolfs II* (exh. cat.) (2 vols.), eds. J. Schultze and H. Fillitz, Kulturstiftung Ruhr, Villa Hügel Essen, Kunsthistorisches Museum Vienna, Lingen, 1988

Prusinovsky 2019: P.R. Prusinovsky OSB, *Benedictine Abbey Ottobeuren. Basilica St. Alexander and Theodor*, Ottobeuren, 2019 [1986]

Pühringer-Zwanowetz 1966: L. Pühringer-Zwanowetz, *Matthias Steinl*, Vienna, 1966

Rasmussen 1975: J. Rasmussen, *Deutsche Kleinplastik der Renaissance und des Barock*, Hamburg, 1975

Rasmussen 1977: J. Rasmussen (ed.), *Barockplastik in Norddeutschland* (exh. cat.), Museum für Kunst und Gewerbe, Hamburg, 1977

Riccardi-Cubitt 2000: M. Riccardi-Cubitt, 'ON THE MARKET: The Duke of Buckingham's "cabinet d'amateur": An aesthetic, religious and political statement', *British Art Journal*, Vol. 1, no. 2, 2000, pp. 77-86

Richard 1998: M. Richard, 'Jacques Callot (1592-1635). Les Misères et les Malheurs de la Guerre (1633): A Work and its Context', in Bussmann and Schilling 1998, Vol. II, pp. 517-23

Ricke 1973: H. Ricke, *Hans Morinck. Ein Wegbereiter der Barockskulptur am Bodensee*, Sigmaringen, 1973

Rinn 2012: B. Rinn, 'Eighteenth-century stucco in Germany' in Casey and Lucey 2012, pp. 111-128

Rococo Art from Bavaria 1954: *Rococo Art from Bavaria* (exh. cat.), Victoria and Albert Museum, London, 1954

Röbbig 2008: G. Röbbig, *Cabinet Pieces. The Meissen Porcelain Birds of Johann Joachim Kändler 1706-1775. Eighteenth-century masterpieces from Private Collections*, Munich, 2008

Roeck 2004: B. Roeck, *Elias Holl: ein Architekt der Renaissance*, Regensburg, 2004

Rösner 1988: C. Rösner, *Andreas Faistenberger (1646-1735) Werk und Stellung eines Münchner Hofbildhauers um 1700*, Munich, 1988

Rückert 1963: R. Rückert, *Franz Anton Bustelli*, Munich, 1963

Rupprecht 1959: B. Rupprecht, *Die Bayerische Rokoko-Kirche*, Munich, 1959

Rupprecht 1987: B. Rupprecht (with photographs by W.-C. von der Mülbe), *Die Brüder Asam. Sinn und Sinnlichkeit im bayerischen Barock*, Regensburg, 1987

Rupprecht and Sauermost 1972: B. Rupprecht and H. J. Sauermost (eds.), *Zwischen Donau und Alpen. Festschrift für Norbert Lieb zum 65. Geburtstag* (Zeitschrift für bayerische Landesgeschichte, Vol. 35, part 1), Munich, 1972

Sandrart [1675-80]: J. Sandrart, *Teutsche Academie der Bau-, Bildhauer- und Maler-Kunst* (eds. C. Klemm and J. Becker) (3 vols.) [Nuremberg, 1675-80], Nördlingen, 1994-5, http://ta.sandrart.net/en/ (accessed during 2020)

Saur 1992-2019: Saur, *Allgemeines Künstlerlexikon. Die Bildenden Künstler aller Zeiten und Völker* (103 vols.), Leipzig, 1992-2019

Sauerlandt 1926: M. Sauerlandt, *Plastik des 18. Jahrhunderts*, Munich, 1926

Sauermost 1988: H.-J. Sauermost, *Die Weilheimer – Große Künstler aus dem Zentrum des Pfaffenwinkels*, Munich, 1988

Schädler 1985: A. Schädler, with contributions by E. Langenstein, *Georg Petel (1601/2-1634). Barockbildhauer zu Augsburg*, Zurich, 1985

Schindler 1976: H. Schindler, *Grosse Bayerische Kunstgeschichte* (2 vols.), Munich, 1976

Schlosser 1908: J. von Schlosser, *Die Kunst- und Wunderkammern der Spätrenaissance: Ein Beitrag zur Geschichte des Sammelwesens*, Leipzig, 1908

Schmidt 1986: W. Schmidt, 'Kunstsammeln im augusteischen Dresden', in *Barock in Dresden* 1986, pp. 191-201

Schmidt 2012: E.D. Schmidt, *Das Elfenbein der Medici*, Munich, 2012

Schreiter and Pyritz 2007: C. Schreiter and A. Pyritz (eds.), *Berliner Eisen. Die Königliche Eisengiesserei Berlin. Zur Geschichte eines preussischen Unternehmens*, Berlin, 2007

Schnell n.d. [1936]: H.K.M. Schnell, *Der baierische Barock. Die volklichen, die geschichtlichen und die religiösen Grundlagen, sein Siegeszug durch das Reich*, Munich, n.d. [1936]

Schnell 1972: H. Schnell, 'Die Bedeutung von Wessobrunn', in Rupprecht and Sauermost 1972, pp. 186-201

Schnell 2016: W. Schnell, *Marienmünster Diessen. Ehemalige Augustinerchorherrenkirche*, Passau, 2016

Schoenberger 1954: A. Schoenberger, *Ignaz Günther*, Munich, 1954

Scholten 2004/5: F. Scholten, 'The Larson Family of Statuary Founders. Seventeenth-Century Reproductive Sculpture for Gardens and Painters' Studios', *Simiolus. Netherlands Quarterly for the History of Art*, Vol. 31, no.1/2, 2004/5, pp. 54-89

Schraut 1990: E. Schraut, 'Bemerkungen zu Leonhard Kerns Skulptur "Szene aus dem Dreissigjährigen Krieg"', in Siebenmorgen 1990, pp. 30-37

Schütz 2000: B. Schütz, *Die Kirchliche Barockarchitektur in Bayern und Oberschwaben 1580-1780*, aufnahmen von A. Hirmer, Munich, 2000

Schwanthaler 1974: Die Bildhauerfamilie Schwanthaler 1633-1748. Vom Barock zum Klassizismus (exh. cat.), Augustinerchorherrenstift, Reichersberg am Inn, 1974

Sculpture 1977: La sculpture au siècle de Rubens dans les Pays-Bas méridionaux et la principauté de Liège (exh. cat.), Musée d'Art Ancien, Brussels, 1977

Sculpture 2008: The Sculpture Collection in the Bode Museum, eds. J. Chapuis, D. Kline, L. Gilbert (tr. M. Hulse), Munich, 2008

Sedlmayr 1930: H. Sedlmayr, *Österreichische Barockarchitektur 1690-1740*, Vienna, 1930

Siebenmorgen 1988: H. Siebenmorgen (ed.), *Leonhard Kern (1558-1662). Meisterwerke der Bildhauerei für die Kunstkammern Europas*, Sigmaringen, 1988

Siebenmorgen 1990: H. Siebenmorgen (ed.), *Leonhard Kern (1558-1662). Neue Forschungsbeiträge*, Sigmaringen, 1990

Sitwell 1938: S. Sitwell (with photographs by A. Ayscough and descriptive notes by N. Pevsner), *German Baroque Sculpture*, London, 1938

Sobotka and Tietze 1927: G. Sobotka and H. Tietze, *Die Bildhauerei der Barockzeit*, Vienna, 1927

Splendor of Dresden 1978-9: The Splendor of Dresden. Five Centuries of Art Collecting (exh. cat.), National Gallery of Art, Washington DC; Metropolitan Museum of Art, New York; Fine Arts Museums of San Francisco, CA; Palace of the Legion of Honour, New York, 1978-9

Statnik 2019: B. Statnik, *Ignaz Günther: Ein bayerischer Bildhauer und Retabel-Architekt im Europa der ausgehenden Barock- und Rokokozeit*, Petersberg, 2019

Stech 1959: V.V. Stech, *Die Barockskulptur in Böhmen*, Prague, 1959

Steinberg 2011: J. Steinberg, *Bismarck. A Life*, Oxford, 2011

Steiner 1974: P. Steiner, *Johann Baptist Straub*, Munich, 1974

Steiner 2007: P.B. Steiner, 'Was bedeutet Barockisierung?', in *Asam in Freising* 2007, pp. 54-66

Steiner 2010: P.B. Steiner, *Die Asamkirche in München*, Lindenburg im Allgäu, 2010

Stiegemann 2010: C. Stiegemann (ed.), *Peter Paul Rubens und der Barock im Norden* (exh. cat.), Diözesanmuseum, Paderborn, Petersberg, 2020

Syndram 2006: D. Syndram (ed.), with contributions by J. Kappel and U. Arnold, *Das Grüne Gewölbe zu Dresden. Führer durch seine Geschichte und seine Sammlungen*, Munich and Dresden, 2006

Syndram and Minning 2012: D. Syndram and M. Minning (eds.), *Die kurfürstlich-sächsische Kunstkammer in Dresden. Geschichte einer Sammlung*, Dresden, 2012

Tacke 1998: A. Tacke, 'Mars, the Enemy of Art', in Bussmann and Schilling 1998, Vol. II, pp. 245-52

Tarnai and Weber 2017: T. Tarnai and D. Weber, 'Turned Geometry: Two Masterpieces by Georg Friedel'. *The Burlington Magazine*, Vol. CLIX July 2017, pp. 544-52

Tatlock 2010: L. Tatlock (ed.), *Enduring Loss in Early Modern Germany. Cross Disciplinary Perspectives*, Leiden and Boston, 2010

Teufel 1962: R. Teufel, *Banz und Vierzehnheiligen*, Berlin, [1936] [3rd ed. 1962]

Theuerkauff 1968: C. Theuerkauff, 'Der "Helffenbeinarbeiter" Ignaz Elhafen', *Wiener Jahrbuch für Kunstgeschichte*, Vol. XXI, 1968, pp. 92-157

Theuerkauff 1975: C. Theuerkauff, 'Zu Francis van Bossuit (1635-1692). "Beeldsnyder in yvoor"', *Wallraf-Richartz Jahrbuch*, Vol. XXXVII, 1975, pp. 119-82

Theuerkauff 1984: C. Theuerkauff, *Elfenbein Sammlung Reiner Winkler* (Vol. 1 of 2 vols.), Munich, 1984

Theuerkauff 1986: C. Theuerkauff, *Die Bildwerke in Elfenbein des 16.-19. Jahrhunderts. Die Bildwerke der Skulpturengalerie Berlin*, Berlin, 1986

Theuerkauff 1991: C. Theuerkauff, 'Johann Ignaz Bendl: Sculptor and Medalist', *Metropolitan Museum Journal*, Vol. 26, 1991, pp. 227-75

Theuerkauff 1994: C. Theuerkauff, *Elfenbein Sammlung Reiner Winkler*, Vol. II, Munich, 1994

Theuerkauff and Möller et al. 1977: C. Theuerkauff and L.L. Möller et al., *Museum für Kunst und Gewerbe Hamburg. Die Bildwerke des 18. Jahrhunderts*, Braunschweig, 1977

Thon 1977: C. Thon, *Johann Baptist Zimmermann als Stukkator*, Munich, 1977

Toman 1997: R. Toman (ed.), *Die Kunst des Barock. Architektur, Skulptur, Malerei*, Cologne, 1997

Trenschel 1969: H.-P. Trenschel, *Die kirchlichen Werke des Würzburger Hofbildhauers Johann Peter Wagner*, Schöningh in Komm, Würzburg, 1969

Trenschel 1980a: H.-P. Trenschel, *Der Würzburger Hofbildhauer Johann Peter Wagner (1730-1809)*, Aschaffenburg, 1980

Trenschel 1980b: H.-P. Trenschel, *Fränkische Plastik am Ende eines goldenen Zeitalters. Werke des Hofbildhauers Johann Peter Wagner im Landkreis Haßberge*, Ebern, 1980

Trusted 1984: M. Trusted, 'Four Amber Statuettes by Christoph Maucher', *Pantheon*, Vol. XLII, no. III, 1984, pp. 245-9

Trusted 1985: M. Trusted, *Catalogue of European Ambers in the Victoria and Albert Museum*, London, 1985

Trusted 1990: M. Trusted, *German Renaissance Medals. A Catalogue of the Collection in the Victoria and Albert Museum*, London, 1990

Trusted 2013: M. Trusted, *Baroque & Later Ivories. Victoria and Albert Museum*, London, 2013

Trusted 2014: M. Trusted, 'The Same but Different. Baroque Ivories and Reproduction', in W. Cupperi (ed.), *Multiples in Pre-Modern Art*, Zurich, 2014, pp. 245-69

Unger 1972: A. Unger, *Joseph Götsch. Ein Bayerischer Bildhauer des Rokoko aus Tirol*, Weissenhorn, 1972

Urban 2015: W. Urban, *Barockkirche Steinhausen. Bedeutungsfülle von Architektur und Kunst*, Lindenberg, 2015

Vogl 1989: H. Vogl, *Joseph Deutschmann 1717-1787: Der Letzter Klosterbildhauer von St Nikola von Passau*, Weissenhorn, 1989

Volk 1980a: P. Volk, *Münchener Rokoko-plastik (Bayerisches Nationalmuseum Bild-führer 7)*, Munich, 1980

Volk 1980b: P. Volk, 'Satyrköpfe mit Geweihenin Maximilians Kammer-galerie', in Glaser 1980, pp. 175-8

Volk 1981: P. Volk (with photographs by A. Hirmer and I. Ernstmeier-Hirmer), *Rokokoplastik in Altbayern, Bayrisch-Schwaben und im Allgäu*, Munich, 1981

Volk 1982/3: P. Volk, 'Zwei kleinplas-tische Arbeiten von Paul Egell', *Pantheon*, Vol. XLI, 1982/3, pp. 104-8

Volk 1984: P. Volk (with photographs by A. Hirmer and I. Ernstmeier-Hirmer), *Johann Baptist Straub 1704-1784*, Munich, 1984

Volk 1986: P. Volk, 'Zum Reliefschmuck von Glocken der Rokokozeit in Alt-bayern', in T. Breuer (ed.), *Lusus Campan-ularum. Beiträge zur Glockenkunde. Sigrid Thurm zum 80. Geburtstag*, Munich, 1986, pp. 99-104

Volk 1991: P. Volk (with photographs by W.-C. von der Mülbe), *Ignaz Günther. Vollendung des Rokoko*, Regensburg, 1991

Volk and Kozyr 2001: P. Volk and O. Kozyr, *Zur Lemberger Rokokoplastik. Bozzetti von Johann Georg Pinsel*, Munich, 2001

Volk and Seling 1986: P. Volk and A. Seling (eds.), *Entwurf und Ausführung in der europäischen Barockplastik: Beiträge zum internationalen Kolloquium des Bayer-ischen Nationalmuseums und des Zentral Instituts für Kunstgeschichte München, 24. bis 26. Juni 1985*, Munich, 1986

Volk-Knüttel 1980: B. Volk-Knüttel, 'Maximilian I. von Bayern als Sammler und Auftraggeber. Seine Korrespondenz mit Philipp Hainhofer 1611-1615', in Glaser 1980, pp. 83-128

Ward-Jackson 1969: P. Ward-Jackson, *Some Main Streams and Tributaries in European Ornament from 1500 to 1750*, London, 1969

Watson 1965: F.J.B. Watson, Review of E. Hempel, *Baroque Art and Architecture . . .*, *Journal of the Royal Society of Arts*, Vol. 113, no. 5111, October 1965, pp. 925-6

Weisbach 1921: W. Weisbach, *Der Barock als Kunst der Gegenreformation*, Berlin, 1921

Weisbach 1941: W. Weisbach, *Spanish Baroque Art. Three Lectures Delivered at the University of London*, Cambridge, 1941

Weitlauff 2011: M. Weitlauff (ed.), *Benediktinerabtei St. Ulrich und Afra in Augsburg (1012-2012) - Geschichte, Kunst, Wirtschaft und Kultur einer ehemaligen Reichsabtei* (2 vols.), Lindenberg im Allgäu, 2011

Welt im Umbruch 1980: *Welt im Umbruch. Augsburg zwischen Renaissance und Barock* (exh. cat.) (2 vols.), Augsburg, 1980

Wendel 2010: L.P. Wendel, 'Locating the Sacred in Biconfessional Augsburg', in L. Tatlock (ed.), *Enduring Loss in Early Modern Germany. Cross Disciplinary Perspectives*, Leiden and Boston, 2010, pp. 307-25

Whaley 2012a: J. Whaley, *Germany and the Holy Roman Empire. Volume I: Maxi-milian I to the Peace of Westphalia 1493-1648*, Oxford, 2012

Whaley 2012b: J. Whaley, *Germany and the Holy Roman Empire. Volume II: The Peace of Westphalia to the Dissolution of the Reich 1648-1806*, Oxford, 2012

Whaley 2018: J. Whaley, *The Holy Roman Empire. A Very Short Introduction*, Oxford, 2018

Wilson 2016: P.H. Wilson, *The Holy Roman Empire. A Thousand Years of Europe's History*, London, 2016

Wittkower 1999a: R. Wittkower, *Art and Architecture in Italy 1600-1750. Vol. I: The Early Baroque* (revised by J. Connors and J. Montagu), New Haven, 1999

Wittkower 1999b: R. Wittkower, *Art and Architecture in Italy 1600-1750. Vol. II: The High Baroque* (revised by J. Connors and J. Montagu), New Haven, 1999

Woeckel 1958: G. Woeckel, *Johann Joseph Christian von Riedlingen: ein ober-schwäbischer Bildhauer des Rokoko*, Lindau, 1958

Woeckel 1975: G.P. Woeckel, *Ignaz Günther. Die Handzeichnungen des kufürst-lich bayerischen Hofbildhauers Franz Ignaz Günther (1725-1775)*, Weissenhorn, 1975

Woeckel 1977: G.P. Woeckel, *Ignaz Günther. Der grosse Bildhauer des bayer-ischen Rokoko*, Regensburg, 1977

Wölfflin 1926: H. Wölfflin, *Renaissance und Barock: Eine Untersuchung über Wesen und Entstehung des Barockstils in Italien* [Munich, 1888], (ed. H. Rose), Munich, 1926

Wölfflin 1984: H. Wölfflin, *Renaissance and Baroque* (tr. K. Simon; introduction P. Murray), London, 1984

Wölfflin 1950: H. Wölfflin, *Principles of Art History. The Problem of the Develop-ment of Style in Later Art* (tr. M.D. Hottinger), New York, 1950 [1932]; [German edition published 1915]

Wölfle 2015: S. Wölfle, 'Die Fugger und Florenz. Aspekte der süddeutschen Rezeption des italienischen Villenideals', in *Bella Figura* 2015, pp. 108-15

Wood 2003: C.S. Wood (ed.), *The Vienna School Reader. Politics and Art Historical Method in the 1930s*, New York, 2003

Wunderwelt 2014: *Wunderwelt: Der Pommersche Kunstschrank* (exh. cat.), Maximilian Museum, Augsburg, 2014

Zeschick 2015: J. Zeschick, *Benedikitiner-abtei Rohr in Niederbayern*, ed. S. Weiss, Lindenberg, 2015

Zikos 2015: D. Zikos, '"longa amities". Giambolognas Kunst und Bayern', in *Bella Figura* 2015, pp. 88-107

Zitzelsperger 2014: P. Zitzelsperger, 'Schlüters Männlich-Grabmal', in *Andreas Schlüter* 2014, pp. 328-39

Zoege von Manteuffel 1969: C. Zoege von Manteuffel, *Die Bildhauer Familie Zürn* (2 vols.), Weissenhorn, 1969

Zoege von Manteuffel 1998: C. Zoege von Manteuffel, *Die Waldseer Bildhauer Zürn* (exh. cat.), Kornhausmuseum, Bad Waldsee, 1998

Zohner 1977: W. Zohner, 'Hans Degler (1564-1634/5)', *Lech-Isar-Land*, 1977, pp. 76-89

Zohner 1993: W. Zohner, *Bartholomäus Steinle um 1580-1629/9. Bildhauer und "Director über den Kirchenbau zu Weilheim"*, Weissenhorn, 1993

INDEX